Burned Palaces and Elite Residences of
AGUATECA: Excavations and Ceramics

Burned Palaces and Elite Residences of Aguateca:
Excavations and Ceramics

Edited by
TAKESHI INOMATA AND DANIELA TRIADAN

Monographs of the Aguateca Archaeological Project First Phase
Takeshi Inomata and Daniela Triadan, General Editors
Volume 1

The University of Utah Press
Salt Lake City

The Defiance House Man colophon is a registered trademark of the
University of Utah Press. It is based upon a four-foot-tall, Ancient Puebloan
pictograph (late PIII) near Glen Canyon, Utah.

14 13 12 11 10   1 2 3 4 5

LIBRARY OF CONGRESS CATALOGING-IN-PUBLICATION DATA

Burned palaces and elite residences of Aguateca : excavations and
ceramics / edited by Takeshi Inomata and Daniela Triadan.
        p. cm.
    Includes bibliographical references and index.
    ISBN 978-1-60781-001-8 (cloth : alk. paper) 1. Aguateca Site
(Guatemala) 2. Excavations (Archaeology)—Guatemala—Aguateca Site.
3. Mayas—Guatemala—Aguateca Site—Antiquities. 4. Mayas—Guatemala—
Aguateca Site—Social life and customs. 5. Mayas—Guatemala—Aguateca
Site—Material culture. 6. Palaces—Guatemala—Aguateca Site. 7. Dwellings—
Guatemala—Aguateca Site. 8. Maya pottery—Guatemala—Aguateca Site.
I. Inomata, Takeshi. II. Triadan, Daniela, 1964
    F1435.1.A37B87 2009
    972.81'2—dc22   2009053807

Printed and bound by Sheridan Books, Inc., Ann Arbor, Michigan.

Contents

Figures

Tables

Acknowledgments

The Aguateca Archaeological Project First Phase was conducted under permits granted by the Instituto de Antropología e Historia de Guatemala. We thank its directors, Dr. Juan Antonio Valdés, Licda. Mercedes Flores, Arq. Arturo Paz, Lic. Salvador López, Dr. Héctor Escobedo, and Maestro Guillermo Díaz Romeu; the heads of the Departamento de Monumentos Prehispánicos y Coloniales, Lic. Edgar Suyuc, Lic. Rene Ugarte, Licda. Nora López, Lic. Paulino Morales, and Lic. Juan Carlos Pérez; and its inspectors, Gustavo Amarra, Hugo Barrera, and Julio López.

Financial support for the project came from the National Science Foundation (BCS-9707950, BCS-9974302, and BCS-9910594), Mitsubishi Foundation, National Geographic Society, Sumitomo Foundation, Foundation for Advancement of Mesoamerican Studies, and H. John Heinz III Charitable Trust. A National Endowment for the Humanities fellowship gave Inomata a one-year leave from teaching obligations, which allowed him to concentrate on the initial preparation of this book. The field work was conducted while Inomata was at Yale University and Triadan at the Smithsonian Institution, whereas the lab seasons took place after we moved to the University of Arizona. We are grateful for their institutional support: Yale gave Inomata a Junior Faculty Fellowship leave and research grants from the Albers Fund; and the University of Arizona offered Inomata and Triadan international travel grants, a Junior Faculty Professional Development leave, and a GIS assistant grant.

We are also indebted to our colleagues for their generous help and intellectual inspiration. Our work was a direct development of Inomata's dissertation research, conducted as part of the Vanderbilt Petexbatun Regional Archaeological Project. We thank its directors, Arthur Demarest, Stephen Houston, and Juan Antonio Valdés, as well as its numerous members.

In recent years publications of excavation data have become increasingly difficult. We recognize the University of Utah Press's decision to publish a three-volume monograph series in this environment and the professional work by John Herbert, Glenda Cotter, Reba Rauch, and Kim Vivier. The National Science Foundation provided a subvention (BCS-0836904) crucial for this publication. David Freidel and Heather McKillop read a draft of this volume and offered thoughtful comments.

This book represents the fruits of hard work by numerous researchers and volunteers, as described in Chapter 1. Our work would not have been possible without the help and understanding of the people of the Petexbatun region. In particular, we express our heartfelt gratitude to the owners of the Chiminos Island Lodge, John and Aurora Schmidt and Mynor Pinto, for their kind support and occasional cold drinks. We are also grateful to our field crews from the Q'eqchi' Maya community of Las Pozas and other nearby villages for their tireless work and cheerful conversations. Special thanks are due to the Xe family and the members of the Comité para la Promoción de Turismo Las Pozas for continuing dialogues on the region's heritage and for their famous *caldo de chunto*.

chapter 1

Introduction

Takeshi Inomata

The Aguateca Archaeological Project conducted fieldwork at the Maya site of Aguateca, Guatemala, from 1996 through 1999, followed by lab seasons from 2000 through 2003. The project developed from Takeshi Inomata's prior research at the site, which revealed evidence of rapid abandonment at the end of the Classic period (ca. AD 810). It appeared that the central part of Aguateca was burned and that the elite residents of the area fled or were taken as captives, leaving a significant portion of their possessions behind. Such sudden desertion is rare in the Maya Lowlands, and Aguateca promised an extraordinary opportunity for examining the daily lives of Maya elites. Taking advantage of this unique situation, the Aguateca Project focused on extensive excavations of rapidly abandoned elite residences to address the following questions:

1. How were Classic Maya elite households organized, and what kind of activities did their members conduct in and around their dwellings?
2. How were elite households articulated with other political, economic, and social organizations, particularly the royal court?
3. How was the royal court as the central political institution of a Maya city organized, and how did it function?

Elite Households and the Royal Court

Archaeological Studies of Domestic Groups

After the pioneering work by Lewis Henry Morgan (1871, 1965 [1881]) and Karl Marx (Engels 1942) that emphasized the family, research in the social sciences and history focused on larger political, economic, and social units and related issues, such as states, communities, and kinship systems. In these studies, domestic groups were characterized as passive entities that lacked enduring structure and whose organization was determined by social norms, including the descent rule and postmarital residence rule. Thus, the family and household were not considered central research subjects. Since the late 1960s, however, social anthropologists, as well as sociologists and historians, have renewed their interest in households and families and have demonstrated that the study of these small groups provides rich information on societies and social change (Hammel 1980; Hammel and Laslett 1974; Laslett 1969; Laslett and Wall 1972; Nakane 1970; Netting 1965, 1993; Netting et al., ed. 1984; Wilk 1983, 1991; Yanagisako 1979).

Under the influence of growing interest in the family and household among social anthropologists and historians, the archaeological study of these groups—household archaeology—has rapidly developed during the last three decades (Bawden 1982; Bermann 1994; Deetz 1982; Drennan 1988; Manzanilla 1993; Santley and Hirth 1993; Schwartz and Falconer 1994; Smith 1987; Tringham 1991; Wilk and Ashmore 1988; Wilk and Rathje 1982). Moreover, developments in activity area studies and spatial analysis (Carr 1984; Kent 1984, 1990), ethnoarchaeology (David and Kramer 2001; Deal 1998; Hayden and Cannon 1983; Kramer 1979; Longacre 1991), and the study of vernacular architecture (Blanton 1994; Glassie 1975; Lawrence and Low 1990; Rapoport 1969, 1982) have provided analytical and interpretive tools.

The forms and functions of domestic groups are diverse among different societies. Most scholars now agree that there are no universal definitions of families and households, but they are culturally defined. Yet there exists the general consensus that families mean groups based on kinship relations while households refer to groups sharing basic economic resources and collaborating in domestic activities (Bender 1967; Goodenough 1970; Netting et al. 1984; Yanagisako 1979). Archaeologists tend to focus on the household rather than on the family, partly because of the difficulty of addressing kinship relations through the analysis of material remains.

It has been suggested that there are three important dimensions of households: activities that household members conduct; morphology, or the composition of households; and ideology, including social norms, symbolism, and concepts of households (Netting et al. 1984:xxxi; Yanagisako 1979). In the early development of household archaeology in the 1980s, scholars placed a strong emphasis on the analysis of activities (e.g., Ashmore and Wilk 1988; Hirth 1993). On the one hand, formation theory and architectural studies brought substantial criticism of work that attempted to relate artifact distributions and architectural forms to specific compositions of households in rather simplistic ways (Deal 1985:264; Hayden and Cannon 1983; Schiffer 1987). On the other hand, material remains were believed to reflect past activities relatively well, despite distortions introduced by formation processes. The focus on activities was also due to the influence of important work by Richard Wilk and Robert Netting (1984), who defined households as action groups that collaborated in various domestic activities.

These ideas were followed by a new development in the 1990s. Archaeologists inspired by gender studies viewed households not as natural, homogeneous units but as culturally constructed entities with internal heterogeneity and contestation (Brumfiel 1991; Joyce 1993). Ruth Tringham (1991:100–103), in particular, argued that the overemphasis on the study of domestic activities reduced households to "faceless, genderless categories." She suggested that gender relations at a domestic level formed a basis for social relations at larger scales. Another source of influence was practice theory, which postulated that large structures of society played out through daily practices (Bourdieu 1977). Domestic groups, as primary social arenas of such practices, present critical fields for inquiry into this issue. Again, an important implication was the political nature inherent in interactions among household members. In these discussions, identities of individuals and groups emerged as a critical issue (Meskell 1999). Scholars began to explore how various identities were constructed and acted out through daily practices (Hendon 1996). These perspectives brought renewed interest in the compositions of households. A study of the actions and decision making of the household as a whole is not enough, and a stronger emphasis on intentions, perceptions, and actions of individual agents is necessary. In other words, in addition to the question of what a household did, we need to examine who within the household did what (Robin 2006).

In this theoretical trend, the issue of ideology associated with domestic groups also received increasing attention (Ashmore 1992; Hodder 1990; Pearson and Richards 1994; Samson 1990). Ideology is not a neutral set of beliefs, but it is what shapes human beings to perceive their positions in a society and their relations with others in specific ways (Gardiner 1992; McGuire 1992; Therborn 1980). One aspect of ideology related to domestic groups is a strong emotional and social value placed on the unity of the family and household, which is observed in many societies (Rapp 1991). The perceived unity of a domestic group, however, may involve inequality and power relations among its members. In this regard, the question of ideology is closely tied to the issues of identity and political relations among household members.

The archaeology of domestic groups now addresses diverse problems, including the unity and heterogeneity of households, as well as their relations with other social organizations and structures (Robin 2003; Yaeger 2003). In exploring these questions, many researchers recognize the importance of examining the interrelations of various aspects of domestic groups, such as their activities, compositions, and ideologies. At the same time, we need to acknowledge the difficulty of understanding various issues through material remains. The archaeological study of ideologies associated with domestic groups is particularly arduous when ethnographic analogy or written records are absent (Douglas 1972; Herbich and Dietler 1993).

Structure and Dynamics of Domestic Groups

We believe that the study of domestic groups requires attention to both the structural properties of such groups and the dynamic processes of change and reproduction through interactions among individual agents. In terms of the analysis of their structures, households may be the most basic units of collaboration and resource sharing in many societies, but they should not be considered the only social unit responsible for domestic activities. There may exist various domestic groups associated with different sets of activities, groups that nest or cross-cut each other. Jack Goody (1958:56) defined domestic groups as units of individuals associated with specific domestic activities, such as reproduction, residence, and food production. In other words, the unit for food storage may not be the same as that for food consumption, co-residence, or reproduction. In Goody's classic ethnographic example of the Lo-Dagaba in West Africa, a nuclear family or a polygynous extended family of three generations lives in a compound, forming a co-residential unit. These co-residential units generally correspond to the religious and judicial units. Within a co-residential group, however, father and sons may form separate units of production or of agricultural activities. A unit of food preparation and consumption is formed by even smaller groups of individuals, including a wife and her offspring (Goody 1958).

This example shows that units of religious activities, co-residence, production, and consumption do not necessarily correspond with one another, and the boundaries of a family and household are not always easily defined. In addition, although households are often considered to be equivalent to co-residential units, it is not always the case (see Freeman 1958 and Horne 1982 for ethnographic examples; Netting et al. 1984). In other words, an architectural remain cannot be simply equated with a household. A clear understanding of households in a given society needs to be achieved through the examination of various units of individuals associated with particular activities, including co-residence. Researchers must examine how different domestic groups articulate with one another, taking into consideration the degree of their variability and fluidity. The structural properties of domestic groups also include specific forms of power relations and the assignment of rights and duties defined by such categories as gender and age group. These patterns tend to perpetuate through time and space to a certain degree, but they always contain a level of variability and fluidity.

These structures of domestic groups shape, and are shaped by, practices and perceptions of individuals, comprising contestation and negotiation (Bourdieu 1977; Giddens 1984). This observation implies that these structures are never static properties. The maintenance of existing structures, as well as the creation of new ones, requires constant attention and action on the part of social agents. We need to examine the dynamic processes involved in the reproduction and production of structures, in which individual agents play critical roles. For the archaeological study of the role of individual agents, in which researchers cannot directly observe people, the analysis of activities conducted by different individuals through their material remains is still an effective strategy (Hendon 1996; Tringham 1991; Wright 1991). We should also note that the same individuals may be at once parts of larger social groups, such as kin-based and non-kin-based associations, male or female groups, and ego-centered personal networks, which may cross-cut domestic groups.

Domestic Groups, Politics, and Royal Courts

The foregoing discussion makes it clear that the relations between household members, as well as those between different domestic groups, are inherently political. It follows that households and other domestic groups should not be considered "domestic" or "private" spheres separated from "political" or "public" spheres (Rapp 1991; Yanagisako 1979). In most traditional societies, in particular, what we call the private and the public merge inseparably, in contrast to modern societies, in which the division between "home" and "work" is relatively common.

The convergence of the domestic and the public becomes particularly evident when we address the issue of the royal court, which is defined as a group of individuals surrounding the sovereign. Archaeological, epigraphic, and iconographic data have made it clear that the royal court was the primary administrative apparatus of each Maya polity (Inomata and Houston 2001; Sanders and Webster 1988; Schele and Miller 1986). The royal court also functioned as the ruler's household, which carried out common domestic activities of food preparation and consumption, sleeping, sex, and child rearing. As suggested for historic European courts (Elias 1983:41–43), the power of the Maya rulers derived partially from their authority as the master of a house, and polity administration was in many respects an extension of household management (Inomata and Houston 2001). In addition, the royal court was an arena where elite ethos, cultural codes, and world views were produced and reproduced as elite children were socialized and courtiers lived a significant part of their daily lives in its domestic setting. In this sense, just as large social structures shape patterns of daily interaction among individuals at intimate levels, the forms and operations of households provide a model for society-wide political organizations. The study of domestic groups concerns not only personal interactions at small levels but also broad social and political processes.

The main issues discussed for households in general apply to the study of the court as well. An important problem is the relationship between its structural properties and its process of change and reproduction. In this regard, any centralized polity involves two overlapping aspects. One is the institutionalized administrative system underlain by its economic basis and political ideologies. A particularly formalized version is commonly called bureaucracy, in which rights and duties are assigned to organizational positions rather than to the officeholders as persons (Weber 1978:956–958). The other aspect is an organization constituted by flesh-and-blood individuals with diverse agendas and fluid personal relations.

It is important to note that these two aspects are not mutually exclusive. Even in the modern nation-state, in which the impersonal bureaucratic institutions are supposed to prevail, power struggles and negotiations among individuals characteristic of court organization strongly color its politics in reality. Nor does a court organization without developed bureaucracy mean the lack of enduring structures. Any court involves certain orders of titles and positions that condition patterns of interaction and power relations. Moreover, operations of the royal court are framed in often conservative systems of symbols and ideas that constitute the notions of rulership and court culture. We need to examine the articulation of these two dimensions to understand the political processes of centralized societies (Inomata 2001b).

Thus, the court is fashioned by numerous conflicting factors, including administrative necessities demanding pragmatic efficiency and an array of symbols that defy rational explanations, along with institutional structures and shifting personal relations. Such organizational characteristics shape, and are shaped by, varying human motivations, and the court always appears to create a fiercely competitive arena, whether aggression is openly played out or kept under the surface and whether internal competition is fueled or kept under control by external rivalry with other courts. The court is at once empowering and dangerous for its members, as it may allow individuals of humble origins to gain prominent power through flexible personal relations and it may strip the most powerful courtier of all honors and privileges overnight (Anglo 1977; Loades 1986). The collision of such diverse forces can lead to both fluidity and inertia.

As in the case of households, the change and reproduction of the court and its structure take place through physical actions of people. The concept of performance is particularly important in this regard (Inomata and Coben 2006). Performance refers to the indissoluble relation between physical actions and intangible notions. Through performance, people act out idealized images of courtiers and their moral values. At the same time, the physical acts create and re-create such meanings and abstract structures (Austin 1962; Hymes 1975). Moreover, performance is the process of physical interaction between these social agents framed in specific historical contexts and material settings. Through performance, the identities of individuals and groups are maintained and transformed, and cultural notions and ideologies are transmitted, negotiated, and resisted.

Another common issue in the study of the royal court and the household is its relations with the rest of society. The court expresses both detachment from and connection with its subject population. On the one hand, the court is an extraordinary sphere distinct from the ordinary realm of daily lives among the masses. It claims communication with supernatural or foreign domains and fosters exclusive culture. Its members consider themselves a select few endowed with special qualities distinct from others (Sahlins 1985; Tambiah 1976). On the other hand, the court emphasizes its role as an exemplary center of society, and the sovereign projects its image as the caring father or mother of the entire society (Geertz 1980). After all, the court as an administrative apparatus has to be constantly alert to what happens outside the palace walls. The court is thus at once at the center of the society and apart from it.

The Study of Domestic Groups and Royal Courts in the Classic Maya Lowlands

Maya archaeologists have been playing an important role in developing household archaeology (Haviland 1985; Lohse and Valdez 2004; McAnany 1995; Rathje 1983; Robin 2003; Tourtellot 1988b; Webster 1989; Wilk and Ashmore 1988; Wilk and Rathje 1982). The active engagement of Mayanists in household archaeology may be due partly to pioneering studies of the household (Wauchope 1934; 1938) and partly to a strong tradition in settlement studies (Ashmore 1981; Willey et al. 1965). Field investigations at various sites have generated a large amount of data on the distribution of house mounds, domestic architecture, domestic activities, and craft specialization at the household level. In addition, the high visibility of house remains and a strong interest in demography have encouraged Maya archaeologists to examine the question of household size and composition (Culbert and Rice 1990; Haviland 1972; Tourtellot 1983). More recently, Maya archaeologists are also exploring the symbolic and ideological domains of the household, as well as gender relations and articulations with other social groups (Ashmore 1992; Gillespie 2000; Hendon 1997; Joyce 2000; Robin 2006; Yaeger 2003).

Still, we have a rather limited understanding about who conducted what activities and how individuals and activities were organized in Classic Maya domestic settings. Maya archaeologists have relied heavily on ethnographic and ethnohistorical analogies rather than hard archaeological data to reconstruct prehispanic households. An issue relatively easy to address archaeologically might be the identification of co-residential groups. Yet our understanding is unsatisfactory even with regard to the relatively simple question of whether single structures were occupied by single nuclear families or extended families. Various figures ranging from 4 to 25 individuals per structure were applied from ethnohistorical and ethnographic data (Adams 1981; see Cogolludo 1971 [1654]; de la Garza et al. 1983; Hellmuth 1977; Puleston 1973; Redfield and Villa Rojas 1934:226–228; Rice and Culbert 1990:17–18; Ringle and Andrews 1990:226–228; Roys et al. 1940, 1959; Villa Rojas 1945, 1969 for ethnographic and ethnohistorical data; Villagutierre 1933 [1701]).

In addition, scholars do not agree on the use of space in multiroom structures, that is, whether single rooms were occupied by nuclear families or whether single nuclear families occupied entire multiroom buildings (Becquelin and Michelet 1994; Harrison 1970; Inomata 1995; Inomata and Stiver 1998; Tourtellot et al. 1990; Webster and Freter 1990). Likewise, although groups of structures around an open space—commonly called patio groups—are often assumed to be important socioeconomic units (Tourtellot 1988a; Willey 1981:389–391), their internal organization is not well understood. We have even more limited understanding of the domestic organization of production and consumption, its relation to larger economic and political systems, and gender and power relations at the domestic level.

The study of the ancient Maya court is still in the incipient stage. Many Mayanists have focused on political organization, administrative systems, and other institutional aspects of Maya political lives, and the issue of royal courts has remained secondary in these studies. After breakthroughs in epigraphic decipherment, research has focused on the reconstruction of dynastic histories and inquiries into the nature of rulership (Culbert 1991; Freidel and Schele 1988; Houston and Stuart 1996), but scholars have paid little attention to other individuals who surrounded the ruler and the complex processes of interaction among them. Archaeological approaches to the court have also been slow to develop. Although archaeologists gradually recognized that some of the buildings that were generally called "palaces" were residences of sovereigns and other high-status groups (Harrison 1970), the activities and interactions that took place there have been rather poorly understood.

This trend began to change gradually. Particularly influential was the pioneering work by Linda Schele and Mary Ellen Miller (1986) that shed more light on courtly lives, mainly through the study of inscriptions and images. Subsequent developments in epigraphy and iconography have added significant information on the royal court

and its members (Houston and Inomata 2009; Jackson 2005, 2009; Miller and Martin 2004; Stuart 2005). From the perspective of anthropological archaeology, William Sanders and David Webster (1988:90) advocated the necessity of examining court dimensions of centralization. The edited volumes by Inomata and Stephen Houston (2001a, 2001b) brought the explicit focus on the royal court to the foreground of Maya studies.

Patterns of Abandonment and the Understanding of Domestic Groups

The difficulties in reconstructing Classic Maya households stem partly from the fact that most Maya settlements were abandoned gradually. When a house is deserted slowly, inhabitants have time to transport a large portion of their possessions to the next residence and leave few objects behind (Baker 1975; Cameron and Tomka 1993; Deal 1985: 268; Inomata and Webb 2003; Lange and Rydberg 1972; Manzanilla and Barba 1990; Schiffer 1976, 1987:89–98; Stevenson 1982). Archaeological assemblages are significantly affected by various formation processes, and durable stone buildings often appear to have been disturbed by later squatters. In these cases, it is difficult to infer how rooms and areas around buildings were used. In contrast, abruptly abandoned sites contain numerous artifacts left in situ, providing rich information about the occupants and their activities. Earthquakes, floods, fire, attacks by enemies, and similar events may cause sudden abandonment (Manzanilla and Barba 1990:41; Schiffer 1987:92), with the most dramatic cases being sites destroyed by volcanic eruptions, such as Pompeii in Italy and Joya de Cerén in El Salvador (Sheets 1992, 2002). Such patterns of abrupt abandonment are extremely rare in the Maya Lowlands. Among the few exceptions are Ceibal Structure C-31a (Tourtellot 1988b:129–138) and Copan Structure 9N-81 (Webster 1989:20–22). These, however, represent rather fortuitous findings in single structures, and other parts of the sites do not exhibit such patterns. Extremely rare examples of more extensive rapid abandonment may include the central part of Caracol (Chase and Chase 2000). Consequently, the numbers of objects left on room floors are quite small at most Classic Maya sites. Moreover, floor assemblages were sometimes disturbed by later squatters. This problem is particularly severe for so-called palace buildings, many of which have durable masonry construction.

Archaeologists have been developing methods and theories to reconstruct past behavior from limited material remains. These include the sophistication of formation theory (Deal 1985; Hayden and Cannon 1983; Schiffer 1976, 1987), development in the analysis of activity areas and site structure (Kent 1984, 1990), and the recovery of microdebitage and the detection of chemical concentrations from floors (Ball and Kelsay 1992; Barba and Ortíz 1992; Fladmark 1982; Manzanilla and Barba 1990; McGovern et al. 1983; Rosen 1986). Although such methodological and theoretical sophistication has considerably augmented our knowledge of household organization and activities, the most direct and richest information still derives from rapidly abandoned sites, where most objects are left in situ (Inomata and Sheets 2000; Inomata and Webb 2003).

The central part of Aguateca presents a rare case of extensive rapid abandonment. Previous investigations (Inomata and Stiver 1998) revealed elite residences that were burned and contained numerous complete and reconstructible objects. While these remains offer an unprecedented opportunity for the study of Maya domestic groups and royal courts, we also need to consider their limitations. First, although these floor assemblages provide remarkable views of Maya daily lives, they are not the same as the original sets of objects that the living residents possessed. At the time of abandonment, the inhabitants and intruders may have removed or added certain items, and the locations of remaining objects may have been changed. In addition, many materials deteriorated during the fire and after the abandonment. In this regard, the preservation of objects in the shallow deposits of Aguateca is substantially worse than the preservation at Cerén, buried under deep volcanic ash. The evaluation of formation processes is still critical.

Second, those floor assemblages represent snapshots of the final moments of this center, and it is difficult to address the dynamic processes of household organization and activity through time. We need to combine the analysis of floor assemblages with other lines of evidence, including midden materials, architectural remains, and chemical residues. Third, rapid abandonment was limited to the central part of Aguateca, and other areas of the site do not exhibit this pattern. The information gained from rapidly deserted elite residences does not directly apply to the non-elite groups that occupied the areas outside the central part. In this regard, the analysis of chemical residues is significant. The rapidly abandoned buildings with rich floor assemblages provide test cases with which to refine our applications and interpretations of floor chemical analysis. This procedure then can be applied to gradually abandoned structures that are devoid of floor objects.

We should add that the study of abandonment patterns is highly productive in its own right. Not only does it provide information with which to evaluate formation processes, but it also sheds light on the nature of social organization, ideological values attached to buildings and places, and causes of abandonment. For this line of inquiry, the edited volume by Catherine Cameron and Steve Tomka (1993), which followed the pioneering work by Michael Schiffer (1987) and Marc Stevenson (1982), is significant. In the Maya area, James Garber (1983), David Freidel (Freidel and Schele 1989), and their colleagues (Freidel et al. 1998) have identified remains of ritual destruction and deposit at the time of abandonment, which they termed termination ritual. Expanding on these works, Inomata and Ronald Webb (2003) specifically examined abandonment as a social process.

Immediately before its abandonment, Aguateca was probably under the threat of enemy attack. We need to evaluate carefully the possibility that in this highly tense circumstance the organization of domestic groups and their activities may have changed substantially from the prior period. This also means that such changes and patterns of abandonment may provide important clues to social organization and political dynamics leading to the fall of the center. Our excavation of the Palace Group of Aguateca did not reveal patterns of rapid abandonment, but the analysis of its abandonment process holds critical information on social conditions during the final days of this center and the symbolic values of this complex and its residences.

Aguateca and Its Settings
Location and Environment

Detailed descriptions of Aguateca's setting were offered in previous publications (Inomata 1995, 2007, 2009), and here we present a brief summary. Aguateca is one of several major centers in the Petexbatun region, which lies in the western part of the Department of El Peten, Guatemala (Figure 1.1). Other important centers in the region include Dos Pilas, Tamarindito, Arroyo de Piedra, and Punta de Chimino. Aguateca is located on top of an escarpment that overlooks Laguneta Aguateca and Riachuelo (Stream) Aguateca (Figure 1.2). Today the primary rain forest around Aguateca is protected as a national

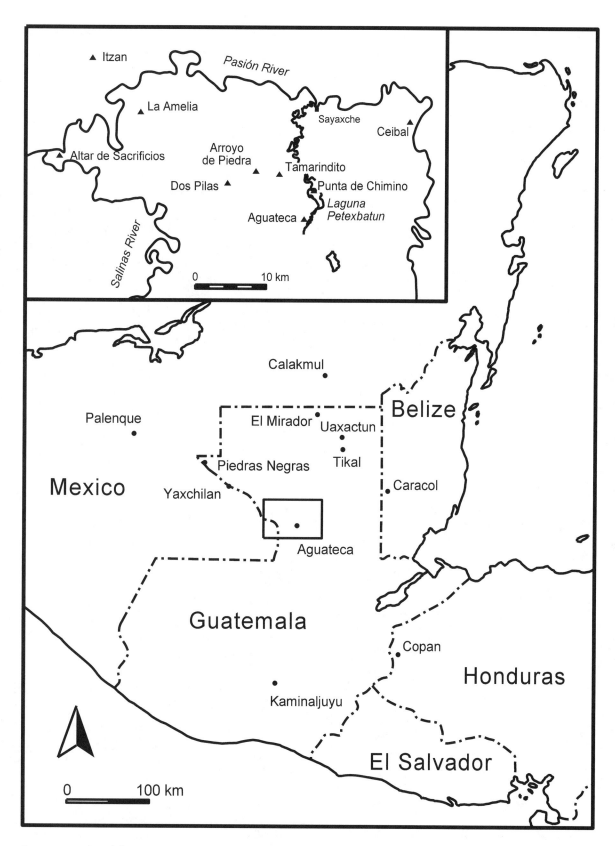

Figure 1.1. Map of the Maya area with the locations of Aguateca and other important sites.

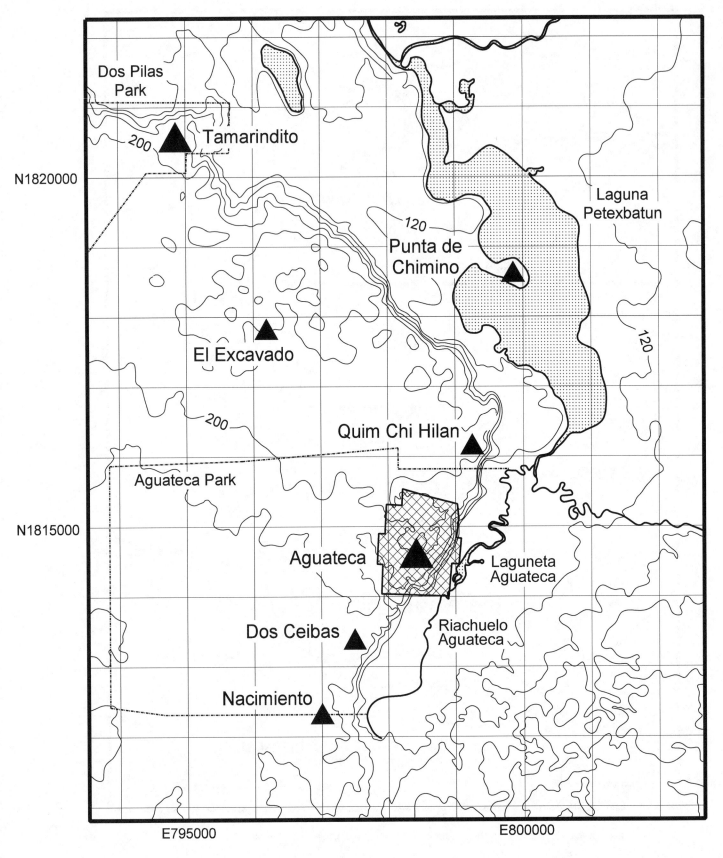

FIGURE 1.2. Map of the area around Aguateca. The crosshatched part indicates the area mapped during the Petexbatun Regional Archaeological Project. 1 km UTM grid and 20-m contour intervals.

park, but the last decade witnessed invasions of squatters, illegal logging, and increased looting of archaeological remains.

Ancient settlements at Aguateca are found in a relatively flat terrain above the escarpment. The most characteristic geological feature at the site is the Grieta, a 70-m-deep chasm running parallel to the escarpment (Figure 1.3). The area exhibits typical karst topography and is densely covered with sinkholes. Most sinkholes have small holes in the bottom where water percolates into the ground. Areas between sinkholes are mostly flat, and the bedrock in these places usually consists of flat solid limestone. The bedrock in most parts is very hard, but some spots contain softer rocks, which the Maya appear to have used to make dressed blocks. Soils in the flat areas are shallow (10–30 cm), and in some places the bedrock is exposed.

The Aguateca center refers to the area demarcated by the escarpment to the east and a ravine to the west and surrounded by concentric defensive walls. Areas outside the center are considered peripheries. Within the center, the monumental core, consisting of the Palace Group, the elite residential area along the Causeway, and the Main Plaza, is called the epicenter.

Previous Work at Aguateca

The Aguateca Archaeological Project First Phase, the results of which are reported in this monograph series, constituted part of a long-term research effort at this center. This series of projects can be summarized as follows:

- Petexbatun Regional Archaeological Project, Aguateca Subproject (1990–1993 field work; 1994 lab work): general director, Arthur Demarest; subproject director, Takeshi Inomata. The establishment of a general chronology, a study of warfare and abandonment.
- Aguateca Archaeological Project First Phase (1996–1999 field work; 2000–2003 lab work): director, Inomata; co-directors, Daniela Triadan, Erick Ponciano, and Kazuo Aoyama. A study of domestic groups and the royal court through extensive excavation of elite buildings.
- Aguateca Restoration Project First Phase (1999–2000): director, Juan Antonio Valdés. Restoration of monumental buildings.
- Aguateca Restoration Project Second Phase (2002–2004): director, Inomata. Restoration of monumental buildings.
- Aguateca Archaeological Project Second Phase

(2004–2005 field work; 2006 lab work): director, Inomata; co-directors, Triadan, Ponciano, and Aoyama. Intersite survey, excavations in the Main Plaza, nonelite residential groups, and the Grieta, and at Punta de Chimino (Inomata et al. 2009).

Here I summarize the work prior to the Aguateca Archaeological Project First Phase and its results to provide a historical background to the project. After its discovery in the late 1950s, Ian Graham (1967) visited Aguateca, recording its monuments and producing a map. A systematic study of Aguateca's inscriptions was done in the 1980s by Houston (1993), who also expanded Graham's map. Inomata's dissertation research from 1990 to 1993 constituted the first systematic archaeological investigation at this site (Inomata 1995, 1997; Inomata and Stiver 1998). The research was conducted as part of the Petexbatun Regional Archaeological Project, directed by Arthur Demarest (Demarest 1997, 2006), which involved investigations at various sites in the region. Following the general goal of the Petexbatun Project, Inomata's research focused on the questions of warfare and the abandonment of the center at the end of the Classic period. Field investigations included the production of a detailed archaeological map of the entire site, the excavation of possible defensive walls that were previously documented by Graham (1967) and Houston (1987, 1993), test excavations in various parts of the site, and extensive excavation in the site epicenter.

The results of the investigations contributed to the establishment of Aguateca's occupation history. Evidence of the earliest occupation dates to the Late Preclassic period (300 BC–AD 250). Large platforms found in the Guacamaya Group in the western part of the center were built during this period. The Early Classic period (AD 250–600), however, is poorly documented. Although the chronology of this era is still problematic, Aguateca appears to have been nearly deserted. The Petexbatun region was dominated by the dynasty seated at the twin capitals of Tamarindito and Arroyo de Piedra (Houston 1993).

The Tamarindito dynasty continued to prosper during the Late Classic period (AD 600–830), and the areas of Dos Pilas and Aguateca may have been under the control of this dynasty during the early part of the Late Classic. The political landscape of the region was transformed with the arrival of a Tikal royal personage, Bahlaj Chan K'awiil, at Dos Pilas apparently under the order and collaboration of his native center (Fahsen 2003; Guenter 2003; Houston 1993; Martin and Grube 2000). Dos Pilas

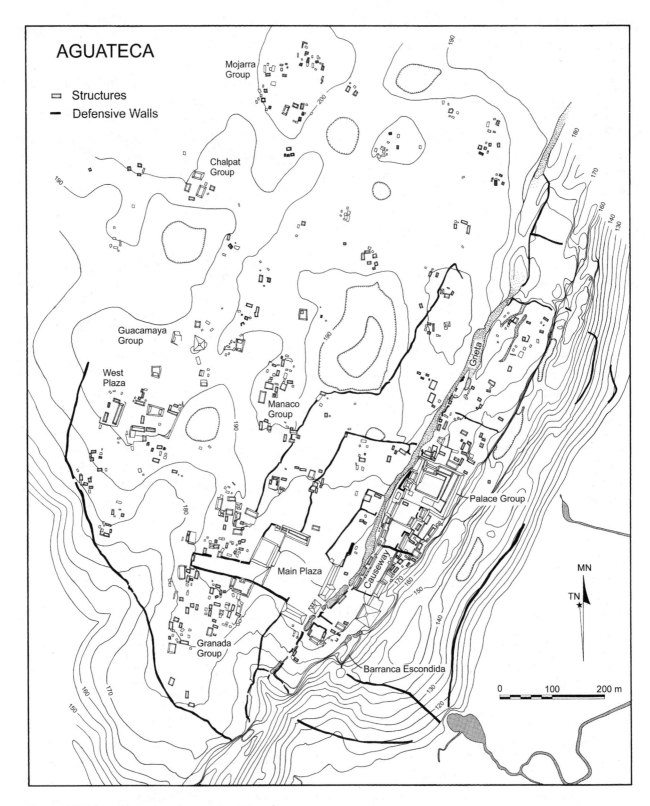

FIGURE 1.3. Map of Aguateca. 5-m contour intervals.

soon started a civil war with Tikal. Bahlaj Chan K'awiil was then defeated by Calakmul and exiled to a place that may have been Aguateca. After this event, Dos Pilas became subordinate to Calakmul and continued the war against Tikal.

Bahlaj Chan K'awiil, also called Ruler 1 of the Dos Pilas dynasty, developed diplomatic relations in the region, forming marriage alliances with the royal families of Tamarindito and Itzan. His son, Ruler 2, Itzamnaaj K'awiil, conducted a ritual, possibly at Aguateca, on 9.14.10.0.0 (AD 721), according to the inscriptions of Stela 15 of Dos Pilas (Houston 1993). It is not clear whether Rulers 1 and 2 already had Aguateca under their control or visited this place when it was still part of the Tamarindito territory.

The earliest stela in the Main Plaza of Aguateca is Stela 3, dedicated by Ruler 3 with the date of 9.15.0.0.0 (AD 731) (Graham 1967). Probably at the beginning of the eighth century Aguateca became an important focus of ceremonial and administrative activities as the twin capital of the Dos Pilas dynasty. Small test pits excavated in the Main Plaza and the patio of the Palace Group revealed only one floor, built directly on the bedrock. It appears that the epicenter of Aguateca was sparsely occupied before the Late Classic period, and its monumental core was built quickly as Aguateca became a new dynasty seat. Ruler 3 defeated Ceibal in AD 735, and the Dos Pilas–Aguateca dynasty enjoyed its heyday (Houston 1993).

Ruler 4, K'awiil Chan K'inich, continued to expand the dynasty's power, but its fortunes turned abruptly. Ruler 4 may have been defeated by Tamarindito on 9.16.9.15.3 (AD 761). The ruling family and elites abandoned Dos Pilas (Demarest 1997; Palka 1997). The next ruler, Tahn Te' K'inich, stayed at Aguateca, which occupied a more defensible location. Inomata's excavation of stone walls at Aguateca showed that they were built for defense. Whereas similar walls at Dos Pilas were built over ruined elite buildings with stones robbed from these constructions, those at Aguateca in most cases abut existing structures (Demarest et al. 1997), which suggests that they were most likely built during the reign of Tahn Te' K'inich. Some walls blocked the passage of the Causeway and run through patios in elite residential areas. Although many elites remained at Aguateca, their lives had been severely disrupted by the threat of enemy attack. This rapid transformation of Aguateca into a fortified center indicated that the residents were facing intensified warfare

that involved destructive attacks on settlements (Demarest et al. 1997; Inomata 2007).

The end of Aguateca appears to have been abrupt and violent. The pattern of rapid abandonment was first detected in the partial excavation of Structure M8-11, along the Causeway, in 1991 (Figure 1.4). Excavators uncovered numerous reconstructible vessels and other artifacts on the room floors, but comparable patterns were not found in areas outside the epicenter. To better understand the process of abandonment, Inomata decided to excavate extensively two elite residences, Structures M7-35 (House of the Niche) and M8-10 (House of the Scribe), in the same residential area along the Causeway in 1993. The two buildings contained numerous reconstructible vessels and grinding stones, as well as substantial numbers of jade ornaments, carved shells, and musical instruments. The presence of carbon and burned artifacts indicated that the structures were burned at the time of abandonment. The distribution of artifacts appears to reflect the patterns of activity and space use. The center rooms contained a relatively small number of objects and may have been used for meetings and visitor reception. Some of the side rooms were full of large jars, grinding stones, and other artifacts, and appear to have been used for storage and food preparation. Some areas with pigment grinders were probably related to courtly artistic work. These patterns suggest that the floor materials were not deposited as ritual objects at the time of abandonment but represent the assemblages that were owned and used by the original residents. Aguateca was probably attacked by enemies, and its elites fled or were taken away, leaving a substantial part of their possessions in their houses.

The lack of diagnostic Terminal Classic ceramics indicated that Aguateca was abandoned at the end of the Late Classic period. Later investigations of the Aguateca Restoration Project in 2002 and 2003 narrowed it down to around AD 810 (Inomata et al. 2004). The areas outside the epicenter were deserted about the same time but somewhat more gradually (Inomata 2003).

OVERVIEW OF THE PROJECT
Research Strategies

We designed the Aguateca Archaeological Project First Phase to take full advantage of the unique condition of the site, that is, the pattern of rapid abandonment. Rich floor assemblages found in the rapidly abandoned buildings in the epicenter present an extraordinary opportunity to

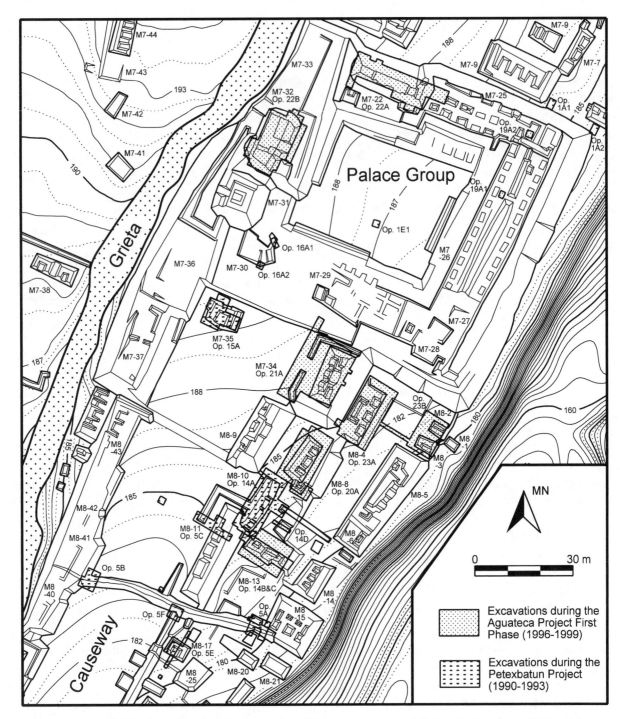

FIGURE 1.4. Map of the Palace Group and the Causeway with the areas excavated during the Petexbatun Regional Archaeological Project and the Aguateca Archaeological Project First Phase.

examine the domestic organization and activity among the elite and the operation of the royal court. For this general purpose, the field work consisted of the following components:

1. Extensive excavations in the elite residential areas along the Causeway (Figure 1.4). Following the excavation of Structures M7-35 and M8-10, we planned

to excavate extensively additional elite residences to expand our data set of floor assemblages. These two buildings were chosen because they did not have large trees growing on them. All other buildings had some trees, but we decided to excavate these potentially disturbed structures to obtain more balanced samples. For this purpose, we completely exposed Structures

M7-34 (House of Metates), M8-4 (House of Mirrors), and M8-8 (House of Axes). We also excavated subfloor levels of Structure M8-10 (House of the Scribe) to examine the presence of burials and its construction sequence. Following the practices in Inomata's dissertation work, we assigned these nicknames to the buildings for easier recognition only, and they are not functional descriptions.

In addition to the elite residences, we proposed to excavate smaller structures, which may have been occupied by lower-status groups or may have served as nonresidential buildings. We hoped to gain an understanding of non-elite members of noble domestic groups and the royal court, as well as a wide range of activities that took place in the elite residential area. We chose Structure M8-13, a medium-sized building, and Structures M8-2 and M8-3, small structures.

Because of our focus on the recovery of floor assemblages at the last occupation level, we did not excavate layers below the floors in most cases. In addition, in 1998 and 1999, a group of squatters, motivated by radical indigenous rights movements after the Peace Accord, illegally occupied parts of the national park. They visited us to demand money and supplies, sometimes threatening to close down our excavations. This charged political atmosphere also discouraged us from excavating burials under the floors.

2. Extensive excavations in the Palace Group (Figure 1.4). The Palace Group was most likely a residential complex of the royal family, and the investigation of this compound was critical for an understanding of the Aguateca royal court. Although previous test pits did not reveal evidence of rapid abandonment of this group, we decided to extensively excavate Structures M7-22 (House of Masks) and M7-32 (House of Bones), possible residential quarters of the royal family. The buildings did not exhibit the pattern of rapid abandonment, but we continued to follow our detailed excavation procedures to record architectural features and processes of abandonment.

3. Test excavations around the Main Plaza (Figures 1.5 and 1.6). We planned test excavations in this area to examine whether it was also rapidly abandoned. Excavations on top of Structure L8-5, a temple pyramid on the eastern side of the Main Plaza, did not reveal patterns of rapid abandonment. In this process Stela 19 was discovered in front of nearby Structure L8-6. Test excavations in the Granada Group, an elite residential area to the west of the Main Plaza, suggested that the area was gradually abandoned. We decided not to conduct extensive excavation in this area.

4. Investigations in the Barranca Escondida (Figure 1.7). The site guards reported looting of new stelae in the Barranca Escondida in the escarpment to the south of the Main Plaza. We decide to conduct an emergency operation in this area to document the monuments and associated deposits.

Methodology

We designed our field methods primarily to recover detailed information on activities and their spatial patterns reflected in dense floor assemblages. Building on the experience of excavating Structures M7-35 and M8-10, we made some modifications to the system of the Petexbatun Project.

In most cases, excavations followed 2-×-2-m grid systems that were aligned to the axis of the buildings. For provenience control, we devised a five-level hierarchical lot system. Each hierarchical level is a subdivision within the higher-level category. An operation refers to the excavation of a mound group, and a suboperation to an individual building. A unit is a basis of horizontal control, usually corresponding to a 2-×-2-m grid. When walls and other architectural features are found, the boundaries of a unit may be modified at a deeper level so that they correspond to such culturally significant divisions. Levels refer to vertical divisions, in most cases corresponding to natural or architectural layers. Level 1 was always used for the top humus layer, Level 2 for the collapse layer, and Level 3 for materials found directly on the last occupation floor. Level 4 and subsequent ones were used for layers below the last floor. Lots are subdivisions within a unit and a level. They may refer to cultural features, such as a niche or a burial. They can also be used for any arbitrary divisions. For example, a 2-×-2-m unit was usually subdivided into four 1-×-1-m lots at the floor level. Thick layers were sometimes subdivided into arbitrary vertical lots. Alphabetical letters were used for suboperations, and numbers for the others. A set of consecutive numbers or alphabetical designations was applied within each division of the higher hierarchical level. In a common way of description, 3A2-1-4 means Lot 4 of Level 1 of Unit 2 of Suboperation A of Operation 3.

In addition, we kept artifact logs by individually numbering artifact bags. We used consecutive numbers, starting with 101 within each suboperation. As a general rule,

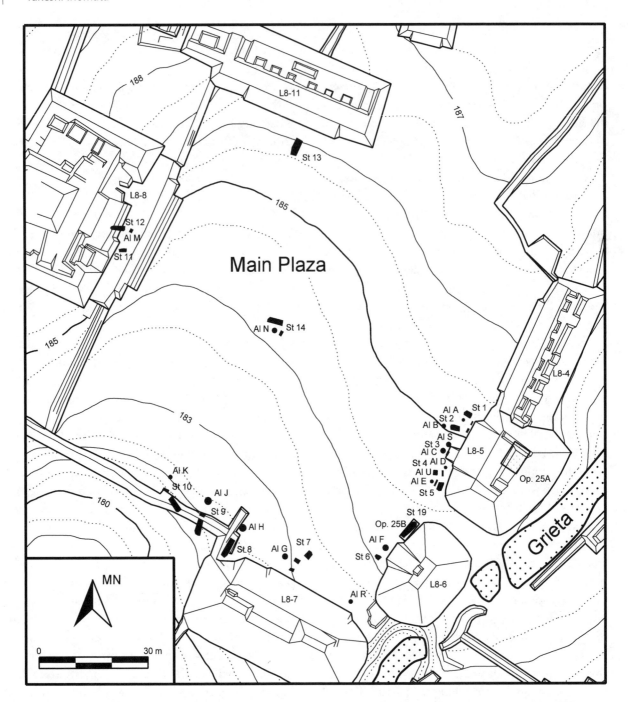

FIGURE 1.5. Map of the Main Plaza with the areas excavated during the Aguateca Archaeological Project First Phase.

we bagged artifacts from each lot by artifact categories, using the following abbreviated artifact codes:

AX	Polished stone axes
BA	Bone artifacts
BS	Black stones (basalt, etc.)
CD	Ceramic disks
DS	Doughnut stones
FG	Figurines
JD	Green stones
LT	Chipped stone artifacts

ML	Malacates (spindle whorls)
MN	Manos
MT	Metates
OA	Other ceramic artifacts
OB	Obsidian artifacts
OM	Other materials
OS	Other stone artifacts
PG	Pigments
PM	Pumice
PR	Pyrite

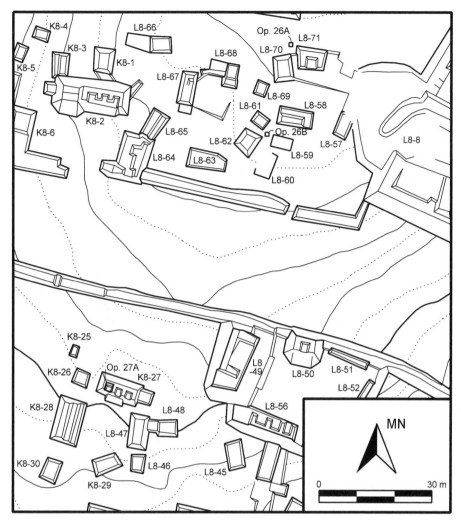

FIGURE 1.6. Map of the Granada Group with the locations of test pits.

PS   Pestles
SA   Shell artifacts
SM   Stone mortars
VS   Ceramic vessels

In the second phase of the project, we combined some of the categories and slightly reduced the number of codes.

When investigators found unique objects, they gave them artifact numbers different from those of other objects of the same category, for better control. In this way, artifact numbers could also serve for provenience control more detailed than that of lots. For example, some small objects were point-plotted with a total station and were given individual artifact numbers. The lot system, artifact codes, and artifact number system were also meant to facilitate the development of a computer database and data input in the field with a data collector.

Excavations proceeded with much care, following natural layers so we could recover delicate objects and record detailed provenience information. In most cases, the general configurations of the buildings with room divisions were recognizable before the excavation. For the excavation of each room, we usually excavated units that covered half the room first, using the unit boundary close to the center axis of the room as a section line. The expansion of excavation areas, however, was adjusted according to the architecture and artifact deposits we found. In most rapidly abandoned structures, there was a relatively small quantity of artifacts on benches, whereas room floors in front of benches were often filled with numerous objects, leaving little room to step. Thus, we usually excavated the rear part of a room first so that the excavators could walk over the unexcavated front part. In most cases, we tried to expose the entire bench surface or the entire room floor so that we could photograph their artifact assemblages together.

A significant portion of collapsed wall materials was found outside the buildings. We usually subdivided these

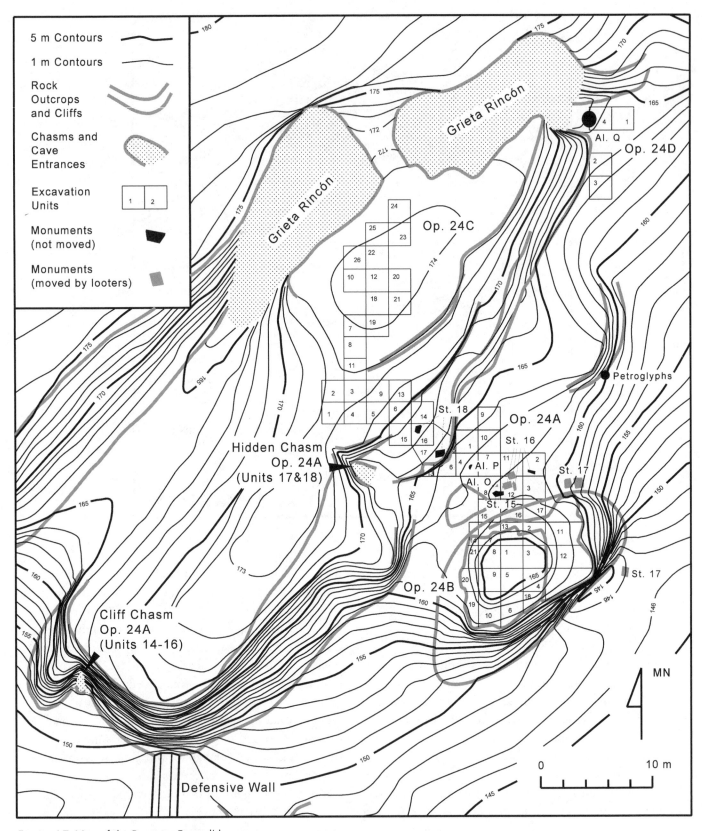

FIGURE 1.7. Map of the Barranca Escondida.

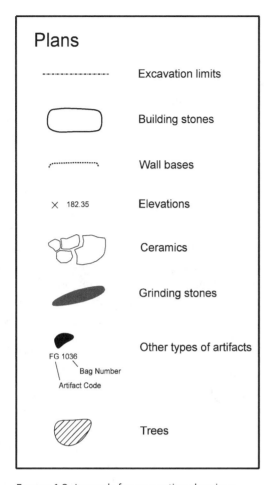

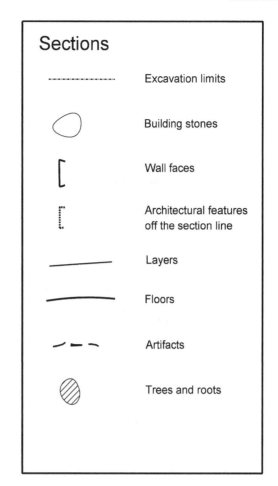

FIGURE 1.8. Legends for excavation drawings.

collapse layers into two vertical lots. Artifacts mixed in the upper part of a collapse layer generally appear to have been placed originally inside the building and to have fallen outside when the structure collapsed. Those in the lower part near the exterior floors were probably stored outside the building.

All the soils, except some areas of collapsed stone roofs with few artifacts, were screened with ¼" or ¹⁄₁₆" mesh. When excavators found artifacts in the humus or collapse layers, they photographed them and point-plotted them with a total station if necessary before they deepened the excavation. In most extensively excavated structures, construction fills contained few artifacts. Thus, we assumed that most artifacts found in collapse layers belonged to the last occupation contexts. At the floor level, most objects were left in situ and were photographed and drawn at ¹⁄₁₀ or ⅓ scales (Figure 1.8). Some small objects, such as obsidian blades, were point-plotted with a total station because their distribution might have been obscured by larger artifacts in conventional drawings. When floors were not well preserved, some artifacts appear to have been mixed in the

surfaces of the floors. In those cases, we scraped the floors to collect these objects. In this manner, we believe that we collected most of the artifacts preserved in the excavated areas that belonged to the last occupation contexts. Still, a small number of artifacts may have fallen through loose fills and may not have been recovered. In addition, excavators collected flotation samples, macrobotanical samples, soil chemistry samples, and soil samples for microdebitage analysis.

During the lab work, we cleaned artifacts, applied conservation treatments if necessary, and analyzed them. When necessary, we assigned catalog numbers to individual artifacts. Catalog numbers are consecutive numbers within each artifact number. For example, Cat. 20A1032-1 refers to Catalog 1 of Artifact 1032 of Suboperation A of Operation 20. Only for bone and shell artifacts were consecutive numbers used within each lot. For cataloging ceramic vessels, we used a different system, which was modified from the system of the Petexbatun Project (Foias 1996). This system uses six-digit numbers independent of operations or artifact numbers. Each reconstructed vessel or each group of sorted sherds received a unique number. This system of vessel numbers was necessary because a single reconstructed vessel typically included fragments from multiple lots and bags.

In the lab analysis, a significant effort was invested in the reconstruction of broken objects because complete or nearly complete artifacts provided unique information that was not available from fragments. In addition, the proveniences of refitted pieces were recorded, which helped clarify the process of abandonment, disturbance, and the original locations of the objects.

Development of the Project Work

The 1996 Season
Inomata, Daniela Triadan, and Erick Ponciano conducted the first season, from June 29 through July 20, 1996, as a small pilot operation to establish the field procedure. The field crew included Shannon Coyston, Bruce Bachand, and Byron Castellanos. We excavated the west room and the western half of the center room of Structure M8-13 as Operation 14B. The presence of dense floor assemblages confirmed our hypothesis that the entire elite residential area along the Causeway was rapidly abandoned. At the beginning of this season, we established a project camp at the site. We also excavated small test pits in Structures M7-25 and M7-26 in the Palace Group as Operation 19A to examine patterns of abandonment.

The 1997 Season
In the second season, from June 5 through July 2, 1997, we expanded the project camp, setting up a water pump and a generator. Ponciano, Estela Pinto, and Julio Antillón continued the excavation of Structure M8-13 while Triadan, Coyston, Ivan Ghezzi, and Stewart Brewer exposed the northern half of Structure M8-8 (House of Axes) as Operation 20A. Bachand excavated subfloor levels of Structure M8-10 (House of the Scribe) as Operation 14A. Yale undergraduate volunteers (Rachel Cane, Helen Chan, Elizabeth Coon, and David Hoffman) also participated. After the field season, lab work was conducted in Salon 3, a warehouse of the Guatemalan Institute of Anthropology and History in Guatemala City.

The 1998 Season
The 1998 season, conducted from February 13 through May 20, was longer than the previous ones. Triadan, Coyston, Markus Eberl, and Jeanette Castellanos excavated the southern half of Structure M8-8 (House of Axes), and Ponciano, Pinto, and Marco Antonio Monroy exposed Structure M7-34 (House of Metates) as Operation 21A. Ramón Puga and Inomata excavated the western half of Structure M7-22 (House of Masks) in the Palace Group as Operation 22A. Richard Terry and Eric Jellen collected and analyzed soil chemistry samples, and Harriet "Rae" Beaubien carried out field conservation treatments of delicate materials.

After the field season, we received a report of looting in the Barranca Escondida, and Inomata, Ponciano, and Kazuo Aoyama returned to the site for salvage operations. We established a project lab in Guatemala City, where Beaubien, Stephanie Hornbeck, and Elizabeth Robertson began systematic conservation work. Aoyama conducted lithic analysis, and Kitty Emery initiated faunal analysis. Terry and Jacob Parnell continued soil analysis at Brigham Young University. An undergraduate volunteer, John Taylor, participated in lab work.

The 1999 Season
We conducted the last field season from March 2 through May 20, 1999. As Ponciano, Pinto, and Monroy completed the excavation of the area in front of Structure M7-34 (House of Metates), they also began the investigation of Structure M7-32 (House of Bones) as Operation 22B. Inomata continued the excavation of Structure M7-22 (House of Masks), and Triadan, Eberl, Jeffrey Buechler, and Jaroslaw Zralka completely exposed Structure M8-4 (House of Mirrors) as Operation 23A. In the Main Plaza, Zralka and Inomata conducted the excavation of Structure L8-5 and Stela 19 as Operation 25, and John Murphy carried out test excavation in the Granada Group as Operations 26 and 27. In addition, a small trench was placed as Operation 14B in the area in front of Structure M8-10. Eberl conducted excavations in the Barranca Escondida as Operation 24 and documented monuments in the area, and Triadan, Castellanos, and Inomata excavated Structures M8-2 and M8-3 as Operation 23B. Terry and Fabian Fernández continued the collection and analysis of soil chemistry samples. In the lab season, Beaubien and Joanne Boyer continued the conservation treatments, Aoyama the lithic analysis, and Emery the faunal studies.

The 2000 through 2003 Seasons
After the completion of the field work, we focused on the lab analysis of excavated materials. Each building contained a large number of artifacts, and treatment of delicate objects and refitting of broken pieces required

substantial effort and time. The lab work involved the analysis of ceramics by Triadan, Inomata, Pinto, Eberl, Monroy, Pablo Rodas, Elisa Jimenez, Diego Guerra, and Yukiko Tonoike; lithic studies by Aoyama; faunal analysis by Emery; the examination of figurines by Triadan; soil analysis by Terry; the analysis of botanical remains by David Lentz; epigraphic studies by Stephen Houston; the study of pyrite artifacts by Marcelo Zamora and Inomata; the analysis of spindle whorls by Inomata and Erin McCracken; the examination of grinding stones and other items by Inomata; and the analysis of human skeletal remains by Lori Wright. Conservation interns who worked under the supervision of Beaubien included Monica Shah and Candis Griggs in 2000, Jill Plitnikas and Sylvia Keochakian in 2001, and Kimberly Machovec-Smith and Margaret Kipling in 2002. Undergraduate volunteers included Catherine Wetmore in 2001 and Helen Raichle in 2002. Ponciano, Pinto, and Anaité Galeotti oversaw administrative matters.

During the field and lab seasons, excavation and lab data were input into computer databases by the field and lab crews. Alfredo Román drew many of the artifacts in the lab, and Rodas digitized field drawings. In the United States, graduate students and undergraduate volunteers, including Tonoike, Bachand, Raichle, A. J. Vonarx, Lindsay Wygant, and Jessica Munson, scanned drawings and photographs and made three-dimensional computer models of buildings and vessels. John Chamblee and Munson digitized the map of Aguateca, and Marijke Stoll digitally traced drawings of monuments.

The Organization and Strategies of the Reports

The reports of the Aguateca Archaeological Project First Phase consist of three volumes. The current volume contains descriptions of excavations and the analysis of ceramics. The second volume (Aoyama 2009) provides the results of lithic analysis by Aoyama. The third volume (Inomata and Triadan in preparation) includes the analysis of other types of artifacts and a synthesis of data.

The section on excavations in the first volume contains general descriptions of architectural features and artifact deposits. Detailed discussions of architectural types, construction techniques, and building materials found at Aguateca are given in previous publications (Inomata 1995, 2007), and we do not repeat them here. Unless otherwise specified, stone blocks used in architecture were made of limestone. Descriptions of artifact depos-

its in this section mainly concern the finds made and recognized during excavation, and in most cases they do not present precise quantified data. The sections on individual artifact types report the more precise results of lab analysis.

The unique finds at Aguateca are so rich that they present the potential for various kinds of research beyond the original theoretical scope of the project. It is thus critical to make these data available to other researchers and the general public. The primary goal of these monographs is to present detailed descriptions of the data obtained through the project, whereas more analytical and theoretical aspects of our work are published in separate articles and other publications (Aoyama 2005, 2007; Emery and Aoyama 2007; Inomata 2001a, 2001c, 2003; Triadan 2007). In these monographs, we try to strike a balance between two distinct strategies. One strategy is to organize our finds into certain classes or types along with the use of quantified data. Such procedures, particularly common in the tradition of American archaeology, help us find "patterns" in complex data sets and facilitate comparisons with data from other sites. However, they reduce the richness of the original finds and limit the possibilities for different ways of viewing the data by other and future researchers. The other strategy is to emphasize detailed descriptions of individual finds. This approach allows us to appreciate the subtleties and nuances of contextual information and provides a basis for open-ended approaches that permit different ways of classification and interpretation by future researchers. In a rough sense, the former strategy tends to help us to address structural properties of domestic groups and the royal court, whereas the latter may facilitate the study of the dynamics, heterogeneity, and fluidity in agents' practices and perceptions. While we search for the best combination of the different approaches, we need to be conscious as well of the economics and efficiency of presentation. Thus, the three volumes are results of certain compromises.

The conclusion and synthesis of these data are presented in the third volume of this monograph series. These volumes constitute the final reports of our research project, but they by no means represent the final words on this data set. Instead, we hope that they provide a step toward richer discussion among researchers and other interested groups on these remarkable episodes of human experience.

EXCAVATION

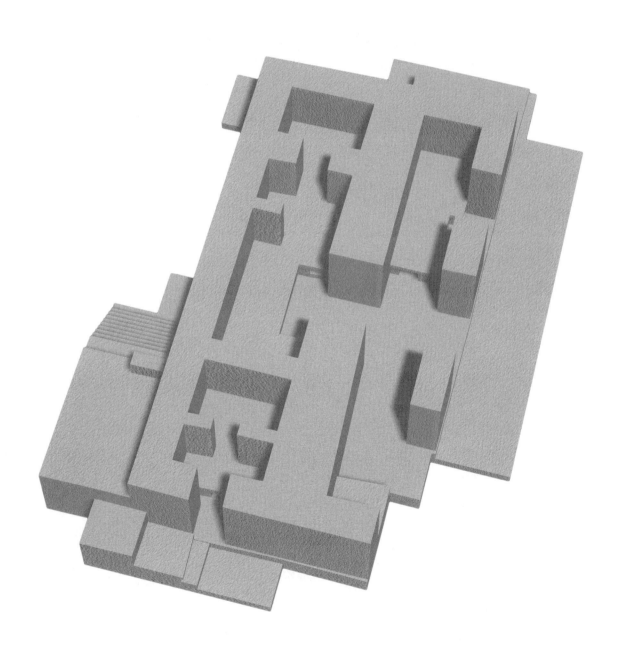

2 | The Palace Group

Takeshi Inomata and Erick Ponciano

THE PALACE GROUP, or Group M7-5, is located at the northern end of the Causeway, and it is the largest complex next to the Main Plaza at the site (see Figure 1.4). Its size, location, and form indicate that it was a residential group for the royal family. A test pit placed near Structure M7-9 behind the Palace Group in 1990 revealed large manos, further supporting the residential function of the complex (Inomata 2007). Moreover, the focus of defense by concentric stone walls appears to have been the Palace Group, which also points to the political and symbolic importance of the compound.

We decided to investigate this group to examine the organization and activity of the royal court and associated symbolism. In 1996 we conducted test excavations in Structures M7-25 and M7-26. Although the test excavations did not reveal evidence of rapid abandonment, we thought that the further investigation of the royal residential complex was critical for our study of the court. We conducted extensive excavations of Structure M7-22 (House of Masks) in 1998 and 1999 and Structure M7-32 (House of Bones) in 1999. The configurations of these buildings are similar to those of other elite dwellings, and they appeared to have been the residential quarters of the royal family. Because many elite residences also served as places for political meetings and audiences, we assumed that these buildings were arenas where the daily lives of the royal family, the politics of the court, and the management of the polity intertwined.

We established a separate grid system for each building. The thick layers of collapsed stone roofs contained few artifacts, and excavators started to screen soils with ¼" mesh when they approached floor levels. When significant deposits of artifacts were encountered, we switched to ¹⁄₁₆" mesh.

STRUCTURES M7-25 AND M7-26 (OPERATION 19A)

To examine the pattern of abandonment in the Palace Group, we placed one test pit each in Structures M7-25 and M7-26 (Figure 1.4). These two buildings were chosen because they appeared to have had relatively shallow collapse layers and it seemed easy to reach the floor level. We did not excavate levels below the floors.

Structure M7-26 (Unit 1)

Unit 1 was a pit 2 1.5 m. Excavators found a grabble floor, or a possible eroded stucco floor, below a relatively small number of collapsed stones. They found few artifacts on the floor.

Structure M7-25 (Unit 2)

Unit 2 consisted of a 2-×-2-m pit placed near the eastern end of Structure M7-25. Excavators reached a grabble floor, or a possible eroded stucco floor, directly below the humus layer. Only a small number of artifacts were found.

Interpretation

The small amount of collapsed stones suggests that Structures M7-25 and M7-26 did not have masonry roofs. Structure M7-26 consisted of rows of columns and entrances to long open halls on both sides of the thick center wall, which probably supported beams for a thatched roof. This open configuration indicates that the building served as a place for meetings, administrative work, or ceremonial activities rather than as a dwelling. The preservation of Structure M7-25 was worse, but it appears to have had a configuration and functions similar to those of Structure M7-26. Although the detection of patterns of rapid abandonment is not easy with small test pits, the small quantity of artifacts points to a gradual process.

Structure M7-26 was later excavated by Juan Antonio Valdés and Mónica Urquizú during the Aguateca Restoration Project First Phase, and the aforementioned interpretations were confirmed (Valdés et al. 1999).

STRUCTURE M7-22 (HOUSE OF MASKS): OPERATION 22A

Before the excavation it was possible to recognize the presence of at least three rooms with respective doorways. In 1998 we excavated the center room and the eastern portion of the building, opening 32 units. Units 33 to 54, excavated in 1999, covered the western part of the structure. The collapse layer contained few artifacts, and we did not screen most soils from this level. Excavators began to screen soils with ¼" mesh when they approached the floors. In most cases the collapse layer was divided into two or three arbitrary levels (Figures 2.1–2.12).

Architecture

Under the humus, excavators reached a thick collapse layer with light yellow soil and limestone blocks, including vault stones and capstones. Vault stone usually measured 60 to 65 cm in length, about 50 cm in width, and 15 cm in height. The capstones had a flat face on one side and a convex face on the other. Collapsed vault stones were often found next to each other, and it appears that the entire roof collapsed at once (Figure 2.13). The wooden lintels had long been lost. The front and back walls had collapsed outward, and the large stones of the vault springs, measuring approximately 80 cm in length, 50 cm in width, and 15 cm in height, had slid outside the building. Their locations give the original height of the vault spring of 1.95 to 2.00 m from the room floor.

The building consisted of five rooms in a single row: the easternmost, east, center, west, and westernmost rooms (Figure 2.14). We call this part the main portion of the building. To the south of the easternmost room, excavators uncovered a small room, the east front room, which was probably added later. The exterior of the main portion of the building was covered with finely cut stones, measuring 20 × 20 to 35 × 35 cm, with little space in between. The Maya builders used homogeneous soft limestone for these blocks. In some places stones were individually shaped into complex forms so they could be fitted without chinking stones (Figure 2.15). In a common construction method of Maya architecture, joints of blocks between different courses were not deliberately broken. These blocks, measuring 15 to 20 cm in depth, served as

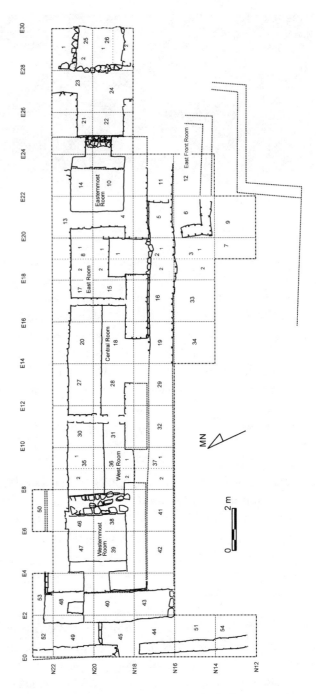

FIGURE 2.1. Plan of Structure M7-22 with the locations of excavation units and lots in Level 1 (humus layer).

veneer stones and did not contribute much to the structural strength of the building. Small pieces of thin stucco were preserved on some areas of the exterior wall.

The interior walls, in contrast, were made of roughly shaped stones of varying sizes with substantial spaces and chinking stones in between (Figure 2.15). Unlike the veneer stones of the exterior, the longer axes of these stones were placed horizontally toward the core of the

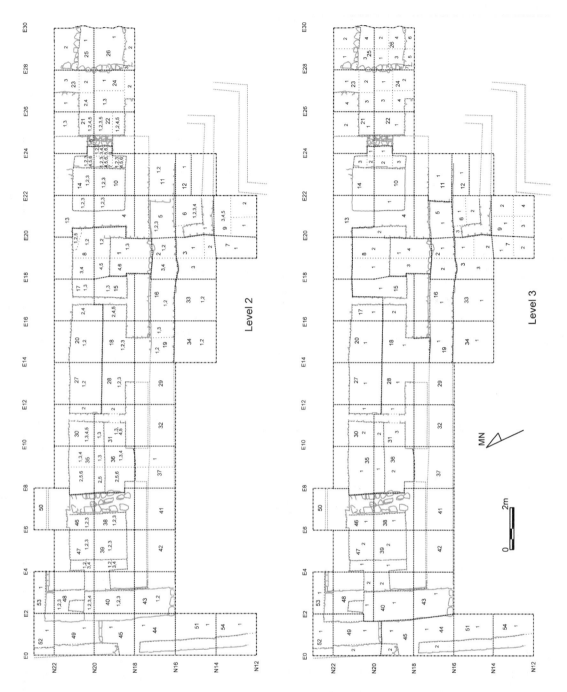

FIGURE 2.2. Lot numbers for Level 2 (wall-fall layer) and Level 3 (on-floor artifacts) in the excavation of Structure M7-22.

walls. They were made of the hard limestone common at Aguateca and were split along the natural horizontal layers. In most rooms, there were no traces of stucco covering the interior walls. The only exception was the easternmost room, as discussed below. The structure appears to have been built rapidly, and the builders focused their limited resources on the exterior of the building to impress visitors and viewers.

Center Room

The center room was larger than the others and had a spacious bench. This chamber was originally connected to the east and west rooms through narrow passages, but the aperture between the central and east rooms was later sealed (Figure 2.16). The room divisions measured roughly 40 cm in thickness. The doorjambs of the openings in the room partitions consisted of cut stones, but

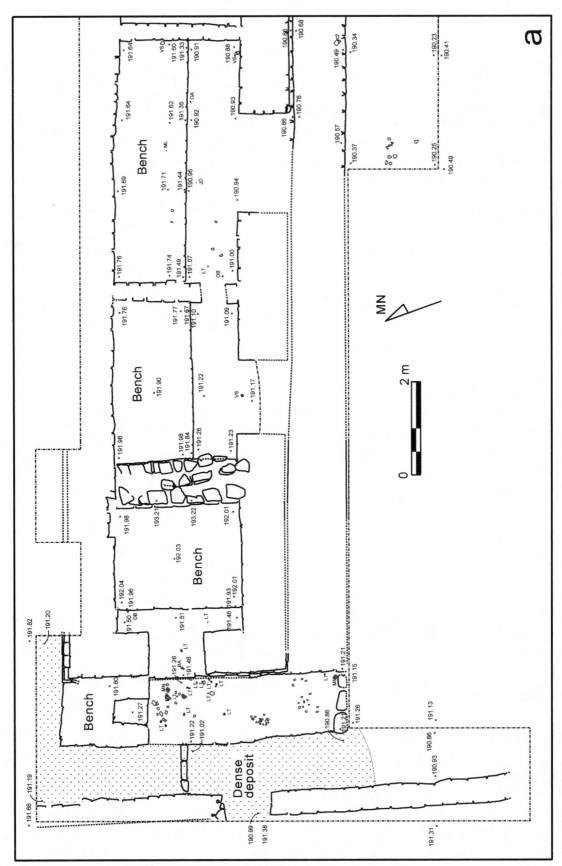

FIGURE 2.3. Distribution of artifacts on the last occupation floor of Structure M7-22. (a) Western half. (b) Eastern half.

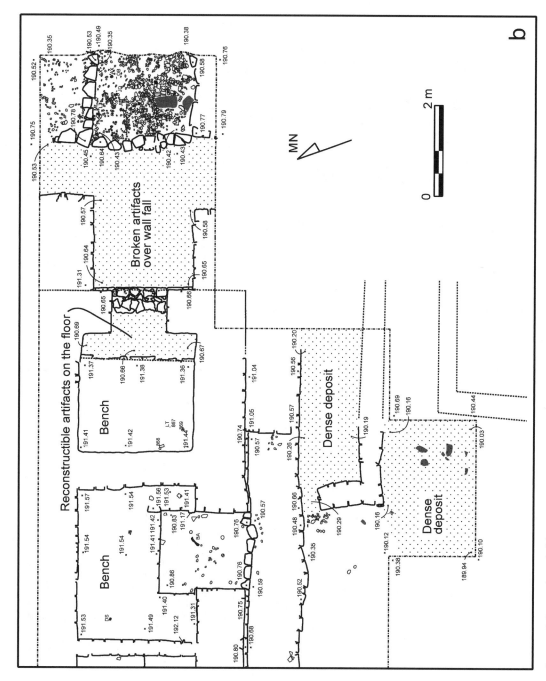

FIGURE 2.3. continued. (b) Eastern half.

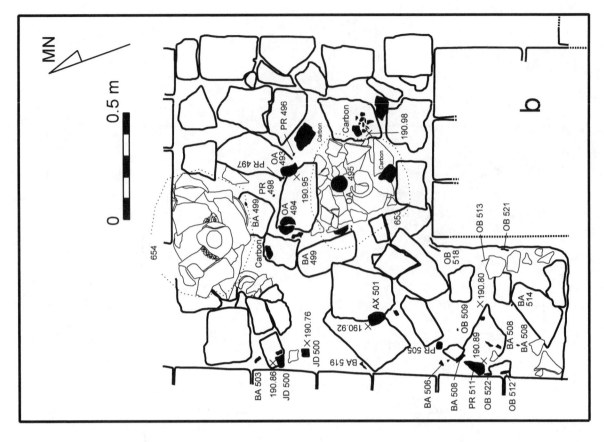

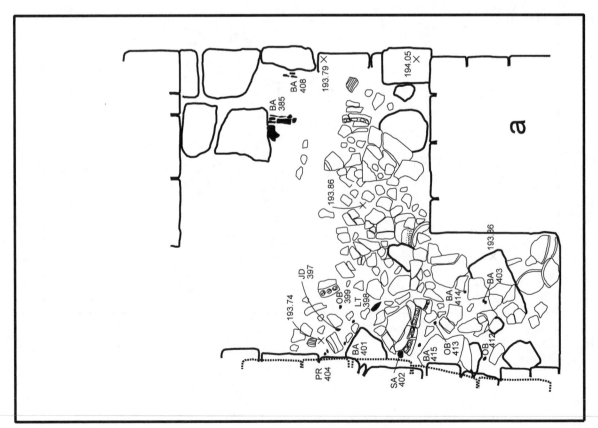

FIGURE 2.4. Reconstructible artifacts found on the room floor in front of the bench of the easternmost room of Structure M7-22. (a) First layer. (b) Second layer. (c) Third layer. (d) Fourth layer.

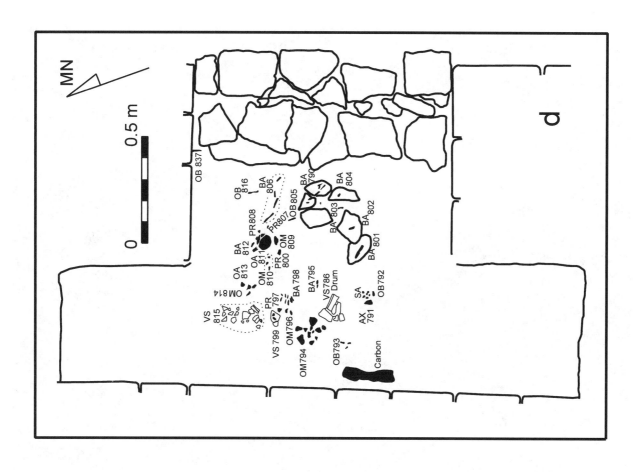

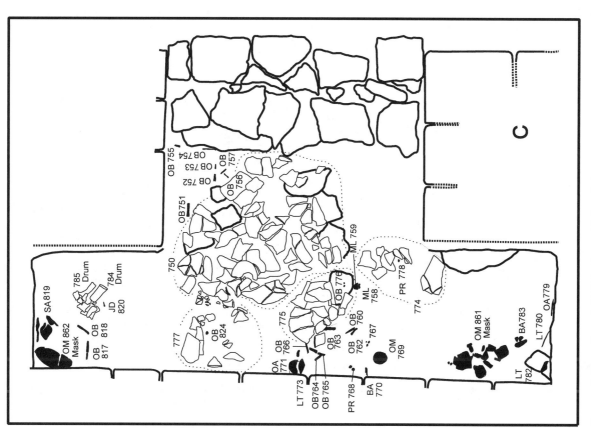

FIGURE 2.4. continued. (c) Third layer. (d) Fourth layer.

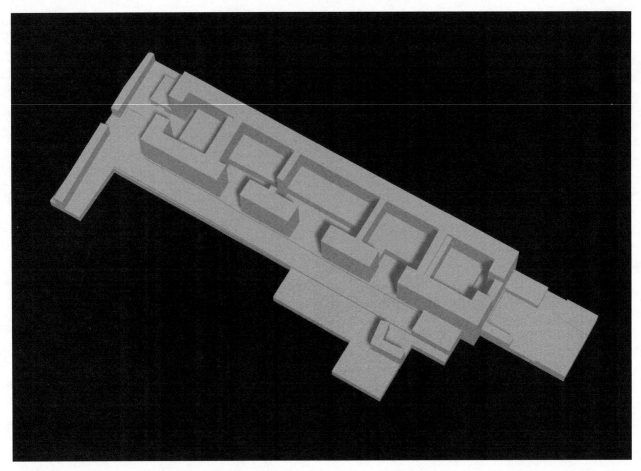

FIGURE 2.5. Reconstruction model of Structure M7-22, viewed from the south. The model shows only the excavated area and does not include the vaulted roof.

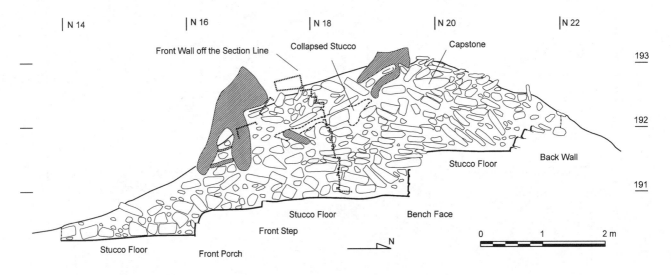

FIGURE 2.6. North-south section of the center room of Structure M7-22 along the E14 line.

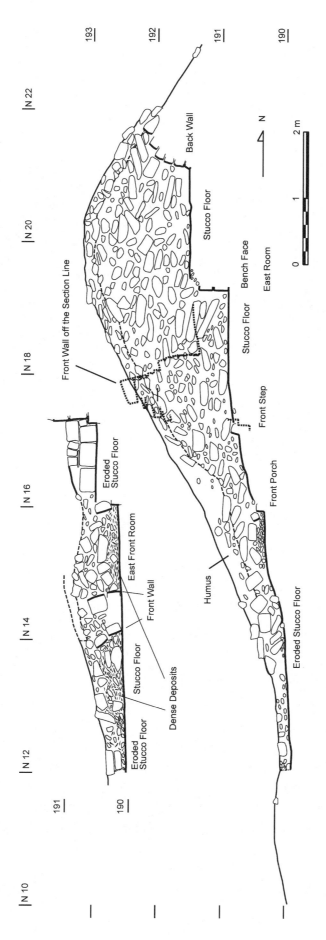

FIGURE 2.7. North-south section of the east room of Structure M7-22 along the E19 line, and north-south section of the east front room along the E22 line.

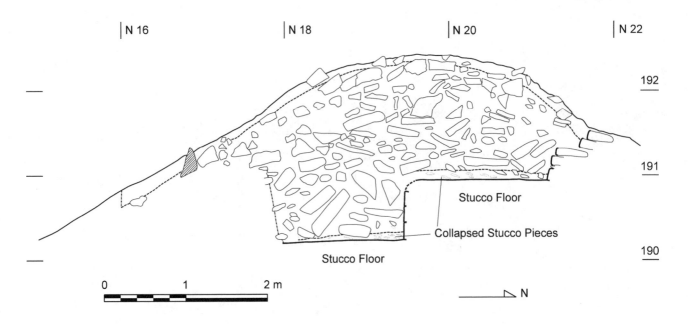

192

191

Stucco Floor

Collapsed Stucco Pieces

190

Stucco Floor

0 1 2 m

N

FIGURE 2.8. North-south section of the west room of Structure M7-22 along the E9 line.

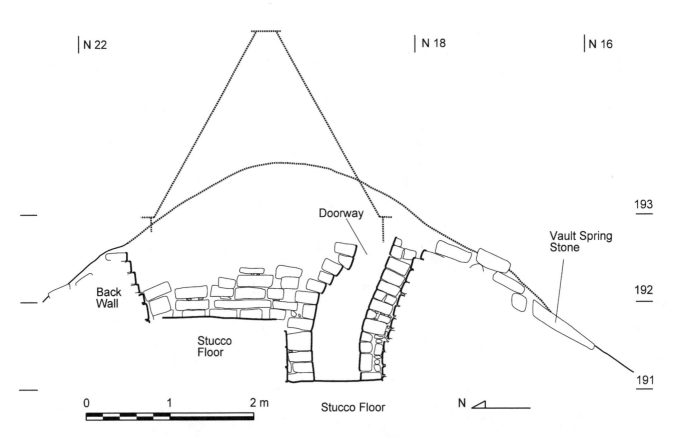

N 22   N 18   N 16

193

Doorway

Vault Spring Stone

192

Back Wall

Stucco Floor

191

Stucco Floor

0 1 2 m

N

FIGURE 2.9. Front view of the east wall of the west room of Structure M7-22 with the reconstruction of the vaulted roof.

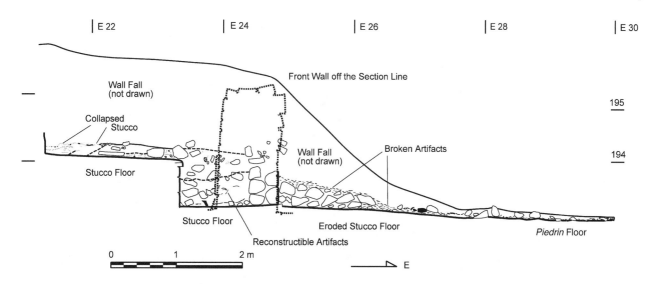

FIGURE 2.10. East-west section of the easternmost room of Structure M7-22 along the N20 line.

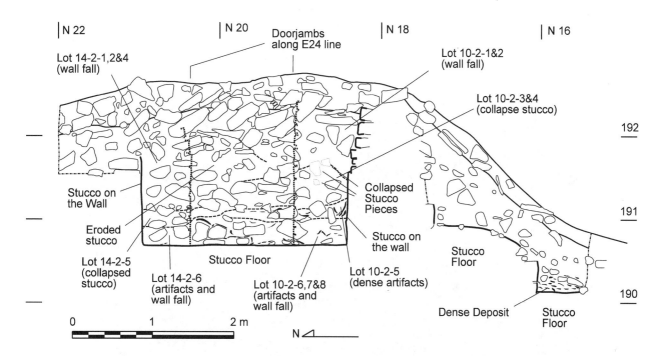

FIGURE 2.11. North-south section of the easternmost room of Structure M7-22 along the E23.7 line.

there were some chinking stones in between. There were small pieces of stucco preserved on these cut blocks, but the rest of the room divisions were apparently not covered with plaster. The bench face was made of finely cut stones, but the top course was missing. The stucco bench floor behind the bench face, however, does not appear to leave enough space for top course blocks. It is possible that the top portion of the bench face was made of stucco, which was damaged when the structure collapsed. The plas-

ter of the bench and room floors was 4 cm thick. These were thickest stucco floors found at Aguateca. There was evidence of a series of thin replastering. The top layer was originally painted red, although it was mostly eroded. We did not find any remains of paint on lower layers.

The room divisions abutted the front and back walls whereas the bench abutted the room partitions. These walls, as well as the bench face, appear to continue under the room floor. As we did not excavate below the floor, the

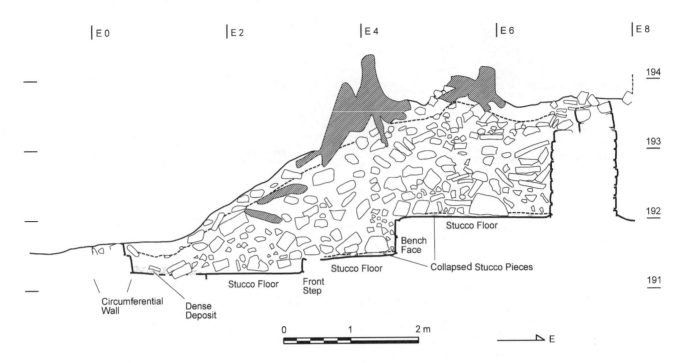

FIGURE 2.12. West-east section of the westernmost room of Structure M7-22 along the N20 line.

FIGURE 2.13. Collapsed vault stones found near the back wall of the east room. Viewed from the east.

FIGURE 2.14. Structure M7-22 after excavation, viewed from the south. *Left:* Western portion. *Right:* Center room and eastern portion.

FIGURE 2.15. Masonry of Structure M7-22. *Left:* Southern doorjamb of the easternmost room with elaborately cut blocks. *Right:* Western doorjamb of the east room. Note the different types of blocks used for the doorjamb and for the interior walls.

FIGURE 2.16. Side walls of the center room of Structure M7-22. *Left:* West wall with an open passage. *Right:* East wall with a closed passage.

FIGURE 2.17. Possible curtain holders found in the east room of Structure M7-22. *Left:* One embedded in the closed passage of the west wall. *Right:* One placed in the east wing of the bench.

precise construction sequence is not clear. It is possible that these architectural elements were built essentially in a single construction episode. The blocks filling the opening in the eastern room division were placed on the stucco floor, indicating that it was closed sometime after the completion of the initial construction.

East Room

The east room was smaller than the center room and had a C-shaped bench. The bench faces consisted of cut stone with a small number of chinking stones. In this regard, the masonry was slightly inferior to that of the other rooms' benches, which did not have chinking. Like the bench of the center room, the top portion of the central bench face appears to have been made of stucco. Whereas the front walls continued below the room floor, the bench faces sat on the floor. It appears that the room was originally equipped with a rectangular bench of the same depth as those of the center and west rooms and which was probably expanded later. The bench face of the eastern wing continued beyond the face of the central portion, but the entire bench extension may have been done at the same time. The plaster of the bench and room floors was 1 cm thick, and there were remains of red paint on the room floor.

A curtain holder made of limestone was embedded in the bench face of the east wing near the front wall (Figure 2.17). The western wing was damaged, and the presence of a curtain holder there was not confirmed. It is not clear whether the west wing was damaged at the time of structure collapse or whether it was intentionally destroyed. Another curtain holder was placed in the blocked opening in the room partition with the center room, but no

corresponding feature was found on the east room division (Figure 2.17). As with the other room partitions, the dividing walls abutted the front and back walls.

West Room

The west room was roughly the same size as the east room and had a rectangular bench of the same depth as that of the center room. The bench face was made of finely cut stones, and blocks in the central part were individually fit into complex shapes. It appears that two groups of stone-cutters were involved, each working on half the bench face and adjusting the difference in the heights of their stone course in the central part. There were remains of thin stucco cover on the bench face.

As mentioned earlier, this room was connected with the center room through a narrow opening in the room division. The walls were constructed in the same way as those of the center and east rooms. The room divisions, consisting of roughly shaped stones, abutted the front and back walls. The front walls continued below the room floor. Although the room-floor stucco went up against the room divisions and the bench faces, these blocks may have sat on the floor fills. There were no traces of stucco on the interior walls, but excavators found some stucco fragments on the bench and the room floor. They probably fell from the ceiling.

Easternmost Room

Unlike the other rooms, the easternmost room had interior walls that were covered with 3-cm-thick stucco. It reached up to the inner corners of the doorjambs of the entrance. It appears that the stucco originally covered the entire height of the walls and the ceiling. At the time of excavation it was preserved up to the height of 0.6 m from the bench surface. A large amount of collapsed stucco pieces covered the bench and the room floor. The stucco was severely burned into gray color. It does not appear to have been painted. The interior walls behind the stucco layer consisted of roughly shaped stones. The room division with the east room was thicker than the other partitions, measuring roughly 0.78 m. In the easternmost room the partition became thinner, making a shelf of 0.18 m depth, at a height of 1.25 m from the bench surface. There were remains of stucco on the wall above the shelf. As discussed below, the room appears to have functioned as a storage space. The thick stucco on the wall was probably for the protection of stored goods, preventing pests from invading the room, rather than for aesthetic purposes.

The wide bench had a face made of finely cut stones with a thin layer of stucco painted in red. The top course of blocks projected forward 4 cm. The bench face covered the stucco on the south and north walls, indicating that it was built after the walls were stuccoed. The plaster of the bench surface and the room floor was 2 to 3 cm thick and was painted in red.

The entrance was sealed with two rows of limestone blocks at some point. The front row consisted of cut stones, but they were not well fit; they were probably reused stones. The back row contained roughly shaped stones. It appears that the entrance was originally completely sealed, but excavators found only two to three courses of blocking stones preserved. The rest of the blocks had collapsed forward. As discussed below, the sealed entrance was probably opened intentionally in ancient times.

In the area in front of the easternmost room, or to the east of it, there were bench-like constructions on both sides of the entrance. Three to four courses of cut stones were preserved, but they were originally higher. They were apparently added after the completion of the front walls of the easternmost room. The exterior floor in front of the doorway was stuccoed, but it was mostly eroded. Farther to the east, excavators exposed the western end of Structure M7-25, which consisted of a rather poorly made low platform one or two courses high. It was not clear whether its floor was plastered. The central part of this platform was added later to the two higher levels on the sides. The poor quality of this platform may point to its late date.

Westernmost Room

The westernmost room had a shape similar to that of the easternmost room, but its interior walls were not covered by stucco. The plaster of the bench surface and the room floor was 1 cm thick and more poorly preserved than that of the easternmost room. As in the case of the easternmost room, its room division with the adjacent chamber had a shelf.

Outside the room, excavators exposed a bench attached to the northern front wall; it was probably added later. Its retaining walls were made of roughly shaped stones. Although the western and northern portions had collapsed, part of a stucco floor was preserved. It had a niche on the southern side, but we did not find its capstone, which may have been removed in ancient times (see the case of Structure M7-32). Alternatively, the capstone may have been made of wood. The bench apparently functioned as outdoor furniture, though it may have been covered by an awning. A small excavation to the north of this bench indicated that there was a narrow leveled floor behind the building.

To the south of the bench along its western wall was a low step made of roughly cut stones. This step and the associated floor were added after the construction of the bench. Part of this step was covered by the floor to the west of the bench and the associated step running east-west. Farther to the west the bench excavators found low, narrow walls made of a few courses of roughly shaped stones. There was an opening between the walls, providing access to the westernmost room.

East Front Room and the Area in Front of the Building

The exterior floor in front of the building appears to have been plastered originally, but it was mostly eroded. To the south of the easternmost room, excavators found a raised terrace two courses high attached to the building wall. It was well built with cut stones, and a portion of its stucco floor was preserved. Its retaining wall sat on the stucco floor in front of the building, indicating that it was added later.

Farther to the south, investigators revealed a small area defined by a low stone wall, which we named the east front room. The southern part of the wall consisted of roughly shaped or naturally shaped stones placed in vertical positions. The western part was made of reused cut stones. Its poor quality may point to its late date.

In the unexcavated area to the south, we could recognize a low stone wall similar to those found to the west of the building. It appears that these walls surrounded the building, although we could not confirm their presence along the front stairway.

Artifact Deposits

Westernmost, West, Center, and East Rooms

Excavators recovered few artifacts in the westernmost, west, center, and east rooms. It appears that the residents cleaned the rooms completely when they abandoned the buildings. A small number of fragmentary artifacts found in the west, center, and east rooms were not directly on the floors but on a layer of calcareous white soil, which measured roughly 2 to 5 cm in thickness. At Cerros and Yaxuna, investigators detected layers of white marl deposited in ritually terminated buildings (Freidel and Robertson 1986; Freidel et al. 1998). It is possible that the white layer in Structure M7-22 was intentionally deposited during the termination ritual.

Easternmost Room

Only the easternmost room contained a large number of reconstructible objects. The artifacts found inside and in front of the room included two carved long bones with hieroglyphic texts (Cat. BA 22A332-2, 22A524-8), a large conch shell incised with a glyphic text (Cat. SA 22A819-1), three probable bone bloodletters (Cat. BA 22A790-109, 22A790-111, 22A803-92), three small ceramic drums (WDR 22A-1, Cat. 310264; WDR 22A-2, Cat. 310265; WDR 22A-3, Cat. 310266), various greenstone ornaments, nine round pyrite mosaic mirrors, two ceramic laminate masks (Cat. OM 22A861-1, 22A862-1), and at least 17 ceramic vessels of Late Classic types. Found among the greenstone ornaments was a fragment of a celt-shaped plaque with a perforation at the narrower end (Cat. JD 22A500-1). It was probably part of the royal attire, hung at the belt, as shown in images of rulers on stelae.

The fact that the entrance to the room was sealed indicates that these items were intentionally stored in this room by the departing royal family. Many objects were on the floor in front of the bench, but some were mixed in with the collapsed stones and may have originally been stored in higher locations, such as the bench surface and rafters (Figure 2.18). The bench surface was devoid of objects when it was excavated. It is not clear whether a large part of the bench surface was kept clean or whether perishable materials were placed there. Numerous fragments of ceramics and other objects found outside the room in front of the doorway were stratigraphically sandwiched between the rubble of the entrance seal and a layer of roof fall. The exterior floor below the collapsed stones was almost clean of artifacts (Figure 2.19). This pattern suggests that most of the objects, including those found in front of the room, were originally stored inside the room behind the completely sealed doorway.

Heavy traces of fire found in the room suggest that the building was burned down after the sealed entrance was opened. If the room had been completely sealed when the fire started, its interior would have been protected from the fire. The results of lab analysis lend further support to this interpretation. Five greenstone fragments were refitted into a pendant with an image of the face of the Maize God (Cat. 22A458-1). Two pieces were found inside the room (Lot 10-2-4) whereas three fragments were recovered outside the room 3–4 m east of the doorway (Lots 23-3-3, 24-3-2, and 24-3-3). This distribution pattern could not have resulted from the collapse of the building during the fire. The enemies who invaded Aguateca probably opened this room and intentionally broke some objects before they set the building on fire. They may have removed some stored items. It is possible that the invaders fed fuel into the room unless the room originally contained a large quantity of flammable materials.

Termination Ritual Deposits

A large number of broken objects were found in the east front room and in the area to the south of it, as well as in the area to the west of the building (Figure 2.20). The test pit excavated in 1990 in front of the west room revealed a similar dense deposit. These deposits measured to 30 cm in thickness and contained ceramic sherds consisting largely of common Late Classic types, fragments of grinding stones, chipped stone tools, shell ornaments, greenstone ornaments, pieces of pyrite mosaic mirrors, and fragments of alabaster vessels with the Aguateca emblem glyph and other hieroglyphic incisions. Unlike the ceramic fragments found in the rapidly abandoned elite residences along the Causeway, these sherds were mostly unreconstructible. Soils mixed in these deposits were black and ashy, and many artifacts exhibited clear traces of burning. It is probable that these objects represent termination ritual deposits dumped by the enemies when they ritually burned and destroyed the buildings, although we do not deny the possibility that the departing royal family or the remaining elites left some refuse in these areas.

STRUCTURE M7-32 (HOUSE OF BONES): OPERATION 22B

Before the excavation the center wall and its vault strings were visible on the surface. In 1999 we excavated 56 units, or an area 220 m², covering almost the entire building (Figures 2.21–2.27).

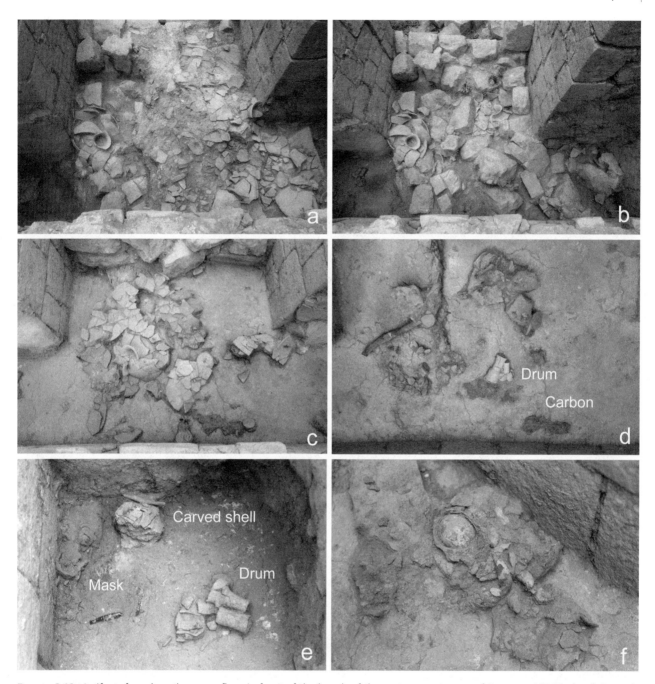

FIGURE 2.18. Artifacts found on the room floor in front of the bench of the easternmost room of Structure M7-22. (a–d) Central part, viewed from the west. (a) First layer (southern half) and second layer (northern half). (b) Second layer. (c) Third layer. (d) Fourth layer. (e) Mask and other artifacts in the northern corner, viewed from the south. (f) Mask in the southwestern corner, viewed from the northeast.

Architecture

Structure M7-32 was even more elaborately built than Structure M7-22. Under the humus, excavators revealed a thick collapse layer with light yellow soil mixed with vault stones and capstones. Lintels above the doorways were apparently made of wood, but all their traces had been lost. The building consisted of two rows of rooms divided by thick center walls (Figure 2.28). The open-hallway-like front room filled the front part of the building, facing forward with three doorways. The center walls were divided by the central doorway, which led to the center room in the back, probably a throne room. The center room led to the north room, which did not have direct entrances from the outside. The south room was separated from the center room and had its own doorway on the south side.

FIGURE 2.19. Area in front of the easternmost room of Structure M7-22, viewed from the east. *Left:* After the wall fall of the building was removed, exposing artifacts deposited over the collapsed stones that had blocked the doorway. *Right:* After the artifacts and collapsed stones were removed.

FIGURE 2.20. Dense deposits possibly associated with termination rituals. *Left:* Area in front of the east front room, viewed from the south. *Right:* East front room, viewed from the west.

The center walls were the best-preserved parts of the building, and their height to the vault spring was 2.4 m from the room floor. With a thickness of 1.1 m, they were more substantial than the front walls (1.0 m thick) and the back wall (0.9 m thick). As in Structure M7-22, the exterior walls were made of finely cut stones without any chinking, but the interior walls consisted of roughly cut stones with chinking stones. The exterior walls appear to have been covered by thin stucco. A cornice made of one course of large cornice stones went around the entire structure. Although most upper portions of the exte-

rior walls had collapsed, the cornice was preserved in the southwestern part of the building.

All the bench and room floors were stuccoed, and small traces of red paint were preserved in some parts.

Center Room

The center room possessed a large C-shaped bench, measuring 0.71 m in height. The bench face was made of finely cut blocks. There was a niche under each wing, but the northern one was destroyed at the time of abandonment. Unlike niches in many other buildings and those in the

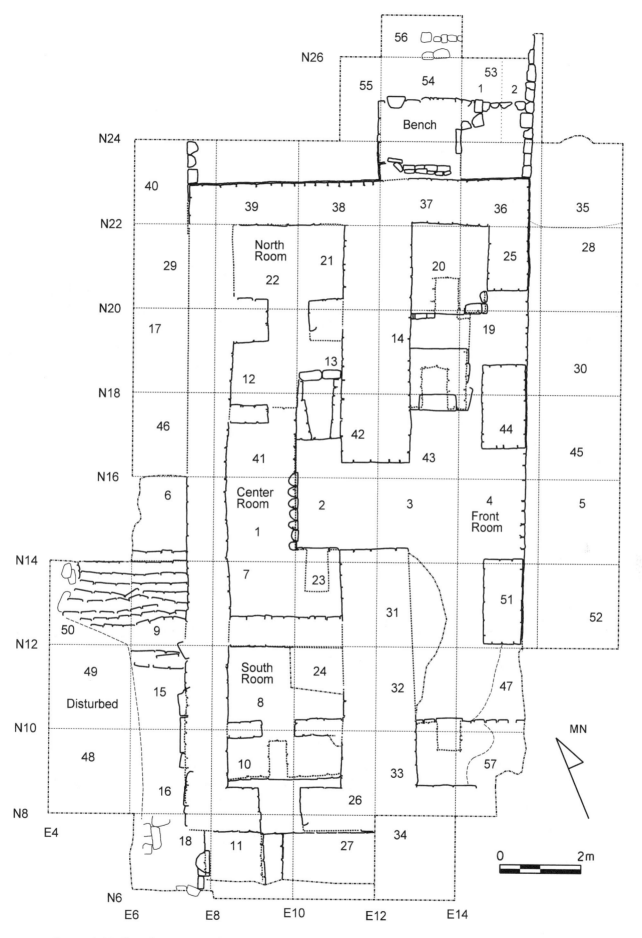

FIGURE 2.21. Plan of Structure M7-32 with the locations of excavation units and lots in Level 1 (humus layer).

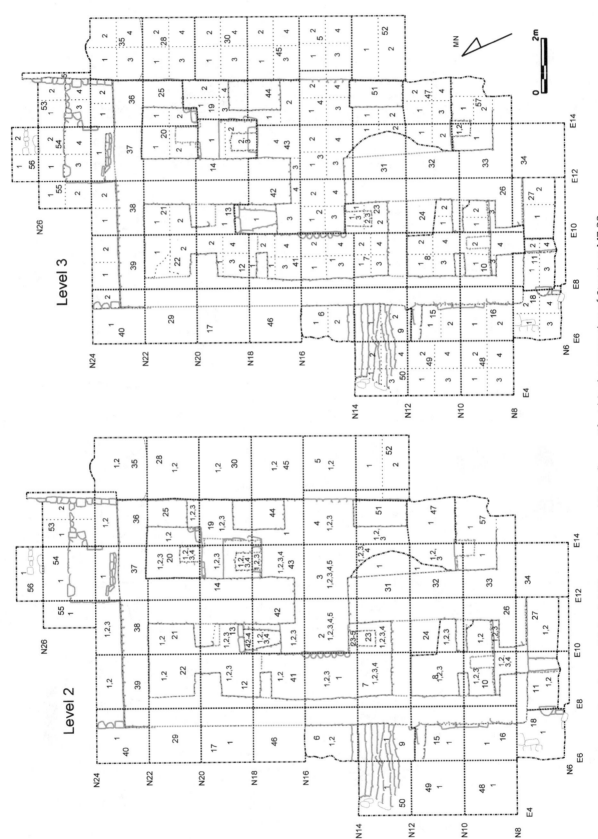

Figure 2.22. Lot numbers for Level 2 (wall-fall layer) and Level 3 (on-floor artifacts) in the excavation of Structure M7-32.

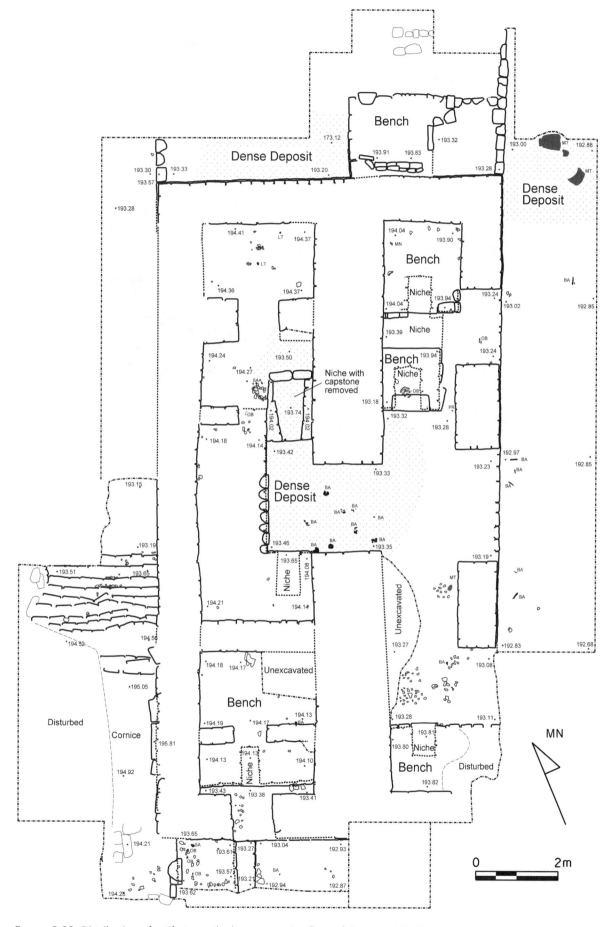

FIGURE 2.23. Distribution of artifacts on the last occupation floor of Structure M7-32.

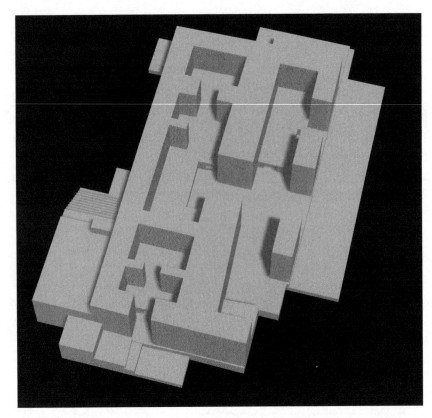

FIGURE 2.24. Reconstruction model of Structure M7-32, viewed from the south. The model shows only the excavated area and does not include the vaulted roof.

front and south rooms of this structure, their bases were higher than the room floor. On the interior parts of the center walls near the doorways, at heights of 0.6 and 1.0 m, there were curtain or cord holders made of limestone (Figure 2.29). There was a thin wall in the northwestern part of the center room, dividing the chamber into two areas. Along the northern face of this wall, a line of cut stones was visible on the bench floor. This line of stones connected with the north-south line of stones along the bench face that was exposed after the capstone of the northern niche was removed. This indicates that the center room originally had a smaller bench of a rectangular or L-shape. At some point during its occupation, a niche, or niches, was added, and the bench was expanded all the way into the north room.

North and South Rooms

The north room was a small room divided from the center room by thick walls. The floor of the room made a single continuous surface with the bench surface of the center room.

A large, 0.71-m-high bench occupied a large portion of the south room. A niche under the bench faced the south-

ern doorway. The room floor continued into the niche. The room was divided into front and back portions by thin walls. Investigators left the northeastern corner of the room unexcavated to support the leaning walls.

Front Room

The front room had two benches, one in the northern part and one in the southern part. The southern bench, measuring 0.66 m in height, was relatively small, and there was a niche on its northern face. The larger northern bench, measuring 0.69 m in height, had a niche on the southern side. In addition, there was a niche on the eastern side. This niche turned north under the bench, making a T-shape. It appears that the bench was originally smaller with a niche facing south. As builders expanded it, they created a niche along the southern face of the original bench. Unlike the niches in the center room, the bases of the front room niches were at the same level as the room floor.

The southeastern corner of the front wall had completely collapsed forward. The southern portion of the center wall was leaning, and part of the collapsed layer along the wall was left unexcavated.

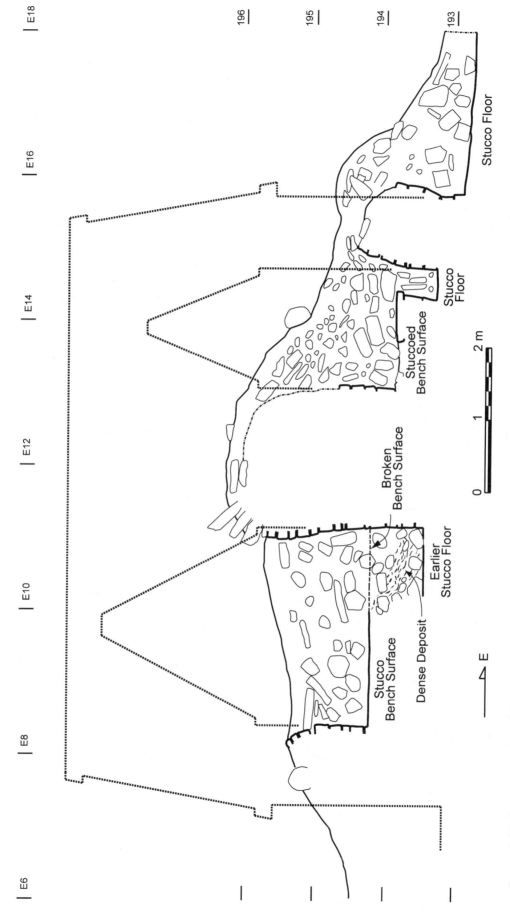

FIGURE 2.25. East-west section of the center and front rooms of Structure M7-32 along the N18 line, the section below the broken bench surface along the N19 line, and the reconstruction of the vaulted roof.

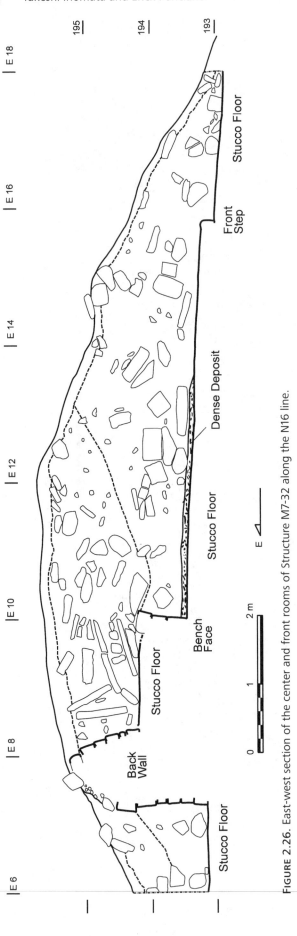

FIGURE 2.26. East-west section of the center and front rooms of Structure M7-32 along the N16 line.

Northern Side

Excavators revealed an outdoor bench attached to the northern wall of the building (Figure 2.30). The bench had a backrest made of flat blocks. Its position indicates that the occupants of the bench were meant to face north.

To the north of the bench there was a line of stones running east to west. Although it was not well preserved, it may be the remains of a circumferential wall similar to those of Structure M7-22.

Western and Southern Sides

In the southern part behind the structure was a 1.8-m-high platform built against the back wall of the building. A stairway with nine steps on its northern side provided access. The stairway was made of finely cut stones. A narrow wall was placed on top of the platform parallel to the stairway. The function of this wall is not clear, but it may have defined a room-like area. The western part of the platform was badly eroded, and its original shape was not clear. The platform apparently faced west toward the Grieta and the area beyond it, but its function remains unclear.

A small excavation south of the building revealed a raised area in front of the west front wall of the south room. Although its entire configuration is not clear, it may have served as an outdoor bench.

Artifact Deposits

Dense deposits comparable to those around Structure M7-22 were found in two areas: the central room extending into the front room, and the northern side of the building west of the outdoor bench. The appearance and the contents of the deposits were similar to those of Structure M7-22, and they were most likely termination ritual deposits.

In the center room the deposit covered the entire room floor in front of the bench and in the doorway in the center walls, as well as in a small area in the front room (Figure 2.31). In the front room the deposits continued into the areas south of the north bench and north of the south bench with a decreasing density. They measured 12 to 15 cm in thickness. As in the Structure M7-22 deposits, artifacts were mixed with black, ashy soils, and traces of burning were visible on many objects. A large portion of the bench surface was clean of artifacts. The capstone of the northern niche, however, was deliberately removed and the bench surface next to it was destroyed (Figure 2.32). Dense deposits of fragmentary objects filled these damaged areas, indicating that the destruction was

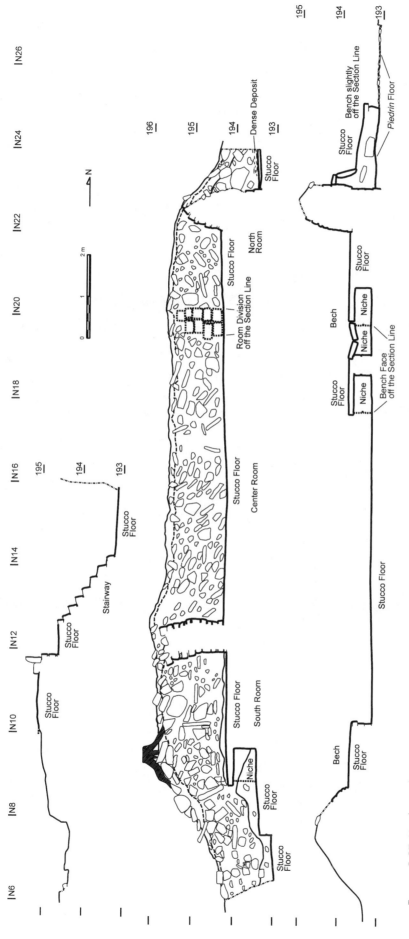

Figure 2.27. North-south sections of Structure M7-32. *Top:* Elevation of the north platform along the E7 line. *Middle:* Section of the north, center, and south rooms along the E9.5 line. *Bottom:* Elevation of the exterior bench and front room along E14 line.

FIGURE 2.28. General views of Structure M7-32 after excavation. *Left:* View from the east. *Right:* View from the west.

FIGURE 2.29. Possible curtain holders on the north face of the southern center wall of the center room, Structure M7-32.

done at the time of abandonment before the deposition of the termination ritual materials and the collapse of the building.

The deposit on the northern side was similar to that in the center room (Figure 2.33). In the area in front of the outdoor bench up to the line of stones there was also a similar artifact deposit, though in a somewhat lower density. Another deposit of moderate density was found on the exterior floor east of the northeastern corner of the building.

In the south room a small number of fragmentary ar-

tifacts were found on the bench. In front of the bench and in the area in front of the south room was a deposit of moderate density.

Interesting finds in these deposits include broken human bones of at least two individuals. According to Lori Wright, they include fragments of crania, mandibles, a scapula, a humerus, an ulna, a radius, fibulae, tibiae, and metatarsi. They were scattered on the floor in front of the central bench, in the broken floor of the bench, in the front room, and on the exterior floors north and south of the building, and some were burned. Although the nature

FIGURE 2.30. The exterior bench built against the northern wall of Structure M7-32. Viewed from the northeast.

FIGURE 2.31. Dense deposit found in front of the bench of the center room of Structure M7-32.

FIGURE 2.32. The northern niche of the bench of the center room of Structure M7-32. Its capstone was removed in antiquity. The bench surface next to it was also intentionally broken. Note that broken artifacts were densely deposited in those damaged parts of the bench.

FIGURE 2.33. Dense deposit along the northern exterior wall of Structure M7-32.

of the deposits associated with the south room is not clear, the presence of human bones appears to point to their deposition during termination rituals.

INTERPRETATION

Functions

The Palace Group was probably built rapidly during the Late Classic period. Later excavation by the Aguateca Project Second Phase showed that the platform of Structure M7-22 was built in one construction episode directly over the bedrock. Inomata's earlier excavation in 1991 in the patio of the Palace Group also found only one floor. The use of finely cut stones on the exteriors and coarser blocks on the interiors of these buildings probably implies that they were built rather hastily.

In Structure M7-22 the central room was larger than other rooms. It is probable that the ruler or his close relative used this room to give audience to his subjects and to receive emissaries from other centers. The west room that connected with the central room may have been a more private space for the ruler or the royal family member who used the central room. The east room may have had comparable functions, but after its access to the central room was closed, it may have been used by other members of the royal family. Likewise, in Structure M7-32 the large central room may have been a throne room of the ruler, and the north room that connected with the central room may have been his private chamber. The south room, with its separate entrance, may have been used by other royal personages. These patterns of space use are similar to those found in rapidly abandoned elite residences (Structures M7-35, M8-4, M8-8, and M8-10). Soil chemistry data from Structure M7-22 also appear consistent with this interpretation (Inomata et al. 2001).

A potential difference between the buildings of the Palace Group and the rapidly abandoned elite residences at Aguateca is the location of food preparation. All the excavated elite residences along the Causeway contained large storage jars and grinding stones, suggesting that food was stored and prepared in the same structures (Triadan 2000). In the case of the Palace Group, we suspect that a possible kitchen facility was located in a nearby structure to the north. The phosphate concentrations inside Structures M7-22 and M7-32 do not vary significantly, which may be due to the lack of food preparation activities in these buildings. This appears to have been a common arrangement for royal palaces at other Maya sites (Inomata et al. 2001).

The Palace Group also functioned as a theatrical space. The central room of Structure M7-22 is located along the axis of the Causeway rather than along the central axis of the Palace Group, sacrificing the Maya obsession with symmetry (Inomata 2001a; Inomata et al. 2001). It is probable that a person sitting on the bench of the central room of Structure M7-22 would have been visible not only to the people standing in the plaza but also to those occupying the northern part of the Causeway.

The elaborate construction of Structure M7-32 suggests that its central room was the main throne room of the ruler. The occupants of Structure M7-22 are more difficult to identify, but it is probable that the ruler used both structures to control his visibility, depending on the nature of his political and ceremonial actions.

The two outdoor benches attached to Structures M7-22 and M7-32 point to a spatial arrangement geared toward even more explicit theatrical performance. In front of these benches was Structure M7-33, a low platform without clear evidence of superstructures. Structure M7-33 may have been an open platform used for dancing, which could have been seen by individuals sitting on the outdoor benches, as well as those occupying the plaza. Later excavations by the Aguateca Restoration Project Second Phase revealed that the front stairway of Structure M7-32 was expanded to the corner with the platform of Structure M7-22. This wide stairway provided access to this possible dancing platform. At Copán, a similar low platform, Structure 10L-25, is also interpreted as a dancing stage (Fash et al. 1992).

Circumferential Walls

The nature of the walls surrounding Structures M7-22 and M7-32 is not well understood. They were roughly 0.5 to 0.6 m wide and may have originally measured around 0.6 m in height. They were made of roughly shaped blocks and possibly reused cut stones. They may have continued in front of the buildings along the edge of the front stairways, although their presence was not confirmed during the excavation of these parts during the Aguateca Restoration Project Second Phase. These walls are probably comparable to those around Structure M7-34 (House of Metates) and around Structure M8-37, which was excavated by Mónica Urquizú and Juan Antonio Valdés during the Aguateca Restoration Project First Phase (Valdés et al. 1999). In the case of Structure M8-37, the central entrance between the walls was substantially narrower than the width of the stairway, indicating that the addition of these walls changed the accessibility of the building. The use of used cut stones in these walls also points to their late date.

It is possible that these walls were built for defensive purposes toward the end of the Late Classic period, along with other defensive walls, although we should not dismiss other interpretations. Excavations during the Aguateca Restoration Project Second Phase showed that the blocks of the stairway of Structure M7-22 were removed in ancient times. They may have been used for the construction of these walls and other defensive features. It is not clear whether the royal family continued to live in the Palace Group after the construction of the walls.

Abandonment

The royal family that occupied this complex probably evacuated the center before the final attack by enemies. They removed most possessions from the rooms and stored some of them in the sealed easternmost room of Structure M7-22. The storage of important items there suggests that the royal family was hoping to come back to Aguateca.

The invading enemies are probably responsible for the opening of the sealed storage room, the destruction of the central bench of Structure M7-32, and the burning of the two structures. The mutilation of the central bench reflects the symbolic importance of this throne and the building. Similar examples of destroyed thrones include Throne 1 of Piedras Negras and the hieroglyphic bench of the Murciélago Palace of Dos Pilas (Demarest et al. 2003).

In addition, the deposition of termination ritual materials represents a unique treatment of the symbolically and politically charged complex. Later excavations during the Aguateca Archaeological Project Second Phase revealed similar deposits around Structures L8-6 and L8-7, temples in the Main Plaza associated with last ruler of Aguateca, but comparable deposits were not found in elite residences along the Causeway.

We should also note a unique characteristic of the termination ritual deposits in the Aguateca Palace Group. Robin Robertson (1983:112) and Debra Walker (1998) reported that termination ritual deposits at Cerros contained large ceramic fragments, many of which can be fitted together. This pattern suggested to them that complete vessels were used during rituals and were broken at the end of rites. Most sherds from the dense deposits of Structure M7-22, however, could not be refitted and appear to have been brought from other locations in the form of already broken materials. A small portion of sherds found in and around Structure M7-32 appear to be reconstructible, but a substantial quantity of them are not. An intriguing piece of evidence is a ceramic whistle refitted by Triadan. One section came from a deposit in the southern part of the front room of Structure M7-32 (22B51-2-3, Cat. 484-1), and another from the north room of the rapidly abandoned elite residence of Structure M8-4 (23A43-3-5, Cat. 1653-1). Although the data are inconclusive, some materials in termination ritual deposits may have been taken from the nearby elite residential area.

chapter 3

The Elite Residential Area

Takeshi Inomata, Daniela Triadan, and Erick Ponciano

T HE AREA ALONG the Causeway to the south of the Palace Group was an elite residential zone where previous excavations during the Petexbatun Project revealed patterns of rapid abandonment. We extensively excavated probable large, multiroom buildings, Structures M7-34 (House of Metates), M8-4 (House of Mirrors), and M8-8 (House of Axes). We also exposed a medium-sized building, Structure M8-13, and smaller buildings, Structures M8-2 and M8-3 (Figure 1.4). The objectives of these excavations were to test the hypothesis on rapid abandonment and to examine household organization and domestic activities reflected in artifact-rich floor assemblages. The operations constituted the most important focus of the project. In addition, we excavated subfloor levels in Structure M8-10 (House of the Scribe), which was previously excavated during the Petexbatun Project. Through this deeper excavation, we planned to examine its construction sequence and the presence of burials. We also placed a small trench over Structure M8-12.

STRUCTURE M8-4 (HOUSE OF MIRRORS): OPERATION 23A

In 1993 we excavated 51 units, covering an area 204 m² and exposing the entire building (Figures 3.1–3.8). In addition, we excavated a 1-×-10-m trench with five units in the patio in front of the building. The easternmost unit of the trench was excavated as Operation 23B, but its findings are discussed here (Figure 3.4). The configuration of the building—three main rooms—was recognizable before the excavation, but the rear portion of the building was obscured by a thick deposit of collapsed stones from the platform of Structure M7-34 (House of Metates). Its location next to the Palace Group pointed to the residents' high status. The remaining portion of its walls, however, appeared lower than those of Structure M8-8 (House of Axes) and Structure M8-10 (House of the Scribe). We

hoped that a full excavation would clarify the nature of this building. We extended the grid system established originally for Structure M8-8, which was later shared for the excavation of Structures M8-2 and M8-3.

Architecture

The three main rooms were named the north, center, and south rooms (Figures 3.1 and 3.8). Excavators also found an area defined by low lines of stones on the northern side of the structure, which we called the north addition. The back wall measured 40 cm in width whereas the side walls were more substantial with a width of 60 cm. Those walls were made of roughly shaped stones with the common use of chinking stones, and their lower quality in comparison with those of Structures M8-8 and M8-10 was notable. The room divisions were roughly 40 cm wide and consisted mostly of vertically placed slabs. The original height of the masonry portions of the back and side walls was probably 2 to 2.5 m, and they appear to have supported beams directly. The masonry parts of the room divisions probably measured around 80 cm in height from the bench surface.

The center room was slightly wider than the side rooms, but the three rooms were equipped with benches of the same depth. The front faces of the three benches formed a continuous line, which appears to have been constructed before the room divisions were placed. The benches measured roughly 50 cm in height. Like the back and side walls, the bench faces were made of somewhat coarsely cut blocks and did not have niches. The bench surfaces and floors of the main rooms were covered by thin stucco.

In front of the benches was a small step leading to the front areas of the rooms. Narrow walls made of vertically placed slabs were built over this step, leaving the central parts open for access. This configuration of front

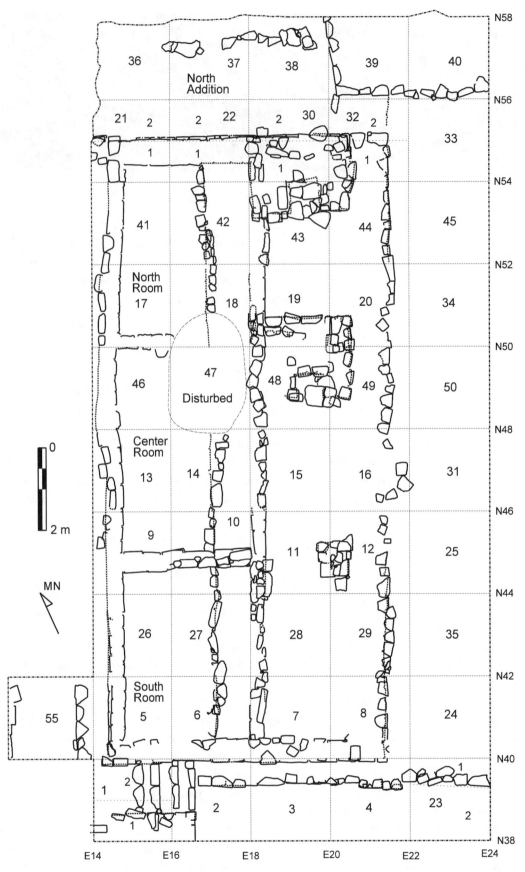

FIGURE 3.1. Plan of Structure M8-4 with the locations of excavation units and lots in Level 1 (humus layer).

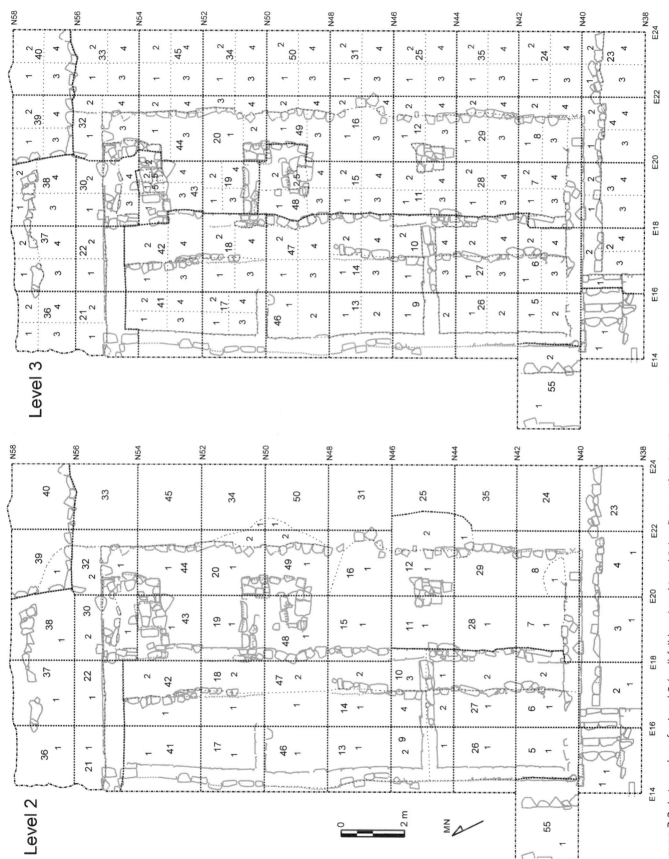

FIGURE 3.2. Lot numbers for Level 2 (wall-fall layer) and Level 3 (on-floor artifacts) in the excavation of Structure M8-4.

Figure 3.3. Distribution of artifacts on the last occupation floor of Structure M8-4. (a) Western part of the north addition. (b) Eastern part of the north addition and the platform. (c) Back bench of the north room. (d) Room floor of the north room. (e) Front area of the north room and the front porch. (f) Back bench of the center room. (g) Room floor of the center room. (h) Front area of the center room and the front porch. (i) Back bench of the south room. (j) Room floor of the south room. (k) Front area of the south room and the front porch. (l) Western part of the center room. (m) Eastern part of the south side. (n) Area behind the structure. (o) Lower layer of artifacts in the front area of the north room (the frame corresponds to that of Figure 3.3e).

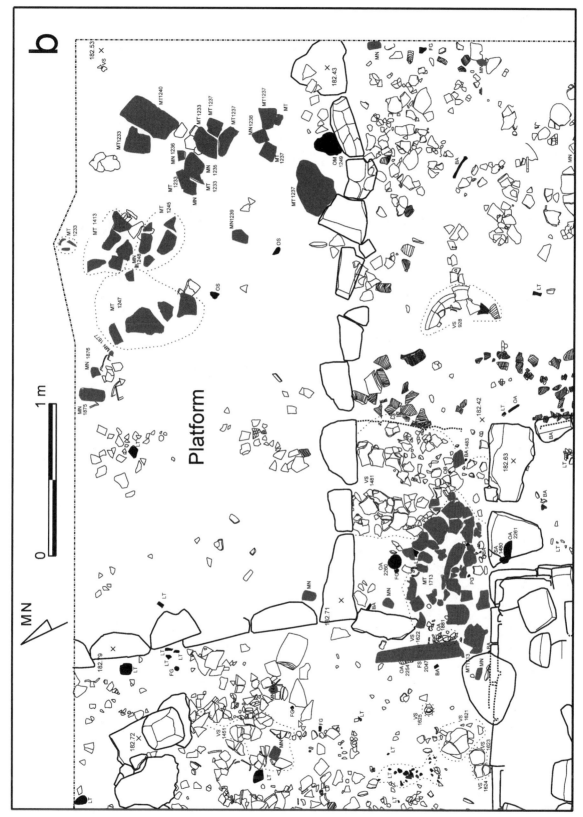

FIGURE 3.3. continued. (b) Eastern part of the north addition and the platform.

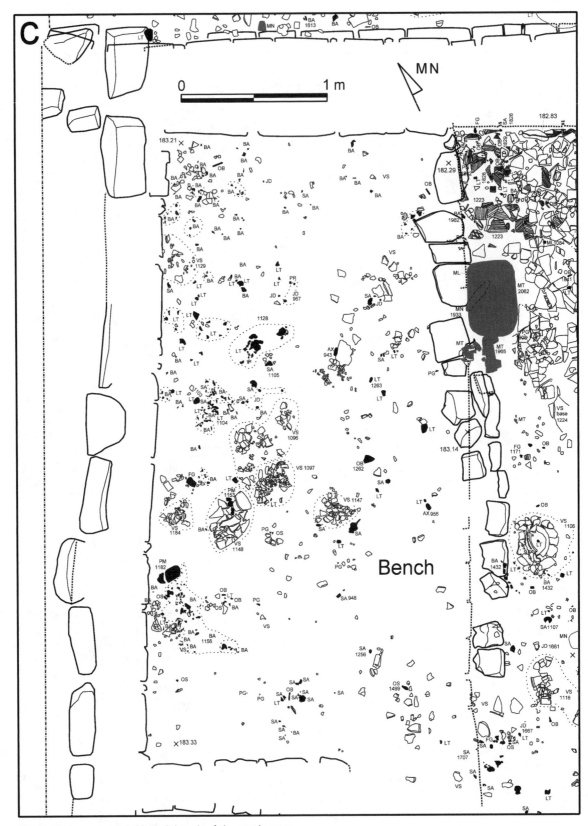

FIGURE 3.3. continued. (c) Back bench of the north room.

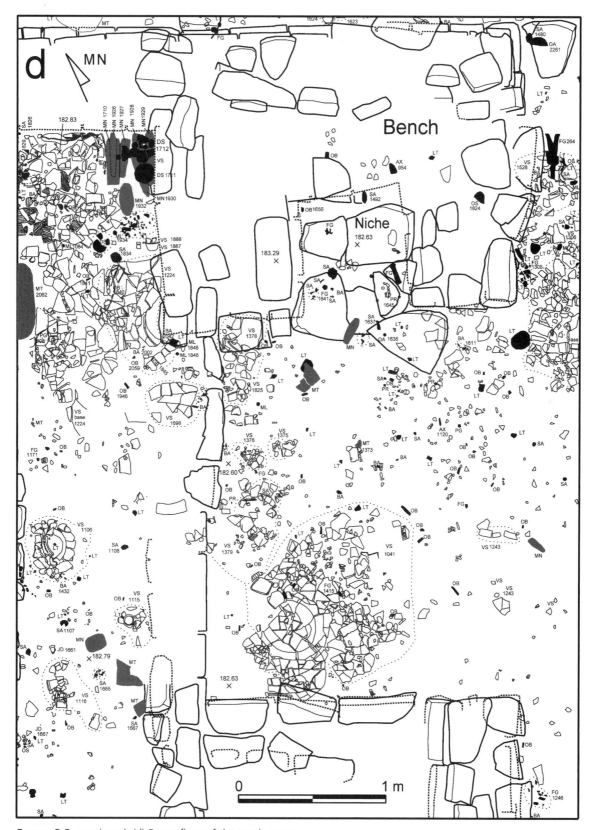

FIGURE 3.3. continued. (d) Room floor of the north room.

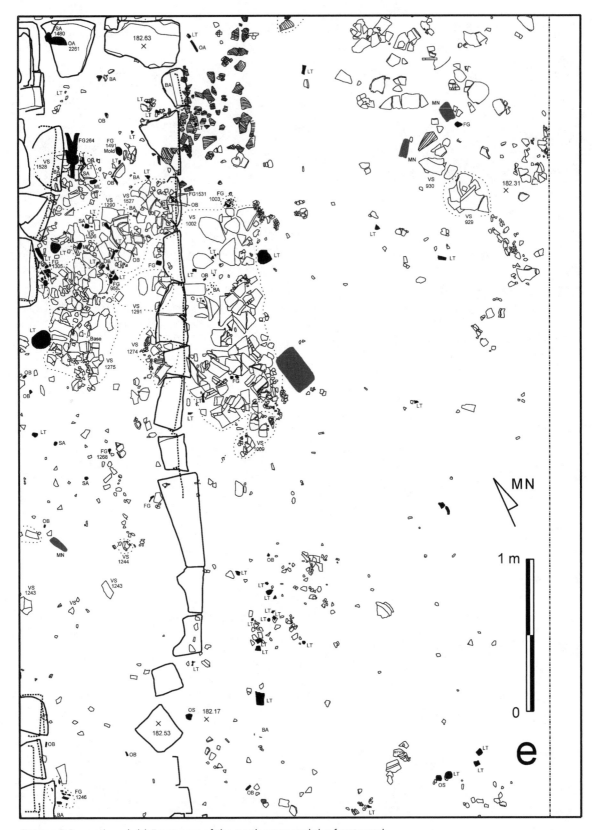

FIGURE 3.3. continued. (e) Front area of the north room and the front porch.

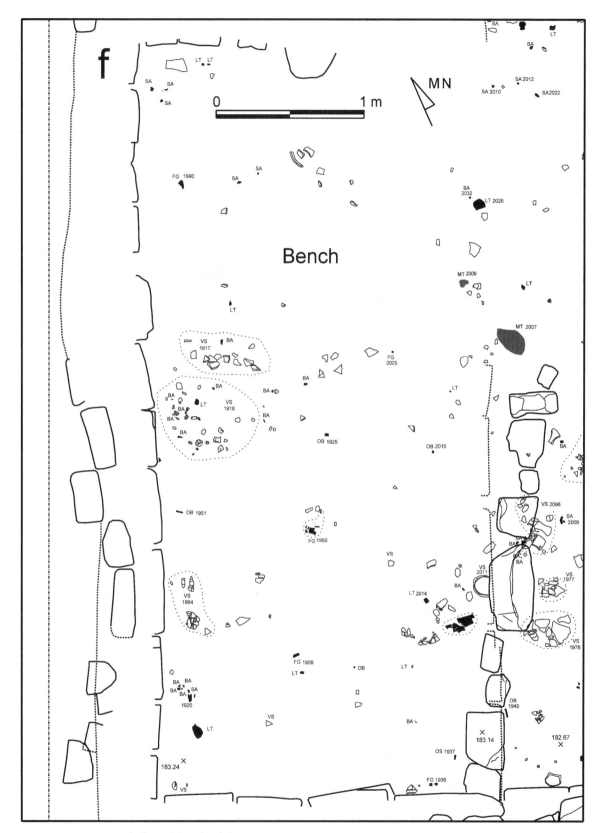

FIGURE 3.3. continued. (f) Back bench of the center room.

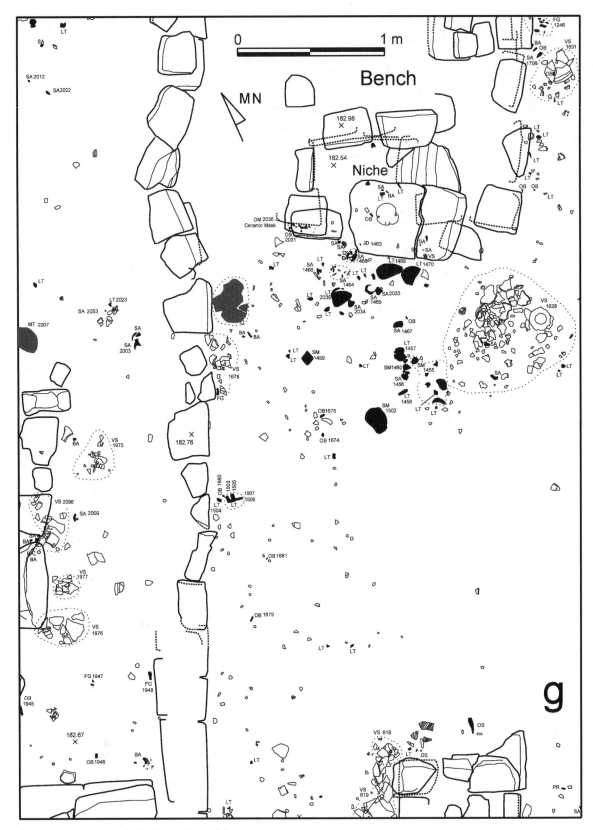

FIGURE 3.3. continued. (g) Room floor of the center room.

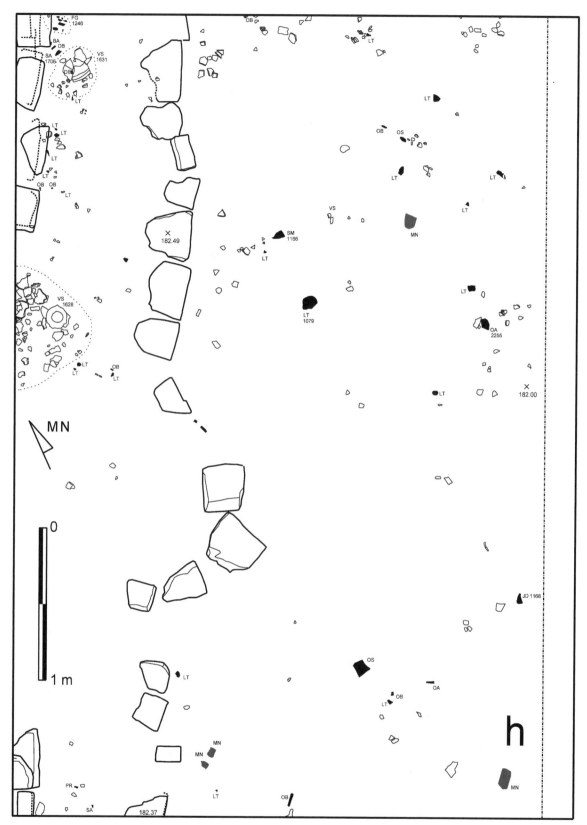

FIGURE 3.3. continued. (h) Front area of the center room and the front porch.

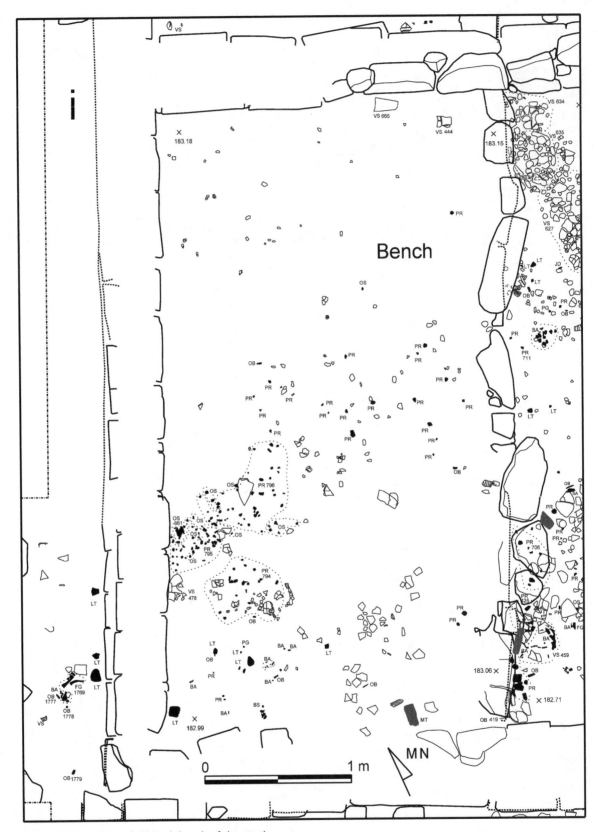

FIGURE 3.3. continued. (i) Back bench of the south room.

FIGURE 3.3. continued. (j) Room floor of the south room.

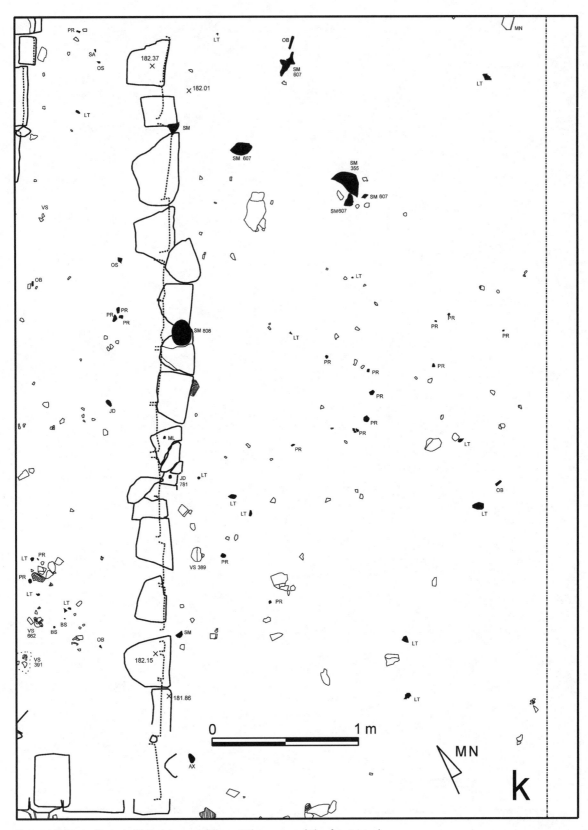

FIGURE 3.3. continued. (k) Front area of the south room and the front porch.

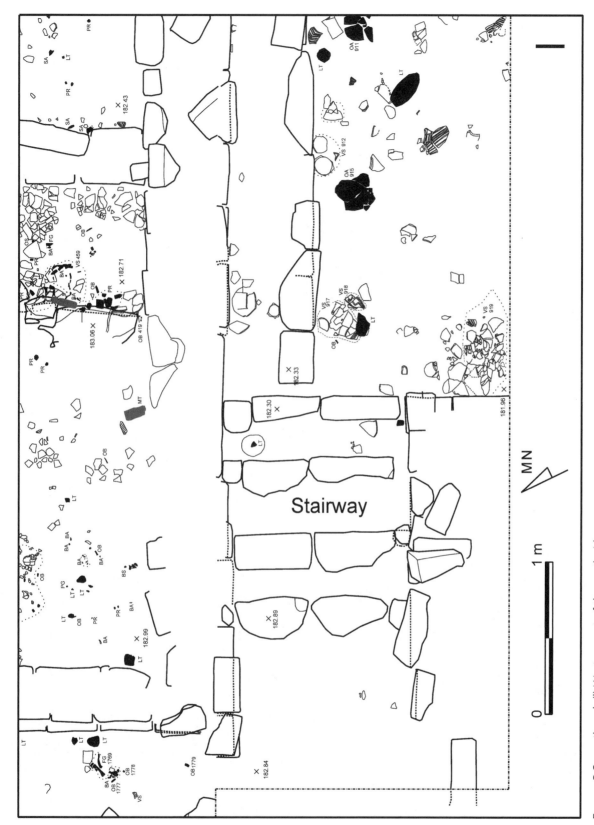

Stairway

MN

0   1 m

FIGURE 3.3. continued. (l) Western part of the south side.

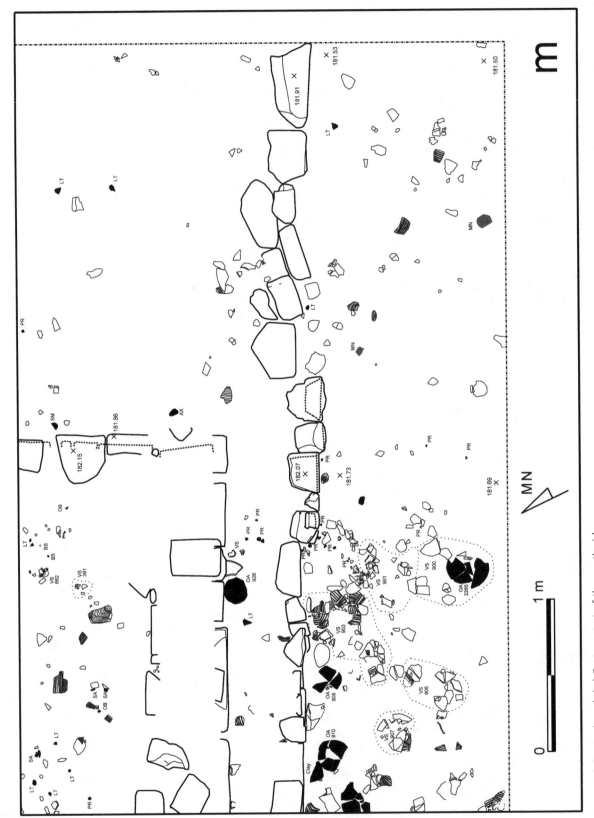

FIGURE 3.3. continued. (m) Eastern part of the south side.

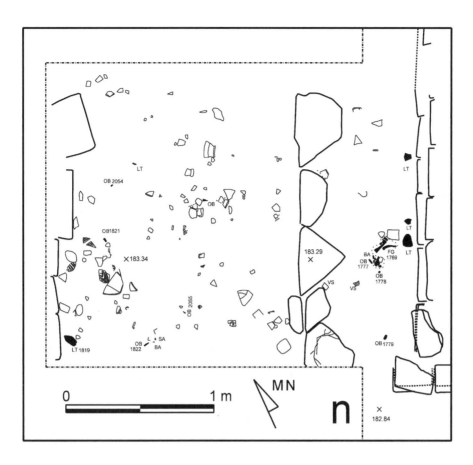

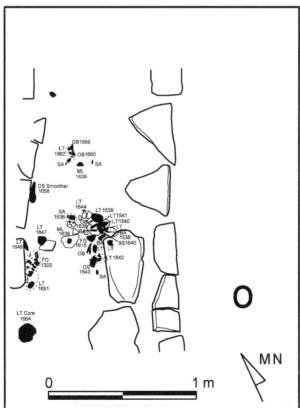

FIGURE 3.3. continued. (n) Area behind the structure. (o) Lower layer of artifacts in the front area of the north room (the frame corresponds to that of Figure 3.3e).

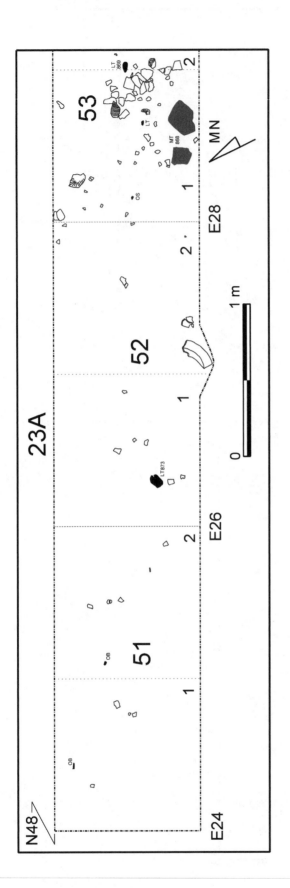

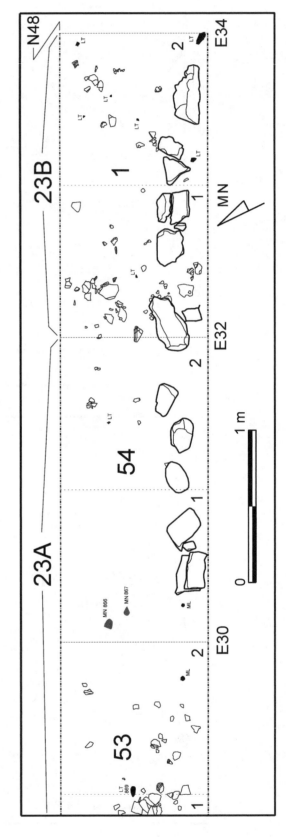

FIGURE 3.4. Plan of the trench placed in the patio in front of Structure M8-4 with the distribution of artifacts on the floor and lot numbers for Level 3 (on-floor artifacts). Level 1 contained one lot for each unit, and there was no Level 2 (wall fall).

FIGURE 3.5. Reconstruction model of Structure M8-4, viewed from the southeast. The model shows only the excavated area.

room division is similar to that of Structures M7-34 and M8-11. The side walls continued into the front portion of the building, and there was a square pillar in the line of each room division, indicating that the front part was covered by a roof. In the front portion of the center and north rooms, side benches were built against the pillar, the side wall, and the front room divisions. These benches were probably added later during the occupation of the building. Each of these benches had a niche. The northeastern portion of the rear bench of the center room was disturbed, probably by an old tree fall. The front room division and a part of the side bench of this chamber were also damaged.

In the northeastern part of the excavated area, we found a low platform made of one course of blocks. The nature of this platform was not clear. It may have been attached to the platform of the Palace Group. The northern addition was defined only by coarse lines of roughly shaped stones. These lines were placed after the construction of the northeastern platform and Structure M8-4. We suspect that the northern addition was covered by a roof or eave, although we did not find direct evidence. Unlike in the main rooms, the floor of the north addition was at the same level as the exterior floor and was not stuccoed.

On the south side of the structure we found a narrow side porch. It is not clear whether the edge of this porch turns north and forms a front porch. The trench across the patio along the central axis of the building did not reveal a step, however. We excavated only a 2-×-2-m area behind the building near its southwestern corner, revealing a narrow back porch and the edge of the platform supporting

Structure M7-34. The exterior floor behind the building was higher than those on the side or in front, probably reflecting the slope of the bedrock. Between the southern side wall of the structure and the platform of Structure M8-8 was a narrow stairway with four steps made of roughly shaped stones.

In 2004, during the second phase of the Aguateca Archaeological Project, we excavated under the floors of this building (Structure M8-4 2nd). Excavators unearthed a partially dismantled earlier structure under the center and south rooms. The back wall of this structure was visible on the bench surface of the south room during the excavation in 1999. Structure M8-4 2nd appears to date to the Tepeu 2 phase of the Late Classic period.

In the eastern part of the trench placed in the patio, excavators found a coarse line of stones, but it is not clear if it was part of a platform.

Artifact Deposits

Structure M8-4 contained numerous artifacts, indicating that the building was abandoned rapidly. Traces of fire were visible on numerous objects, although fire marks were not clear on the building.

Center Room

As in Structures M7-35 (House of the Niche) and M8-10 (House of the Scribe), the quantity of artifacts in the center room was relatively small (Figure 3.3f–h). On the back bench and in front of it were a few small concentrations of ceramic sherds, which probably represented reconstructible serving vessels. Later analysis showed that

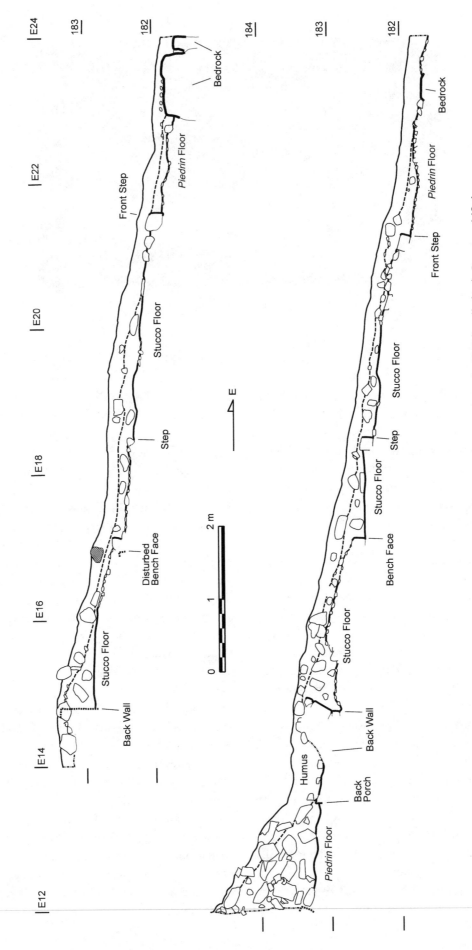

FIGURE 3.6. East-west sections of the north room along the N52 line (*above*) and the south room along the N42 line (*below*), Structure M8-4.

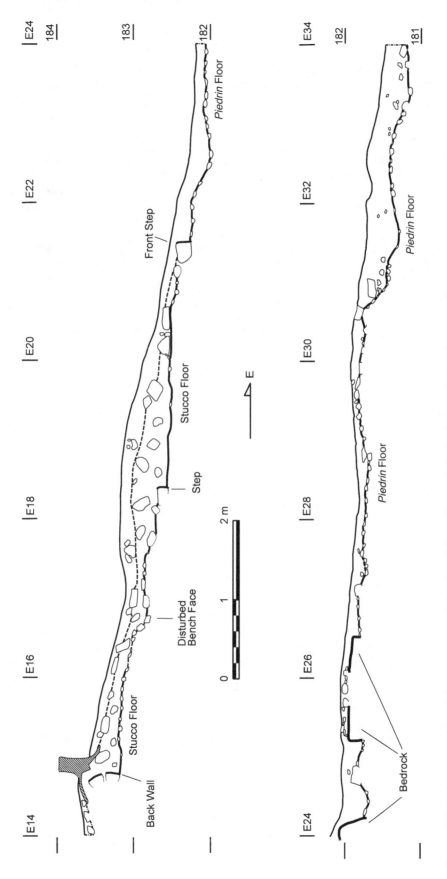

FIGURE 3.7. East-west sections of the center room (*above*) and the patio trench (*below*) along the E48 line, Structure M8-4.

FIGURE 3.8. Structure M8-4 (House of Mirrors) after excavation, viewed from the east.

two of them were possible incense burners (WVS 23A-40, Cat. 310276; WVS 23A-41, Cat. 310319). Two fragments of carved bones uncovered on the back bench of this room had glyphic texts with the Aguateca emblem glyph, pointing to the high status of the residents (Cat. BA 23A1121-7, BA 23A1121-12). In front of the opening in the room division, excavators unearthed fragmented large chert knives. They exhibited severe fire damage, but their exceptional quality of production was notable. They may have fallen from the rear part of the room.

In front of and on the front bench were one stone pestle and seven stone mortars, each of which fits nicely in one's hand. Five mortars and the pestle were made of chert whereas the two other mortars were made of sandstone and possible metamorphic rock. Three more chert mortars and one pestle were found near the pillar dividing the central and south rooms and in front of the south room. These objects were probably used for the preparation of pigments, although the analysis of five mortars by Beaubien (2001) at the Smithsonian Center for Materials Research and Education did not detect unambiguous residues of pigments. There were 12 to 14 unworked riverine bivalve shells in the same area. It is suggestive that the central room of Structure M8-10 (House of the Scribe) contained similar shells along with stone mortars. These shells may have been used as ink pots. It appears that a scribe worked sitting on the front bench of this room.

A small bowl left in the niche under the front bench

of this room survived as a complete piece (WVS 23A-43, Cat. 310168) (Figure 3.9). A concentration of sherds in front of the front bench was recognizable as a reconstructible Pantano jar (WVS 23A-42, Cat. 310359). Excavators also found badly fragmented clay-textile laminates pressed against the face of the front bench. The material was similar to that of the masks found in Structure M7-22 (House of Masks), but it was so badly damaged that we were not able to reconstruct it.

North Room

The north room contained numerous lithic tools and ceramic vessels (Figure 3.3c–e, o). On the back bench there was a moderate amount of ceramic sherds, which represented several reconstructible serving vessels. In the northern part of the area between the back bench and the front room division was a dense concentration of ceramics. Later analysis showed that it contained three storage jars and three serving vessels. In the same area, excavators unearthed nine manos and three doughnut stones that were neatly stored on the floor (Figure 3.10).

The front part of the room contained one large Manteca Incised storage jar (WVS 23A-2, Cat. 310393) and a few serving vessels. A find of interest in the north room was a large plate (WVS 23A-1, Cat. 310164) (Figure 3.11). Although its shape is similar to that of a *comal*, or a griddle for cooking tortillas, its function remains unclear. Fragments of a reconstructible ceramic flute were found in the

FIGURE 3.9. The niche under the front bench of the center room of Structure M8-4, viewed from the south.

FIGURE 3.10. Manos and doughnut stones found in the north room of Structure M8-4. *Left:* Before doughnut stones were removed. *Right:* After doughnut stones were removed.

niche of the front bench. This object may have been stored originally on the bench. There was a dense concentration of ceramics on the room floor east of the front bench, and a part of it was spilling over the adjacent exterior floor. It contained four Tinaja/Pantano jars, two Chaquiste bowls, and four other serving vessels. In the same area, excavators found a large, finely made figurine depicting a high-status male, which may represent an ancestral figure of this family (Cat. FG23A 264-1) (Figure 3.12) (Triadan 2007). A possible stucco smoother made of chert was also found nearby.

Three more Subin/Chaquiste bowls and one storage jar were found on the exterior floor between the north room and the platform to the north. A large limestone metate, most likely used for grinding maize, sat on the exterior floor next to the northeastern corner of the room. Along with the stored manos and numerous storage and cooking vessels, this object suggests that the room was used for food preparation.

Excavators also unearthed shell ornaments and greenstone beads in this room. A concentration of spindle whorls in the room points to its association with spinning.

FIGURE 3.11. Ceramics in the southwestern corner of the front area of the north room of Structure M8-4. *Left:* Manteca Incised storage jar (WVS 23A-2, Cat. 310393). Note the turned-over base next to the photo arrow. *Right: Comal*-like vessel found under the Manteca Incised jar (WVS 23A-1, Cat. 310164).

FIGURE 3.12. Large figurine found in the north room of Structure M8-4 during excavation (Cat. FG 23A264-1).

South Room

One of the most remarkable finds of the project was an alabaster ornament unearthed on the bench of the south room (Cat. OS 23A661-1)(Figures 3.3i–k and 3.13). Houston identified it as an image of the Jester God, or a symbol of rulership (see Freidel 1990). Two holes in the back of the Jester God head were probably for attachment to a headband. Small perforations in the nose and chin were probably used for attaching beads. Associated with

this ornament were 11 or 12 square alabaster plaques, also with small perforations for attachment. They most likely formed a diadem.

The same room contained more than three hundred mosaic pieces of pyrite mirrors. Some pieces were found attached to fragments of a stone mirror back, although the glue had been lost. The analysis of these materials by Marcelo Zamora and Inomata showed that some mosaic mirror pieces were in the process of being reworked into

Figure 3.13. The Jester God ornament (Cat. OS 23A661-1) and other alabaster and pyrite pieces found on the bench of the south room of Structure M8-4, viewed from the east.

possible ornaments of rectangular shape. Finished rectangular ornaments were found next to the Jester God diadem whereas pieces in the process of reworking were unearthed 30 to 70 cm away. Mosaic mirror pieces that had not been reworked were also found mixed with these reworked objects and in the surrounding areas.

Next to the Jester God ornament, excavators also found four pieces of possible siltstone and one fragment of ceramic that had similar shapes to those of the reworked pyrite objects. In addition, a concentration of 10 pieces of worked bone, each measuring roughly 2 cm in length, was found on the same bench about 1 m to the southeast of the Jester God diadem. One end of each piece was rounded whereas the other end was not smoothed after it was cut and snapped. Interestingly, the rounded ends of most pieces were more severely burned than the unsmoothed ends. It appears that these worked bones were embedded in perishable materials on the unsmoothed ends, which were thus protected from fire. These objects, including the reworked pyrite pieces, siltstone objects, and worked bones, were probably parts of complex composite ornaments, such as headdresses, which were meant to be used along with the Jester God headband.

The amount of ceramic sherds found on the bench of the south room was relatively small, and they represented a few small, reconstructible serving vessels. Denser concentrations of ceramics were found near the northern and southern ends of the area between the bench and the front room divisions. They were fragments of two large Encanto Striated jars, one Subin bowl, and three Pantano jars. Excavators also unearthed another concentration of sherds east of the opening in the front room division. They represented another large storage jar, which may have fallen from the area between the bench and the front room division.

A moderate amount of ceramic sherds were scattered in the front area of the room. Project members reconstructed four serving vessels and one Pantano jar from these pieces but noted that the fragments were dispersed over several units.

North Addition and Outside the Building

The north addition contained numerous artifacts, including ceramic vessels and stone tools (Figure 3.3a, b). Reconstructible pots were mostly serving vessels. This area may have been a work or storage space. Marco Antonio Monroy, who analyzed ceramics from this structure, recognized four round reworked sherds, each measuring 10 to 15 cm in diameter, which were unearthed in the southeastern corner of the north addition and in the nearby areas. Nine similar objects were also found in the area to the south of the structure (Figure 3.3l, m). Eight of these reworked sherds were made from bases of large bowls or jars, some with concave cross sections, and could not have been mirror backs. Burned clay was caked on the exteriors of some pieces, which may be related to a chunk of burned clay found on the southern side. Only two similar reworked sherds were found in the rest of the excavated structures in the Causeway area, and the high number of round reworked sherds appears to be related to a unique activity conducted in and around Structure M8-4. Activities involving the use of clay were probably carried out in these areas, but their precise nature remains unclear.

On the platform north of the building, we unearthed numerous fragments of metates and manos. It is not clear whether these grinding stones were used by the residents of Structure M8-4. On the south side of the building, excavators recovered several reconstructible vessels, including serving vessels and storage jars (Figure 3.3l, m). It appears that this area also had work and storage functions. A modest amount of ceramics and other artifacts were found behind the structure, but we could not reconstruct any vessels (Figure 3.3n). This may be because of the limited area of excavation.

In the trench in the patio, excavators found a relatively small quantity of artifacts (Figure 3.4). Most sherds were severely eroded, and it is not clear whether any of them were reconstructible. It does not appear that the patio was swept clean at the time of abandonment.

Interpretation

Structure M8-4 was most likely a residence occupied by an elite household. The north room, and possibly the north addition, were related to food storage and preparation. The central room, with a relatively small number of artifacts, may have been used for meetings and the reception of visitors. The soil phosphate levels in the north room and the north addition are moderately higher than those in the central and south rooms, reflecting this pattern of space use (Terry et al. 2004). A resident also seems to have engaged in scribal or artistic work in the central room (Inomata 2001c). Another important task performed in and around this structure was the preparation and maintenance of possible royal attires, such as a Jester God headband and a headdress.

Stela 19 of Aguateca, recently discovered in the Main Plaza by the Aguateca Project, as well as Stela 7, depicts Ruler 5 of Aguateca, Tahn Te' K'inich—possibly the last king of this center—wearing a Jester God headband, with small beads on the nose and chin of the Jester God and square plaques along the band. The depictions of the Jester God on the stelae appear identical to the excavated piece,

and one may entertain the thought that the excavated alabaster ornament was the very piece worn by the last ruler of Aguateca and depicted on the stelae. A resident of this structure may have been a high courtier responsible for maintaining royal regalia. Alternatively, the Jester God diadem may have been owned and used by a resident of this building. Although in most cases the use of Jester God images was reserved for rulers, Miller (1986:63) points out that some nobles depicted in the Bonampak murals wear Jester God headbands.

A resident of this structure, and possibly assistants, appears to have been preparing new royal attires or refurbishing existing ones for the next ceremony. The level of iron in the floor of the south room, however, was relatively low. Nor did we find debitage from the reworking of pyrite pieces. Interestingly, soil chemistry analysis detected an area of high iron concentration 2 m to the southeast of the structure (Terry et al. 2004). If the manufacturer cut and polished pyrite pieces in the south room, he must have thoroughly collected manufacturing refuse and thrown it outside. Or he may have worked outdoors and brought back unfinished pieces to the south room.

Many of the artifacts excavated in and around this building form reconstructible objects, and their distribution closely reflects the original use of space. Fragments of the vessels excavated from the south room, however, were often scattered over a wide area of the room floor, and a significant number of pyrite mosaic pieces were also dispersed in this area and on the exterior floor in front of it. It appears that the floor assemblage of the south room was more disturbed than others. Invading enemies or fleeing residents may have thrown and broke these objects at the time of abandonment.

STRUCTURE M8-8 (HOUSE OF AXES): OPERATION 20A

In 1997 we excavated the north half of this building, and in 1998 its southern half. In total the excavation covered 48 units and an area of 192 m², exposing the entire building (Figures 3.14–3.20). The structure sits on a modified natural terrace, and a wide front stairway provided access from the lower level on the east. Although two large trees stood in the southern part of the structure, its configuration with three main rooms was visible before the excavation. The excavation proceeded without cutting these two trees. We established a new grid system different from that of Structure M8-10. This grid system was later expanded for the excavation of Structures M8-2, M8-3, and M8-4.

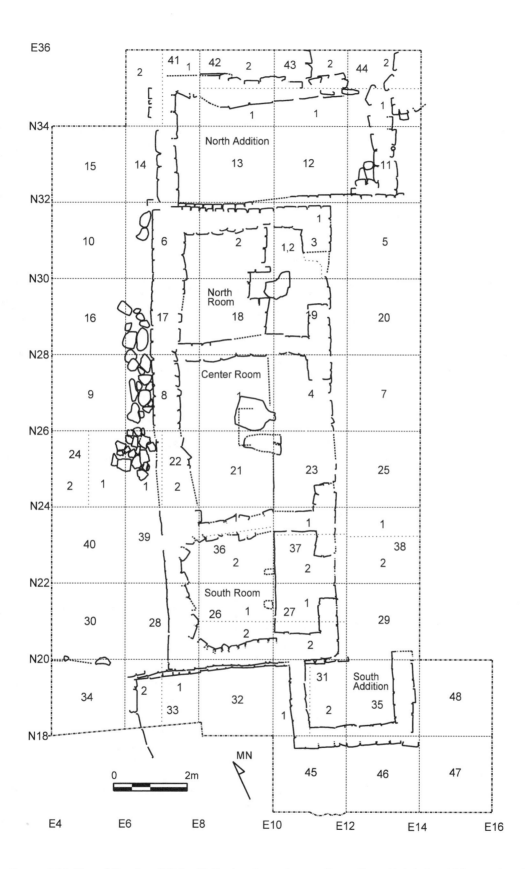

FIGURE 3.14. Plan of Structure M8-8 with the locations of excavation units and lots in Level 1 (humus layer).

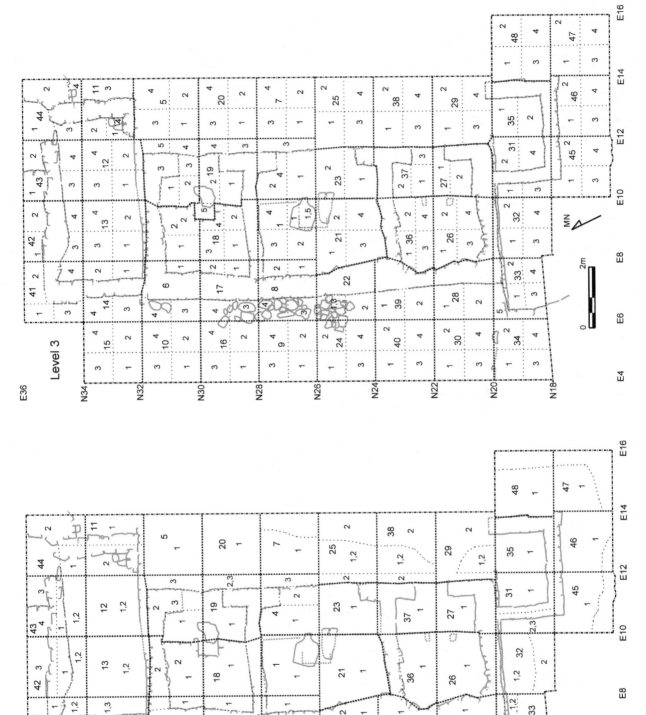

FIGURE 3.15. Lot numbers for Level 2 (wall-fall layer) and Level 3 (on-floor artifacts) in the excavation of Structure M8-8.

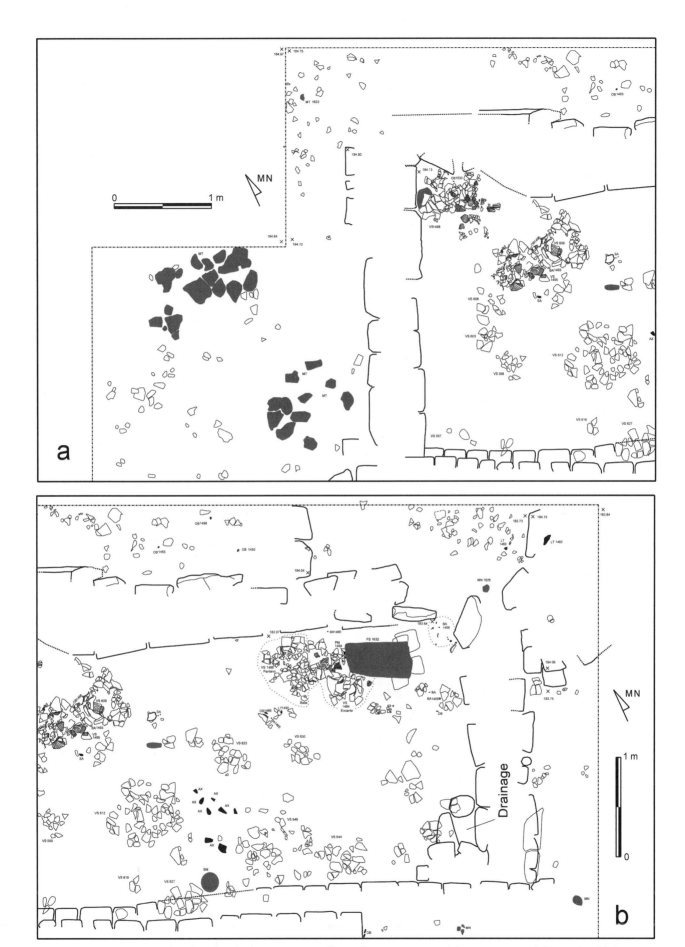

FIGURE 3.16. Distribution of artifacts on the last occupation floor of Structure M8-8. (a) Western part of the north addition. (b) Eastern part of the north addition. (c) Western part of the north room and the area behind it. (d) Eastern part of the north room and the area in front of it. (e) Western part of the center room and the area behind it. (f) Eastern part of the center room and the area in front of it. (g) Western part of the south room and the area behind it. (h) Eastern part of the south room and the area in front of it. (i) South side of the building. (j) South addition.

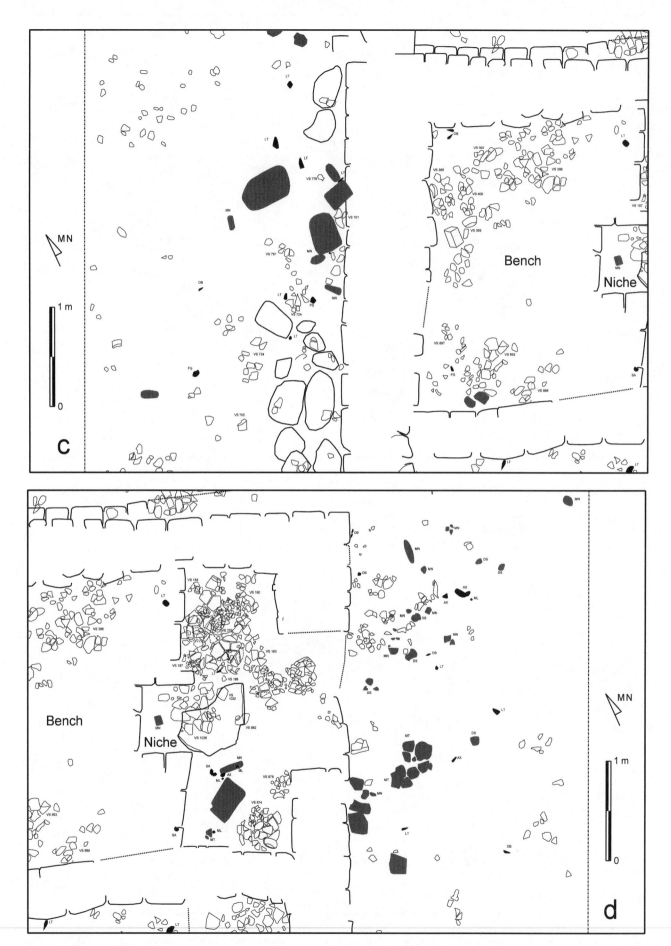

FIGURE 3.16. continued. (c) Western part of the north room and the area behind it. (d) Eastern part of the north room and the area in front of it.

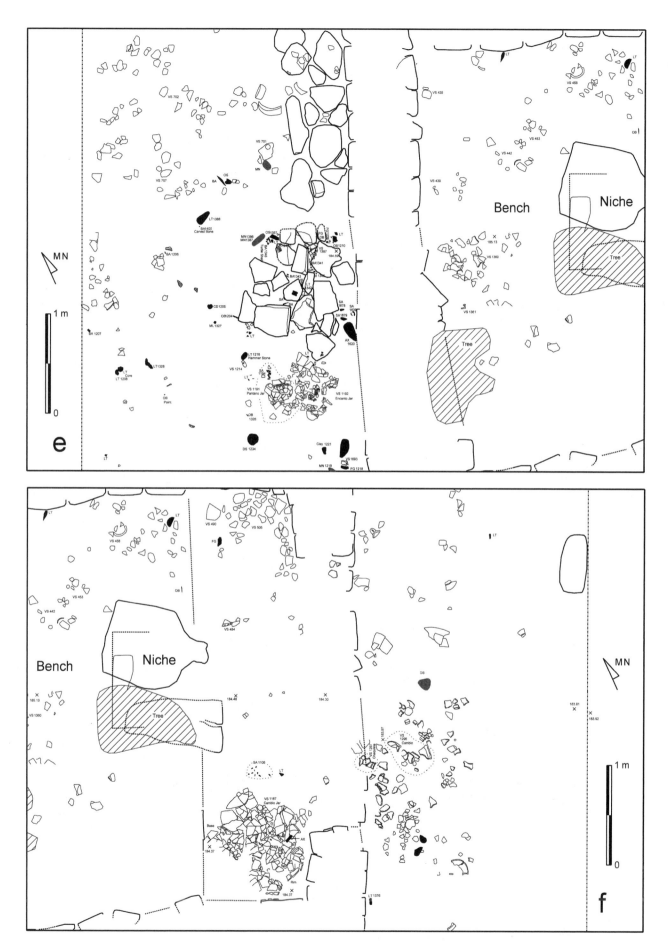

FIGURE 3.16. continued. (e) Western part of the center room and the area behind it. (f) Eastern part of the center room and the area in front of it.

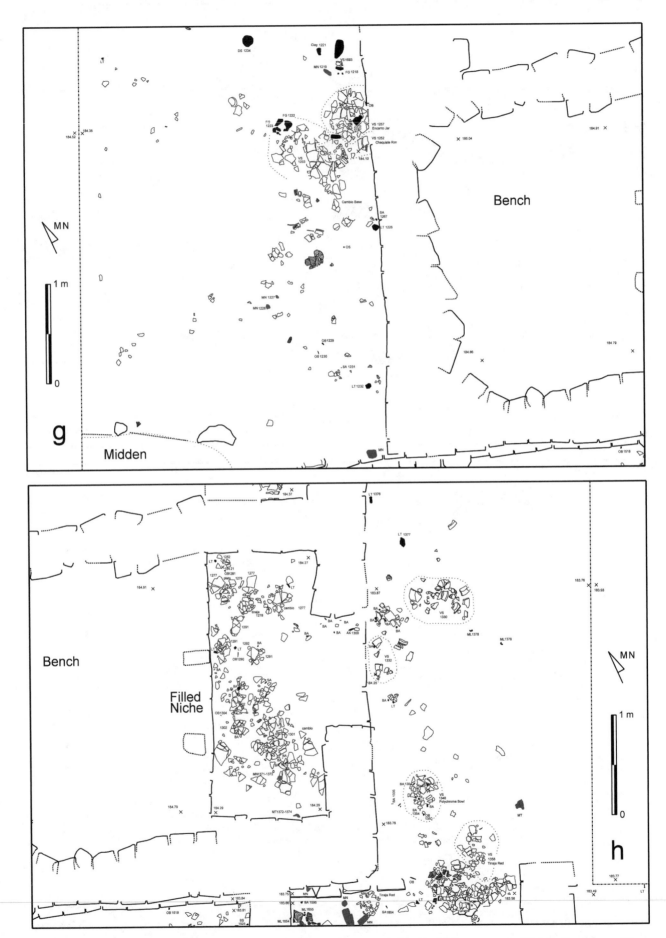

Figure 3.16. continued. (g) Western part of the south room and the area behind it. (h) Eastern part of the south room and the area in front of it.

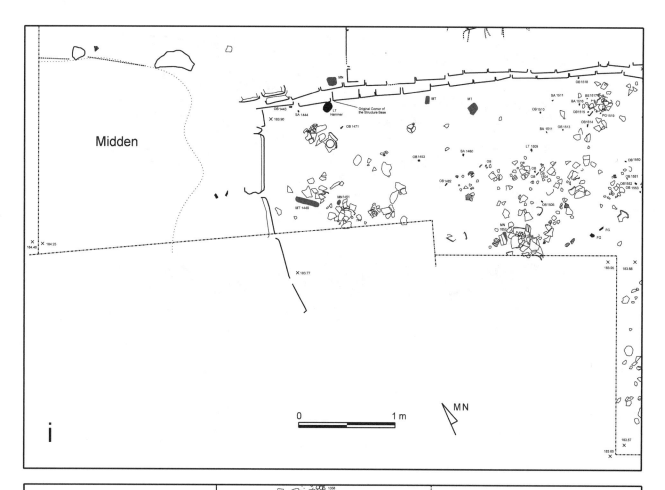

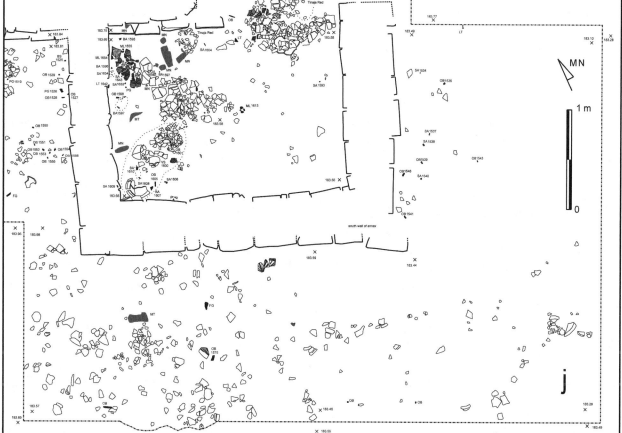

Figure 3.16. continued. (i) South side of the building. (j) South addition.

FIGURE 3.17. Reconstruction model of Structure M8-8, viewed from the east. The model shows only the excavated area.

Architecture

Structure M8-8 consisted of three main rooms, which we called the north, central, and south rooms, and of the north and south additions. As in Structure M8-4, the main part of this building had elevated floors whereas the floors of the north and south additions were at the same level as the exterior floor. The main rooms had their doorways in the front, but the north and south additions opened sideways. The interiors of the north and south additions were not visible from the lower terrace in front of the building. Each room of the main part of the building had a spacious bench in its rear part. The bench of the north room measured 45 cm in height, and those of the center and south rooms 65 cm. The floors and bench surfaces of the main rooms and the north addition had thin stucco, but the floor of the south addition consisted of gravel.

The walls of the main rooms and bench faces consisted of finely cut blocks without chinking stones (Figure 3.21). Unlike most other residential buildings, which had room divisions made of vertically placed slabs, the room partitions of Structure M8-8 consisted of finely cut blocks. The back, side, and front walls of the main portion of the building measured 70 to 75 cm in thickness whereas the room divisions were 40 to 50 cm thick. The masonry walls of the main rooms and the north addition appear to have supported the beams, but it was not clear whether the masonry portion of the room divisions reached this height. The walls of the north and south additions were made of roughly shaped stones and vertically placed blocks, and measured roughly 50 cm in thickness. The masonry part

of the walls of the south addition probably measured 1 to 1.5 m in height. An area behind the center and north rooms was raised with an irregular slab. Although it was not a formal porch, it probably served as a work area.

The main portion of the building was constructed first. The room divisions were placed after the benches were built, but the three-room configuration was most likely the original form of the building. Originally, each bench of the three rooms had a niche in its center covered by a wide, thin slab. The niche of the south room, however, was filled at some point. The north and south addition were added later during the occupation. After the north addition was built, the exterior floors on its side and behind the building were raised, covering a part of the walls.

In 2005, during the second phase of the Aguateca Archaeological Project, we excavated under the floors of the center and north rooms. The excavation revealed construction fills placed directly on the bedrock, showing that the main portion of the structure was built in one construction episode.

Artifact Deposits

This building also contained numerous complete and reconstructible objects. Many of them were burned, and traces of fire were recognizable on the stucco floor of the north addition and the stuccoed exterior floor in front of the building, as well as some parts of the walls. This building appears to exhibit fire damage more clearly than the other excavated structures. It is not clear whether Structure M8-8 suffered more severe fire or whether this is due to its construction materials. The relatively well preserved

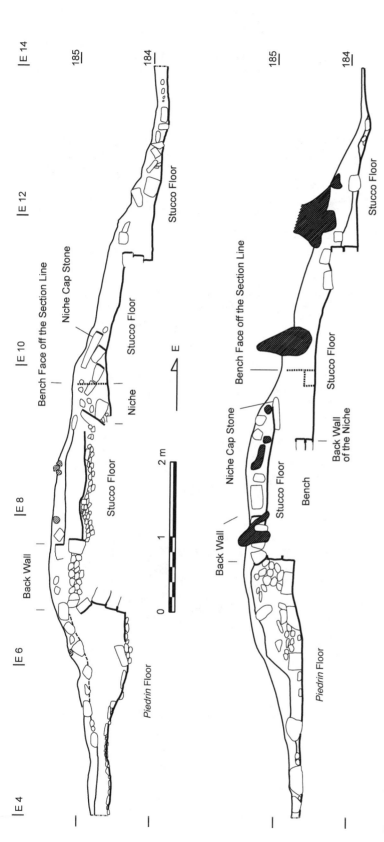

FIGURE 3.18. East-west sections of the north room along the N30 line (*above*) and the center room along the N26 line (*below*), Structure M8-8.

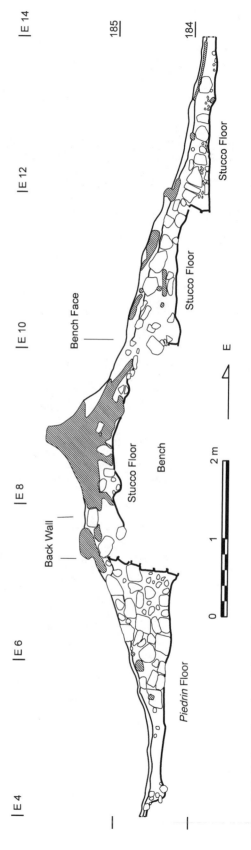

FIGURE 3.19. East-west section of the south room along the N22 line, Structure M8-8.

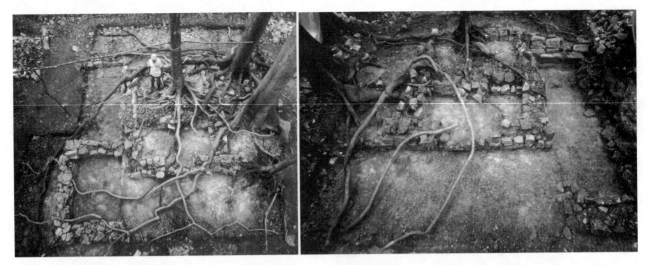

FIGURE 3.20. Structure M8-8 (House of Axes) after excavation, viewed from the east. *Left:* Southern half, excavated in 1998. *Right:* Northern half, excavated in 1997. (The northern edge of the north addition was not excavated until 1998.)

FIGURE 3.21. The southwestern corner of the north addition of Structure M8-8. Note that the wall of the main portion of the building on the viewer's left consists of finely cut stones whereas the wall of the north addition on the right is made of rough blocks.

stucco floor of the north addition and soft limestone blocks of the wall may retain and show fire marks more clearly than eroded floors and roughly shaped stones made of harder dolomitic stone.

Center and South Rooms

Although the southern part of the bench of the center room was not excavated because of a tree, the number of artifacts placed on or over the bench appears to have been relatively small (Figure 3.16e, f). They include reconstructible serving vessels and Tinaja/Pantano jars. A larger density of sherds was found in the northern and southern corners of the area between the bench and the front walls. A large Manteca Impressed storage jar was placed on the southwestern corner of the room floor (WVS 20A-24, Cat. 310179) (Figure 3.22). Some artifacts found in front

FIGURE 3.22. Fragments of a Manteca Impressed storage jar found in the southwestern corner of the room floor of the center room of Structure M8-8 (WVS 20A-24, Cat. 310179).

FIGURE 3.23. Artifacts found on the room floor of the north room, Structure M8-8. *Left:* Southern part. *Right:* Northern part.

of the center room probably fell off from the inside. The niche under the bench was mostly filled by a large root, and we could not confirm whether any artifact was placed there.

The number of artifacts in the south room was relatively small, although a part of the bench was not excavated because of a tree (Figure 3.16g, h). This room might have been a sleeping and resting space. A moderate amount of ceramic sherds, representing a few reconstructible vessels, was found in the front part of the bench, on the room floor, and in front of the room.

North Room

The north room contained numerous artifacts, including large storage jars, serving vessels, and grinding stones (Figures 3.16c and d, 3.23). In front of this room there was

FIGURE 3.24. A complete bowl found in the niche of the north room of Structure M8-8 (WVS 20A-21, Cat. 310020).

FIGURE 3.25. Fragments of an Encanto Striated jar found in the north addition.

a large metate that was probably used for grinding corn. Thus, the north room appears to have been associated with food storage and preparation. As in the north room of Structure M8-4, there was a concentration of spindle whorls inside and in front of this room. The niche under the bench housed a complete bowl (WVS 20A-21, Cat. 310020) (Figure 3.24). Also found in front of the north room were forty greenstone beads, which were probably parts of a necklace. In the same area, excavators unearthed five polished stone axes. We also found several reconstructible vessels in front of the northern front wall. It appears that these vessels were placed outside the room, possibly protected by an eave.

North and South Additions

The north addition probably served as a storage and work space (Figure 3.16a, b). It contained numerous artifacts, including storage jars, obsidian blades, and grinding stones (Figure 3.25). Excavators found a large limestone slab placed on limestone blocks in the northeastern corner of the room (Cat. OS 20A1632-1) (Figure 3.26). The presence of numerous fine incisions on the upper surface indicates that the stone was used as a work surface for cutting. There was a drainage hole in the southeastern corner of the north addition, suggesting the use of water in the

FIGURE 3.26. A flat limestone block with fine incisions (Cat. OS 20A1632-1) and fragments of ceramic vessels found in the north addition of Structure M8-8, viewed from the south.

room. A notable find was a concentration of 11 polished stone axes in the central part of the north addition (Figure 3.27).

The south addition contained storage jars and grinding stones (Figures 3.16j, 3.28). The relatively low level of phosphate in the soil points to the storage function of this room rather than food preparation (Terry et al. 2004).

Outside the Building

Behind the structure, we found numerous artifacts, including ceramic vessels, figurines, and grinding stones, concentrated on and around the area raised with slabs (Figure 3.16). The area along the back wall of the structure was probably covered by an eave and served as a storage and work space. Excavators also found numerous fragments of grinding stones behind the north addition. They may have fallen from Structure M7-34 (House of Metates), which contained numerous manos and metates.

On the south side of the structure we found a few reconstructible vessels (Figure 3.16i). This area also appears to have served as a work and storage area.

Interpretation

Structure M8-8 was most likely a residence where an elite household slept and prepared its food. The use of space in

this building was similar to that of Structure M8-4 and the other elite residences. The center room was geared to meetings and receptions, whereas the north room was closely associated with food preparation and storage.

Unique finds from this structure were the polished stone axes. Although other excavated structures usually contained polished stone axes, the number from Structure M8-8 was particularly large. The stone axes from Structure M8-8 varied in size and shape, and they appear to have formed a carver's tool kit. Use-wear analysis by Aoyama (2000, 2007, 2009) indicates that they were used for carving stones. Carved stones besides stelae are scarce at Aguateca, despite our extensive excavations in the royal palace, elite residences, and a temple, so perhaps a resident of Structure M8-8 was a carver of stelae and other stone monuments who worked for the ruler. If so, the carver used the axes mostly in the Main Plaza or other places outside the structure and stored them in the north addition.

STRUCTURE M8-10 (HOUSE OF THE SCRIBE): OPERATION 14A AND D

Structure M8-10 was excavated down to the last occupation floors in 1991. Excavators noted a depression in the north room, possibly caused by an old tree. They cleaned this depression but did not find older structures or burials.

FIGURE 3.27. Polished stone axes found in the north addition of Structure M8-8.

FIGURE 3.28. Artifacts found in the south addition of Structure of M8-8, viewed from the east.

In 1997 we returned to this building to excavate levels below the floors in the center and south rooms (Figure 3.29).

Under the floor in front of the bench of the center room, excavators unearthed Burial 9 (Figures 3.30, 3.31). Its cist was placed directly on the bedrock and within a loose fill, and its side walls and capstones consisted of irregular stones. It was a primary extended burial of an adult male placed face-up and with the head to the north. His right arm was placed on the abdomen, and his left arm was behind the back. The right leg was crossed over

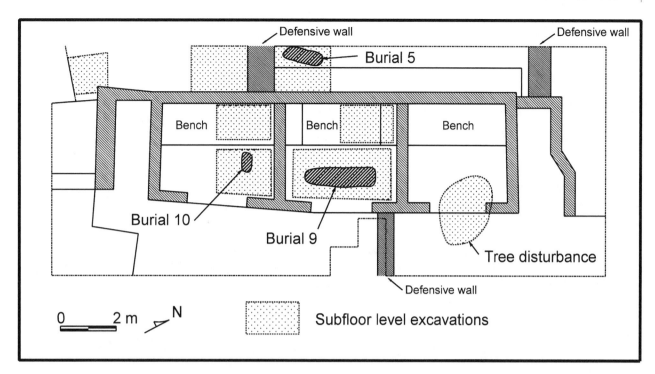

FIGURE 3.29. Locations of burials associated with Structure M8-10.

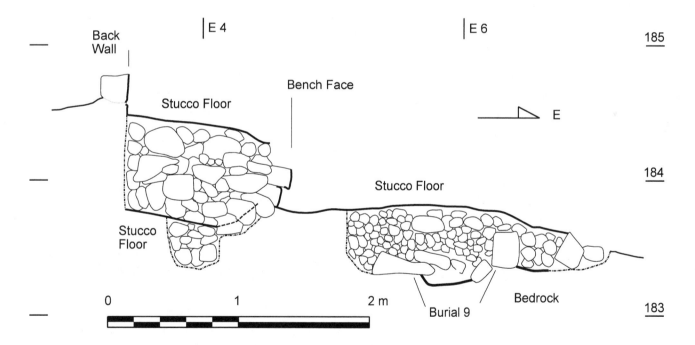

FIGURE 3.30. East-west section of the center room below the floor of Structure M8-10.

the left leg. The burial contained only one Saxche-Palmar Polychrome bowl near the head. Protected under the stucco floor, the skeleton was fairly well preserved compared with other burials found at Aguateca.

Below the bench surface of the center room excava-

tors found a loose fill and then a continuation of the room floor. The stucco of this floor was poorly preserved. It appears that this room originally did not have a bench. Under this floor was also a loose fill, but we did not reach bedrock in this part.

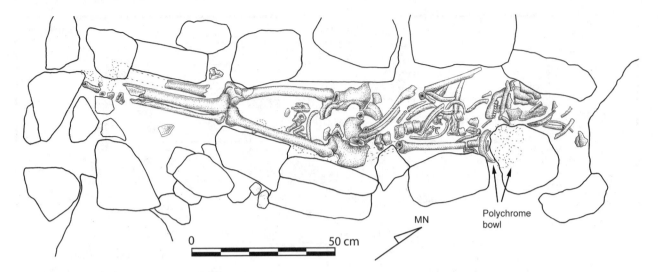

FIGURE 3.31. Plan view of Burial 9, found under the room floor of the center room of Structure M8-10.

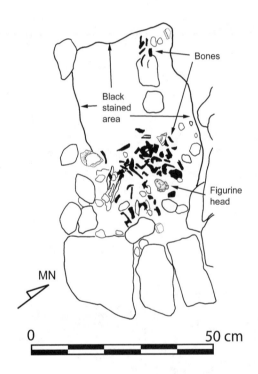

FIGURE 3.32. Plan view of Burial 10, found under the room floor of the south room of Structure M8-10.

In the south room, under the room floor in front of the bench, excavators found Burial 10, which contained the poorly preserved bones of an infant (Figure 3.32). The burial was placed in a loose fill and did not have a formal structure. A broken-off figurine head found near the skeleton may have been an offering. We excavated 50 cm below the bench surface, but it was not clear whether the room floor continued under the bench.

If we assume that the locations of burials generally correspond to the spaces that these individuals mainly used, these results appear to support our original interpretation of space use. The distribution of the floor assemblages in Structure M8-10 suggested to us that the center room was used mainly by the male head of the household whereas the south room was primarily a female space. The male burial found in the center room may have been the former head of the household who used this room. If infants spent substantial time with females, it is possible that they tended to be buried in spaces used commonly by women.

Operation 14D refers to a 1-×-6-m trench excavated across a possible small platform, Structure M8-12, in the patio in front of Structures M8-10 and M8-13. We revealed rocks that appear to have been disturbed by roots but no clear remains of architecture. A relatively small number of artifacts were recovered.

STRUCTURE M8-13: OPERATION 14B AND C

Structure M8-13 formed a patio group with Structure M8-10 (the House of the Scribe), which was excavated in 1993. The building was disturbed by tree falls, but it appeared to have been smaller and more coarsely built than Structure M8-10 and other elite residences. We expected that the excavation of this structure would provide information on a lower-status household. In 1996 we excavated the west room and part of the center room. In 1997 we exposed the rest of the center room, but the most severely disturbed eastern portion was left unexcavated. Juan Antonio Valdés and Monica Urquizú of the Guatemalan Restoration Project First Phase later excavated this part,

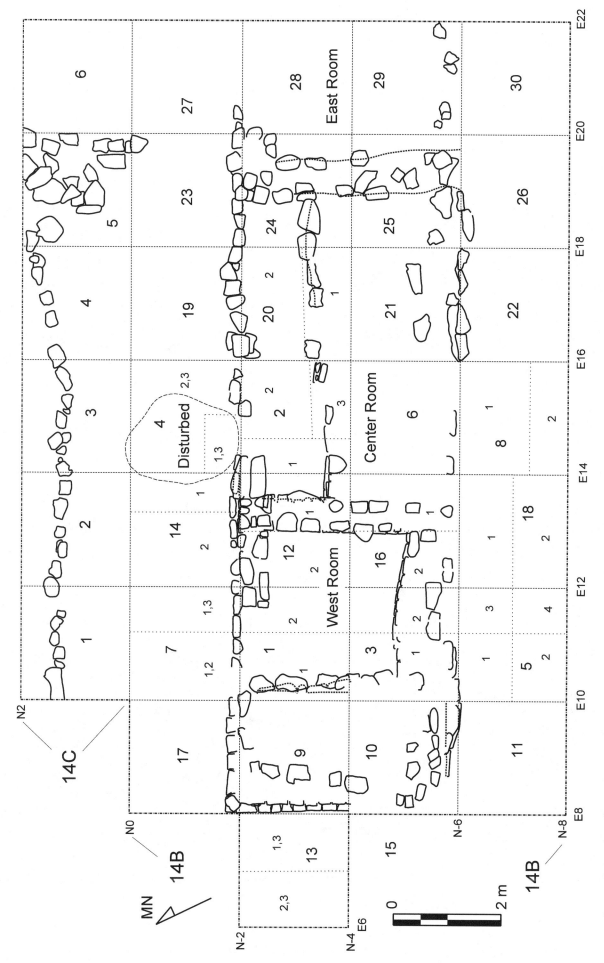

FIGURE 3.33. Plan of Structure M8-13 with the locations of excavation units and lots in Level 1 (humus layer).

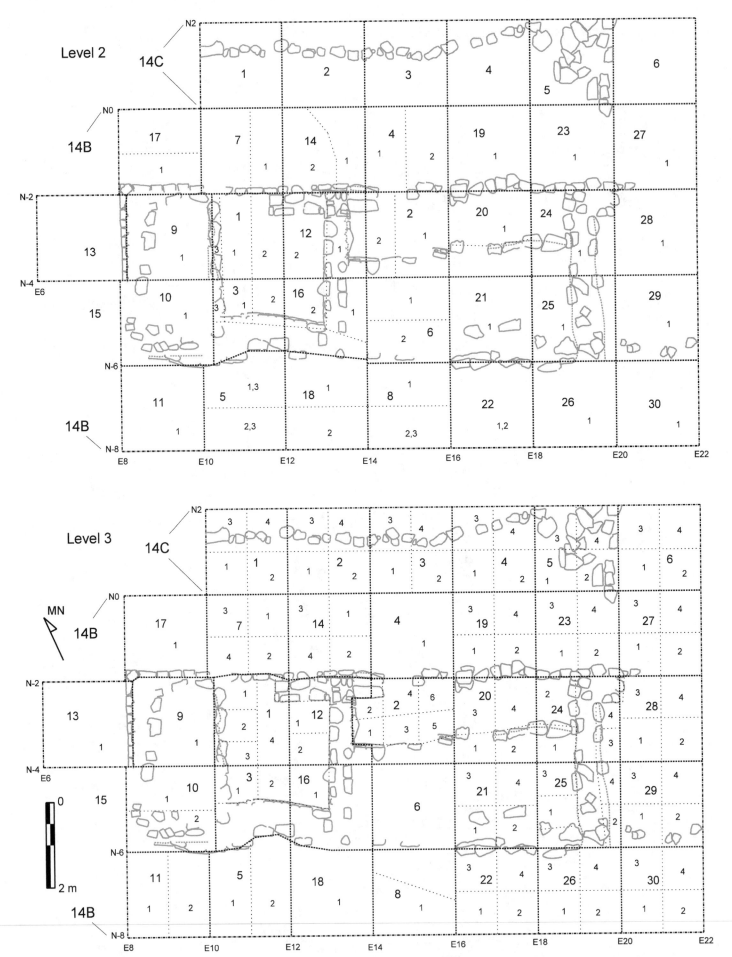

Figure 3.34. Lot numbers for Level 2 (wall-fall layer) and Level 3 (on-floor artifacts) in the excavation of Structure M8-13.

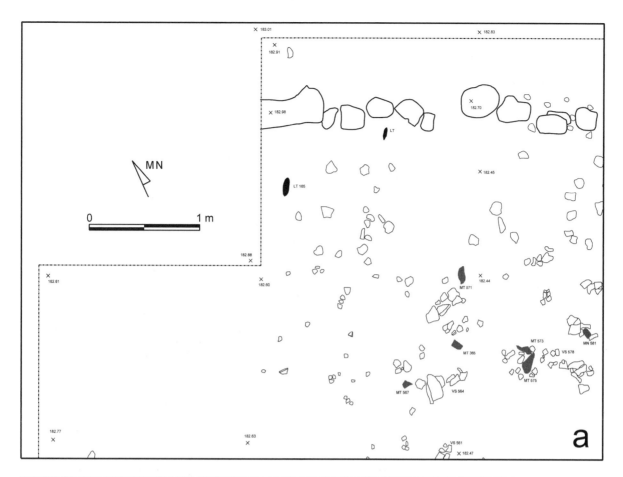

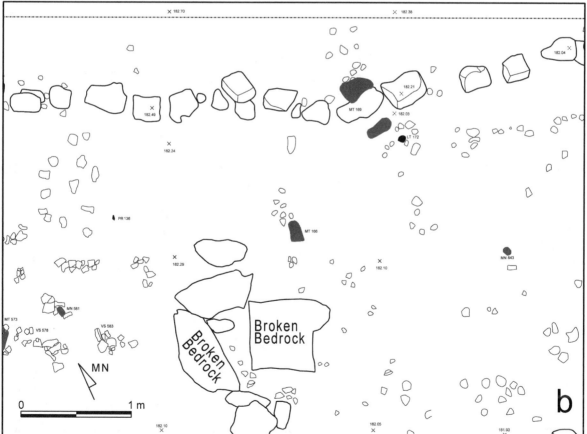

FIGURE 3.35. Distribution of artifacts on the last occupation floor of Structure M8-13. (a) Patio floor in front of the west room. (b) Patio floor in front of the western portion of the center room. (c) Patio floor in front of the eastern portion of the center room and the east room. (d) West room. (e) Western portion of the center room. (f) Eastern portion of the center room and western portion of the east room. (g) Area behind the west room. (h) Area behind the western portion of the center room. (i) Area behind the eastern portion of the center room and the east room.

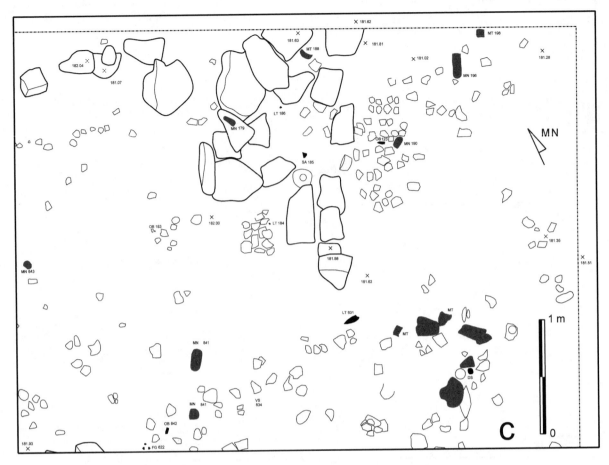

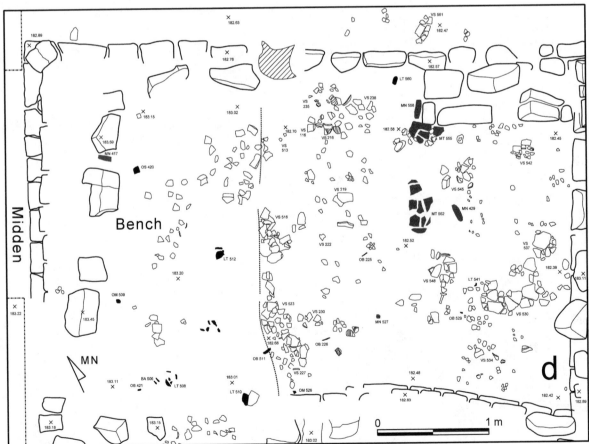

FIGURE 3.35. continued. (c) Patio floor in front of the eastern portion of the center room and the east room.
(d) West room.

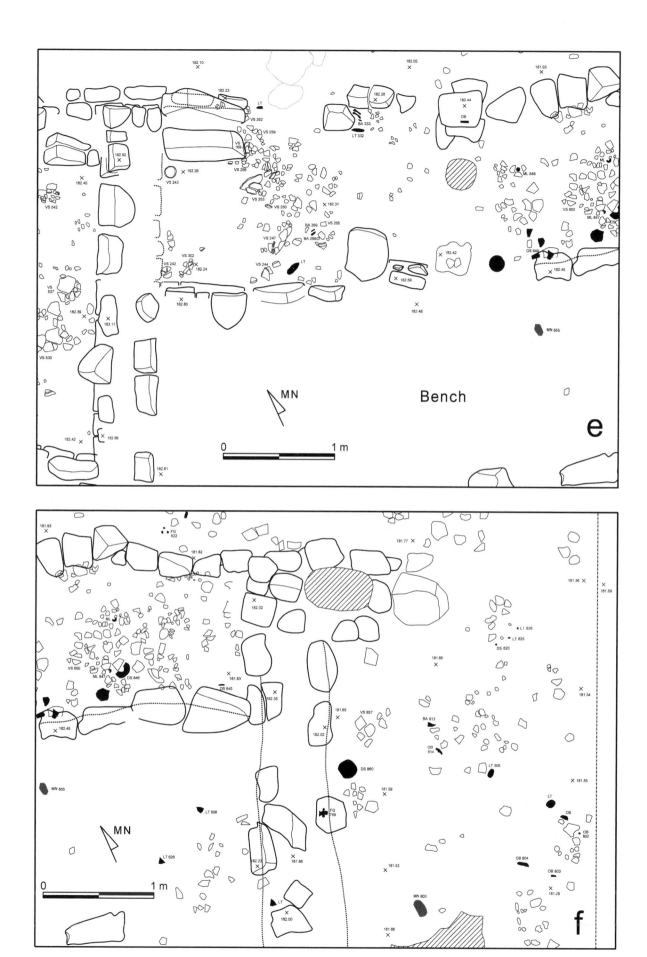

FIGURE 3.35. continued. (e) Western portion of the center room. (f) Eastern portion of the center room and western portion of the east room.

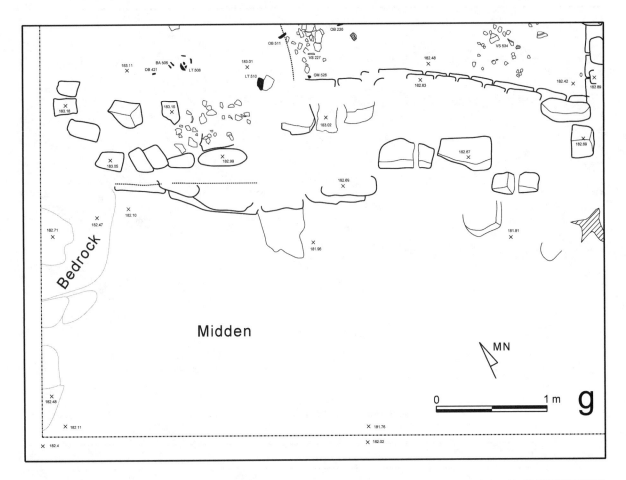

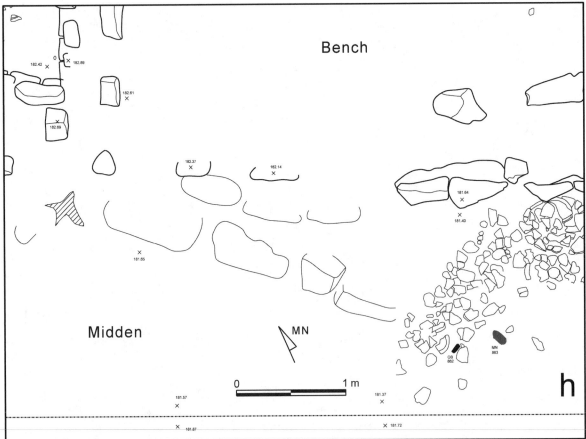

FIGURE 3.35. continued. (g) Area behind the west room. (h) Area behind the western portion of the center room.

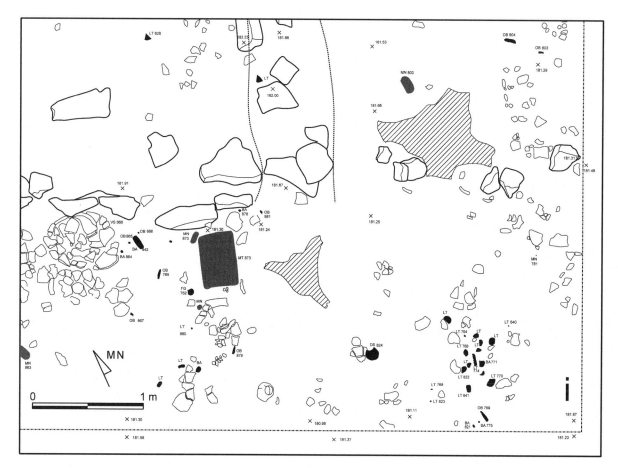

FIGURE 3.35. continued. (i) Area behind the eastern portion of the center room and the east room.

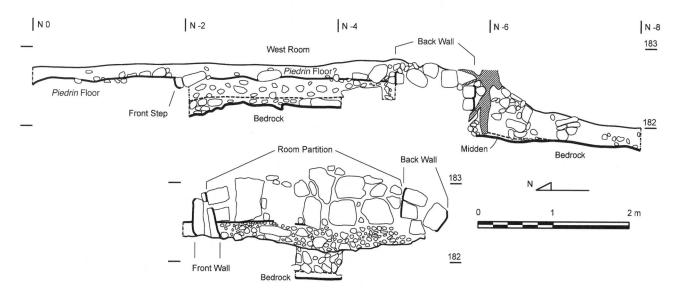

FIGURE 3.36. North-south section of the west room of Structure M8-13. *Above:* Room floor along the 11.2 line. *Below:* Front view of the room partition and the section of layers below the floor along the 13 line.

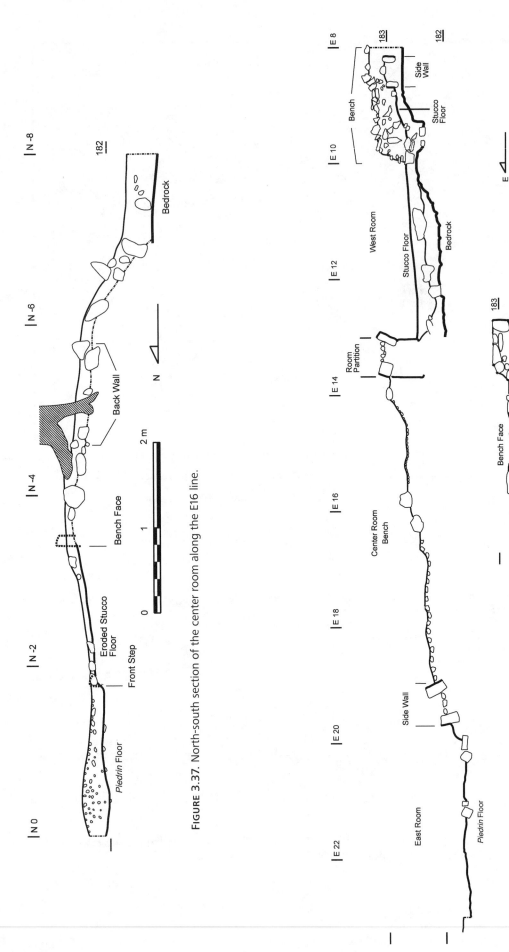

FIGURE 3.37. North-south section of the center room along the E16 line.

FIGURE 3.38. East-west section of Structure M8-13. *Above:* Section along the N-4 line. *Below:* Front view of the center room bench face and the section of layers below the floor.

FIGURE 3.39. Structure M8-13 after excavation, viewed from the north. *Left:* Center room, excavated in 1997. *Right:* West room and the western part of the center room, excavated in 1996.

revealing the east room (Valdés et al. 1999). In total, we excavated 35 units, exposing an area of 140 m². We used the same grid system as that of Structure M8-10 (Figures 3.33–3.39).

Architecture

The masonry parts of the walls appear to have originally measured roughly 1 m in height from the room floor. The back wall had mostly collapsed, but the relatively well preserved portion behind the west room measured 80 cm in thickness. It was built with roughly shaped blocks. The room divisions and front walls were roughly 55 cm thick, and they consisted mostly of vertically placed flat blocks. In the center of the wide doorway of the center room, a stone block was placed on the front step, which may have served as a base for a wooden post.

Unlike the other residences excavated in this area, the west room had a bench on its western side. The bench of the center room was closer to the Aguateca residence norm and filled the rear part of the room. The east room apparently did not have a bench. The face of the west room bench was made of horizontally placed roughly shaped blocks whereas that of the center room consisted of vertically placed slabs. Plaster was preserved in some parts of the floors of the central and west rooms, but it was not clear whether the bench floors were stuccoed. In particular, the surface of the center room bench was severely eroded because its back wall had collapsed backward.

The exterior floor in front of the building appears to have consisted of grabble, and we did not find traces of stucco. In front of the center room, large broken pieces of the bedrock were exposed, which may have been caused by a tree fall. Near the northern edge of the excavation, we

found a step of a low terrace extending to the north. The step was made of roughly shaped blocks. At the southern corner of the terrace, excavators found a pile of stone blocks. It was not clear whether they represented a formal structure.

In the western half of the excavated area behind the building, the bedrock was exposed. The eastern half was covered by a thin layer of grabbles.

In 1997 we excavated subfloor levels in the center room (Unit 2) and the west room (Units 1, 3, 9, 12, and 16). Excavators found construction fills made of loose blocks with little soil under floor fills consisting of grabbles (Figures 3.36–3.38). Underneath the construction fill in Units 1, 3, 12, and 16, we found a layer of black soil measuring 30 cm in thickness and resting on the bedrock. In other areas loose construction fills were placed directly on the bedrock.

We did not excavate under the room divisions and the center room bench, but they appeared to sit on the stucco floors. In excavating under the west room bench, we uncovered the continuation of the stucco floor. The front and walls, in contrast, were placed on the bedrock or construction fills. It is not clear whether the room divisions and the center room bench were added later during the occupation or whether they belonged to the original construction episode. We can be more confident that the bench of the west room was a later addition. These subfloor excavations did not reveal burials or caches.

Artifact Deposits

Numerous complete and reconstructible objects were found in and around this building, pointing to its rapid abandonment. Many objects were burned, but traces of

FIGURE 3.40. Artifacts found on the room floor in the western part of the center room of Structure M8-13.

fire were not so clear on architectural elements, which may be due to the eroded state of the floors and the hard stone materials. The artifact assemblage from Structure M8-13 appears similar to those from the excavated elite residences (Structures M7-35, M8-4, M8-8, and M8-10) in terms of objects related to essential domestic activities, such as food storage and preparation. Yet the number of valuable goods, such as jade beads and fine shell ornaments, was extremely small, in contrast with the abundance of such materials in the elite residences. Along with the lower quality of the construction, these artifact assemblages may point to the lower status of the residents.

Center Room

The bench of the center room was relatively clean of artifacts. Because the bench surface was severely eroded, some objects may have fallen into the fill or outside the structure. Still, the quantity of artifacts originally placed on this bench was probably small. A significantly larger quantity of artifacts was found on the room floor in front of the bench (Figures 3.35e, f). Near the room partition with the west room, excavators found a dense concentration of artifacts, including reconstructible storage jars, Subin/Chaquiste bowls, and serving vessels (Figure 3.40). The deposit on the eastern part of the room floor was somewhat less dense but involved several Tinaja/Pantano jars and serving vessels. Some of those vessels appear to have

fallen out of the room when the structure collapsed. The central part of the room was probably kept clean of artifacts originally.

There were three spindle whorls in the center room and in the area in front of it whereas the west room contained only one. This distribution pattern contrasts with those in the other residential buildings.

West Room

The west room contained storage jars, Tinaja/Pantano jars, and possible cooking vessels (Figure 3.35d). Some of these vessels were found on the bench, indicating that this bench was not a sleeping space. Fragments of two large limestone metates were found associated with this room. Two manos that fit these metates were found nearby, suggesting that these grinding stones were originally used in this room as complete pieces (Figure 3.41). Interestingly, one metate was nearly worn through whereas the other one was thick. The residents probably had just obtained a new metate to replace their old, worn one (Inomata 2003). Fragments of thick metate were found inside the room on the floor, while pieces of worn-down metate were found in front of the room on the collapsed stones of the front wall that fell forward. It appears that the metates were placed inside the room near the front wall on a table or supports made of perishable material (see Sheets 1992: 54; 2002). As the burning structure collapsed, the worn-down metate probably fell forward with the front wall,

FIGURE 3.41. Grinding stones and ceramic vessels found in the eastern part of Structure M8-13.

and the thick metate fell inside the room. In other words, this distribution pattern most likely resulted from the fire that began while these objects were still in their locations of use or storage. These grinding stones were most likely used for grinding corn, and the room appears to have been closely associated with food preparation.

East Room and Outside the Building

The portion of the east room excavated by the Aguateca Project contained a few serving vessels. The materials recovered by the Restoration Project First Phase were not refitted (Valdés et al. 1999), and the function of this room remains unclear.

On the west side of the building was a dense midden, which continued to the southern wall of Structure M8-10. It appears that most materials of this midden were discarded by the residents of Structure M8-10. The drainage coming from behind Structure M8-10 opened up to this midden, suggesting that it was constantly wet and probably stank. The terrain of this area sloped to the east. The water and garbage of this midden was contained by a low wall built from the southeastern corner of Structure M8-10 to the south, but some trash had spilled over to the area in front of Structure M8-13. The place of the higher-status residence on higher ground and the lower-status one down the slope was not only symbolic but appears to have had practical consequences.

Most trash and water were directed to the area be-

hind Structure M8-13 around its southwestern corner. Some trash was washed down to the area behind the west room. The trash apparently did not reach the area behind the eastern half of the center room and the east room. The water was probably diverted away from the building in this part. In this area, excavators unearthed several Tinaja/Pantano jars, Subin/Chaquiste bowls, and serving vessels (Figures 3.35g–i). This part appears to have been used as a work and storage space. A large flat limestone block found in this area may have been used as a work surface (Figures 3.35i, 3.42).

Interpretation

The artifact assemblage from Structure M8-13 appears similar to those from the excavated elite residences, Structures M7-35, M8-4, M8-8, and M8-10, in terms of objects related to essential domestic activities, such as food storage and preparation. Yet the number of valuable goods, such as jade beads and fine shell ornaments, was extremely small, which stands in contrast with the abundance of such materials in the elite residences. In addition, the quality of construction of Structure M8-13 was lower. These data indicate that Structure M8-13 was used as a residence but the status of its residents was lower than those of Structures M7-35, M8-4, M8-8, and M8-10.

The general pattern of space use is similar to that of the elite residences, with the center room oriented toward presentation and reception and one of the side rooms

FIGURE 3.42. Flat limestone block found behind the center room of Structure M8-13, viewed from the south.

geared to food preparation. Nonetheless, the presence of spindle whorls in the center room distinguishes Structure M8-13 from the elite residences. If the distribution of spindle whorls indeed reflects the use of space by females, this may indicate that the head of this household was a female. A possible interpretation is that Structure M8-13 was occupied by one of the wives of the male head, who primarily lived in Structure M8-10. It is also possible that Structure M8-10 was occupied by a conjugal family but that the division of male and female spaces in lower-status households was less strict than in elite residences.

A unique feature of Structure M8-13 is the side bench in the west room, a contrast with the rear benches commonly found in Aguateca residences. The occupants of this bench were mostly shielded from outside views, and this configuration appears to accord with the room's functions for food preparation rather than presentation to visitors and viewers.

STRUCTURES M8-2 AND M8-3: OPERATION 23B

Two small one-room structures, M8-2 and M8-3, were located to the east of Structure M8-4 (House of Mirrors). We expected that the excavation of these buildings would provide information on lower-status households or work-storage areas associated with elite residences. We excavated 24 units and an area of 96 m², exposing the two

buildings completely (Figures 3.43–3.47). We extended the grid system of Operation 23A over these structures.

Architecture

These buildings had C-shape walls made mostly of vertically placed slabs. The walls measured 50 to 70 cm in thickness, and the original heights of the masonry parts appear to have been about 1 m. The front parts of the buildings were wide open without front walls. The floors do not seem to have been stuccoed. Whereas Structure M8-2 did not have benches, Structure M8-3 was furnished with a C-shaped bench with its faces made of vertically placed blocks. On the exterior floor in front of Structure M8-2, we noted a feature defined by irregular stone blocks. Some bones were visible inside this feature. It was most likely a burial without capstones, but we did not excavate it. In 2005, during the second phase of the Aguateca Project, Ponciano excavated levels below the bench surface of Structure M8-3 (Figure 3.46). He encountered a fill mixed with compact soil placed on the bedrock. There were no burials or earlier constructions.

Artifact Deposits

The buildings were associated with complete and reconstructible objects, but their quantity, particularly that of prestige goods, was smaller than those of the elite

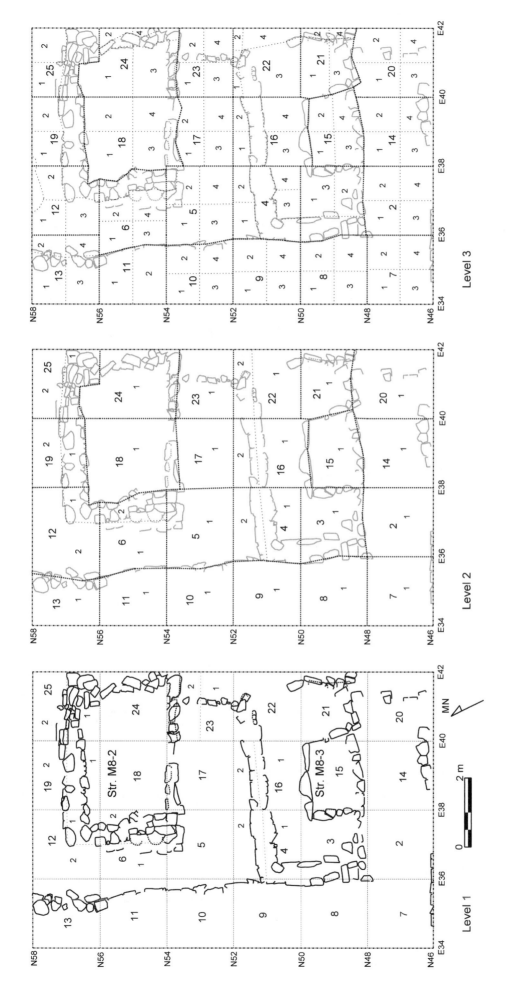

FIGURE 3.43. Plan of Structures M8-2 and M8-3 with the locations of excavation units and lots in Level 1 (humus layer), Level 2 (wall-fall layer), and Level 3 (on-floor artifacts).

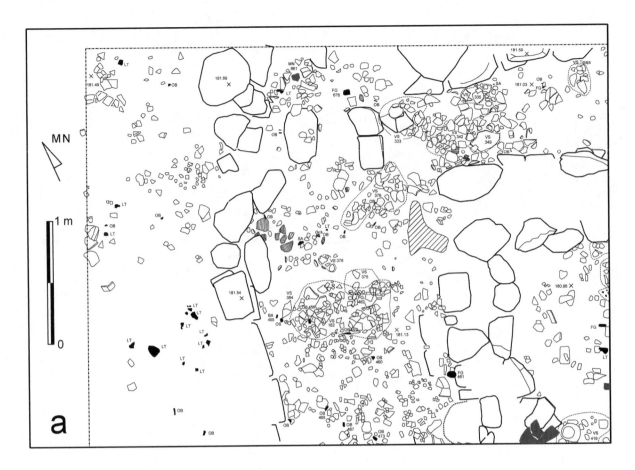

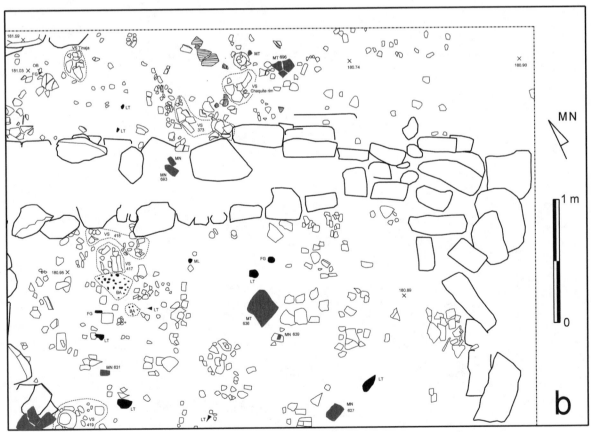

Figure 3.44. Distribution of artifacts on the last occupation floor of Structures M8-2 and M8-3. (a) Northwestern corner of Structure M8-2 and the area around it. (b) Northern part of Structure M8-2. (c) Southwestern corner of Structure M8-2 and the area around it. (d) Southern part of Structure M8-2 and the area in front of it. (e) Northwestern corner of Structure M8-3 and the area around it. (f) Northern part of Structure M8-3. (g) Southwestern corner of Structure M8-3 and the area around it. (h) Southern part of Structure M8-3 and the area in front of it.

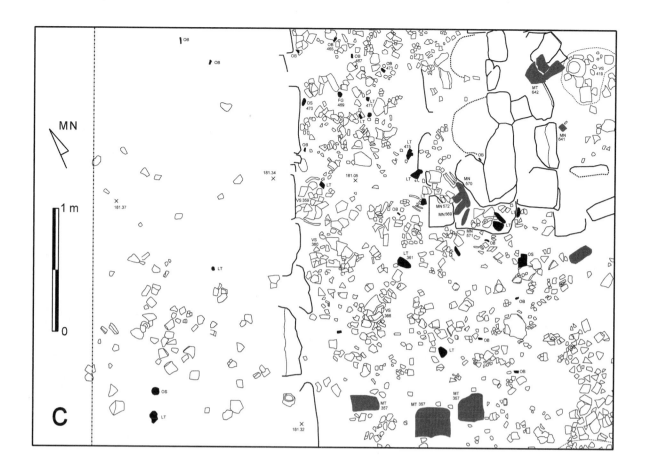

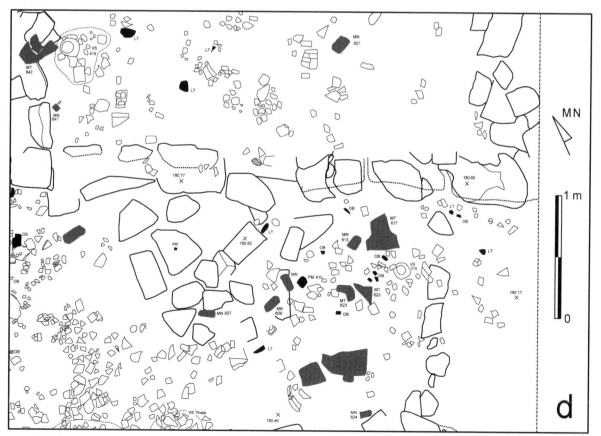

FIGURE 3.44. continued. (c) Southwestern corner of Structure M8-2 and the area around it. (d) Southern part of Structure M8-2 and the area in front of it.

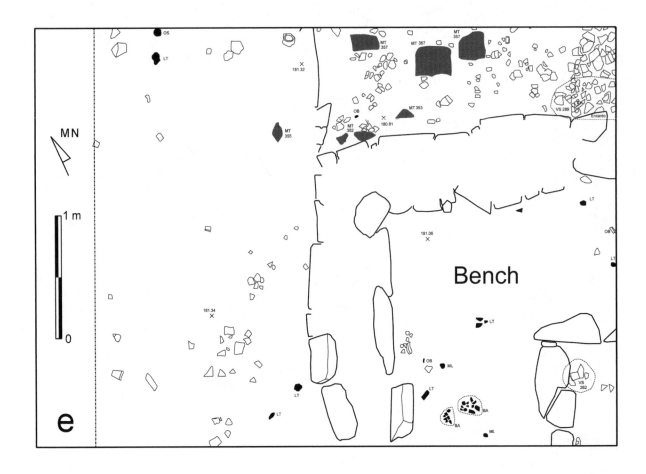

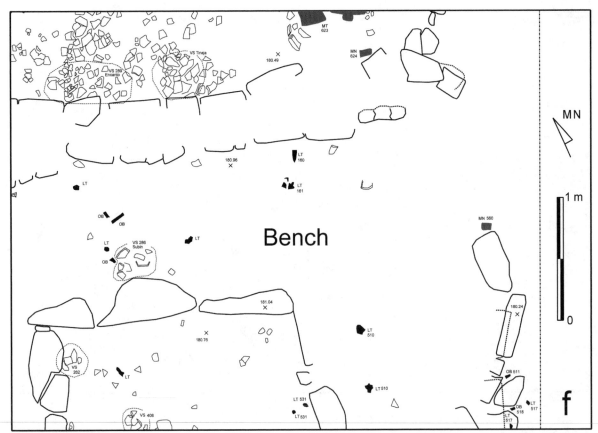

FIGURE 3.44. continued. (e) Northwestern corner of Structure M8-3 and the area around it. (f) Northern part of Structure M8-3.

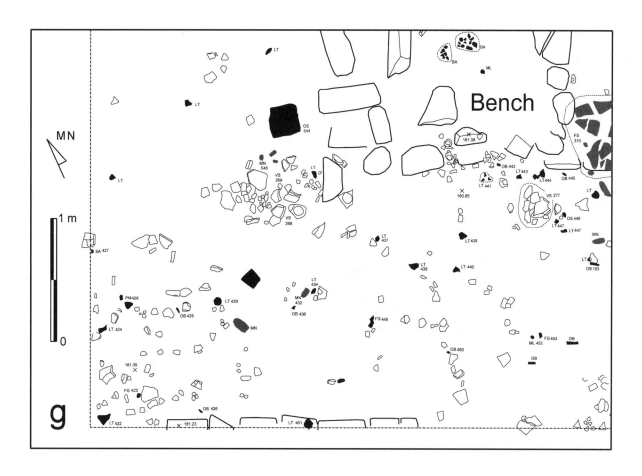

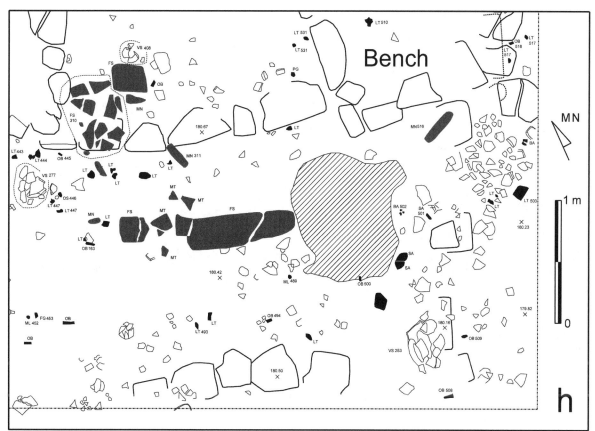

FIGURE 3.44. continued. (g) Southwestern corner of Structure M8-3 and the area around it. (h) Southern part of Structure M8-3 and the area in front of it.

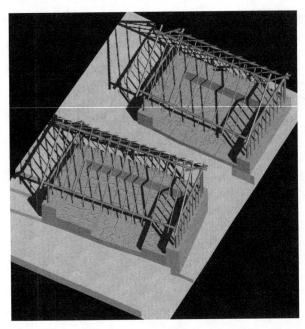

FIGURE 3.45. Reconstruction model of Structures M8-2 and M8-3, viewed from the south. The model shows only the excavated area.

residences. Many artifacts were burned, but traces of fire were not clear on architectural elements.

Structure M8-2

Structure M8-2 contained a relatively small number of stone tools, including Tinaja/Pantano jars and serving vessels (Figure 3.44a–d). Excavators unearthed a large number of artifacts in a deposit to the west of the structure. This area showed high concentrations of phosphate and appears to have been a midden (Terry et al. 2004). In the areas behind the building, excavators found several partial Tinaja/Pantano jars and Subin/Chaquiste bowls, as well as numerous shell ornaments. Since Structures M8-2 and M8-3 contained few shell artifacts or other ornaments, these materials found behind Structure M8-2 may have fallen from the Palace Group. Near the southwestern corner of the building, we uncovered a reconstructible storage jar and serving vessels, together with four manos (Figure 3.48). In front of the building there were two reconstructible metates.

Structure M8-3

The number of artifacts found in Structure M8-3 was relatively small (Figure 3.44e–h). A unique find was a small ball (roughly 3 cm in diameter) of red pigment made of specular hematite (Figure 3.49). Excavators found two rectangular flat limestone blocks and two long flat lime-

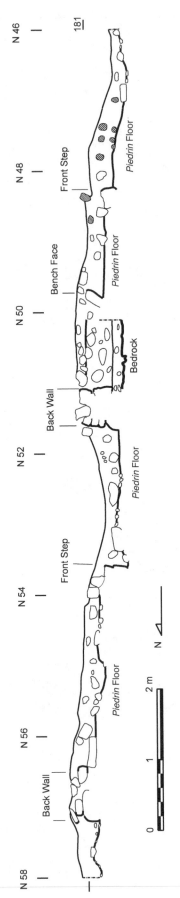

FIGURE 3.46. North-south section of Structures M8-2 and M8-3 along the E40 line.

FIGURE 3.47. Structures M8-2 (*back*) and M8-3 (*front*) after excavation, viewed from the south.

FIGURE 3.48. Artifacts found near the southwestern corner of Structure M8-2.

stone pieces, along with three manos. These stones appear to have been used for grinding, pounding, or pressing some materials, but their precise function is not clear. Excavators also found a *comal*-like vessel, Tinaja/Pantano jars, and serving vessels associated with this structure. Behind the building we unearthed a storage jar and a Subin/ Chaquiste bowl placed against the back wall, but it was not clear whether they were used by the users/occupants of Structure M8-3 or by those of Structure M8-2, if they were different groups. A few reconstructible vessels were found near the southern edge of the excavation. They may have fallen from Structure M8-5.

FIGURE 3.49. Ball of specular hematite pigment found in Structure M8-3.

Interpretation

The function of Structures M8-2 and M8-3 remains unclear. One possibility is that they were residences of low-status individuals. This hypothesis may be supported by the presence of a burial in front of Structure M8-2, a possible midden west of the structure, and its association with grinding stones. Another possibility is that they were manufacturing areas. The presence of unique grinding stones and pigment associated with Structure M8-3, as well as high levels of iron and copper in soils to the east of Structure M8-3, may point to this function (Terry et al. 2004). It is also possible that Structure M8-2 was a residence of low-status individuals who used M8-3 as a work space.

STRUCTURE M7-34 (HOUSE OF METATES): OPERATION 21A

Structure M7-34 faced the Causeway and was surrounded by stone walls. Its location and shape reminded us of Structure M8-11, which was partially excavated in 1991. In 1998 we excavated the main portion of the building, and in 1999 we expanded the excavation to the area in front of it, exposing small platforms, Structures M7-91 and M7-92. We laid out a grid system specific to this building. In total we excavated 82 units, exposing an area of 320 m² (Figures 3.50–3.59). The eastern and southern sides of the build-

ing were steep slopes leading to the level where Structures M8-4 and M8-8 stood. We did not excavate these sloped parts. We originally assumed that Structure M7-34 was an elite residence, but the results of excavation compelled us to consider the possibility that it was used for feasting and meetings by groups larger than a single household.

Architecture

Structure M7-34 consisted of three rooms, which we called the north, center, and south rooms. Each room was divided into front and rear parts by walls placed parallel to the axis of the building, and the partitions between the rooms abutted these front divisions. The large part of the rear section of each room was filled with a bench 60 to 70 cm high. The benches did not have niches. The front, side, and back walls, as well as bench faces, were made of cut stones with some chinking, whereas the room partitions consisted of vertically placed slabs and roughly shaped blocks. The front, side, and back walls appear to have reached the beams, but the masonry portions of the room partitions were probably lower. The front, side, and back walls measured roughly 70 cm in thickness, and the room divisions were approximately 50 cm thick. The floors appear to have had thin stucco, but large parts were eroded. It appears that the benches were raised after the side and back walls were built, and then the room

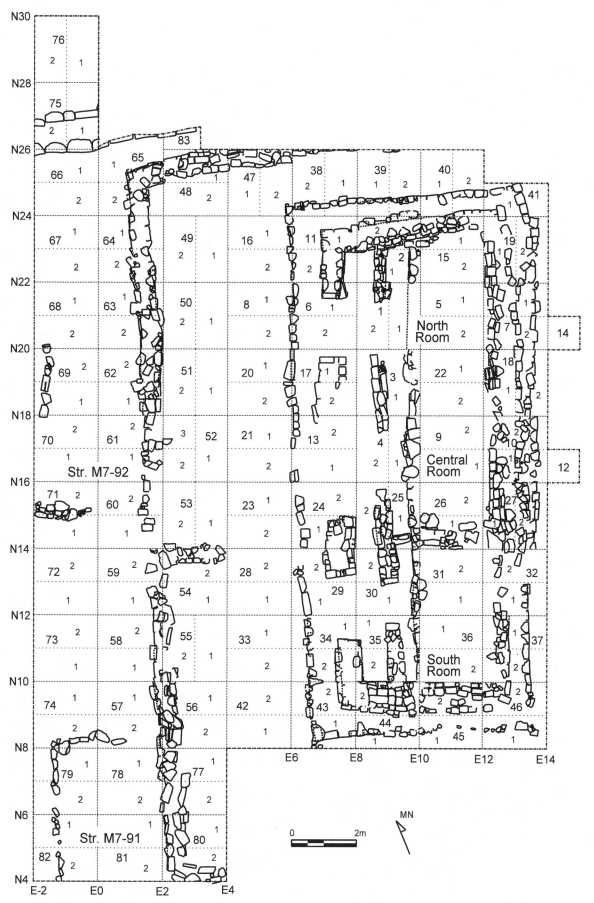

FIGURE 3.50. Plan of Structures M7-34, M7-91, and M7-92 with the locations of excavation units and lots in Level 1 (humus layer).

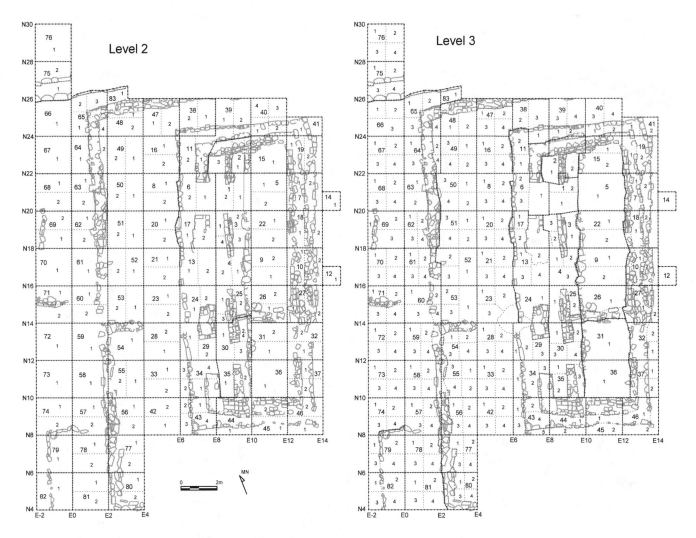

FIGURE 3.51. Lot numbers for Level 2 (wall-fall layer) and Level 3 (on-floor artifacts) in the excavation of Structures M7-34, M7-91, and M7-92.

divisions were placed. The front face of the north room bench and the room division between the north and center rooms were damaged, possibly by an old tree fall.

The building was constructed on a low platform that formed front, side, and back porches. The area in front of the building was a *piedrín* floor, or it may have been an eroded stucco floor. Walls M7-9 and M7-10 surrounded the building on the northern and western sides, leaving an opening of 4.2 m in front of the center room. These circumferential walls measured roughly 60 cm in thickness and consisted of vertically placed slabs and roughly shaped blocks. Their original height may have been approximately 80 to 100 cm. The walls were built along the edges of a low terrace that supported the building. It appears that the terrace existed at one point without the walls, which were added later during the occupation of the building.

The late construction date of the walls is also suggested by their relation to a stairway of the Causeway. In the northern part of the excavated area, we unearthed two wide steps made of large rectangular blocks. They were probably parts of a wide stairway that spanned the Causeway. Wall M7-9 stood in front of the eastern end of this stairway, leaving a space of only 60 cm between them and reducing the access to the stairway. In other words, the circumferential walls of Structure M7-34, and possibly the terrace underneath them as well, were added later than the stairway of the Causeway.

In front of Walls M7-9 and M7-10, excavators uncovered low platforms defined by coarse lines of roughly shaped blocks. Although we did not have direct evidence of perishable walls and roofs over these platforms, the presence of abundant artifacts suggested that they were

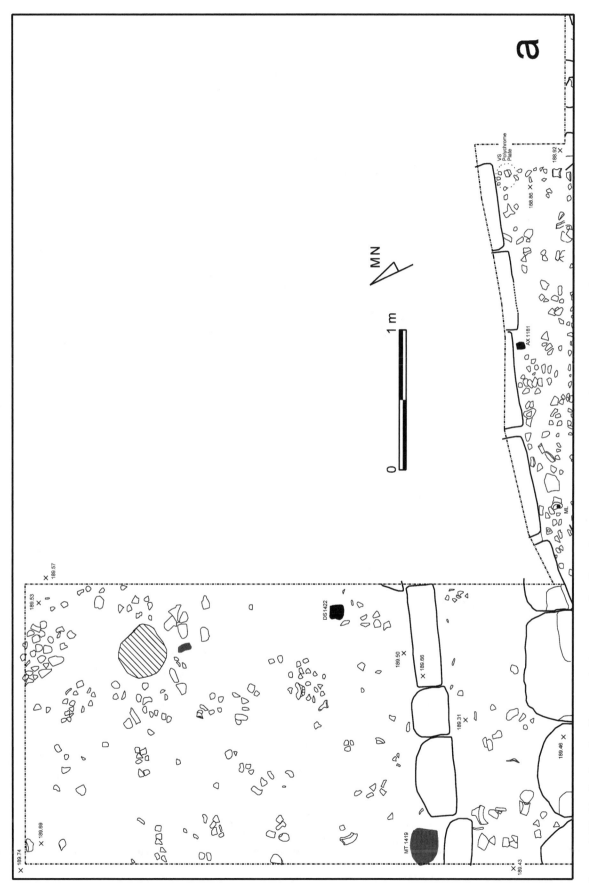

FIGURE 3.52. Distribution of artifacts on the last occupation floor of Structures M7-34, M7-91, and M7-92. (a) Terrace of the Palace Group. (b) Area north of Structure M7-92. (c) Area in front of the north room. (d) Front portion of the north room. (e) Bench of the north room. (f) Structure M7-92. (g) Area in front of the center room. (h) Front portion of the center room. (i) Bench of the center room. (j) Area between Structures M7-91 and M7-92. (k) Area in front of the south room. (l) Front portion of the south room. (m) Bench of the south room. (n) Structure M7-91.

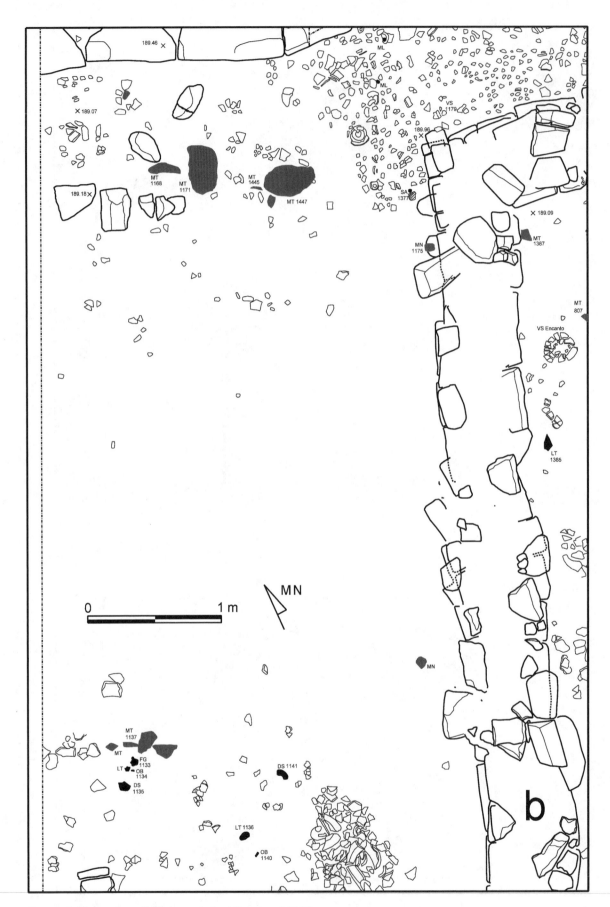

FIGURE 3.52. continued. (b) Area north of Structure M7-92.

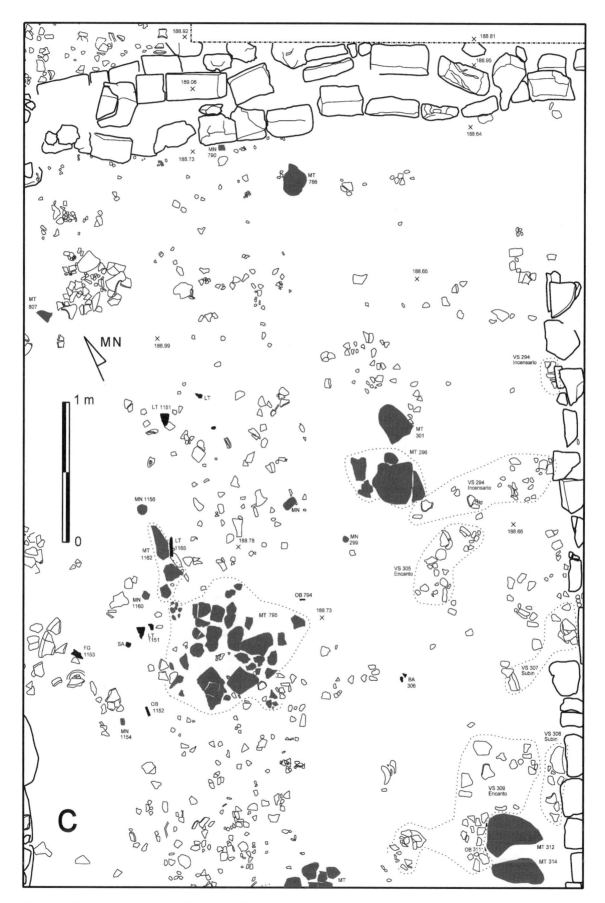

FIGURE 3.52. continued. (c) Area in front of the north room.

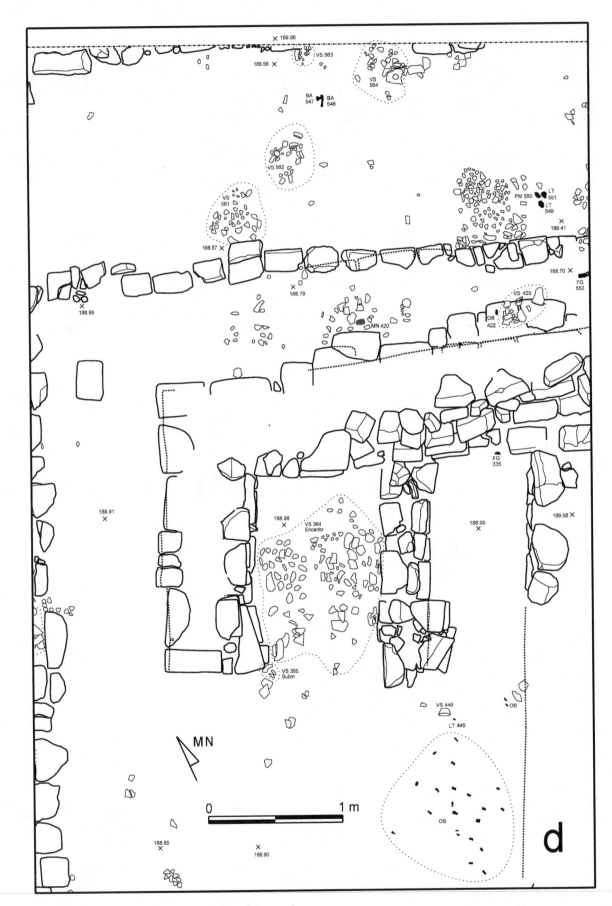

FIGURE 3.52. continued. (d) Front portion of the north room.

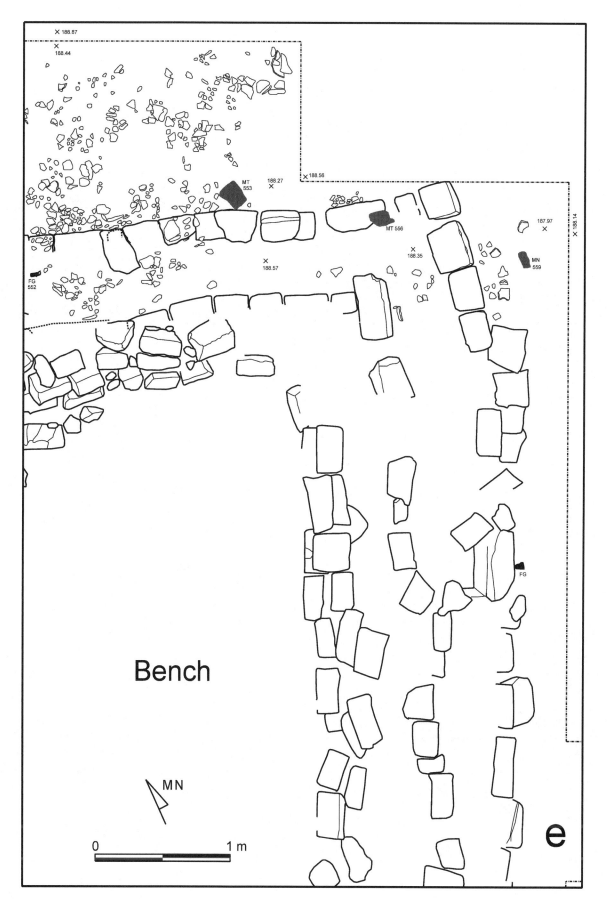

Bench

MN

0   1 m

FIGURE 3.52. continued. (e) Bench of the north room.

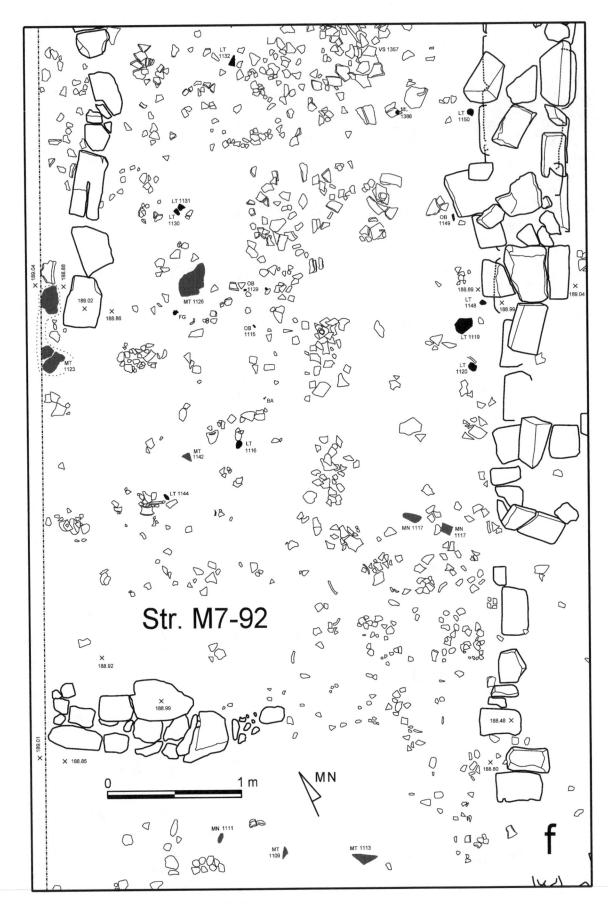

FIGURE 3.52. continued. (f) Structure M7-92.

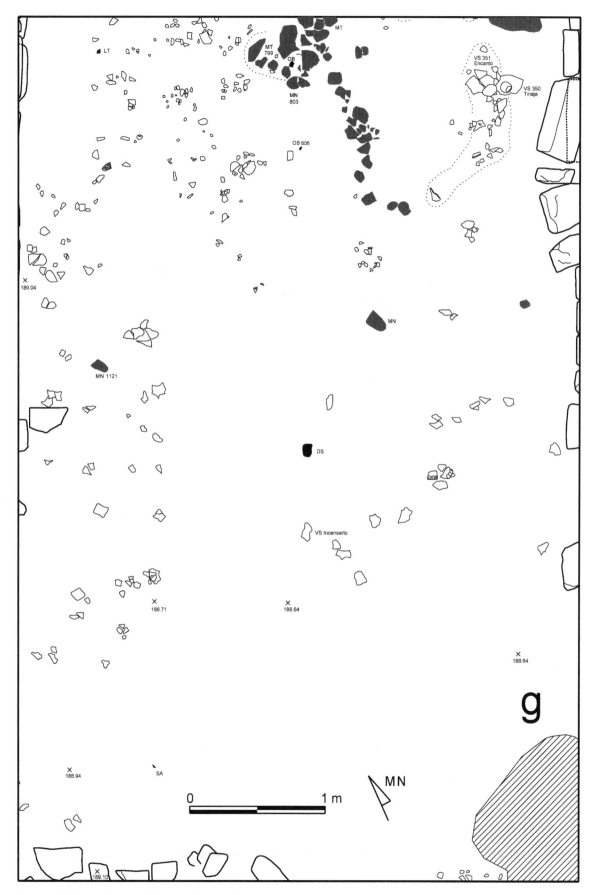

FIGURE 3.52. continued. (g) Area in front of the center room.

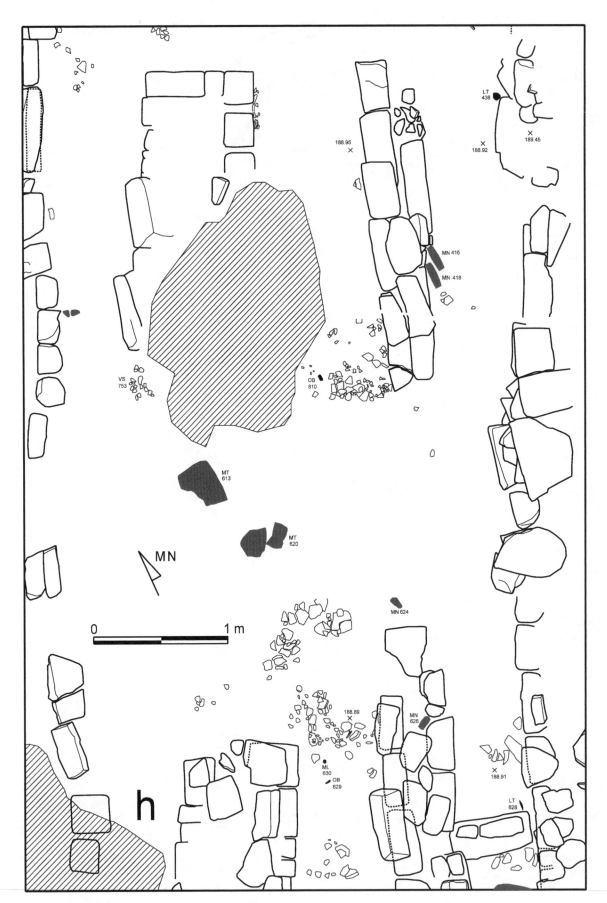

FIGURE 3.52. continued. (h) Front portion of the center room.

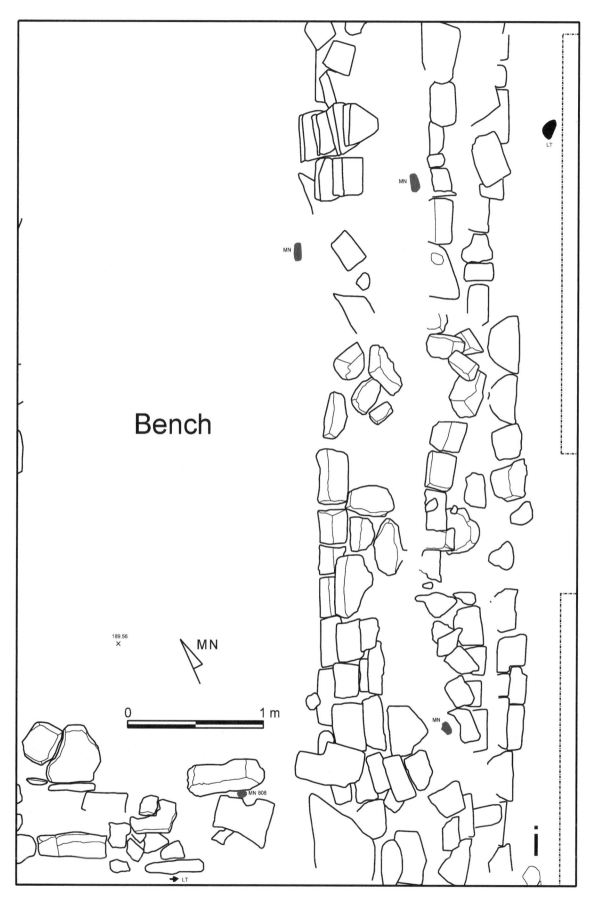

Bench

189.56
×

MN

0   1 m

MN 808

LT

i

FIGURE 3.52. continued. (i) Bench of the center room.

FIGURE 3.52. continued. (j) Area between Structures M7-91 and M7-92.

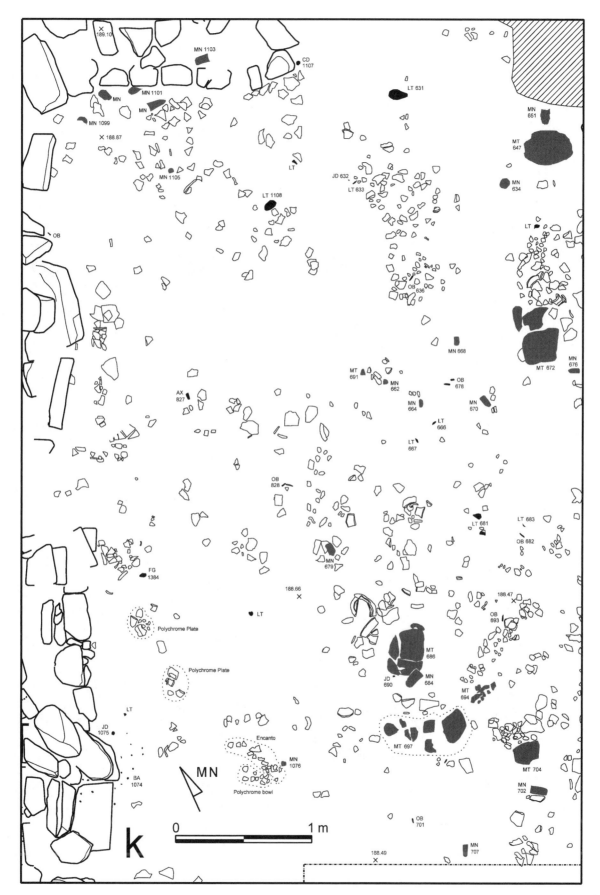

FIGURE 3.52. continued. (k) Area in front of the south room.

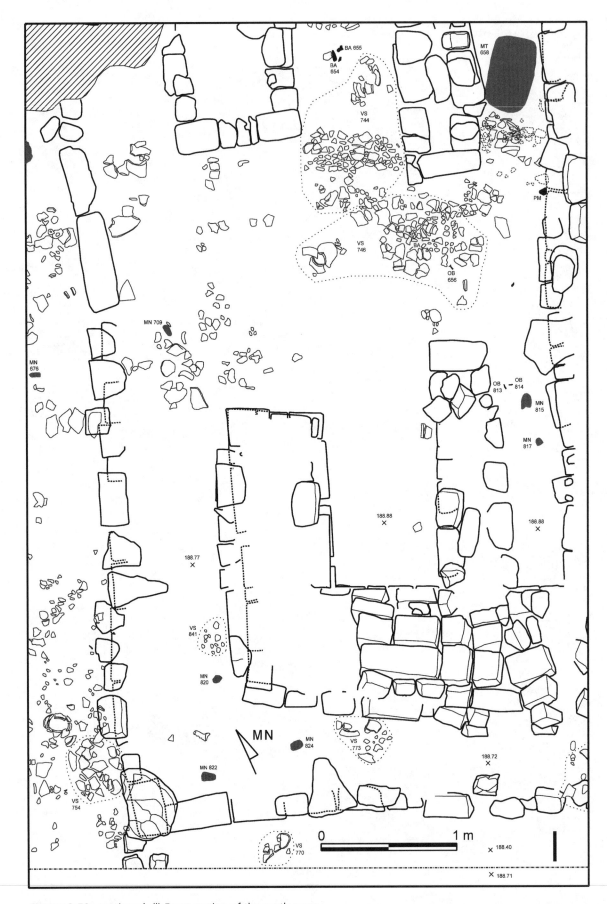

FIGURE 3.52. continued. (l) Front portion of the south room.

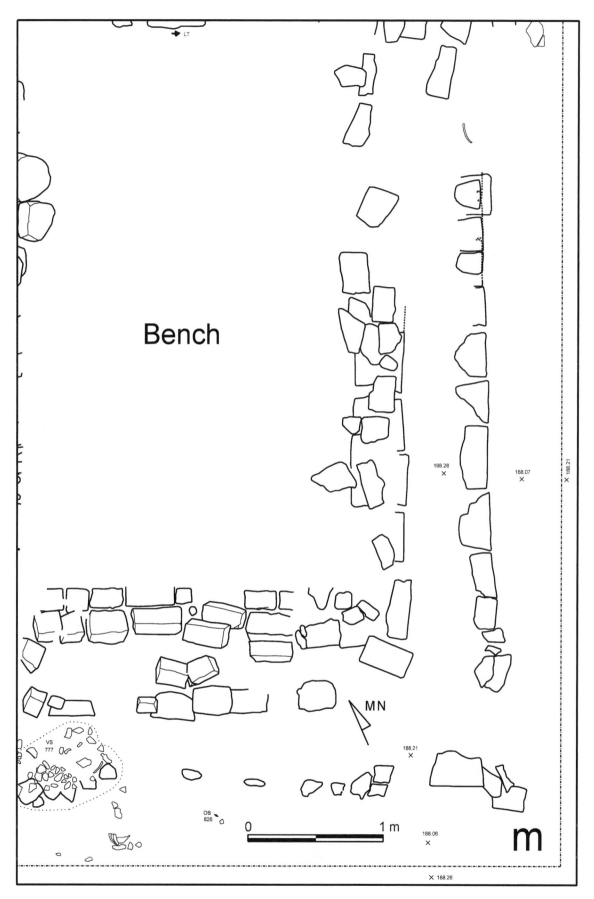

FIGURE 3.52. continued. (m) Bench of the south room.

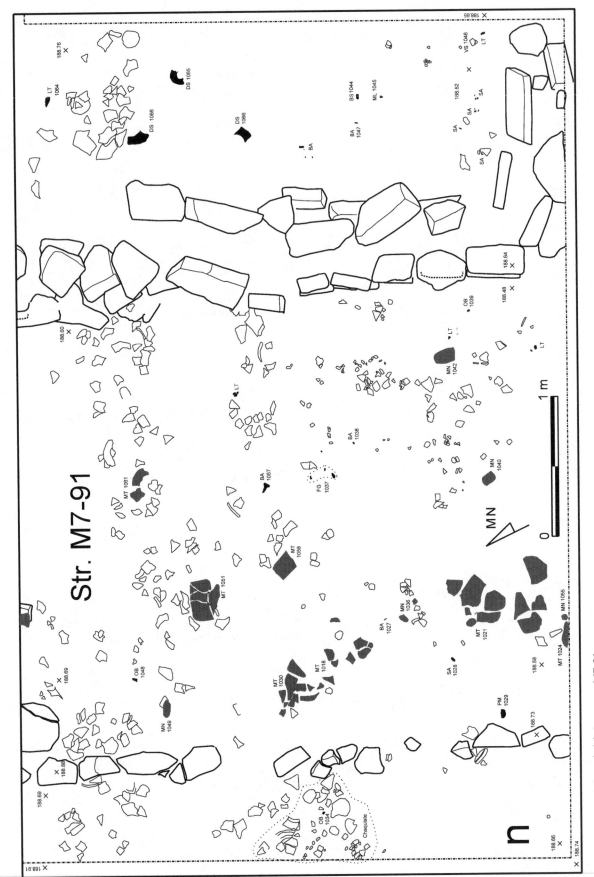

FIGURE 3.52. continued. (n) Structure M7-91.

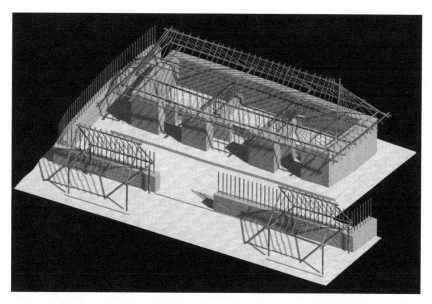

FIGURE 3.53. Reconstruction model of Structures M7-34, M7-91, and M7-92, viewed from the southwest.

work or storage areas protected from the elements. We named them Structures M7-91 and M7-92.

Artifact Deposits

A significant quantity of artifacts was found associated with Structure M7-34. Many objects exhibited traces of fire, but burning marks were not clear on architectural elements.

Inside Structure M7-34

The quantity of objects found inside the building was smaller than in the elite residences (Figure 3.52). In particular, the benches were mostly clean of artifacts. Most of the reconstructible ceramic vessels were found in narrow areas between the front walls and the front room divisions. Only in the south room was the northern part of the area between the bench and the front division filled with sherds, derived from a storage jar and a Pantano jar. A complete metate was also found face-down near the northern end of this part (Figure 3.60). Fragments of a reconstructible metate were unearthed in the doorway of the center room. Findings of interest include numerous small obsidian blades uncovered in the disturbed area in front of the bench of the north room.

Area Outside the Building and Inside Walls M7-9 and M7-10

We found a larger quantity of objects outside Structure M7-34 than inside (Figure 3.52). On the northern side, ex-

cavators uncovered storage jars, Tinaja/Pantano jars, serving vessels, and two pitchers. In the front area a substantial quantity of ceramics, including storage jars, Tinaja/Pantano jars, Subin/Chaquiste bowls, and serving vessels, was scattered over a wide area, but the central access between the opening of the circumferential walls and the center room was kept relatively clean of objects. Finds of interest include an incense burner with an old-man face discovered in front of the north room (WVS 21A-20, Cat. 310050). Also found in this area were seven reconstructible large limestone metates (Figure 3.61).

The south side was not completely excavated because it was near the edge of the terrace. A small number of vessels were found, indicating that this area was also used as a storage or work space. Some objects, including the metates found behind Structure M8-8 (House of Axes), may have fallen down the slope from this part. Unlike the case with the other elite residences, the number of objects found behind the structure was small. This is probably because there was only a narrow area between the back wall of the building and the edge of the terrace.

Structures M7-91 and M7-92 and the Area Outside Walls M7-9 and M7-10

Numerous objects found in Structures M7-91 and M7-92 and outside Walls M7-9 and 10 were badly eroded, but many of the ceramic sherds appear to form reconstructible vessels, including storage jars, Tinaja/Pantano jars, Subin/Chaquiste bowls, and serving vessels. These ceramics were

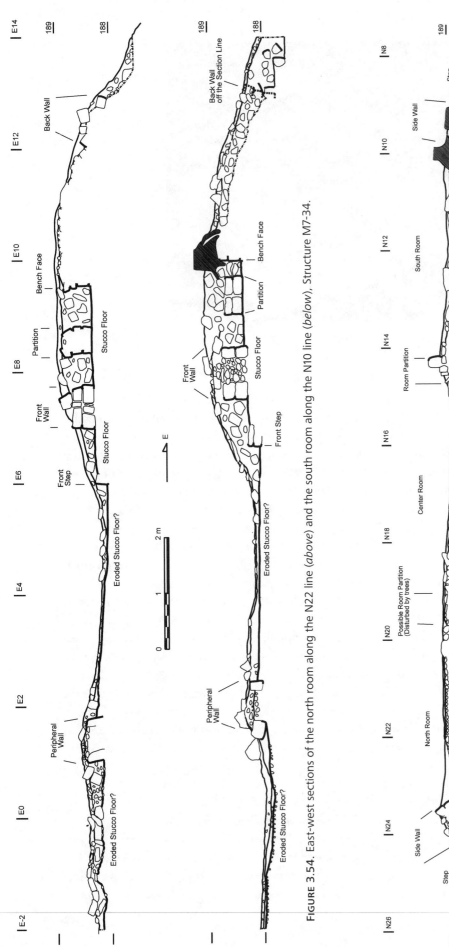

FIGURE 3.54. East-west sections of the north room along the N22 line (above) and the south room along the N10 line (below), Structure M7-34.

FIGURE 3.55. North-south section along the E10 line (above) and east-west section of the center room along the N18 line (below), Structure M7-34.

FIGURE 3.56. Structure M7-34 after excavation, viewed from the west. *Top left:* North room. *Top right:* Center room. *Left:* South room.

FIGURE 3.57. Structure M7-34 and the area in front of it, viewed from the north. *Left:* Structure M7-34, excavated in 1998. *Right:* Circumferential walls and Structures M7-91 and M7-92, excavated in 1999.

FIGURE 3.58. Structure M7-91, viewed from the west.

FIGURE 3.59. Structure M7-92, viewed from the west.

found in Structures M7-91 and M7-92, as well as the area between them (Figures 3.58, 3.59). Metates were also abundant in this area. Excavators found four of them associated with Structure M7-91 and one in Structure M7-92. A reconstructible storage jar was found in front of the stair-

way of the Causeway, and a few serving vessels were on the terrace above the stairway. These objects suggest that the stairway and the Causeway had lost much of their function as a public and ceremonial street. In the small space between the eastern part of the stairway of the Cause-

FIGURE 3.60. Face-down metate and other artifacts found in the north part of the area in front of the bench of the south room, Structure M7-34, viewed from the south.

way and Wall M7-9, excavators found a dense deposit of ceramics and other artifacts (Figure 3.62). They included partially reconstructible Tinaja/Pantano jars and a Subin/Chaquiste bowl. It is not clear whether this was a midden or a storage area.

Interpretation

The pattern of artifact distribution in and around Structure M7-34 is different in several respects from those of the elite residences, Structures M7-35, M8-4, M8-8, and M8-10. First, the number of reconstructible vessels and other artifacts found in Structure M7-34 is smaller. A larger quantity of objects, however, was unearthed outside the building. Second, functional differences between the rooms of this building were not clear. We did not find metates and other objects closely associated with food preparation in the center rooms of the elite residences, and these spaces appear to have served for meetings and the reception of visitors. The center room of Structure M7-34, in contrast, contained a large limestone metate. Third, the large number of metates distinguishes the artifact assemblage of Structure M7-34 from those of the elite residences. The quantity appears to exceed the needs of a common household. Fourth, the presence of an incense burner is unique, or nearly so. Although Structure M8-4 contained incense burners, we did not find this type of vessel in the other elite residences. A simpler incense burner was uncovered in Structure M8-17, a possible shrine (Inomata and Stiver 1998).

The circumferential walls of Structure M7-34 are similar to those of Structures M7-22 (House of Masks), M7-32 (House of Bones), M8-11, and M8-37. Although

FIGURE 3.61. Grinding stones and other artifacts found in the area in front of the north room of Structure M7-34.

FIGURE 3.62. Dense artifact deposit found between the terrace stairway and Wall M7-9.

the precise timing of their construction is not clear, they most likely belong to the latter part of the occupation of the buildings. One possibility is that the occupants or users of these structures tried to shield the buildings from public view. Alternatively, these walls may have had defensive functions. The latter explanation appears to apply better to the walls in the Palace Group. If so, these walls may have been contemporaneous with other defensive walls. The presence of numerous objects in the area between Structure M7-34 and these walls leads us to wonder whether this area was roofed, but we did not find any direct evidence.

Structures M7-91 and M7-92 were most likely built toward the end of the Late Classic occupation of Aguateca. By that time, defensive walls had probably blocked the Causeway, and the Causeway may have lost its original function.

These considerations lead to two possible interpretations of Structure M7-34's functions. One possibility is that Structure M7-34 originally served as an elite residence similar to Structures M7-35, M8-4, M8-8, and M8-10, but its use drastically changed after the construction of defensive walls. Structure M7-34 may have served to provide food to the new residents who moved into the epicenter of Aguateca, which was the best-protected area. Alternatively, it may have been meant to supply food to warriors at the time of enemy attacks.

Another possible explanation is that the artifact assemblage reflects the original function of the building relatively well. In this case, Structure M7-34 may have functioned as a communal house used by groups larger than a single household. A large number of metates may have been used for communal feasting. The presence of an incense burner may point to this interpretation. William Ringle and George Bey (2001:276) suggest that the colonnaded halls of Mayapan, which had abundant remains of incense burners, were *popol nah* (council houses documented in Colonial sources) (Fash et al. 1992). Although we are reluctant to equate Structure M7-34 of Aguateca with Colonial-period *popol nah*, this similarity is significant. In addition, seven reconstructible ceramic drums were found in this operation. These musical instruments may also have been used during communal rituals. Although the nature of Structure M7-34 is still not clear, the presence of an incense burner and musical instruments appears to support the latter interpretation.

4

chapter

The Barranca Escondida

Takeshi Inomata and Markus Eberl

The Barranca Escondida is located 150 m south of the Main Plaza in the middle of a steep escarpment, and its northern part is demarcated by the Grieta Rincón (Figures 1.3 and 1.7). Because of its rugged topography, the area was not mapped during Inomata's 1990–1993 survey. The site's government guards reported the presence of carved monuments in this area to the members of the Petexbatun Regional Archaeological Project in 1996, and Héctor Escobedo visited the area (Escobedo, personal communication 2004), but we were not informed of this finding. After our field season of 1998, some of the monuments in the Barranca Escondida were looted. On hearing this news, Inomata and Ponciano made an emergency trip to examine the damage. They photographed and plotted the remaining fragments of monuments (Figure 4.1).

During the following field season, in 1999, Eberl conducted excavations in the Barranca Escondida (Figures 4.2–4.8). He also documented monuments and moved some pieces to the guardhouse for protection. Excavations focused on the following areas: (1) the area around the stelae (Operation 24A), (2) the rock outcrop behind the stelae (Operation 24B), (3) the hill north of the stelae (Operation 24C), (4) the eastern entrance to the Grieta Rincón (Operation 24D), (5) the Hidden Chasm (Operation 24A Units 17 and 18), and (6) the Cliff Chasm (Operation 24A Units 14–16).

EXCAVATIONS

Area around the Stelae

The three stelae (Stelae 15, 16, and 17) were found on a leveled area filled with fist-sized and larger rocks. The lack of sediments in the fill suggests that it was artificial construction. The looters disturbed a large part of the stela area. They left the eroded fragments of the three stelae behind, and only the lower part of Stela 15 was still in place, set into the loose fill in front of the rock outcrop, facing north.

The looters had thrown three large fragments of Stela 17 over the eastern escarpment, and the surfaces of the two fragments found at the foot of the escarpment bore heavy and recent abrasion marks. These three pieces made the monument complete. Stela 17 was most likely placed originally in the leveled part of the stela area.

When we excavated the loose fill around Stela 15, we noticed that the part below the surface was roughly carved and unpolished. It is likely that Stela 15 was placed originally in this location and that the carving was finished after its erection. If the stela had been reset in antiquity, its weight would have made it difficult to place it at the same depth as before. The lower left side of Stela 15 had an incision with an eroded U-shaped profile measuring several centimeters in length and 1.5 cm in depth (visible in Figure 4.4). It may represent an ancient attempt to cut down the monument. The fill around the butt of Stela 15 did not contain ceramics. A fragment with glyphic inscriptions found during the 1998 visit most likely belongs to Stela 15 because of its calligraphic style and the crystalline quality of the limestone. Several plain limestone fragments with a similar consistency bore marks of the chainsaw that the looters used to remove better-preserved parts of Stela 15.

The looters also moved pieces of Stela 16. The excavation revealed its top portion with inscriptions, which made this monument complete (Figure 4.7). The eroded condition of this stela apparently discouraged the looters. The extensive excavation of the stela area revealed fragments of two plain altars (O and P). Altar O measured 0.60 m in diameter and 0.12 m in height, and Altar P had a diameter of 0.54 m and a height of 0.12 m (Figure 4.8). They were noticeably smaller than other altars at Aguateca (Graham 1967). These altars were buried underneath 10–15-cm-thick humus topsoil and embedded in rubble. The vicinity of the stelae was heavily disturbed by the looters, and we encountered an undisturbed section

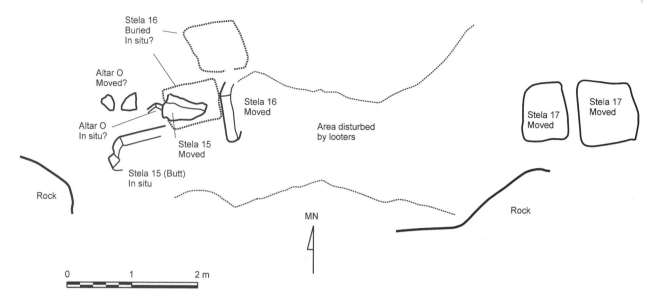

FIGURE 4.1. Monument pieces found in the stela area of the Barranca Escondida.

FIGURE 4.2. The stela area of the Barranca Escondida during the 1999 excavation, viewed from the northwest.

only in the eastern part of the excavated area. There the looters piled 10 cm of loose back dirt, containing almost 300 sherds, on top of very dark grayish-brown humus and gravel measuring 20 cm in thickness. This undisturbed layer contained close to 200 ceramic sherds, along with the inscribed top part of Stela 16. Below it was the artifact-free fill that leveled the stela area. Farther north, the humus-gravel layer abutted sterile, reddish-brown humus.

Roughly 3,000 ceramic sherds and other artifacts were recovered from the looters' back dirt and the humus-gravel layer around the stelae, the foot of the rock outcrop, and toward the entrance to the Hidden Chasm. Given the absence of artifacts in the fill around Stela 15 and in the eastern part, nearly all the artifacts found in the looters' back dirt were probably deposited originally on the surface or in the humus-gravel layer.

FIGURE 4.3. The stela area and the rock outcrop during the 1999 excavation, viewed from the north.

FIGURE 4.4. The butt of Stela 15 and fragments of Stela 16 and Altar O, as found in 1998.

Rock Outcrop

To the south of the stelae was a circular rock outcrop, roughly 3 m higher than the stela area (Figures 4.9–4.11). From the stela area one can easily ascend the outcrop, although we did not find any remains of artificial stairs. All other sides were nearly vertical cliffs of 20 m. On the flat top of the outcrop, measuring 60 m², excavators found a very thin layer of densely rooted humus. Underneath it was a dark-brown layer of loose sand and gravel over bedrock. The sand-gravel layer formed a level surface, being thicker to the south as the bedrock declined. All artifacts were found on top of or in the first centimeters of this

FIGURE 4.5. The hill to the north of the stela area of the Barranca Escondida, viewed from the southeast. The white rock that is split in half on the viewer's left of the person in the lowest location is the butt of Stela 18.

FIGURE 4.6. The midsection of Stela 18, found on the rock ledge to the northwest of the stela area of the Barranca Escondida. The stela area with monument fragments is visible in the background.

layer. This stratigraphy differed markedly from the dense clayey humus commonly found at Aguateca. The loose sand-gravel layer resembled floors in some residences and appears to have been laid as a floor. The chemical analysis of soil samples did not detect particular concentrations of trace elements that could have helped to define activity areas.

Several rocks and some cut stones were found on top of the sand-gravel floor. Although they did not form clear wall foundations, their distribution showed roughly square alignment, suggesting that a structure (Structure M9-1) once stood there; it was probably destroyed in ancient times (Figure 4.12). The in situ Stela 15 stood in front of the outcrop, facing north, and it is likely that Stelae 16 and 17 were originally placed in similar positions. This lay-

out resembles the temple-stela complexes found in the Aguateca Main Plaza and at other centers. The structure on the outcrop probably served as a shrine or temple before it was destroyed.

The Hill North of the Stela Area

A survey around the stela area led to the discovery of Stela 18 on the rock ledge northwest of the entrance to the Hidden Chasm. The stela butt was in its original location, though it had fallen face-down and had been split by a boulder. Stela 18 originally faced the rock outcrop and Stela 15. The broken-off midsection of the stela was found at the edge of the rock ledge. We assumed that the top section had fallen off the ledge, although an intense search failed to uncover it, except for several small fragments.

FIGURE 4.7. The top portion of Stela 16, found during the 1999 excavation.

FIGURE 4.8. Altar O (*left*) and Altar P (*right*).

The discovery of Stela 18 prompted an extensive excavation of the hill north of the stela area. Except for a small quantity of ceramics found around Stela 18, the area was nearly devoid of artifacts. We did not find any other remains of constructions in this area.

Eastern Entrance to the Grieta Rincón

Excavations in the eastern entrance to the Grieta Rincón uncovered a circular rock measuring 1.4 m in diameter and 0.4 m in height. It was large enough to block the entrance to the chasm. We suspected that this might be a human-made monument and tentatively named it Altar Q. However, the rock was plain, not perfectly round, and had crude edges. It was probably a natural rock, although it may have been placed in this location purposefully.

During the second phase of the Aguateca Project, Reiko Ishihara further investigated the Grieta Rincón (Ishihara 2007, 2009). In addition, Hiro Iwamoto

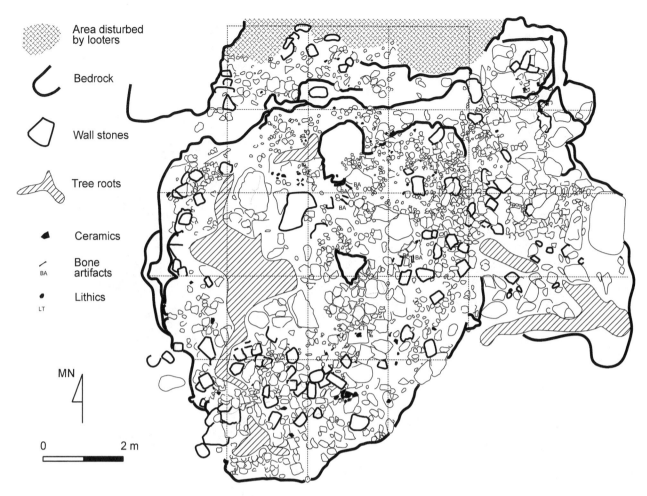

Area disturbed
by looters

Bedrock

Wall stones

Tree roots

Ceramics

Bone
artifacts
BA

Lithics
LT

MN

0   2 m

FIGURE 4.9. Plan of the rock outcrop of the Barranca Escondida.

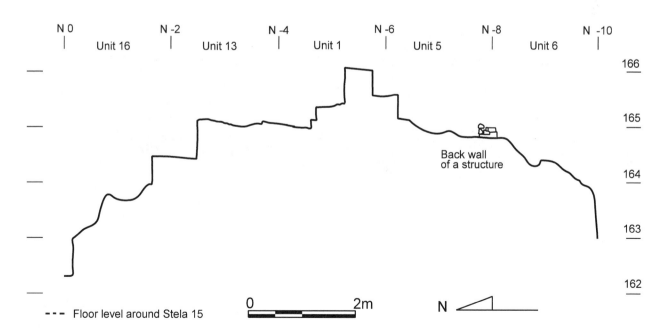

N 0   N -2   N -4   N -6   N -8   N -10

Unit 16   Unit 13   Unit 1   Unit 5   Unit 6

166

165

Back wall
of a structure

164

163

162

- - - Floor level around Stela 15   0   2m   N

FIGURE 4.10. Elevation of the rock outcrop of the Barranca Escondida.

FIGURE 4.11. The rock outcrop of the Barranca Escondida, viewed from the west.

FIGURE 4.12. The alignment of cut stones on the rock outcrop (Units 24B6 and 10), viewed from the east.

discovered petroglyphs northeast of the stela area on a flat panel under an overhanging rock (Iwamoto and Inomata 2009). Their date and relations to the stelae are not clear.

Hidden Chasm

The entrance to the Hidden Chasm was found 12 m to the west of the stela area (Figure 4.13). The chasm was no more than 2.5 m wide and at least 25 m deep. Filled-in rocks and sediments created at least three levels where one can walk (Figure 4.14). Several fissures in the bedrock, some of them wide enough to crawl through, formed a three-dimensional maze of walkways and fresh-air channels. Because of the restricted interior space, only a few people could have congregated inside the chasm. Dur-

FIGURE 4.13. Entrance to the Hidden Chasm.

ing the tape-and-compass mapping of the interior, Eberl noted various artifacts, including greenstone and shell ornaments, on the surface and several wall sections that were darkened by soot at floor level. We collected the artifacts around the entrance and on the first level. The eastern end of the first level, which had a high density of materials, was designated Operation 24A Unit 17.

We placed a test pit on the second level (Operation 24A Unit 18), excavating through thick layers of bat excrement and sediments washed in from outside (Figure 4.15). Most artifacts were found in depths between 0.2 m and 0.5 m. Among the artifacts from the lowermost level were three complete vessels, including two identical heart-shaped miniature vessels with stoppers (WVS 24A-2, Cat. 310221; WVS 24A-3, Cat. 310291; WVS 24A-4, Cat. 310222; WVS 24A-5, Cat. 310461; WVS 24A-6, Cat. 310220), seven complete bifacial points, and a complete greenstone axe.

Cliff Chasm

A large fissure marked the southwestern face of the cliff. Rocks and boulders filled the fissure, but we were able to follow it for a few meters. This fissure may be connected to the Hidden Chasm. We collected ceramic sherds from two spots in the interior of the fissure (Operation 24A Units 15 and 16). In an excavation unit placed at the mouth of the fissure (Operation 24A Unit 14), we recovered a complete flint biface, roughly 150 ceramic sherds, and other artifacts in the thin topsoil layer above bedrock. The ceramic assemblage consisted mostly of Early Classic types, including Quintal Unslipped, Triunfo Striated, Balanza Black, and Dos Arroyos Polychrome, which corresponded chronologically to the early ceramic materials found in the stela area. One beautifully preserved Dos Arroyos plate sherd found in the interior of the fissure fitted to a fragment found in the excavation.

MONUMENTS AND ARTIFACTS

Drawings and discussions of the monuments are presented in Volume 3 (Inomata and Triadan, in preparation). Artifact types and their distributions at Aguateca are discussed in the second part of this volume (ceramics), in Volume 2 (Aoyama 2009) (lithics and cave stones), and in Volume 3 (fossilized wood and other artifacts). Here we present a summary of these data.

Stela 15 shows stylistic similarities to Stela 5 of Tamarindito and probably dates to the early sixth century (Eberl 2007:63). Stela 16 appears to record the dates of 9.9.13.0.0 (AD 626) and 9.10.0.0.0 (AD 633). Stelae 17 and 18 do not show calendrical dates, but their style appears to correspond to those of the seventh century and the early eighth century. All the stelae were broken, and the figure on Stela 16 was defaced. It is possible that the monuments were mutilated in ancient times. Fragments of Stelae 16 and 17 could be refitted into complete monuments. Some pieces of Stela 15, and possibly those of Stela 18, appear to have been removed by looters.

Ceramics were found in substantial quantities in the stela area, on the rock outcrop, and inside the chasms. These ceramic assemblages are characterized by the high proportions of plates and *incensarios* and the low percentage of jars compared with those found in residential areas (see Table 7.2). This pattern most likely reflects the predominantly ritual use of the Barranca Escondida. A substantial portion of the ceramics found in the Barranca Escondida appears to belong to the Jordan complex of the Early Classic period and to the early facet of

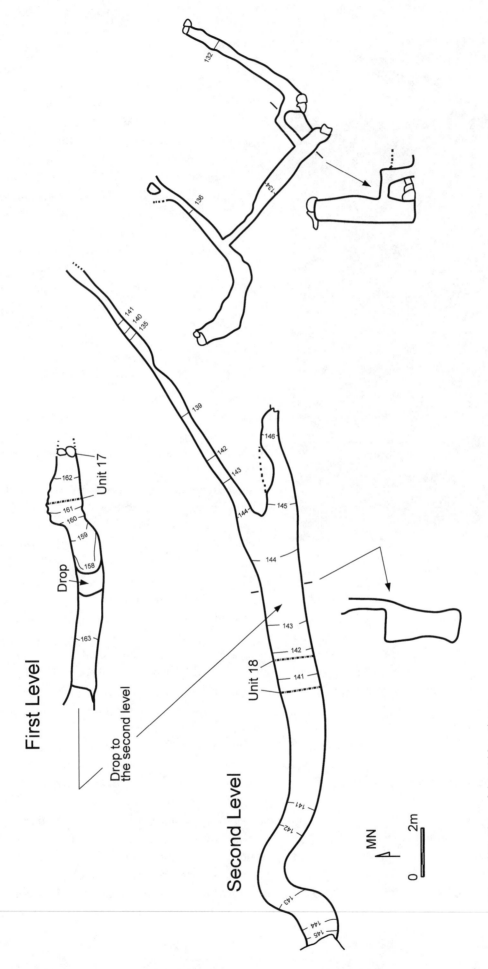

First Level

Second Level

Unit 17

Unit 18

Drop

Drop to
the second level

MN

0   2m

FIGURE 4.14. Plans of the Hidden Chasm.

FIGURE 4.15. Mapping and excavation in the second level of the Hidden Chasm (Operation 24A Unit 18).

the Late Classic Nacimiento complex, which is contemporaneous with the Tepeu 1 phase of Uaxactun (see Table 7.1). Although ceramics dating to the middle facet of the Nacimiento complex are present, diagnostic markers of the late facet were absent. This ceramic chronology correlates well with the estimated dates of the stelae. Nonetheless, since we did not find well-defined stratigraphy in any of the excavation units, the specific association and sequence among the excavated samples is not clear. We cannot determine whether the use of the Barranca Escondida was discontinued after the intrusion of the Dos Pilas–Aguateca dynasty around AD 730 or whether the area continued to be used, albeit less intensively. Despite this ambiguity, it appears reasonable to assume that this location was used primarily during the latter part of the Early Classic period and the early part of the Late Classic.

Of the 73 greenstone ornaments found in the Barranca Escondida, 68 came from the rock outcrop. Three were found in the Hidden Chasm, and the two pieces

TABLE 4.1. Cave Stone Distribution in the Barranca Escondida.

| | CAVE STONE | | | |
| | SPELEOTHEM | | INDETERMINATE | |
	NO.	WEIGHT	NO.	WEIGHT
Stela area	29.4%	34.0%	20.2%	26.6%
Rock outcrop	60.3%	63.2%	17.5%	11.9%
Other contexts	10.3%	2.8%	62.3%	61.5%
Total	68	10,650.5 g	228	9,564.0 g

found near Stelae 15 and 16 may have fallen from the outcrop. Clearly, the rock outcrop was the focus of the deposition of greenstone artifacts. Forty-four pieces are broken. The high percentage of broken pieces stands in contrast with the greenstone artifacts found in the Causeway area. Pieces from the Barranca Escondida were probably broken intentionally and deposited during rituals (see Garber 1983).

We recovered almost 300 cave stones weighing more than 20 kg from the Barranca Escondida (Table 4.1). They include speleothems and other layered stones of translucent brown-yellowish color. One-third of all Barranca Escondida cave stones were found on the rock outcrop, deposited on its ancient floor. Stalagmites or stalactites were almost exclusively concentrated on the rock outcrop, representing half the cave stones found in this part (19 stems and 22 tips). We found hardly any loose cave stones in the test pit inside the Hidden Chasm. Nor did we note any speleothems or damaged walls inside the fissure. The cave stones found in the Barranca Escondida were probably brought in from other areas. Five fragments that refitted into two speleothems came from different areas of the rock outcrop. It is probable that they were intentionally broken and scattered. Alternatively, they may have been dispersed when the building was destroyed.

Among the surprising finds in the Barranca Escondida were 74 fragments of fossilized wood, weighing just less than 1 kg in total. They were found exclusively on the rock outcrop and in a northern adjacent area. More than half the fragments came from units along the northern edge of the outcrop. Eighteen pieces fit together into six larger sticks. Most of these refitted fragments were not from the same or even adjacent units. For example, two fragments from the northern edge of the rock outcrop fit to three fragments from the center and to one fragment from the southeastern edge. It is likely that these objects were brought in from other locations and were intentionally broken and scattered.

INTERPRETATIONS

The placement of stelae in a rugged escarpment is unique. Two hypotheses are possible. One is that these monuments, originally placed in other locations, were moved to the Barranca Escondida. The other is that they were erected there originally.

Resetting of stelae was common among the Maya, and in some cases monuments may have been moved from one center to another as war trophies. For example, the Naranjo Hieroglyphic Stairway appears to have been set originally at Caracol, but many of its carved blocks were moved to Naranjo after the latter's victory over the former, and one block was taken to Ucanal (Graham 1978; Martin 2000). Because Stelae 15 and 16 were most likely dedicated by the Tamarindito–Arroyo de Piedras dynasty, we need to consider the possibility that they were originally placed in the centers of this dynasty. It may also be possible that Aguateca was part of the territory or the sphere of control of the Tamarindito dynasty, which erected these monuments in the Main Plaza or other locations of Aguateca.

Archaeological evidence, however, appears to support the other hypothesis. Stela 15 seems to have been set in the current location and then carved. In addition, many ceramics from the Barranca Escondida date to the same periods as the carving of the stelae. No substantial deposits or constructions dating to the Early Classic have been found at Aguateca. Excavations at the Main Plaza have shown that its floor was not laid until the early eighth century. The Barranca Escondida was probably the most important ritual location at Aguateca before it became the second capital of the Dos Pilas dynasty.

The absence of artifacts in the floor fill around Stela 15 is significant, given the fact that Early Classic and early Nacimiento ceramics were densely deposited on the floor of the stela area. If the stela was reset there, we would expect a substantial amount of artifacts to be mixed in the fill. Stela 15, most likely the earliest monument in the area, was probably set when the floor was clean of artifacts or at the same time as the floor construction. Artifacts were probably deposited after the stela erection in rituals associated with the monuments. It thus appears likely that Stelae 15, 16, and 17 were placed originally in this location, forming a stela-temple complex along with Structure M9-1, built on the rock outcrop.

Stela 18 appears stylistically latest in the area, probably dating to the early eighth century. Stela 15 of Dos Pilas records the erection of a stela in AD 721, possibly at Aguateca (Houston 1993). We may entertain the possibility that it refers to Stela 18 because the earliest stela found in the Main Plaza of Aguateca dates to AD 731. The Dos Pilas dynasty may have used this sacred place jointly with the Tamarindito around AD 720, leading to the complete takeover of Aguateca roughly ten years later.

The ritual conducted in the Barranca Escondida was probably associated with religious meanings of caves. This is indicated by the placement of the stelae in front of an entrance to a cave-like chasm, the abundance of cave stones, and artifact deposits inside the chasms. The difficult access and the small space of the Barranca Escondida suggest that the ceremonies were most likely exclusive ones mainly for elites. Even though the general arrangement of monuments and a building was similar to those of common stela-temple complexes, the makeup of ritual participants and possibly the political implications of the rite appear to have been significantly different from those held in open plazas.

It is not clear when Structure M9-1, on the rock outcrop, was destroyed. One possibility is that the destruction occurred when Aguateca was taken over by the Dos Pilas–Aguateca dynasty shortly before AD 731. Stelae 15 and 16, associated with the Tamarindito dynasty, may have been mutilated at the same time. If this interpretation is correct, the termination of the ritual location was possibly meant to sever the symbolic tie of the Tamarindito dynasty with Aguateca. The takeover may have been antagonistic or violent. The lack of Late Nacimiento ceramics in the area appears to support this hypothesis. Alternatively, the structure and the monuments may have been destroyed when Aguateca was attacked and abandoned around AD 810.

Either way, some of the artifacts may have been deposited during the termination rituals associated with the destruction of the structure. In particular, the marked concentration of greenstone artifacts and speleothems on the outcrop, as opposed to the wider distribution of ceramics, may have resulted from termination rituals. A significant number of greenstone artifacts were also found in termination ritual deposits in the Palace Group whereas they were absent in Structure L8-5, a temple in the Main Plaza. The high ratio of broken pieces, however, distinguishes the greenstone assemblage of the Barranca Escondida from that of the Palace Group.

5

chapter

Test Pits in Other Locations

Takeshi Inomata

MAIN PLAZA: OPERATION 25

In the Main Plaza we excavated Structure L8-5 and Stela 19, found in front of Structure L8-6 (Figure 1.5). Structure L8-5 was a temple pyramid measuring 7 m in height and located on the eastern side of the Main Plaza. Graham (1967) identified Stelae 1, 2, 3, 4, and 5 and associated altars in front of this building. Stela 3, dedicated by Ruler 3 on 9.15.0.0.0 (AD 731), was the earliest monument in the Main Plaza, and Stela 2 commemorated the victory over Ceibal by the same ruler. Stela 1 was erected by Ruler 4 but mentioned the death of Ruler 3 (Houston 1993). It appears that Structure L8-5 was closely associated with Ruler 3 and may have been one of the earliest temples built by the Dos Pilas–Aguateca dynasty. Our objective was to examine whether this temple showed traces of burning or ritual destruction, as seen in the elite residences. It is well documented that the Maya and other Mesoamerican groups destroyed or burned temples of defeated enemies. Given the burning and destruction of the elite residential area and the Palace Group, the treatment of temples by enemies was of major interest. The building was more extensively excavated later by the Aguateca Restoration Project First Phase, directed by Valdés, and was restored by the Aguateca Restoration Project Second Phase.

Structure L8-6 was located to the south of Structure L8-5. Inomata had noted the presence of a stela-like stone half-buried in front of this temple. In the previous year Stelae 15, 16, and 17 were looted before archaeologists could fully record them. Wishing to avoid a similar disaster, we decided to excavate and to document this possible stela. We excavated three units around the stone as Operation 25B. The excavation revealed a beautifully carved stela, which we registered as Stela 19. Ponciano excavated the front part of this building more extensively in 2005 during the second phase of the Aguateca Archaeological Project (Ponciano et al. 2009).

Structure L8-5: Operation 25A

In 1999 we excavated eight units of Structure L8-5, covering an area 7 × 4 m, in the northern half of the top of the pyramid (Figures 5.1–5.3). The excavation was limited to the levels above the last floor. We exposed the floor, which was under a humus layer 20 cm thick, and the side and back walls. The walls consisted of roughly cut stones, and only two courses were preserved. Their masonry parts appear to have measured roughly 1.5 m in height, and the upper parts of the walls and the roof were probably made of perishable materials. We did not find room divisions. The front part of the room was open and had three low steps, leading to a wide terrace. The room floor was badly eroded, but it may have originally been stuccoed.

The quantity of recovered artifacts was small, but they include a complete obsidian point, a complete small ceramic plate, a partially reconstructible vase, and two partially reconstructible small *incensarios*. We did not find clear traces of burning.

We could not determine the structure's mode of abandonment with reasonable certainty. Still, the presence of complete and partially reconstructible objects is notable. The excavated *incensarios* probably reflect the original use of the building as a temple. At the very least, the temple was not completely cleaned of objects before the abandonment. The temple might originally have contained a far smaller quantity of objects than residential buildings. It is also possible that some artifacts had been moved to the more heavily defended area on the other side of the chasm before the final attack. We could not determine confidently whether the temple was ritually destroyed by enemies. Subsequent excavations of this temple by Ponciano and colleagues during the Aguateca Restoration Project did not reveal termination ritual deposits comparable to those found in the Palace Group. In contrast, the

149

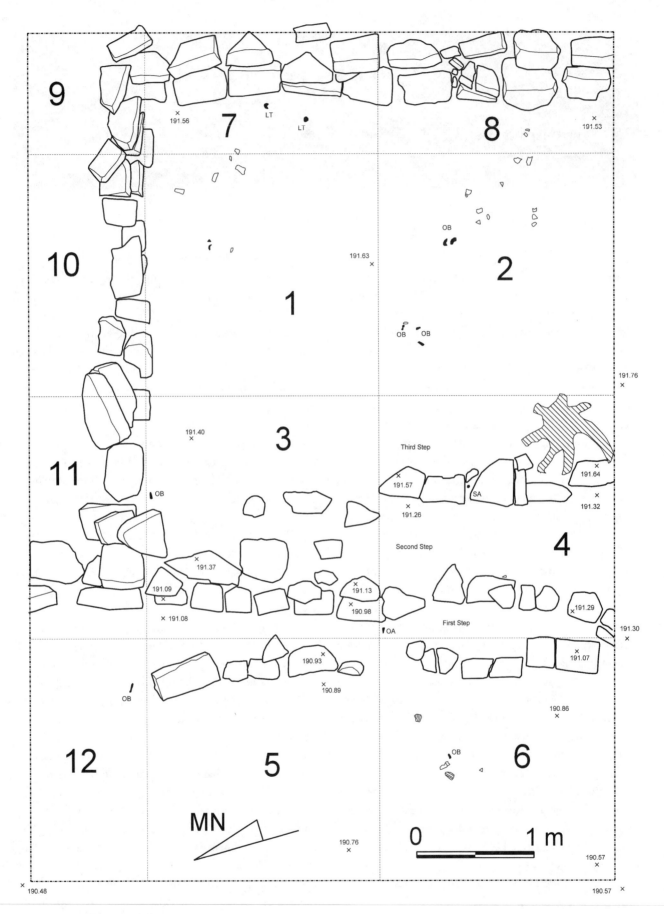

Figure 5.1. Plan of the excavation of Structure L8-5.

excavation of Structure L8-6 during the Aguateca Project Second Phase unearthed dense ritual deposits in front of it. This temple appears to have been commissioned by Tahn Te' K'inich, and the enemy may have selectively destroyed temples associated with the last ruler, leaving Structure L8-5 intact.

Stela 19: Operation 25B

We placed three units in 1999 and excavated around the possible stela down to the plaza floor (Figures 5.4 and 5.5). A small amount of artifacts was recovered. The stela lay facedown and was broken into three large pieces. Its back was not carved. We pulled up the stela fragments with a rope, protecting its carved surface with blankets. Though slightly eroded, the stela was elaborately carved. Underneath the stela we found the plaza floor, made of *piedrín*. There was also a line of stones, which probably formed a step in front of Structure L8-6.

It is unusual to find a stela lying parallel to the front edge of the temple with all its pieces together. Moreover, we did not find a hole in which the monument was placed. Most stelae collapsed forward or backward, lying perpendicular to the front walls of the associated buildings. Their butts often remained in their original location with their upper portions broken off. It is probable that Stela 19 was toppled intentionally in ancient times or was placed on a terrace of Structure L8-6.

Stela 19 was dedicated by Ruler 5, Tahn Te' K'inich. Next to this monument, Graham (1967) had documented Stela 6, which was erected by the same ruler. Structure L8-6 appears to have been associated with this last ruler of Aguateca. Ponciano's excavation in 2005 in front of Structure L8-6 revealed the front walls of the building, with their facing stones dismantled and dense termination ritual deposits (Ponciano et al. 2009).

THE GRANADA GROUP: OPERATIONS 26 AND 27

The Granada Group was an elite residential area located to the west of the Main Plaza. In 1999 we excavated test pits with the objectives of (1) comparing the distribution of artifacts with the results of soil phosphate analysis, and (2) examining whether this area was abandoned rapidly. We placed two units in Group L8-9 as Operation 26 and one unit in Structure K8-27 of Group K8-3 as Operation 27 (Figure 1.6). The excavations were limited to levels above the last occupation floors.

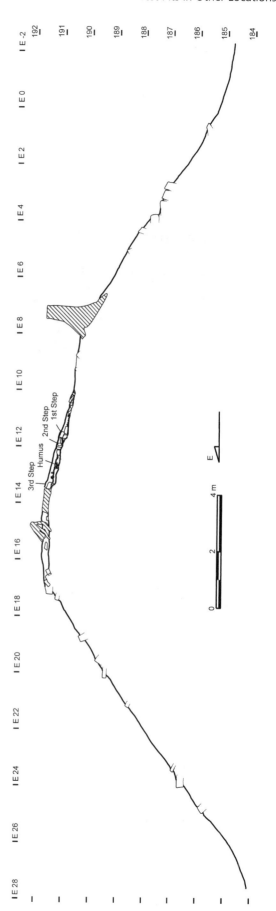

FIGURE 5.2. East-west section of Structure L8-5.

FIGURE 5.3. Structure L8-5 after excavation, viewed from the west.

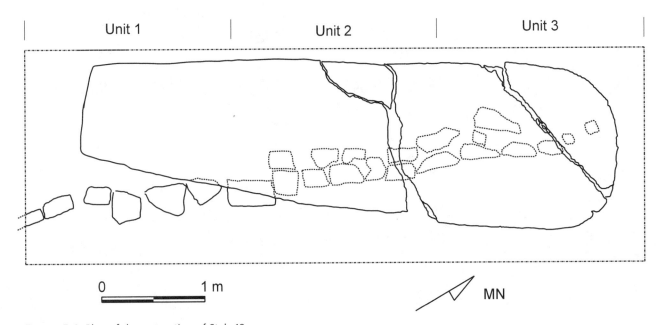

Unit 1   Unit 2   Unit 3

0   1 m   MN

FIGURE 5.4. Plan of the excavation of Stela 19.

Group L8-9: Operation 26

Group L8-9 was located behind Structure L8-8. It consisted of small mounds around a patio and appeared to have been a residential group. In 1998 Richard Terry analyzed soil phosphate levels in this group and in Group L8-8 to the west. We placed two 1-×-1-m pits in locations where particularly high phosphate concentrations were

detected. Unit 1 of Operation 26A was placed behind Structures L8-70 and L8-71, and Unit 1 of Operation 26B was excavated behind Structures L8-61 and L8-62.

In Unit 1 of Operation 26A, excavators found a dense deposit of artifacts at a depth of 25 cm, directly on the surface of the bedrock. This probably represented a midden. In Unit 1 of Operation 26B, excavators also revealed a

FIGURE 5.5. Structure L8-6 and Stela 19 during excavation, viewed from the north.

dense deposit of artifacts at a depth of 25 cm, including numerous fragments of lithics. These artifacts were directly on the surface of bedrock and seemed to represent a midden. The presence of possible middens in two units accorded well with the results of the phosphate analysis.

Structure K8-27: Operation 27

Structure K8-27 of Group K8-3 appeared to be a three-room building, a common configuration for an elite residence. In the excavations in the Causeway area, we found particularly large amounts of artifacts in the side rooms of elite residences. We placed a 2-×-2-m unit in the west room of Structure K8-27, which appeared to be a good location to detect a pattern of rapid abandonment. We excavated down to the floor but recovered only a small quantity of artifacts. It was not clear whether the building was burned. Given the lack of evidence for rapid abandonment, we decided not to continue excavations in the Granada Group.

Ceramics

Introduction to the Ceramic Study at Aguateca

Chapter 6

Takeshi Inomata

ALL CERAMICS EXCAVATED during the Aguateca Archaeological Project First Phase were analyzed during our lab seasons. This part of the monograph deals with remains of ceramic vessels. Other ceramic artifacts, such as reworked sherds, figurines, and beads, are described in the third volume of the monograph series (Inomata and Triadan in preparation). Ceramic drums are also included in this part because in many cases fragments of drums and those of vessels are difficult to distinguish.

Our ceramic analysis consisted of two levels. The first was the study of all ceramic remains according to the type-variety system. Chapter 7 reports the results of this study, providing an overview of the ceramic chronology and typology at Aguateca. The second level refers to the more detailed analysis of complete, reconstructible, and partial vessels, which is discussed in Chapter 8. All ceramic figures are on a scale of ¼ unless otherwise noted.

TYPE-VARIETY ANALYSIS

The ceramic analysis based on the type-variety system at Aguateca builds on the previous work by Richard Adams (1971) at Altar de Sacrificios, Jeremy Sabloff (1975) at Ceibal, and Antonia Foias (1996) in the Petexbatun region (Figure 6.1). In particular, Foias conducted an exhaustive study of Petexbatun ceramics, including those from Aguateca excavated during the Petexbatun Project. Chapter 7 thus focuses on the distribution of ceramics by area and describes classes of ceramics that were not discussed by Foias.

The analytical method followed the one used by Foias (1996) for the Petexbatun Project materials, with minor modifications. All ceramic remains excavated during the Aguateca Archaeological Project First Phase were sorted by types and varieties, counted, and weighed. We should note that our analysis emphasized type-level classification rather than variety-level, or subdivisions within each type. Because fragments from a single vessel may sometimes be classified into different categories in too detailed sorting, such divisions may obscure overall patterns of ceramic distribution. Investigators analyzed ceramics by individual bags, representing lots or smaller subdivisions within a lot. To each sorted group of sherds a unique six-digit ceramic catalog number was given. Complete, reconstructible, and partial vessels were given separate catalog numbers.

A few points of modification from Foias's method need to be mentioned. Foias sorted sherds by type varieties and by parts of vessels, such as rims, bases, ridges, and modeled pieces. In other words, rims and body sherds of the same type from the same lot were given different catalog numbers. In our analysis, we deemphasized classification by vessel part. Except for miniature vessels and lids, which were sorted separately from other sherds of the same type, one catalog number was given to rim and body sherds of the same type from the same lot. This speeded up the process of recording.

In recording sherd frequencies, Foias counted fragments belonging to the same vessel as one, but we counted them separately unless they were broken during or after excavation. Our collection involves numerous reconstructible vessels from rapidly abandoned structures and nonreconstructible fragments from middens, fills, and ritual deposits. Thus, this counting method provides better data for comparison across different contexts. After counting the total number of sherds for each sorted group in this manner, we also counted rims, bases, and modeled pieces. In this case, we counted those belonging to the same vessel as one. In this manner, the numbers of rims and bases serve as better indicators of the original number of vessels represented in the sample.

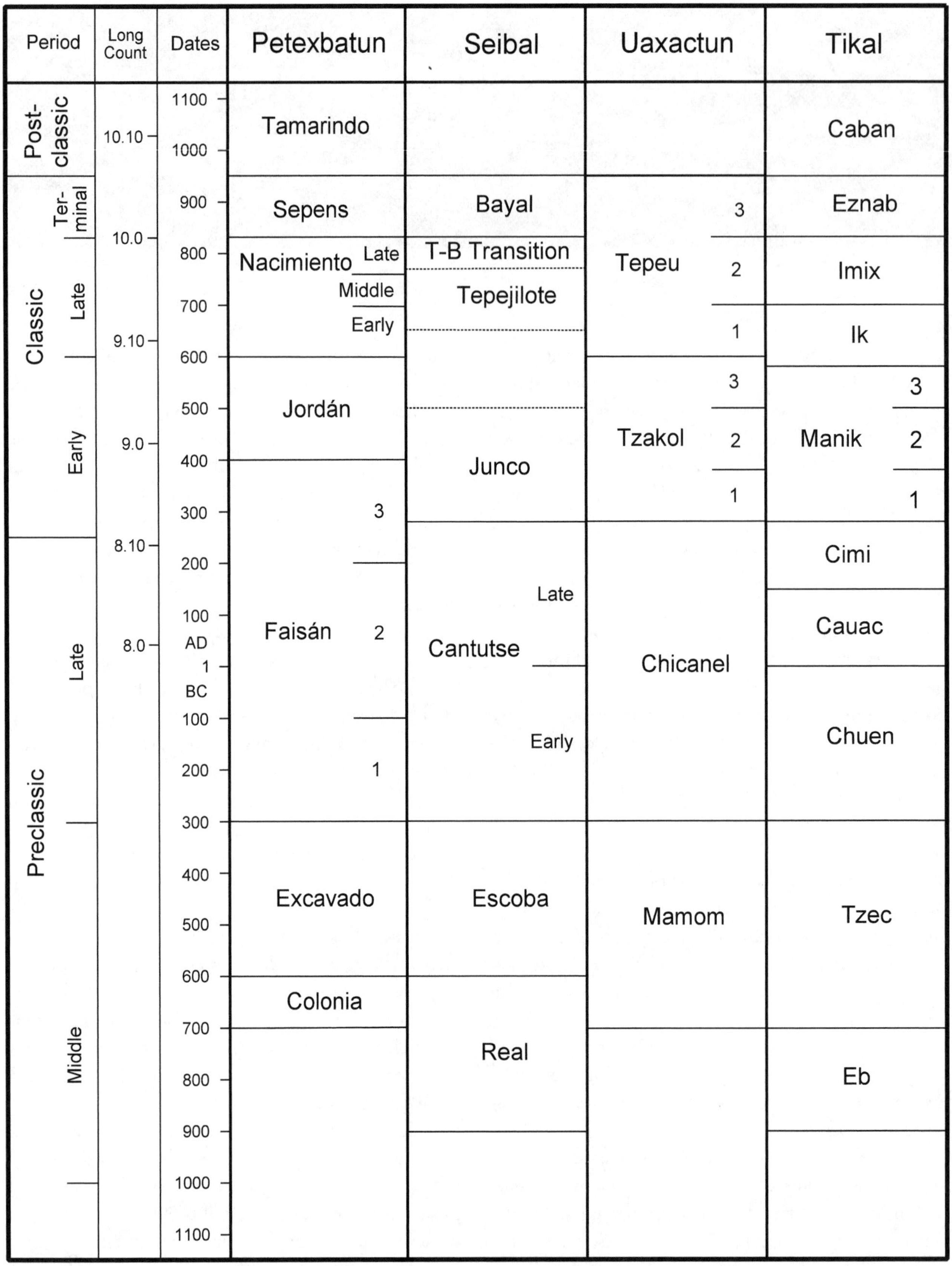

Period		Long Count	Dates	Petexbatun	Seibal	Uaxactun		Tikal	
Post-classic		10.10	1100 / 1000	Tamarindo				Caban	
Classic	Terminal	10.0	900	Sepens	Bayal	Tepeu	3	Eznab	
Classic	Late	10.0	800	Nacimiento — Late	T-B Transition	Tepeu	2	Imix	
Classic	Late		700	Middle	Tepejilote	Tepeu			
Classic	Late	9.10		Early		Tepeu	1	Ik	
Classic	Early		600 / 500	Jordán		Tzakol	3	Manik	3
Classic	Early	9.0	400	Jordán	Junco	Tzakol	2	Manik	2
Classic	Early		300	Faisán 3	Junco	Tzakol	1	Manik	1
Preclassic	Late	8.10	200	Faisán 3	Cantutse Late	Chicanel		Cimi	
Preclassic	Late		100 AD	Faisán 2	Cantutse	Chicanel		Cauac	
Preclassic	Late	8.0	1 BC	Faisán 2	Cantutse	Chicanel		Cauac	
Preclassic	Late		100	Faisán	Cantutse	Chicanel		Chuen	
Preclassic	Late		200	Faisán 1	Cantutse Early	Chicanel		Chuen	
Preclassic	Middle		300 / 400 / 500	Excavado	Escoba	Mamom		Tzec	
Preclassic	Middle		600 / 700	Colonia	Real	Mamom		Eb	
Preclassic	Middle		800 / 900		Real	Mamom		Eb	
Preclassic	Middle		1000 / 1100						

FIGURE 6.1. Ceramic chronology of Aguateca and the Petexbatun region. The Petexbatun sequence is modified from Foias (1996) and Bachand (2006). The Seibal, Uaxactun, and Tikal sequences are after Sabloff (1975), Smith (1955), and Culbert (1993).

ANALYSIS OF COMPLETE, RECONSTRUCTIBLE, AND PARTIAL VESSELS

Complete, reconstructible, and partial vessels are the particularly unique and important data obtained at Aguateca, and their analysis was the primary focus of our lab work. Sorting and refitting broken fragments of ceramic vessels found in the floor level were extremely time consuming, and a substantial effort was dedicated to this work during the lab seasons following field work from 1996 through 1999, as well as during the continuous lab work from 2000 through 2003. Most of the ceramic studies in the Maya area are based on fragments of ceramic vessels that are from contexts not directly related to daily use. The common use of the type-variety system, heavily emphasizing surface treatments, partially reflects these conditions of ceramic remains. The Aguateca ceramic assemblages of complete and reconstructible vessels from primary use or storage contexts present new possibilities for the understanding of Maya ceramic function and meaning. As noted in the introductory chapter of this volume, qualitative data organized into classificatory schemes such as the type-variety system facilitate the extraction of overall patterns but limit the possibility of analysis from different perspectives. Detailed descriptions conveying the subtlety and nuance of contextual and qualitative information, in contrast, allow researchers to pursue open-ended inquiries into how various groups and individuals produced and used these objects in specific settings. For this reason, the discussion of these assemblages in Chapter 8 emphasizes detailed descriptions of individual vessels with close attention to their modal attributes and their contexts. Their implications for the study of domestic organization and activity are discussed in the third volume of the monograph series, combined with the distributions of other classes of artifacts.

Definitions of Complete, Reconstructible, and Partial Vessels

The complete, reconstructible, and partial vessels discussed in Chapter 8 include those found in the floor levels, as well as objects in burials and ritual deposits. The identification of reconstructible vessels, particularly those in the floor levels, is often quite difficult. Most vessels were badly smashed when the masonry walls of the structures collapsed. Since a room or an area often contained a significant number of vessels, their broken fragments were usually mixed together. Although we dedicated considerable time and effort to the reconstruction of broken ceramic artifacts, many of them remained incomplete. For the materials found in rapidly abandoned structures, in particular, we are mainly interested in vessels that appear to have been used or stored in usable condition, either complete or partially broken, immediately before the abandonment of the structures. A problem we need to take into account is that some vessels or fragments may have been used in broken condition (Sheets 1992, 2002).

In considering the condition of Aguateca artifacts, we define complete, reconstructible, and partial vessels as follows. A *complete vessel* generally refers to an object of which more than 80 percent is unbroken and more than 90 percent can be reconstructed. *Reconstructible vessels* are those that were found in broken condition but can be restored in a significant portion. Many reconstructible vessels are believed to have been originally—that is, immediately before the abandonment—complete. Those also include vessels that may have been used in broken condition but retained their original function. For example, a jar with broken neck may have continued to serve the same function. Nonetheless, when a vessel cannot be restored completely, the preservation condition at Aguateca makes it nearly impossible in most cases to determine whether it was originally complete and some pieces were lost or misidentified, or whether it was used in a broken condition. Partial vessels are generally restored in smaller portions than most reconstructible vessels. They are less likely, though still possible, to have been originally complete than reconstructible vessels. It is also probable that some of them were used or stored as broken objects. Some of these broken items may have been reused for functions different from their original ones. For instance, the lower body of a broken jar might have been reused as a bowl or plate. When we judge that such reuse is likely, we classify the object as a partial vessel rather than reconstructible vessel. It is necessary to note that the residents might have kept broken objects in and around their houses temporarily before discarding them (Deal 1985, 1998; Schiffer 1987). It is possible that such objects were classified as reconstructible or partial vessels. In addition, we should note that large broken pieces of bowls or jars that are too small or incomplete to be recognized as partial vessels might have been reused as lids or plates. It is nearly impossible to distinguish these reused fragments from refuse at Aguateca, and they are not included in this list.

Complete vessels can be easily identified. Criteria for a reconstructible vessel are more problematic and often remain rather subjective since various factors affect the likelihood of successful reconstruction. One of the factors is the preservation condition of fragments. Many sherds from Aguateca are badly eroded. In particular, those that were near the surface have often lost decorations and their edges are rounded. Small fragments may even have disintegrated. Such poor preservation hinders not only reconstruction but also the identification of fragments belonging to the same vessel. The second factor is the condition and the type of the structure. For example, in a room defined by well-preserved walls, fragments of a reconstructible vessel tend to remain in a relatively small area. In some cases, the original shapes of vessels, though fragmented, are recognizable in the field. In extramural areas and in structures with perishable walls, however, fragments tend to be scattered in wider areas and to be more disturbed.

The third factor is the completeness of excavation and the proximity to unexcavated areas. When we find a potential reconstructible vessel near the edge of an excavation area or in a location where there were tree falls, we always need to consider the possibility that parts of the vessel remained unexcavated. The fourth factor is the type of vessel. When a vessel has complex designs over a wide area, it is relatively easy to identify pieces belonging to the same vessel and to glue them together. Restoring unslipped or monochrome ceramics without decorative designs is often quite difficult. When more than one similar vessel of these types is found in close proximity, even determining which fragments belong to which vessel is not easy. Moreover, the sizes of the vessels matter. Miniature vessels have a higher chance of surviving as complete or nearly complete objects whereas restoring and identifying large reconstructible vessels is extremely difficult. Thus, we need to determine the identification of a reconstructible or partial vessel case by case, evaluating these factors. Under favorable circumstances many reconstructible vessels can be restored around 80 percent, but in poor conditions those with restored portions as low as 30 percent might be considered reconstructible.

Definitions of Other Terms

The following terminology is used for the descriptions of complete and reconstructible vessels.

Catalog No.: This is the same system of cataloging discussed above for the type-variety analysis. Each complete/reconstructible/partial vessel is given a unique catalog number.

WVS No./WDR No.: These are identification numbers given to complete/reconstructible/partial objects in addition to the catalog numbers for the sake of easy and concise descriptions. They are used for items found in the final floor levels, particularly those recovered from rapidly abandoned structures. These numbers are not given to artifacts found in burials, caches, or middens. WVS numbers are used for ceramic vessels, and WDR numbers are for ceramic drums. They are consecutive numbers for each structure or area.

Bag No.: Bag numbers are assigned in the field and are used for the control of provenience. Different parts of a vessel often come from different lots or smaller spatial subdivisions, and thus from different bags. This information helps us estimate the original location of vessels and the processes of disturbance at the time of or after abandonment. For example, fragments of a large storage vessel are often found close together, indicating that the vessel was placed on the floor. In this case, the provenience of base fragments approximates the original location of the vessel. Fragments of small to medium-sized vessels are sometimes scattered in wider areas. These vessels may have fallen from high places, such as shelves and rafters. In some cases, fragments are found in even wider areas, which may have been caused by disturbance at the time of abandonment. Descriptions list bag numbers and their lots for rim, body, and base parts in the order of the amount of pieces belonging to each bag.

Provenience: This term generally refers to the most representative location where fragments of the vessel were found. In the case of a large storage vessel that was probably placed on the floor, we usually use the lot where its base was found. For a smaller vessel, the provenience generally refers to the lot where the largest portion of fragments was found. In other words, the provenience, in many cases, is not the location where the vessel was originally placed but the place where it fell.

Context: We describe the context where fragments of the vessel were found. In some cases, we also discuss the possible location where the vessel was originally stored.

Condition: We identify the vessel as complete, reconstructible, or partial, as discussed above. We then estimate what portion of the original complete vessel is represented by the sample that was recovered and recognized as part of this vessel in terms of weight percentage. The state of preservation and traces of burning may also be discussed.

Dimensions: All the dimensions refer to those of the original shape of the vessels when they were complete, not to those of the present parts. The exterior rim diameter is measured at the exterior edges of the rim for vessels with vertical, flared, or outcurved walls. The interior rim diameter is measured at the interior edges of the rim for vessels with incurved walls. The top rim diameter is measured at the highest point for most types of lip and at the middle point for flat lips. When less than half the rim is present, only the exterior or interior diameter is measured. The maximum diameter is measured at the widest point of the vessel. For vessels with flared or outcurved walls, the maximum diameter is the same as the exterior rim diameter. For vessels with noncircular sections, measurements are taken for the largest cross-section. The minimum opening is measured only for jars, at the narrowest point of the neck. If the horizontal section is not circular, the diameter is measured at the narrowest and widest points. The height refers to the distance between the rim and the lowest point of the base or supports. We always measure from the rim, even when some appendages, such as spouts and handles, are higher than the rim. For vessels with supports, the height without feet is also measured from the rim to the lowest point of the base. For jars with a neck that forms a sharp angle with the body, the neck height is measured from the rim to the neck-body juncture on the outside.

For those dimensions, the accuracy of the measurement is noted. *Measured* means that the distance between two points was measured directly. In the case of diameter measurements, this means that more than half a circumference is present. The range of error is generally around 0.1 cm. *Estimate* means that the distance was estimated based on less than complete parts, and the measurements have an error range of 0.5 to 2 cm, depending the size of the vessel. Estimated diameters are measured by placing small pieces along a series of circles with different diameters. *Rough estimate* is primarily used for the measurements of maximum diameters and heights. When the vessels are incomplete, the maximum diameters and heights are sometimes estimated based on the curvature of the walls. These measurements may have errors larger than 2 cm.

Wall thicknesses are measured at the thinnest and thickest parts of the wall pieces that are present, not including the thickened or folded rim, ridges, and appliqués.

The sample weight refers to the weight of the pieces that are present. The original weight is calculated based on the estimated ratio of the present pieces to the original complete vessel.

Volume refers to the vessel's capacity to hold liquids. We created three-dimensional models of vessels with Microstation CAD software (Bentley Systems, Inc.), which calculated the volume of liquids held up to the neck-body junctures of jars or up to 85 percent of the depths of bowls, plates, and vases. This method provides accurate volumes for complete and reconstructed items, which can be used for comparisons among vessels. For poorly reconstructed objects, however, the values can have substantial ranges of error. We calculated values for these incomplete vessels, mainly for comparisons of storage capacities between different rooms and structures.

Type: Types are classified according to the type-variety system, discussed above.

Paste, temper, and firing: The paste color is indicated according to the Munsell Soil Color Charts, and color names follow the Munsell scheme. Pastes are classified into fine, medium grain, and coarse categories through visual inspection. The identification of tempers was made through naked-eye observation, and remains preliminary. The size descriptions of temper, such as 0.2–2.0 mm diameter, means that roughly 80 percent of temper falls into this range by naked-eye examination. The presence of temper smaller than 0.1 mm is usually disregarded.

Surface finish and decoration: The terms used here follow the definitions established by Robert Smith (Smith 1955:chap. 4; 1971:chap. 5). The Munsell Soil Color Charts were not used for the descriptions of paint and slip colors because good matches were often not found.

Form: The definitions of many terms follow those established by Sabloff and Willey for Ceibal ceramic analysis (Sabloff 1975:22–32), with minor modifications. The modifications are as follows. (1) Although Sabloff divides plates and dishes, we combine them into the category of plate. (2) We use the classificatory term *jar* for what is generally called miniature bottles. (3) For the classification of jars, we added jars with insloped necks. (4) For the classification of bowls, we added bowls with outcurved upper sides and incurved lower sides. (5) For the classification of lip, we added flat lip, which is a type of beveled-in lip with a horizontal surface. (6) Beveled-in and beveled-out lips are determined in relation to the direction of the rim, not in relation to the vertical line. (7) For the classification of base, we added the hollow rattle base, which is a type of hollow base that contains rattles inside. We also added the flat base with ridge, which is similar to the ring base but the entire base is flat. (8) For the description of handles, we added the category of hollow whistle handle. These handles are hollow with small openings and are generally used for pitchers. As liquid was poured, such a handle probably made a whistling sound. (9) For the classification of feet, we added the category of hollow cylinder feet, which have rectangular or slightly trapezoidal shapes in cross section. We make distinctions between solid and hollow feet, and then describe shapes according to the Ceibal classifications for hollow feet. One of the resulting new categories is solid oven feet. We also note whether or not rattles are present.

Use-wear: Patterns of wear possibly resulting from use are described.

The Temporal and Spatial Distributions of Ceramics

Takeshi Inomata

CERAMIC CHRONOLOGY AND TYPOLOGY

Table 7.1 presents the distribution of ceramic types in different areas at Aguateca. All three tables in this chapter are based on sherds and reconstructible vessels found during the Aguateca Archaeological Project First Phase. The Palace Group includes Operations 19 and 22; the Causeway area, Operations 14, 20, 21, and 23; the Barranca Escondida, Operation 24; and the Main Plaza–Granada Group, Operations 25, 26, and 27.

Late Preclassic Faisan Chicanel Complex (300 BC–AD 400)

A small quantity of Preclassic ceramics was found, all of them mixed with Classic period materials. Virtually all were classified into the Paso Caballo Waxy ware of the Late Preclassic Faisan Chicanel complex, which dates from 300 BC to AD 400 (Bachand 2006, 2007; Foias 1996) chronology. Because our Preclassic collection is small and fragmentary, it is virtually impossible to distinguish types of the Paso Caballo Waxy ware from those of the Flores Waxy ware, dating to the Middle Preclassic period. Likewise, unslipped types of the Late Preclassic period were impossible to separate from Classic period materials.

Despite these problems in identifying Preclassic ceramics, it is reasonable to say that Preclassic occupations in the Aguateca epicenter were extremely small. We did not find any Preclassic buildings in this area, and the floors of the Main Plaza and the Palace Group plaza, as well as all the deeply excavated structures, were built directly on the bedrock during the Late Classic period. The center of Preclassic occupations was found around the Guacamaya Group, in the western part of the Aguateca center, where a pyramid and platforms dating to the Late Preclassic period were found (Bachand 2006; Inomata et al. 2009).

Early Classic Jordan Tzakol Complex (AD 400–600)

The quantity of Early Classic ceramics of the Jordan Tzakol complex (AD 400–600) is small. A small number of fragments of plates with basal flanges were found in the Causeway area, mixed with Late Classic materials. It is probable that body sherds of unslipped Early Classic ceramics were not distinguished from Late Classic types, but Early Classic occupations in the epicenter were most likely limited.

Most of our Early Classic samples came from the Barranca Escondida. This ceramic chronology accords well with the estimated date of Stela 15 found in the same area. Nonetheless, since we did not find well-defined stratigraphy in any of the excavation units in the Barranca Escondida, the specific association and sequence among the excavated samples is not clear. Early Classic ceramic types from the Barranca Escondida include Dos Arroyos Polychrome (Figure 7.1a–d), Aguila Orange (Figure 7.1e and f), and Balanza Black (Figure 7.1g). Many were plates or bowls with characteristic basal flanges. Also excavated were unslipped types, such as Quintal Unslipped (Figure 7.1h and k) and Triunfo Striated.

Common forms of Quintal Unslipped and Triunfo Striated found at Ceibal (Sabloff 1975) include jars with short vertical or outcurved necks. A substantial portion of unslipped jars from the Barranca Escondida possess taller necks, which appear to represent transitional forms from typical Quintal and Triunfo to Late Classic Cambio Unslipped and Encanto Striated. In addition, striations on some jars show intermediate patterns between the fine striations typical of Triunfo and the wider, deeper ones of Encanto (Figure 7.1l and m). These observations suggest that ceramics from the Barranca Escondido were deposited mostly during the late part of the Early Classic

TABLE 7.1. Distribution of Ceramic Types by Area (weight in grams).

	TOTAL FOR ALL AREAS				PALACE GROUP				CAUSEWAY AREA				BARRANCA ESCONDIDA				MAIN PLAZA–GRANADA GROUP			
	FREQ	%	WT	%	FREQ	%	WT	%	FREQ	%	WT	%	FREQ	%	WT	%	FREQ	%	WT	%
Late Preclassic Faisan Chicanel (300 BC–AD 400)																				
Paso Caballo Waxy Ware																				
Sierra Ceramic Group																				
Sierra Red	16	0.01	151	0.00	11	0.01	87	0.01	5	0.00	64	0.00	0	0.00	0	0.00	0	0.00	0	0.00
Mateo Red-on-cream	1	0.00	6	0.00	0	0.00	0	0.00	1	0.00	6	0.00	0	0.00	0	0.00	0	0.00	0	0.00
Flor Ceramic Group																				
Flor Cream	38	0.02	189	0.01	7	0.01	56	0.00	31	0.03	133	0.01	0	0.00	0	0.00	0	0.00	0	0.00
Polvero Ceramic Group																				
Polvero Black	1	0.00	4	0.00	0	0.00	0	0.00	1	0.00	4	0.00	0	0.00	0	0.00	0	0.00	0	0.00
Undetermined																				
Paso Caballo Waxy undetermined	14	0.01	111	0.00	6	0.01	55	0.00	7	0.01	44	0.00	1	0.02	12	0.02	0	0.00	0	0.00
Subtotal	70	0.03	461	0.01	24	0.02	198	0.01	45	0.04	251	0.01	1	0.02	12	0.02	0		0	
Early Classic Jordan Tzakol (AD 400–600) (Some types continue into the Late Classic)																				
Uaxactun Unslipped Ware																				
Quintal Ceramic Group																				
Quintal Unslipped: White wash v.	30	0.01	552	0.02	0	0.00	0	0.00	0	0.00	0	0.00	30	0.65	552	0.71	0	0.00	0	0.00
Quintal/Triunfo	7	0.00	359	0.01	0	0.00	0	0.00	0	0.00	0	0.00	7	0.15	359	0.46	0	0.00	0	0.00
Quintal-Cambio transition	233	0.10	13825	0.39	0	0.00	0	0.00	0	0.00	0	0.00	233	5.05	13825	17.80	0	0.00	0	0.00
Quintal-Cambio (rough surface)	79	0.04	2255	0.06	0	0.00	0	0.00	0	0.00	0	0.00	79	1.71	2255	2.90	0	0.00	0	0.00
Quintal-Cambio (impressed)	1	0.00	10	0.00	0	0.00	0	0.00	0	0.00	0	0.00	1	0.02	10	0.01	0	0.00	0	0.00
Triunfo-Encanto transition	751	0.34	7651	0.21	0	0.00	0	0.00	0	0.00	0	0.00	751	16.29	7651	9.85	0	0.00	0	0.00
Peten Gloss Ware																				
Aguila Ceramic Group																				
Aguila Orange	5	0.00	226	0.01	0	0.00	0	0.00	0	0.00	0	0.00	5	0.11	226	0.29	0	0.00	0	0.00
Balanza Ceramic Group																				
Balanza Black	8	0.00	1150	0.03	0	0.00	0	0.00	0	0.00	0	0.00	8	0.17	1150	1.48	0	0.00	0	0.00

Dos Arroyos Ceramic Group

	N	%	N	%	N	%	N	%	N	%	N	%	N	%	N	%	N	%	N	%
Dos Arroyos Orange Polychrome	25	0.01	570	0.02	0	0.00	0	0.00	17	0.01	200	0.01	8	0.17	370	0.48	0	0.00	0	0.00
Subtotal	1139	0.51	26598	0.75	0	0.00	0	0.00	17	0.01	200	0.01	1122	24.33	26398	33.98	0	0.00	0	0.00

Late Classic Nacimiento Tepeu Early Facet (AD 600–720)

Peten Gloss Ware

Saxche-Palmar Ceramic Group

	N	%	N	%	N	%	N	%	N	%	N	%	N	%	N	%	N	%	N	%
Saxche Polychrome	32	0.01	795	0.02	0	0.00	0	0.00	15	0.01	374	0.02	16	0.35	413	0.53	1	0.05	8	0.02

Late Classic Nacimiento Tepeu General (AD 600–810)

Uaxactun Unslipped Ware

Cambio Ceramic Group

	N	%	N	%	N	%	N	%	N	%	N	%	N	%	N	%	N	%	N	%
Cambio Unslipped	1406	0.63	33611	0.94	339	0.35	11997	0.79	1033	0.86	20695	1.07	8	0.17	303	0.39	26	1.37	616	1.81
Encanto Striated	59413	26.53	1022642	28.68	24431	24.95	408873	27.02	34487	28.85	605238	31.19	17	0.37	540	0.70	478	25.17	7991	23.52
Encanto Striated: Impressed v.	1091	0.49	25628	0.72	598	0.61	10438	0.69	490	0.41	15162	0.78	0	0.00	0	0.00	3	0.16	28	0.08
Cambio/Encanto	7686	3.43	217768	6.11	2723	2.78	82066	5.42	4815	4.03	132273	6.82	20	0.43	704	0.91	128	6.74	2725	8.02
Cambio/Encanto (with red or white wash)	672	0.30	14729	0.41	134	0.14	5032	0.33	531	0.44	8556	0.44	7	0.15	1141	1.47	0	0.00	0	0.00
Pedregal Modeled	155	0.07	6296	0.18	0	0.00	0	0.00	10	0.01	617	0.03	145	3.14	5679	7.31	0	0.00	0	0.00
Miseria Appliqued	33	0.01	2320	0.07	0	0.00	0	0.00	0	0.00	0	0.00	33	0.72	2320	2.99	0	0.00	0	0.00
Cambio Group undetermined	1875	0.84	53033	1.49	1210	1.24	35244	2.33	513	0.43	14535	0.75	139	3.01	2997	3.86	13	0.68	257	0.76

Peten Gloss Ware

Tinaja Ceramic Group

	N	%	N	%	N	%	N	%	N	%	N	%	N	%	N	%	N	%	N	%
Tinaja Red	908	0.41	13142	0.37	318	0.32	5406	0.36	383	0.32	4519	0.23	204	4.42	3182	4.10	3	0.16	35	0.10
Pantano Impressed	10399	4.64	212486	5.96	1066	1.09	36527	2.41	9296	7.78	175034	9.02	9	0.20	407	0.52	28	1.47	518	1.52
Tinaja/Pantano	23392	10.44	326682	9.16	8005	8.18	126476	8.36	15007	12.55	195497	10.07	99	2.15	1181	1.52	281	14.80	3528	10.39
Subin Red	2072	0.93	58836	1.65	618	0.63	16574	1.10	1386	1.16	39045	2.01	58	1.26	2890	3.72	10	0.53	327	0.96
Chaquiste Impressed	6917	3.09	201378	5.65	2925	2.99	101913	6.74	3943	3.30	97676	5.03	9	0.20	320	0.41	40	2.11	1469	4.32
Subin/Chaquiste	10047	4.49	180772	5.07	4803	4.91	93641	6.19	4960	4.15	79837	4.11	57	1.24	1238	1.59	227	11.95	6056	17.83

TABLE 7.1. (continued) Distribution of Ceramic Types by Area (weight in grams).

	TOTAL FOR ALL AREAS				PALACE GROUP				CAUSEWAY AREA				BARRANCA ESCONDIDA				MAIN PLAZA–GRANADA GROUP			
	FREQ	%	WT	%	FREQ	%	WT	%	FREQ	%	WT	%	FREQ	%	WT	%	FREQ	%	WT	%
Nanzal Red	14	0.01	53	0.00	0	0.00	0	0.00	14	0.01	53	0.00	0	0.00	0	0.00	0	0.00	0	0.00
Corozal Incised	875	0.39	7159	0.20	23	0.02	111	0.01	848	0.71	7029	0.36	3	0.07	18	0.02	1	0.05	1	0.00
Corozal Incised: Grooved-incised v.	48	0.02	275	0.01	2	0.00	3	0.00	46	0.04	272	0.01	0	0.00	0	0.00	0	0.00	0	0.00
Zopilote Smudged Black	16	0.01	408	0.01	12	0.01	330	0.02	4	0.00	78	0.00	0	0.00	0	0.00	0	0.00	0	0.00
Unnamed fluted-incised	25	0.01	127	0.00	1	0.00	9	0.00	21	0.02	103	0.01	1	0.02	3	0.00	2	0.11	12	0.04
Unnamed incised-punctuated	6	0.00	192	0.01	0	0.00	0	0.00	5	0.00	14	0.00	1	0.02	178	0.23	0	0.00	0	0.00
Unnamed impressed	22	0.01	556	0.02	7	0.01	55	0.00	0	0.00	0	0.00	15	0.33	501	0.64	0	0.00	0	0.00
Tinaja Group undetermined	919	0.41	8501	0.24	24	0.02	394	0.03	473	0.40	3641	0.19	422	9.15	4466	5.75	0	0.00	0	0.00
Infierno Ceramic Group																				
Infierno Black	63	0.03	356	0.01	15	0.02	79	0.01	41	0.03	176	0.01	2	0.04	84	0.11	5	0.26	17	0.05
Carmelita Incised	89	0.04	599	0.02	28	0.03	295	0.02	54	0.05	258	0.01	0	0.00	0	0.00	7	0.37	46	0.14
Carmelita Incised: Grooved v.	29	0.01	600	0.02	0	0.00	0	0.00	25	0.02	570	0.03	4	0.09	30	0.04	0	0.00	0	0.00
Chilar Fluted	8	0.00	32	0.00	2	0.00	6	0.00	5	0.00	24	0.00	1	0.02	2	0.00	0	0.00	0	0.00
Unnamed carved-incised	2	0.00	39	0.00	0	0.00	0	0.00	1	0.00	10	0.00	1	0.02	29	0.04	0	0.00	0	0.00
Infierno Group undetermined	124	0.06	884	0.02	59	0.06	272	0.02	58	0.05	532	0.03	7	0.15	80	0.10	0	0.00	0	0.00
Azote Ceramic Group (Orange slip)																				
Torres Incised	38	0.02	955	0.03	36	0.04	889	0.06	2	0.00	66	0.00	0	0.00	0	0.00	0	0.00	0	0.00
Salada Fluted	286	0.13	2250	0.06	115	0.12	1056	0.07	171	0.14	1194	0.06	0	0.00	0	0.00	0	0.00	0	0.00
Azote Group undetermined	82	0.04	1042	0.03	74	0.08	598	0.04	8	0.01	444	0.02	0	0.00	0	0.00	0	0.00	0	0.00
Saxche-Palmar Ceramic Group																				
Saxche-Palmar Polychrome	10936	4.88	165186	4.63	2795	2.85	48023	3.17	7721	6.46	111408	5.74	320	6.94	4736	6.10	100	5.27	1019	3.00

Type	n	%	n	%	n	%	n	%	n	%	n	%	n	%	n	%	n	%	n	%
Saxche-Palmar (incised)	331	0.15	4968	0.14	48	0.05	271	0.02	281	0.24	4693	0.24	0	0.00	0	0.00	2	0.11	4	0.01
Saxche-Palmar (fluted/incised and fluted)	94	0.04	1421	0.04	23	0.02	897	0.06	71	0.06	524	0.03	0	0.00	0	0.00	0	0.00	0	0.00
Saxche-Palmar (impressed)	2	0.00	133	0.00	0	0.00	0	0.00	2	0.00	133	0.01	0	0.00	0	0.00	0	0.00	0	0.00
Unnamed																				
Unnamed cream or buff slipped	4	0.00	13	0.00	3	0.00	10	0.00	1	0.00	3	0.00	0	0.00	0	0.00	0	0.00	0	0.00
Unnamed white slipped	100	0.04	864	0.02	36	0.04	362	0.02	64	0.05	502	0.03	0	0.00	0	0.00	0	0.00	0	0.00
Unnamed white slipped-incised	17	0.01	136	0.00	4	0.00	86	0.01	3	0.00	4	0.00	10	0.22	46	0.06	0	0.00	0	0.00
Undetermined																				
Peten Gloss undetermined	500	0.22	4760	0.13	167	0.17	1097	0.07	209	0.17	2263	0.12	85	1.84	1070	1.38	39	2.05	331	0.97
Unnamed Ware																				
Unnamed volcanic ash undetermined	679	0.30	7155	0.20	175	0.18	2445	0.16	494	0.41	4565	0.24	6	0.13	97	0.12	4	0.21	48	0.14
Unnamed striated	2	0.00	21	0.00	1	0.00	9	0.00	1	0.00	12	0.00	0	0.00	0	0.00	0	0.00	0	0.00
Unnamed impressed	9	0.00	87	0.00	0	0.00	0	0.00	9	0.01	87	0.00	0	0.00	0	0.00	0	0.00	0	0.00
Unnamed modeled-carved	3	0.00	12	0.00	0	0.00	0	0.00	2	0.00	5	0.00	1	0.02	7	0.01	0	0.00	0	0.00
Unnamed carved-incised	2	0.00	6	0.00	0	0.00	0	0.00	2	0.00	6	0.00	0	0.00	0	0.00	0	0.00	0	0.00
Unnamed unslipped and painted	2	0.00	25	0.00	0	0.00	0	0.00	2	0.00	25	0.00	0	0.00	0	0.00	0	0.00	0	0.00
Unnamed stuccoed	13	0.01	367	0.01	13	0.01	367	0.02	0	0.00	0	0.00	0	0.00	0	0.00	0	0.00	0	0.00
Other/Undefined	105	0.05	2003	0.06	13	0.01	153	0.01	92	0.08	1850	0.10	0	0.00	0	0.00	0	0.00	0	0.00
Subtotal	141511	63.18	2580508	72.38	50846	51.93	992004	65.56	87584	73.26	1529228	78.80	1684	36.52	34249	44.09	1397	73.57	25028	73.68

TABLE 7.1. (continued) Distribution of Ceramic Types by Area (weight in grams).

	TOTAL FOR ALL AREAS				PALACE GROUP				CAUSEWAY AREA				BARRANCA ESCONDIDA				MAIN PLAZA–GRANADA GROUP			
	FREQ	%	WT	%	FREQ	%	WT	%	FREQ	%	WT	%	FREQ	%	WT	%	FREQ	%	WT	%
Late Classic Nacimiento Tepeu Late Facet (AD 761–810)																				
Uaxactun Unslipped Ware																				
Cambio Ceramic Group																				
Cambio Unslipped (angled neck)	3	0.00	639	0.02	3	0.00	639	0.04	0	0.00	0	0.00	0	0.00	0	0.00	0	0.00	0	0.00
Cambio Unslipped (angled neck and scratched)	496	0.22	11612	0.33	58	0.06	1854	0.12	438	0.37	9758	0.50	0	0.00	0	0.00	0	0.00	0	0.00
Encanto Striated (striation band)	188	0.08	5091	0.14	10	0.01	1025	0.07	178	0.15	4066	0.21	0	0.00	0	0.00	0	0.00	0	0.00
Encanto Striated (striation band and impressions)	274	0.12	8301	0.23	41	0.04	1616	0.11	233	0.19	6685	0.34	0	0.00	0	0.00	0	0.00	0	0.00
Manteca Impressed	739	0.33	16695	0.47	249	0.25	6442	0.43	488	0.41	10205	0.53	0	0.00	0	0.00	2	0.11	48	0.14
Manteca Impressed (red or white wash)	28	0.01	507	0.01	26	0.03	436	0.03	2	0.00	71	0.00	0	0.00	0	0.00	0	0.00	0	0.00
Manteca Impressed (angled neck)	32	0.01	1207	0.03	4	0.00	345	0.02	28	0.02	862	0.04	0	0.00	0	0.00	0	0.00	0	0.00
Manteca Impressed: Ridged v.	3693	1.65	114408	3.21	98	0.10	3471	0.23	3595	3.01	110937	5.72	0	0.00	0	0.00	0	0.00	0	0.00
Manteca Impressed: Ridged v. (red or white wash)	131	0.06	7099	0.20	120	0.12	6631	0.44	11	0.01	468	0.02	0	0.00	0	0.00	0	0.00	0	0.00
Peten Gloss Ware																				
Tinaja Ceramic Group																				
Cameron Incised	27	0.01	496	0.01	25	0.03	475	0.03	2	0.00	21	0.00	0	0.00	0	0.00	0	0.00	0	0.00

Fine Gray Ware

Chablekal Ceramic Group																				
Chablekal Gray	450	0.20	1993	0.06	0	0.00	0	0.00	1993	0.10	450	0.38	0	0.00	0	0.00	0	0.00	0	0.00
Chicxulub Incised	231	0.10	994	0.03	16	0.02	97	0.01	897	0.05	215	0.18	0	0.00	0	0.01	0	0.00	0	0.00
Telchac Composite	11	0.00	191	0.01	0	0.00	0	0.00	191	0.01	11	0.01	0	0.00	0	0.00	0	0.00	0	0.00
Chablekal Undetermined	391	0.17	1302	0.04	12	0.01	26	0.00	1276	0.07	379	0.32	0	0.00	0	0.00	0	0.00	0	0.00
Unnamed Volcanic Ash Ware																				
Andres Ceramic Group																				
Andres Red	378	0.17	6740	0.19	265	0.27	5352	0.35	1388	0.07	113	0.09	0	0.00	0	0.00	0	0.00	0	0.00
Matu Incised	145	0.06	802	0.02	9	0.01	120	0.01	682	0.04	136	0.11	0	0.00	0	0.00	0	0.00	0	0.00
Unnamed Ware																				
Unnamed red-orange paste	819	0.36	2412	0.07	232	0.24	1212	0.08	1182	0.06	583	0.49	3	0.07	16	0.02	1	0.05	2	0.01
Unnamed micaceous paste	222	0.10	2794	0.08	77	0.08	1441	0.10	1353	0.07	145	0.12	0	0.00	0	0.00	0	0.00	0	0.00
Unnamed quartz tempered	158	0.07	1563	0.04	23	0.02	656	0.04	907	0.05	135	0.11	0	0.00	0	0.00	0	0.00	0	0.00
Other unnamed	197	0.09	1983	0.06	147	0.15	1028	0.07	825	0.04	38	0.03	0	0.00	0	0.00	12	0.63	130	0.38
Subtotal	8613	3.85	186829	5.24	1415	1.45	32866	2.17	153767	7.92	7180	6.01	16	0.02	16	0.79	15	0.79	180	0.53
Undetermined																				
Eroded/ Undetermined	72606	32.42	770209	21.60	45627	46.60	487949	32.25	256916	13.24	24708	20.67	1785	38.71	16590	21.36	486	25.59	8754	25.77
Total	223971	100.00	3565400	100.00	97912	100.00	1513017	100.00	1940736	100.00	119549	100.00	4611	100.00	77678	100.00	1899	100.00	33970	100.00

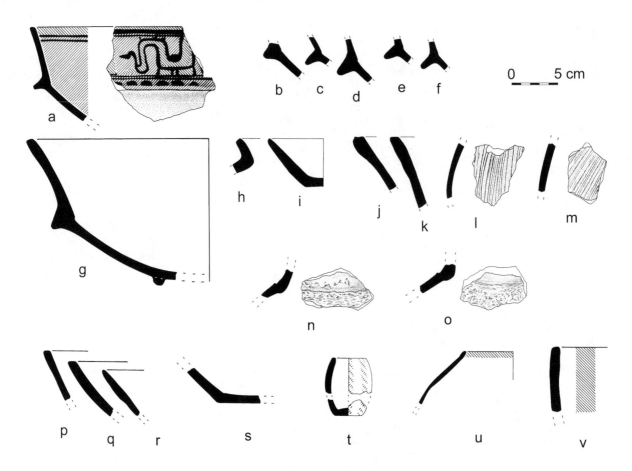

FIGURE 7.1. Jordan Tzakol ceramics from the Barranca Escondida. (a–d) Dos Arroyos polychrome. (a) 24A14-1-1, Cat. 360032. (b) 24A16-1-1, Cat. 360044. (c) 24B19-1-1, Cat. 360341. (d) 24A4-2-1, Cat. 360292. (e, f) Aguila Orange. (e) 24A414-1-1, Cat. 360095. (f) 24C8-1-1, Cat. 360296. (g) Blanza Black. 24A16-1-1, Cat. 360049. (h–k) Quintal Unslipped. (h) 24A (looter's back dirt), Cat. 360005. (i) 24A (looter's back dirt), Cat. 3600326. (j) 24B16-1-1, Cat. 360172. (k) 24B4-1-1, Cat. 360160. (l, m) Triunfo Striated–Encanto Striated transition. (l) 24A16-1-1, Cat. 360046. (m) 24A3-1-1, Cat. 360082. (n, o) Quintal Unslipped with rough surface. (n) 24A16-1-1, Cat. 360048. (o) 24A (looter's back dirt), Cat. 360007. (p–s) Quintal Unslipped White Wash variety. (p, r) 24A-18-1, Cat. 360061. (q) 24A (looter's back dirt), Cat. 360026. (s) 24B18-1-1, Cat. 360062. (t) Quintal Unslipped White Wash variety with a green band on the interior rim and green vertical stripes. (u, v) Tinaja Red? (u) 24B6-2-1, Cat. 360109. (v) 24B6-2-1, Cat. 360108.

and the early part of the Late Classic, that is, roughly from AD 500 to 720. This ceramic chronology would accord well with the estimated dates of the stelae found in this area.

A unique variation of Quintal Unslipped found in the Barranca Escondida includes jars with rough, unsmoothed exterior body surfaces and short smoothed necks (Figure 7.1n and o). Sabloff (1975) and Foias (1996:369) note that their Quintal Unslipped samples from Ceibal and the Petexbatun region have smoothed surfaces. Also notable are plates and bowls made of calcite-tempered reddish paste (2.5YR5/8–6/8, 5YR6/8), similar to that of Pedregal Modeled, and with thick, dull white slip (Figure 7.1p–s). Foias (1996:373) established Quintal Unslipped White

Wash variety for samples found at Arroyo de Piedra, and our materials were tentatively classified into this category. We should, however, note that the Barranca Escondida samples have relatively thick white material, which may be called slip rather than wash. One miniature vessel has greenish blue paint over white slip along the interior rim and is vertically striped on the exterior (Figure 7.1t). Foias (1996:374) suggests their function as *incensarios*. Among the Barranca Escondida samples, two vessels show traces of burning in the interior, but the others do not. Thus, their functions remain inconclusive. Some red-slipped vessels have forms uncommon for Tinaja Red, and they may date to the Early Classic period or the early facet of the Late Classic (Figure 7.1u and v).

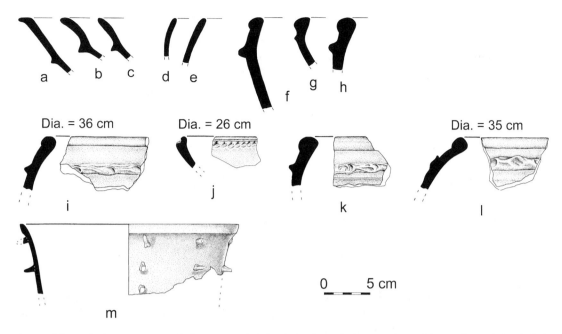

FIGURE 7.2. Possible Nacimiento Tepeu early facet ceramics. (a–c) Saxche Polychrome plates. (a) 24A (looter's back dirt), Cat. 360528. (b) 24A2-1-1, Cat. 360098. (c) 24A2-1-3, Cat. 360220. (d, e) Saxche Polychrome vases. (d) 24A2-1-1, Cat. 360099. (e) 24A11-1-1, Cat. 360195. (f–h) Subin Red bowls. (f) 24A (looter's back dirt), Cat. 360011. (g) 24A3-1-1, Cat. 360091. (h) 24A (looter's back dirt), Cat. 360011. (i–l) Chaquiste Impressed with impressed designs. (i) 24A3-1-1. Cat. 360093. (j) 24B2-2-2, Cat. 360463. (k, l) 24A (looter's back dirt), Cat. 360013. (m) Miseria Appliquéd (possibly Jordan-Tzakol or Nacimiento-Tepeu early facet), 24B6-1-1, Cat. 360579.

Late Classic Nacimiento Tepeu Complex: Early Facet (AD 600–720)

Foias (1996:428) divides the Late Classic ceramic chronology of the Petexbatun region into the early and late facets, with their division corresponding to the possible defeat of Ruler 4, K'awiil Chan K'inich, in AD 761. Our analysis of the Aguateca chronology suggests that her early facet can be further divided into two. In our refined chronology, the early facet dates to AD 600–720, corresponding to the Tepeu 1 phase at Uaxactun (Smith 1955) and the Imix complex at Tikal (Culbert 1993). The middle facet, AD 720–761, is contemporaneous with the early part of the Tepeu 2 phase. The late facet dates to AD 761–810, corresponding to the late part of the Tepeu 2 phase.

The division between the early and middle facets is not easy to make, and Sabloff (1975) and Foias (1996) do not make this distinction in their studies of Ceibal and Petexbatun ceramics. Changes can be recognized mostly in terms of certain modes, particularly the shapes of polychrome vessels, rather than in terms of types. Saxche Polychrome plates of the early facet are characterized by markedly flared or outcurved sides, small basal ridges, and rounded bases (Figure 7.2a–c). Later Tepeu 2 corresponding polychrome plate forms are dominated by those with

flat bases, and their sides tend to be less flared or less outcurved. In addition, round-sided polychrome bowls or vases (Figure 7.2d and e) generally date to the early facet. Bowls and vases from the later facets mostly have straight or outcurved sides, although these shapes may also occur during the early facet. This sequence of polychrome vessels parallels those at Uaxactun (Smith 1955:Fig. 36) and Tikal (Culbert 1993:Figs. 42–44).

Both round-based, outflared plates and flat-based ones were found in Burial 30, located in Structure L5-1 at Dos Pilas, a possible tomb of the ruler, Itzamnaaj K'awiil, who died in AD 726 (Foias 1996:1088). It is probable that common plate forms shifted gradually from the late seventh century through the early eighth century. We tentatively place the division between the early and middle facets around AD 720, as this date roughly corresponds with the establishment of Aguateca as the second capital of the Dos Pilas dynasty. The ceramic change, however, was most likely continuous with some period of overlap of different forms (see Eberl 2007:80–118).

The identification of the early facet ceramics shown in Table 7.1 was done conservatively, and it includes only the aforementioned polychrome vessels. A substantial number of sherds that potentially belong to the early facet were classified into the Nacimiento General category. Early facet Saxche polychromes are found in the Causeway area and in the Barranca Escondida. The Causeway area samples were found mostly in Structure M8-4. It appears that the fills of this building contained materials from middens or construction fills dating to the early facet. The presence of the early facet materials in the Barranca Escondida suggests that the use of this area continued from the Early Classic period. It is probable that the quantity of early facet materials from the Barranca Escondida is considerably larger than indicated in Table 7.1.

As discussed above, we found a significant amount of transitional forms from Quintal Unslipped to Cambio Unslipped and from Triunfo Striated to Encanto Striated. Some of them may date to the early facet of the Nacimiento phase. Likewise, some part of the Cambio ceramic group classified as Nacimiento General most likely date to the early facet. A comparison of ceramics from the Barranca Escondida and those from the other areas points to other potential chronological changes not reflected in Table 7.1.

Among monochrome types that are common throughout the Late Classic period are Subin Red and Chaquiste Impressed, which are red-slipped bowls with incurved sides, exteriorly thickened rim, and a ridge below the rim. The following four points suggest the early dates of Subin and Chaquiste vessels excavated from the Barranca Escondida area. First, most examples from this area are relatively open bowls, while in the later period bowls with markedly incurved walls also become common. It is likely that the relatively open forms of these vessels tend to suggest their early dates (Foias, personal communication 2000). Second, Subin Red vessels from this area exhibit more marked thickening of the rim and higher ridges than later samples (Figure 7.2f–h). Third, in the collection from the Barranca Escondida area, the proportion of Subin Red to Chaquiste Impressed is significantly higher than in those from other parts of Aguateca. Fourth, a considerable portion of Chaquiste Impressed vessels from this area have impressions made with tools or fingers (Figure 7.2i–l), while in later collections stamped impressions are most common (see Foias 1996:Figs. 6.33–6.37; Sabloff 1975:Fig. 329).

Another common category of Late Classic monochrome vessels includes red-slipped jars of Tinaja Red and Pantano Impressed types. Jars of the two types have essentially identical shapes and are distinguished by the presence and absence of stamped impressions. In the Barranca Escondida collection the number of Tinaja Red is substantially larger than that of Pantano Impressed whereas in other areas the latter is far more common than the former. It is possible that this represents a chronological trend from the early to middle-late facets.

We should reiterate that these differences between the ceramics of the early and middle facets of the Nacimiento phase are not clear-cut. Whereas round-based polychrome plates with smooth wall-base junctures (see Foias 1996: Fig. 6.53) can most likely date to the early facet, other forms of round-based plates may also appear during the later period (Foias 1996:1116, 1117). Changes in the forms of Subin Red bowls are even less clear-cut. The aforementioned early forms still appear in the later period, though in a smaller quantity. Thus, in many cases it is not possible to date individual pieces securely. Nonetheless, the composition of the ceramic assemblage from the Barranca Escondida area as a whole is markedly different from that of assemblages from other areas of Aguateca, and it is most likely that a significant portion of ceramics from this area was deposited during the Early Classic and the early part of the Late Classic.

Late Classic Nacimiento Tepeu Complex General (AD 600–810)

Previous studies by Sabloff (1975) and Foias (1996) show that the types listed under the heading of Nacimiento General in Table 7.1 were the main components of the middle facet of the Nacimiento phase (AD 720–761). We should note, however, that most of them were used throughout the Late Classic period. The majority of our samples classified in this category were indeed recovered from termination ritual deposits or floor assemblages of rapidly abandoned buildings, which were deposited or used at the end of the Late Classic Aguateca occupation around AD 810. In addition, a considerable amount of early facet ceramics are probably included in this group, as discussed above. In particular, the Cambio group undetermined category most likely includes not only body sherds of early facet unslipped jars but also those of Early Classic Quintal Unslipped and Preclassic Achiote Unslipped.

Most of those types were thoroughly discussed by Foias (1996), but a few of them require additional comments. Miseria Appliquéd is a spiked censor type dated to the Terminal Classic period at Uaxactun (Smith and Gifford 1966) and at Ceibal (Sabloff 1975), but Foias (1996: 465) points out that it appears during the Late Classic period. Similar spiked censors called Corriental Appliquéd are found in Late Preclassic or Protoclassic levels at Altar de Sacrificios (Adams 1971:53–54) and Uaxactun (Smith 1955:Figs. 16g1, 70d4). Bachand (Bachand 2006: 298) also found this type from Protoclassic contexts at Punta de Chimino, and Eberl (2007:467) found it at Dos Ceibas. At Aguateca spiked censors are recovered only in the Barranca Escondida (Figure 7.2m). Although we cannot securely determine their chronological place at Aguateca, their association with Early Classic and early Late Classic materials suggests that these censors were already in use during these early periods.

Smith and Gifford (1966) originally used the name Saxche Polychrome for Tepeu 1 materials and Palmar Polychrome for Tepeu 2 ones. The difficulty of distinguishing them, however, led Sabloff (1975) to combine the two names, calling it Saxche-Palmar Polychrome, and Foias (1996:183) to use the name Palmar Polychrome for materials from both Tepeu 1 and 2 corresponding facets. As discussed above, it is possible to recognize changes in vessel forms from early facet polychromes to middle facet ones. Although we agree that these changes do not represent differences at the typological level, we prefer to use Saxche Polychrome for the early facet materials to make its chronological position clearer. We use the name Saxche-Palmar Polychrome for the Nacimiento General category because, owing to the difficulty of recognizing chronological changes in small fragments and in vessel forms other than plates, these vessels most likely include both early facet and later facet materials.

Foias (1996:557, 558) notes that the Petexbatun ceramic collection includes a small amount of Zacatal Polychrome with cream background slip in addition to Saxche-Palmar Polychrome with orange slip. Because of the poor preservation of many sherds, however, it is often impossible to make this distinction. Following Sabloff (1975), we included possible Zacatal Polychrome in the Saxche-Palmar Polychrome category.

Saxche-Palmar Polychrome vessels commonly have calcite temper, but a small portion of them contain volcanic ash temper (Foias 1996:559). Some of them appear to have paste similar to that of the Andres ceramic group (see below) and may date to the late facet. Highly eroded volcanic ash tempered sherds were classified into the category of unnamed volcanic ash undetermined of the Late Classic Nacimiento Tepeu General. They probably include pieces of Saxche-Palmar Polychrome and the Andres ceramic group.

Relatively well preserved examples, including recon-

structible drums from Structure M7-22 (WDR 22A-1 and 22A-2), indicate that white or cream slipped monochrome vessels existed. However, many of them are difficult to distinguish from eroded polychromes, and these categories may include a substantial number of eroded polychromes.

A small number of sherds from the Palace Group and the Causeway area were decorated with painted stucco. In many cases, however, the fragile stucco was probably eroded after deposition.

The deposits at the Barranca Escondida contain a significant number of sherds belonging to the Late Classic Nacimiento Tepeu General. Present among these samples, albeit in a relatively small quantity, are varieties and forms typical of the middle facet. It is likely that the Barranca Escondida continued to be used, though less intensively, during the mid-eighth century.

Late Classic Nacimiento Tepeu Complex: Late Facet (AD 761–810)

Foias (1996:428) originally defined the late facet through the analysis of ceramics that appear only in contexts postdating the possible defeat of Ruler 4, K'awiil Chan K'inich, such as the squatters' village and defense walls at Dos Pilas and the late occupation at Aguateca. In our analysis of ceramics from the rapidly abandoned structures along the Causeway and the termination deposits in the Palace Group, we recognized additional kinds of ceramics that probably date to this facet. The end date of AD 810 reflects our estimated date of the abandonment of Aguateca based on the inscription on the unfinished Altar M, associated with the unfinished Temple L8-8 (Inomata et al. 2004).

Some jars have pastes identical to those of common Cambio Unslipped but exhibit angled neck-body junctures, as in Preclassic and Early Classic jars (Figure 7.3a and b). Many of these jars had thick body walls and rough surfaces scratched vertically, probably with pointed sticks (Figure 7.3c). A small number of Encanto Striated jars had one or more horizontal bands of striation, interspaced by smoothed, undecorated surfaces (Figure 7.3d). The edges of the striation bands are often defined by a series of fingernail-like impressions. Other unique examples of Encanto Striated include those with sparse striation, bowls with markedly incurved sides, and plates with no sides (Figure 7.3e–j).

Manteca Impressed vessels commonly have shapes and pastes of Cambio Unslipped jars with horizontal bands

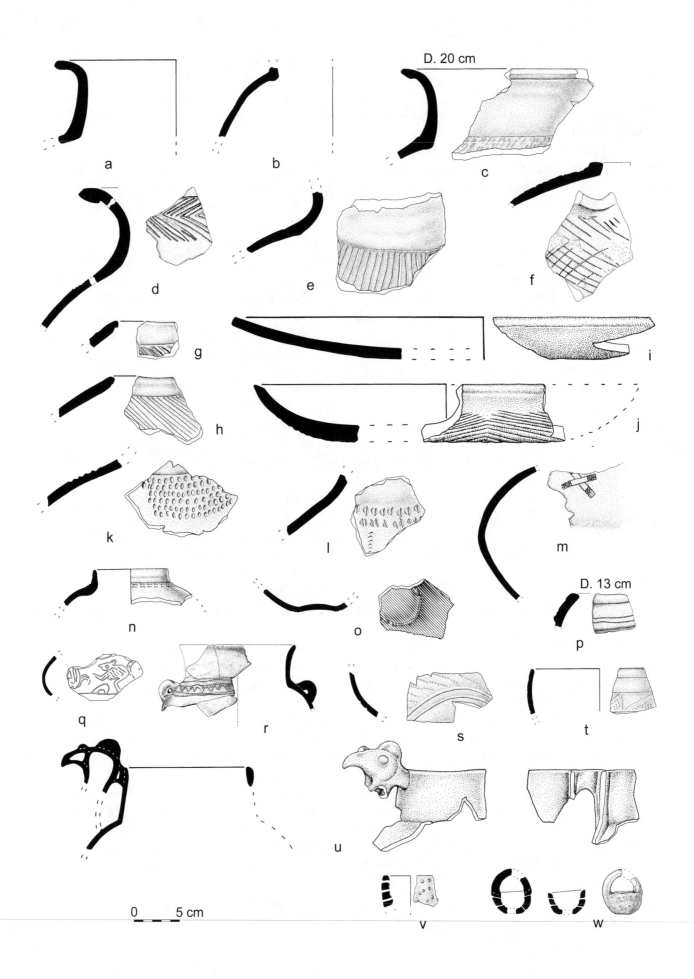

D. 20 cm

D. 13 cm

a

b

c

d

e

f

g

h

i

j

k

l

m

n

o

p

q

r

s

t

u

v

w

0   5 cm

of impressions on the shoulders. Impressions are often fingernail-like (Figure 7.3k and l), but a small number of vessels had stamped impressions similar to those of Pantano Impressed. A small portion of Manteca Impressed jars have angled neck-body junctures. Manteca Impressed Ridged variety is a common class of large storage jars found in residential structures. These vessels have rims and necks similar to those of Cambio Unslipped and Encanto Striated, smoothed surfaces, and flat bases. A characteristic attribute is a pronounced horizontal ridge with braid-design impressions. Some of them have red or white wash, particularly on the neck and shoulder. The floor assemblages from the rapidly abandoned structures contained a considerable number of reconstructible Manteca Impressed jars, and their body sherds were relatively securely identified. In the ceramic collections from the termination deposits of the Palace Group, only shoulder sherds with ridges were confidently classified into this category whereas numerous other body and rim sherds of Manteca Impressed jars were probably classified into Cambio Undetermined. This factor most likely contributed to the small quantity of Manteca Impressed from the Palace Group compared with that from the Causeway area.

Tinaja Red and Pantano Impressed jars are among the most common vessel types, but unique examples include a Pantano Impressed jar with a short neck and a possible jar with impressions on the base (Figure 7.3n and o). A small number of Pantano Impressed have incised motifs on the shoulder (Figure 7.3m). Corozal Incised and Carmelita Incised often occur as bowls or vases with incised motifs of monkeys. Less common examples include jars with incisions and motifs of squirrels (Figure 7.3p and q). Sabloff (1975) and Foias (1996:644) date Cameron Incised to the Terminal Classic period, but a small quantity of these vessels are present in the floor assemblages of the rapidly abandoned structures along the Causeway and the termination deposits in the Palace Group (Figure 7.3r). Since other Terminal Classic materials are absent in these contexts, Cameron Incised most likely began to be used

at Aguateca at the end of the Classic period. Foias (1996: 648) notes that at Uaxactun, Cameron Incised is defined for the Tepeu 3 phase, but identical materials are illustrated for the Tepeu 1 and 2 phases. Although Foias (1996: 644) proposes to classify the Petexbatun Terminal Classic materials as Corozal Incised Cameron variety, these vessels are associated most closely with Subin Red, and we prefer to use the original type name of Cameron Incised.

Vessels of Fine Gray ware Chablekal ceramic group are relatively common in the floor assemblages found in the Causeway area but much less common in the Palace Group. The implications of this pattern are not clear. A significant portion of the Chablekal group consists of Chicxulub Incised. A less common type is Telchac Composite, which has incisions and punctuations (Figure 7.3s and t).

Some vessels of unique shape deserve comment. Several examples of pitchers with whistle handles have been found at Aguateca (Figure 7.4u). Some of them have red slip and are tentatively classified as Tinaja Red or Corozal Incised, but their walls are generally thinner than those of common Tinaja vessels. A hollow handle with a whistle opening is attached to the globular body, and it probably made sound as one poured liquid. Small vessels with multiple perforations have been called colander-like objects, or candeleros (Figure 7.4v and w), and have been found at Altar de Sacrificios (Adams 1971:fig. 104d), Ceibal (Willey 1978:Fig. 48k and l), Tikal (Moholy-Nagy 2003:Fig. 141g–o), and Dos Ceibas (Eberl 2007:Fig. 10.41). Their functions are unclear although their use as small incensarios has been suggested.

Andres Red and related volcanic ash tempered types were defined by Foias (1996) and were probably imported from other regions. Common shapes include plates and bowls (Figure 7.4a–k). A small number of them show black paint over red slip or other polychrome decorations (Figure 7.4l–m). Other unnamed types were most likely imported from other regions, and a significant portion of them were found in the Palace Group. Most of the

FIGURE 7.3. (opposite) Nacimiento Tepeu late facet ceramics. (a, b) Cambio Unslipped jars with angled neck-body juncture. (a) 22B35-2-1, Cat. 395648. (b) 22B2-3-3, Cat. 390088. (c) Cambio Unslipped with angled neck-body juncture and scratched surface, 23B13-3-1, Cat. 350400. (d) Encanto Striated with horizontal bands of striation, 21A41-3-2, Cat. 371149. (e) Encanto Striated with sparse striation, 22B3-2-4, Cat. 400015. (f–h) Encanto Striated bowls with markedly incurved sides. (f) 23A55-3-2, Cat. 382158. (g) 22A1-3-4, Cat. 346214. (h) 22A9-2-2, Cat. 340176. (i) Cambio Unslipped plate with no sides, 22A10-2-5, Cat. 343052. (j) Encanto Striated plate with no sides, 22B53-3-3, Cat. 395569. (k, l) Manteca Impressed. (k) 22A45-3-1, Cat. 346541. (l) 22A45-3-1, Cat. 346540. (m–o) Pantano Impressed. (m) 22A6-3-1, Cat. 346013. (n) 22B2-3-2, Cat. 390070. (o) 23A55-2-1, Cat. 382137. (p) Corozal Incised, 23B16-3-4, Cat. 351372. (q) Carmelita Incised, 22A9-1-1, Cat. 346064. (r) Cameron Incised, 23A35-1-1, Cat. 382035. (s–t) Telchac Composite. (s) 23B6-3-3, Cat. 350291. (t) 23B13-3-1, Cat. 350414. (u) Whistle-handle pitcher, 22A45-3-1, Cat. 346567. (v, w) Small vessels with multiple perforations. (v) 22B43-3-4, Cat. 390272. (w) 22A6-2-4, Cat. 340075.

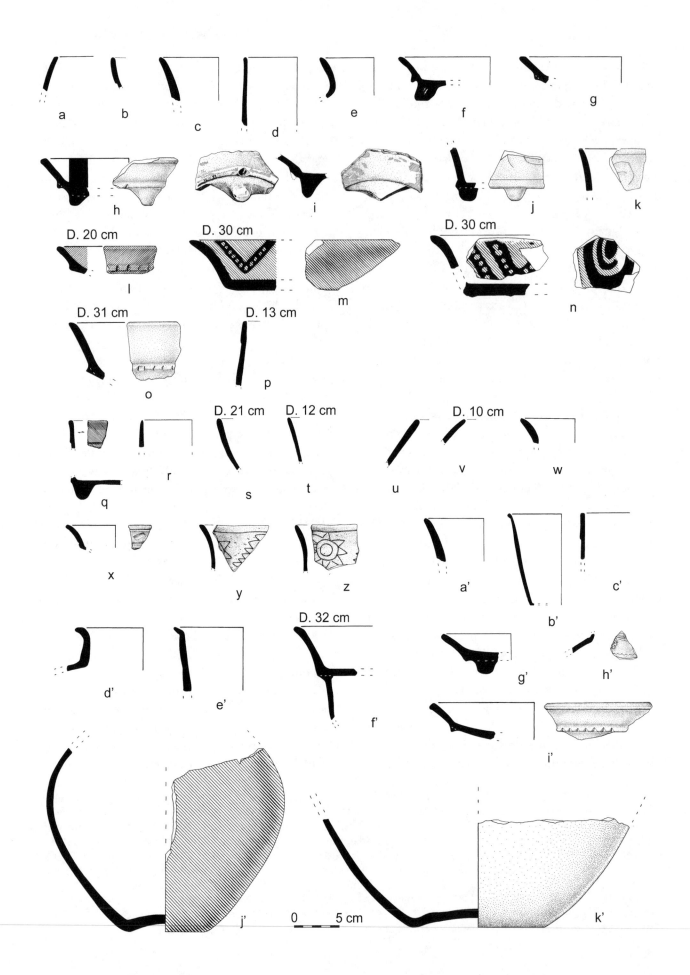

D. 20 cm

D. 30 cm

D. 30 cm

D. 31 cm

D. 13 cm

D. 21 cm

D. 12 cm

D. 10 cm

D. 32 cm

a

b

c

d

e

f

g

h

i

j

k

l

m

n

o

p

q

r

s

t

u

v

w

x

y

z

a'

b'

c'

d'

e'

f'

g'

h'

i'

j'

k'

0   5 cm

unnamed red-orange paste vessels are not reconstructible, but they appear to be predominantly cylinder vases and vases or bowls with slightly incurved sides, but bowls or plates with outflared walls are also present (Figure 7.3q–z). Their pastes are hard and compact, and their walls are thin. Their pastes and forms exhibit some resemblance to those of the Fine Orange ware, but a small amount of temper inclusions distinguish them from true Fine Orange. Some have red slip preserved on the surface, and others have incisions. According to personal observation by Inomata, some materials from the Palenque region appear nearly identical to red-orange paste vessels from Aguateca. A rare example of this type is a reconstructible bowl with rattles in the base, incised and painted with black and white, which was found in Structure M8-8. The presence of a small quantity of the red-orange paste ware at the Barranca Escondida is peculiar in the absence of other late facet materials. Typological definitions of the red-orange paste ware are still not well established, and different materials may be included in this tentative category.

The unnamed compact brown paste ware typically occurs as thin-walled bowls and vases (Figure 7.4a'–c'). Rare types include the unnamed micaceous paste ware (Figure 7.4d'–f') and the unnamed quartz sand tempered ware (Figure 7.4g'–i'). Their pastes are substantially different from those of other Aguateca ceramics. A small number of micaceous tempered vessels are polychrome. Some of these types share common modes, including thin-walled vases with slightly thickened rims for the unnamed red-orange paste ware and the unnamed compact brown paste ware. Plates with a ridge slightly above the wall-base juncture occur in Andres Red and related volcanic ash tempered types, as well as the quartz sand tempered wares. Those shared modes may indicate that they originated from the same general region, possibly the lower or middle Usumacinta drainage.

Some ceramics found in the Palace Group appear

unique and different from those excavated from the rapidly abandoned structures along the Causeway. For example, a reconstructible Chaquiste Impressed bowl (WVS 22A-7, Cat. 310254) has a flat base with ridge and rough exterior, and a nonreconstructible Tinaja or Pantano jar (Cat. 310257, Figure 7.4j') has an incurved base, the edge of which is rounded, as opposed to the angled edges commonly found in other vessels. Cat. 310297 has only a base and a lower body, but it appears to have been a jar (Figure 7.4k'). It exhibits a mixture of characteristics of Cambio and Tinaja/Pantano. Its paste is like Cambio with very coarse temper, although it has a slightly incurved base, common for Tinaja/Pantano jars. WVS 22A-2 (Cat. 310298) exhibits a jar neck common for Cambio but has a slight ridge and triangular impression along the shoulder, as well as an incurved base. Another reconstructible Cambio jar (WVS 22A-3, Cat. 310299) also shows an appearance quite different from other Cambio Unslipped vessels. These two jars have similar pastes, which are different from those of common Cambio jars.

Terminal Classic and Postclassic Periods

No ceramics confidently dated to the Terminal Classic or Postclassic periods were found during the Aguateca Archaeological Project First Phase, although a small number of Plumbate and Fine Orange vessels were recovered during the Aguateca Subproject of the Petexbatun Project and the Aguateca Reconstruction Project. It appears that Aguateca was completely abandoned sometime around AD 810 and only a small number of individuals visited this place during the Terminal Classic and Postclassic periods.

VESSEL FORMS AND FUNCTIONAL IMPLICATIONS

Table 7.2 shows the distribution of different vessel forms by area. The Main Plaza and the Granada Group are treated separately because vessel forms illustrate the difference between them more clearly than types. In Table

FIGURE 7.4. (*opposite*) Nacimiento Tepeu late facet ceramics. (a–i) Andres Red. (a) 22A45-3-1, Cat. 346570. (b) 23A21-3-1, Cat. 381388. (c) 22A7-1-1, Cat. 340045. (d) 22A9-1-1, Cat. 346083. (e) 22A44-1-1, Cat. 340555. (f) 22A9-1-1, Cat. 346085. (g) 22B54-3-1, Cat. 395497. (h) 22B3-3-3, Cat. 400086. (i) 22A9-2-5, Cat. 340044. (j, k) Matu Incised. (j) 22B35-3-3, Cat. 395711. (k) 22B35-3-2, Cat. 395703. (l–n) Unnamed volcanic ash tempered polychrome. (l) 22B56-2-1, Cat. 405218. (m) 22A9-1-1, Cat. 346084. (n) 22A6-3-1, Cat. 346020. (o, p) Unnamed volcanic ash tempered undetermined. (o) 22A25-3-2, Cat. 343392. (p) 23A54-1-1, Cat. 382238. (q–w) Unnamed red-orange paste ware. (q) 22A9-1-1, Cat. 346077. (r) 22B53-2-2, Cat. 395541. (s) 23A21-2-1, Cat. 381367. (t) 22A53-3-1, Cat. 346401. (u) 22A9-2-3, Cat. 346102. (v) 22A6-3-1, Cat. 346021. (w) 22A9-1-1, Cat. 346078. (x–z) Unnamed red-orange paste ware incised type. (x) 22A9-1-1, Cat. 346076. (y) 23A1-1-2, 380011. (z) 23A55-1-1, Cat. 382130. (a'–c') Unnamed compact brown paste ware. (a') 22A7-1-1, Cat. 340045. (b') 22A49-3-1, Cat. 346498. (c') 22A9-2-5, Cat. 346120. (d', e') Unnamed micaceous paste ware. (d') 22A6-3-1, Cat. 346017. (e') 22A45-3-1, Cat. 346563. (f') Unnamed micaceous paste polychrome. 22A26-3-2, Cat. 343484. (g'–i') Unnamed quartz sand tempered paste ware. (g') 22A9-1-1, Cat. 346039. (h') 22A9-1-1, Cat. 346585. (i') 22B2-3-4, Cat. 390107. (j') Tinaja Red or Pantano Impressed jar with a rounded-edge incurved base. 22A10-2-5, Cat. 310257. (k') Probable Cambio Unslipped jar with a Tinaja/Pantano-like incurved base. 22A22-3-1, Cat. 310297.

TABLE 7.2. Distribution of Ceramic Vessel Forms by Area (weight in grams).

	TOTAL FOR ALL AREAS				PALACE GROUP				CAUSEWAY AREA			
	FREQ	%	WT	%	FREQ	%	WT	%	FREQ	%	WT	%
Jars	112162	76.45	2071204	75.17	39034	76.44	732923	72.25	71380	76.81	1309070	77.81
Bowls	22738	15.50	481365	17.47	9167	17.95	224835	22.16	13060	14.05	240338	14.29
Plates	6726	4.58	149001	5.41	1989	3.89	47044	4.64	4519	4.86	97312	5.78
Vases	2904	1.98	25026	0.91	438	0.86	4320	0.43	2404	2.59	20184	1.20
Pitchers	335	0.23	3119	0.11	44	0.09	704	0.07	291	0.31	2415	0.14
Incensarios	570	0.39	14744	0.54	204	0.40	3290	0.32	185	0.20	3520	0.21
Drums	1285	0.88	10802	0.39	192	0.38	1270	0.13	1092	1.18	9526	0.57
Total of identified	146720	100.00	2755261	100.00	51068	100.00	1014386	100.00	92931	100.00	1682365	100.00
Identified	146720	65.51	2755260	77.28	51068	52.16	1014385	67.04	92931	77.73	1682365	86.69
Unidentified	77251	34.49	810138	22.72	46844	47.84	498631	32.96	26618	22.27	258369	13.31
Grand Total	223971	100.00	3565399	100.00	97912	100.00	1513017	100.00	119549	100.00	1940734	100.00

	BARRANCA ESCONDIDA				MAIN PLAZA				GRANADA GROUP			
	FREQ	%	WT	%	FREQ	%	WT	%	FREQ	%	WT	%
Jars	815	59.49	14031	41.37	802	68.31	13603	60.34	131	74.01	1577	77.00
Bowls	196	14.31	8013	23.62	286	24.36	7917	35.12	29	16.38	262	12.79
Plates	172	12.55	3967	11.70	29	2.47	469	2.08	17	9.60	209	10.21
Vases	18	1.31	142	0.42	44	3.75	380	1.69	0	0.00	0	0.00
Pitchers	0	0.00	0	0.00	0	0.00	0	0.00	0	0.00	0	0.00
Incensarios	169	12.34	7766	22.90	12	1.02	168	0.75	0	0.00	0	0.00
Drums	0	0.00	0	0.00	1	0.09	6	0.03	0	0.00	0	0.00
Total of identified	1370	100.00	33919	100.00	1174	100.00	22543	100.00	177	100.00	2048	100.00
Identified	1370	29.71	33919	43.67	1174	76.28	22543	79.78	177	49.17	2048	35.84
Unidentified	3241	70.29	43759	56.33	365	23.72	5712	20.22	183	50.83	3667	64.16
Grand Total	4611	100.00	77678	100.00	1539	100.00	28255	100.00	360	100.00	5715	100.00

7.3 closed vessels consist of jars, pitchers, and drums whereas open ones include plates, vases, and *incensarios* (Foias 1996:189). Many bowls are included in open forms, but those with markedly incurved walls are classified as closed. Even when fragments are too small to be assigned to specific vessel shapes, the identification of closed or open forms is sometimes possible on the basis of rim shape and treatment of the interior and exterior surfaces. A substantial portion of closed-form vessels, including jars and some of the closed bowls, were used for storage and for containing liquid. Many of the open-form pots, particularly vases and small open bowls, were most likely serving vessels. The identification of cooking vessels is difficult, but they probably include large bowls of both closed and open forms. The unidentified category consists mostly of small and eroded fragments but also includes an extremely small number of forms other than those listed, such as lids.

In both Tables 7.2 and 7.3, the compositions of ceramic assemblages from the Palace Group and the Causeway area are similar, although we should note the substantial portion of unidentified pieces in the former due to erosion. The percentage of bowls is somewhat higher for the Palace Group, particularly in terms of weight. This is probably because the thickened rims of Subin/Chaquiste bowls can be identified relatively confidently even for eroded sherds, and they tend to weigh more than other sherds. The quantity of other vessel forms in relation to that of bowls might have been slightly higher if they had not been so eroded. It appears that the original composition of the Palace Group assemblage was fairly close to that of the Causeway.

The nature of the termination ritual deposits that which make up a large part of the Palace Group assemblage is not clear. These data, however, may suggest that

TABLE 7.3. Distribution of Closed and Open Ceramic Vessels by Area (weight in grams).

	TOTAL FOR ALL AREAS				PALACE GROUP				CAUSEWAY AREA			
	FREQ	%	WT	%	FREQ	%	WT	%	FREQ	%	WT	%
Closed forms	115420	77.03	2108056	75.65	39488	76.11	735989	71.82	74140	77.97	1342887	78.96
Open forms	34411	22.97	678710	24.35	12395	23.89	288728	28.18	20947	22.03	357916	21.04
Total of identified	149831	100.00	2786766	100.00	51883	100.00	1024717	100.00	95087	100.00	1700803	100.00
Identified	149831	66.90	2786766	78.16	51883	52.99	1024716	67.73	95087	79.54	1700803	87.64
Unidentified	74140	33.10	778633	21.84	46029	47.01	488300	32.27	24462	20.46	239932	12.36
Grand Total	223971	100.00	3565399	100.00	97912	100.00	1513017	100.00	119549	100.00	1940735	100.00

	BARRANCA ESCONDIDA				MAIN PLAZA				GRANADA GROUP			
	FREQ	%	WT	%	FREQ	%	WT	%	FREQ	%	WT	%
Closed forms	833	57.05	13765	38.02	817	68.08	13768	60.36	142	70.65	1648	73.80
Open forms	627	42.95	22440	61.98	383	31.92	9041	39.64	59	29.35	585	26.20
Total of identified	1460	100.00	36205	100.00	1200	100.00	22809	100.00	201	100.00	2233	100.00
Identified	1460	31.66	36205	46.61	1200	77.97	22809	80.73	201	55.83	2233	39.07
Unidentified	3151	68.34	41473	53.39	339	22.03	5446	19.27	159	44.17	3482	60.93
Grand Total	4611	100.00	77678	100.00	1539	100.00	28255	100.00	360	100.00	5715	100.00

they were originally the domestic refuse of this center. If the termination ritual deposits consist of vessels that were used during the rituals and feastings and then were broken and scattered, as suggested for some other cases of termination ritual deposits, we would expect higher proportions of serving vessels and *incensarios*. In addition, the Palace Group deposits consist mostly of nonreconstructible materials (see Chapter 8). The finding that a fragment of a ceramic flute found in Structure M7-32 was refitted with a piece from Structure M8-4 may also support this interpretation (see Volume 3 [Inomata and Triadan in preparation]). We should note that a significant presence of greenstone and shell ornaments in the Palace Group deposits distinguishes them from common domestic middens and that certain materials may have been added during the termination rituals.

Many of the Barranca Escondida materials were found near the surface and are heavily eroded, but we can note the low percentage of jars and the high quantities of *incensarios* and plates. This pattern reflects the ritual, nondomestic nature of the area. Plates were probably used for offerings, and it is not clear if they are related to feasting. The composition of the Granada Group assemblage is similar to that of the Causeway area, although less common forms are not well represented in this small sample. This confirms the interpretation that it represents domestic refuse. The percentages of forms in the Main Plaza sample, however, show values between those of the Palace Group–Causeway area assemblages and those of the Barranca Escondida. This is because it combines different types of materials from Structures L8-5 and L8-6. Structure L8-5's assemblage is associated with temple rituals, with strong representations of incense burners and other ritual objects, and is similar to that of the Barranca Escondida. Structure L8-6's assemblage resulted from termination rituals comparable to those of the Palace Group.

Complete, Reconstructible, and Partial Vessels

8

chapter

Takeshi Inomata, Daniela Triadan, and Estela Pinto

Table 8.1 shows a summary of the data in this chapter. Figures 8.60 and 8.61 show close-up drawings of impressed motifs.

STRUCTURE M7-22 (HOUSE OF MASKS): OPERATION 22A

WVS No.: 22A-1; Catalog No.: 310293 (Figure 8.1a)
Bag No.: Rim: 455 (24-3-2), 472 (24-3-2); Body: 455, 472; Base: 455, 472. Provenience: 22A24-3-2. Context: Floor. On the floor in front of the easternmost room where the layer of stones collapsed from the wall sealing the entrance thinned off. The fragments were found in an area 1 × 1 m. It is probable that the vessel was originally stored inside the easternmost room. Condition: Reconstructible (98% present). Well preserved. Only a small part of the interior rim is slightly darkened. Dimensions: Rim diameter: [exterior] 10.9 cm, [top] 10.3 cm (measured); Height: 4.2 cm (measured); Wall thickness: 0.7–0.9 cm; Sample weight: 185 g; Original weight: 189 g; Volume: 126 cm³. Coordinates: (18.36, 27.72) (estimate). Type: Cambio Unslipped. Paste, temper, and firing: Reddish yellow paste (5YR6/6). Medium grain. A medium amount of calcite temper (0.3–1.0 mm diameter) and a small amount of ferruginous temper (0.5–1.5 mm diameter). The paste is completely oxidized. Surface finish and decoration: The exterior is smoothed. The interior is slightly better smoothed than the exterior. Form: Bowl with flared sides. Direct rim and rounded lip. Flat base. Use-wear: No clear use-wear despite the relatively good preservation. No clear indication of use as an incense burner.

WVS No.: 22A-2; Catalog No.: 310298 (Figure 8.1b)
Bag No.: Rim: 472 (24-3-2); Body: 472, 424 (24-3-1), 422 (23-3-2), 273 (24-3-3), 473 (24-3-3); Base: 472, 424. Provenience: 22A24-3-2. Context: Floor. On the floor in front of the easternmost room where the layer of stones col-

lapsed from the wall sealing the entrance thinned off. The fragments were found in an area 2 × 1.5 m. It is probable that the vessel was originally stored inside the easternmost room. Condition: Reconstructible (80% present). Eroded. Parts of the exterior wall are blackened. Dimensions: Rim diameter: [exterior] 13.1 cm, [top] 12.7 cm (measured); Maximum diameter: 18.5 cm (measured); Minimum opening: 8.0 cm (measured); Height: 18.7 cm (measured); Neck height: 4.1 cm (measured); Wall thickness: 0.8–2.3 cm; Sample weight: 2,038 g; Original weight: 2,548 g; Volume: 1,712 cm³. Coordinates: (19.87, 27.25) (estimate). Type: Manteca Impressed (it has characteristics of both Cambio Unslipped and Pantano Impressed). Paste, temper, and firing: Reddish yellow paste (5YR6/8). Coarse grain. A large amount of quartz temper (1.0–3.0 mm long, some as large as 7.0 mm long), a medium amount of calcite temper (0.3–2.5 mm diameter), and a small amount of ferruginous temper (0.5–2.0 mm diameter). The paste is completely oxidized. Surface finish and decoration: The exterior is smoothed. It appears to have been unslipped. Slight ridge and a line of triangular impressions along the body-neck juncture. Form: Jar with outcurved neck with very thick walls. Direct rim and rounded lip. Incurved base. Use-wear: Not clear because of erosion.

WVS No.: 22A-3; Catalog No.: 310299 (Figure 8.1c and 8.1d)
Bag No.: Rim: 472 (24-3-2), 299 (24-2-3); Body: 472, 299, 424 (24-3-1), 520 (10-2-6), 391 (10-2-5); Base: 299, 391, 424, 473 (24-3-3). Provenience: 22A24-3-2. Context: Floor. Most fragments were found on the floor in an area 2 × 1 m in front of the easternmost room where the layer of stones collapsed from the wall sealing the entrance thinned off. A few pieces were recovered from the wall-fall layer inside the easternmost room. The vessel appears to have

TABLE 8.1. Summary of Reconstructible Vessel Data.

WVS	CATALOG	PROV.	PRESENT PORTION (%)	RIM DIA. Ex/In (cm)	RIM DIA. Top (cm)	MAX DIA. (cm)	MIN OPEN. (cm)	HT. (cm)	NECK HT. (cm)	HT. W/O F. (cm)	WALL THIN (cm)	WALL THICK (cm)	WEIGHT SAMPLE (g)	WEIGHT ORIGINAL (g)	VOLUME (cm³)	TYPE	FORM
M7-22 (House of Masks)																	
22A-1	310293	22A24-3-2	98	10.9	10.3			4.2			0.7	0.9	185	189	126	Cambio Unslipped	bowl
22A-2	310298	22A24-3-2	80	13.1	12.7	18.5	8.0	18.7	4.1		0.8	2.3	2038	2548	1712	Manteca Impressed	jar
22A-3	310299	22A24-3-2	60	21.3	20.1	36.1	14.9	32.0	6.1		0.7	1.5	4386	7310		Cambio Unslipped scratched	jar
22A-4	310036	22A14-2-6	99	14.5	14.3	34.5	7.8	34.1	5.1		0.8	1.4	5485	5540	17061	Pantano Impressed	jar
22A-5	310052	22A10-3-1	98	14.8	14.8	38.8	8.1	39.7	5.7		0.8	1.3	6077	6201	22352	Pantano Impressed	jar
22A-6	310053	22A10-2-8	95	14.2	13.7	41.4	8.1	40.3	5.8		0.7	1.1	6129	6451	25156	Pantano Impressed	jar
22A-7	310254	22A10-2-5	40	42.0		47.0	40.0	21.1			0.8	1.0	1765	4413	13575	Chaquiste Impressed	bowl
22A-8	310256	22A10-2-5	90	46.7	47.3	52.1	46.7	18.9			0.8	0.9	4381	4868	13271	Chaquiste Impressed	bowl
22A-9	310295	22A23-3-1	40	14.4	14.8	16.7	14.4	7.8			0.7	1.0	217	543	577	Chaquiste Impressed	bowl
22A-10	310296	22A21-2-4	55	29.4	29.9	32.7		15.3			0.6	1.0	1214	2207	5314	Chaquiste Impressed	bowl
22A-11	310294	22A24-3-1	65	32.6	31.6			9.5		4.3	0.7	1.1	934	1437	1505	Saxche-Palmar Poly.	plate
22A-12	310397	22A24-2-3	95	11.4	11.0			17.4			0.6		721	759		Saxche-Palmar Poly.	vase
22A-13	310415	22A26-3-4	90	29.3	28.8			10.0		4.9	0.4	0.6	1215	1350	1538	Saxche-Palmar Poly.	plate
22A-14	310423	22A24-2-3	30	27.0				11.0		4.2	0.5	0.8	485	1616		Saxche-Palmar Poly.	plate
22A-15	310424	22A10-2-5	30	28.0				9.2		4.0	0.7	1.0	457	1523		Saxche-Palmar Poly.	plate
22A-16	310426	22A23-3-2	30	30.0				10.3		5.5	0.8	0.9	516	1720		Saxche-Palmar Poly.	plate
22A-17	310255	22A10-2-5	45	16.0		17.0		8.8			0.5	0.8	376	836	910	Saxche-Palmar Poly.	bowl
M7-32 (House of Bones)																	
22B-1	310483	22B55-3-2	95	19.3	20.3	37.8		22.7			0.8	1.0	2237	2355		Chaquiste Impressed	bowl
22B-2	310247	22B43-3-4	70		13.8	14.3		7.3			0.8	0.9	300	428	386	Cameron Incised	bowl
22B-3	310244	22B42-3-3	95	28.5	27.9			9.5		4.3	0.7	0.8	1136	1196	1248	Saxche-Palmar Poly.	plate
22B-4	310468	22B55-3-2	70	23.0				7.6		3.6	0.7	0.8	537	767		Saxche-Palmar Poly.	plate
22B-5	310467	22B38-3-2	95	10.8	10.4			6.3		5.3	0.6		187	197		Torres Incised	bowl
M8-4 (House of Mirrors)																	
North room																	
23A-1	310164	23A19-3-3	93	45.5	44.3			6.3			0.7		2200	2365		Cambio Unslipped	comal
23A-2	310393	23A19-3-2	50			75.0		85.0			0.9	1.1	15829	31658	225326	Manteca Impressed Ridged	jar
23A-3	310396	23A42-3-2	90	42.0		65.0	28.5	72.0	12.3		0.9	1.2	19872	22080	126992	Manteca Impressed Ridged	jar
23A-4	310364	23A42-3-2	95	35.3	33.8	55.0	24.4	64.0	11.3		0.7	1.1	19574	20604	131466	Encanto Striated	jar
23A-5	310406	23A42-3-2	70	29.0		33.0	17.0	42.0	11.0		0.8	1.0	3850	5500	15707	Encanto Striated impressed	jar
23A-6	310285	23A18-3-3	65	9.6	9.3	14.1	8.0	11.9	2.2		0.4	0.9	308	474	848	Tinaja Red	jar
23A-7	310279	23A18-3-2	93	16.0	15.5	24.6	9.7	21.9	5.6		0.6	1.0	1892	2034	4446	Pantano Impressed	jar

TABLE 8.1. (continued) Summary of Reconstructible Vessel Data.

STRUCTURES AREAS WVS	CATALOG	PROV.	PRESENT PORTION (%)	RIM DIA. (cm) Ex/In	RIM DIA. (cm) Top	MAX DIA. (cm)	MIN OPEN. (cm)	HT. (cm)	NECK HT. (cm)	HT. W/O F. (cm)	WALL THICK. (cm) THIN	WALL THICK. (cm) THICK	WEIGHT (g) SAMPLE	WEIGHT (g) ORIGINAL	VOLUME (cm³)	TYPE	FORM
23A-8	310165	23A42-3-2	93	5.0		10.5	3.7	8.2			0.4	0.8	277	298	623	Pantano Impressed	mini jar
23A-9	310166	23A19-2-1	98	7.0	6.8	10.4	3.7	10.0			0.4	0.6	236	241	236	Pantano Impressed	mini jar
23A-10	310277	23A18-3-2	98	7.1	6.9	10.9	4.2	10.6			0.6	0.8	228	233	351	Pantano Impressed	mini jar
23A-11	310301	23A44-3-1	85	15.1	14.6	25.2	9.3	23.0	5.2		0.6	0.8	1550	1823	5066	Pantano Impressed	jar
23A-12	310347	23A44-3-1	50	14.9	14.5	21.0	9.5	23.0	5.2		0.4	1.0	615	1230	3499	Pantano Impressed	jar
23A-13	310357	23A44-3-1	60	13.6	13.3	36.0	7.7	33.0	4.4		0.5	0.7	2324	3873	15257	Pantano Impressed	jar
23A-14	310300	23A43-3-3	70	16.7	16.2	25.6	12.6	24.9	4.9		0.7	0.8	1395	1992	6974	Pantano Impressed	jar
23A-15	310310	23A17-3-2	90	8.7	8.5	11.7	5.7	10.8	2.3		0.4	0.7	308	342	492	Pantano Impressed	jar
23A-16	310370	23A44-3-1	50	14.1	13.8	30.0	8.0	31.0	5.7		0.5	0.7	1538	3076	9813	Pantano Impressed	jar
23A-17	310360	23A44-3-4	50	10.0		19.0		20.0	4.2		0.5	0.6	672	1344	2878	Tinaja undetermined	pitcher
23A-18	310349	23A33-3-3	50	13.8	14.4	21.0		15.0			0.7	0.8	554	1108	2655	Chaquiste Impressed	bowl
23A-19	310361	23A44-3-1	90	13.5	14.3	29.0		23.6			0.7	1.1	2213	2459	9741	Chaquiste Impressed	bowl
23A-20	310421	23A33-3-2	30	38.0		60.0		33.0			0.8	0.9	3355	11183	58450	Chaquiste Impressed	bowl
23A-21	310419	23A44-3-2	80	43.0		68.0		47.0			0.8	1.2	7613	9516	96661	Chaquiste Impressed	bowl
23A-22	310159	23A42-3-2	98	9.7	9.3			4.3			0.7		156	159	167	Saxche-Palmar Poly.	bowl
23A-23	310275	23A17-3-1	98	30.0	29.1			9.1		5.3	0.8	1.0	1395	1423	1795	Saxche-Palmar Poly.	plate
23A-24	310322	23A42-3-4	75	12.8				23.2			0.4	0.6	846	1128	2169	Saxche-Palmar Poly.	vase
23A-25	310345	23A18-3-3	85	13.0	12.3			6.7			0.4	0.7	264	311	427	Saxche-Palmar Poly.	bowl
23A-26	310327	23A44-3-1	90	28.4	27.7			9.4		4.2	0.7	0.8	969	1076	1368	Saxche-Palmar Poly.	plate
23A-27	310479	23A44-3-2	50	29.0				10.0		4.3	0.6	0.8	959	1918	1456	Saxche-Palmar Poly.	plate
23A-28	310223	23A19-3-1	80	26.0	25.7			25.2			0.6	1.2	2218	2773	8359	Corozal Incised	vase
23A-29	310224	23A18-3-4	100	3.0	2.8	5.4		5.1			0.4	0.5	53	53	52	Corozal Incised	mini jar
23A-30	310286	23A43-3-3	90	11.1	10.9			13.0			0.4	0.8	274	304	826	Salada Fluted	vase
23A-31	310318	23A41-3-4	70	15.0				13.8			0.3	0.5	380	542	1177	Chablekal Gray	vase
23A-32	310363	23A42-3-1	30	15.0				13.0			0.4	0.5	160	533	1033	Chablekal Gray	bowl
23A-33	310351	23A17-3-1	65	13.0				9.5		8.7	0.4	0.5	210	323	386	Chicxulub Incised	bowl
23A-34	310352	23A41-3-1	40	14.0		15.0		10.0			0.4	0.5	119	298	949	Chablekal Gray	bowl
23A-35	310354	23A41-3-4	30	15.0				13.0			0.5		172	573	740	Chablekal Gray	bowl
23A-36	310355	23A44-3-1	20	13.0				10.0		8.5	0.4	0.6	82	410	291	Chicxulub Incised	bowl
23A-37	310225	23A41-3-4	95	14.9	15.2	17.6		11.5		10.9	0.4	0.6	470	495	1000	Unnamed Volcanic Ash	bowl
23A-38	310284	23A18-3-3	95	14.0	14.7	16.0		10.2		9.3	0.4	0.6	365	384	1006	Unnamed Volcanic Ash	bowl
23A-39	310278	23A42-3-4	95	34.3	33.0			12.0		5.5	0.7	0.9	1327	1397	2832	Unnamed Volcanic Ash	plate

Center room

23A-40	310276	23A14-3-3	85	13.0	12.5			5.1	4.8		0.5	0.8	224	264	235	Cambio Unslipped	bowl
23A-41	310319	23A10-3-2	70	10.7	10.0			4.9			0.6	0.9	160	228	152	Cambio Unslipped	bowl
23A-42	310359	23A49-3-3	60	14.5	14.0	31.0		29.0			0.6	0.9	1853	3088	9399	Pantano Impressed	jar
23A-43	310168	23A48-3-5	99	13.1	12.8		8.2	7.2		5.1	0.5	0.8	355	359	410	Saxche-Palmar Poly.	bowl
23A-44	310372	23A14-3-4	65	14.6	14.2			6.2			0.5	0.7	186	286	403	Saxche-Palmar Poly.	bowl
23A-45	310338	23A14-3-3	65	10.0	9.7	15.0	7.6	11.7		2.0	0.6	0.7	403	620	1214	Undetermined	jar
23A-46	310337	23A13-3-2	20	9.8				20.0			0.4	0.5	88	440	1367	Corozal Incised	vase
23A-47	310330	23A15-2-1	60	10.5				17.8			0.3	0.7	295	491	1336	Salada Fluted	vase
23A-48	310348	23A11-2-1	30	8.0				6.5	5.3		0.4	0.6	34	113	79	Chicxulub Incised	bowl

South room

23A-49	310407	23A10-3-4	50	33.8	32.8	48.0	19.0	58.0		11.0	0.9	1.1	7837	15674	49384	Encanto Striated	jar
23A-50	310381	23A27-2-2	50	44.3	43.3	68.0	29.4	77.0		11.0	0.9	1.2	16176	32352	155681	Encanto Striated	jar
23A-51	310380	23A6-3-2	50	36.3	34.4	56.0	24.1	65.0		12.5	1.0	1.2	11152	22304	74798	Encanto Striated	jar
23A-52	310320	23A11-3-4	50	13.0		17.9	9.0	15.3		3.7	0.6	0.7	327	654	1389	Pantano Impressed	jar
23A-53	310321	23A6-3-2	60	9.3	8.9	15.2	5.4	14.0		2.8	0.6	0.8	445	741	907	Pantano Impressed	jar
23A-54	310333	23A10-3-4	65	11.9	11.5	19.1	7.0	19.0		3.9	0.6	0.9	722	1110	2492	Pantano Impressed	jar
23A-55	310373	23A10-2-1	40	10.5		18.0	7.6	17.0		3.4	0.5	0.6	370	925	1816	Pantano Impressed	jar
23A-56	310376	23A10-2-1	50	44.0	44.0	46.0		18.1			0.8	1.2	2411	4822	14258	Subin Red	bowl
23A-57	310288	23A27-3-1	80	13.6	13.3	13.9		23.5			0.5	0.6	785	981	2783	Corozal Incised	vase
23A-58	310328	23A11-3-3	50	13.5	13.2			24.0			0.4	0.5	512	1024	2790	Saxche-Palmar Poly.	vase
23A-59	310353	23A5-3-2	80	17.6	17.2	18.1		30.9			0.5	0.7	1518	1898	5839	Saxche-Palmar Poly.	vase
23A-60	310289	23A5-3-1	92	18.3	17.9			10.1			0.5	0.6	433	471	1495	Unnamed Volcanic Ash	bowl
23A-61	310312	23A8-3-3	90	2.5				5.6			0.2	0.4	34	38	22	Tinaja Red	mini jar
23A-62	310356	23A8-3-3	50	13.0		21.0		19.0		5.5	0.6	0.9	590	1180	2800	Undetermined	pitcher

North addition

23A-63	310369	23A32-3-1	70	25.6	24.5	41.0	14.3	37.0		10.5	0.6	1.0	2522	3603	20647	Encanto Striated	jar
23A-64	310167	23A21-3-2	98	4.3	3.8	8.6		7.5			0.4	0.8	186	190	92	Pantano Impressed	mini jar
23A-65	310290	23A30-3-2	85	7.3	7.2	12.0	4.4	12.1		2.9	0.5	0.8	365	429	432	Pantano Impressed	mini jar
23A-66	310334	23A30-3-2	65	13.0	12.3	17.0	7.3	18.0		3.0	0.8	1.1	442	680	1395	Pantano Impressed	jar
23A-67	310366	23A32-3-1	60	33.5	34.2	54.2		31.0	16.6		0.7	0.8	5496	9160	44821	Chaquiste Impressed	bowl
23A-68	310287	23A36-3-4	95	12.9	12.5	13.3		18.3	4.7		0.5	0.6	696	733	1944	Saxche-Palmar Poly.	vase
23A-69	310329	23A30-3-2	70	28.2	27.2			9.5			0.7	0.8	639	912	1119	Saxche-Palmar Poly.	plate
23A-70	310339	23A21-3-2	95	21.0	20.0			8.0	4.1		0.7	0.8	512	538	672	Saxche-Palmar Poly.	plate
23A-71	310325	23A22-3-1	70	12.5	12.2			23.2			0.3	0.6	635	907	2380	Saxche-Palmar Poly.	vase
23A-72	310459	23A38-3-4	90	36.0	34.0			11.1	5.0		0.7	0.9	1650	1833	2159	Saxche-Palmar Poly.	plate
23A-73	310331	23A22-2-2	55	19.0				9.9			0.4	0.6	272	494	1184	Chablekal Gray	bowl
23A-74	310350	23A30-3-2	50	14.0				7.1	6.6		0.4	0.5	111	222	393	Unnamed White Slipped	bowl

TABLE 8.1. (continued) Summary of Reconstructible Vessel Data.

STRUCTURES AREAS WVS	CATALOG	PROV.	PRESENT PORTION (%)	RIM DIA. (cm) Ex/In	RIM DIA. (cm) Top	MAX DIA. (cm)	MIN OPEN. (cm)	HT. (cm)	NECK HT. (cm)	HT. w/o F. (cm)	WALL THICK. (cm) THIN	WALL THICK. (cm) THICK	WEIGHT (g) SAMPLE	WEIGHT (g) ORIGINAL	VOLUME (cm³)	TYPE	FORM
South exterior																	
23A-75	310386	23A2-3-1	20	29.0		35.0	15.0	40.0	10.0		0.9	1.1	2318	11590	16306	Encanto Striated	jar
23A-76	310378	23A4-3-3	40			57.0	25.0	66.0			0.8	1.0	7843	19607	72211	Encanto Striated	jar
23A-77	310341	23A4-3-3	70	20.0				5.5		3.0	0.5	0.7	252	360	277	Tinaja Red	plate
23A-78	310336	23A3-3-2	65	14.9	13.7	19.1	8.9	17.2	4.9		0.5	1.1	675	1038	1916	Pantano Impressed	jar
23A-79	310358	23A2-2-1	50	13.5		26.0	6.8	26.0	5.8		0.5	0.8	1379	2758	6234	Pantano Impressed	jar
23A-80	310340	23A4-3-3	70	28.6	28.1			10.2		4.8	0.7	0.9	875	1250	1043	Saxche-Palmar Poly.	plate
23A-81	310346	23A3-3-1	50	28.5	28.0			10.3		4.9	0.8	1.0	743	1486	1506	Saxche-Palmar Poly.	plate
23A-82	310401	23A2-3-3	40								0.5	0.8	1456	3640		Tinaja or Pantano	jar
23A-83	310343	23A2-3-3	65	15.6	15.3			16.1			0.4	0.7	357	549	714	Chablekal Gray	bowl
23A-84	310323	23A3-3-4	95	19.2	18.6			5.6		3.3	0.5	0.6	340	358	531	Andres Red	plate
Patio																	
23A-85	310324	23A52-3-2	60	29.5	28.6			6.1			0.7	1.0	797	1328	1947	Unnamed Volcanic Ash	plate
M8-8 (House of Axes)																	
North room																	
20A-1	310055	20A3-3-1	85			76.5		83.0			0.8	0.9	25914	30487	212581	Manteca Impressed Ridged	jar
20A-2	310126	20A2-3-1	90	36.0	34.4	58.0	22.0	65.0	11.0		0.6	1.2	20223	22470	77709	Encanto Striated	jar
20A-3	310155	20A17-3-1	50	22.0		35.0	12.0	35.0	9.0		0.6	0.8	1388	2776	13162	Encanto Striated	jar
20A-4	310173	20A13-2-1	50	32.0		48.0	20.0	48.0	10.0		0.6	0.9	5812	11624	41474	Encanto Striated	jar
20A-5	310017	20A3-3-5	99	3.5	3.0	8.4		8.7			0.6		141	142	167	Tinaja Red	mini jar
20A-6	310016	20A18-2-1	99	3.8	3.6	6.9		7.9			0.7		158	159	91	Pantano Impressed	mini jar
20A-7	310002	20A19-3-1	93	12.4	12.0	17.7	8.5	15.4	3.4		0.6	0.8	785	844	1486	Pantano Impressed	jar
20A-8	310022	20A19-3-1	95	14.6	14.3	40.0	8.0	39.8	5.4		0.5	1.2	4748	4998	26164	Pantano Impressed	jar
20A-9	310027	20A18-3-1	70	13.9	13.1	24.2	8.3	23.5	5.9		0.7	0.9	1787	2552	4734	Pantano Impressed	jar
20A-10	310149	20A6-3-1	40	27.0		28.0		10.5			0.7	0.8	685	1713	2182	Subin Red	bowl
20A-11	310127	20A18-3-1	30	40.0		40.0		19.0			0.7	0.9	1130	3767	12176	Chaquiste Impressed	bowl
20A-12	310128	20A3-3-4	30	31.0		46.0		30.0			0.8	1.5	867	2890	23656	Chaquiste Impressed	bowl
20A-13	310023	20A3-3-2	95	15.2	16.2	30.5		24.1			0.7	0.8	2908	3061	8790	Chaquiste Impressed	bowl
20A-14	310004	20A6-3-1	95	25.0	24.6					4.9	0.7	0.9	894	941	996	Saxche-Palmar Poly.	plate
20A-15	310009	20A3-3-5	90	19.7	19.2			5.8		3.9	0.6	0.8	445	494	418	Saxche-Palmar Poly.	plate
20A-16	310013	20A5-3-3	89	27.5	26.6					5.0	0.6	0.9	971	1091	1115	Saxche-Palmar Poly.	plate
20A-17	310021	20A17-3-2	93	29.8	29.3			10.9		5.8	0.3	0.8	990	1065	1372	Saxche-Palmar Poly.	plate
20A-18	310139	20A1-3-2	70	13.0		17.0	12.0	14.0	3.3		0.4	0.6	316	451	1637	Saxche-Palmar Poly.	jar
20A-19	310001	20A3-3-2	80	14.2	14.0			10.9		9.2	0.4	0.6	350	438	918	Unnamed Red-Orange	bowl
20A-20	310014	20A3-3-5	60	28.0				9.0		5.5	0.7	0.8	712	1187	1842	Unnamed Quartz Tempered	plate
20A-21	310020	20A19-3-5	99	14.1	13.8			10.3		10.0	0.5		438	442	587	Undetermined	bowl
20A-22	310031	20A6-3-1	60	8.2	8.6	12.4		9.4		9.0	0.4	0.7	316	527	432	Undetermined	bowl

																Ware	Form
Center room																	
20A-23	310134	20A4-3-2	60	36.3	34.5	49.0	18.0	53.0	16.0		0.7	0.9	5622	9370	50657	Manteca Impressed Ridged	jar
20A-24	310179	20A23-3-1	90	43.0		78.0	30.0	83.0	15.0		0.8	1.2	28691	31878	177627	Manteca Impressed Ridged	jar
20A-25	310129	20A1-3-4	70	34.0		42.0	22.0	45.0	9.0		0.7	1.2	8804	12577	28296	Encanto Striated	jar
20A-26	310135	20A1-3-2	30	13.5	13.1	30.0	7.8	29.0	5.3		0.6	1.2	849	2830	9684	Pantano Impressed	jar
20A-27	310138	20A8-3-1	50	12.0		32.0	8.2	32.0	5.1		0.7	0.9	1532	3064	11692	Pantano Impressed	jar
20A-28	310140	20A21-3-1	70	15.0		39.0	8.6	38.0	5.8		0.6	0.9	2774	3963	19834	Pantano Impressed	jar
20A-29	310038	20A25-3-1	60	25.0		27.0		10.9		10.8	0.4	0.7	610	1017	2578	Chaquiste Impressed	bowl
20A-30	310000	20A1-3-4	99	12.9	12.6			5.8			0.3	0.8	301	304	341	Saxche-Palmar Poly.	bowl
20A-31	310005	20A4-3-2	96	18.8	17.9			5.5		3.5	0.5	0.9	455	474	338	Saxche-Palmar Poly.	plate
20A-32	310008	20A4-3-3	95	31.9	30.6			11.6		6.3	0.7	0.9	1674	1762	2290	Saxche-Palmar Poly.	plate
20A-33	310030	20A4-3-1	30	20.0				6.1		3.1	0.6	0.8	224	747	631	Saxche-Palmar Poly.	plate
20A-34	310039	20A21-3-1	40	17.0				24.8			0.7	0.7	628	1570	4259	Saxche-Palmar Poly.	vase
South room																	
20A-35	310158	20A37-3-2	80	28.0		35.0	18.0	40.0	8.5		0.7	0.9	4850	6062	17310	Cambio Unslipped	jar
20A-36	310162	20A36-3-4	35	30.0		30.0		13.0			0.6	0.8	1141	3260	10068	Tinaja or Pantano	jar
20A-37	310037	20A38-3-3	95	28.0	27.0			10.4		4.8	0.9	1.1	1248	1314	1398	Saxche-Palmar Poly.	plate
20A-38	310040	20A29-3-3	99	16.9	16.4			6.4			0.5		396	400	684	Saxche-Palmar Poly.	bowl
20A-39	310160	20A37-3-2	85	26.8	25.7			8.3		4.2	0.7	0.8	857	1008	783	Saxche-Palmar Poly.	plate
North addition																	
20A-40	310170	20A13-3-2	90	30.0		45.0	18.0	46.0	10.0		0.8	1.2	12302	13668	63468	Encanto Striated	jar
20A-41	310171	20A42-3-3	80	32.0		48.0	19.0	48.0	11.0		0.5	1.1	12452	15565	39050	Encanto Striated	jar
20A-42	310172	20A12-3-1	90	25.0		43.0	13.0	42.0	10.0		0.7	1.0	6901	7667	43487	Encanto Striated	jar
20A-43	310177	20A43-3-4	70	33.0		54.0	19.8	49.0	9.0		0.7	1.0	9167	13095	73155	Encanto Striated	jar
20A-44	310268	20A11-3-2	65	38.0				6.0			0.9	1.3	1618	2489	3224	Encanto Striated	plate
20A-45	310176	20A41-3-4	60	16.2	15.9	40.0	8.6	40.0	5.8		0.5	0.8	2334	3890	22033	Pantano Impressed	jar
20A-46	310174	20A13-3-3	70	38.0		41.0		13.0			0.6	0.7	1317	1881	8028	Chaquiste Impressed	bowl
20A-47	310029	20A13-3-4	70	4.0	3.2	6.9		8.9			0.6		98	140	100	Tinaja undetermined	mini jar
20A-48	310175	20A43-3-3	90	15.9	15.0	27.0	9.2	27.0	6.4		0.6	0.8	2763	3070	6589	Pantano Impressed	jar
20A-49	310010	20A12-3-1	80	26.0	25.3					4.9	0.7	0.9	718	898	1061	Saxche-Palmar Poly.	plate
20A-50	310011	20A12-3-1	90	11.8	11.6	12.6		22.1			0.6	0.7	715	794	2066	Saxche-Palmar Poly.	vase
20A-51	310054	20A13-3-2	60	10.0				15.8			0.3	0.4	175	292	991	Chixclub Incised	vase
20A-52	310019	20A14-3-1	65	3.5	3.0	6.1		5.7			0.5		56	86	53	Undetermined	mini jar
South addition and south exterior																	
20A-53	310309	20A35-3-1	18			46.0		45.0			0.7	0.8	1604	8911	36849	Cambio Unslipped red w.	jar
20A-54	310274	20A31-3-2	85	31.0	29.3	49.0	20.4	47.0	9.5		0.8	1.1	9175	10794	30265	Encanto Striated	jar
20A-55	310307	20A32-3-2	40	29.5	28.6	45.0	17.8	50.0	10.5		0.6	0.8	3360	8400	38600	Encanto Striated	jar
20A-56	310311	20A35-3-1	70	24.4	23.4	36.0	15.9	40.0	9.5		0.6	1.4	3701	5287	18100	Encanto Striated	jar

TABLE 8.1. (continued) Summary of Reconstructible Vessel Data.

STRUCTURES / AREAS (WVS)	CATALOG	PROV.	PRESENT PORTION (%)	RIM DIA. (cm) EX/IN	RIM DIA. (cm) TOP	MAX DIA. (cm)	MIN OPEN. (cm)	HT. (cm)	NECK HT. (cm)	HT. W/O F. (cm)	WALL THICK. (cm) THIN	WALL THICK. (cm) THICK	WEIGHT (g) SAMPLE	WEIGHT (g) ORIGINAL	VOLUME (cm³)	TYPE	FORM
20A-57	310305	20A31-3-2	90	10.7	10.1	14.7	7.6	12.4	2.1		0.3	0.5	502	558	969	Tinaja Red	jar
20A-58	310163	20A29-3-4	35	15.0		24.0		24.0			0.5	0.6	775	2214	5081	Pantano Impressed	jar
20A-59	310313	20A33-3-1	50	15.4	15.0	46.0	8.9	43.0	5.6		0.6	0.9	3385	6770	40761	Pantano Impressed	jar
20A-60	310308	20A31-3-2	20	25.0		46.0		33.0			0.7	0.9	2250	11250	31428	Chaquiste Impressed	bowl
20A-61	310314	20A33-2-1	40	36.0		64.0		40.0			0.7	0.9	3672	9180	75422	Chaquiste Impressed	bowl
20A-62	310304	20A31-3-4	60	12.4	12.1			22.0			0.5	0.7	552	920	2395	Matu Incised	vase
Behind the structure																	
20A-63	310169	20A39-3-2	90	19.6	17.6	44.0	12.5	49.0	6.3		0.8	1.3	4993	5547	23182	Manteca Impressed red w.	jar
20A-64	310156	20A8-3-4	30	36.9	35.1	60.0	23.7	65.0	12.0		0.9	1.5	7235	24116	85492	Encanto Striated	jar
20A-65	310151	20A17-3-4	70	25.0		33.0	15.0	35.0	8.0		0.8	1.0	2869	4099	12781	Encanto Striated	jar
20A-66	310157	20A9-2-1	70	3.6	3.1	8.8	2.7	12.9	4.1		0.6	0.9	299	427	266	Tinaja Red	jar
20A-67	310018	20A6-3-3	98	2.9	2.5	4.9		6.4			0.4		56	57	28	Tinaja Red	mini jar
20A-68	310051	20A22-3-2	98	14.8	14.5	26.3	8.9	26.2	5.3		0.5	0.8	2226	2271	6335	Pantano Impressed	jar
20A-69	310178	20A17-3-3	90	13.5	13.0	40.0	8.2	40.0	5.9		0.7	0.8	4268	4742	27666	Pantano Impressed	jar
20A-70	310012	20A9-3-3	95	34.4	33.4			10.7		5.4	0.6	0.8	1727	1818	2200	Saxche-Palmar Poly.	plate
20A-71	310015	20A6-3-3	92	30.8	30.3			11.1		6.3	0.8	1.0	1432	1557	1980	Saxche-Palmar Poly.	plate
20A-72	310033	20A10-3-1	60	26.1	25.4					4.6	0.5	0.7	503	838	908	Saxche-Palmar Poly.	plate
20A-73	310042	20A22-3-1	75	8.8	8.4	9.5		19.7			0.4	0.5	346	461	839	Saxche-Palmar Poly.	vase
20A-74	310046	20A24-3-4	100	2.6	2.4	4.2		6.4			0.4	0.5	60	60	28	Saxche-Palmar Poly.	mini jar
20A-75	310032	20A17-2-2	40	18.0				7.5			0.7	0.8	264	660	814	Undetermined	bowl
20A-76	310047	20A17-3-4	60	3.4	2.9	3.6		4.4			0.4	0.7	36	60	12	Undetermined	mini vase
20A-77	310049	20A39-3-1	80	4.5		7.0		7.5			0.4	0.6	133	166	113	Undetermined	mini jar
M8-10 (House of the Scribe)																	
	310006	14A4-4-2	94	16.5	16.2	16.5		9.0			0.4	0.5	566	602		Saxche-Palmar Poly.	bowl
M8-13																	
West room																	
14B-1	310144	14B7-3-2	40	34.0		34.0		5.5			0.8	1.3	684	1,710	1720	Encanto Striated	comal
14B-2	310136	14B9-3-1	20	36.0		49.0	20.0				0.7	1.2	2029	10145	57249	Encanto Striated	jar
14B-3	310107	14B16-3-1	10			52.0					0.7	1.0	1439	14,390		Encanto Striated	jar
14B-4	310152	14B14-3-3	20	25.0		42.0	16.0	42.0			0.7	0.8	1534	7670	26739	Encanto Striated	jar
14B-5	310098	14B3-3-1	30			40.0		40.0			0.6	1.0	1178	3,927	24277	Tinaja or Pantano	jar
14B-6	310099	14B3-3-1	80	14.0		39.0	6.3	41.0	4.9		0.5	0.8	3368	4210	25244	Pantano Impressed	jar
14B-7	310100	14B1-3-3	80			38.0		43.0			0.5	0.8	4170	5,213	25960	Pantano Impressed	jar
14B-8	310147	14B9-3-1	70	14.0	13.7	40.0	8.5	38.0	5.1		0.6	1.1	2915	4164	20253	Pantano Impressed	jar

14B-9	310043	14B1-3-4	90	23.5	24.1	26.3	23.5	11.7			0.6	0.7	1110	1,233	2627	Chaquiste Impressed	bowl
14B-10	310045	14B12-3-2	85	22.0	22.3	23.8	22.0	8.2			0.4	0.7	730	859	1964	Chaquiste Impressed	bowl
14B-11	310024	14B10-3-1	40	24.0	23.1			9.1		4.2	0.7	0.8	292	730	726	Saxche-Palmar Poly.	plate
14B-12	310141	14B14-2-1	80	23.7				9.5		4.6	0.6	0.9	550	688	1053	Saxche-Palmar Poly.	plate
14B-13	310142	14B14-2-1	40	33.0				9.5		5.1	0.9	1.2	549	1,373	2044	Saxche-Palmar Poly.	plate
14B-14	310154	14B1-3-3	50	28.0				9.5		5.5	0.7	0.8	455	910	1555	Saxche-Palmar Poly.	plate
Center room																	
14B-15	310066	14B2-2-2	7	36.0	35.4		22.5	47.0			1.1	1.5	1582	22600		Cambio or Encanto	jar
14B-16	310094	14B24-3-2	50	24.0		40.0	16.0				0.7	0.9	3547	7094	24900	Encanto Striated	jar
14B-17	310079	14B2-3-4	30	21.0		42.0	13.7				0.7	1.4	1337	4457	33060	Manteca Impressed	jar
14B-18	310115	14B2-3-4	30	20.0		43.0					0.8	1.1	1555	5183	27132	Encanto Striated	jar
14B-19	310057	14B20-2-1	60	17.5	16.9			5.7		3.7	0.6	1.0	257	428	319	Tinaja Red	plate
14B-20	310059	14B6-2-2	30	8.0	7.6	8.4					0.5	0.7	87	290	402	Tinaja Red	vase
14B-21	310114	14B2-3-4	40			40.0		43.0			0.6	1.0	2248	5620	28320	Tinaja or Pantano	jar
14B-22	310073	14B19-3-4	40	9.5	9.0	25.0	5.7	20.0	3.0		0.7	0.8	490	1225	5049	Pantano Impressed	jar
14B-23	310090	14B2-3-4	75	13.6	12.8	26.0	7.5	27.2	5.0		0.7	0.9	2286	3048	6465	Pantano Impressed	jar
14B-24	310091	14B20-2-1	50	9.5	9.0	15.0	6.1	15.0	3.4		0.7	0.9	565	1130	1874	Pantano Impressed	jar
14B-25	310092	14B20-3-4	40	12.8	11.4	23.0	8.7	20.0	5.1		0.8	1.1	434	1085	3129	Pantano Impressed	jar
14B-26	310095	14B19-3-1	30	14.8	14.1	36.0	9.2		5.4		0.9	1.1	1239	4130	15541	Pantano Impressed	jar
14B-27	310096	14B19-3-1	40	14.0		28.0	9.2		5.5		0.9	1.1	1073	2683	8289	Pantano Impressed	jar
14B-28	310025	14B20-3-4	25	14.3	13.8	24.0	8.9	27.0	5.3		0.5	0.7	471	1884	7261	Pantano Impressed	jar
14B-29	310083	14B2-3-3	50	44.0		47.0	44.0	16.0			0.7	0.9	2031	4062	12985	Subin Red	bowl
14B-30	310082	14B2-3-4	50	25.0	26.0	30.0	25.0	15.0			0.8	0.9	587	1174	5245	Chaquiste Impressed	bowl
14B-31	310084	14B2-3-4	50	27.0		33.0	27.0	17.0			0.7	0.9	1025	2050	6306	Chaquiste Impressed	bowl
14B-32	310058	14B2-3-6	30	10.0				6.5		6.0	0.4	0.6	53	177	169	Nanzal Red	bowl
14B-33	310056	14B2-1-2	70	25.1	24.0			8.2		4.2	0.6	0.9	456	651	874	Saxche-Palmar Poly.	plate
14B-34	310061	14B19-3-2	80	38.0	37.4			11.0		5.6	0.9	1.1	1674	2093	3275	Saxche-Palmar Poly.	plate
14B-35	310063	14B2-3-4	90	25.5	24.5					4.2	0.7	0.8	678	753	1042	Saxche-Palmar Poly.	plate
14B-36	310075	14B20-3-3	70	33.0	32.0			14.0		6.0	0.8	1.0	669	956	2631	Saxche-Palmar Poly.	plate
14B-37	310076	14B21-1-1	50	32.7	31.8			14.0		6.9	0.9	1.0	698	1396	2479	Saxche-Palmar Poly.	plate
14B-38	310088	14B8-2-1	35	12.1	11.6			18.0			0.4	0.6	256	731	1428	Saxche-Palmar Poly.	vase
14B-39	310097	14B19-1-1	50	14.0		14.0		23.0			0.6	0.8	491	982	2218	Saxche-Palmar Poly.	vase
14B-40	310110	14B2-3-2	20								0.7	0.7	88	440		Fine Gray	bowl
14B-41	310109	14B2-3-1	40								0.5	0.5	196	490		Unnamed Red-Orange	bowl
14B-42	310108	14B20-2-1	20	20.0				12.0			0.6	0.7	180	900	1422	Undetermined	bowl
14B-43	310048	14B6-1-1	80	3.8		4.7	2.4	7.3	2.1		0.6	0.7	63	79	76	Undetermined	mini jar
East room																	
14B-44	310026	14B24-3-3	50	27.0				9.8		5.5	0.6	0.9	720	1440	1260	Saxche-Palmar Poly.	plate
14B-45	310102	14B29-3-4	30	27.0						4.7	0.9	1.2	259	863	1072	Saxche-Palmar Poly.	plate
14B-46	310104	14B28-2-1	30	16.0		16.0					0.5	0.6	234	780	2837	Unnamed Volcanic Ash	vase

TABLE 8.1. (continued) Summary of Reconstructible Vessel Data.

STRUCTURES/AREAS WVS	CATALOG	PROV.	PRESENT PORTION (%)	RIM DIA. (cm) Ex/In	RIM DIA. (cm) Top	MAX DIA. (cm)	MIN OPEN. (cm)	HT. (cm)	NECK HT. (cm)	HT. w/o F. (cm)	WALL THICK. (cm) Thin	WALL THICK. (cm) Thick	WEIGHT (g) Sample	WEIGHT (g) Original	VOLUME (cm³)	TYPE	FORM
In front of the structure																	
14B-47	310101	14B23-3-2	35	31.0	29.0	51.0		26.0			0.8	0.9	1412	4034	30142	Chaquiste Impressed	bowl
14B-48	310124	14C6-3-1	50	31.0		35.0		12.0			0.8	1.0	731	1462	4179	Chaquiste Impressed	bowl
Behind the structure																	
14B-49	310077	14B22-3-3	85	11.9	11.5	20.5	7.9	19.0	3.1		0.8	1.1	1152	1355	3082	Pantano Impressed	jar
14B-50	310078	14B22-3-4	80	13.0	12.5	37.0	7.5	34.0	5.2		0.6	0.9	2740	3425	16647	Pantano Impressed	jar
14B-51	310080	14B30-3-3	20	12.0	11.6	36.0	6.7	36.0	5.1		0.6	0.7	846	4230	18994	Pantano Impressed	jar
14B-52	310081	14B30-3-4	50	13.0		28.0	8.0	30.0			0.6	1.0	1651	3302	8547	Pantano Impressed	jar
14B-53	310130	14B30-3-3	40			33.0		33.0			0.6	0.9	1555	3888	13511	Pantano Impressed	jar
14B-54	310085	14B26-3-1	20	40.0		44.0		21.0			0.6	0.7	631	3155	9500	Subin Red	bowl
14B-55	310003	14B22-3-4	85	39.5	41.5	44.2	39.5	18.2			0.8	0.9	4220	4964	11396	Subin Red	bowl
14B-56	310131	14B26-3-4	15	11.0		18.0	10.0	25.0	4.9		0.3	0.6	210	1400	2974	Corazal Incised	pitcher
14B-57	310062	14B26-3-2	30	21.0				7.2			0.5	0.6	262	873	1084	Saxche-Palmar Poly.	plate
14B-58	310064	14B30-3-1	35	33.0				10.3		5.8	0.8	0.9	577	1649	3368	Saxche-Palmar Poly.	plate
14B-59	310065	14B26-3-1	50	27.0				10.4		5.6	0.7	0.8	758	1516	1376	Saxche-Palmar Poly.	plate
14B-60	310089	14B8-2-1	60	15.0		15.0		20.8			0.6	0.9	786	1310	2352	Saxche-Palmar Poly.	vase
14B-61	310133	14B26-2-1	40	8.0				11.0			0.4	0.5	103	258	621	Chixclub Incised	vase
14B-62	310071	14B26-3-3	20	10.0		15.0		16.0			0.4	0.7	135	675	1797	Undetermined	bowl
M8-2 and M8-3																	
Inside M8-2																	
23B-1	310212	23B24-3-4	20	31.0		50.0	19.0	48.0			0.5	0.9	3003	15015	44071	Encanto Striated	jar
23B-2	310194	23B18-3-1	25	14.4	14.0	32.0	8.9	33.0	6.0		0.7	0.9	591	2364	12050	Pantano Impressed	jar
23B-3	310196	23B24-3-2	90	13.9	13.6	38.0	8.0	38.0	5.5		0.6	0.9	3604	4004	21871	Pantano Impressed	jar
23B-4	310183	23B24-3-2	90	20.5	19.7			4.5		3.5	0.7	0.9	480	533	419	Saxche-Palmar Poly.	plate
23B-5	310192	23B18-3-1	55	26.5	26.0			8.7		4.2	0.6	0.9	501	911	1188	Saxche-Palmar Poly.	plate
23B-6	310207	23B18-3-3	20	20.1	19.6						0.8	0.9	440	2200	3100	Unnamed Volcanic Ash	vase
West of M8-2																	
23B-7	310215	23B5-3-1	80	33.0		49.0	21.0	47.0	12.0		1.0	1.2	7691	9613	39232	Encanto Striated	jar
23B-8	310218	23B10-3-4	90	14.0	13.8	36.0	8.6	36.0	5.6		0.6	1.0	3507	3897	16260	Pantano Impressed	jar
23B-9	310182	23B6-3-1	100	3.3	2.6			7.8			0.4		43	43	34	Salada Fluted	mini vase
23B-10	310184	23B5-3-1	65	19.8	19.4			4.5		3.3	0.6	0.6	234	360	379	Saxche-Palmar Poly.	plate
23B-11	310189	23B5-3-1	85	16.1	15.9			10.8			0.5	0.6	380	447	731	Saxche-Palmar Poly.	bowl
23B-12	310191	23B13-3-1	40	18.0				11.3			0.3	0.5	171	428	996	Unnamed Red-Orange	bowl

Behind M8-2

Sample	Cat. No.	Provenience	n													Type	Form
23B-13	310198	23B12-3-1	40	14.8	14.1	36.0	8.4	34.0	5.2		0.6	0.9	1290	3225	15874	Tinaja or Pantano	jar
23B-14	310199	23B12-3-2	50	13.3	12.9	29.0	7.9	31.0	5.3		0.7	0.8	1443	2886	9881	Pantano Impressed	jar
23B-15	310282	23B12-3-1	45	12.3	12.1	40.0	8.5	40.0	5.0		0.7	1.2	2120	4711	22759	Pantano Impressed	jar
23B-16	310460	23B12-3-3	25	14.0	13.4	34.0	7.9	34.0	5.4		0.6	0.8	1213	4852	14761	Pantano Impressed	jar
23B-17	310203	23B19-3-2	60	40.0	39.0	43.5		14.0			0.6	1.0	1644	2740	16317	Subin Red	bowl
23B-18	310195	23B19-3-2	20	16.9	18.5	43.0		29.0			0.6	0.8	527	2635	17561	Chaquiste Impressed	bowl
23B-19	310206	23B19-3-2	50	10.6	10.2						0.4	0.5	210	420	1390	Salada Fluted	vase

In front of M8-2 and behind M8-3

Sample	Cat. No.	Provenience	n													Type	Form
23B-20	310283	23B16-3-1	60	35.0		48.0	25.0	46.0			0.6	1.2	5349	8915	39283	Encanto Striated	jar
23B-21	310205	23B16-3-1	40	35.0		38.0		17.0			0.7	0.9	1451	3628	9015	Subin Red	bowl

Inside M8-3

Sample	Cat. No.	Provenience	n													Type	Form
23B-22	310211	23B16-3-3	70	44.0	19.1			3.5			0.7	0.8	1414	2020	2183	Cambio Unslipped	plate
23B-23	310181	23B16-3-3	80	20.1				6.7			0.4	0.6	476	595	706	Subin Red	bowl
23B-24	310188	23B21-3-3	55	14.1	13.8	23.8	9.2	21.0	5.3		0.4	0.7	943	1715	4294	Pantano Impressed	jar
23B-25	310200	23B15-3-1	93	11.0		36.0	8.7	36.0	5.7		0.7	0.9	3622	3894	17849	Pantano Impressed	jar
23B-26	310201	23B3-3-2	60	12.0		13.0		9.5		9.0	0.5		259	432	481	Saxche-Palmar Poly.	bowl

In front of M8-3

Sample	Cat. No.	Provenience	n													Type	Form
23B-27	310209	23B20-3-3	25			41.0		42.0			0.7		1503	6012	23295	Encanto Striated	jar
23B-28	310210	23B7-3-2	20			53.0					0.8		1698	8490	57443	Encanto Striated	jar
23B-29	310202	23B20-3-3	50	15.5	14.9	25.0	10.1	25.0	4.9		0.7	0.8	794	1588	5668	Pantano Impressed	jar
23B-30	310193	23B20-3-2	45	28.0		46.0		40.0			0.8	1.0	3680	8178	29174	Chaquiste Impressed	bowl
23B-31	310190	23B7-3-2	50	29.5	28.9			11.0		4.5	0.7	0.9	647	1294	1735	Saxche-Palmar Poly.	plate
23B-32	310186	23B2-3-2	80	12.2	11.8	19.4	10.8	16.6	3.8		0.5	0.7	692	865	3016	Andres Red	jar
23B-33	310204	23B2-3-3	40	10.0		24.0		20.0			0.4	0.7	378	945	3883	Unnamed Volcanic Ash	bowl

M7-34 (House of Metates)

North room

Sample	Cat. No.	Provenience	n													Type	Form
21A-1	310240	21A2-3-1	30	38.0		57.0	21.0	53.0	12.0		0.8	1.1	4502	15006	58565	Encanto Striated red w.	jar
21A-2	310437	21A8-3-3	25	35.0		54.0	25.0	50.0	10.5		0.7	0.8	3833	15332	49001	Encanto Striated	jar
21A-3	310418	21A20-3-2	35	30.3	29.3	46.0	19.9	54.0	9.0		0.7	0.9	3284	9383	37997	Encanto Striated	jar
21A-4	310438	21A8-3-4	10	35.0		35.0	21.0		10.0		0.8	1.0	1881	18810		Cambio or Encanto	jar
21A-5	310431	21A50-3-3	80	14.8	14.5	18.6	8.0	16.9			0.7	0.8	1068	1335	2114	Tinaja Red	jar
21A-6	310262	21A3-2-1	35	16.0	14.8	22.0	9.0	24.0	5.2		0.5	1.0	923	2637	4265	Pantano Impressed	jar
21A-7	310239	21A2-2-3	70	15.1	14.3	23.1	9.8	21.9	5.2		0.5	0.9	1247	1781	3716	Pantano Impressed	jar
21A-8	310429	21A47-3-4	60	11.4	11.2	28.0	7.3	26.0	4.6		0.4	0.8	1512	2520	7754	Pantano Impressed	jar
21A-9	310430	21A48-3-1	40	13.4	13.3	33.0	7.9	33.0	5.1		0.5	0.8	1523	3807	13790	Pantano Impressed	jar
21A-10	310420	21A20-3-2	35	14.4	14.3	33.0	8.0	33.0	4.7		0.6	0.8	1268	3622	13300	Pantano Impressed	jar
21A-11	310241	21A2-3-1	20	41.0		44.0		18.2			0.7	0.9	1110	5550	10080	Subin Red	bowl
21A-12	310427	21A49-3-2	25	44.0				24.0			0.8	0.9	1254	5016	25069	Subin Red	bowl
21A-13	310422	21A8-3-2	55	38.7	40.0	41.9		15.7			0.7	0.9	2140	3890	9160	Subin Red	bowl

Table 8.1. (continued) Summary of Reconstructible Vessel Data.

Structures Areas WVS	Catalog	Prov.	Present Portion (%)	Rim Dia. (cm) Ex/In	Rim Dia. (cm) Top	Max Dia. (cm)	Min Open. (cm)	Ht. (cm)	Neck Ht. (cm)	Ht. w/o F. (cm)	Wall Thick. (cm) Thin	Wall Thick. (cm) Thick	Weight (g) Sample	Weight (g) Original	Volume (cm³)	Type	Form
21A-14	310344	21A17-2-2	60	43.0		46.0		22.0			0.6	1.0	3011	5018	18853	Chaquiste Impressed	bowl
21A-15	310435	21A50-3-2	50	9.5				19.0			0.3	0.5	349	698	919	Corozal Incised	vase
21A-16	310044	21A1-3-2	97	11.6	11.2			5.5			0.7		231	238	276	Saxche-Palmar Poly.	bowl
21A-17	310433	21A50-2-2	80	28.4	28.1			8.5			0.6	0.8	636	795	1066	Saxche-Palmar Poly.	plate
21A-18	310434	21A50-3-3	70	10.3							0.8		118	169		Peten Gloss group	lid
21A-19	310365	21A7-2-2	25	15.0				15.3			0.5	0.7	264	1056	1775	Unnamed Micaceous	vase
21A-20	310050	21A16-3-4	95	11.6	12.1	20.7		23.8		14.7	0.5		1658	1745	5932	Unnamed modeled	incensario
Center room																	
21A-21	310269	21A4-3-1	40	19.6	19.5	30.0	12.8	30.0	3.2		0.4	0.7	1164	2910	11445	Cambio Unslipped	jar
21A-22	310263	21A3-2-4	40			42.0	16.0				0.8	1.0	2044	5110	28483	Encanto Striated angular	jar
21A-23	310270	21A25-3-1	70	15.8	15.2	27.2	9.3	27.4	5.8		0.7	1.1	1727	2467	6734	Pantano Impressed	jar
21A-24	310229	21A25-3-1	55	41.0		46.0		21.3			0.8	0.9	2758	5015	15703	Subin Red	bowl
21A-25	310342	21A4-3-1	30	22.0		24.0		9.8			0.5	0.6	558	1860	1544	Subin Red	bowl
21A-26	310432	21A20-1-2	60	20.0				12.2			0.6	0.8	548	913	1461	Saxche-Palmar Poly.	bowl
21A-27	310385	21A21-3-3	70	11.3		17.3		16.0			0.9		1163	1661	2590	Peten Gloss group	incensario
South room																	
21A-28	310273	21A30-3-3	40	41.0	38.9	60.0	26.4	70.0	12.0		0.9	1.1	10351	25878	93194	Cambio Unslipped red w.	jar
21A-29	310416	21A43-3-3	50	17.0		40.0	11.5	48.0	7.0		0.7	1.2	2565	5130	33947	Cambio Unslipped angled	jar
21A-30	310417	21A43-3-3	30	22.5	21.0	42.0	15.5	51.0	10.4		0.6	0.7	1571	5236	32869	Encanto Striated	jar
21A-31	310267	21A30-2-3	70	34.5	33.5	54.0	19.8	58.0	11.5		0.8	1.1	9231	13187	58002	Encanto Striated	jar
21A-32	310228	21A42-3-1	20	31.4	30.4	53.0	21.4	62.0	10.0		0.8	1.0	3698	18490	70061	Encanto Striated	jar
21A-33	310404	21A55-33-3	20	17.3	16.6	32.0	11.4	32.0	4.0		0.7	0.8	655	3275	13668	Encanto Striated	jar
21A-34	310394	21A42-3-4	15	30.0		42.0	22.0	45.0	10.0		0.7	1.3	1512	10080	30001	Encanto Striated	jar
21A-35	310482	21A33-1-1	85	17.4	16.7	30.8	11.7	29.0	6.0		0.5	0.6	2641	3107	12131	Encanto Striated	jar
21A-36	310402	21A55-3-3	50	13.8	13.5	40.0	8.2	39.0	5.4		0.5	1.1	1938	3876	23647	Pantano Impressed	jar
21A-37	310280	21A30-2-4	85	15.5	14.5	37.9	8.0	35.3	5.4		0.6	1.1	4004	4711	18942	Pantano Impressed	jar
21A-38	310272	21A34-3-2	70	13.4	12.9	36.3	7.2	33.7	5.2		0.6	1.7	3681	5258	15452	Pantano Impressed	jar
21A-39	310410	21A43-3-2	35	14.5	14.3	30.0	8.7	30.0	4.4		0.5	0.7	1054	3011	10541	Pantano Impressed	jar
21A-40	310409	21A43-3-3	40	48.0		50.0		16.7			0.7	0.8	2370	5925	14987	Chaquiste Impressed	bowl
21A-41	310271	21A36-1-1	65	12.3	12.0			6.7			0.4	0.5	140	215	485	Saxche-Palmar Poly.	bowl
21A-42	310387	21A33-3-2	40	28.6	28.1			10.0		4.1	0.7	0.9	534	1335	1250	Saxche-Palmar Poly.	plate
21A-43	310375	21A56-3-2	80	25.7	25.2			8.9		5.1	0.6	0.8	640	800	1256	Saxche-Palmar Poly.	plate
21A-44	310374	21A56-3-2	50	40.0				11.9		6.5	0.9	1.4	1649	3298	4161	Saxche-Palmar Poly.	plate
21A-45	310389	21A54-3-4	40	32.0				10.0		5.4	0.7	0.8	656	1640	1597	Saxche-Palmar Poly.	plate
21A-46	310379	21A56-3-4	50	15.0				7.0			0.5	0.6	155	310	648	Saxche-Palmar Poly.	bowl

North of the structure

Sample	Cat. No.	Lot	n	a	b	c	d	e	f	g	t1	t2	N1	N2	N3	Type	Form
21A-47	310367	21A38-3-3	60	26.0		35.0		39.0	11.5		0.6	0.7	2162	3543	17082	Manteca Impressed	jar
21A-48	310231	21A40-3-3	50	32.1	30.6	55.0	21.8	60.0	5.6		0.8	1.0	8449	16898	64595	Encanto Striated	jar
21A-49	310395	21A39-3-3	30	13.5		30.0	7.1	30.0	5.6		0.7	1.1	1104	3680	9337	Pantano Impressed	jar
21A-50	310398	21A39-3-4	70	13.5	12.9	34.0	7.3	33.0	4.6		0.5	0.8	2356	3365	13907	Pantano Impressed	jar
21A-51	310226	21A39-3-3	95	8.0	6.6	18.3	3.6	18.2	3.6		0.9	1.1	1195	1258	2016	Pantano Impressed	jar
21A-52	310392	21A40-3-3	75	13.5		31.0	8.2	29.0	6.1		0.6	1.0	2475	3300	9686	Pantano Impressed	jar
21A-53	310399	21A39-3-3	80	16.5	16.1			10.6		9.0	0.6		393	491	904	Corozal Incised	bowl
21A-54	310368	21A38-3-3	60	12.5				5.6		5.0	0.4	0.6	153	255	358	Infierno Black	bowl
21A-55	310400	21A40-3-3	60	23.8	22.7	21.0		7.0		3.8	0.7	0.8	505	841	615	Saxche-Palmar Poly.	plate
21A-56	310326	21A39-3-2	85	13.0	12.5	21.0	10.0	20.5	5.0		0.5	0.7	1124	1322	3468	Undetermined	pitcher
21A-57	310391	21A40-3-4	37			21.0		21.0			0.5	0.7	491	1327	3317	Undetermined	pitcher

South of the structure

Sample	Cat. No.	Lot	n	a	b	c	d	e	f	g	t1	t2	N1	N2	N3	Type	Form
21A-58	310408	21A77-3-2	45	16.0		34.0	11.0	33.2	6.7		0.6	1.2	1675	3722	12789	Pantano Impressed	jar
21A-59	310230	21A45-3-1	30	41.0		45.0		15.0			0.8	1.0	1237	4123	7949	Chaquiste Impressed	bowl
21A-60	310238	21A44-3-1	90	26.7	25.7			9.3		5.3	0.6	1.0	1031	1146	1148	Saxche-Palmar Poly.	plate

M7-91

Sample	Cat. No.	Lot	n	a	b	c	d	e	f	g	t1	t2	N1	N2	N3	Type	Form
21A-61	310451	21A81-3-2	50	25.1	23.8	37.0	15.6	43.0	7.5		0.7	0.8	3235	6470	21988	Encanto Striated	jar
21A-62	310466	21A82-3-4	20	33.1	31.7	40.0	19.0	47.0	10.5		0.7	1.0	2161	10805	26150	Encanto Striated	jar
21A-63	310465	21A82-3-2	30	27.4	26.6	38.0	17.0	41.0	9.0		0.7	0.8	2759	9197	21845	Encanto Striated	jar
21A-64	310440	21A73-3-3	40	14.8	14.3	35.0	7.0	35.0	4.8		0.7	0.8	1520	3800	14662	Pantano Impressed	jar
21A-65	310441	21A57-3-1	25	14.5	15.0	33.0	8.1	33.0	5.3		0.6	1.1	867	3468	13335	Pantano Impressed	jar
21A-66	310476	21A78-3-3	40	15.3	15.0	27.0	9.5	27.0	4.3		0.7	0.8	643	1607	7131	Pantano Impressed	jar
21A-67	310243	21A79-3-2	70			39.3		42.0			0.7	0.8	2819	4027	27403	Tinaja or Pantano	jar
21A-68	310445	21A59-2-1	50	20.2	20.6	22.4		7.0			0.5	0.6	349	698	1160	Chaquiste Impressed	bowl
21A-69	310453	21A82-3-1	60	31.0		44.0		28.0			0.5	0.7	3661	6102	47504	Chaquiste Impressed	bowl
21A-70	310444	21A81-3-2	50	12.0				10.0			0.4	0.6	242	484	435	Corozal Incised	bowl
21A-71	310234	21A78-3-2	80	25.9	25.3	23.5		8.1		4.3	0.5	0.9	701	876	1015	Saxche-Palmar Poly.	plate
21A-72	310235	21A78-3-2	40								0.7		834	2085		Saxche-Palmar Poly.	plate
21A-73	310236	21A78-3-2	80	18.7	18.3					3.0	0.6	0.8	375	469	225	Saxche-Palmar Poly.	plate
21A-74	310442	21A59-3-4	40	30.0				9.7		5.5	0.8	0.9	622	1555	1876	Saxche-Palmar Poly.	plate

M7-92

Sample	Cat. No.	Lot	n	a	b	c	d	e	f	g	t1	t2	N1	N2	N3	Type	Form
21A-75	310443	21A72-3-1	50	31.0		52.0	21.0	58.0	7.0		1.0	1.5	8037	16074	65104	Manteca Impressed Ridged	jar
21A-76	310458	21A63-3-2	60	26.6	24.7	40.0	17.2	45.0	7.9		0.6	1.0	3367	5611	28429	Cambio Unslipped angled	jar
21A-77	310481	21A64-3-2	20	24.2	22.7	40.0	12.0	38.0	10.0		0.8	1.1	1153	5765	18996	Cambio or Encanto	jar
21A-78	310450	21A70-3-2	60	14.1	13.6	21.1	9.1	17.8	4.2		0.7	0.8	1071	1785	2612	Pantano Impressed	jar
21A-79	310449	21A70-3-4	60	13.0		24.0	9.0	22.0	4.4		0.6	0.9	1381	2302	4353	Pantano Impressed	jar
21A-80	310456	21A63-3-2	35	13.0		34.0	7.4	34.0	5.4		0.6	0.7	1360	3885	16184	Pantano Impressed	jar
21A-81	310233	21A63-3-2	85	34.6	33.8			11.1		5.3	0.9	1.3	1923	2262	2231	Saxche-Palmar Poly.	plate

TABLE 8.1. (continued) Summary of Reconstructible Vessel Data.

STRUCTURES AREAS — WVS	CATALOG	PROV.	PRESENT PORTION (%)	RIM DIA. (cm) Ex/In	RIM DIA. (cm) Top	MAX DIA. (cm)	MIN OPEN. (cm)	HT. (cm)	NECK HT. (cm)	HT. w/o F. (cm)	WALL THICK. (cm) THIN	WALL THICK. (cm) THICK	WEIGHT (g) SAMPLE	WEIGHT (g) ORIGINAL	VOLUME (cm³)	TYPE	FORM
21A-82	310455	21A61-3-1	75	27.0	26.5			9.2		4.9	0.5	0.6	742	989	1276	Saxche-Palmar Poly.	plate
21A-83	310232	21A62-3-3	45	30.1	29.3			10.4		4.9	0.6	0.8	641	1424	1752	Saxche-Palmar Poly.	plate
21A-84	310454	21A62-3-1	45	15.5				6.7			0.3	0.6	122	271	667	Saxche-Palmar Poly.	bowl
21A-85	310446	21A71-3-4	50	11.0				4.1		3.5	0.3	0.5	55	110	196	Peten Gloss group	bowl
Around the stairway to the north																	
21A-86	310469	21A83-3-1	70	18.8						3.0	1.1		569	813		Cambio group	lid
21A-87	310480	21A66-3-1	30	31.0		67.0	21.0	70.0	11.0		1.2	1.6	8815	29383	225186	Manteca Impressed Ridged	jar
21A-88	310261	21A83-3-1	70	15.1	14.8	38.0	9.8	38.0	4.8		0.6	1.0	2753	3933	19422	Pantano Impressed	jar
21A-89	310471	21A66-3-2	50	15.3	14.9	22.0	10.0	24.0	5.2		0.5	0.7	813	1626	4262	Pantano Impressed	jar
21A-90	310473	21A65-3-1	90	14.0	13.7	36.2	8.2	36.1	5.5		0.6	0.9	4181	4645	17544	Pantano Impressed	jar
21A-91	310475	21A65-3-2	90	14.2	14.0	38.0	9.0	38.0	6.0		0.7	1.1	4532	5035	20448	Pantano Impressed	jar
21A-92	310242	21A65-3-2	80	35.0		37.0		15.2			0.7	1.0	2220	2775	8061	Subin Red	bowl
21A-93	310472	21A76-3-4	70	15.2	14.8	15.4		8.1			0.5	0.7	237	339	686	Saxche-Palmar Poly.	bowl
21A-94	310470	21A75-3-4	50	33.0				10.8		5.0	0.9	1.0	851	1702	2082	Saxche-Palmar Poly.	plate
21A-95	310237	21A65-3-2	98	1.9	1.7	3.8	1.4	4.0			0.5		38	39	10	Unslipped undetermined	mini jar
Barranca Escondida																	
Knoll																	
24A-1	310219	24B6-2-1	100		2.3			5.0			0.4		71	71		Pedregal Modelado	bowl
Chasm																	
24A-2	310221	24A18-1-1	100	2.4	2.1			5.0			0.6		51	51		Cambio Unslipped	mini jar
24A-3	310291	24A18-1-1	100			2.0		3.3					8	8		Cambio Unslipped	lid
24A-4	310222	24A18-1-1	100	2.6	2.4			4.7			0.6		48	48		Cambio Unslipped	mini jar
24A-5	310461	24A18-1-1	100			2.1		3.6					12	12		Cambio Unslipped	lid
24A-6	310220	24A18-1-1	100	2.4	2.6	7.2		6.8			0.4	0.5	167	167	93	Encanto Striated	mini bowl
24A-7	310292	24A18-1-1	95			3.5		3.0					21	22		Cambio Unslipped	lid
L8-5																	
25A-1	310484	25A5-2-1	100	8.8	8.4			3.0			0.4		82	82		Cambio Unslipped	mini bowl
25A-2	310487	25A1-2-1	40	11.5	11.2			4.3			0.5	0.7	99	248		Cambio Unslipped	incensario
25A-3	310488	25A6-1-1	40	8.2				4.9			0.6	0.8	40	100	43	Cambio Unslipped	incensario
25A-4	310486	25A1-3-1	50	8.8	8.3	9.0		17.2			0.5	0.6	260	520	771	Peten Gloss group	vase

*For diameters and heights of irregular-shaped vessels, this table lists their average values whereas the text describes their ranges.

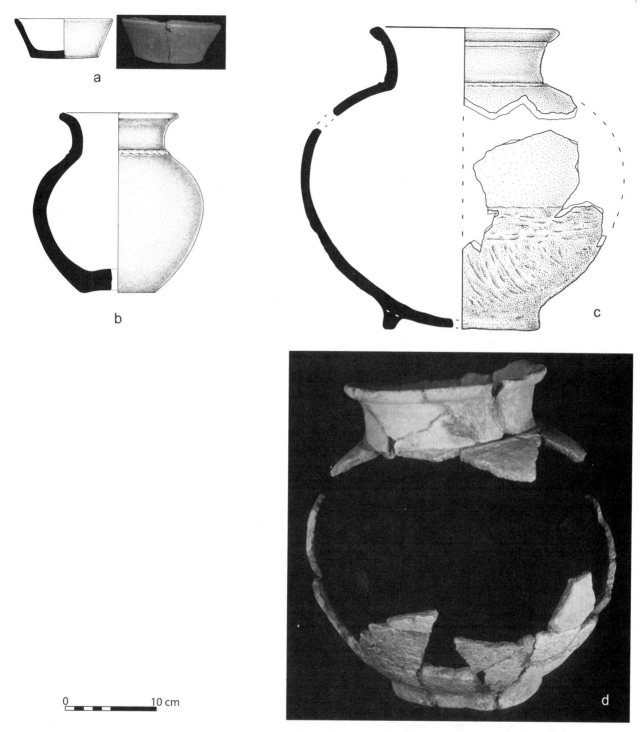

FIGURE 8.1. Complete and reconstructible vessels from Structure M7-22. (a) Cambio Unslipped, 22A24-3-2, Cat. 310293, WVS 22A-1. (b) Manteca Impressed, 22A24-3-2, Cat. 310298, WVS 22A-2. (c, d) Cambio Unslipped, 22A24-3-2, 310299, WVS 22A-3.

been stored originally inside the easternmost room. Condition: Reconstructible (60% present). Eroded. No clear traces of burning. Dimensions: Rim diameter: [exterior] 21.3 cm, [top] 20.1 cm (measured); Maximum diameter: 36.1 cm (measured); Minimum opening: 14.9 cm (measured); Height: 32 cm (estimate); Neck height: 6.1 cm

(measured); Wall thickness: 0.7–1.5 cm; Sample weight: 4,386 g; Original weight: 7,310 g; Volume: not calculated. Coordinates: (18.86, 27.60) (estimate). Type: Cambio Unslipped, scratched. Paste, temper, and firing: Reddish yellow paste (7.5YR7/8). Coarse grain. A large amount of quartz temper (1.0–4.0 mm long, some as large as

7.0 mm long), a medium amount of calcite temper (0.3–2.5 mm diameter), and a small amount of ferruginous temper (0.5–2.0 mm diameter). The paste is completely oxidized. Surface finish and decoration: The exterior neck and the exterior upper body are smoothed. The interior neck is slightly smoothed. The exterior lower body is very rough. It appears to have been deliberately scratched with a comb-like implement. Form: Jar with outcurved neck. Small ridge along the neck-body juncture. Exterior-folded rim and rounded lip. Prominent ring base. Use-wear: Not clear because of erosion.

WVS No.: 22A-4; Catalog No.: 310036 (Figures 8.2a, 8.5a, and 8.60a)
Bag No.: Rim: 654 (14-2-6), 833 (10-3-2), 750 (10-3-1); Body: 654; Base: 654. Provenience: 22A14-2-6. Context: Floor. In the northern part of the room floor near the doorway in the easternmost room. All fragments were found in one concentration, and the shape of a jar was recognizable in the field. Condition: Reconstructible (99% present). Some parts are slightly blackened, which may have been caused by the burning of the structure. Fragments were mixed with the collapsed stones. The vessel was probably stored in a high location inside the room. Dimensions: Rim diameter: [exterior] 14.5 cm, [top] 14.3 cm (measured); Maximum diameter: 34.5 cm (measured); Minimum opening: 7.8 cm (measured); Height: 34.1 cm (measured); Neck height: 5.1 cm (measured); Wall thickness: 0.8–1.4 cm; Sample weight: 5,485 g; Original weight: 5,540 g; Volume: 17,061 cm^3. Coordinates: (20.20, 23.96) (measured). Type: Pantano Impressed. Paste, temper, and firing: Reddish yellow paste (5YR7/6). Medium grain. A medium amount of calcite temper (0.5–1.5 mm diameter) and a small amount of ferruginous temper (0.5–1.5 mm diameter). The paste is completely oxidized. Surface finish and decoration: The entire exterior, including the base, has red slip, but the interior of the neck is not slipped. The body and base are polished, but the neck is roughly smoothed. A band of scroll impressions below the neck-body juncture, and a line of triangular impressions below it. Form: Jar with outcurved neck. Direct rim with squared lip. Incurved base. Use-wear: Little wear on the base. Slight use-wear on the edge of the base. No indication of use for cooking.

WVS No.: 22A-5; Catalog No.: 310052 (Figures 8.2b, 8.5b, and 8.60b)
Bag No.: Rim: 750 (10-3-1); Body: 750, 775 (10-3-2), 777 (14-3-2), 774 (10-3-2), 833 (10-3-2); Base: 750, 737 (14-2-6),

827 (10-3-1), 799 (10-3-2), 259 (10-2-4), 654 (14-2-6), 653 (10-2-8). Provenience: 22A10-3-1. Context: Floor. In front of the bench of the easternmost room. Although it was broken into many fragments, the shape of a jar was recognizable in the field. Fragments were mixed in collapsed stones. The vessel was probably stored in a high location inside the room. Condition: Reconstructible (98% present). Relatively well preserved. Some fragments are darkened from fire. The vessel was exposed to fire after it broke. Dimensions: Rim diameter: [exterior] 14.8 cm, [top] 14.8 cm (measured); Maximum diameter: 38.8 cm (measured); Minimum opening: 8.1 cm (measured); Height: 39.7 cm (measured); Neck height: 5.7 cm (measured); Wall thickness: 0.8–1.3 cm; Sample weight: 6,077 g; Original weight: 6,201 g; Volume: 22,352 cm^3. Coordinates: (19.89, 23.98) (measured). Type: Pantano Impressed. Paste, temper, and firing: Red paste (2.5YR5/6). Medium grain. A medium amount of calcite temper (0.1–0.5 mm diameter) and a small amount of ferruginous temper (0.4–0.7 mm diameter). The paste is completely oxidized. Surface finish and decoration: Red slip on the entire exterior, including the base. No slip on the interior of the neck. Three lines of triangular impressions below the neck-body juncture. Form: Jar with outcurved neck. Direct rim and squared lip. Incurved base. Use-wear: The entire exterior base is heavily worn, most likely from use. One side of the lower body next to the base (3 cm wide) is heavily worn, while the other side is undamaged. The lip appears to be slightly worn. No indication of use for cooking.

WVS No.: 22A-6; Catalog No.: 310053 (Figures 8.2c, 8.5c–e, and 8.60c)
Bag No.: Rim: 653 (10-2-8), 774 (10-3-2); Body: 653, 774, 750 (10-3-1), 654 (14-2-6); Base: 653. Provenience: 22A10-2-8. Context: Floor. In the wall fall near the floor in front of the bench of the easternmost room. Although it was broken into many fragments, the shape of a jar was recognizable in the field. Fragments were mixed in collapsed stones. The vessel was probably stored in a high location inside the room. Condition: Reconstructible (95% present). Relatively well preserved. Some fragments are slightly darkened from fire. Dimensions: Rim diameter: [exterior] 14.2 cm, [top] 13.7 cm (measured); Maximum diameter: 41.4 cm (measured); Minimum opening: 8.1 cm (measured); Height: 40.3 cm (measured); Neck height: 5.8 cm (measured); Wall thickness: 0.7–1.1 cm; Sample weight: 6,129 g; Original weight: 6,451 g; Volume: 25,156 cm^3. Coordinates: (19.46, 24.18) (measured). Type: Pantano Impressed. Paste, temper, and firing: Light red-

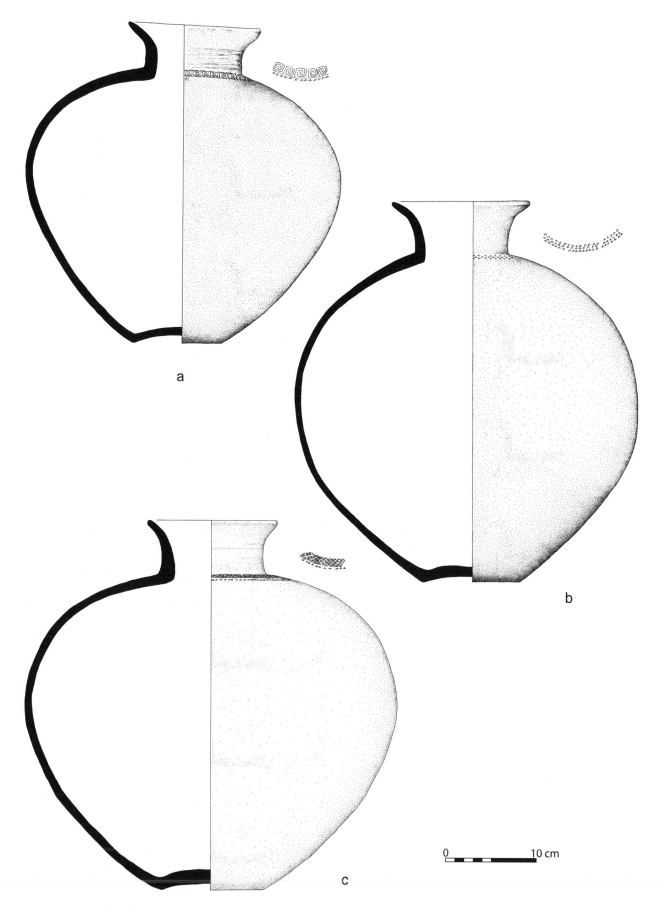

FIGURE 8.2. Complete and reconstructible vessels from Structure M7-22. Pantano Impressed. (a) 22A14-2-6, Cat. 310036, WVS 22A-4. (b) 22A10-3-1, Cat. 310052, WVS 22A-5. (c) 22A10-2-8, Cat. 310053, WVS 22A-6.

dish brown (2.5YR7/4). Medium grain. A large amount of calcite temper (0.1–1.0 mm diameter) and a small amount of ferruginous temper (0.4–0.7 mm diameter). The paste is completely oxidized. Surface finish and decoration: Red slip on the entire exterior, including the base. No slip on the interior of the neck. Crosshatch impressions and a line of triangular impressions below the neck-body juncture. Form: Jar with outcurved neck. Direct rim and squared lip. Incurved base. Use-wear: The edge of the exterior base is worn from use. No indication of use for cooking.

WVS No.: 22A-7; Catalog No.: 310254 (Figures 8.4a and 8.5f)

Bag No.: Rim: 223 (10-2-3), 391 (10-2-5), 392 (10-2-5), 390 (10-2-5), 520 (10-2-6); Body: 390, 391, 223, 395 (10-2-5), 396 (10-2-5); Base: 396, 395. Provenience: 22A10-2-5. Context: Floor. In the wall fall in front of the bench of the easternmost room. Most fragments were found closed together. It is probable that the vessel was smashed and its fragments scattered after the room was opened. The missing part may have been thrown outside the room. Condition: Partial (40% present). Slightly eroded. A part of the rim is reddened and a part of the interior wall is blackened, probably from burning. Dimensions: Rim diameter: 42 cm (estimate); Maximum diameter: 47 cm (estimate); Minimum opening: 40 cm (estimate); Height: 21.1 cm (measured); Wall thickness: 0.8–1.0 cm; Sample weight: 1,765 g; Original weight: 4,413 g; Volume: 13,575 cm³. Coordinates: (19.08, 23.68) (estimate). Type: Chaquiste Impressed. Paste, temper, and firing: Reddish yellow paste (5YR6/6). Medium grain. A moderate amount of calcite temper (0.3–1.0 mm diameter), a small amount of ferruginous temper (0.5–1.3 mm diameter), and a small amount of quartz temper (0.1 mm diameter). The paste appears to have been completely oxidized originally. Surface finish and decoration: Red slip on the exterior rim (above the ridge); rest of the vessel is unslipped. The exterior wall is slightly smoothed. The interior wall is smoothed. Nail impressions on the ridge. Form: Bowl with incurved walls and slightly restricted orifice. Exterior-thickened rim and rounded lip. Ridge below the rim. Flat base with ridge. Use-wear: No clear use-wear or evidence of use for cooking.

WVS No.: 22A-8; Catalog No.: 310256 (Figures 8.4b, 8.5g, and 8.60d)

Bag No.: Rim: 384 (10-2-5), 386 (10-2-5), 389 (10-2-5);

Body: 384, 386, 389, 808 (14-3-1); Base: 384, 808. Provenience: 22A10-2-5. Context: Floor. In the wall fall in front of the bench of the easternmost room. Most fragments were found close together. It is probable that the vessel was stored in a high location or was deliberately smashed after the room was opened. Condition: Reconstructible (90% present). Eroded. A large part of the interior is blackened, but it is not clear whether the clouding resulted from the burning of the structure. Dimensions: Rim diameter: [interior] 46.7 cm (measured), [top] 47.3 cm (measured); Maximum diameter: 52.1 cm (measured); Minimum opening: 46.7 cm (measured); Height: 18.9 cm (measured); Wall thickness: 0.8–0.9 cm; Sample weight: 4,381 g; Original weight: 4,868 g; Volume: 13,271 cm³. Coordinates: (19.32, 24.19) (estimate). Type: Chaquiste Impressed. Paste, temper, and firing: Reddish yellow paste (5YR6/6). Medium grain. A large amount of calcite temper (0.1–1.0 mm diameter) and a small amount of ferruginous temper (0.5–2.0 mm diameter). The paste is completely oxidized. Surface finish and decoration: Red slip on the exterior rim (above the ridge). The exterior and interior walls are unslipped and smoothed. A line of stamps with five dots on the ridge. Form: Bowl with incurved walls and slightly restricted orifice. Exterior-thickened rim and rounded lip. Ridge below the rim. Ring base. Use-wear: No clear use-wear or evidence of use for cooking.

WVS No.: 22A-9; Catalog No.: 310295 (Figures 8.4c and 8.60e)

Bag No.: Rim: 419 (25-3-1), 263 (23-2-3), 392 (10-2-5), 393 (10-2-5); Body: 419, 263, 392, 393; Base: 419. Provenience: 22A23-3-1. Context: Floor. Most fragments were found in an area 1 × 1 m on the floor in front of the easternmost room where the layer of stones collapsed from the wall sealing the entrance thinned off. Two fragments of the rim came from the wall-fall layer inside the easternmost room (10-2-5). This indicates that the vessel was originally stored inside the room as a complete vessel, which was deliberately broken and scattered after the sealed room was opened. Condition: Partial (40% present). Pieces from outside the room are eroded whereas those from inside the room are slightly better preserved. Some fragments are darkened. Dimensions: Rim diameter: [interior] 14.4 cm, [top] 14.8 cm (measured); Maximum diameter: 16.7 cm (measured); Minimum opening: 14.4 cm (measured); Height: 7.3–8.2 cm (measured); Wall thickness: 0.7–1.0 cm; Sample weight: 217 g; Original weight:

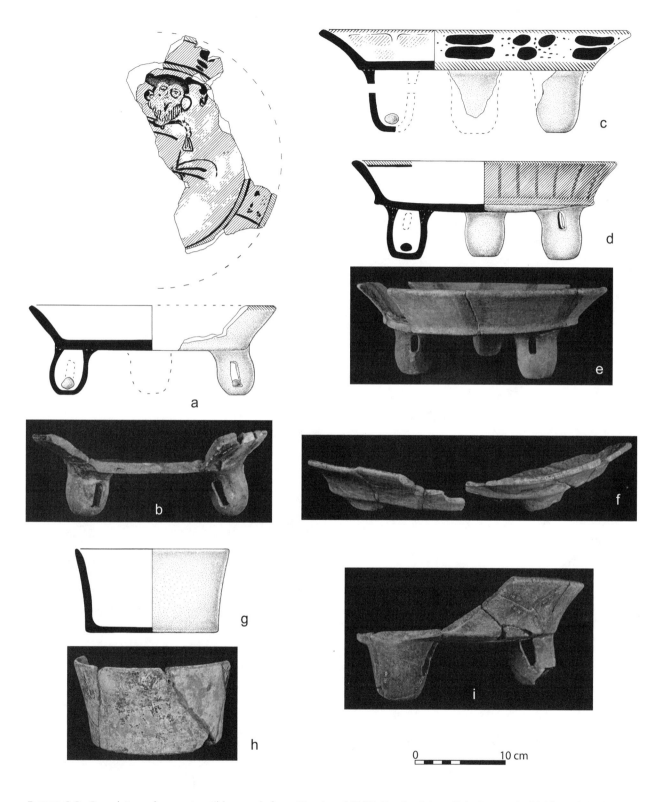

FIGURE 8.3. Complete and reconstructible vessels from Structure M7-22. Saxche-Palmar Polychrome. (a, b) 22A10-2-5, Cat. 310424, WVS 22A-15. (c) 22A24-3-1, Cat. 310294, WVS 22A-11. (d, e) 22A26-3-4, Cat. 310415, WVS 22A-13. (f) 22A24-2-3, Cat. 310423, WVS 22A-14. (g, h) 22A10-2-5, Cat. 310255, WVS 22A-17. (i) 22A23-3-2, Cat. 3100426, WVS 22A-16.

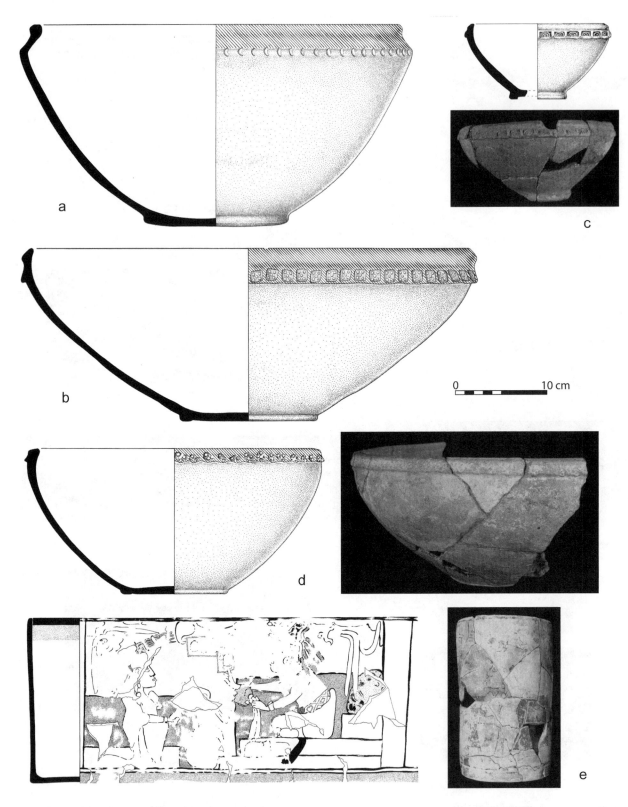

FIGURE 8.4. Complete and reconstructible vessels from Structure M7-22. (a–d) Chaquiste Impressed. (a) 22A10-2-5, Cat. 310254, WVS 22A-7. (b) 22A10-2-5, Cat. 310256, WVS 22A-8. (c) 22A23-3-1, Cat. 310295, WVS 22A-9. (d) 22A21-2-4, Cat. 310296, WVS 22A-10. (e) Saxche-Palmar Polychrome, 22A24-2-3, Cat. 310397, WVS 22A-12.

0   10 cm

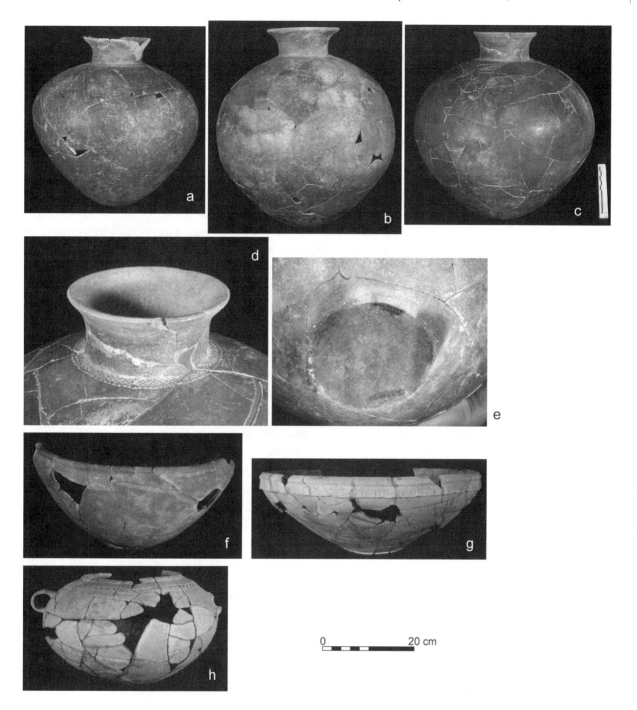

FIGURE 8.5. Complete and reconstructible vessels from Structures M7-22 and M7-32. (⅛ scale for a–c and f–g; d and e are not to scale.) (a–e) Pantano Impressed. (a) 22A14-2-6, Cat. 310036, WVS 22A-4. (b) 22A10-3-1, Cat. 310052, WVS 22A-5. (c–e) 22A10-2-8, Cat. 310053, WVS 22A-6. (d) Close-up of the neck. (e) Close-up of the base. (f–h) Chaquiste Impressed. (f) 22A10-2-5, Cat. 310254, WVS 22A-7. (g) 22A10-2-5, Cat. 310256, WVS 22A-8. (h) 22B55-3-2, Cat. 310483, WVS 22B-1.

543 g; Volume: 577 cm³. Coordinates: (21.02, 27.18) (estimate). Type: Chaquiste Impressed. Paste, temper, and firing: Reddish yellow paste (7.5YR6/6). Medium grain. A medium amount of calcite temper (0.1–0.3 mm diameter). The paste is completely oxidized. Surface finish and decoration: The interior is well smoothed and slipped with red. Red slip on the exterior rim (above the ridge). The rest of the exterior is slightly rougher than the interior and appears to be unslipped. Stamps with scroll patterns on the ridge. Form: Bowl with incurved sides. Exterior-thickened rim and rounded lip. Ridge below the rim. Ring base. Use-wear: Not clear because of erosion.

WVS No.: 22A-10; Catalog No.: 310296 (Figures 8.4d and 8.6of)

Bag No.: Rim: 263 (23-2-3), 288 (21-2-4); Body: 268 (21-2-4), 288; Base: 268. Provenience: 22A21-2-4. Context: Floor. In front of the easternmost room over the stones collapsed from the wall sealing the entrance of the easternmost room. Fragments were found close together. Condition: Partial (55% present). Eroded. Although some pieces are darkened, it is not clear whether the darkening was caused by the burning of the structure. Dimensions: Rim diameter: [interior] 29.4 cm, [top] 29.9 cm (measured); Maximum diameter: 32.7 cm (measured); Height: 15.3 cm (measured); Wall thickness: 0.6–1.0 cm; Sample weight: 1,214 g; Original weight: 2,207 g; Volume: 5,314 cm^3. Coordinates: (20.66, 25.20) (estimate). Type: Chaquiste Impressed. Paste, temper, and firing: Reddish yellow paste (7.5YR7/6). Medium grain. A medium amount of calcite temper (0.3–1.0 mm diameter) and a small amount of ferruginous temper (0.5–2.0 mm diameter). The paste is completely oxidized. Surface finish and decoration: Remains of red slip on the exterior rim and on the ridge. The interior is well smoothed, but the exterior below the ridge is poorly smoothed. The interior and the exterior below the ridge appear to have been unslipped. Stamps with five-dot patterns on the ridge. Form: Bowl with incurved sides. Exterior-thickened rim and rounded lip. Ridge immediately below the rim. Ring base. Use-wear: The interior, except the area immediately below the rim, is heavily worn and pitted from use.

WVS No.: 22A-11; Catalog No.: 310294 (Figure 8.3c)

Bag No.: Rim: 424 (24-3-1), 472 (24-3-2); Body: 472; Base: 424, 472. Provenience: 22A24-3-1. Context: Floor. On the floor in front of the easternmost room where the layer of stones collapsed from the wall sealing the entrance thinned off. Most fragments were found in an area 2 × 1 m. It is probable that the vessel was originally stored inside the easternmost room. Condition: Reconstructible (65% present). Eroded. No clear traces of burning. Dimensions: Rim diameter: [exterior] 32.6 cm, [top] 31.6 cm (measured); Height: 9.5 cm (estimate); Height without feet: 4.3 cm (measured); Wall thickness: 0.7–1.1 cm; Sample weight: 934 g; Original weight: 1,437 g; Volume: 1,505 cm^3. Coordinates: (19.53, 27.62) (estimate). Type: Saxche-Palmar Polychrome. Paste, temper, and firing: Reddish yellow paste (5YR7/6). Fine grain. A medium amount of calcite temper (0.1 mm diameter) and a small amount of ferruginous temper (0.3–0.8 mm di-

ameter). The paste is completely oxidized. Surface finish and decoration: Remains of black, red, and orange paints over cream underslip on the exterior wall and the interior. Form: Plate with slightly outcurved sides. Direct rim and flat lip. Flat base. Use-wear: Not clear because of poor preservation.

WVS No.: 22A-12; Catalog No.: 310397 (Figure 8.4e)

Bag No.: Rim: 299 (24-2-3), 288 (21-2-4); Body: 299, 290 (22-2-3), 473 (24-3-3), 288; Base: 473, 290, 299. Provenience: 22A24-2-3. Context: Floor. Area in front of the easternmost room. Fragments were scattered in an area 2 × 3 m. Many were found on the layer of collapsed stones that were sealing the room entrance, and some were found on the exterior floor where the collapsed stone layer thinned out. This pattern indicates that the vessel was thrown there after the entrance of the room was opened. It is probable that the vessel was originally stored in the sealed room as a complete piece. Condition: Reconstructible (95% present). Eroded. The vessel appears to be slightly burned and darkened. Dimensions: Rim diameter: [exterior] 11.4 cm, [top] 11.0 cm (measured); Height: 17.4 cm (measured); Wall thickness: 0.6 cm; Sample weight: 721 g; Original weight: 759 g; Volume: not calculated. Coordinates: (19.30, 26.33) (measured). Type: Saxche-Palmar Polychrome. Paste, temper, and firing: Reddish yellow paste (7.5YR7/6). Fine grain. A medium amount of calcite temper (0.1–0.2 mm diameter) and a small amount of ferruginous temper (0.3–0.7 mm diameter). The paste is completely oxidized. Surface finish and decoration: Black and red paints over orange slip. It depicts a court scene with a lord seated on a low bench, facing a person seated on the floor. There is a short text with probably four glyphs, possibly of the lord's name, but it is badly eroded. No paint or slip on the exterior base. Black band over the exterior and interior rim. A red band below the interior rim. Form: Cylinder vase with vertical sides. Direct rim and rounded lip. Flat base. Use-wear: Not clear because of erosion.

WVS No.: 22A-13; Catalog No.: 310415 (Figure 8.3d and 8.3e)

Bag No.: Rim: 659 (26-3-4), 618 (26-3-2); Body: 659, 618; Base: 618, 659. Provenience: 22A26-3-4. Context: Floor. On the floor of Structure M7-25. It is not clear whether the vessel was stored in the easternmost room of Structure M7-22 and thrown there or whether it was originally stored in Structure M7-25. Condition: Reconstructible

(90% present). Badly eroded. Some parts of the vessel are darkened, but it is not clear whether it was burned. Dimensions: Rim diameter: [exterior] 29.3 cm, [top] 28.8 cm (measured); Height: 10.0 cm (measured); Height without feet: 4.9 cm (measured); Wall thickness: 0.4–0.6 cm; Sample weight: 1,215 g; Original weight: 1,350 g; Volume: 1,538 cm³. Coordinates: (19.22, 28.78) (measured). Type: Saxche-Palmar Polychrome. Paste, temper, and firing: Reddish yellow paste (7.5YR7/6). Fine grain. A small amount of calcite temper (0.1–0.3 mm diameter) and a small amount of ferruginous temper (0.3–1.2 mm diameter). The paste is completely oxidized. Surface finish and decoration: The surface is mostly eroded, but there are some remains of red and orange paints over cream underslip on the interior surface and on the rim. Weak red vertical stripes over thin cream underslip on the exterior wall. The exterior base and feet are not painted. Form: Plate with outflared sides. Direct rim and rounded lip. Flat base. Ridge along the body-base juncture. Three oven-shaped feet with two openings and a rattle. Use-wear: Not clear because of erosion.

WVS No.: 22A-14; Catalog No.: 310423 (Figure 8.3f)
Bag No.: Rim: 299 (24-2-3), 301 (24-2-2); Body: 299, 301; Base: 299, 301. Provenience: 22A24-2-3. Context: Floor. On the exterior floor in front of the easternmost room. In the layer of dense artifacts above the collapsed stones of the wall sealing the room. Fragments were found in an area 2 × 1 m. Condition: Reconstructible (30% present). Relatively well preserved. No recognizable traces of burning. Dimensions: Rim diameter: 27 cm (estimate); Height: 11 cm (estimate); Height without feet: 4.2 cm (measured); Wall thickness: 0.5–0.8 cm; Sample weight: 485 g; Original weight: 1,616 g; Volume: not calculated. Coordinates: (18.68, 26.71) (estimate). Type: Saxche-Palmar Polychrome. Paste, temper, and firing: Light red paste (2.5YR6/8). Medium grain. A medium amount of calcite temper (0.1–0.5 mm diameter) and a small amount of ferruginous temper (0.5–2.0 mm diameter). The paste is completely oxidized. Surface finish and decoration: The interior wall is polished and has orange slip. Black tong motifs on the rim and red band on the lip. The exterior is casually smoothed and has thin orange slip. Form: Plate with outcurved sides. Direct rim and rounded lip. Flat base. Three hollow oven feet with two openings and a rattle. Use-wear: The interior base and the lower part of the interior wall are heavily worn and pitted, probably from use.

WVS No.: 22A-15; Catalog No.: 310424 (Figure 8.3a and 8.3b)
Bag No.: Rim: 391 (10-2-5), 392 (10-2-5); Body: 391, 392, 390 (10-2-5); Base: 391, 392, 520 (10-2-6), 386 (10-2-5). Provenience: 22A10-2-5. Context: Floor. In the wall fall in front of the bench in the southern portion of the easternmost room. Other parts of the vessel may have been thrown outside when the sealed room was opened. Condition: Reconstructible (30% present). Relatively well preserved. The exterior is burned and blackened. The interior is slightly darkened. Most of the recovered fragments were glued together. Dimensions: Rim diameter: 28 cm (estimate); Height: 9.2 cm (measured); Height without feet: 4.0 cm (measured); Wall thickness: 0.7–1.0 cm; Sample weight: 457 g; Original weight: 1,523 g; Volume: not calculated. Coordinates: (18.93, 23.63) (estimate). Type: Saxche-Palmar Polychrome. Paste, temper, and firing: Reddish yellow paste (5YR7/6). Fine grain. A small amount of calcite temper (0.1–0.5 mm diameter), a small amount of ferruginous temper (0.5–1.5 mm diameter), and a very small amount of volcanic ash temper (0.1 mm length). The paste is completely oxidized. Surface finish and decoration: The interior surface is polished and has weak red slip. Red bands with black outlines on the lip and the wall-base juncture. Black motifs on the interior wall. A front view of an owl drawn in black lines on the base. The exterior surface is smoothed and unslipped. Form: Plate with outflared sides. Direct rim and rounded side. Flat base. Three hollow oven feet with two openings and a rattle. Use-wear: The painting on the interior base is worn, possibly from use. The interior wall is well preserved. Use-wear on the feet is not clear.

WVS No.: 22A-16; Catalog No.: 310426 (Figure 8.3i)
Bag No.: Rim: 422 (23-3-2); Body: 422; Base: 422. Provenience: 22A23-3-2. Context: Floor. On the exterior floor in front of the easternmost room, where the layer of stones collapsed from the wall sealing the entrance thinned out. Fragments were found in an area 1 × 1 m. Condition: Reconstructible (30% present). Eroded. Burned and darkened. All the recovered fragments were glued together. Dimensions: Rim diameter: 30 cm (estimate); Height: 10.3 cm (measured); Height without feet: 5.5 cm (measured); Wall thickness: 0.8–0.9 cm; Sample weight: 516 g; Original weight: 1,720 g; Volume: not calculated. Coordinates: (20.27, 27.59) (estimate). Type: Saxche-Palmar Polychrome. Paste, temper, and firing: Reddish yellow paste (5YR7/6). Fine grain. A small amount of calcite temper

(0.1–0.4 mm diameter) and a small amount of ferruginous temper (0.3–1.0 mm). The paste is completely oxidized. Surface finish and decoration: Orange and weak red slips on the interior. Human profile in black lines and red paints on the base. Red band on the lip. The exterior is eroded, but there are some remains of red and orange colors. Form: Plate with outflared sides. Direct rim and rounded lip. Flat base. Three hollow oven feet with two openings and a rattle. Use-wear: Not clear because of erosion.

WVS No.: 22A-17; Catalog No.: 310255 (Figure 8.3g and 8.3h)
Bag No.: Rim: 388 (10-2-5), 391 (10-2-5); Body: 388; Base: 388, 391, 390 (10-2-5), 259 (10-2-4). Provenience: 22A10-2-5. Context: Floor. In the wall fall in front of the bench of the easternmost room. Most fragments were found close together. It is probable that the vessel was smashed and its fragments scattered after the room was opened. The missing part may have been thrown outside the room. Condition: Partial (45% present). Heavily eroded. It is not clear whether the vessel was burned. Dimensions: Rim diameter: 16 cm (estimate); Maximum diameter: 17 cm (estimate); Height: 8.8 cm (measured); Wall thickness: 0.5–0.8 cm; Sample weight: 376 g; Original weight: 836 g; Volume: 910 cm³. Coordinates: (19.17, 23.98) (estimate). Type: Saxche-Palmar Polychrome. Paste, temper, and firing: Reddish yellow paste (5YR6/6). Fine grain. A moderate amount of volcanic ash temper (0.1 mm long) and a small amount of black nodules (0.3–0.8 mm diameter). The paste is completely oxidized. Surface finish and decoration: Remains of black and red paints over cream underslip on the exterior wall. The interior is eroded. Form: Bowl with slightly outcurved sides. Direct rim and rounded lip. Flat base. Use-wear: Not clear because of poor preservation.

STRUCTURE M7-32 (HOUSE OF BONES): OPERATION 22B

WVS No.: 22B-1; Catalog No.: 310483 (Figures 8.5h and 8.6a)
Bag No.: Rim: 588 (55-3-2), 593 (38-3-2); Body: 588, 507, 593 (39-3-2), 493 (55-2-1), 585 (55-3-1), 580 (38-3-1); Base: 588, 593, 493. Provenience: 22B55-3-2. Context: Floor. On the exterior floor north of the structure, west of the exterior bench. Most fragments were found in one concentration. Condition: Reconstructible (95% present). Eroded. The interior lower body is darkened, and the exterior lower body is slightly darkened. It is not clear whether this was caused by burning after use. Dimensions: Rim diameter: [interior] 19.3 cm, [top] 20.3 cm (measured); Maximum diameter: 37.8 cm (measured); Height: 22.7 cm (measured); Wall thickness: 0.8–1.0 cm; Sample weight: 2,237 g; Original weight: 2,355 g; Volume: not calculated. Coordinates: (24.28, 11.66) (estimate). Type: Chaquiste Impressed. Paste, temper, and firing: Reddish yellow paste (7.5YR7/6). Relatively fine grain. A small amount of quartz temper (0.1–0.3 mm length), a small amount of mica temper (0.2–0.4 mm length), a small amount of calcite temper (0.3–0.5 diameter), and a small amount of ferruginous temper (0.5–1.3 mm diameter), including some chunks of hematite (5–13 mm diameter). In the lower body the core near the interior surface is dark. The paste is different from that of common Subin/Chaquiste vessels, suggesting that this was an imported object. Surface finish and decoration: Red slip on the exterior above the ridge. Red slip on the upper interior surface. Circular stamps above the ridge. Form: Bowl with markedly incurved sides and restricted orifice. Exterior-thickened rim and rounded lip. Subtle ridge below the rim. Flat base (slightly incurved) without ring. Two strap handles. The decoration and form are different from those of common Chaquiste bowls found in elite residences. Use-wear: The edge of the base appears to be worn. It is not clear whether the dark color of the lower body is related to its use.

WVS No.: 22B-2; Catalog No.: 310247 (Figure 8.6b)
Bag No.: Rim: 540 (43-3-4), 163 (3-3-1); Body: 540; Base: 540, 163. Provenience: 22B43-3-4. Context: Floor. On the floor near the doorway to the rear center room. Condition: Reconstructible (70% present). Slightly eroded. Traces of burning not clear. Dimensions: Rim diameter: [top] 13.8 cm (measured); Maximum diameter: 14.3 cm (measured); Height: 7.3 cm (measured); Wall thickness: 0.8–0.9 cm; Sample weight: 300 g; Original weight: 428 g; Volume: 386 cm³. Coordinates: (16.29, 13.09) (estimate). Type: Cameron Incised. Paste, temper, and firing: Pink paste (5YR6/4). Coarse grain. A large amount of calcite temper (0.3–1.0 mm diameter) and a small amount of ferruginous temper (0.3–1.0 mm diameter). The paste is completely oxidized. Surface finish and decoration: Weak red slip on the interior surface. The interior rim has dark red slip. The exterior surface is unslipped. Shallow groove on the exterior rim. Form: Bowl with slightly incurved sides. Direct rim and pointed lip. Ring base. Use-wear:

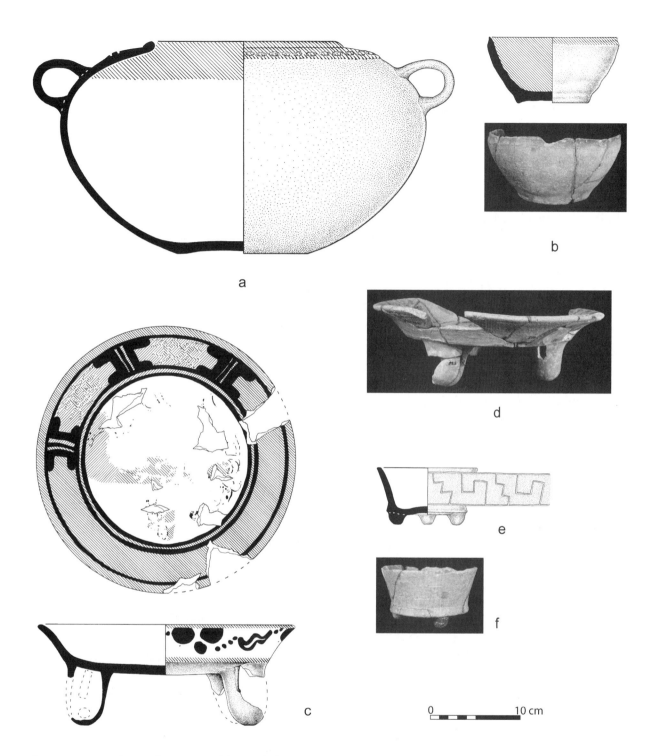

FIGURE 8.6. Complete and reconstructible vessels from Structure M7-32. (a) Chaquiste Impressed, 22B55-3-2, Cat. 310483, WVS 22B-1. (b) Cameron Incised, 22B43-3-4, Cat. 310247, WVS 22B-2. (c) Saxche-Palmar Polychrome, 22B42-3-3, Cat. 310244, WVS 22B-3. (d) Saxche-Palmar Polychrome, 22B55-3-2, Cat. 310468, WVS 22B-4. (e, f) Torres Incised, 22B38-3-2, Cat. 310467, WVS 22B-5.

The interior base appears to be worn from use. Use-wear on the exterior is not clear because of erosion.

WVS No.: 22B-3; Catalog No.: 310244 (Figure 8.6c)
Bag No.: Rim: 433 (42-3-3), 119 (2-2-4), 516 (42-3-4), 385 (42-2-4), 406 (43-2-4), 187 (2-3-4), 500 (13-3-1); Body: 387 (42-2-3), 516; Base: 433, 194 (2-3-1), 455 (42-3-1), 406, 185 (2-3-2), 433, 530 (43-3-3), 392 (42-2-4), 382 (42-2-4), 500. Provenience: 22B42-3-3. Context: Floor. In the termination deposit of the center room. Some fragments were on the floor in front of the bench, and others were in the broken northern niche of the bench and in the broken floor north of the niche. This distribution of fragments shows that materials in the broken floor were deposited at the same time as those on the floor. The nearly completely reconstructible state of the vessel suggests that this plate was broken during the ritual and scattered. It was probably not redeposited midden material. Condition: Reconstructible (95% present). Slightly eroded. Traces of burning not clear. Dimensions: Rim diameter: [exterior] 28.5 cm, [top] 27.9 cm (measured); Height: 9.5 cm (estimate); Height without feet: 4.3 cm (measured); Wall thickness: 0.7–0.8 cm; Sample weight: 1,136 g; Original weight: 1,196 g; Volume: 1,248 cm^3. Coordinates: (16.64, 10.62) (estimate). Type: Saxche-Palmar Polychrome. Paste, temper, and firing: Pink paste (5YR7/4). Fine grain. A small amount of calcite temper (0.1–0.5 mm diameter) and a small amount of ferruginous temper (0.5–1.5 mm diameter). The paste is completely oxidized. Surface finish and decoration: Red, black, and orange paints over cream underslip on the interior. Figural motifs on the interior base are eroded. Red band and black jaguar pelt motifs painted directly on the paste on the exterior wall. Form: Plate with slightly outcurved sides. Direct rim and rounded lip. Flat base. Three hollow oven feet with two openings and possibly a rattle. Use-wear: The interior base is heavily worn and pitted. The interior wall is well preserved, which suggests that this condition of the interior base is due not to erosion but to use.

WVS No.: 22B-4; Catalog No.: 310468 (Figure 8.6d)
Bag No.: Rim: 588 (55-3-2), 593 (38-3-2), 330 (38-2-3); Body: 593 (38-3-2), 507 (39-3-2), 330; Base: 588, 507, 593, 585 (55-3-1). Provenience: 22B55-3-2. Context: Floor. On the exterior floor north of the structure. Fragments were scattered in the 1-×-4-m area along the wall, as well as the 2-×-1-m area east of the exterior bench. Condition: Reconstructible (70% present). Eroded. Traces of burning

not clear. Most fragments were refitted. Dimensions: Rim diameter: 23 cm (estimate); Height: 7.6 cm (measured); Height without feet: 3.6 cm (measured); Wall thickness: 0.7–0.8 cm; Sample weight: 537 g; Original weight: 767 g; Volume: not calculated. Coordinates: (24.58, 11.40) (estimate). Type: Saxche-Palmar Polychrome. Paste, temper, and firing: Light red paste (2.5YR7/6). Medium grain. A medium amount of calcite temper (0.3–1.0 mm diameter) and a small amount of ferruginous temper (0.3–1.0 mm diameter). The paste is completely oxidized. Surface finish and decoration: Some remains of black and red paints over cream underslip. Form: Plate with slightly outcurved sides. Direct rim and rounded lip. Flat base. Three hollow oven feet with two openings and a rattle. Use-wear: The interior base is heavily worn and pitted.

WVS No.: 22B-5; Catalog No.: 310467 (Figure 8.6e and 8.6f)
Bag No.: Rim: 593 (38-3-2); Body: 593; Base: 593. Provenience: 22B38-3-2. Context: Floor. On the exterior floor north of the structure. Condition: Reconstructible (95% present). Eroded. It appears that the vessel was burned and some pieces were broken off by heat. The blackening of the interior, however, may have been caused by use as an incense burner. Dimensions: Rim diameter: [exterior] 10.8 cm, [top] 10.4 cm (measured); Height: 6.3 cm (measured); Height without feet: 5.3 cm (measured); Wall thickness: 0.6 cm; Sample weight: 187 g; Original weight: 197 g; Volume: not calculated. Coordinates: (23.67, 11.36) (estimate). Type: Torres Incised. Paste, temper, and firing: Reddish yellow paste (5YR7/6). Relatively fine grain. A small amount of calcite temper (0.1–0.5 mm diameter) and a very small amount of volcanic ash temper (0.1 mm length). The paste is completely oxidized. Surface finish and decoration: Incised motifs on the exterior wall. Orange to cream surface, which appears to be the color of the paste. Form: Bowl with outflared sides. Direct rim and squared lip. Ridge at the base. Flat base. Three solid nubbin feet. Use-wear: The interior base is black, which may have resulted from the burning of organic material.

STRUCTURE M8-4 (HOUSE OF MIRRORS): OPERATION 23A

North Room
WVS No.: 23A-1; Catalog No.: 310164 (Figure 8.7a)
Bag No.: Rim: 1501 (19-3-3); Body: 1501; Base: 1501. Provenience: 23A19-3-3. Context: Floor. On the floor near the southwestern corner of the front part of the north room.

Most fragments were in one concentration in the shape of a skewed circle, partly covered with fragments of a large Manteca Impressed vessel. Fragments from one section of the vessel were found in the humus layer of the same unit and in Unit 20, roughly 2 m apart from the large concentration. A small section near the center was not recovered. The vessel appears to have been stored in a high location. When it fell, it was probably impacted in the central part and one section of the vessel broke off. Condition: Reconstructible (93% present). A large portion is well preserved, but the broken-off section is heavily eroded. A section of the rim is darkened. It is not clear whether it is from fire. Dimensions: Rim diameter: [exterior] 45.5 cm, [top] 44.3 cm (measured); Height: 6.3 cm (measured); Wall thickness: 0.7 cm; Sample weight: 2,200 g; Original weight: 2,365 g; Volume: N/A. Coordinates: (50.94, 18.91) (measured). Type: Cambio Unslipped. Paste, temper, and firing: Reddish yellow paste (5YR6/6). Medium grain. A large amount of calcite temper (1.0–2.5 mm diameter) and a very small amount of ferruginous temper (1.0–3.0 mm diameter). The paste is completely oxidized. Surface finish and decoration: Unslipped. The interior is well polished. The exterior was roughly smoothed when the clay was still soft. Coarse temper particles were moved, leaving small striations. Form: Plate with no sides (*comal*). Slightly rounded base. Interior-thickened rim and squared lip. Use-wear: The center of the exterior base is slightly worn. There is no clear use-wear on other parts of the exterior. No clear use-wear on the interior. There is no soot on the exterior. Unless soot was burned away in the fire at the time of abandonment, the vessel does not appear to have been used as a griddle. For a griddle, wear by contact with hearth stones in the exterior sections between the center and the rim is expected.

WVS No.: 23A-2; Catalog No.: 310393
Bag No.: Body: 1041 (19-3-2); Base: 1041. Provenience: 23A19-3-2. Context: Floor. On the floor of the front area of the north room. Fragments were found in one concentration. The base was found upside-down during the excavation. The vessel was probably placed on the floor near the southwestern corner of the front area. It may have been pushed down intentionally or by the collapsing stone wall. Condition: Partial (50% present). Eroded. Some fragments are burned and darkened. The rim and the neck of the vessel were not recovered, and the fillet on the shoulder is not complete. The vessel may have been used as a partial jar after the neck broke off. Alternatively,

when the vessel tumbled, the neck may have broken off and rolled away from the body part. The curvature of the fillet appears to be about the same as in the reconstructed large jar from the north room of Structure M8-8 (WVS 20A-1, Cat. 310055). Dimensions: Maximum diameter: 75 cm (rough estimate); Height: 85 cm (rough estimate); Wall thickness: 0.9–1.1 cm; Sample weight: 15,829 g; Original weight: 31,658 g; Volume: 225,326 cm^3. Coordinates: (51.11, 18.83) (measured). Type: Manteca Impressed Ridged variety. Paste, temper, and firing: Reddish yellow paste (7.5YR7/6). Coarse grain. A large amount of calcite temper (0.5–3.0 mm diameter). The paste is completely oxidized. Surface finish and decoration: The exterior and interior are unslipped and smoothed. A thick fillet (3 cm wide, 1 cm high) was attached to the shoulder. Large braid design impressions on the fillet. Form: Jar. Flat base. Use-wear: None clear on the exterior base.

WVS No.: 23A-3; Catalog No.: 310396 (Figure 8.12a)
Bag No.: Rim: 1224 (42-3-2); Body: 1224, 1231 (42-3-4), 1378 (43-3-3); Base: 1231, 240 (42-1-1), 1110 (18-3-2). Provenience: 23A42-3-2. Context: Floor. On the floor in front of the rear bench of the north room. Fragments were found in one concentration. The vessel was probably placed on the floor. Condition: Reconstructible (90% present). Eroded. Some fragments are burned and darkened. Dimensions: Rim diameter: 42 cm (estimate); Maximum diameter: 65 cm (rough estimate); Minimum opening: 28.5 cm (estimate); Height: 72 cm (rough estimate); Neck height: 12.3 cm (estimate); Wall thickness: 0.9–1.2 cm; Sample weight: 19,872 g; Original weight: 22,080 g; Volume: 126,992 cm^3. Coordinates: (53.23, 17.75) (measured). Type: Manteca Impressed Ridged variety. Paste, temper, and firing: Reddish yellow paste (5YR7/6). Coarse grain. A large amount of calcite temper (0.5–2.0 mm diameter). The paste is completely oxidized. Surface finish and decoration: The exterior and interior are unslipped and smoothed. Thick fillet with impressions on the shoulder. Form: Jar with outcurved neck. Exterior-folded rim and beveled-in lip. Flat base. Use-wear: Not clear because of erosion.

WVS No.: 23A-4; Catalog No.: 310364 (Figure 8.12b)
Bag No.: Rim: 1223 (42-3-2); Body: 1223, 1224 (42-3-2); Base: 1223. Provenience: 23A42-3-2. Context: Floor. On the floor in front of the rear bench of the north room. Only the rim and neck parts were restored in the lab, but most fragments appear to have been in one concentration.

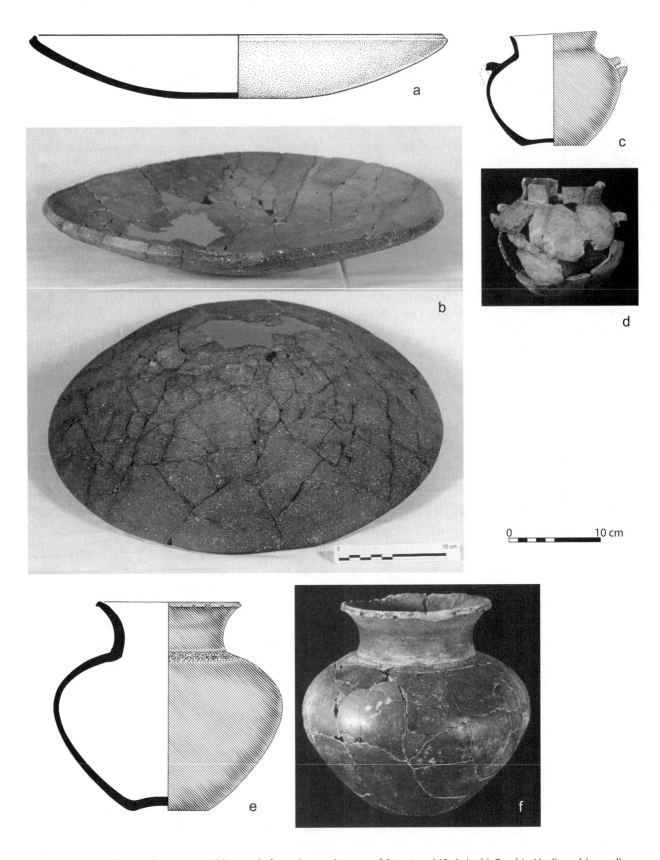

FIGURE 8.7. Complete and reconstructible vessels from the north room of Structure M8-4. (a, b) Cambio Unslipped (*comal*), 23A19-3-3, Cat. 310164, WVS 23A-1. (c, d) Tinaja Red, 23A18-3-3, Cat. 310285, WVS 23A-6. (e, f) Pantano Impressed, 23A18-3-2, Cat. 310279, WVS 23A-7.

The vessel was probably placed on the floor near the northern corner in front of the bench. Condition: Reconstructible (95% present). Slightly eroded. Traces of burning are not clear. Dimensions: Rim diameter: [exterior] 35.3 cm, [top] 33.8 cm (measured); Maximum diameter: 55 cm (estimate); Minimum opening: 24.4 cm (measured); Height: 64 cm (rough estimate); Neck height: 11.3 cm (measured); Wall thickness: 0.7–1.1 cm; Sample weight: 19,574 g; Original weight: 20,604 g; Volume: 131,466 cm³. Coordinates: (54.11, 17.25) (measured). Type: Encanto Striated. Paste, temper, and firing: Pink paste (7.5YR7/4). Coarse grain. A large amount of calcite temper (0.5–3.0 mm diameter). The paste is completely oxidized. Surface finish and decoration: Striation on the exterior body below the neck. Form: Jar with outcurved neck. Exterior-folded rim and beveled-in lip. Rounded base. Use-wear: The base appears to be slightly worn.

WVS No.: 23A-5; Catalog No.: 310406
Bag No.: Rim: 1224 (42-3-2), 1223 (42-3-2), 1149 (17-3-1), 152 (18-1-1), 1070 (42-2-2), 1231 (42-3-4), 240 (42-1-1); Body: 1223, 1224; Base: 1223. Provenience: 23A42-3-2. Context: Floor. On the floor in front of the rear bench. Most fragments were found in one concentration. The vessel was probably placed on the bench or on the floor in front of it. Condition: Reconstructible (70% present). Eroded. Traces of burning are not clear. Dimensions: Rim diameter: 29 cm (measured); Maximum diameter: 33 cm (rough estimate); Minimum opening: 17 cm (estimate); Height: 42 cm (rough estimate); Neck height: 11 cm (estimate); Wall thickness: 0.8–1.0 cm; Sample weight: 3,850 g; Original weight: 5,500 g; Volume: 15,707 cm³. Coordinates: (53.64, 17.19) (measured). Type: Encanto Striated with impressions. Paste, temper, and firing: Pink paste (7.5YR7/4). Coarse grain. A large amount of calcite temper (0.5–2.0 mm diameter). The paste is completely oxidized. Surface finish and decoration: Striation on the body and base below the shoulder. A line of small impressions made with a finger or a round stick where striation starts. The neck and interior are unslipped and smoothed. Form: Jar with outcurved neck. Exterior-folded rim and beveled-in lip. Rounded base. Use-wear: Not clear because of erosion.

WVS No.: 23A-6; Catalog No.: 310285 (Figure 8.7c and 8.7d)
Bag No.: Rim: 1498 (18-3-3), 1254 (18-3-1), 1255 (18-3-3); Body: 1498, 1254, 1255; Base: 1498, 1254, 1255. Prove-

nience: 23A18-3-3. Context: Floor. In the southern part of the rear bench near the room partition with the central room. Most fragments were found in an area 1 × 1 m on the bench and in the humus layer. The vessel was probably placed on the floor. Condition: Reconstructible (65% present). Badly eroded. Severely burned in reddish and dark colors. Dimensions: Rim diameter: [exterior] 9.6 cm, [top] 9.3 cm (measured); Maximum diameter: 14.1 cm (measured); Minimum opening: 8.0 cm (measured); Height: 11.9 cm (measured); Neck height: 2.2 cm (measured); Wall thickness: 0.4–0.9 cm; Sample weight: 308 g; Original weight: 474 g; Volume: 848 cm³. Coordinates: (50.86, 16.38) (estimate). Type: Tinaja Red. Paste, temper, and firing: Reddish yellow paste (7.5YR7/6). Medium grain. A medium amount of calcite temper (0.3–1.3 mm diameter) and a small amount of ferruginous temper (0.5–1.5 mm diameter). The interior is dark, which may have been caused by fire at the time of abandonment. Surface finish and decoration: The exterior is red-slipped. It is not clear whether the interior neck and the exterior base were slipped. Form: Small jar with slightly outcurved neck and incurved base. Direct rim and rounded lip. Two strap handles. Use-wear: Not clear because of erosion.

WVS No.: 23A-7; Catalog No.: 310279 (Figures 8.7e, 8.7f, and 8.60g)
Bag No.: Rim: 1106 (18-3-2); Body: 1106, 1426 (42-3-2); Base: 1106. Provenience: 23A18-3-2. Context: Floor. In the southern part of the room floor in front of the rear bench, near the central axis of the bench. Most fragments were found in one concentration. The shape of a jar placed on the floor was recognizable in the field. The vessel was probably placed on the floor. Condition: Reconstructible (93% present). Slightly eroded. A large part of the vessel is burned in a dark color. Dimensions: Rim diameter: [exterior] 16.0 cm, [top] 15.5 cm (measured); Maximum diameter: 24.6 cm (measured); Minimum opening: 9.7 cm (measured); Height: 21.8–22.0 cm (measured); Neck height: 5.6 cm (measured); Wall thickness: 0.6–1.0 cm; Sample weight: 1,892 g; Original weight: 2,034 g; Volume: 4,446 cm³. Coordinates: (51.72, 17.37) (measured). Type: Pantano Impressed. Paste, temper, and firing: Reddish yellow paste (7.5YR6/6). Medium grain. A medium amount of calcite temper (0.1–1.2 mm diameter) and a medium amount of ferruginous temper (0.5–1.2 mm diameter). The paste is completely oxidized. Surface finish and decoration: Red slip on the exterior, including the base. Thin red slip on the interior neck. The exterior

body is polished, but the interior and exterior neck surfaces are smoothed. Notches and vertical incisions on the lip. Cross-and-dots stamps and triangular impressions below the neck-body juncture. Form: Small jar with outcurved neck and incurved base. Exterior-thickened rim and squared lip. Use-wear: The edge of the exterior base is heavily worn from use.

WVS No.: 23A-8; Catalog No.: 310165 (Figure 8.8a and 8.8b)
Bag No.: Rim: 1888 (42-3-2); Body: 1888; Base: 1888. Provenience: 23A42-3-2. Context: Floor. On the floor in front of the rear bench of the north room. Fragments were found together. Condition: Reconstructible (93% present). Slightly eroded. Part of the vessel is slightly darkened, probably from fire. Dimensions: Rim diameter: 5 cm (estimate); Maximum diameter: 10.5 cm (measured); Minimum opening 3.7 cm (measured); Height: 8.2 cm (estimate); Wall thickness: 0.4–0.8 cm; Sample weight: 277 g; Original weight: 298 g; Volume: 623 cm³. Coordinates: (53.72, 18.02) (measured). Type: Pantano Impressed. Paste, temper, and firing: Reddish yellow paste (5YR6/6). Medium grain. A medium amount of calcite temper (0.1–1.0 mm diameter) and a small amount of ferruginous temper (0.3–1.5 mm diameter). The paste is completely oxidized. Surface finish and decoration: Red slip on the entire exterior. Two lines of triangular impressions below the neck-body juncture. Form: Miniature jar with outcurved neck. The rim was not recovered. Slightly incurved base. Two strap handles. Use-wear: The exterior base is worn. No visible residues inside.

WVS No.: 23A-9; Catalog No.: 310166 (Figure 8.8d and 8.8e)
Bag No.: Rim: 851 (19-2-1); Body: 851; Base: 851. Provenience: 23A19-2-1. Context: Floor. In an area disturbed by a tree fall in the front part of the north room. Condition: Complete (98% present). Eroded and burned. Dimensions: Rim diameter: [exterior] 7.0 cm, [top] 6.8 cm (measured); Maximum diameter: 10.4 cm (measured); Minimum opening 3.7 cm (measured); Height: 10.0 cm (measured); Wall thickness: 0.4–0.6 cm; Sample weight: 236 g; Original weight: 241 g; Volume: 236 cm³. Coordinates: (51.53, 19.74) (estimate). Type: Pantano Impressed. Paste, temper, and firing: Reddish yellow paste (7.5YR7/6). Medium grain. A medium amount of calcite temper (0.1–1.0 mm diameter) and a small amount of ferruginous temper (0.3–1.0 mm diameter). The paste is

completely oxidized. Surface finish and decoration: Specular ferruginous red slip on the entire exterior. Two lines of triangular impressions below the neck-body juncture. Form: Miniature jar with outcurved neck. Direct rim and rounded lip. Incurved base. A small hole (0.8 cm diameter) on one side. The purpose of the hole is not clear. Use-wear: Not clear because of erosion. Red color in some parts of the interior. The vessel probably contained red pigment.

WVS No.: 23A-10; Catalog No.: 310277 (Figure 8.8f and 8.8g)
Bag No.: Rim: 1115 (18-3-2); Body: 1115; Base: 1115. Provenience: 23A18-3-2. Context: Floor. On the southern part of the room floor in front of the rear bench of the north room. All fragments were found in one concentration. Condition: Complete (98% present). Slightly eroded. Parts of the vessel are blackened from fire. Dimensions: Rim diameter: [exterior] 7.1 cm, [top] 6.9 cm (measured); Maximum diameter: 10.9 cm (measured); Minimum opening 4.2 cm (measured); Height: 10.6 cm (measured); Wall thickness: 0.6–0.8 cm; Sample weight: 228 g; Original weight: 233 g; Volume: 351 cm³. Coordinates: (51.26, 17.91) (measured). Type: Pantano Impressed. Paste, temper, and firing: Reddish yellow paste (7.5YR7/6). Medium grain. A medium amount of calcite temper (0.1–1.2 mm diameter) and a small amount of ferruginous temper (0.5–1.0 mm diameter). The paste is completely oxidized. Surface finish and decoration: Red slip on the entire exterior, including the base, and on the interior neck. The exterior body is polished, but the exterior and interior neck surfaces are smoothed. Two lines of punctuation below the neck-body juncture. Form: Miniature jar with outcurved neck. Direct rim and rounded lip. Incurved base. Use-wear: The edge of the base appears to be worn.

WVS No.: 23A-11; Catalog No.: 310301 (Figures 8.8h, 8.8i, and 8.60h)
Bag No.: Rim: 1275 (44-3-1); Body: 1275, 1272 (44-3-3); Base: 1275. Provenience: 23A44-3-1. Context: Floor. On the floor of the front porch of the north room. All fragments were found in one concentration. Condition: Reconstructible (85% present). Eroded. Some parts are blackened, probably from burning. Dimensions: Rim diameter: [exterior] 15.1 cm, [top] 14.6 cm (measured); Maximum diameter: 25.2 cm (measured); Minimum opening: 9.3 cm (measured); Height: 23.0 cm (measured); Neck height: 5.2 cm (measured); Wall thickness: 0.6–0.8 cm;

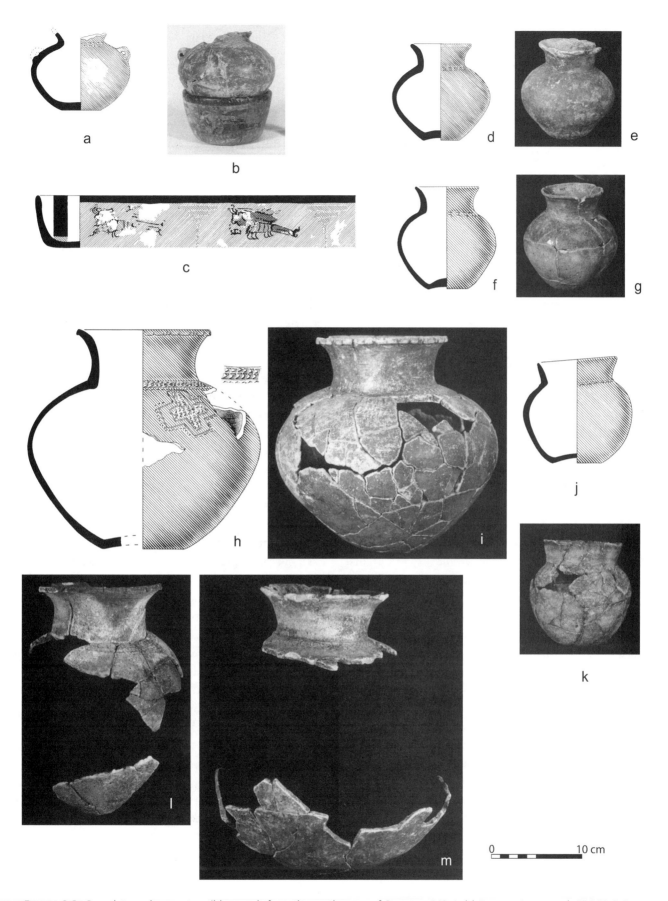

FIGURE 8.8. Complete and reconstructible vessels from the north room of Structure M8-4. (a) Pantano Impressed, 23A42-3-2, Cat. 310165, WVS 23A-8. (b) WVS 23A-8 and 23A-22 in the positions found during excavation. (c) Saxche-Palmar Polychrome, 23A42-3-2, Cat. 310159, WVS 23A-22. (d–m) Pantano Impressed. (d, e) 23A19-2-1, Cat. 310166, WVS 23A-9. (f, g) 23A18-3-2, Cat. 310277, WVS 23A-10. (h, i) 23A44-3-1, Cat. 310301, WVS 23A-11. (j, k) 23A17-3-2, Cat. 310310, WVS 23A-15. (l) 23A44-3-1, Cat. 310347, WVS 23A-12. (m) 23A44-3-1, Cat. 310357, WVS 23A-13.

Sample weight: 1,550 g; Original weight: 1,823 g; Volume: 5,066 cm³. Coordinates: (53.38, 20.69) (measured). Type: Pantano Impressed. Paste, temper, and firing: Pink paste (7.5YR8/4). Medium grain. A large amount of calcite temper (0.3–1.0 mm diameter) and a small amount of ferruginous temper (0.8–2.0 mm diameter). The paste is completely oxidized. Surface finish and decoration: Red slip over the entire exterior, including the base. The interior neck is also slipped. A series of cross-and-dots stamps and triangular punctuations below the neck-body juncture. Cross-shaped incised motif filled with stamps on two sides of the shoulder. Notched along the exterior rim. Form: Jar with outcurved neck. Exterior-thickened rim and squared lip. Incurved base. Use-wear: Edge of the exterior base is worn from use.

WVS No.: 23A-12; Catalog No.: 310347 (Figure 8.8l)
Bag No.: Rim: 1527 (44-3-1), 1275 (44-3-1); Body: 1527, 1003 (44-3-2); Base: 1527, 1002 (44-3-2). Provenience: 23A44-3-1. Context: Floor. On the front porch of the north room. Most fragments were found in one concentration. Condition: Reconstructible (50% present). Badly eroded. Some parts are blackened, probably from burning. Dimensions: Rim diameter: [exterior] 14.9 cm, [top] 14.5 cm (measured); Maximum diameter: 21 cm (estimate); Minimum opening: 9.5 cm (measured); Height: 23 cm (estimate); Neck height: 5.2 cm (measured); Wall thickness: 0.4–1.0 cm; Sample weight: 615 g; Original weight: 1,230 g; Volume: 3,499 cm³. Coordinates: (53.95, 21.32) (measured). Type: Pantano Impressed. Paste, temper, and firing: Reddish yellow paste (5YR7/6). Medium grain. A large amount of calcite temper (0.3–2.0 mm diameter) and a small amount of ferruginous temper (0.8–1.5 mm diameter). The paste is oxidized in most parts, but in the neck where the wall is thick, the core is slightly dark. Surface finish and decoration: Red slip on the exterior. The interior neck also appears to have been slipped. It is not clear whether the exterior base was slipped. Cross-and-dots stamps and triangular punctuations below the neck-body juncture. Notched on the exterior rim. Form: Jar with outcurved neck. Exterior-thickened rim and squared lip. Incurved base. Use-wear: Not clear because of erosion.

WVS No.: 23A-13; Catalog No.: 310357 (Figure 8.8m)
Bag No.: Rim: 1274 (44-3-3); Body: 1275 (44-3-1), 1285 (44-2-1), 245 (44-1-1), 1267 (44-3-3), 1292 (44-3-1); Base: 1275. Provenience: 23A44-3-1. Context: Floor. On the front porch of the north room. A significant portion was

found in one concentration. Other fragments were found in an area 1 × 1 m. Condition: Reconstructible (60% present). Some fragments are badly eroded, and others are better preserved. Some are darkened, but it is not clear whether it is due to burning. Dimensions: Rim diameter: [exterior] 13.6 cm, [top] 13.3 cm (measured); Maximum diameter: 36 cm (rough estimate); Minimum opening: 7.7 cm (measured); Height: 33 cm (rough estimate); Neck height: 4.4 cm (measured); Wall thickness: 0.5–0.7 cm; Sample weight: 2,324 g; Original weight: 3,873 g; Volume: 15,257 cm³. Coordinates: (53.11, 20.75) (measured). Type: Pantano Impressed. Paste, temper, and firing: Pink paste (7.5YR7/4). Medium grain. A large amount of calcite temper (0.1–1.0 mm diameter) and a small amount of ferruginous temper (0.8–2.0 mm diameter). The paste is completely oxidized. Surface finish and decoration: Red slip on the entire exterior, including the base. It is not clear whether the interior neck was slipped. Cross-hatch stamps and triangular punctuations below the neck-body juncture. Form: Jar with outcurved neck. Direct rim and rounded lip. Incurved base. Use-wear: Heavy along the edge of the exterior base.

WVS No.: 23A-14; Catalog No.: 310300 (Figures 8.9a, 8.9b, and 8.60i)
Bag No.: Rim: 1368 (43-3-3), 1825 (43-3-3); Body: 1825, 1170 (42-3-4), 1278 (43-2-1), 1368 (43-3-3), 158 (20-1-1), 155 (19-1-1), 1042 (19-2-1), 1416 (19-3-1); Base: 1825. Provenience: 23A43-3-3. Context: Floor. In the front part of the north room in front of the front bench. A significant portion of the vessel was found in one concentration. Other fragments were scattered in an area 2 × 3 m. Condition: Reconstructible (70% present). Eroded. Burned and darkened. Dimensions: Rim diameter: [exterior] 16.7 cm, [top] 16.2 cm (measured); Maximum diameter: 25.6 cm (measured); Minimum opening: 12.6 cm (measured); Height: 24.9 cm (measured); Neck height: 4.9 cm (measured); Wall thickness: 0.7–0.8 cm; Sample weight: 1,395 g; Original weight: 1,992 g; Volume: 6,974 cm³. Coordinates: (52.88, 18.65) (measured). Type: Pantano Impressed. Paste, temper, and firing: Red paste (2.5YR5/6). Medium grain. A large amount of calcite temper (0.3–1.5 mm diameter) and a small amount of ferruginous temper (0.5–2.0 mm diameter). The paste is completely oxidized. Surface finish and decoration: Red slip on the entire exterior, as well as on the exterior base and the interior neck. Triangular punctuations below the neck-body junction. On the shoulder there are incisions defining a rectangular area filled with X-and-dots stamps and cross-and-dots stamps.

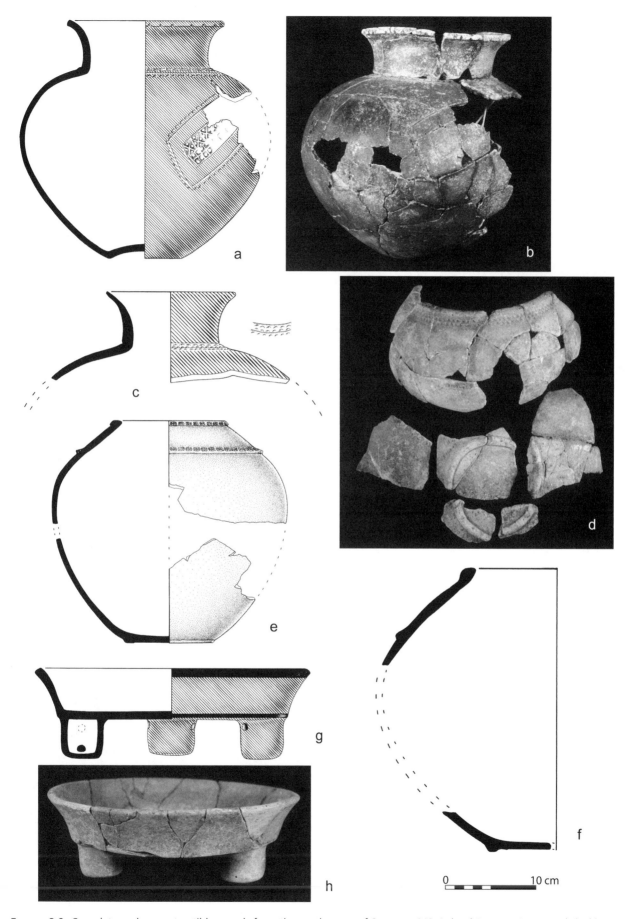

FIGURE 8.9. Complete and reconstructible vessels from the north room of Structure M8-4. (a–c) Pantano Impressed. (a, b) 23A43-3-3, Cat. 310300, WVS 23A-14. (c) 23A44-3-1, Cat. 310370, WVS 23A-16. (d–f) Chaquiste Impressed. (d) 23A33-3-3, Cat. 310349, WVS 23A-18. (e) 23A44-3-1, Cat. 310361, WVS 23A-19. (f) 23A33-3-2, Cat. 310421, WVS 23A-20. (g, h) Saxche-Palmar Polychrome, 23A17-3-1, Cat. 310275, WVS 23A-23.

Notches on the thickened exterior rim. Form: Jar with outcurved neck. Exterior-thickened rim and squared lip. Incurved base. Use-wear: Heavy along the edge of the exterior base.

WVS No.: 23A-15; Catalog No.: 310310 (Figure 8.8j and 8.8k)
Bag No.: Rim: 1147 (17-3-2); Body: 1147; Base: 1147. Provenience: 23A17-3-2. Context: Floor. In the southern part of the rear bench of the north room. Fragments were found in one concentration. Condition: Reconstructible (90% present). Badly eroded. Burned, and some parts are darkened. Dimensions: Rim diameter: [exterior] 8.7 cm, [top] 8.5 cm (measured); Maximum diameter: 11.7 cm (measured); Minimum opening: 5.7 cm (measured); Height: 10.8 cm (measured); Neck height: 2.3 cm (measured); Wall thickness: 0.4–0.7 cm; Sample weight: 308 g; Original weight: 342 g; Volume: 492 cm^3. Coordinates: (51.92, 15.99) (measured). Type: Pantano Impressed. Paste, temper, and firing: Reddish yellow paste (5YR6/6). Medium grain. A medium amount of calcite temper (0.1–1.2 mm diameter). The paste is completely oxidized. Surface finish and decoration: Red slip on the exterior. It is not clear whether the interior neck and the exterior base were slipped. Triangular punctuations below the neck-body juncture. Form: Jar with outflared neck. Direct rim and rounded lip. Incurved base. Use-wear: Not clear because of erosion.

WVS No.: 23A-16; Catalog No.: 310370 (Figures 8.9c and 8.60j)
Bag No.: Rim: 1275 (44-3-1), 1292 (44-3-1); Body: 1275; Base: 1527 (44-3-1). Provenience: 23A44-3-1. Context: Floor. On the front porch in front of the north room. Most of the recovered fragments were found in one concentration. Condition: Reconstructible (50% present). Eroded. Burned, and some fragments are blackened. Dimensions: Rim diameter: [exterior] 14.1 cm, [top] 13.8 cm (measured); Maximum diameter: 30 cm (estimate); Minimum opening: 8.0 cm (measured); Height: 31 cm (rough estimate); Neck height: 5.7 cm (measured); Wall thickness: 0.5–0.7 cm; Sample weight: 1,538 g; Original weight: 3,076 g; Volume: 9,813 cm^3. Coordinates: (53.25, 21.00) (measured). Type: Pantano Impressed. Paste, temper, and firing: Pink paste (5YR7/4). Medium grain. A medium amount of calcite temper (0.5–3.0 mm diameter) and a small amount of ferruginous temper (0.8–2.0 mm diameter). The paste is completely oxidized. Surface finish and

decoration: Red slip on the exterior. It is not clear whether the exterior base and the interior neck were slipped. Triangular punctuations below the neck-body juncture. Form: Jar with outcurved neck. Direct rim and squared lip. A large part of base is missing. Use-wear: Not clear because of erosion.

WVS No.: 23A-17; Catalog No.: 310360
Bag No.: Rim: 1009 (44-3-4), 1013 (44-3-4); Body: 1009, 1013, 1242 (20-3-3). Provenience: 23A44-3-4. Context: Floor. On the patio floor in front of the north room. Most fragments were found in one concentration. The vessel is broken into small pieces, and many small fragments were probably not recovered in the field. Condition: Reconstructible (50% present). Eroded. Some parts appear to have been burned. Dimensions: Rim diameter: 10 cm (rough estimate); Maximum diameter: 19 cm (rough estimate); Height: 20 cm (rough estimate); Neck height: 4.2 cm (measured); Wall thickness: 0.5–0.6 cm; Sample weight: 672 g; Original weight: 1,344 g; Volume: 2,878 cm^3. Coordinates: (52.45, 21.99) (measured). Type: Tinaja undetermined. Paste, temper, and firing: Red paste (2.5YR5/6). Medium grain. A large amount of calcite temper (0.1–0.3 mm diameter) and a small amount of ferruginous temper (0.5–2.0 mm diameter). The paste is completely oxidized. The paste is redder and slightly coarser than common Tinaja Red/Pantano Impressed paste. Surface finish and decoration: Red slip on the exterior. No recognizable incisions. Form: Whistle pitcher with globular body and vertical neck. Open spout. Whistle handle. Use-wear: Not clear because of the fragmentary state of the vessel.

WVS No.: 23A-18; Catalog No.: 310349 (Figure 8.8d)
Bag No.: Rim: 949 (33-3-3), 934 (33-3-2); Body: 949, 934, 206 (33-1-1), 944 (33-3-4), 931 (33-3-1); Base: 949, 931, 206. Provenience: 23A33-3-3. Context: Floor. On the patio floor in front of the north room. Most fragments were found in an area 1 × 1 m. Some fragments are relatively large and do not seem to have been tramped over; thus, they are probably not trash thrown in the patio. Missing fragments may be in unexcavated areas. Condition: Reconstructible (50% present). Many sherds are badly eroded. Traces of burning are not clear. Dimensions: Rim diameter: [interior] 13.8 cm, [top] 14.4 cm (measured); Maximum diameter: 21 cm (estimate); Height: 15 cm (measured); Wall thickness: 0.7–0.8 cm; Sample weight: 554 g; Original weight: 1,108 g; Volume: 2,655 cm^3. Coor-

dinates: (54.92, 22.99) (measured). Type: Chaquiste Impressed. Paste, temper, and firing: Reddish yellow paste (5YR7/6). Medium grain. A medium amount of calcite temper (0.1–1.2 mm diameter) and a small amount of ferruginous temper (0.8–1.5 mm diameter). The paste is completely oxidized. Surface finish and decoration: Red slip on the entire exterior except the base. Triangular punctuations below the rim. The interior is smoothed but not slipped. Form: Bowl with markedly incurved sides and restricted orifice. Exterior-thickened rim and rounded lip. Ring base. Use-wear: Part of the interior base is blackened, and red material is attached. It is not clear whether this red material is the remains of pigment stored or mixed in this vessel or whether it was attached to the sherds postdepositionally.

WVS No.: 23A-19; Catalog No.: 310361 (Figures 8.9e and 8.60k)
Bag No.: Rim: 1290 (44-3-1), 1288 (44-2-1); Body: 1290, 1688; Base: 1290. Provenience: 23A44-3-1. Context: Floor. On the front porch of the north room. Most fragments were found in one concentration. Condition: Reconstructible (90% present). Badly eroded. It is darkened, probably because of burning. The vessel may have been placed on the floor. Dimensions: Rim diameter: [interior] 13.5 cm, [top] 14.3 cm (measured); Maximum diameter: 29 cm (estimate); Height: 23.6 cm (measured); Wall thickness: 0.7–1.1 cm; Sample weight: 2,213 g; Original weight: 2,459 g; Volume: 9,741 cm³. Coordinates: (53.72, 21.00) (measured). Type: Chaquiste Impressed. Paste, temper, and firing: Pink paste (7.5YR8/4). Coarse grain. A very large amount of calcite temper (0.3–1.2 mm diameter) and a very small amount of ferruginous temper (0.5–2.0 mm diameter). The paste is completely oxidized. Surface finish and decoration: Some remains of red slip on the exterior, including the rim, the upper body above the ridge, the ridge, and the lower body below the ridge. X-and-dots stamps on the ridge. Slightly smaller stamps of the same motif on the exterior-thickened rim, unlike common Chaquiste Impressed vessels, which have stamps below the thickened rim. Form: Bowl with markedly incurved sides and restricted orifice. Exterior-thickened rim and rounded lip. Subtle ring base. Use-wear: Not clear because of erosion.

WVS No.: 23A-20; Catalog No.: 310421 (Figure 8.9f)
Bag No.: Rim: 934 (33-3-2), 931 (33-3-1); Body: 934, 931, 949 (33-3-3), 944 (33-3-4), 206 (33-1-1), 1013 (44-3-4); Base: 934. Provenience: 23A33-3-2. Context: Floor. On the patio floor in front of the north room. Most fragments were found in an area 1 × 2 m. Missing pieces may be in unexcavated areas. The vessel may have originally been placed on the platform northeast of Structure M8-4, or it may have fallen from the Palace Group. Condition: Reconstructible (30% present). Badly eroded. Some fragments are blackened, but it is not clear whether the vessel was burned. Dimensions: Rim diameter: 38 cm (rough estimate); Maximum diameter: 60 cm (rough estimate); Height: 33 cm (rough estimate); Wall thickness: 0.8–0.9 cm; Sample weight: 3,355 g; Original weight: 11,183 g; Volume: 58,450 cm³. Coordinates: (55.69, 23.28) (estimate). Type: Chaquiste Impressed. Paste, temper, and firing: Pink paste (7.5YR7/4). Medium grain. A large amount of calcite temper (0.1–1.0 mm diameter) and a very small amount of ferruginous temper (0.5–0.8 mm diameter). The paste is completely oxidized. Surface finish and decoration: The surface is mostly eroded, but there are some remains of red slip on the exterior wall above the ridge and on the interior surface. The ridge appears to have been stamped, but the motif is not clear. Form: Bowl with markedly incurved sides and restricted orifice. Exterior-thickened rim and rounded lip. Ring base. Use-wear: Not clear because of erosion.

WVS No.: 23A-21; Catalog No.: 310419
Bag No.: Rim: 1002 (44-3-2), 934 (33-3-2); Body: 1002; Base: 1002, 1013 (44-3-4). Provenience: 23A44-3-2. Context: Floor. On the patio floor right in front of the step of the front porch of the north room. Condition: Reconstructible (80% present). Most fragments are badly eroded, but some parts are relatively well preserved. The exterior base and parts of the lower body are blackened, probably from burning. Dimensions: Rim diameter: 43 cm (rough estimate); Maximum diameter: 68 cm (rough estimate); Height: 47 cm (rough estimate); Wall thickness: 0.8–1.2 cm; Sample weight: 7,613 g; Original weight: 9,516 g; Volume: 96,661 cm³. Coordinates: (53.20, 21.85) (measured). Type: Chaquiste Impressed. Paste, temper, and firing: Reddish yellow paste (5YR6/6). Coarse grain. A large amount of calcite temper (0.2–1.0 mm diameter) and a small amount of ferruginous temper (0.8–1.5 mm diameter). The paste is completely oxidized. Surface finish and decoration: Red slip on the exterior surface above the ridge and on the entire interior. Cross-and-dots stamps below the thickened rim and on the ridge. Form: Bowl with markedly incurved sides and restricted orifice.

Exterior-thickened rim and rounded lip. Ridge below the rim. Ring base. Use-wear: Not clear because of erosion. The ring base appears to be worn.

WVS No.: 23A-22; Catalog No.: 310159 (Figures 8.8b and 8.8c)
Bag No.: Rim: 1887 (42-3-2); Body: 1887; Base: 1887. Provenience: 23A42-3-2. Context: Floor. On the floor in front of the rear bench of the north room. All fragments were found in one concentration near the wall of the front bench. Condition: Reconstructible (98% present). Relatively well preserved. Part of the exterior wall is slightly darkened from fire. Dimensions: Rim diameter: [exterior] 9.7 cm, [top] 9.3 cm (measured); Height: 4.3 cm (measured); Wall thickness: 0.7 cm; Sample weight: 156 g; Original weight: 159 g; Volume: 167 cm^3. Coordinates: (53.68, 18.02) (measured). Type: Saxche-Palmar Polychrome. Paste, temper, and firing: Very pale brown paste (10YR7/4). Fine. A small amount of calcite temper (0.3–0.5 mm diameter) and a very small amount of shiny, glass-like particles (0.1 mm length). The paste is completely oxidized. Surface finish and decoration: The interior and exterior are well polished. Black paint on the interior wall and exterior rim. Red paint on the interior base. Two designs of fish or insects in red, black, and white paints over orange slip on the exterior wall. The exterior base is not slipped. The vessel does not seem to have underslip. Form: Open bowl with flared sides and flat base. Direct rim and rounded lip. Use-wear: The exterior base appears to be slightly worn. The interior is not worn.

WVS No.: 23A-23; Catalog No.: 310275 (Figure 8.9g and 8.9h)
Bag No.: Rim: 1148 (17-3-1), 853 (17-2-1); Body: 1148, 853; Base: 1148, 853. Provenience: 23A17-3-1. Context: Floor. On the bench surface of the north room, near the back wall along the center axis of the room. Half the vessel was found in one concentration on the bench, and the other half was in the wall-fall layer. The vessel was probably stored in a higher location. Condition: Reconstructible (98% present). Eroded. Part of the vessel is darkened from fire. Dimensions: Rim diameter: [exterior] 30.0 cm, [top] 29.1 cm (measured); Height: 9.1 cm (measured); Height without feet: 5.3 cm (measured); Wall thickness: 0.8–1.0 cm; Sample weight: 1,395 g; Original weight: 1,423 g; Volume: 1,795 cm^3. Coordinates: (51.91, 15.22) (measured). Type: Saxche-Palmar Polychrome. Paste, temper, and firing: Light brown paste (7.5YR6/4). Fine.

A small amount of white temper (0.3–1.3 mm diameter) and a small amount of shiny, glass-like particles (0.1 mm length). The paste and temper do not react to weak acid. The paste appears slightly different from that of common Saxche-Palmar Polychrome. The paste is completely oxidized. Surface finish and decoration: The surface is mostly eroded. The entire vessel appears to have cream underslip. Red slip on the exterior, including the base and feet. Black paint on the rim and above the wall-base juncture on the exterior. Remains of red paint on the interior. Form: Plate with slightly outcurved sides and flat base. Direct rim and flat lip. Three hollow cylinder feet with two round openings and a rattle. Use-wear: The feet are worn. Use-wear on the interior is not clear because of erosion.

WVS No.: 23A-24; Catalog No.: 310322 (Figure 8.10a and 8.10b)
Bag No.: Rim: 1773 (42-3-4), 1117 (18-3-4), 1426 (42-3-2); Body: 1773, 1426, 1066 (20-2-1), 1170 (42-3-4); Base: 1773. Provenience: 23A42-3-4. Context: Floor. On the floor in front of the back bench of the north room. A significant portion of the vessel was found in one concentration. Other fragments were found in an area 3 × 1 m. Condition: Reconstructible (75% present). Badly eroded. Severely burned and reoxidized. The burning caused many fragments to break off. Dimensions: Rim diameter: 12.8 cm (estimate); Height: 23.2 cm (measured); Wall thickness: 0.4–0.6 cm; Sample weight: 846 g; Original weight: 1,128 g; Volume: 2,169 cm^3. Coordinates: (53.00, 17.52) (measured). Type: Saxche-Palmar Polychrome. Paste, temper, and firing: Red paste (2.5YR6/6). Fine grain. A small amount of calcite temper (0.3–0.5 mm diameter). The paste is completely oxidized. Surface finish and decoration: The surface is mostly eroded, but there are remains of red paint and black lines over orange slip. Black bland over the lip. Form: Cylinder vase with vertical sides. Direct rim and rounded lip. Flat base. Use-wear: Not clear because of erosion.

WVS No.: 23A-25; Catalog No.: 310345 (Figure 8.10c)
Bag No.: Rim: 1255 (18-3-3), 1117 (18-3-4), 204 (46-1-1); Body: 152 (18-1-1); Base: 1255, 1117, 1049 (18-2-2). Provenience: 23A18-3-3. Context: Floor. On the bench surface of the north room near the room division with the central room and in the area in front of the bench. Most fragments were found in an area 1 × 1.5 m. The vessel was probably stored on the bench or a higher location near the room division. Condition: Reconstructible (85%

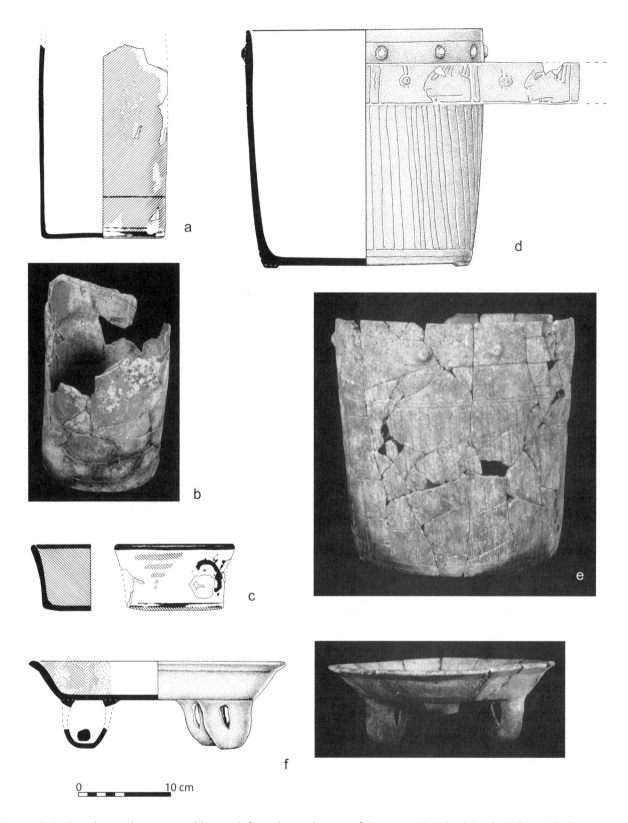

FIGURE 8.10. Complete and reconstructible vessels from the north room of Structure M8-4. (a–c) Saxche-Palmar Polychrome. (a, b) 23A42-3-4, Cat. 310322, WVS 23A-24. (c) 23A18-3-3, Cat. 310345, WVS 23A-25. (d, e) Corozal Incised, 23A19-3-1, Cat. 310223, WVS 23A-28. (f) Saxche-Palmar Polychrome, 23A44-3-1, Cat. 310327, WVS 23A-26.

present). Eroded. Severely burned and darkened. The vessel was broken by heat. Dimensions: Rim diameter: [exterior] 13.0 cm, [top] 12.3 cm (measured); Height: 6.7 cm (measured); Wall thickness: 0.4–0.7 cm; Sample weight: 264 g; Original weight: 311 g; Volume: 427 cm³. Coordinates: (50.50, 16.51) (measured). Type: Saxche-Palmar Polychrome. Paste, temper, and firing: Reddish yellow paste (7.5YR7/6). Fine grain. A small amount of calcite temper (0.1–0.5 mm diameter). The paste is completely oxidized. Surface finish and decoration: Black band on the rim. Black and red paint on orange background on the exterior. Two images, probably of fish. Red radiating stripes on the interior base. Form: Bowl with slightly outcurved sides. Direct rim and rounded lip. Flat base. Use-wear: None clear.

WVS No.: 23A-26; Catalog No.: 310327 (Figure 8.10f)
Bag No.: Rim: 1291 (44-3-1), 1526 (32-3-3), 207 (32-1-1), 1267 (44-3-3), 206 (32-1-1), 1001 (32-3-4); Body: 1291; Base: 1291, 1001, 259 (45-1-1), 1526, 207. Provenience: 23A44-3-1. Context: Floor. On the front porch in front of the north room. Most fragments were found in one concentration. Condition: Reconstructible (90% present). Eroded. Burned, and a part is blackened. Dimensions: Rim diameter: [exterior] 28.4 cm, [top] 27.7 cm (measured); Height: 9.4 cm (measured); Height without feet: 4.2 cm (measured); Wall thickness: 0.7–0.8 cm; Sample weight: 969 g; Original weight: 1,076 g; Volume: 1,368 cm³. Coordinates: (53.40, 21.28) (measured). Type: Saxche-Palmar Polychrome. Paste, temper, and firing: Reddish yellow paste (7.5YR7/6). Fine grain. A medium amount of calcite temper (0.1–0.5 mm diameter) and a small amount of ferruginous temper (0.3–1.0 mm diameter). The paste is completely oxidized. Surface finish and decoration: There are some remains of red and black paints over orange slip on the interior surface. There are no recognizable remains of slip on the exterior. Form: Plate with outflared sides. Outflared everted rim and rounded lip. Flat base. Use-wear: Not clear because of erosion.

WVS No.: 23A-27; Catalog No.: 310479
Bag No.: Rim: 245 (44-1-1), 1292 (44-3-1), 1267 (44-3-3), 1002 (44-3-2), 1241 (20-3-1), 1013 (44-3-4); Body: 245, 998 (20-3-2), 1267, 1241, 207; Base: 245, 207 (32-1-1), 1292, 1267. Provenience: 23A44-3-2. Context: Floor. On the front porch of the north room. Most fragments were found in an area 1 × 1 m. The vessel may have been stored in a higher

location. Condition: Reconstructible (50% present). Badly eroded. It appears to be burned and reoxidized. Dimensions: Rim diameter: 29 cm (estimate); Height: 10 cm (estimate); Height without feet: 4.3 cm (measured); Wall thickness: 0.6–0.8 cm; Sample weight: 959 g; Original weight: 1,918 g; Volume: 1,456 cm³. Coordinates: (52.69, 21.18) (estimate). Type: Saxche-Palmar Polychrome. Paste, temper, and firing: Reddish yellow paste (5YR7/8). Fine grain. A small amount of calcite temper (0.1–0.5 mm diameter) and a small amount of ferruginous temper (0.5–2.0 mm diameter). The paste is completely oxidized. Surface finish and decoration: The surface is completely eroded. Form: Plate with slightly outcurved sides. Direct rim and rounded lip. Flat base. Three hollow oven feet with two openings and a rattle. Use-wear: Not clear because of erosion.

WVS No.: 23A-28; Catalog No.: 310223 (Figure 8.10d and 8.10e)
Bag No.: Rim: 1379 (19-3-1); Body: 1379, 235 (43-1-1), 1042 (19-2-1), 155 (19-1-1), 1368 (43-3-3), 1278 (43-2-1), 1375 (43-3-3), 1170 (42-3-4), 1041 (19-3-2), 152 (18-1-1); Base: 1379. Provenience: 23A19-3-1. Context: Floor. In the front area of the north room along its central axis (along the division of Units 19 and 43). Most fragments were found in one concentration. Condition: Reconstructible (80% present). Eroded. Although the presence of fire clouds from the original firing makes the recognition of traces of burning difficult, some parts of the rim appear to be burned. The interior is also darkened, possibly from fire. Dimensions: Rim diameter: [exterior] 26.0 cm, [top] 25.7 cm (measured); Height: 25.2 cm (measured); Wall thickness: 0.6–1.2 cm; Sample weight: 2,218 g; Original weight: 2,773 g; Volume: 8,359 cm³. Coordinates: (51.91, 18.74) (measured). Type: Corozal Incised. Paste, temper, and firing: Light brown paste (7.5YR6/4). Medium grain. A large amount of calcite temper (0.3–1.0 mm diameter) and a small amount of ferruginous temper (0.5–1.5 mm diameter). The paste is completely oxidized. The exterior and a section of the lower body are blackened from the original firing (the black surface on the base and feet is worn from use). Surface finish and decoration: The entire exterior, except the base, has red slip. Incised motifs below the rim, including faces, vertical lines, and zigzag lines. Vertical incised lines below them. Nubbins (possibly eight) below the rim. No red slip in incised lines. It appears that the exterior was slipped and then incised while the clay was still soft. Form:

Vase with slightly flaring sides with flat base. Direct rim and rounded lip. Four small nubbin feet. Use-wear: The center of the base and the feet are worn from use.

WVS No.: 23A-29; Catalog No.: 310224 (Figure 8.11a)
Bag No.: Rim: 1657 (18-3-4); Body: 1657; Base: 1657. Provenience: 23A18-3-4. Context: Floor. In a disturbed area in front of the bench of the north room where the room partition with the central room used to be. Condition: Complete (100% present). Eroded. Burned (some parts are darkened and some parts are oxidized). Dimensions: Rim diameter: [exterior] 3.0 cm, [top] 2.8 cm (measured); Maximum diameter: 5.4 cm (measured); Height: 5.1 cm (measured); Wall thickness: 0.4–0.5 cm; Sample weight: 53 g; Original weight: 53 g; Volume: 52 cm³. Coordinates: (50.10, 17.22) (measured). Type: Corozal Incised. Paste, temper, and firing: Reddish yellow paste (7.5YR6/6). Medium grain. A medium amount of calcite temper (0.2–0.8 mm diameter). Because the vessel is complete, it is not clear whether the paste is oxidized. Surface finish and decoration: It appears to have had red slip on the entire exterior, including the base. Horizontal band of very fine incisions on the upper body. Form: Miniature jar with outflared neck. Direct rim and squared lip. Slightly incurved base. Use-wear: Not clear because of erosion.

WVS No.: 23A-30; Catalog No.: 310286 (Figure 8.11b)
Bag No.: Rim: 1375 (43-3-3), 1071 (42-2-2), 259 (45-1-1), 1278 (43-2-1); Body: 1071, 1260 (42-3-3), 1117 (18-3-4), 1375, 240 (42-1-1), 235 (43-1-1); Base: 1267 (44-3-3), 1259 (42-3-1), 240. Provenience: 23A43-3-3. Context: Floor. In the front area of the north room in front of the front bench. Fragments were found in an area 1 × 4 m, including the wall-fall layer. It is probable that the vessel was originally placed on the front bench or in a higher location. Condition: Reconstructible (90% present). Badly eroded. Severely burned in reddish color. Dimensions: Rim diameter: [exterior] 11.1 cm, [top] 10.9 cm (measured); Height: 13.0 cm (measured); Wall thickness: 0.4–0.8 cm; Sample weight: 274 g; Original weight: 304 g; Volume: 826 cm³. Coordinates: (52.39, 18.90) (estimate). Type: Salada Fluted. Paste, temper, and firing: Reddish yellow paste (5YR6/8). Fine, compact, and hard. A small amount of white particles (0.5–1.0 mm diameter). The paste and temper do not react to weak acid. The paste is completely oxidized. Surface finish and decoration: The surface is mostly eroded. Remains of orange slip on the entire exterior, including the exte-

rior base, and on the upper interior wall. Vertical (slightly slanted) flutes on the body, and horizontal grooves below the rim. Form: Vase with vertical sides and slightly incurved base. Exterior-thickened rim and rounded rim. Use-wear: The base is worn.

WVS No.: 23A-31; Catalog No.: 310318 (Figure 8.11d)
Bag No.: Rim: 1097 (41-3-4); Body: 1097; Base: 1097. Provenience: 23A41-3-4. Context: Floor. On the bench (near its center) of the north room. Most fragments were found in one concentration. Condition: Reconstructible (70% present). Relatively well preserved. It is not clear whether the vessel is burned. Dimensions: Rim diameter: 15 cm (estimate); Height: 13.8 cm (measured); Wall thickness: 0.3–0.5 cm; Sample weight: 380 g; Original weight: 542 g; Volume: 1,177 cm³. Coordinates: (52.14, 15.56) (measured). Type: Chablekal Gray. Paste, temper, and firing: Yellow paste (10YR7/6). Fine grain. A small amount of rectangular black and white inclusions (0.5 mm length). The paste is completely oxidized. Surface finish and decoration: Black slip over the entire exterior and interior surface. Horizontal bands with grooving in the midsection and at the bottom. Form: Vase with outcurved sides. Exterior-thickened rim and rounded lip. Flat base. Use-wear: None clearly recognizable.

WVS No.: 23A-32; Catalog No.: 310363 (Figure 8.11c)
Bag No.: Rim: 1259 (42-3-1), 1070 (42-2-2), 1260 (42-3-3), 1254 (18-3-1); Body: 1259, 240 (42-1-1), 1260, 1070, 1646 (43-3-5); Base: 1259, 240, 1646. Provenience: 23A42-3-1. Context: Floor. On the rear bench of the north room. Fragments were found in an area 2 × 1 m. The vessel was probably stored in a high location and fell. Some small fragments were probably not recovered in the field. Condition: Reconstructible (30% present). Eroded. Severely burned and reoxidized. Dimensions: Rim diameter: 15 cm (estimate); Height: 13 cm (rough estimate); Wall thickness: 0.4–0.5 cm; Sample weight: 160 g; Original weight: 533 g; Volume: 1,033 cm³. Coordinates: (53.20, 16.34) (estimate). Type: Chablekal Gray. Paste, temper, and firing: Gray paste (7.5YR6/1). Fine grain. A very small amount of quartz temper (0.3–0.7 mm length) and a small amount of volcanic ash temper (0.1 mm length). The paste is completely oxidized. Many fragments are burned into light red (10R6/8). Surface finish and decoration: Remains of black slip on the exterior wall. Some vertical incisions near the base. Form: Bowl with outcurved sides.

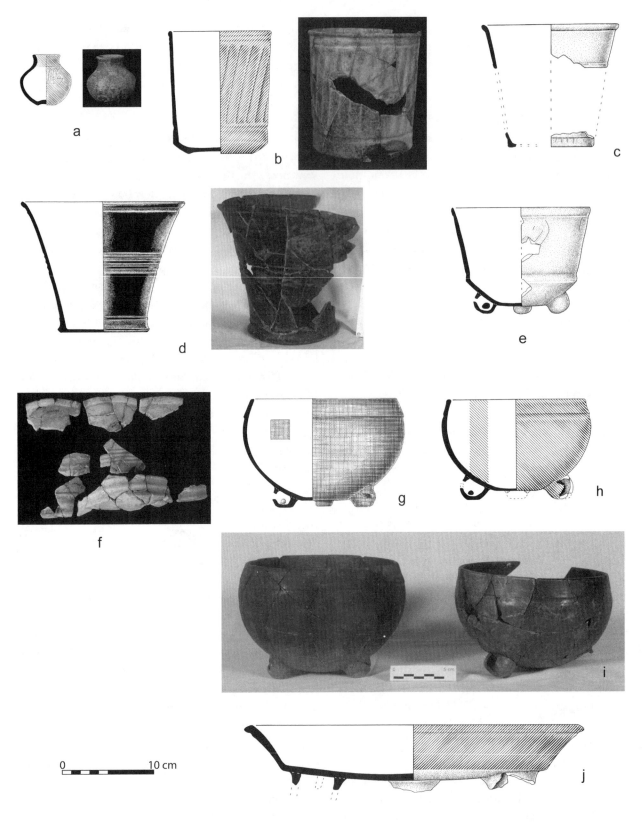

FIGURE 8.11. Complete and reconstructible vessels from the north room of Structure M8-4. (a) Corozal Incised, 23A18-3-4, Cat. 310224, WVS 23A-29. (b) Salada Fluted, 23A43-3-3, Cat. 310286, WVS 23A-30. (c–f) Chablekal Gray. (c) 23A42-3-1, Cat. 310363, WVS 23A-32. (d) 23A41-3-4, Cat. 310318, WVS 23A-31. (e) 23A17-3-1, Cat. 310351, WVS 23A-33. (f) 23A41-3-4, Cat. 310354, WVS 23A-35. (g–j) Unnamed volcanic ash undetermined. (g) 23A41-3-4, Cat. 310225, WVS 23A-37. (h) 23A18-3-3, Cat. 310284, WVS 23A-38. (i) WVS 23A-37 and 23A-38. (j) 23A42-3-4, Cat. 310278, WVS 23A-39.

Exterior-thickened rim and rounded lip. Flat base. Use-wear: Not clear because of erosion.

WVS No.: 23A-33; Catalog No.: 310351 (Figure 8.11e)
Bag No.: Rim: 1184 (17-3-1), 1128 (41-3-4), 1260 (42-3-3); Body: 1184; Base: 1184. Provenience: 23A17-3-1. Context: Floor. On the back bench of the north room near the back wall. Most fragments were found in one concentration. Condition: Reconstructible (65% present). Badly eroded. Severely burned. Dimensions: Rim diameter: 13 cm (estimate); Height: 9.5 cm (measured); Height without feet: 8.7 cm (measured); Wall thickness: 0.4–0.5 cm; Sample weight: 210 g; Original weight: 323 g; Volume: 386 cm³. Coordinates: (51.91, 14.91) (measured). Type: Chicxulub Incised. Paste, temper, and firing: Light gray paste (7.5YR7/1). Fine grain. A very small amount of quartz temper (0.3 mm length) and a very small amount of volcanic ash temper (0.1 mm length). The paste is completely oxidized. Some pieces are burned into light red (10R7/8). Surface finish and decoration: Incisions on the exterior wall, probably depicting monkeys. No remains of slip. Form: Bowl with outflared sides. Exterior-thickened rim and rounded lip. Rounded base. Slight Z-angle along the wall-base juncture. Three hollow hemispherical feet with one opening and a rattle. Use-wear: Not clear because of erosion.

WVS No.: 23A-34; Catalog No.: 310352
Bag No.: Rim: 1129 (41-3-1); Body: 1129, 1130 (41-3-1); Base: 1129. Provenience: 23A41-3-1. Context: Floor. On the back bench of the north room near the back wall. Most fragments were found in one concentration. It is broken into many small pieces, and some may not have been recovered in the field. The vessel may have fallen from a higher location where it was stored. Condition: Reconstructible (40% present). Badly eroded and severely burned. Dimensions: Rim diameter: 14 cm (estimate); Maximum diameter: 15 cm (estimate); Height: 10 cm (rough estimate); Wall thickness: 0.4–0.5 cm; Sample weight: 119 g; Original weight: 298 g; Volume: 949 cm³. Coordinates: (53.60, 14.88) (measured). Type: Chablekal Gray. Paste, temper, and firing: Light gray paste (7.5YR7/1). Fine grain. A small amount of ferruginous temper (0.3 mm diameter) and a very small amount of volcanic ash temper. The paste is completely oxidized. Some pieces are burned into red (2.5YR6/8). Surface finish and decoration: No remains of slip. Form: Bowl with incurved wall. Direct rim and rounded lip. Flat base. Use-wear: Not clear because of erosion.

WVS No.: 23A-35; Catalog No.: 310354 (Figure 8.11f)
Bag No.: Rim: 1128 (41-3-4), 1129 (41-3-1); Body: 1128, 1129; Base: 1129. Provenience: 23A41-3-4. Context: Floor. On the bench of the north room. Half the fragments were found in one concentration; others were scattered in an area 0.8 × 0.8 m. It is probable that the vessel fell from a higher location. Condition: Reconstructible (30% present). Eroded. Burned and reoxidized. The burning made the vessel brittle, and thus many small fragments were probably not recovered in the field. Dimensions: Rim diameter: 15 cm (estimate); Height: 13 cm (rough estimate); Wall thickness: 0.5 cm; Sample weight: 172 g; Original weight: 573 g; Volume: 740 cm³. Coordinates: (53.05, 15.49) (measured). Type: Chablekal Gray. Paste, temper, and firing: Light gray paste (7.5YR7/1). Fine grain. A small amount of ferruginous temper (0.2 mm diameter), a very small amount of calcite temper (0.2–0.5 mm diameter), and a very small amount of volcanic ash temper (0.1 mm length). The paste is completely oxidized. Many fragments are burned into reddish yellow color (7.5YR7/6). Surface finish and decoration: Some remains of black slip on the exterior. Horizontal bands with groovings on the exterior wall and above the base. Form: Bowl with out-curved sides. Exterior-thickened rim and rounded lip. Flat base. Use-wear: Not clear because of erosion.

WVS No.: 23A-36; Catalog No.: 310355
Bag No.: Rim: 1306 (44-3-1); Body: 1306; Base: 1306. Provenience: 23A44-3-1. Context: Floor. On the front porch of the north room. The recovered fragments were found in one concentration. Condition: Reconstructible (20% present). Eroded. Severely burned and reoxidized. Many fragments are extremely small, and many were probably not recovered in the field. Dimensions: Rim diameter: 13 cm (estimate); Height: 10 cm (rough estimate); Height without feet: 8.5 cm (rough estimate); Wall thickness: 0.4–0.6 cm; Sample weight: 82 g; Original weight: 410 g; Volume: 291 cm³. Coordinates: (53.69, 20.83) (measured). Type: Chicxulub Incised. Paste, temper, and firing: Light gray paste (7.5YR7/1). Fine grain. A very small amount of ferruginous temper (0.2 mm diameter), a very small amount of quartz temper (0.5 mm length), and a very small amount of volcanic ash temper (0.1 mm length). The core of the paste is slightly dark. Some fragments are burned into reddish yellow (7.5YR7/8). Surface finish and decoration: Incisions on the exterior wall, probably depicting monkeys. Two horizontal grooves below the rim. No remains of slip. Form: Bowl with outflared sides. Direct rim and rounded lip. Rounded base. Probably three

hollow hemispherical feet with one opening and a rattle. Use-wear: Not clear because of erosion.

WVS No.: 23A-37; Catalog No.: 310225 (Figure 8.11g and 8.11i)

Bag No.: Rim: 1096 (41-3-4); Body: 1096; Base: 1096. Provenience: 23A41-3-4. Context: Floor. Near the center of the rear bench of the north room. All fragments were found in one concentration. It is not clear whether the vessel was placed on the bench surface or fell from a higher location. Condition: Reconstructible (95% present). Relatively well preserved. Part of the upper body and part of the rim are blackened, which may have been caused by fire at the time of abandonment. Dimensions: Rim diameter: [interior] 14.9 cm, [top] 15.2 cm (measured); Maximum diameter: 17.6 cm (measured); Height: 11.5 cm (measured); Height without feet: 10.9 cm (measured); Wall thickness: 0.4–0.6 cm; Sample weight: 470 g; Original weight: 495 g; Volume: 1,000 cm^3. Coordinates: (52.57, 15.66) (measured). Type: Unnamed volcanic ash undetermined. Paste, temper, and firing: Light red paste (2.5YR7/6). Fine and hard. A medium amount of volcanic ash temper (0.1 mm length). The paste and temper do not react to weak acid. Where the vessel is not blackened, the paste is completely oxidized. The paste and firing appear different from those of common Andres Red. Surface finish and decoration: The interior and exterior are well polished. The entire surface seems to be slipped. Although the slip color appears brown, it may be due to burning. A similar vessel, WVS23A-38 (Cat. 310284), suggests that the original color was probably red. Form: Open bowl with round sides and rounded base. Slightly exterior-thickened rim and rounded lip. Three small hollow oven feet with an opening and a rattle. Use-wear: Although the feet are worn from use, the interior is not worn. There are speckles of bright red pigments on some fragments, including their breaks, but there are no residues of pigment on the interior. When the structure collapsed, the vessel likely was sprinkled with pigment that was stored nearby. Comment: Identical to WVS 23A-38 (Cat. 310284), from the same room.

WVS No.: 23A-38; Catalog No.: 310284 (Figures 8.11h and 8.11i)

Bag No.: Rim: 1255 (18-3-3), 1117 (18-3-4), 232 (47-1-1), 1048 (18-2-1), 1400 (15-2-1); Body: 1255, 232, 152 (18-1-1), 1048; Base: 1255, 232. Provenience: 23A18-3-3. Context: Floor. On the rear bench near the room partition with the cen-

tral room, in an area disturbed by a tree fall. Although a significant portion of the vessel was found in an area 1 × 1 m, other fragments were up to 3 m apart in Units 47 and 15. These pieces were probably disturbed postdepositionally. Condition: Reconstructible (95% present). Relatively well preserved. Many fragments are burned in black color. Many pieces were exposed to fire after the vessel broke. Dimensions: Rim diameter: [interior] 14.0 cm, [top] 14.7 cm (measured); Maximum diameter: 16.0 cm (measured); Height: 10.2 cm (measured); Height without feet: 9.3 cm (measured); Wall thickness: 0.4–0.6 cm; Sample weight: 365 g; Original weight: 384 g; Volume: 1,006 cm^3. Coordinates: (50.37, 16.54) (estimate). Type: Unnamed volcanic ash undetermined. Paste, temper, and firing: Red paste (2.5YR5/8). Fine and hard. A small amount of volcanic ash temper (0.1 mm length). The paste and temper do not react to weak acid. The paste is completely oxidized. The paste and firing appear different from those of common Andres Red. Surface finish and decoration: The interior and exterior are well polished. The entire surface, including feet, is red-slipped. Form: Open bowl with round sides and rounded base. Slightly exterior-thickened rim and rounded lip. Three small hollow oven feet with an opening and possibly a rattle. Use-wear: None clearly recognizable. Comment: Identical to WVS23A-37 (Cat. 310225), from the same room.

WVS No.: 23A-39; Catalog No.: 310278 (Figure 8.11j)

Bag No.: Rim: 1698 (42-3-4); Body: 1698; Base: 1698, 1646 (43-3-5), 245 (44-1-1). Provenience: 23A42-3-4. Context: Floor. In the northern part of the room floor in front of the rear bench of the north room, in the access to the bench. Almost all fragments were found in one concentration. Condition: Reconstructible (95% present). Badly eroded. A large part of the vessel is burned in a dark color. Although the vessel is nearly complete, its feet were not recovered. It is probable that the plate was used with broken feet. Dimensions: Rim diameter: [exterior] 34.3 cm, [top] 33.0 cm (measured); Height: 12 cm (rough estimate); Height without feet: 5.5 cm (measured); Wall thickness: 0.7–0.9 cm; Sample weight: 1,327 g; Original weight: 1,397 g; Volume: 2,832 cm^3. Coordinates: (52.66, 18.12) (measured). Type: Unnamed volcanic ash undetermined. Paste, temper, and firing: Reddish yellow paste (5YR6/8). Fine. A medium amount of volcanic ash temper (0.1 mm length), a small amount of calcite temper (0.3–0.6 mm diameter), a small amount of ferruginous temper (0.4–1.3 mm diameter), and a small amount of white particles

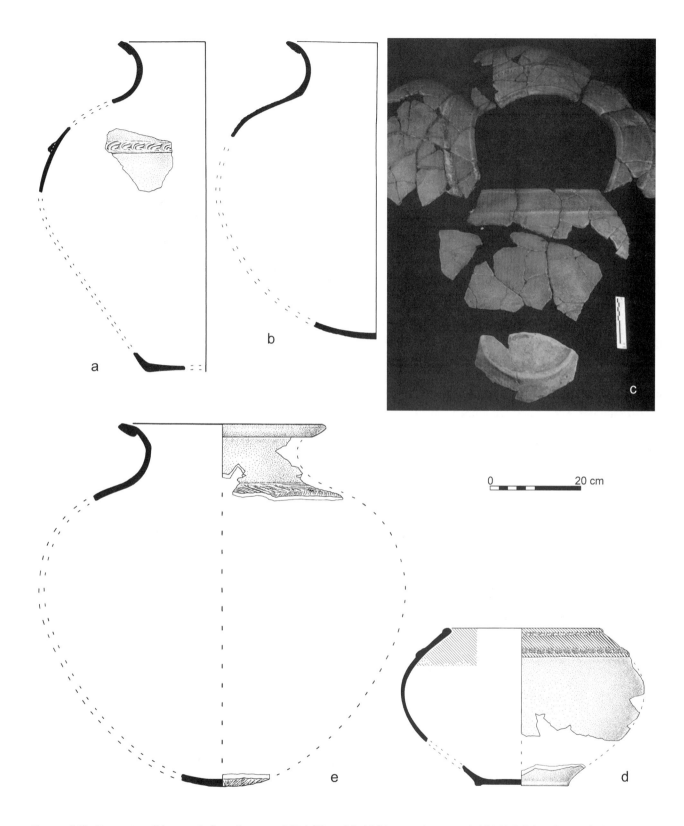

Figure 8.12. Reconstructible vessels from Structure M8-4 (⅛ scale). (a) Manteca Impressed, 23A42-3-2 (north room), Cat. 310396, WVS 23A-3. (b) Encanto Striated, 23A42-3-2 (north room), Cat. 310364, WVS 23A-4. (c, d) Chaquiste Impressed, 23A32-3-1 (north addition), Cat. 310366, WVS 23A-67. (e) Encanto Striated, 23A27-2-2 (south room), Cat. 310381, WVS 23A-50.

that do not react to weak acid (0.5–1.0 mm diameter). The thin layers of the surfaces are oxidized, leaving a wide dark core. The paste is harder than that of common Andres Red. Surface finish and decoration: Remains of red and orange paints over cream underslip on the exterior wall. Remains of cream underslip on the interior. Form: Plate with slightly outcurved sides and flat base. Direct rim and beveled-in lip. Remains of three hollow feet with two openings. Use-wear: Not clear because of erosion.

Center Room

WVS No.: 23A-40; Catalog No.: 310276 (Figures 8.13a and 8.13c)

Bag No.: Rim: 2011 (14-3-3), 1973 (14-3-3); Body: 2011; Base: 2011. Provenience: 23A14-3-3. Context: Floor. In the southern part of the rear bench surface of the central room. A significant portion of the vessel was found in one concentration. Condition: Reconstructible (85% present). Eroded. The exterior base has fire clouding. It is not clear whether the fire clouding was caused during the original firing of the vessel. Dimensions: Rim diameter: [exterior] 13.0 cm, [top] 12.5 cm (measured); Height: 4.9–5.2 cm (measured); Height without feet: 4.6–4.9 cm (measured); Wall thickness: 0.5–0.8 cm; Sample weight: 224 g; Original weight: 264 g; Volume: 235 cm³. Coordinates: (46.40, 16.96) (measured). Type: Cambio Unslipped. Paste, temper, and firing: Strong brown paste (7.5YR5/6). Medium grain. A medium amount of calcite temper (0.1–0.6 mm diameter). The paste is completely oxidized. The paste looks more like that of Tinaja Red than that of Cambio Unslipped. Surface finish and decoration: The interior and exterior surfaces are smoothed and uneven. No traces of slip. Notches and punctuation on the pedestal. Form: Bowl with flared sides. Direct rim and squared lip. Flat base with pedestal. The vessel may have been an incense burner. Use-wear: No clear use-wear on the rim, interior, or base. There is no soot or fire smudge on the interior, but it is possible that such indications of use as an incense burner were lost when the vessel was burned.

WVS No.: 23A-41; Catalog No.: 310319 (Figure 8.13b and 8.13c)

Bag No.: Rim: 1966 (10-3-2), 1140 (13-2-1), 1955 (13-3-2); Body: 1966; Base: 1140. Provenience: 23A10-3-2. Context: Floor. On the floor of the central room in front of the back bench. Fragments were found in an area 1 × 1 m. Condition: Partial (70% present of the bowl-shaped part,

not including a possible attachment). Slightly eroded. Traces of burning are not clear. It was probably used as a partial vessel after a handle or a modeled decoration broke off. Dimensions: Rim diameter: [exterior] 10.7 cm, [top] 10.0 cm (measured); Height of the bowl-shaped part: 4.9 cm (measured); Wall thickness: 0.6–0.9 cm; Sample weight: 160 g; Original weight of the bowl-shaped part: 228 g; Volume: 152 cm³. Coordinates: (45.13, 17.44) (measured). Type: Cambio Unslipped (it may have been Pedregal Modeled with an appendage). Paste, temper, and firing: Reddish yellow paste (5YR7/6). Medium grain. A medium amount of calcite temper (0.1–0.3 mm diameter) and a small amount of ferruginous temper (0.3–1.3 mm diameter). The paste is completely oxidized. The paste is more like that of Tinaja Red than that of most Cambio/Encanto vessels. Surface finish and decoration: The interior and exterior are smoothed and unslipped. Form: Bowl with outflared sides. Direct rim and squared lip. Flat base. A trace of an appendage on the exterior wall near the base. It may have been attached to a modeled portion (see, for example, Demarest et al. 2003: Fig. 5.11). The vessel may have been used as an incense burner. Use-wear: No signs of soot or blackening. Such indications of use as an incense burner may have been lost when the vessel was burned.

WVS No.: 23A-42; Catalog No.: 310359 (Figure 8.13d)

Bag No.: Rim: 1628 (49-3-3); Body: 1628; Base: 1628. Provenience: 23A49-3-3. Context: Floor. On the floor of the front part of the center room, in front of the front bench. All recovered fragments were found in one concentration. The complete neck and base are present. Missing body sherds may be too eroded to be recognized as part of this vessel. Condition: Reconstructible (60% present). Badly eroded. Some parts appear to be burned. Some parts are blackened, but it is not clear whether that is due to burning. Dimensions: Rim diameter: [exterior] 14.5 cm, [top] 14.0 cm (measured); Maximum diameter: 31 cm (rough estimate); Minimum opening: 8.2 cm (measured); Height: 29 cm (rough estimate); Neck height: 5.1 cm (measured); Wall thickness: 0.6–0.9 cm; Sample weight: 1,853 g; Original weight: 3,088 g; Volume: 9,399 cm³. Coordinates: (48.16, 20.31) (measured). Type: Pantano Impressed. Paste, temper, and firing: Pink paste (7.5YR8/4). Medium grain. A medium amount of calcite temper (0.1–1.5 mm diameter) and a small amount of ferruginous temper (0.5–2.0 mm diameter). The paste is completely oxidized. Surface finish and decoration: The surface is mostly eroded, but there are some remains of red slip. It is not

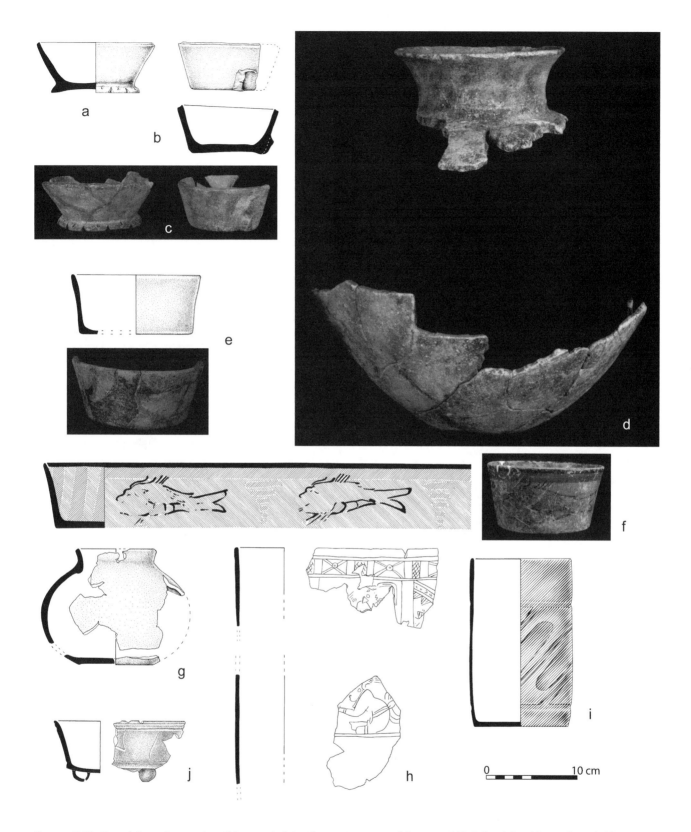

FIGURE 8.13. Complete and reconstructible vessels from the center room of Structure M8-4. (a–c) Cambio Unslipped. (a) 23A14-3-3, Cat. 310276, WVS 23A-40. (b) 23A10-3-2, Cat. 310319, WVS 23A-41. (c) WVS 23A-40 and 23A-41. (d) Pantano Impressed. 23A49-3-3, Cat. 310359, WVS 23A-42. (e, f) Saxche-Palmar Polychrome. (e) 23A-14-3-4, Cat. 310372, WVS 23A-44. (f) 23A48-3-5, Cat. 310168, WVS 23A-43. (g) Undetermined (probably Saxche-Palmar Polychrome), 23A14-3-3, Cat. 310338, WVS 23A-45. (h) Corozal Incised, 23A13-3-2, Cat. 310337, WVS 23A-46. (i) Salada Fluted, 23A15-2-1, Cat. 310330, WVS 23A-47. (j) Chicxulub Incised, 23A11-2-1, Cat. 310348, WVS 23A-48.

clear whether the exterior base and the interior neck were slipped. Form: Jar with outcurved neck. Direct rim and pointed lip. Incurved base. Arc-shaped stamps below the neck-body juncture. Use-wear: Not clear because of erosion.

WVS No.: 23A-43; Catalog No.: 310168 (Figure 8.13f)
Bag No.: Rim: 1423 (48-3-5); Body: 1423; Base: 1423. Provenience: 23A48-3-5. Context: Floor. In the niche under the front bench of the center room. Although the vessel was broken, it retained its shape when excavated. The vessel was originally stored in the niche. Condition: Reconstructible (99% present). Eroded, but a significant part of the painting is still visible. No traces of burning. Placed in a niche, the vessel was probably protected from fire. Dimensions: Rim diameter: [exterior] 13.1 cm, [top] 12.8 cm (measured); Height: 7.2 cm (measured); Wall thickness: 0.5–0.8 cm; Sample weight: 355 g; Original weight: 359 g; Volume: 410 cm^3. Coordinates: (48.82, 19.63) (measured). Type: Saxche-Palmar Polychrome. Paste, temper, and firing: Pink paste (7.5YR7/4). Fine. A shiny glass-like temper (volcanic ash? 0.1–0.3 mm length) and a small amount of calcite temper (0.1–0.3 mm diameter). The paste is completely oxidized. Surface finish and decoration: Orange slip on the entire surface, except the exterior base. Vertical red lines on the interior wall and red paint on the interior base. Black and red bands on the rim. Two paintings of fish on the exterior wall. Form: Bowl with flared sides and flat base. Direct rim and rounded lip. Use-wear: The rim and the interior base are heavily worn. It is not clear whether that is from use or from postdepositional erosion. Use-wear on the exterior base is not clear.

WVS No.: 23A-44; Catalog No.: 310372 (Figure 8.13e)
Bag No.: Rim: 1977 (14-3-4), 1126 (46-2-1), 1408 (16-2-1); Body: 1977; Base: 1977, 2096 (14-3-4), 1947 (10-3-2). Provenience: 23A14-3-4. Context: Floor. In front of the rear bench. A significant portion was in one concentration. Other fragments were scattered in an area 4 × 4 m. It is probable that the vessel was originally placed on the bench or in a higher location. Condition: Reconstructible (65% present). Eroded. Burned. Dimensions: Rim diameter: [exterior] 14.6 cm, [top] 14.2 cm (measured); Height: 6.2 cm (measured); Wall thickness: 0.5–0.7 cm; Sample weight: 186 g; Original weight: 286 g; Volume: 403 cm^3. Coordinates: (46.39, 17.39) (measured). Type: Saxche-Palmar Polychrome. Paste, temper, and firing: Reddish yellow paste (5YR6/6). Medium grain. A medium amount

of calcite temper (0.1–1.0 mm diameter), a medium amount of volcanic ash temper (0.1 mm length), and a small amount of ferruginous temper (0.5–1.5 mm diameter). The paste is completely oxidized. The paste is coarser and redder than that of common Saxche-Palmar vessels. The paste feels sandy. Surface finish and decoration: The surface is mostly eroded, but there are some remains of red paint over cream underslip on the exterior and interior. Form: Bowl with outflared sides. Direct rim and rounded lip. Flat base. Use-wear: Not clear because of erosion.

WVS No.: 23A-45; Catalog No.: 310338 (Figure 8.13g)
Bag No.: Rim: 1973 (14-3-3); Body: 1973, 1218 (14-2-2), 2096 (14-3-4), 146 (14-1-1), 1972 (14-3-2); Base: 1973. Provenience: 23A14-3-3. Context: Floor. On the bench of the central room. A significant portion of the vessel was found in an area 1 × 1 m. Other fragments were found in an area roughly 2 × 2 m. The vessel may have been stored on the bench surface or in a higher location. Condition: Reconstructible (65% present). Badly eroded. It is slightly darkened and appears to have been burned. Dimensions: Rim diameter: [exterior] 10.0 cm, [top] 9.7 cm (measured); Maximum diameter: 15.0 cm (estimate); Minimum opening: 7.6 cm (measured); Height: 11.7 cm (measured); Neck height: 2.0 cm (measured); Wall thickness: 0.6–0.7 cm; Sample weight: 403 g; Original weight: 620 g; Volume: 1,214 cm^3. Coordinates: (46.14, 16.60) (estimate). Type: Undetermined (probably Saxche-Palmar Polychrome). Paste, temper, and firing: Very pale brown paste (10YR7/4). Fine grain. A small amount of calcite temper (0.1–0.8 mm diameter) and a small amount of ferruginous temper (0.3–0.6 mm). The paste is completely oxidized. Surface finish and decoration: The surface appears to have been painted or slipped, but it is completely eroded. Form: Jar with outflared neck. Direct rim and rounded lip. Flat base. It does not appear to have handles. Use-wear: Not clear because of erosion.

WVS No.: 23A-46; Catalog No.: 310337 (Figure 8.13h)
Bag No.: Rim: 1964 (13-2-1), 1140 (13-2-1), 1966 (10-3-2); Body: 1964, 1966. Provenience: 23A13-3-2. Context: Floor. On the bench of the central room near the back wall. Most recovered fragments were found in one concentration. Other sherds came from the area in front of the bench 2 m away from the first concentration. The vessel may have been stored in a high location along the back wall, and missing parts may have fallen in the unexcavated area behind the structure, or perhaps the residents kept

some fragments. Condition: Reconstructible (20% present). The fragments from the first concentration are relatively well preserved whereas others are eroded. All fragments are burned. Dimensions: Rim diameter: 9.8 cm (estimate); Height: 20 cm (measured); Wall thickness: 0.4–0.5 cm; Sample weight: 88 g; Original weight: 440 g; Volume: 1,367 cm^3. Coordinates: (46.28, 14.96) (measured). Type: Corozal Incised. Paste, temper, and firing: Red paste (2.5YR5/8). Fine grain. A small amount of calcite temper (0.3–0.8 mm diameter) and a small amount of ferruginous temper (0.5–1.5 mm diameter). A large part of the paste except the surface remains dark. Surface finish and decoration: The paste was polished and then incised at a leather-hard stage. The incisions show horizontal and vertical bands and a seated figure. Red slip appears to have covered the entire exterior surface. Form: Cylinder vase with vertical sides. Direct rim and rounded lip. Use-wear: Not clear.

WVS No.: 23A-47; Catalog No.: 310330 (Figure 8.13i)
Bag No.: Rim: 1401 (15-2-1), 1975 (14-3-2), 146 (14-1-1); Body: 1401, 1975, 1400 (15-2-1), 1218 (14-2-2), 146; Base: 1401. Provenience: 23A15-2-1. Context: Floor. In the center room. Most fragments were found in the wall-fall layer in an area 2 × 2 m around the central axis of the room and a step in front of the back bench. One piece was found on the floor in front of the bench. The vessel was probably stored on the back bench or in a higher location. Condition: Reconstructible (60% present). Badly eroded and severely burned. Dimensions: Rim diameter: 10.5 cm (estimate); Height: 17.8 cm (measured); Wall thickness: 0.3–0.7 cm; Sample weight: 295 g; Original weight: 491 g; Volume: 1,336 cm^3. Coordinates: (47.01, 18.21) (estimate). Type: Salada Fluted. Paste, temper, and firing: Reddish yellow paste (5YR6/8). Fine grain. A small amount of calcite temper (0.1–0.4 mm diameter), a very small amount of ferruginous temper (0.5–1.0 mm diameter), and a very small amount of volcanic ash temper (0.1 mm length). In some parts of the vessel the paste core has a slightly dark color. Surface finish and decoration: Diagonal fluting on the exterior wall. Some remains of orange slip. Form: Cylinder vase with vertical sides. Direct rim and rounded lip. Flat base. Use-wear: Not clear because of erosion.

WVS No.: 23A-48; Catalog No.: 310348 (Figure 8.13j)
Bag No.: Rim: 309 (11-2-1); Body: 309; Base: 309. Provenience: 23A11-2-1. Context: Floor. Fragments were found in an area 2 × 2 m in the wall-fall layer in the front part in front of the central and south rooms. The vessel was probably placed in a high location in the rear part of the central or south room near the room division. Condition: Reconstructible (30% present). Very eroded. Small fragments probably disintegrated or could not be recognized as parts of this vessel. Dimensions: Rim diameter: 8 cm (estimate); Height: 6.5 cm (measured); Height without feet: 5.3 cm (measured); Wall thickness: 0.4–0.6 cm; Sample weight: 34 g; Original weight: 113 g; Volume: 79 cm^3. Coordinates: (45.30, 19.11) (estimate). Type: Chicxulub Incised. Paste, temper, and firing: Dark bluish gray paste (10B4/1) on the surface and yellow paste (2.5Y8/6) in the core. Very fine grain. No visible temper. The paste is completely oxidized. Surface finish and decoration: Horizontal grooves on the exterior below the rim and above the body-base juncture. Vertical incisions on the exterior body. Black slip on the exterior in the areas defined by grooves and incisions. Form: Bowl with slightly outcurved sides. Direct rim and beveled-in lip. Slightly rounded base. Three small hollow hemispherical feet. Use-wear: Not clear because of erosion.

South Room

WVS No.: 23A-49; Catalog No.: 310407
Bag No.: Rim: 635 (10-3-4); Body: 635. Provenience: 23A10-3-4. Context: Floor. On the floor in front of the rear bench of the south room. Half the recovered fragments were found in one concentration, and others were in the wall-fall layer in an area 0.7 × 1 m. The rim was found on the floor whereas many body sherds were in the wall-fall layer. The base does not appear to have been recovered. The vessel may have been placed upside-down or may have fallen from the bench. Only the rim was partially restored. Condition: Reconstructible (50% present). Eroded. Some fragments appear to have been burned and blackened. Dimensions: Rim diameter: [exterior] 33.8 cm, [top] 32.8 cm (measured); Maximum diameter: 48 cm (rough estimate); Minimum opening: 19.0 cm (measured); Height: 58 cm (rough estimate); Neck height: 11 cm (rough estimate); Wall thickness: 0.9–1.1 cm; Sample weight: 7,837 g; Original weight: 15,674 g; Volume: 49,384 cm^3. Coordinates: (44.22, 17.33) (measured). Type: Encanto Striated. Paste, temper, and firing: Pink paste (7.5YR7/4). Coarse grain. A very large amount of calcite temper (0.5–3.0 mm diameter). The paste is completely oxidized. Surface finish and decoration: The body below the shoulder is striated. Its striations are slightly finer than those of common Encanto vessels. The neck and interior are unslipped and

smoothed. Form: Jar with outcurved neck. Exterior-folded rim and beveled-in, grooved lip. Use-wear: Not clear because of the incomplete state of the vessel.

WVS No.: 23A-50; Catalog No.: 310381 (Figure 8.12e)
Bag No.: Rim: 265 (28-2-1), 292 (26-2-1), 273 (5-2-1); Body: 266 (27-2-2), 265, 417 (6-3-4), 416 (6-3-3), 408 (7-3-3), 128 (6-1-1), 414 (6-3-1), 211 (27-1-1), 461 (28-3-3), 592 (28-3-2), 457 (28-3-1), 424 (27-3-4), 267 (10-2-1), 285 (7-2-1), 309 (11-2-1), 140 (11-1-1); Base: 266, 309, 422 (27-3-1). Provenience: 23A27-2-2. Context: Floor. A significant part of the vessel was found in the wall-fall layer in front of the rear bench of the south room near the central axis of the room. A small amount of pieces were on the southern half of the floor in front of the bench. Others were scattered on the bench and in the western half of the front area of the room. It is possible that the vessel was originally placed on the bench or on the floor in front of it and that fragments were scattered due to disturbance at the time of abandonment. Condition: Reconstructible (50% present). Eroded. Traces of burning not clear. Dimensions: Rim diameter: [exterior] 44.3 cm, [top] 43.3 cm (measured); Maximum diameter: 68 cm (rough estimate); Minimum opening: 29.4 cm (rough estimate); Height: 77 cm (rough estimate); Neck height: 11.0 cm (measured); Wall thickness: 0.9–1.2 cm; Sample weight: 16,176 g; Original weight: 32,352 g; Volume: 155,681 cm^3. Coordinates: (42.37, 17.80) (estimate). Type: Encanto Striated. Paste, temper, and firing: Reddish yellow paste (5YR6/6). Coarse grain. A very large amount of calcite temper (0.5–3.0 mm diameter). The paste is completely oxidized in most parts, but in the base the core is dark. Surface finish and decoration: Striation on the body and base below the shoulder. The neck and interior are unslipped and smoothed. Form: Jar with outcurved neck. Exterior-folded rim and rounded lip. Rounded base. Use-wear: The center of the exterior base does not appear to have much wear.

WVS No.: 23A-51; Catalog No.: 310380 (Figure 8.14a)
Bag No.: Rim: 309 (11-2-1), 382 (8-3-1), 592 (28-3-2), 406 (7-3-1), 461 (28-3-3), 168 (28-1-1); Body: 309, 461, 382 (8-3-1), 106 (7-1-1), 460 (28-3-4), 596 (29-3-4), 184 (29-1-1), 388 (8-3-4), 168, 459 (28-3-3), 595 (29-3-3), 387 (8-3-3), 117 (8-1-1), 289 (8-2-1), 140 (11-1-1), 407 (7-3-2), 128 (6-1-1), 415 (6-3-2), 422 (27-3-1), 461, 285 (7-2-1), 457 (28-3-1), 267 (10-2-1); Base: 409 (7-3-4). Provenience: 23A6-3-2. Context: Floor. Fragments were scattered over the entire south room, including the rear bench, the floor in front of the bench, and

the front area. Significant concentrations of sherds were in the southern part of the floor in front of the bench and in the northern part of the bench. Another concentration that included most of the neck part was in the wall-fall layer in the front area between the internal division and a front pillar. Most parts of the vessel have not been restored, and it is not clear whether all the fragments indeed belong to the same vessel. Condition: Reconstructible (50% present). Eroded. Traces of burning are not clear. Dimensions: Rim diameter: [exterior] 36.3 cm, [top] 34.4 cm (measured); Maximum diameter: 56 cm (rough estimate); Minimum opening: 24.1 cm (measured); Height: 65 cm (rough estimate); Neck height: 12.5 cm (measured); Wall thickness: 1.0–1.2 cm; Sample weight: 11,152 g; Original weight: 22,304 g; Volume: 74,798 cm^3. Coordinates: (41.95, 17.65) (estimate). Type: Encanto Striated. Paste, temper, and firing: Pink paste (7.5YR7/4). Coarse grain. A large amount of calcite temper (0.5–3.0 mm diameter). The paste is completely oxidized. Surface finish and decoration: Striation on the body and base below the shoulder. The neck and interior are unslipped and smoothed. Form: Jar with outcurved neck. Exterior-folded rim and beveled-in lip. Rounded base. Use-wear: Not clear because of the fragmentary state of the vessel.

WVS No.: 23A-52; Catalog No.: 310320 (Figure 8.14c)
Bag No.: Rim: 620 (11-3-4); Body: 620; Base: 620. Provenience: 23A11-3-4. Context: Floor. On the floor in the front area between the south and central rooms, next to the front pillar. All fragments were found in one concentration, but a significant part of the vessel is missing. One possibility is that it was used as a partial vessel. It is also possible that the south room was disturbed at the time abandonment. Condition: Reconstructible (50% present). Badly eroded. Some parts are severely burned and reoxidized. Dimensions: Rim diameter: 13 cm (estimate); Maximum diameter: 17.9 cm (measured); Minimum opening: 9 cm (estimate); Height: 15.3 cm (measured); Neck height: 3.7 cm (measured); Wall thickness: 0.6–0.7 cm; Sample weight: 327 g; Original weight: 654 g; Volume: 1,389 cm^3. Coordinates: (44.73, 19.64) (measured). Type: Pantano Impressed. Paste, temper, and firing: Reddish yellow paste (7.5YR7/6). Medium grain. A medium amount of calcite temper (0.1–1.5 mm diameter) and a small amount ferruginous temper (0.5–2.0 mm diameter). The paste is completely oxidized. Surface finish and decoration: Red slip on the exterior. The interior neck is not slipped. It is not clear whether the exterior base was

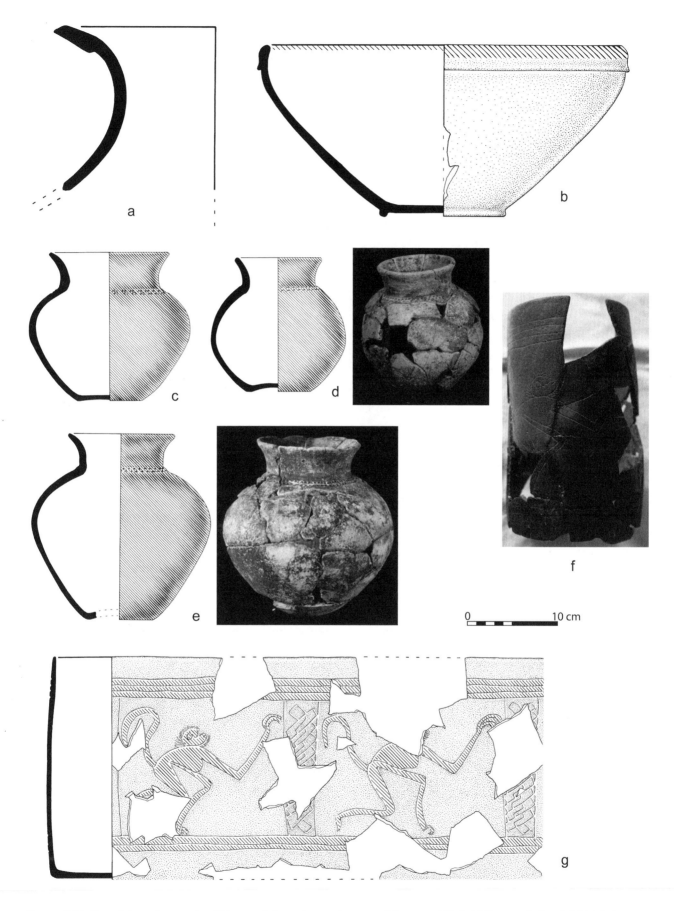

FIGURE 8.14. Complete and reconstructible vessels from the south room of Structure M8-4. (a) Encanto Striated, 23A6-3-2, Cat. 310380, WVS 23A-51. (b) Subin Red, 23A10-2-1, Cat. 310376, WVS 23A-56. (c–e) Pantano Impressed. (c) 23A11-3-4, Cat. 310320, WVS 23A-52. (d) 23A6-3-2, Cat. 310321, WVS 23A-53. (e) 23A10-3-4, Cat. 310333, WVS 23A-54. (f, g) Corozal Incised, 23A27-3-1, Cat. 310288, WVS 23A-57.

slipped. Form: Jar with outcurved neck. Direct rim and rounded lip. Use-wear: Not clear because of erosion.

WVS No.: 23A-53; Catalog No.: 310321 (Figure 8.14d)
Bag No.: Rim: 422 (27-3-1); Body: 415 (6-3-2), 168 (28-1-1), 422 (27-3-1), 417 (6-3-4), 421 (27-3-1), 297 (27-2-2), 283 (6-2-2), 290 (26-2-1); Base: 415, 283, 128 (6-1-1). Provenience: 23A6-3-2. Context: Floor. On the bench and floor of the south room. Fragments were scattered in an area 4 × 3 m, including the bench surface and floor in front of it. The vessel was probably broken and scattered at the time of abandonment. Condition: Reconstructible (60% present). Eroded. No clear traces of burning. Dimensions: Rim diameter: [exterior] 9.3 cm, [top] 8.9 cm (measured); Maximum diameter: 15.2 cm (measured); Minimum opening: 5.4 cm (measured); Height: 14.0 cm (measured); Neck height: 2.8 cm (measured); Wall thickness: 0.6–0.8 cm; Sample weight: 445 g; Original weight: 741 g; Volume: 907 cm³. Coordinates: (41.92, 17.67) (estimate). Type: Pantano Impressed. Paste, temper, and firing: Reddish yellow paste (7.5YR7/6). Medium grain. A medium amount of calcite temper (0.1–0.8 mm diameter) and a small amount of ferruginous temper (0.5–2.0 mm diameter). The paste is completely oxidized. Surface finish and decoration: Red slip over the exterior. It is not clear whether the exterior base and the interior neck were slipped. Triangular punctuations below the neck-body juncture. Form: Jar with outflared neck. Direct rim and rounded lip. Incurved base. Use-wear: Not clear because of erosion.

WVS No.: 23A-54; Catalog No.: 310333 (Figure 8.14e)
Bag No.: Rim: 634 (10-3-4); Body: 634, 633 (10-3-4); Base: 634. Provenience: 23A10-3-4. Context: Floor. On the floor of the south room in front of the bench. Most fragments were found in one concentration. Condition: Reconstructible (65% present). Eroded. The vessel appears to have been burned and reoxidized. Dimensions: Rim diameter: [exterior] 11.9 cm, [top] 11.5 cm (measured); Maximum diameter: 19.1 cm (measured); Minimum opening: 7.0 cm (measured); Height: 19.0 cm (measured); Neck height: 3.9 cm (measured); Wall thickness: 0.6–0.9 cm; Sample weight: 722 g; Original weight: 1,110 g; Volume: 2,492 cm³. Coordinates: (44.53, 17.25) (measured). Type: Pantano Impressed. Paste, temper, and firing: Reddish yellow paste (7.5YR7/6). Medium grain. A large amount of calcite temper (0.1–1.5 mm diameter) and a small amount of ferruginous temper (0.8–1.5 mm diameter).

The paste is completely oxidized. Surface finish and decoration: Red slip on the exterior. It is not clear whether the exterior base is slipped. The interior neck is not slipped. Triangular punctuations below the neck-body juncture. Form: Jar with outcurved neck. Direct rim and rounded lip. Incurved base. Use-wear: Not clear because of erosion.

WVS No.: 23A-55; Catalog No.: 310373
Bag No.: Rim: 422 (27-3-1), 211 (27-1-1); Body: 272 (10-2-1); Base: 272. Provenience: 23A10-2-1. Context: Floor. Most fragments were found in the wall-fall layer in front of the back bench near the northeastern corner of the rear part of the south room. A few pieces were found on the floor in front of the bench. The vessel may have fallen from the bench or a higher location where it was stored. Missing fragments may have been mixed with those of other vessels and misidentified. Condition: Reconstructible (40% present). Eroded. Some fragments are darkened, but it is not clear whether that was caused by burning. Dimensions: Rim diameter: 10.5 cm (estimate); Maximum diameter: 18 cm (estimate); Minimum opening: 7.6 cm (measured); Height: 17 cm (estimate); Neck height: 3.4 cm (measured); Wall thickness: 0.5–0.6 cm; Sample weight: 370 g; Original weight: 925 g; Volume: 1,816 cm³. Coordinates: (44.08, 17.48) (estimate). Type: Pantano Impressed. Paste, temper, and firing: Reddish yellow paste (7.5YR7/6). Medium grain. A medium amount of calcite temper (0.1–1.0 mm diameter) and a small amount of ferruginous temper (0.8–1.5 mm diameter). The paste is completely oxidized. Surface finish and decoration: Red slip over the entire exterior, including the base. The interior neck is not slipped. Triangular punctuations below the neck-body juncture. Form: Jar with outcurved neck. Direct rim and rounded lip. Slightly incurved base. Use-wear: Not clear.

WVS No.: 23A-56; Catalog No.: 310376 (Figure 8.14b)
Bag No.: Rim: 268 (10-2-1), 307 (10-2-2), 459 (28-3-3), 466 (5-3-2), 445 (10-3-3); Body: 268, 459, 267 (10-2-1); Base: 268. Provenience: 23A10-2-1. Context: Floor. Most fragments were found in the wall-fall layer in the northeast corner (in front of the rear bench) of the rear part of the south room in an area 0.5 × 0.5 m. A small number of pieces were scattered in the rear part of the room. Condition: Reconstructible (50% present). Some fragments are relatively well preserved whereas others are eroded. Some fragments are darkened, but it is unclear whether the darkening was caused by the fire at the time of abandonment.

It is not clear whether the vessel was kept as a partial bowl or whether missing fragments were thrown to other areas at the time of abandonment. Dimensions: Rim diameter: 44 cm (estimate); Maximum diameter: 46 cm (estimate); Height: 18.1 cm (measured); Wall thickness: 0.8–1.2 cm; Sample weight: 2,411 g; Original weight: 4,822 g; Volume: 14,258 cm³. Coordinates: (44.40, 17.69) (estimate). Type: Subin Red. Paste, temper, and firing: Reddish yellow paste (7.5YR7/6). Medium grain. A large amount of calcite temper (0.3–0.8 mm diameter) and a small amount of ferruginous temper (0.8–1.3 mm diameter). The paste is completely oxidized. Surface finish and decoration: Red slip on the exterior rim. No slip on the exterior wall below the thickened rim. Very weak red slip on the interior surface. Form: Open bowl with slightly incurved sides. Exterior-thickened rim and rounded lip. Ring base. Use-wear: The interior is smooth and there is no recognizable use-wear. The ring base appears to be slightly worn.

WVS No.: 23A-57; Catalog No.: 310288 (Figure 8.14f and 8.14g)
Bag No.: Rim: 423 (27-3-2), 665 (10-3-3), 408 (7-3-3), 406 (7-3-1), 457 (28-3-1); Body: 406, 407 (7-3-2), 422 (27-3-1), 423 (27-3-2), 290 (26-2-1), 309 (11-2-1), 609 (26-3-2), 608 (26-3-1), 409 (7-3-4), 415 (6-3-2), 459 (28-3-3), 457 (28-3-1); Base: 408, 357 (24-3-3), 422. Provenience: 23A27-3-1. Context: Floor. In the southern room. Fragments were scattered over an area 4 × 4 m, including the bench, the floor in front of the bench, and the front area. Fragments may have been scattered intentionally or unintentionally by the fleeing residents or by the invading enemies. The vessel may have been stored on the bench or in a higher location. Condition: Reconstructible (80% present). Eroded. Severely burned in black color. Fragments were exposed to fire after the vessel broke. Dimensions: Rim diameter: [exterior] 13.6 cm, [top] 13.3 cm (measured); Maximum diameter: 13.9 cm (measured); Height: 23.5 cm (measured); Wall thickness: 0.5–0.6 cm; Sample weight: 785 g; Original weight: 981 g; Volume: 2,783 cm³. Coordinates: (43.64, 16.23) (estimate). Type: Corozal Incised. Paste, temper, and firing: Reddish yellow paste (7.5YR6/6). Medium grain. A medium amount of white particles (0.3–1.0 mm diameter) and a small amount of shiny, glass-like particles (0.1 mm length). The paste and temper do not react to weak acid. The paste is completely oxidized. Surface finish and decoration: Incisions on the exterior walls. Incisions were made when the clay was already hard. Two designs of monkeys divided by panels of mat motifs. The

monkeys and other areas outlined by incisions are filled with red paint. It is not clear whether other parts are slipped. Form: Vase with vertical sides and flat base. Direct rim and rounded lip. Use-wear: Not clear because of erosion and burning.

WVS No.: 23A-58; Catalog No.: 310328 (Figure 8.15a)
Bag No.: Rim: 616 (11-3-3), 174 (25-1-1), 124 (12-1-1), 112 (9-1-1), 458 (28-3-2); Body: 616, 422 (27-3-1), 385 (8-3-2), 117 (8-1-1), 108 (1-1-1), 465 (5-3-1), 285 (7-2-1), 843 (4-2-1), 459 (28-3-3), 106 (7-1-1), 460 (28-3-4), 595 (29-3-3), 188 (35-1-1), 427 (6-3-2), 168 (28-1-1), 458, 596 (29-3-4), 906 (3-3-4), 389 (8-3-2); Base: 188 (35-1-1), 459, 385 (8-3-2), 354 (35-3-4), 460, 106 (7-1-1), 909 (3-3-3), 388 (8-3-4), 594 (29-3-2). Provenience: 23A11-3-3. Context: Floor. On the floor of the south room. Fragments were scattered in the entire south room, including the bench and the patio in front of the room. The largest portion was found in the front area near the central room. Since some fragments could be glued together and some broken edges were relatively well preserved, fragments do not appear to have come from fill or middens. They were probably broken and scattered because of the disturbance at the time of abandonment. Condition: Reconstructible (50% present). Badly eroded. It is not clear whether fragments were burned. Dimensions: Rim diameter: [exterior] 13.5 cm, [top] 13.2 cm (measured); Height: 24 cm (rough estimate); Wall thickness: 0.4–0.5 cm; Sample weight: 512 g; Original weight: 1,024 g; Volume: 2,790 cm³. Coordinates: (44.23, 18.86) (estimate). Type: Saxche-Palmar Polychrome. Paste, temper, and firing: Reddish yellow paste (5YR6/8). Fine grain. A small amount of calcite temper (0.2–1.3 mm diameter), a small amount of ferruginous temper (0.8–2.0 mm diameter), and a very small amount of volcanic ash temper (0.1 mm length). A large part of the paste is dark, except 0.5-mm layers below the surface. Surface finish and decoration: Remains of red paint over cream slip on the exterior, but the surface is mostly eroded. Form: Cylinder vase with vertical sides. Direct rim and rounded lip. Flat base. Use-wear: Not clear because of erosion.

WVS No.: 23A-59; Catalog No.: 310353 (Figure 8.15d–h)
Bag No.: Rim: 304 (10-2-1), 415 (6-3-2), 444 (10-3-3); Body: 466 (5-3-2), 273 (5-2-1), 268 (10-2-1), 306 (10-2-2), 633 (10-3-4), 128 (6-1-1), 126 (5-1-1), 288 (7-2-1), 444 (10-3-3), 422 (27-3-1), 306, 304, 305 (10-2-1), 272 (10-2-1), 297 (27-2-2), 478 (5-3-1), 309 (11-2-1), 415 (6-3-2), 457 (28-3-1), 281 (6-2-1), 465 (5-3-1); Base: 466, 465, 273 (5-2-1), 126, 306.

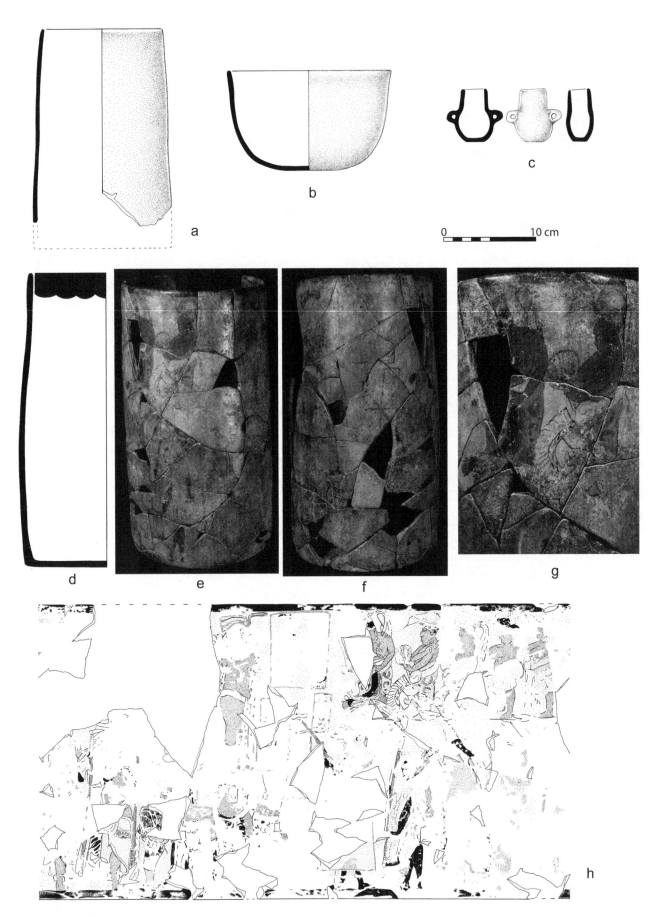

FIGURE 8.15. Reconstructible vessels from the south room of Structure M8-4. (a) Saxche-Palmar Polychrome, 23A11-3-3, Cat. 310328, WSV 23A-58. (b) Unnamed volcanic ash undetermined, 23A5-3-1, Cat. 310289, WVS 23A-60. (c) Tinaja Red, 23A8-3-3, Cat. 310312, WVS 23A-61. (d–h) Saxche-Palmar Polychrome, 23A5-3-2, Cat. 310353, WVS 23A-59. (g) Close-up of WVS 23A-59 (not to scale).

Provenience: 23A5-3-2. Context: Floor. On the rear bench of the south room. A quarter of the vessel was found in an area 1 × 1 m in the southwestern corner of the bench. Other fragments were scattered in the entire rear part of the room (4-×-4-m area). The room was probably disturbed at the time of abandonment. Condition: Reconstructible (80% present). Badly eroded. Burned. Some fragments received fire after the vessel broke. Dimensions: Rim diameter: [exterior] 17.6 cm, [top] 17.2 cm (measured); Maximum diameter: 18.1 cm (measured); Height: 30.9 cm (measured); Wall thickness: 0.5–0.7 cm; Sample weight: 1,518 g; Original weight: 1,898 g; Volume: 5,839 cm³. Coordinates: (41.09, 15.74) (measured). Type: Saxche-Palmar Polychrome. Paste, temper, and firing: Reddish yellow paste (5YR6/6). Fine grain. A small amount of calcite temper (0.3–1.5 mm diameter) and a small amount of volcanic ash temper (0.1 mm length). The paste is completely oxidized. Surface finish and decoration: Extremely fine and elaborate painting on the exterior wall. Black, strong orange, red, and white paints over weak orange slip. Black band on the exterior and interior rims. Glyph blocks in the central part of the scene, but the glyphs are almost completely eroded. Infrared photography did not reveal more. Glyphs were painted on a pink background. The painting depicts a court scene with numerous people in two registers. Karl Taube (personal communication, 2002) has pointed out that the people in the lower register are carrying blowguns. Some of them are painted in black. The style suggests that it was one of the "Ik Site" vessels. Form: Cylinder vase of a slightly barrel-like shape. Direct rim and rounded lip. Flat base. Use-wear: Not clear because of erosion.

WVS No.: 23A-60; Catalog No.: 310289 (Figure 8.15b)
Bag No.: Rim: 478 (5-3-1), 283 (6-2-2), 128 (5-1-1); Body: 478, 618 (11-3-2), 417 (6-3-4), 465 (5-3-1); Base: 618. Provenience: 23A5-3-1. Context: Floor. In the southern room. Most (70%) of the rim and body was found in one concentration in the southern part of the bench near the back wall. The rest of the rim and body was on the southern part of the room floor in front of the bench. The base was found in the front part near the pillar that divided the central and southern rooms. Fragments from different areas are burned differently. Fragments may have been scattered intentionally or unintentionally by the fleeing residents or by the invading enemies. The vessel may have been stored on the bench or in a higher location. Condition: Reconstructible (92% present). Eroded. The base is severely burned in red color. Other parts are burned in dark color. Fragments were exposed to fire after the vessel broke. Dimensions: Rim diameter: [exterior] 18.3 cm, [top] 17.9 cm (measured); Height: 10.1 cm (measured); Wall thickness: 0.5–0.6 cm; Sample weight: 433 g; Original weight: 471 g; Volume: 1,495 cm³. Coordinates: (41.38, 14.87) (measured). Type: Unnamed volcanic ash undetermined. Paste, temper, and firing: Yellow paste (10YR7/8). Fine. A small amount of possible volcanic ash (0.1 mm length). The paste is completely oxidized. Surface finish and decoration: The surface is mostly eroded. Remains of white underslip on the exterior wall. Form: Bowl with rounded sides and small flat base. Direct rim and rounded lip. Use-wear: Not clear because of erosion and burning.

WVS No.: 23A-61; Catalog No.: 310312 (Figure 8.15c)
Bag No.: Rim: 662 (8-3-3); Body: 662; Base: 662. Provenience: 23A8-3-3. Context: Floor. In the front part of the south room near the side wall. All fragments were found in one concentration. Condition: Reconstructible (90% present). Eroded. The vessel is burned in dark color. Dimensions: Rim diameter: 2.5 cm (estimate); Height: 5.6 cm (measured); Wall thickness: 0.2–0.4 cm; Sample weight: 34 g; Original weight: 38 g; Volume: 22 cm³. Coordinates: (41.17, 20.52) (measured). Type: Tinaja Red. Paste, temper, and firing: Red paste (2.5YR5/6). The paste color appears to have been changed by burning. Medium grain paste. A medium amount of calcite temper (0.1–0.2 mm diameter). Surface finish and decoration: The entire exterior surface appears to have been red-slipped, although it is darkened by fire. Form: Miniature jar with vertical neck. Direct rim and squared lip. Two strap handles. Use-wear: Not clear because of erosion and burning.

WVS No.: 23A-62; Catalog No.: 310356
Bag No.: Rim: 595 (29-3-3), 458 (28-3-2); Body: 391 (8-3-3), 382 (8-3-1), 340 (23-3-3), 387 (8-3-3), 458, 459 (28-3-3); Base: 382. Provenience: 23A8-3-3. Context: Floor. On the floor of the front area of the south room. Condition: Reconstructible (50% present). Badly eroded. Severely burned and reoxidized. Dimensions: Rim diameter: 13 cm (rough estimate); Maximum diameter: 21 cm (rough estimate); Height: 19 cm (rough estimate); Neck height: 5.5 cm (estimate); Wall thickness: 0.6–0.9 cm; Sample weight: 590 g; Original weight: 1,180 g; Volume: 2,800 cm³. Coordinates: (40.92, 20.43) (measured). Type: Undetermined. Paste, temper, and firing: Reddish yellow paste

(7.5YR6/6). Medium grain. A medium amount of calcite temper (0.3–2.0 mm diameter) and a small amount of ferruginous temper (0.5–2.0 mm diameter). The paste is completely oxidized. Surface finish and decoration: The surface is completely eroded. No recognizable slip or incisions. Form: Pitcher. Outflared neck and globular body. Open spout. Whistle handle with a modeled bird head decoration. Direct rim and rounded lip. Flat base. Similar to other whistle pitchers. Use-wear: Not clear because of erosion.

North Addition

WVS No.: 23A-63; Catalog No.: 310369

Bag No.: Rim: 1001 (32-3-4), 1000 (32-3-2), 931 (33-3-1), 207 (32-1-1); Body: 1001, 1000, 931, 192 (32-1-2); Base: 1001. Provenience: 23A32-3-1. Context: Floor. On the exterior floor east of the north addition, north of the front porch of the north room. Most fragments were found in an area 2 × 1 m. The vessel may have been placed on the floor. Condition: Reconstructible (70% present). Some fragments are eroded while others are relatively well preserved. Some pieces appear to be burned and blackened. Dimensions: Rim diameter: [exterior] 25.6 cm, [top] 24.5 cm (measured); Maximum diameter: 41 cm (estimate); Minimum opening: 14.3 cm (measured); Height: 37 cm (estimate); Neck height: 10.5 cm (measured); Wall thickness: 0.6–1.0 cm; Sample weight: 2,522 g; Original weight: 3,603 g; Volume: 20,647 cm^3. Coordinates: (55.76, 21.39) (estimate). Type: Encanto Striated. Paste, temper, and firing: Reddish yellow paste (7.5YR6/6). Coarse grain. A large amount of calcite temper (0.5–2.0 mm diameter). The paste is completely oxidized. Surface finish and decoration: Striation on the body and base below the shoulder. The neck and interior are unslipped and smoothed. Form: Jar with outcurved neck. Thin-walled and relatively light. Exterior-folded rim and beveled-in lip. Rounded base. Use-wear: The exterior base appears to be slightly worn from use.

WVS No.: 23A-64; Catalog No.: 310167 (Figure 8.16a and 8.16c)

Bag No.: Rim: 1277; Body: 1277; Base: 1277. Provenience: 23A21-3-2. Context: Floor. On the floor of the north addition. The vessel was found as a complete piece. Condition: Complete (98% present). Burned and reoxidized from fire. Slightly eroded. Dimensions: Rim diameter: [exterior] 4.3 cm, [top] 3.8 cm (measured); Maximum diameter: 8.6 cm (measured); Height: 7.5 cm (measured); Wall

thickness: 0.4–0.8 cm; Sample weight: 186 g; Original weight: 190 g; Volume: 92 cm^3. Coordinates: (55.09, 15.64) (measured). Type: Pantano Impressed. Paste, temper, and firing: Reddish yellow paste (5YR6/6). Coarse. A large amount of calcite temper (0.3–2.0 mm diameter) and a small amount of round ferruginous temper (0.5–2.5 mm diameter). The paste is completely oxidized. Surface finish and decoration: Red slip on the entire exterior, including the base. An incision along the neck-body juncture and triangular impressions below it. Form: Miniature jar with outflared neck. Direct rim and rounded lip. Flat base. Two strap handles. Use-wear: Not clear because of erosion.

WVS No.: 23A-65; Catalog No.: 310290 (Figure 8.16b and 8.16c)

Bag No.: Rim: 1625 (30-3-2); Body: 1619 (30-3-1), 1624 (30-3-2), 1314 (30-2-2), 1620 (30-3-2); Base: 1624, 1619. Provenience: 23A30-3-2. Context: Floor. On the floor of the north addition near the wall of the north room. The lower part of the vessel was found in one concentration. Other fragments were in an area 0.5 × 0.5 m. Condition: Reconstructible (85% present). Eroded. Some fragments were darkened or reoxidized in fire. Dimensions: Rim diameter: [exterior] 7.3 cm, [top] 7.2 cm (measured); Maximum diameter: 12.0 cm (measured); Minimum opening: 4.4 cm (measured); Height: 12.1 cm (measured); Neck height: 2.9 cm (measured); Wall thickness: 0.5–0.8 cm; Sample weight: 365 g; Original weight: 429 g; Volume: 432 cm^3. Coordinates: (55.21, 19.19) (measured). Type: Pantano Impressed. Paste, temper, and firing: Pink paste (7.5YR7/4). Medium grain. A medium amount of calcite temper (0.1–2.0 mm diameter) and a small amount of ferruginous temper (0.5–1.5 mm diameter). The paste is completely oxidized. Surface finish and decoration: Red slip on the exterior, including the base. The interior neck is not slipped. Circle and flat triangle impressions below the neck-body juncture. Form: Miniature jar. Direct rim and pointed lip. Incurved base. Use-wear: The edge of the incurved base is worn from use. The rest of the exterior base is well preserved.

WVS No.: 23A-66; Catalog No.: 310334 (Figure 8.16d)

Bag No.: Rim: 1622 (30-3-2), 1620 (30-3-2); Body: 1622, 1620; Base: 1622, 1620. Provenience: 23A30-3-2. Context: Floor. On the eastern edge of the floor of the north addition. Most fragments were found in one concentration. Condition: Reconstructible (65% present). Very eroded. It appears to be burned and oxidized. Dimensions: Rim

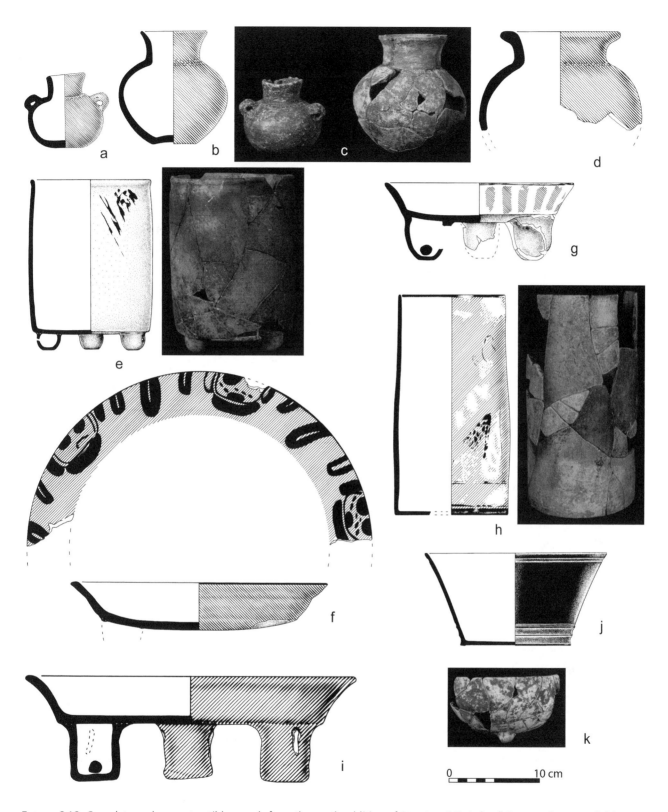

FIGURE 8.16. Complete and reconstructible vessels from the north addition of Structure M8-4. (a–d) Pantano Impressed. (a) 23A21-3-2, Cat. 310167, WVS 23A-64. (b) 23A30-3-2, Cat. 310290, WVS 23A-65. (c) WVS 23A-64 and 23A-65. (d) 23A30-3-2, Cat. 310334, WVS 23A-66. (e–i) Saxche-Palmar Polychrome. (e) 23A36-3-4, Cat. 310287, WVS 23A-68. (f) 23A30-3-2, Cat. 310329, WVS 23A-69. (g) 23A21-3-2, Cat. 310339, WVS 23A-70. (h) 23A22-3-1, Cat. 310325, WVS 23A-71. (i) 23A38-3-4, Cat. 310459, WVS 23A-72. (j) Chablekal Gray, 23A22-3-2, Cat. 310331, WVS 23A-73. (k) Unnamed white slipped, 23A30-3-2, Cat. 310350, WVS 23A-74.

diameter: [exterior] 13.0 cm, [top] 12.3 cm (measured); Maximum diameter: 17.0 cm (measured); Minimum opening: 7.3 cm (measured); Height: 18 cm (rough estimate); Neck height: 3.0 cm (measured); Wall thickness: 0.8–1.1 cm; Sample weight: 442 g; Original weight: 680 g; Volume: 1,395 cm³. Coordinates: (55.53, 20.09) (measured). Type: Pantano Impressed. Paste, temper, and firing: Reddish yellow paste (7.5YR7/6). Medium grain. A large amount of calcite temper (0.3–1.5 mm diameter) and a small amount of ferruginous temper (0.8–1.3 mm diameter). The paste is completely oxidized. Surface finish and decoration: Remains of red slip on the exterior. Two lines of triangular impressions below the neck-body juncture. Form: Jar with markedly outcurved neck. Direct rim and squared lip. Incurved base. Use-wear: Not clear because of erosion.

WVS No.: 23A-67; Catalog No.: 310366 (Figures 8.12c, 8.12d, and 8.60l)
Bag No.: Rim: 1481 (32-3-1); Body: 1481; Base: 1002 (44-3-2). Provenience: 23A32-3-1. Context: Floor. On the exterior floor east of the north addition and north of the front porch of the north room. Most of the recovered fragments were found in one concentration. The vessel appears to have broken in an upside-down position in this place. The base was not recovered in this concentration. A part of a base found in Lot 32-3-2 located 2 m to the southeast of the concentration was tentatively associated with this vessel in the lab. The vessel may have originally been placed on the front bench of the north room or on a wooden table and may have broken into two parts when it fell on the front porch. The upper body may have rolled to the north of the porch, and the vase may have fallen in front of the porch. Condition: Reconstructible (60% present). Eroded. Burned and partially darkened. Dimensions: Rim diameter: [interior] 33.5 cm, [top] 34.2 cm (measured); Maximum diameter: 54.2 cm (measured); Height: 31 cm (estimate); Wall thickness: 0.7–0.8 cm; Sample weight: 5,496 g; Original weight: 9,160 g; Volume: 44,821 cm³. Coordinates: (55.59, 21.13) (measured). Type: Chaquiste Impressed. Paste, temper, and firing: Reddish yellow paste (5YR7/6). Medium grain. A medium amount of calcite temper (0.1–1.2 mm diameter) and a small amount of ferruginous temper (0.5–1.5 mm diameter). The paste is completely oxidized. Surface finish and decoration: Red slip on the exterior wall above the ridge and on the interior. Quincunx stamps below the thickened rim and on the ridge. Form: Bowl with markedly incurved sides and restricted orifice. Exterior-thickened rim and rounded lip. Ring base. Use-wear: Not clear because of erosion.

WVS No.: 23A-68; Catalog No.: 310287 (Figure 8.16e)
Bag No.: Rim: 1484 (36-3-4), 1560 (21-3-1); Body: 1484, 1560, 1320 (36-2-1), 1487 (36-3-4); Base: 1484, 1560. Provenience: 23A36-3-4. Context: Floor. On the floor of the north addition. A significant portion of fragments was found in one concentration. Another smaller concentration was 1.5 m to the southwest of the first one. Condition: Reconstructible (95% present). Badly eroded. Severely burned in dark and reddish colors. Dimensions: Rim diameter: [exterior] 12.9 cm, [top] 12.5 cm (measured); Maximum diameter: 13.3 cm (measured); Height: 18.3 cm (measured); Height without feet: 16.6 cm (measured); Wall thickness: 0.5–0.6 cm; Sample weight: 696 g; Original weight: 733 g; Volume: 1,944 cm³. Coordinates: (56.55, 15.58) (measured). Type: Saxche-Palmar Polychrome. Paste, temper, and firing: Reddish yellow paste (7.5YR7/6). Fine. A small amount of calcite temper (0.3–1.0 mm diameter) and a small amount of ferruginous temper (0.8–1.5 mm diameter). The paste is completely oxidized. Surface finish and decoration: The surface is mostly eroded. There seem to have been red, orange, and black paints, although their original colors are difficult to see because of burning. Remains of paint on the interior rim. Form: Vase with vertical sides. Exterior-thickened rim and rounded lip. Flat base with three small, hollow hemispherical feet with a small opening and a rattle. Use-wear: Not clear because of erosion.

WVS No.: 23A-69; Catalog No.: 310329 (Figure 8.16f)
Bag No.: Rim: 1621 (30-3-2); Body: 1621; Base: 1621. Provenience: 23A30-3-2. Context: Floor. On the floor of the northern addition near the wall of the north room. All the fragments were found in one concentration. It was probably used as a partial vessel. The feet are broken off cleanly, and it appears that the vessel was used without feet. Condition: Partial (70% present). Slightly eroded. It is not clear whether it was burned. Dimensions: Rim diameter: [exterior] 28.2 cm, [top] 27.2 cm (measured); Height: 9.5 cm (rough estimate); Height without feet: 4.7 cm (measured); Wall thickness: 0.7–0.8 cm; Sample weight: 639 g; Original weight: 912 g; Volume: 1,119 cm³. Coordinates: (55.36, 19.39) (measured). Type: Saxche-Palmar Polychrome. Paste, temper, and firing: Very pale brown paste (10YR8/4). Fine grain. A medium amount of calcite

temper (0.1 mm diameter), a small amount of ferruginous temper (0.5–1.0 mm diameter), and a very small amount of large, angular inclusions (3.0–4.0 mm diameter). The paste is completely oxidized. Surface finish and decoration: Motifs painted in weak black and red paints over orange slip on the interior wall. Some remains of orange slip on the interior base, though it is mostly eroded. While the interior is polished, the exterior wall is rough. Red slip on the exterior wall. Some weak red slip on the exterior base. Form: Plate with slightly outflared sides. Direct rim and flat lip. Flat base. Use-wear: Most paint on the interior base is lost, possibly because of use. The base is not pitted, and it appears to have been only abraded. The use-wear on the exterior is not clear. A small amount of burned clay is caked on the exterior wall near the rim, but the interior is clean. It may have been used in a manner similar to the other reused sherds found in the same area, perhaps in some kind of craft work involving the use of clay.

WVS No.: 23A-70; Catalog No.: 310339 (Figure 8.16g)
Bag No.: Rim: 1524 (21-3-2); Body: 1524; Base: 1524. Provenience: 23A21-3-2. Context: Floor. On the floor of the north addition. The shape of the vessel lying face-down was recognizable in the field. It appears that the vessel fell and then was broken by the impact or pressure of materials that fell from above. Condition: Reconstructible (95% present). Eroded. The vessel, particularly some parts of the rim, appears to be burned and reoxidized. This may suggest that it was not placed face-down on the floor originally but was stored in a higher location. Dimensions: Rim diameter: [exterior] 21.0 cm, [top] 20.0 cm (measured); Height: 8.0 cm (measured); Height without feet: 4.1 cm (measured); Wall thickness: 0.7–0.8 cm; Sample weight: 512 g; Original weight: 538 g; Volume: 672 cm^3. Coordinates: (55.54, 15.48) (measured). Type: Saxche-Palmar Polychrome. Paste, temper, and firing: Reddish yellow paste (7.5YR7/6). Fine grain. A small amount of calcite temper (0.1–1.0 mm diameter) and a small amount of ferruginous temper (0.5–2.0 mm diameter). The paste is completely oxidized. Surface finish and decoration: Black band on the interior rim. Black lines over red paint on the interior surface. They seem to show figural motifs. Orange vertical stripes over thin cream slip or the natural paste color on the exterior wall. The exterior base and feet are not slipped. Form: Plate with outflared sides. Direct rim and rounded lip. Flat base. Three hollow oven-shaped feet with two openings and possibly a rattle. Use-wear: Not clear because of erosion.

WVS No.: 23A-71; Catalog No.: 310325 (Figure 8.16h)
Bag No.: Rim: 1547 (22-3-1), 1544 (21-3-1), 1545 (21-3-2), 1616 (22-3-1), 1619 (30-3-1), 1446 (38-3-3); Body: 1547, 1616, 1435 (37-3-3), 1321, 1446, 1619; Base: 1547, 1616. Provenience: 23A22-3-1. Context: Floor. On the floor of the north addition. Many fragments of the low part of the vessel were found in one concentration, but others were scattered over nearly the entire north addition (2-×-4-m area). The vessel may have been stored in a higher location and fell. Condition: Reconstructible (70% present). Badly eroded and badly burned. Some fragments were burned after the vessel broke. Dimensions: Rim diameter: [exterior] 12.5 cm, [top] 12.2 cm (measured); Height: 23.2 cm (measured); Wall thickness: 0.3–0.6 cm; Sample weight: 635 g; Original weight: 907 g; Volume: 2,380 cm^3. Coordinates: (55.40, 16.22) (measured). Type: Saxche-Palmar Polychrome. Paste, temper, and firing: Reddish yellow paste (5YR7/6). Fine grain. A small amount of calcite temper (0.1–0.3 mm diameter), a small amount of ferruginous temper (0.3–0.8 mm diameter), and a very small amount of volcanic ash temper (0.1 mm length). The paste is completely oxidized. Surface finish and decoration: Black and red paints over orange slip on the exterior. It appears to show a palace scene, but the rendering is not clear because of erosion. The exterior base is not slipped. Black band on the rim. The interior surface has cream slip. Form: Cylinder vase with vertical sides. Direct rim and rounded lip. Flat base. Use-wear: Not clear because of erosion.

WVS No.: 23A-72; Catalog No.: 310459 (Figure 8.16i)
Bag No.: Rim: 1451 (38-3-4); Body: 1451; Base: 1451. Provenience: 23A38-3-4. Context: Floor. On the floor of the north addition, near its northeastern corner. All fragments were found in one concentration. Condition: Reconstructible (90% present). Eroded. Burned and darkened. Dimensions: Rim diameter: [exterior] 36.0 cm, [top] 34.0 cm (measured); Height: 11.1 cm (measured); Height without feet: 5.0 cm (measured); Wall thickness: 0.7–0.9 cm; Sample weight: 1,650 g; Original weight: 1,833 g; Volume: 2,159 cm^3. Coordinates: (56.71, 19.42) (measured). Type: Saxche-Palmar Polychrome. Paste, temper, and firing: Reddish yellow paste (5YR6/8). Fine grain. A medium amount of volcanic ash temper (0.1 mm length) and a very small amount of dark red particles (0.1 mm length). The core of the paste is dark. Surface finish and decoration: Remains of orange and red paints over cream underslip on the interior. Orange paint over thin cream underslip on the exterior wall and base. Form: Plate

with slightly outcurved sides. Direct rim and flat lip. Flat base. Three hollow cylindrical feet with two openings and a rattle. Use-wear: Feet are worn from use.

WVS No.: 23A-73; Catalog No.: 310331 (Figure 8.16j)
Bag No.: Rim: 1618 (22-3-2); Body: 1618; Base: 1618. Provenience: 23A22-3-2. Context: Floor. On the floor of the north addition near the wall of the north room. All the recovered fragments are from an area 1 × 1 m. Condition: Reconstructible (55% present). Eroded. Traces of burning are not clear. Dimensions: Rim diameter: 19 cm (estimate); Height: 9.9 cm (measured); Wall thickness: 0.4–0.6 cm; Sample weight: 272 g; Original weight: 494 g; Volume: 1,184 cm^3. Coordinates: (55.55, 17.56) (estimate). Type: Chablekal Gray. Paste, temper, and firing: Gray paste (10YR6/1). Fine grain. A small amount of quartz temper (0.3–1.0 mm length) and a small amount of volcanic ash temper (0.1 mm length). The core of the paste is black. Surface finish and decoration: Black slip on the exterior wall and below the interior rim. The exterior base and the interior do not seem to be slipped and are black from reduced firing. Fluted band above the base. Form: Bowl with outcurved sides. Exterior-thickened rim and rounded lip. Flat base. Use-wear: None recognizable on the interior or the exterior base.

WVS No.: 23A-74; Catalog No.: 310350 (Figure 8.16k)
Bag No.: Rim: 1620 (30-3-2); Body: 1620; Base: 1620, 1618 (22-3-2). Provenience: 23A30-3-2. Context: Floor. On the floor of the north addition. Most fragments were found in an area 1 × 1 m. Condition: Reconstructible (50% present). Badly eroded. Severely burned and reoxidized. Dimensions: Rim diameter: 14 cm (estimate); Height: 7.1 cm (measured); Height without feet: 6.6 cm (measured); Wall thickness: 0.4–0.5 cm; Sample weight: 111 g; Original weight: 222 g; Volume: 393 cm^3. Coordinates: (55.63, 19.10) (estimate). Type: Unnamed white slipped (or Saxche-Palmar Polychrome). Paste, temper, and firing: Reddish yellow paste (7.5YR7/8). Medium grain. A medium amount of calcite temper (0.1–1.3 mm diameter) and a small amount of ferruginous temper (0.5–0.8 mm diameter). The paste is completely oxidized. Surface finish and decoration: White slip on the exterior wall and feet. The exterior base and the entire interior do not seem to have been slipped. The surface of white slip appears different from that of eroded polychrome. Form: Bowl with incurved sides. Direct rim and rounded lip. Rounded base. Three solid nubbin feet. Use-wear: Not clear because of erosion.

Southern Exterior

WVS No.: 23A-75; Catalog No.: 310386 (Figure 8.17a)
Bag No.: Rim: 830 (2-2-1); Body: 919 (2-3-3), 922 (2-3-1), 906 (3-3-4). Provenience: 23A2-3-1. Context: Floor. On the exterior floor south of the structure. Most of the recovered fragments were found in one concentration near the edge of excavation. Other fragments probably remained in the nearby unexcavated area. It is not clear whether the vessel was kept in partial condition. Condition: Reconstructible (20% present). Relatively well preserved. Some fragments are darkened, but it is not clear whether they are burned. Dimensions: Rim diameter: 29 cm (estimate); Maximum diameter: 35 cm (rough estimate); Minimum opening: 15 cm (estimate); Height: 40 cm (rough estimate); Neck height: 10.0 cm (measured); Wall thickness: 0.9–1.1 cm; Sample weight: 2,318 g; Original weight: 11,590 g; Volume: 16,306 cm^3. Coordinates: (38.14, 16.86) (measured). Type: Encanto Striated. Paste, temper, and firing: Reddish yellow paste (5YR6/6). Coarse grain. A very large amount of calcite temper (0.3–2.0 mm diameter), a small amount of quartz sand temper (0.8–1.5 mm length), and a small amount of ferruginous temper (0.5–1.5 mm diameter). The paste is completely oxidized. Surface finish and decoration: Striation below the shoulder. The interior and the neck are smoothed. Form: Jar with outcurved neck. Exterior-folded rim and beveled-in lip. Use-wear: Not clear.

WVS No.: 23A-76; Catalog No.: 310378
Bag No.: Body: 903 (4-3-3), 905 (3-3-4), 909 (3-3-3), 838, 102 (2-1-1), 830 (2-2-1), 101 (3-1-1), 906 (3-3-4), 914 (3-3-2), 926 (4-3-1), 920 (2-3-3), 115 (4-1-1); Base: 905, 909, 102. Provenience: 23A4-3-3. Context: Floor. On the exterior floor south of the structure. A significant portion of the vessel was found in one concentration in front of the side porch. Other fragments were scattered in an area 1 × 2 m. The vessel was not restored in the lab, but it appears to have most of the body parts, including the base. The rim and neck were not recovered. It is not clear whether the vessel was used without a neck or whether the rim and neck remained in the nearby unexcavated area. Condition: Reconstructible (40% present). Some fragments are relatively well preserved while others are eroded. Some fragments are burned and blackened. Dimensions: Maximum diameter: 57 cm (rough estimate); Minimum opening: 25 cm (rough estimate); Height: 66 cm (rough estimate); Wall thickness: 0.8–1.0 cm; Sample weight: 7,843 g; Original weight: 19,607 g; Volume: 72,211 cm^3. Coordinates: (39.11, 20.18) (measured). Type: Encanto

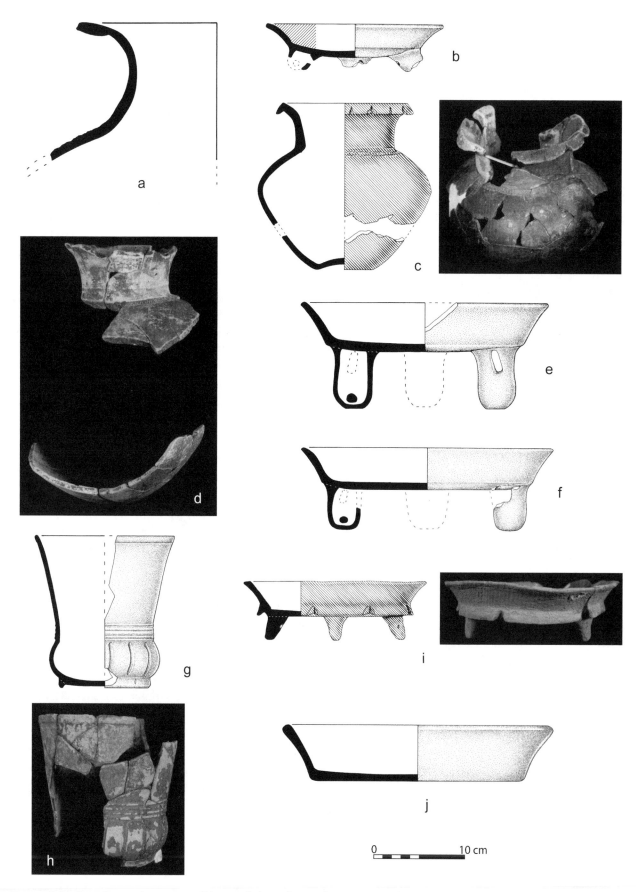

FIGURE 8.17. Complete and reconstructible vessels from the southern exterior of Structure M8-4. (a) Encanto Striated, 23A2-3-1, Cat. 310386, WVS 23A-75. (b) Tinaja Red, 23A-4-3-3, Cat. 310341, WVS 23A-77. (c, d) Pantano Impressed. (c) 23A3-3-2, Cat. 310336, WVS 23A-78. (d) 23A2-2-1, Cat. 310358, WVS 23A-79. (e, f) Saxche-Palmar Polychrome. (e) 23A4-3-3, Cat. 310340, WVS 23A-80. (f) 23A3-3-1, Cat. 310346, WVS 23A-81. (g, h) Chablekal Gray, 23A2-3-3, Cat. 310343, WVS 23A-83. (i) Andres Red, 23A3-3-4, Cat. 310323, WVS 23A-84. (j) Unnamed volcanic ash undetermined, 23A52-3-2, Cat. 310324, WVS 23A-85.

Striated. Paste, temper, and firing: Very pale brown paste (10YR7/4). Coarse grain. A large amount of calcite temper (0.5–2.5 mm diameter) and a small amount of ferruginous temper (0.8–1.3 mm diameter). The paste is completely oxidized. Surface finish and decoration: Striation on the exterior body and base below the shoulder. The interior is smoothed. Form: Jar. Rounded base. Relatively thin-walled. Use-wear: Little wear on the exterior base. Some sherds have some burned clay caked on the exterior as in the reworked sherds found in the same area, but most fragments are clean.

WVS No.: 23A-77; Catalog No.: 310341 (Figure 8.17b)
Bag No.: Rim: 902 (4-3-3); Body: 902; Base: 902. Provenience: 23A4-3-3. Context: Floor. On the exterior floor south of the structure. Fragments were found in an area 1 × 1 m. Condition: Reconstructible (70% present). Very eroded and heavily burned. Many fragments were reoxidized. Most fragments are small. Most of the base and one-third of the wall are present. It is not clear if the vessel was complete at the time of abandonment or was used in partial condition, as were the reused sherds found in the same area. Dimensions: Rim diameter: 20 cm (estimate); Height: 5.5 cm (estimate); Height without feet: 3.0 cm (measured); Wall thickness: 0.5–0.7 cm; Sample weight: 252 g; Original weight: 360 g; Volume: 277 cm³. Coordinates: (39.10, 20.66) (estimate). Type: Tinaja Red. Paste, temper, and firing: Very pale brown paste (10YR7/4). Fine grain. A small amount of sand temper consisting of quartz and other angular minerals (0.1–2.5 mm diameter). The paste is completely oxidized. The paste is different from that of common Tinaja Red or Saxche-Palmar vessels. Surface finish and decoration: Orange slip over the interior wall. Other parts are eroded. Form: Plate with slightly outcurved sides. Direct rim and rounded lip. Flat base. Three hollow oven feet with two openings and possibly a rattle. Use-wear: Not clear because of erosion. A small amount of burned clay is caked on the exterior base, as in the reused sherds found in the same area. The vessel may have been used for some kind of craftwork involving the use of clay.

WVS No.: 23A-78; Catalog No.: 310336 (Figure 8.17c)
Bag No.: Rim: 914 (3-3-2), 905 (3-3-4), 902 (4-3-3), 821 (1-2-1); Body: 914, 902, 905; Base: 914, 905. Provenience: 23A3-3-2. Context: Floor. On the side porch and the exterior floor south of the structure. Most fragments were scattered in an area 1 × 1 m. The vessel was probably

placed on the porch or in a higher location. Condition: Reconstructible (65% present). Some fragments are relatively well preserved whereas others are severely burned and eroded. Some fragments received fire after the vessel broke. Dimensions: Rim diameter: [exterior] 14.9 cm, [top] 13.7 cm (measured); Maximum diameter: 19.1 cm (measured); Minimum opening: 8.9 cm (measured); Height: 17.2 cm (estimate); Neck height: 4.9 cm (measured); Wall thickness: 0.5–1.1 cm; Sample weight: 675 g; Original weight: 1,038 g; Volume: 1,916 cm³. Coordinates: (39.58, 19.62) (measured). Type: Pantano Impressed. Paste, temper, and firing: Reddish yellow paste (5YR6/6). Medium grain. A medium amount of calcite temper (0.1–1.2 mm diameter) and a small amount of ferruginous temper (0.5–2.0 mm diameter). The paste is completely oxidized. Surface finish and decoration: Red slip on the entire exterior, including the base. The interior neck is not slipped. Punctuations below the neck-body juncture. Notched on the exterior rim. Form: Jar with outcurved neck. Exterior-thickened rim and pointed lip. Incurved base. Use-wear: The edge along the exterior base is worn from use.

WVS No.: 23A-79; Catalog No.: 310358 (Figure 8.17d)
Bag No.: Rim: 830 (2-2-1); Body: 830, 838 (3-2-1), 902 (4-3-3), 916 (2-3-4), 905 (3-3-4), 921 (2-3-3), 914 (3-3-2), 909 (3-3-3), 912 (3-3-3), 920 (2-3-3), 843 (4-2-1), 830, Base: 838. Provenience: 23A2-2-1. Context: Floor. On the exterior floor south of the structure. A significant portion was in the wall-fall layer. Fragments were found in an area 2 × 3 m. Missing pieces are probably in unexcavated areas. The vessel was probably stored in a high location along the wall. Condition: Reconstructible (50% present). Eroded and burned. Some fragments received fire after the vessel broke. Dimensions: Rim diameter: 13.5 cm (measured); Maximum diameter: 26 cm (rough estimate); Minimum opening: 6.8 cm (measured); Height: 26 cm (measured); Neck height: 5.8 cm (measured); Wall thickness: 0.5–0.8 cm; Sample weight: 1,379 g; Original weight: 2,758 g; Volume: 6,234 cm³. Coordinates: (38.47, 17.75) (measured). Type: Pantano Impressed. Paste, temper, and firing: Light reddish brown paste (5YR6/4). Medium grain. A medium amount of calcite temper (0.1–2.0 mm diameter) and a small amount of ferruginous temper (0.5–2.0 mm diameter). The paste is completely oxidized. Surface finish and decoration: Red slip on the entire exterior, including the base. It is not clear whether the interior neck was slipped. Cross-hatch stamps and triangular punctua-

tions below the neck-body juncture. Form: Jar with out-curved neck. Direct rim and rounded lip. Incurved base. Use-wear: The edge of the exterior base is worn. Burned clay is caked on a part of the low body near the base and on some body sherds.

WVS No.: 23A-80; Catalog No.: 310340 (Figure 8.17e)
Bag No.: Rim: 901 (4-3-3), 902 (4-3-3); Body: 901, 902; Base: 901, 902. Provenience: 23A4-3-3. Context: Floor. On the exterior floor south of the structure. A quarter of the vessel was found in one concentration. Other fragments were in an area 1 × 2 m. Missing fragments may be in the adjacent unexcavated area. The vessel appears to have been placed on a high location along the exterior wall of the structure. Condition: Partial (70% present). Very eroded and heavily burned. Some fragments are darkened. Some fragments were burned after the vessel broke. Dimensions: Rim diameter: [exterior] 28.6 cm, [top] 28.1 cm (measured); Height: 10.2 cm (measured); Height without feet: 4.8 cm (measured); Wall thickness: 0.7–0.9 cm; Sample weight: 875 g; Original weight: 1,250 g; Volume: 1,043 cm³. Coordinates: (38.85, 20.52) (measured). Type: Saxche-Palmar Polychrome. Paste, temper, and firing: Reddish yellow paste (7.5YR7/6). Medium grain. A medium amount of calcite temper (0.1–2.0 mm diameter) and a small amount of ferruginous temper (0.5–1.0 mm diameter). The paste is completely oxidized. Surface finish and decoration: Remains of red paint over cream underslip on the rim, exterior, and interior. Form: Plate with slightly outcurved sides. Direct rim and rounded lip. Flat base. Three hollow oven feet with a rattle and two openings. Use-wear: Not clear because of erosion.

WVS No.: 23A-81; Catalog No.: 310346 (Figure 8.17f)
Bag No.: Rim: 913 (3-3-1), 909 (3-3-3), 838 (3-2-1), 905 (3-3-4); Body: 913, 909, 838, 905; Base: 913, 909, 905, 902 (4-3-3), 916 (2-3-4). Provenience: 23A3-3-1. Context: Floor. On the exterior floor south of the structure. Fragments were found in an area 1.2 × 3.0 m. The vessel was probably placed originally outside the structure. Condition: Reconstructible (50% present). Very eroded. Part of the interior base is blackened, probably from the burning of the structure. Missing parts may have remained in the adjacent unexcavated area. Dimensions: Rim diameter: [exterior] 28.5 cm, [top] 28.0 cm (measured); Height: 10.3 cm (measured); Height without feet: 4.9 cm (measured); Wall thickness: 0.8–1.0 cm; Sample weight: 743 g; Original weight: 1,486 g; Volume: 1,506 cm³. Coordi-

nates: (38.90, 18.51) (estimate). Type: Saxche-Palmar Polychrome. Paste, temper, and firing: Reddish yellow paste (7.5YR7/6). Fine grain. A medium amount of calcite temper (0.1–0.4 mm diameter) and a small amount of ferruginous temper (0.3–0.8 mm diameter). The paste is completely oxidized. Surface finish and decoration: Remains of red and orange paint over cream underslip. Form: Plate with flared sides. Direct rim and rounded lip. Flat base. Use-wear: Not clear because of erosion.

WVS No.: 23A-82; Catalog No.: 310401
Bag No.: Rim: 920 (2-3-3); Body: 920; Base: 920. Provenience: 23A2-3-3. Context: Floor. On the exterior floor south of the structure. The recovered fragments were found in one concentration. Condition: Partial (40% present). Eroded. Burned and darkened. Only the base and lower body were found. It may have been used as a partial vessel, along with other reworked sherds found in the same area. It is possible that other pieces are in unexcavated areas. Dimensions: The remaining part is 30 cm in diameter and 11 cm in height. Wall thickness: 0.5–0.8 cm; Sample weight: 1,456 g; Original weight: 3,640 g; Volume: not calculated. Coordinates: (38.53, 16.74) (measured). Type: Tinaja Red or Pantano Impressed. Paste, temper, and firing: Pink paste (7.5YR7/4). Medium grain. A medium amount of calcite temper (0.3–1.3 mm diameter) and a small amount of ferruginous temper (0.3–1.3 mm diameter). The paste is completely oxidized. Surface finish and decoration: Red slip on the exterior, including the base. Form: Jar. Incurved base. Use-wear: The edge of the exterior base is heavily worn. No remains of burned clay.

WVS No.: 23A-83; Catalog No.: 310343 (Figure 8.17g and 8.17h)
Bag No.: Rim: 917 (2-3-3), 830; Body: 917, 915 (2-3-4), 830 (2-2-1); Base: 917. Provenience: 23A2-3-3. Context: Floor. On the exterior floor south of the structure. Most fragments were found in one concentration. A small number of fragments were found in an area 1 × 1 m. The vessel may have been placed on the side porch along the wall of the structure. Condition: Reconstructible (65% present). Very eroded. Heavily burned, and some parts of the thickened rim broke off in the heat. The surface appears to have been oxidized by the fire. Dimensions: Rim diameter: [exterior] 15.6 cm, [top] 15.3 cm (measured); Height: 16.1 cm (measured); Wall thickness: 0.4–0.7 cm; Sample weight: 357 g; Original weight: 549 g; Volume: 714 cm³.

Coordinates: (39.15, 17.05) (measured). Type: Chablekal Gray. Paste, temper, and firing: Dark bluish gray paste (10B4/1) in the core and reddish yellow paste (5YR7/6) on the surface. The surface color is probably due to reoxidation in the fire. Very fine grain. A very small amount of red and black temper (0.4–0.8 mm diameter). Surface finish and decoration: Small horizontal ridge on the mid-body and vertical grooves on the lower body. It is not clear whether the vessel was slipped. Form: Bowl with outcurved upper sides and incurved lower sides. Exterior-thickened rim and rounded lip. Ring base. Use-wear: Not clear because of erosion.

WVS No.: 23A-84; Catalog No.: 310323 (Figure 8.17i)
Bag No.: Rim: 907 (3-3-4), 905 (3-3-4); Body: 907, 905; Base: 907, 905. Provenience: 23A3-3-4. Context: Floor. On the exterior floor south of the structure. Most fragments were found in one concentration. The vessel may have been on a porch or in a high location along the exterior wall of the structure. Condition: Reconstructible (95% present). Very eroded and heavily burned. Some parts are darkened, and some are oxidized. The vessel appears to have received fire as a complete piece. Dimensions: Rim diameter: [exterior] 19.2 cm, [top] 18.6 cm (measured); Height: 5.2–5.9 cm (measured); Height without feet: 3.3 cm (measured); Wall thickness: 0.5–0.6 cm; Sample weight: 340 g; Original weight: 358 g; Volume: 531 cm³. Coordinates: (38.73, 19.49) (measured). Type: Andres Red. Paste, temper, and firing: Reddish yellow paste (7.5YR7/6). Burned parts may be light red (2.5YR6/8) or bluish gray (5PB6/1). Fine grain. A small amount of volcanic ash temper (0.1 mm long), and a small amount of ferruginous temper (1.0–1.5 mm diameter). Dark core. Surface finish and decoration: Red to cream slip on the entire interior and on the exterior wall. Notched on the basal ridge. Form: Plate with flared sides. Slightly outflared everted rim and flat lip. Flat base. Three hollow conical feet with one opening. Use-wear: Not clear because of erosion.

Patio

WVS No.: 23A-85; Catalog No.: 310324 (Figure 8.17j)
Bag No.: Rim: 862 (52-3-2), 327 (53-1-1), 859 (53-3-1); Body: 862, 859; Base: 862, 859, 326 (52-1-1), 860 (53-3-2). Provenience: 23A52-3-2. Context: Floor. Exterior floor in the middle of the patio. Fragments were found in an area 0.5 × 1.0 m. It is not clear whether they are large fragments discarded in the patio or whether a complete vessel orig-

inally stored in the structure was thrown at the time of abandonment. Condition: Partial (60% present). Very eroded. No clear traces of burning. Dimensions: Rim diameter: [exterior] 29.5 cm, [top] 28.6 cm (measured); Height: 6.1 cm (measured); Wall thickness: 0.7–1.0 cm; Sample weight: 797 g; Original weight: 1,328 g; Volume: 1,947 cm³. Coordinates: (47.04, 27.11) (measured). Type: Unnamed volcanic ash undetermined. Paste, temper, and firing: Reddish yellow paste (5YR7/8). Medium grain. A small amount of volcanic ash temper (0.1 mm long) and a small amount of calcite temper (0.3–1.0 mm diameter). The paste is completely oxidized. Surface finish and decoration: It is not clear whether the vessel was slipped originally. Form: Plate with outcurved sides. Direct rim and squared lip. Flat base. No feet. Use-wear: Not clear because of erosion.

STRUCTURE M8-8 (HOUSE OF AXES): OPERATION 20A

North Room

WVS No.: 20A-1; Catalog No.: 310055 (Figure 8.18a and 8.18b)
Bag No.: Body: 187 (3-3-1), 184 (3-3-1), 193 (3-3-2), 190 (3-3-1), 1032 (19-3-5), 202 (3-3-3), 917 (19-2-3), 920 (19-3-4), 378 (3-3-2); Base: 187, 909 (19-3-2). Provenience: 20A3-3-1. Context: Floor. In the northern part of the floor in front of the bench in the north room. The recovered fragments were found in one concentration. There were two to three layers of sherds, and some base fragments were found in an upper layer. It appears that the vessel was originally placed near the north wall. The vessel probably broke after it rolled forward. Condition: Reconstructible (85% present). Slightly eroded. Some parts appear to be burned and darkened. Although the most of the body was reconstructed, the rim was not found. It is probable that the vessel was used without the rim after it broke off. Alternatively, the rim may have rolled away when it broke off at the time of abandonment. Dimensions: Maximum diameter: 75–78 cm (measured); Height: 83 cm (estimate); Wall thickness: 0.8–0.9 cm; Sample weight: 25,914 g; Original weight: 30,487 g; Volume: 212,581 cm³. Coordinates: (30.75, 10.10) (measured). Type: Manteca Impressed Ridged variety. Paste, temper, and firing: Very pale brown paste (10YR7/4). Coarse grain. A large amount of calcite temper (0.5–1.3 mm diameter). The paste is completely oxidized. Surface finish and decoration: Unslipped, smoothed body. A thick fillet (2.5 cm wide) on the shoulder with impressions. Form: Jar, probably with

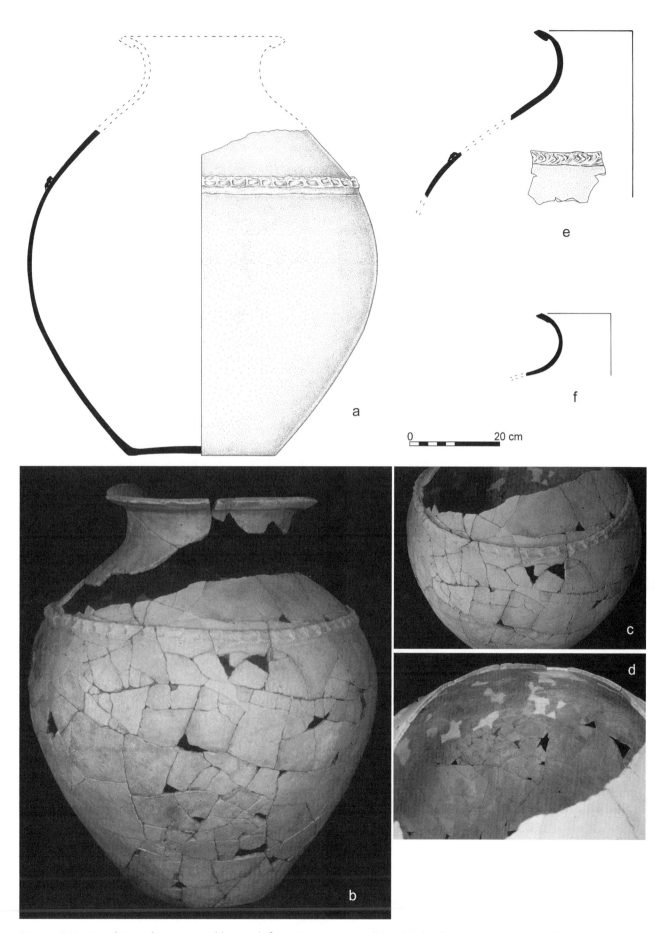

FIGURE 8.18. Complete and reconstructible vessels from Structure M8-8 (⅛ scale). (a–d) Manteca Impressed, 20A3-3-1 (north room), Cat. 310055, WVS 20A-1. (b) Possible reconstruction with a rim portion belonging to a different vessel. (c, d) Close-ups of WVS 20A-1 (not to scale). (e) Manteca Impressed, 20A23-3-1 (center room), Cat. 310179, WVS 20A-24. (f) Encanto Striated, 20A1-3-4 (center room), Cat. 310129, WVS 20A-25.

outcurved neck. Flat base. The upper edge of the fillet is 59–60 cm high. The highest point of the reconstructed part is 69 cm high. Use-wear: Not clear.

WVS No.: 20A-2; Catalog No.: 310126
Bag No.: Rim: 392 (2-3-1), 396 (2-3-2), 544; Body: 392, 396, 400 (6-3-1), 544 (6-2-2), 786 (6-3-3), 103 (2-1-1), 392; Base: 392. Provenience: 20A2-3-1. Context: Floor. On the bench of the north room, near the north wall. Most fragments were found in an area 1.5 × 1.5 m. Condition: Reconstructible (90% present). Eroded. Some parts are burned and slightly darkened. Only half the rim was reconstructed. Body sherds may be mixed with those of other Encanto vessels. Dimensions: Rim diameter: [exterior] 36.0 cm, [top] 34.4 cm (measured); Maximum diameter: 58 cm (rough estimate); Minimum opening: 22 cm (estimate); Height: 65 cm (rough estimate); Neck height: 11.0 cm (measured); Wall thickness: 0.6–1.2 cm; Sample weight: 20,223 g; Original weight: 22,470 g; Volume: 77,709 cm^3. Coordinates: (30.55, 8.44) (measured). Type: Encanto Striated. Paste, temper, and firing: Pink paste (7.5YR7/4). Coarse grain. A very large amount of calcite temper (0.3–2.0 mm diameter). The paste is completely oxidized. Surface finish and decoration: Striation on the body below the shoulder. Unslipped, smoothed neck. Form: Jar with outcurved neck. Exterior-folded rim and beveled-in lip. Rounded base. Use-wear: The base appears to be worn from use.

WVS No.: 20A-3; Catalog No.: 310155
Bag No.: Rim: 913 (17-3-1); Body: 913; Base: 353 (17-2-2). Provenience: 20A17-3-1. Context: Floor. On the bench of the north room, near its southwestern corner. Most fragments were found in an area 1 × 1 m. Condition: Reconstructible (50% present). Eroded. Traces of burning are not clear. Fragments were not refitted. Body sherds may be mixed with those of other Encanto vessels. Dimensions: Rim diameter: 22 cm (estimate); Maximum diameter: 35 cm (rough estimate); Minimum opening: 12 cm (estimate); Height: 35 cm (rough estimate); Neck height: 9.0 cm (measured); Wall thickness: 0.6–0.8 cm; Sample weight: 1,388 g; Original weight: 2,776 g; Volume: 13,162 cm^3. Coordinates: (28.78, 7.83) (estimate). Type: Encanto Striated. Paste, temper, and firing: Light brown paste (7.5YR6/4). Coarse grain. A large amount of calcite temper (0.3–1.5 mm diameter). The core of the paste is dark in some parts. Surface finish and decoration: Striations on the body below the shoulder. Unslipped, smoothed neck. Relatively rough execution.

Form: Jar with outcurved neck. Exterior-folded rim and rounded lip. Rounded base. Use-wear: Not clear because of erosion.

WVS No.: 20A-4; Catalog No.: 310173
Bag No.: Rim: 620 (13-3-4), 416 (13-2-2), 170 (13-2-1); Body: 416, 170, 620, 612 (13-3-2), 211 (14-2-1); Base: 416. Provenience: 20A13-2-1. Context: Floor. Most fragments were found in the wall-fall layer of Unit 13 in the north addition. Roughly half the recovered fragments were in the upper layer of the wall fall, and the other half were in the lower layer. A small number of sherds were on the floor. It is probable that the vessel was originally stored in the north room, along its north wall, and that it fell with the wall into the north addition. Yet since most fragments were not refitted, fragments of other Encanto vessels may be mixed. Condition: Reconstructible (50% present). Slightly eroded. Traces of burning are not clear on most sherds. The base and the lower body appear to be blackened on the exterior, but it is not clear whether that is due to burning or to use. Dimensions: Rim diameter: 32 cm (estimate); Maximum diameter: 48 cm (rough estimate); Minimum opening: 20 cm (estimate); Height: 48 cm (rough estimate); Neck height: 10 cm (estimate); Wall thickness: 0.6–0.9 cm; Sample weight: 5,812 g; Original weight: 11,624 g; Volume: 41,474 cm^3. Coordinates: (33.45, 9.42) (estimate). Type: Encanto Striated. Paste, temper, and firing: Reddish yellow paste (7.5YR7/6). Coarse grain. A large amount of calcite temper (0.3–1.5 mm diameter). The paste is completely oxidized. Surface finish and decoration: Striations on the body below the shoulder. Unslipped, smoothed neck. Form: Jar with outcurved neck. Exterior-folded rim and beveled-in lip. Rounded base. Use-wear: Not clear because of the fragmentary state. It is not clear whether the darkening of the exterior base is related to use.

WVS No.: 20A-5; Catalog No.: 310017 (Figures 8.19a and 8.25f)
Bag No.: Rim: 340 (3-3-5); Body: 340; Base: 340. Provenience: 20A3-3-5. Context: Floor. On the exterior floor in front of the north room. All fragments were found in one concentration. Condition: Reconstructible (99% present). Broken into small fragments. One side is blackened from fire. It appears that it was burned after it fell on the floor and then was smashed by a stone. Eroded. Dimensions: Rim diameter: [exterior] 3.5 cm, [top] 3.0 cm (measured); Maximum transversal measurement: 8.4 cm (measured); Height: 8.7 cm (measured); Wall thickness:

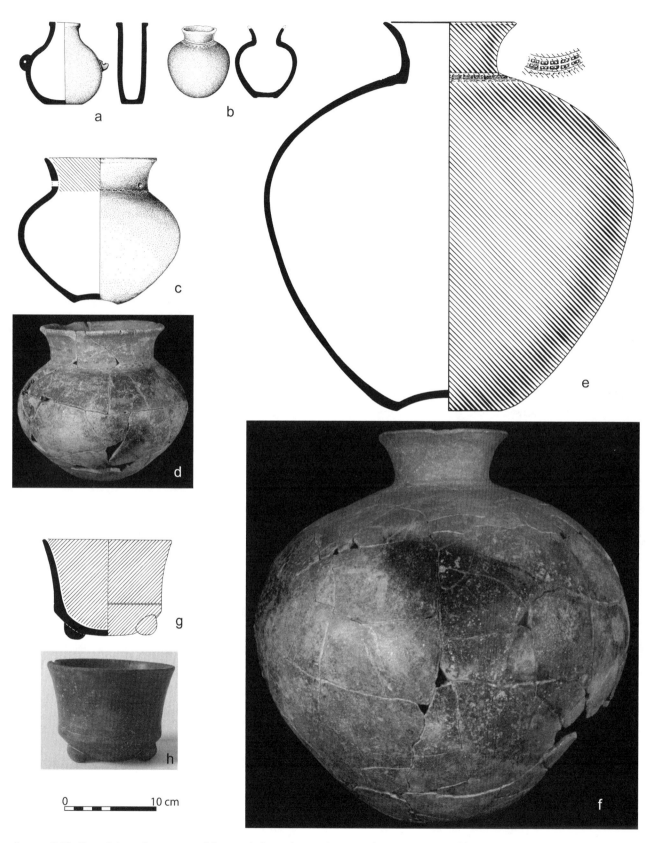

FIGURE 8.19. Complete and reconstructible vessels from the north room of Structure M8-8. (a) Tinaja Red, 20A3-3-5, Cat. 310017, WVS 20A-5. (b) Pantano Impressed, 20A18-2-1, Cat. 310016, WVS 20A-6. (c–f) Pantano Impressed. (c, d) 20A19-3-1, Cat. 310002, WVS 20A-7. (e, f) 20A19-3-1, Cat. 310022, WVS 20A-8. (g, h) Undetermined, 20A19-3-5, Cat. 310020, WVS 20A-21.

o.6 cm; Sample weight: 141 g; Original weight: 142 g; Volume: 167 cm³. Coordinates: (31.59, 11.52) (measured). Type: Tinaja Red. Paste, temper, and firing: Very pale brown paste (10YR7/4). Fine. A small amount of calcite temper (0.1 mm diameter), a small amount of ferruginous temper (0.1–0.2 mm diameter), and a very small amount of black particles (0.1–0.2 mm). The core is not oxidized. Surface finish and decoration: Orange slip on the entire exterior. The slip is more orange than common Tinaja Red. Form: Miniature jar with insloped neck. Body with lenticular cross section. Exterior-thickened rim with squared lip. Flat base. Two strap handles. Use-wear: Not clear due to erosion.

WVS No.: 20A-6; Catalog No.: 310016 (Figures 8.19b and 8.25f)
Bag No.: Rim: 470 (18-2-1); Body: 470; Base: 470. Provenience: 20A18-2-1. Context: Floor. Found in the wall-fall layer over the southern half of the bench of the north room. It was probably placed in a higher location originally. Condition: Complete (99% present). Heavily eroded. No clear traces of burning. Dimensions: Rim diameter: [exterior] 3.8 cm, [top] 3.6 cm (measured); Maximum diameter: 6.9 cm (measured); Height: 7.9 cm (measured); Wall thickness: 0.7 cm; Sample weight: 158 g; Original weight: 159 g; Volume: 91 cm³. Coordinates: (28.14, 8.09) (measured). Type: Pantano Impressed. Paste, temper, and firing: Pink paste (5YR7/4). Medium grain. A large amount of calcite temper (0.1–0.3 mm diameter), a small amount of ferruginous temper (1.0–2.0 mm diameter), and a small amount of quartz temper (1.0–1.5 mm). Because it is complete, it is not clear whether the paste is oxidized. Surface finish and decoration: It probably had red slip on the exterior, but it is mostly eroded. An incision along the neck-body juncture. Triangular impressions below the neck-body juncture. Form: Miniature jar with outcurved neck. Direct rim with rounded lip. Incurved base. No handles. Use-wear: Not clear due to erosion.

WVS No.: 20A-7; Catalog No.: 310002 (Figure 8.19c and 8.19d)
Bag No.: Rim: 878 (19-3-1); Body: 878, 864 (19-2-1), 662 (19-2-2); Base: 878. Provenience: 20A19-3-1. Context: Floor. In the southern part of the room floor near the doorway in the north room. All fragments were found in one concentration. Condition: Reconstructible (93% present). Some parts are blackened from fire, and the lower body part is very eroded. Most fragments were found in one concentration. It is not clear whether the

vessel was stored on the floor or in a higher place. Dimensions: Rim diameter: [exterior] 12.4 cm, [top] 12.0 cm (measured); Maximum diameter: 17.7 cm (measured); Minimum Opening: 8.5 cm (measured); Height: 15.4 cm (measured); Neck height: 3.4 cm (measured); Wall thickness: 0.6–0.8 cm; Sample weight: 785 g; Original weight: 844 g; Volume: 1,486 cm³. Coordinates: (29.17, 10.82) (measured). Type: Pantano Impressed. Paste, temper, and firing: Reddish yellow paste (5YR7/8). Medium grain. A medium amount of calcite temper (0.3–2.0 mm diameter) and a small amount of ferruginous temper (0.5–2.0 mm). Surface finish and decoration: Red slip on the exterior and the interior neck. It is not clear whether the base was slipped. Triangular impressions below the neck-body juncture. Form: Jar with outcurved neck and incurved base. Direct rim and rounded lip. Two perforations on the opposite sides of the lower neck, probably for hanging. It is not clear whether they were made pre- or post-firing. Two small, unfinished perforations: One from inside above one of the finished perforations, and the other from outside between the two finished ones. Use-wear: Not clear because of erosion.

WVS No.: 20A-8; Catalog No.: 310022 (Figures 8.19e, 8.19f, and 8.60m)
Bag No.: Rim: 874 (19-3-1); Body: 874; Base: 874. Provenience: 20A19-3-1. Context: Floor. In the southeastern corner of the room floor in front of the bench of the north room. All fragments were found in one concentration, and the shape of a jar was recognizable in the field. The vessel was probably placed on the floor originally. Condition: Reconstructible (95% present). The vessel appears to have been burned while it was complete. Eroded. Dimensions: Rim diameter: [exterior] 14.6 cm, [top] 14.3 cm (measured); Maximum diameter: 40 cm (measured); Minimum opening: 8.0 cm (measured); Height: 39.8 cm (measured); Neck height: 5.4 cm (measured): Wall thickness: 0.5–1.2 cm; Sample weight: 4,748 g; Original weight: 4,998 g; Volume: 26,164 cm³. Coordinates: (28.72, 10.60) (measured). Type: Pantano Impressed. Paste, temper, and firing: Reddish yellow paste (5YR6/6). Medium grain. A large amount of calcite temper (0.3–2.0 mm diameter) and a small amount of ferruginous temper (0.5–1.5 mm). Surface finish and decoration: Red slip on the entire exterior. Thin red slip on the exterior base. Very thin red wash on the interior neck. The exterior body is polished, and the exterior neck is smoothed. A band of cross-and-dots stamps below the neck-body juncture. Triangular impressions below it. Form: Jar with outcurved neck and in-

curved base. Direct rim and squared lip. Use-wear: Not clear on the base because of erosion and burning.

WVS No.: 20A-9; Catalog No.: 310027 (Figures 8.20a and 8.60n)
Bag No.: Rim: 888 (18-3-1); Body: 888; Base: 906. Provenience: 20A18-3-1. Context: Floor. On the bench surface of the north room next to the room partition with the central room. Most fragments were found in an area 1 × 1 m. It is not clear whether the vessel was placed on the bench or stored in a higher location. Condition: Reconstructible (70% present). Some pieces are darkened from fire. Eroded. Dimensions: Rim diameter: [exterior] 13.9 cm, [top] 13.1 cm (measured); Maximum diameter: 24.2 cm (measured); Minimum opening: 8.3 cm (measured); Height: 23.5 cm (estimate); Neck height: 5.9 cm (measured): Wall thickness: 0.7–0.9 cm; Sample weight: 1,787 g; Original weight: 2,552 g; Volume: 4,734 cm^3. Coordinates: (28.65, 8.63) (measured). Type: Pantano Impressed. Paste, temper, and firing: Reddish yellow paste (7.5YR6/6). Medium grain. A large amount of calcite temper (0.3–1.0 mm diameter) and a very small amount of ferruginous temper (0.3–1.5 mm). Surface finish and decoration: Red slip on the entire exterior. It is not clear whether the exterior base was slipped. The interior neck also seems to have thin red slip. The exterior body is polished, but the exterior neck is roughly smoothed. An incision along the neck-body juncture. A band of cross-hatch stamps and triangular impressions below it. Vertical incisions on the rim. Form: Jar with outcurved neck and incurved base. Exterior-thickened rim and squared lip. Use-wear: The edge of the base appears to be worn. Other use-wear is not clear because of erosion.

WVS No.: 20A-10; Catalog No.: 310149 (Figure 8.20c)
Bag No.: Rim: 544 (6-2-2), 410 (6-3-1), 256 (6-2-2); Body: 544, 256, 410; Base: 256. Provenience: 20A6-3-1. Context: Floor. Although a significant portion of the vessel was found in the wall-fall layer behind the structure, a small number of sherds were in the northwestern corner of the bench surface of the north room. The vessel was probably stored in a high location near the northwestern corner of the room. Condition: Reconstructible (40% present). Slightly eroded. The central part of the interior and a part of the exterior body are darkened. It is not clear whether the darkening is from the original firing or the burning at the time of abandonment. Dimensions: Rim diameter: 27 cm (estimate); Maximum diameter: 28 cm (estimate); Height: 10.5 cm (measured); Wall thickness: 0.7–

0.8 cm; Sample weight: 685 g; Original weight: 1,713 g; Volume: 2,182 cm^3. Coordinates: (30.80, 7.77) (estimate). Type: Subin Red. Paste, temper, and firing: Reddish yellow paste (5YR6/8). Medium grain. A large amount of calcite temper (0.1–0.4 mm diameter) and a very small amount of ferruginous temper (0.4–0.8 mm diameter). The paste is completely oxidized. Surface finish and decoration: Red slip on the exterior rim above the ridge. It is not clear whether the interior was slipped. The interior is well smoothed whereas the exterior is roughly smoothed. Form: Open bowl with incurved sides. Exterior-thickened rim and rounded lip. Rounded base with ring. Ridge below the rim. Use-wear: None recognizable on the interior or the base.

WVS No.: 20A-11; Catalog No.: 310127 (Figure 8.20d)
Bag No.: Rim: 905 (18-3-1); Body: 891 (18-3-1), 905, 674 (18-2-1), 912 (18-3-4); Base: 891, 905. Provenience: 20A18-3-1. Context: Floor. Near the southwest corner of the bench surface of the north room. Most fragments were found in one concentration. Others were found in the same unit (Unit 18). Condition: Partial (30% present). Although we recovered fragments from one large section of a vessel, other parts are absent. The section comprises a significant portion of the base and one side of the vessel, including the rim. One side of the base, the side where the rim is present, is significantly more worn than the other side, indicating that the residents reused this broken fragment. Eroded. No clear traces of burning. Dimensions: Rim diameter: 40 cm (estimate); Maximum diameter: 40 cm (estimate); Height: 19 cm (estimate); Wall thickness: 0.7–0.9 cm; Sample weight: 1,130 g; Original weight: 3,767 g; Volume: 12,176 cm^3. Coordinates: (28.70, 8.13) (measured). Type: Chaquiste Impressed. Paste, temper, and firing: Reddish yellow paste (5YR6/6). Medium grain. A large amount of calcite temper (0.2–1.2 mm diameter). The paste is completely oxidized. Surface finish and decoration: Red slip on the interior and on the exterior rim above the ridge. Cross-hatch stamps on the ridge. Form: Open bowl with incurved sides. Exterior-thickened rim and rounded lip. Flat base with ring. Ridge below the rim. Use-wear: One side of the ring base is worn. No indication of use for cooking.

WVS No.: 20A-12; Catalog No.: 310128 (Figures 8.20e and 8.60o)
Bag No.: Rim: 333 (3-3-4); Body: 333, 269 (3-3-4), 163 (3-2-3); Base: 571 (3-3-4). Provenience: 20A3-3-4. Context: Floor. In the northern part of the floor in front of the bench of

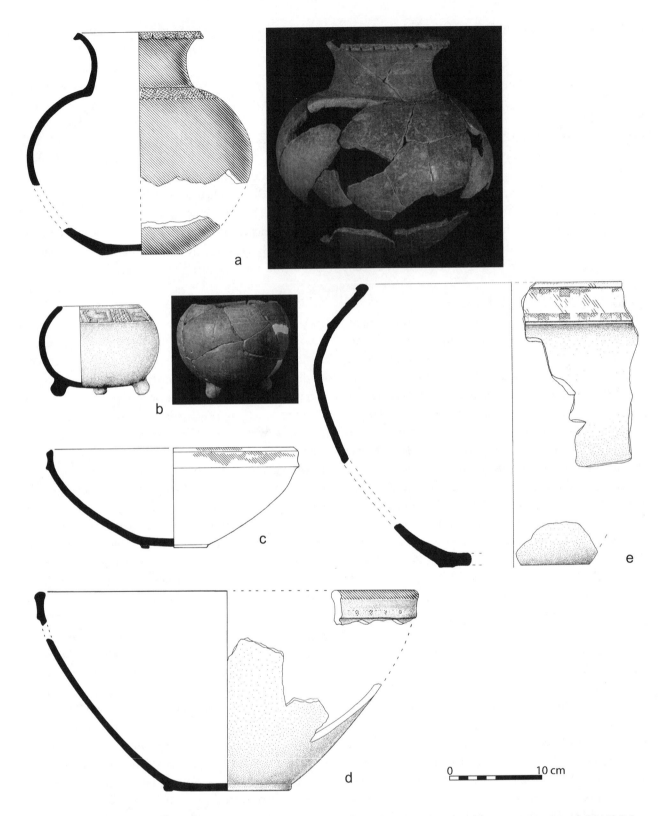

FIGURE 8.20. Complete and reconstructible vessels from the north room of Structure M8-8. (a) Pantano Impressed, 20A18-3-1, Cat. 310027, WVS 20A-9. (b) Undetermined, 20A6-3-1, Cat. 310031, WVS 20A-22. (c) Subin Red, 20A6-3-1, Cat. 310149, WVS 20A-10. (d, e) Chaquiste Impressed. (d) 20A18-3-1, Cat. 310127, WVS 20A-11. (e) 20A3-3-4, Cat. 310128, WVS 20A-12.

the north room. Condition: Partial (30% present). Although we recovered fragments from one large section of a vessel, other parts are absent. The section comprises a part of the base and a part of the rim. It is probable that the large fragment was reused. A significant part is darkened, which may be from burning or from the original firing of the vessel. On the base there is use-wear over the darkened surface. Dimensions: Rim diameter: 31 cm (estimate); Maximum diameter: 46 cm (estimate); Height: 30 cm (rough estimate); Wall thickness: 0.8–1.5 cm; Sample weight: 867 g; Original weight: 2,890 g; Volume: 23,656 cm³. Coordinates: (30.68, 11.77) (measured). Type: Chaquiste Impressed. Paste, temper, and firing: Yellow paste (10YR7/6). Medium grain. A large amount of calcite temper (0.1–0.5 mm diameter). The paste is completely oxidized. Fire clouding on the base. Surface finish and decoration: Red slip on the exterior rim above the ridge. It is not clear whether the interior is slipped. Cross-hatch stamps below the thickened rim and on the ridge. Form: Open bowl with incurved sides. Exterior-thickened rim and rounded lip. Flat base with ring. Ridge below the rim. Use-wear: The ring base is heavily worn. Because the worn part of the base is not darkened, the vessel was probably not used on fire.

WVS No.: 20A-13; Catalog No.: 310023 (Figures 8.21a and 8.60p)
Bag No.: Rim: 378 (3-3-2); Body: 378, 1001 (19-3-5), 1032 (19-3-5), 213 (3-3-2), 382 (3-3-3), 909 (19-3-2), 193 (3-3-2); Base: 1032. Provenience: 20A3-3-2. Context: Floor. On the floor in front of the bench. A significant portion of the vessel was found in one concentration. Other fragments were found in an area 1 × 1 m on the floor. The vessel may have been placed on the bench or in a higher place. Condition: Reconstructible (95% present). Relatively well preserved. The interior surface of the lower body burned black after the vessel broke. Dimensions: Rim diameter: [interior] 15.2 cm, [top] 16.2 cm (measured); Maximum diameter: 30.5 cm (measured); Height: 24.1 cm (measured); Wall thickness: 0.7–0.8 cm; Sample weight: 2,908 g; Original weight: 3,061 g; Volume: 8,790 cm³. Coordinates: (30.65, 10.07) (measured). Type: Chaquiste Impressed. Paste, temper, and firing: Light red paste (2.5YR6/6). Medium grain. A medium amount of calcite temper (0.2–0.8 mm diameter) and a small amount of ferruginous temper (0.5–1.0 mm diameter). The paste is completely oxidized. Surface finish and decoration: Red slip on the exterior surface above the ridge. The exterior surface below the ridge is un-

slipped and smoothed, as is the interior surface. Quincunx stamps below the thickened rim, and X-and-dots stamps on the upper part of the ridge. Form: Deep bowl with markedly incurved sides and restricted orifice. Exterior-thickened rim and rounded lip. Flat base with ring. Use-wear: Ring base appears to be slightly worn.

WVS No.: 20A-14; Catalog No.: 310004 (Figure 8.21b)
Bag No.: Rim: 366 (6-3-1), 916 (17-3-2); Body: 366; Base: 366. Provenience: 20A6-3-1. Context: Floor. A large portion of the vessel was found in one concentration on the bench of the north room next to the back wall. Condition: Reconstructible (95% present). Broken into five large fragments and some small ones. The exterior and half the interior are very eroded. Missing feet. A small part of the interior is blackened from fire. Dimensions: Rim diameter: [exterior] 25.0 cm, [top] 24.6 cm (measured); Height without feet: 4.9 cm (measured); Wall thickness: 0.7–0.9 cm; Sample weight: 894 g; Original weight: 941 g; Volume: 996 cm³. Coordinates: (30.46, 7.69) (measured). Type: Saxche-Palmar Polychrome. Paste, temper, and firing: Reddish yellow paste (5YR7/8). Slightly coarser paste than most other polychrome vessels. A small amount of calcite temper (0.1–1.0 mm diameter), as well as round ferruginous particles (0.5–1.5 mm diameter). The paste is completely oxidized. Surface finish and decoration: The interior and the exterior wall are slipped in orange. The exterior base is not slipped. A black band on the lip and a tong-shaped line below it on the interior. There appear to be some black lines on the orange slip on the interior base, but they are very eroded. On the exterior there is a band of black painting right above the corner of the wall. Form: Plate with outcurved sides and slightly rounded base. Direct rim and flat lip. Three hollow feet, but their shape is unknown. Use-wear: None recognizable.

WVS No.: 20A-15; Catalog No.: 310009 (Figure 8.21c)
Bag No.: Rim: 316 (5-3-1), 319 (3-3-5); Body: 316, 319; Base: 316, 319. Provenience: 20A3-3-5. Context: Floor. On the exterior floor under the wall fall in front of the north room. Fragments were found in two groups roughly 20 cm apart. It was probably placed outside the room near the front wall. Condition: Reconstructible (90% present). Paint is almost completely eroded. Some fragments are burned in light orange color. Dimensions: Rim diameter: [exterior] 19.7 cm, [top] 19.2 cm (measured); Height: 5.8 cm (measured); Height without feet: 3.9 cm (measured); Wall thickness: 0.6–0.8 cm; Sample weight:

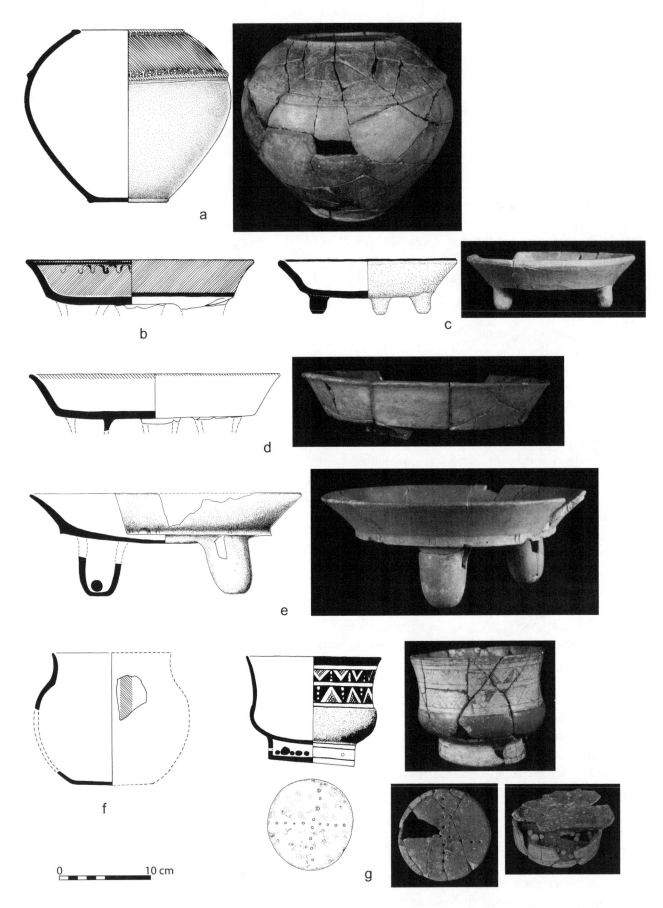

Figure 8.21. Complete and reconstructible vessels from the north room of Structure M8-8. (a) Chaquiste Impressed, 20A3-3-2, Cat. 310023, WVS 20A-13. (b–f) Saxche-Palmar Polychrome. (b) 20A6-3-1, Cat. 310004, WVS 20A-14. (c) 20A3-3-5, Cat. 310009, WVS 20A-15. (d) 20A5-3-3, Cat. 310013, WVS 20A-16. (e) 20A17-3-2, Cat. 310021, WVS 20A-17. (f) 20A1-3-2, Cat. 310139, WVS 20A-18. (g) Unnamed red-orange paste with incisions and black and white paints, 20A3-3-2, Cat. 310001, WVS 20A-19.

445 g; Original weight: 494 g; Volume: 418 cm³. Coordinates: (31.19, 11.95) (measured). Type: Saxche-Palmar Polychrome? Paste, temper, and firing: Reddish yellow paste (5YR6/6). Fine. A small amount of white and black mineral particles (0.2–1.0 mm diameter) as temper. The particles do not react to diluted HCl. The paste is completely oxidized. Surface finish and decoration: Small traces of orange slip on the interior and a black band on the lip. The outside wall appears to be painted in red. Form: Plate with slightly outcurved sides and slightly rounded base. Direct rim and flat lip. Three small solid oven feet. Use-wear: None recognizable.

WVS No.: 20A-16; Catalog No.: 310013 (Figure 8.21d)
Bag No.: Rim: 303 (5-3-3); Body: 303; Base: 303. Provenience: 20A5-3-3. Context: Floor. On the exterior floor under wall fall in front of the north room. All fragments were found close together. It was probably placed outside in a high location near the front wall. Condition: Reconstructible (89% present). The paint is almost completely eroded. The nearly entire interior and some part of the exterior are blackened from fire. Some fitted fragments show different burning patterns, indicating that the vessel also received fire after it broke. Large parts of the feet are missing. Dimensions: Rim diameter: [exterior] 27.5 cm, [top] 26.6 cm (measured); Height without feet: 5.0 cm (measured); Wall thickness: 0.6–0.9 cm; Sample weight: 971 g; Original weight; 1,091 g; Volume: 1,115 cm³. Coordinates: (31.59, 12.48) (measured). Type: Saxche-Palmar Polychrome. Paste, temper, and firing: Red paste (2.5YR6/8). Slightly coarser paste than most other polychrome vessels. A small amount of calcite temper (0.1–2.0 mm diameter), as well as round ferruginous particles (0.5–1.5 mm diameter). The paste is completely oxidized. Surface finish and decoration: Some traces of red paint on the lip and orange paint on the interior wall. Form: Plate with flared sides and flat base. Slightly outflared everted rim and flat lip. Three hollow feet with unknown shape. Use-wear: None recognizable.

WVS No.: 20A-17; Catalog No.: 310021 (Figure 8.21e)
Bag No.: Rim: 897 (17-3-2), 369 (6-3-1), 882 (19-3-2), 672 (17-2-1), 419 (18-1-1); Body: 897, 369, 882, 672, 419; Base: 897, 369, 882, 674 (18-2-1), 672, 916 (17-3-2). Provenience: 20A17-3-2. Context: Floor. In the north room. Fragments were scattered over an area 4 × 2 m (Units 6, 17, 18, and 19). Three-fourths of the vessel was in Lot 17-3-2 (on the bench near the center of the back wall). One-fifth was in Lot

6-3-1 (on the room floor near the center of the doorway). Some fragments were mixed in wall fall. It is probable that the vessel was originally placed in a high location next to the back wall or the south room partition. Condition: Reconstructible (93% present). The paint is almost completely eroded. One piece is chewed by rodents. Missing one foot. Dimensions: Rim diameter: [exterior] 29.8 cm, [top] 29.3 cm (measured); Height: 10.9 cm (measured); Height without feet: 5.8 cm (measured); Wall thickness: 0.3–0.8 cm; Sample weight: 990 g; Original weight: 1,065 g; Volume: 1,372 cm³. Coordinates: (29.74, 7.96) (estimate). Type: Saxche-Palmar Polychrome. Paste, temper, and firing: Light red paste (2.5YR7/6). Slightly coarser paste than other polychrome vessels. A small amount of calcite temper (0.1–1.2 mm diameter), as well as round ferruginous particles (0.5–1.0 mm diameter). The paste is completely oxidized. Surface finish and decoration: Small traces of red paint on the interior rim, of orange paint on the interior wall, and of red paint on the exterior wall. No slip is visible under these layers of paint. Incisions on the basal ridge. Probably 15 pairs of two incisions 0.5 cm apart. Form: Plate with slightly outcurved sides and rounded base. Basal ridge with five arc-shaped notches. Direct rim and slightly beveled-in lip. Three hollow oven feet with two openings and a rattle. Use-wear: None recognizable.

WVS No.: 20A-18; Catalog No.: 310139 (Figure 8.21f)
Bag No.: Rim: 453 (1-3-2), 156; Body: 453, 481 (1-3-2), 156 (1-2-1), 500 (1-3-3), 501 (1-3-4), 442 (1-3-2), 681 (1-3-5); Base: 453. Provenience: 20A1-3-2. Context: Floor. In the northern part of the bench surface of the central room. A significant portion of the vessel was found in one concentration. Other fragments were in an area 2 × 2 m. The vessel may have been stored in a higher location. Condition: Reconstructible (70% present). Eroded. Many pieces appear to have laminated due to fire. Some pieces are burned. Dimensions: Rim diameter: 13 cm (estimate); Maximum diameter: 17 cm (estimate); Minimum opening: 12 cm (estimate); Height: 14 cm (rough estimate); Neck height: 3.3 cm; Wall thickness: 0.4–0.6 cm; Sample weight: 316 g; Original weight: 451 g; Volume: 1,637 cm³. Coordinates: (27.07, 8.70) (measured). Type: Saxche-Palmar Polychrome. Paste, temper, and firing: Reddish yellow paste (5YR6/8). Fine. A small amount of calcite temper (0.1–0.3 mm diameter) and a very small amount of shiny glass-like particles (0.1 mm length). The core is slightly dark. Surface finish and decoration: Paintings are mostly eroded. Cream slip on the exterior. Traces of red paint in

vertical stripes are preserved in some parts. Form: Jar with outcurved neck. Direct rim and rounded lip. Flat base. Use-wear: Not clear because of erosion.

WVS No.: 20A-19; Catalog No.: 310001 (Figure 8.21g)
Bag No.: Rim: 199 (3-3-2); Body: 199; Base: 199. Provenience: 20A3-3-2. Context: Floor. On the floor in front of the bench of the north room near the niche. Condition: Reconstructible (80% present). Fragments were found in one concentration. Dimensions: Rim diameter: [exterior] 14.2 cm, [top] 14.0 cm (measured); Height: 10.4–11.4 cm (measured); Height without feet: 8.7–9.7 cm (measured); Wall thickness: 0.4–0.6 cm; Sample weight: 350 g; Original weight: 438 g; Volume: 918 cm³. Coordinates: (30.33, 10.27) (measured). Type: Unnamed red-orange paste with incisions and black and white paints. Paste, temper, and firing: Red paste (10R4/8). Relatively fine and hard. A small amount of white and black particles, which are not attacked by weak acid (0.1 mm diameter). The paste is completely oxidized. Surface finish and decoration: The surface is well polished. Incisions and white paint on the upper exterior body and the side of the hollow base. The incised triangular patterns are filled with black paint on white. Three are three white dots in the black triangles. Under a low-power microscope the white dots appear to be negative designs. Form: Bowl with incurved lower sides and outcurved upper sides. Direct rim and rounded lip. Hollow base probably with rattles. Perforations through the lower base and the sides of the base. Use-wear: Numerous small pits on the interior base. Part of the rim is worn, which may be due to use.

WVS No.: 20A-20; Catalog No.: 310014
Bag No.: Rim: 322 (3-3-5); Body: 322; Base: 322. Provenience: 20A3-3-5. Context: Floor. On the exterior floor in front of the north room. Fragments were found in one concentration. Condition: Reconstructible (60% present). Heavily eroded. The edges of the broken pieces are so eroded that it is difficult to glue them together. Fragments are darkened or reoxidized from fire. Dimensions: Rim diameter: 28 cm (estimate); Height: 9 cm (estimate); Height without feet: 5.5 cm (estimate); Wall thickness: 0.7–0.8 cm; Sample weight: 712 g; Original weight: 1,187 g; Volume: 1,842 cm³. Coordinates: (31.70, 11.55) (measured). Type: Unnamed quartz tempered. Paste, temper, and firing: Red paste (2.5YR5/8). In some parts the paste is gray (10YR6/1). This variation in color, depending on the degree of oxidation, is similar to Fine Paste ware. Fine. The paste is coarser than Fine Paste ware and feels sandy when eroded. It contains a medium amount of shiny silica-based mineral temper (quartz or volcanic ash? 0.1–0.3 mm length) and a small amount of mica (0.1–0.4 mm length). Unlike Andres Red, the paste is completely oxidized. Surface finish and decoration: A large portion of the surface is eroded, but in preserved parts the surface is polished and has thin red slip. Form: Plate with flared sides and slightly rounded base. Direct rim and pointed lip. Three oven feet with two openings and without rattle. Use-wear: Not clear because of erosion.

WVS No.: 20A-21; Catalog No.: 310020 (Figure 8.19g and 8.19h)
Bag No.: Rim: 1026 (19-3-5); Body: 1026; Base: 1026. Provenience: 20A19-3-5. Context: Floor. In the niche under the bench of the north room. Condition: Complete (99% present). It was protected in the niche and remained complete. Traces of burning. Dimensions: Rim diameter: [exterior] 14.1 cm, [top] 13.8 cm (measured); Height: 9.9–10.6 cm (measured); Height without feet: 10.0 cm (measured); Wall thickness: 0.5 cm; Sample weight: 438 g; Original weight: 442 g; Volume: 587 cm³. Coordinates: (29.75, 10.01) (measured). Type: Undetermined. Paste, temper, and firing: Red paste (2.5YR5/6). Fine, compact, and hard. Contains very fine, shiny particles (0.1 mm diameter). Since it is a complete vessel, examination of the paste is difficult. Surface finish and decoration: The surface is well polished. The entire vessel, including the interior, base, and feet, is slipped with orange. The vessel was fired in reduced atmosphere, and a large portion of the surface has dark brown color. It is not clear whether the reduced firing occurred in the production process or during the fire at the time of structure abandonment. A shallow and narrow groove over the basal angle. Form: Bowl with outcurved sides and rounded base. The center of the base is flat. Direct rim and rounded lip. Three solid nubbin feet. Basal angle. On the interior it is visible that the wall and the base are put together at the basal angle. Use-wear: None recognizable.

WVS No.: 20A-22; Catalog No.: 310031 (Figure 8.22b)
Bag No.: Rim: 674 (18-2-1), 905 (18-3-1), 501 (1-3-4), 419 (18-1-1); Body: 905, 364 (6-3-1), 674, 912 (18-3-4), 501; Base: 1001 (19-3-5). Provenience: 20A6-3-1. Context: Floor. On the bench of the north room. Fragments were found over a wide area of the bench. The vessel was probably stored in a high location near the northwestern corner of the bench.

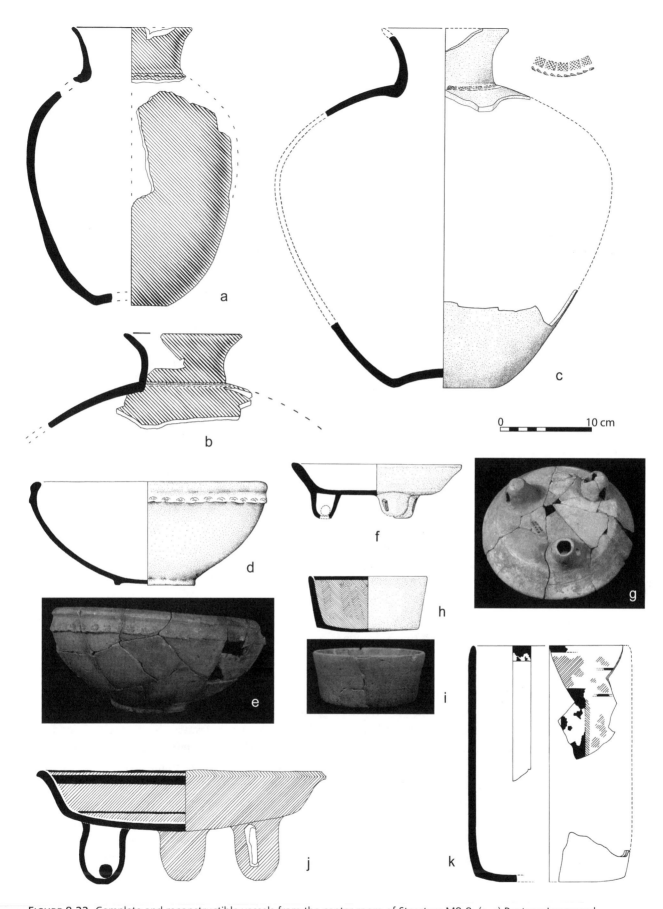

FIGURE 8.22. Complete and reconstructible vessels from the center room of Structure M8-8. (a–c) Pantano Impressed. (a) 20A1-3-2, Cat. 310135, WVS 20A-26. (b) 20A8-3-1, Cat. 310138, WVS 20A-27. (c) 20A21-3-1, Cat. 310140, WVS 20A-28. (d, e) Chaquiste Impressed, 20A25-3-1, Cat. 310038, WVS 20A-29. (f–k) Saxche-Palmar Polychrome. (f, g) 20A4-3-2, Cat. 310005, WVS 20A-31. (Note that the base of one foot is worn through while the others are relatively well preserved.) (h, i) 20A1-3-4, Cat. 310000, WVS 20A-30. (j) 20A4-3-3, Cat. 310008, WVS 20A-32. (k) 20A21-3-1, Cat. 310039, WVS 20A-34.

Condition: Reconstructible (60% present). Slightly eroded. Some fragments are darkened from fire. Dimensions: Rim diameter: [interior] 8.2 cm, [top] 8.6 cm (measured); Maximum diameter: 12.4 cm (measured); Height: 9.4 cm (measured); Height without feet: 9.0 cm (measured); Wall thickness: 0.4–0.7 cm; Sample weight: 316 g; Original weight: 527 g; Volume: 432 cm³. Coordinates: (30.65, 7.87) (measured). Type: Undetermined. Paste, temper, and firing: Red paste (2.5YR5/8). Fine, compact, and hard. A small amount of calcite temper (0.1–0.8 mm diameter). The paste is completely oxidized. Surface finish and decoration: The interior and exterior surfaces are unslipped but well polished. An incised band below the rim. Form: Bowl with round sides and rounded base. The center of the base is flat. Direct rim and flat lip. Three solid nubbin feet. Use-wear: The feet and rim are slightly worn. The interior base is not worn.

Center Room

WVS No.: 20A-23; Catalog No.: 310134
Bag No.: Rim: 521 (7-3-1), 222 (7-2-1), 182 (4-2-3); Body: 490 (4-3-2), 493 (4-3-3), 521, 505 (4-3-2), 513 (4-3-2), 527 (7-3-1), 222, 487 (4-3-2), 182, 124 (7-1-1), 483 (4-3-1), 487 (4-3-2); Base: 513, 490. Provenience: 20A4-3-2. Context: Floor. On the floor in front of the bench, near the northern room division. Most fragments were found in one concentration, although some pieces were found on the exterior floor in front of the room. Condition: Reconstructible (60% present). Eroded. Some parts are blackened, but it is not clear whether that was caused by burning. Dimensions: Rim diameter: [exterior] 36.3 cm, [top] 34.5 cm (measured); Maximum diameter: 49 cm (rough estimate); Minimum opening: 18.0 cm (measured); Height: 53 cm (rough estimate); Neck height: 16.0 cm (measured); Wall thickness: 0.7–0.9 cm; Sample weight: 5,622 g; Original weight: 9,370 g; Volume: 50,657 cm³. Coordinates: (27.72, 10.23) (measured). Type: Manteca Impressed Ridged variety. Paste, temper, and firing: Pink paste (7.5YR7/3). Coarse grain. A large amount of calcite temper (0.3–2.0 mm diameter). In some parts the core of the paste is dark. Surface finish and decoration: Smoothed, unslipped surface. Fillet on the shoulder with impressions of rope-like pattern. Form: Jar with outcurved neck. Exterior-folded rim and grooved lip. Ring base with prominent ring. Use-wear: The ring base does not seem to be worn much.

WVS No.: 20A-24; Catalog No.: 310179 (Figure 8.18e)
Bag No.: Rim: 521 (7-3-1), 1309 (25-3-3), 1133 (25-2-1), 493

(4-3-3), 1167 (23-3-1), 1296 (25-3-1); Body: 1167, 1162 (25-2-2), 1296, 1309, 1074 (23-1-1), 1133, 493, 1077 (25-1-1), 1147 (23-2-1), 1329 (25-3-4); Base: 1167. Provenience: 20A23-3-1. Context: Floor. Near the southwestern corner of the floor in front of the bench of the center room. Most fragments were found in one concentration. Part of the rim had fallen to the outside of the room. The vessel was probably placed on the floor and broke when the structure collapsed. Some fragments probably remained unexcavated under tree roots. Condition: Reconstructible (90% present). Eroded. Traces of burning not clear. Only parts of the rim and base were reconstructed. Dimensions: Rim diameter: 43 cm (estimate); Maximum diameter: 78 cm (rough estimate); Minimum opening: 30 cm (estimate); Height: 83 cm (rough estimate); Neck height: 15.0 cm (measured); Wall thickness: 0.8–1.2 cm; Sample weight: 28,691 g; Original weight: 31,878 g; Volume: 177,627 cm³. Coordinates: (24.47, 10.20) (measured). Type: Manteca Impressed Ridged variety. Paste, temper, and firing: Pink paste (5YR7/4). Coarse grain. A very large amount of calcite temper (0.3–2.0 mm diameter). The paste is completely oxidized. Surface finish and decoration: Unslipped, smoothed surface. Fillet 2.5 cm wide with impressions. The exterior base is also smooth, and there are no recognizable impressions. Form: Jar with outcurved neck. Exterior-folded rim and beveled-in lip. Flat base. Use-wear: Not clear.

WVS No.: 20A-25; Catalog No.: 310129 (Figure 8.18f)
Bag No.: Rim: 462 (1-3-4), 490 (4-3-2); Body: 462, 513 (4-3-2), 490; Base: 462. Provenience: 20A1-3-4. Context: Floor. In the northeastern corner of the bench of the central room. Two-thirds of the fragments were found in one concentration on the bench. Others were on the floor in front of the bench. The vessel was probably placed on the bench near the northern wall. Condition: Reconstructible (70% present). Eroded. Some parts are darkened. Only the rim sherds were refitted. Dimensions: Rim diameter: 34 cm (estimate); Maximum diameter: 42 cm (rough estimate); Minimum opening: 22 cm (estimate); Height: 45 cm (rough estimate); Neck height: 9.0 cm (measured); Wall thickness: 0.7–1.2 cm; Sample weight: 8,804 g; Original weight: 12,577 g; Volume: 28,296 cm³. Coordinates: (27.57, 9.43). Type: Encanto Striated. Paste, temper, and firing: Reddish yellow paste (7.5YR7/6). Coarse. A very large amount of calcite temper (0.5–1.5 mm diameter) and probably a small amount of organic temper, which had left hollow impressions (1.0–10.0 mm long). The paste is completely oxidized. Surface finish and decoration: Striation

below the shoulder. The interior and the exterior neck are smoothed. Form: Jar with outcurved neck. Exterior-folded rim and beveled-in lip. Rounded base. Use-wear: The center of the base is barely worn. Because the vessel was not reconstructed, it is not clear whether the upper part of the base is worn. Roughly 70% of the striated sherds, including the base, have dark exterior (but no recognizable soot), but the neck and the rim are completely oxidized. Probably the entire lower part of the body and the base have dark exterior. It is not clear whether the dark color is due to use for cooking, the original firing, or burning at the time of abandonment.

WVS No.: 20A-26; Catalog No.: 310135 (Figure 8.22a)
Bag No.: Rim: 442 (1-3-2), 481 (1-3-2); Body: 442, 500 (1-3-3), 435 (8-3-2); Base: 482 (8-3-2), 500. Provenience: 20A1-3-2. Context: Floor. In the northwestern area of the bench surface of the central room. Condition: Reconstructible (30% present). Eroded. Traces of burning not clear (fire clouds from the original firing). Some fragments may have remained in unexcavated areas under trees. Dimensions: Rim diameter: [exterior] 13.5 cm, [top] 13.1 cm (estimate); Maximum diameter: 30 cm (estimate); Minimum opening: 7.8 cm (measured); Height: 29 cm (estimate); Neck height: 5.3 cm (measured); Wall thickness: 0.6–1.2 cm; Sample weight: 849 g; Original weight: 2,830 g; Volume: 9,684 cm^3. Coordinates: (26.95, 8.19) (measured). Type: Pantano Impressed. Paste, temper, and firing: Pink paste (5YR7/4). Medium grain. A large amount of calcite temper (0.1–1.3 mm diameter) and a very small amount of ferruginous temper (0.5–1.5 mm diameter). The core is completely oxidized. Probable fire clouding on the exterior base. Surface finish and decoration: Red slip on the exterior. It is not clear whether the exterior base was slipped. No slip on the interior neck. The exterior body is polished whereas the exterior neck is smoothed. The neck-body juncture is broken, and impression patterns are not clear. Form: Jar with outcurved neck. Direct rim and rounded lip. Incurved base. Use-wear: The base is worn along the edge.

WVS No.: 20A-27; Catalog No.: 310138 (Figure 8.22b)
Bag No.: Rim: 1363 (21-3-3), 676 (21-1-1); Body: 439 (8-3-1), 1686 (21-3-3). Provenience: 20A8-3-1. Context: Floor. On the bench surface of the central room. A significant portion of the vessel was found in the northern part of the bench near the back wall. Other fragments were scattered in an area 2 × 3 m. Condition: Reconstructible (50% present). Badly eroded. Traces of burning not clear. Some

fragments, including the base, may have remained in unexcavated areas under trees. Dimensions: Rim diameter: 12 cm (estimate); Maximum diameter: 32 cm (rough estimate); Minimum opening: 8.2 cm (measured); Neck height: 5.1 cm (measured): Wall thickness: 0.7–0.9 cm; Sample weight: 1,532 g; Original weight: 3,064 g; Volume: 11,692 cm^3. Coordinates: (26.45, 7.84) (measured). Type: Pantano Impressed. Paste, temper, and firing: Pink paste (7.5YR7/4). Medium grain. A large amount of calcite temper (0.2–1.0 mm diameter) and a small amount of ferruginous temper (0.5–2.0 mm diameter). The core is completely oxidized. Surface finish and decoration: Red slip on the exterior. No slip on the interior neck. The exterior body is polished whereas the exterior neck is smoothed. Cross-and-dots stamps between incised lines next to the neck-body juncture. Form: Jar with outcurved neck. Direct rim and rounded lip. Use-wear: Not clear.

WVS No.: 20A-28; Catalog No.: 310140 (Figures 8.22c and 8.60q)
Bag No.: Rim: 1360 (21-3-1); Body: 1360, 442 (1-3-2), 439 (8-3-1), 435 (8-3-2); Base: 1360. Provenience: 20A21-3-1. Context: Floor. On the bench surface of the center room, near the back wall and near the central axis of the bench. The vessel was probably placed on the bench surface. Condition: Reconstructible (70% present). Eroded. Traces of burning not clear (fire clouding from the original firing). Dimensions: Rim diameter: 15 cm (estimate); Maximum diameter: 39 cm (rough estimate); Minimum opening: 8.6 cm (measured); Height: 38 cm (rough estimate); Neck height: 5.8 cm (measured); Wall thickness: 0.6–0.9 cm; Sample weight: 2,774 g; Original weight: 3,963 g; Volume: 19,834 cm^3. Coordinates: (25.72, 7.98) (measured). Type: Pantano Impressed. Paste, temper, and firing: Pink paste (7.5YR7/4). Medium grain. A large amount of calcite temper (0.3–1.0 mm diameter) and a small amount of ferruginous temper (0.5–1.3 mm diameter). The core is completely oxidized. Surface finish and decoration: Red slip on the entire exterior, including the base. No slip on the interior neck. The exterior body and base are polished whereas the exterior neck is smoothed. A band of cross-hatch stamps below the neck-body juncture and triangular impressions below it. Form: Jar with outcurved neck. Direct rim and rounded lip. Incurved base. Use-wear: The base is worn along the edge.

WVS No.: 20A-29; Catalog No.: 310038 (Figures 8.22d, 8.22e, and 8.60r)
Bag No.: Rim: 1297 (25-3-1), 1310 (25-3-3); Body: 1297, 1310;

Base: 1297, 1162 (25-2-2). Provenience: 20A25-3-1. Context: Floor. On the exterior floor in front of the central room. Most fragments were found in one concentration. Condition: Reconstructible (60% present). Some parts are darkened from fire. Some fragments were exposed to fire after the vessel broke. Dimensions: Rim diameter: 25 cm (estimate); Maximum diameter: 27 cm (estimate); Height: 10.9 cm (measured); Height without feet: 10.8 cm (measured); Wall thickness: 0.4–0.7 cm; Sample weight: 610 g; Original weight: 1,017 g; Volume: 2,578 cm^3. Coordinates: (25.28, 11.73) (measured). Type: Chaquiste Impressed. Paste, temper, and firing: Yellowish red paste (5YR5/6). Medium grain. A medium amount of calcite temper (0.1–0.3 mm diameter) and a small amount of ferruginous temper (0.7–1.3 mm diameter). The paste is completely oxidized. Surface finish and decoration: The interior is polished and has thin red slip. The red slip also covers the thickened exterior rim. The rest of the exterior surface is smoothed and unslipped. Cross-and-point stamps on the ridge. Form: Open bowl with slightly incurved sides. Direct rim and rounded lip. Exterior-thickened rim and rounded lip. Ridge below the rim. Rounded base with ring. Use-wear: The ring base is worn. The interior and rim do not appear to be worn. No clear traces of use for cooking.

WVS No.: 20A-30; Catalog No.: 310000 (Figure 8.22h and 8.22i)
Bag No.: Rim: 458 (1-3-4); Body: 458; Base: 458. Provenience: 20A1-3-4. Context: Floor. On the bench of the central room. Found upside-down. Although the vessel was broken, the original shape was visible. Condition: Reconstructible (99% present). Paint on the outside is completely eroded but on the inside is relatively well preserved. The outside base is in light color, which may have resulted from oxidation in fire. The outside base is chewed by rodents. Dimensions: Rim diameter: [exterior] 12.9 cm, [top] 12.6 cm (measured); Height: 5.8 cm (measured); Wall thickness: 0.3–0.8 cm; Sample weight: 301 g; Original weight: 304 g; Volume: 341 cm^3. Coordinates: (27.62, 9.12) (measured). Type: Saxche-Palmar Polychrome? (Bichrome?). Paste, temper, and firing: Reddish yellow paste (5YR6/8). Very fine. A very small amount of white mineral particles (0.2–0.5 mm diameter) as temper. The particles do not react to diluted HCl. The paste is completely oxidized. Surface finish and decoration: The outside is completely eroded, and no traces of paint are visible. Red paint on the entire inside. Horizontal

bands of thicker red consisting of the same paint along the rim and the corner of the base, as well as a series of vertical bands on the wall. A band of black paint over the red on the lip. Form: Bowl with slightly outcurved sides and slightly rounded base. Direct rim and rounded lip. Use-wear: None recognizable.

WVS No.: 20A-31; Catalog No.: 310005 (Figure 8.22f and 8.22g)
Bag No.: Rim: 505 (4-3-2); Body: 505; Base: 505. Provenience: 20A4-3-2. Context: Floor. On the room floor of the center room next to the north room partition. Although the vessel was broken, it retained the original shape of a plate. Condition: Reconstructible (96% present). Very eroded. Only small traces of paint remain. Dimensions: Rim diameter: [exterior] 18.8 cm, [top] 17.9 cm (measured); Height: 5.0–6.0 cm (measured); Height without feet: 3.5 cm (measured); Wall thickness: 0.5–0.9 cm; Sample weight: 455 g; Original weight: 474 g; Volume: 338 cm^3. Coordinates: (27.83, 10.65) (measured). Type: Saxche-Palmar Polychrome. Paste, temper, and firing: Reddish yellow paste (5YR6/8). Fine. A small amount of fine calcite temper (0.1–0.5 mm diameter). The paste is completely oxidized. Surface finish and decoration: Orange slip over cream slip on the interior. Small traces of red paint in some parts. The exterior is severely eroded, but the exterior wall appears to have cream slip. The exterior base and feet are unslipped. Form: Plate with outcurved sides and slightly rounded, almost flat, base. Direct rim and flat lip. Three hollow oven feet with two openings and a rattle. Use-wear: The base of one foot is worn through, but others are well preserved. It is not clear if this wear is from use or if the foot was intentionally ground down. No recognizable use-wear on the interior.

WVS No.: 20A-32; Catalog No.: 310008 (Figure 8.22j)
Bag No.: Rim: 497 (4-3-3), 524 (7-3-3); Body: 497, 524; Base: 524, 497, 483 (4-3-1). Provenience: 20A4-3-3. Context: Floor. On the exterior floor under wall fall in front of the center room. About half the vessel was in Lot 4-3-3, and the other half was in Lot 7-3-3. The two concentrations were about 60 cm apart. It is probable that the vessel was originally placed in a high location next to the north front room. Condition: Reconstructible (95% present). Pieces from Lot 7-3-3 are severely burned and eroded, while fragments from Lot 4-3-3 retain some paint. Dimensions: Rim diameter: [exterior] 31.9 cm, [top] 30.6 cm (measured); Height: 11.1–12.1 cm (measured); Height

without feet: 6.3 cm (measured); Wall thickness: 0.7–0.9 cm; Sample weight: 1,674 g; Original weight: 1,762 g; Volume: 2,290 cm³. Coordinates: (27.53, 11.75)(measured). Type: Saxche-Palmar Polychrome. Paste, temper, and firing: Reddish yellow paste (5YR6/6). Fine. A very small amount of calcite temper (0.1–1.0 mm diameter). The paste is completely oxidized. Surface finish and decoration: The entire interior and the exterior walls have cream underslip. Orange slip on the entire interior and on the exterior walls. A red band on the lip and a black band on the rim. The interior base does not seem to have any design. The exterior base is painted in red without underslip. No paint on feet. Form: Plate with outcurved sides and slightly rounded base. Direct rim and squared lip. Three hollow oven feet with two openings and a rattle. Use-wear: None recognizable.

WVS No.: 20A-33; Catalog No.: 310030
Bag No.: Rim: 532 (4-3-3), 527 (7-3-1), 143 (16-1-1), 222 (7-2-1), 483 (4-3-1); Body: 143; Base: 483, 527. Provenience: 20A4-3-1. Context: Floor. On the room in front of the bench of the center room. Most fragments were found in an area 1 × 2 m, including the room (Unit 4) and the exterior floor (Units 4 and 7) in front of the room. Two pieces were found in the humus layer behind the structure (Unit 16). Two interpretations are possible. One is that the residents kept the large fragments after the vessel broke, and the other is that the complete vessel was kept in a high location along the back wall and its fragments scattered when the structure collapsed. Some fragments may have remained in unexcavated areas under trees in the central room. Condition: Partial (30% present). Eroded. Traces of burning are not clear. Dimensions: Rim diameter: 20 cm (estimate); Height: 6.1 cm (measured); Height without feet: 3.1 cm (measured); Wall thickness: 0.6–0.8 cm; Sample weight: 224 g; Original weight: 747 g; Volume: 631 cm³. Coordinates: (26.76, 11.01) (estimate). Type: Saxche-Palmar Polychrome. Paste, temper, and firing: Reddish yellow paste (5YR7/6). Fine. A small amount of calcite temper (0.1–0.7 mm diameter) and a small amount of ferruginous temper (0.3–0.5 mm diameter). The core is slightly dark. Surface finish and decoration: In some parts of the interior and exterior walls, orange paint over cream underslip is preserved. Red band on the rim. Form: Plate with flared sides and flat base. Direct rim and rounded lip. Three relatively small, hollow oven feet with two openings and a rattle. Use-wear: Not clear because of erosion.

WVS No.: 20A-34; Catalog No.: 310039 (Figure 8.22k)
Bag No.: Rim: 1361 (21-3-1); Body: 1361, 1117 (21-2-1); Base: 1361, 1686 (21-3-3). Provenience: 20A21-3-1. Context: Floor. On the bench surface of the center room. Near the back wall and near the central axis of the bench. Condition: Reconstructible (40% present). Some fragments probably remained in unexcavated areas under trees. Badly eroded. Traces of burning not clear. Dimensions: Rim diameter: 17 cm (estimate); Height: 24.8 cm (measured); Wall thickness: 0.7 cm; Sample weight: 628 g; Original weight: 1,570 g; Volume: 4,259 cm³. Coordinates: (25.25, 7.95) (measured). Type: Saxche-Palmar Polychrome. Paste, temper, and firing: Reddish yellow paste (7.5YR8/6). Very fine. A very small amount of calcite temper (0.1–0.5 mm diameter) and a very small amount of shiny glass-like particles (0.1 mm length). The core is slightly dark. Surface finish and decoration: Polished surface with cream underslip. Black, red, and orange paints are mostly eroded. Form: Vase with vertical sides. Direct rim and rounded lip. Slightly rounded base. Use-wear: Not clear because of erosion.

South Room

WVS No.: 20A-35; Catalog No.: 310158 (Figure 8.23a)
Bag No.: Rim: 1277 (37-3-2), 1291 (37-3-1); Body: 1291, 1301 (27-3-1), 1277, 1307 (27-3-2). Provenience: 20A37-3-2. Context: Floor. On the floor in front of the bench of the south room. Fragments were found in an area 2 × 1 m. Condition: Reconstructible (80% present). Eroded. Some parts are darkened. Fragments were not refitted. Dimensions: Rim diameter: 28 cm (estimate); Maximum diameter: 35 cm (rough estimate); Minimum opening: 18 cm (estimate); Height: 40 cm (rough estimate); Neck height: 8.5 cm (estimate); Wall thickness: 0.7–0.9 cm; Sample weight: 4,850 g; Original weight: 6,062 g; Volume: 17,310 cm³. Coordinates: (22.80, 10.70) (measured). Type: Cambio Unslipped. Paste, temper, and firing: Pink paste (7.5YR7/4). Coarse grain. A large amount of calcite temper (0.3–2.0 mm diameter) and a small amount of black particles (0.3–1.0 mm diameter). The paste is completely oxidized. Surface finish and decoration: Unslipped, smoothed surface. Form: Jar with outcurved neck. Exterior-folded rim and beveled-in lip. The base was not identified, but it may have been rounded. Use-wear: Not clear because of the fragmentary state.

WVS No.: 20A-36; Catalog No.: 310162
Bag No.: Body: 1379 (36-3-4), 1142 (36-2-1); Base: 1379.

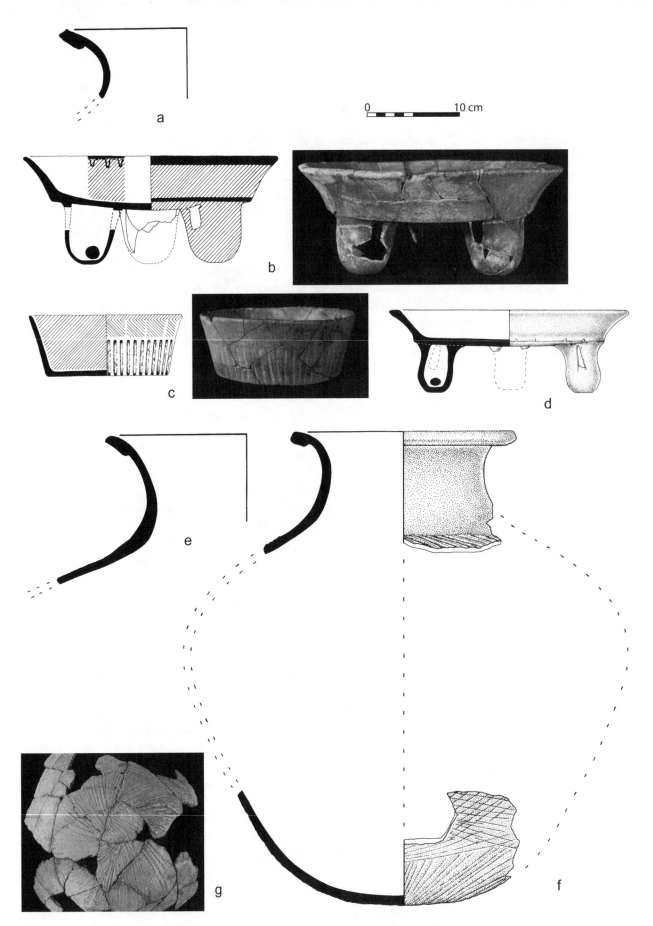

FIGURE 8.23. Complete and reconstructible vessels from the south room and the north addition of Structure M8-8. (a–d) South room. (a) Cambio Unslipped, 20A37-3-2, Cat. 310158, WVS 20A-35. (b–d) Saxche-Palmar Polychrome. (b) 20A36-3-3, Cat. 310037, WVS 20A-37. (c) 20A29-3-3, Cat. 310040, WVS 20A-38. (d) 20A37-3-2, Cat. 310160, WVS 20A-39. (e–g) North addition, Encanto Striated. (e) 20A13-3-2, Cat. 310170, WVS 20A-40. (f) 20A12-3-1, Cat. 310172, WVS 20A-42. (g) Base of WVS 20A-42 (not to scale).

Provenience: 20A36-3-4. Context: Floor. On the bench of the south room. Fragments were found in an area 1 × 1 m. Condition: Partial (35% present). Eroded. Traces of burning not clear. Only fragments of the lower body were found. It may have been used as a partial vessel after it broke. Dimensions: Maximum diameter of the partial vessel: 30 cm (rough estimate); Height of the partial vessel: 13 cm (rough estimate); Wall thickness: 0.6–0.8 cm; Sample weight: 1,141 g; Original weight: 3,260 g; Volume: 10,068 cm^3. Coordinates: (22.34, 9.50) (estimate). Type: Tinaja Red or Pantano Impressed. Paste, temper, and firing: Reddish yellow paste (5YR7/6). Medium grain. A medium amount of calcite temper (0.3–1.0 mm diameter) and a small amount of ferruginous temper (0.3–1.5 mm diameter). The paste is completely oxidized. Surface finish and decoration: Red slip on the exterior surface, including the base. Form: Jar. Incurved base. Use-wear: The edge of the base is heavily worn.

WVS No.: 20A-37; Catalog No.: 310037 (Figure 8.23b)
Bag No.: Rim: 1330 (38-3-3); Body: 1330; Base: 1330. Provenience: 20A38-3-3. Context: Floor. On the exterior floor in front of the south room. Fragments were found in one concentration. Condition: Reconstructible (95% present). Heavily eroded. Slightly darkened from fire. Most parts of the feet with their rattles are present. Dimensions: Rim diameter: [exterior] 28.0 cm, [top] 27.0 cm (measured); Height: 10.4 cm (measured); Height without feet: 4.8 cm (measured); Wall thickness: 0.9–1.1 cm; Sample weight: 1,248 g; Original weight: 1,314 g; Volume: 1,398 cm^3. Coordinates: (22.91, 12.44) (measured). Type: Saxche-Palmar Polychrome. Paste, temper, and firing: Reddish yellow paste (7.5YR7/6). Fine. A small amount of calcite temper (0.3–1.0 mm diameter). The paste is completely oxidized. Surface finish and decoration: The entire surface, including the exterior base and feet, has orange slip. A black band on the rim. Paintings on the interior surface are almost completely eroded. Form: Plate with outcurved sides and slightly rounded base. Direct rim and flat lip. Three hollow oven feet with two openings and a rattle. Use-wear: Not clear due to erosion.

WVS No.: 20A-38; Catalog No.: 310040 (Figure 8.23c)
Bag No.: Rim: 1348 (29-3-3); Body: 1348; Base: 1348. Provenience: 20A29-3-3. Context: Floor. On the exterior floor in front of the south room and the south addition. All fragments were found in one concentration. Condition: Reconstructible (99% present). Some parts are blackened from fire. Dimensions: Rim diameter: [exterior] 16.9 cm, [top] 16.4 cm (measured); Height: 6.4 cm (measured); Wall thickness: 0.5 cm; Sample weight: 396 g; Original weight: 400 g; Volume: 684 cm^3. Coordinates: (20.94, 12.25) (measured). Type: Saxche-Palmar Polychrome. Paste, temper, and firing: Reddish yellow paste (5YR6/8). Fine and compact. Relatively well fired and hard. A small amount of calcite temper (0.3–1.0 mm diameter) and a small amount of black particles (0.1–1.0 mm diameter). The paste is completely oxidized. Surface finish and decoration: The surface is polished. Orange slip on the entire interior and on the upper exterior wall. A band of red squares on the upper exterior wall. The lower exterior wall and the exterior base are unslipped. Vertical grooves on the lower exterior wall. Form: Bowl with flared sides and flat base. Direct rim and rounded lip. Use-wear: Numerous small pits on the interior base, probably from use. No recognizable use-wear on the exterior base or the rim.

WVS No.: 20A-39; Catalog No.: 310160 (Figure 8.23d)
Bag No.: Rim: 1279 (37-3-2), 1338 (38-3-1); Body: 1279; Base: 1279, 1152 (38-2-1), 1163 (38-2-2). Provenience: 20A37-3-2. Context: Floor. On the room floor in front of the bench of the south room. Near the bench face and the room partition with the central room. A significant portion of the vessel was found in one concentration. Several fragments were found in front of the south room across the front wall. It is probable that the vessel was stored in a high location near the front wall and that it broke when the structure collapsed. Condition: Reconstructible (85% present). Badly eroded. Some parts are darkened from fire. Dimensions: Rim diameter: [exterior] 26.8 cm, [top] 25.7 cm (measured); Height: 8.3 cm (measured); Height without feet: 4.2 cm (measured): Wall thickness: 0.7–0.8 cm; Sample weight: 857 g; Original weight: 1,008 g; Volume: 783 cm^3. Coordinates: (22.99, 10.18) (measured). Type: Saxche-Palmar Polychrome. Paste, temper, and firing: Light brown paste (7.5YR6/4). Fine. A medium amount of calcite temper (0.3–1.2 mm diameter) and a small amount of ferruginous temper (0.5–1.0 mm diameter). In some parts the core is dark. Surface finish and decoration: Cream underslip and red paint are preserved in some parts. Form: Plate with outcurved sides and flat base. Direct rim and flat lip. Basal ridge with a series of two notches. Three hollow oven feet with two openings and a rattle. Use-wear: Not clear because of erosion.

North Addition

WVS No.: 20A-40; Catalog No.: 310170 (Figure 8.23e)
Bag No.: Rim: 612 (13-3-2), 1495 (42-3-3), 620 (13-3-4); Body: 612, 620, 606 (13-3-3); Base: 612. Provenience: 20A13-3-2. Context: Floor. On the floor of the north addition. The majority of fragments were found in one concentration. Condition: Reconstructible (90% present). Eroded. Some parts appear to be burned and darkened. Most fragments were not refitted. Dimensions: Rim diameter: 30 cm (estimate); Maximum diameter: 45 cm (rough estimate); Minimum opening: 18 cm (estimate); Height: 46 cm (rough estimate); Neck height: 10 cm (estimate); Wall thickness: 0.8–1.2 cm; Sample weight: 12,302 g; Original weight: 13,668 g; Volume: 63,468 cm^3. Coordinates: (32.92, 9.31) (measured). Type: Encanto Striated. Paste, temper, and firing: Yellow paste (10YR7/6). Coarse grain. A large amount of calcite temper (0.3–1.5 mm diameter). The paste is completely oxidized. Surface finish and decoration: Striations on the body below the shoulder. Unslipped, smoothed neck. Form: Jar with outcurved neck. Exterior-thickened rim and squared lip. Rounded base. Use-wear: Not clear because of the fragmentary state.

WVS No.: 20A-41; Catalog No.: 310171
Bag No.: Rim: 1495 (42-3-3); Body: 1495, 1547 (41-3-4), 606 (13-3-3), 1406 (42-2-2), 1407 (41-2-2), 609 (13-3-3), 1364 (42-2-1), 416 (13-2-2), 1497 (42-3-3), 679 (12-3-1); Base: 1547. Provenience: 20A42-3-3. Context: Floor. On the floor of the north addition. The majority of fragments were found in one concentration. Others were found in an area 2 × 2 m. Condition: Reconstructible (80% present). Eroded. Burned and darkened. Fragments were not refitted. Dimensions: Rim diameter: 32 cm (estimate); Maximum diameter: 48 cm (rough estimate); Minimum opening: 19 cm (estimate); Height: 48 cm (rough estimate); Neck height: 11 cm (estimate); Wall thickness: 0.5–1.1 cm; Sample weight: 12,452 g; Original weight: 15,565 g; Volume: 39,050 cm^3. Coordinates: (33.85, 8.65) (measured). Type: Encanto Striated. Paste, temper, and firing: Brownish yellow paste (10YR6/6). Coarse grain. A large amount of calcite temper (0.3–2.0 mm diameter). The paste is completely oxidized. Surface finish and decoration: Striations on the body below the shoulder. Unslipped, smoothed neck. Form: Jar with outcurved neck. Exterior-folded rim and beveled-in lip. Rounded base. Relatively thick walled. Use-wear: Not clear because of the fragmentary state.

WVS No.: 20A-42; Catalog No.: 310172 (Figure 8.23f and 8.23g)
Bag No.: Rim: 804 (12-3-1), 627 (13-3-2), 216; Body: 804, 627, 216 (12-2-2), 808 (12-3-1), 630 (12-3-4), 679 (12-3-1), 164 (12-2-1), 623 (12-3-3), 1495 (42-3-3), 1464 (43-3-4); Base: 804. Provenience: 20A12-3-1. Context: Floor. On the floor of the northern addition. Most fragments were found in a loose concentration in an area 1 × 2 m near the southern wall. Condition: Reconstructible (90% present). Some pieces are relatively well preserved, but others are eroded. Some parts are burned. Some fragments were darkened after the vessel broke. A significant portion were refitted, but most were not glued together, except the base. Dimensions: Rim diameter: 25 cm (estimate); Maximum diameter: 43 cm (estimate); Minimum opening: 13 cm (estimate); Height: 42 cm (estimate); Neck height: 10 cm (estimate); Wall thickness: 0.7–1.0 cm; Sample weight: 6,901 g; Original weight: 7,667 g; Volume: 43,487 cm^3. Coordinates: (32.67, 10.69) (measured). Type: Encanto Striated. Paste, temper, and firing: Reddish yellow paste (7.5YR7/6). Coarse grain. A very large amount of calcite temper (0.3–2.5 mm diameter). The paste is completely oxidized. Surface finish and decoration: Striations on the body below the shoulder. Unslipped, smooth neck. Form: Jar with outcurved neck. Exterior-folded rim and squared lip. Rounded base. Use-wear: Not clear because of erosion.

WVS No.: 20A-43; Catalog No.: 310177 (Figure 8.24a–c)
Bag No.: Rim: 1464 (43-3-4), 1398 (43-2-2), 1466 (43-3-3), 1467 (43-3-3); Body: 1464, 804 (12-3-1), 623 (12-3-3), 630 (12-3-4), 1466, 226 (5-3-1), 644 (12-3-2), 1467, 808 (12-3-1), 627 (13-3-2); Base: 804, 623. Provenience: 20A43-3-4. Context: Floor. On the floor of the north addition. Roughly a quarter of the vessel, including the rim, neck, and a part of the upper body, was found in one concentration in Unit 43. Other parts were scattered in an area to the south, all the way to the southern wall. It is not clear whether the vessel fell from a higher location or whether fragments were scattered in disturbance. Condition: Reconstructible (70% present). Eroded. Some parts are burned and blackened. Of the recovered fragments, 70%, including the rim, neck, base, and one side of the body, were glued together. Dimensions: Rim diameter: 33 cm (estimate); Maximum diameter: 54 cm (estimate); Minimum opening: 19.8 cm (measured); Height: 49.0 cm (measured); Neck height: 9.0 cm (measured); Wall thickness: 0.7–1.0 cm; Sample weight: 9,167 g; Original weight: 13,095 g;

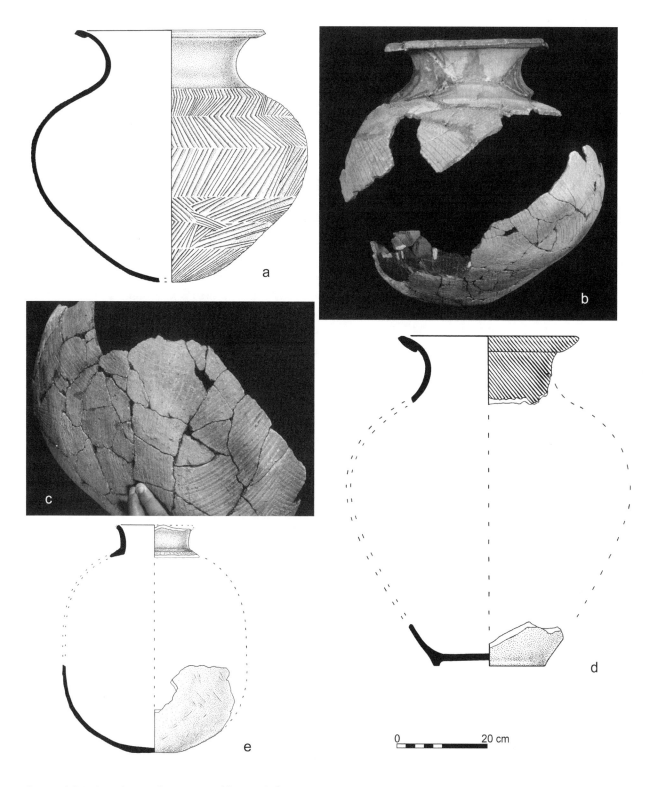

FIGURE 8.24. Complete and reconstructible vessels from Structures M8-8 and M7-34 (⅛ scale). (a, b) Encanto Striated, 20A3-3-4 (Structure M8-8, north addition), Cat. 310177, WVS 20A-43. (c) Base of WVS 20A-43 (not to scale). (d, e) Structure M7-34, south room, Cambio Unslipped. (d) 21A30-3-3, Cat. 310273, WVS 21A-28. (e) 21A43-3-3, Cat. 310416, WVS 21A-29.

Volume: 73,155 cm³. Coordinates: (34.29, 11.29) (measured). Type: Encanto Striated. Paste, temper, and firing: Reddish yellow paste (7.5YR7/6). Coarse grain. A large amount of calcite temper (0.3–2.0 mm diameter). The paste is completely oxidized. Surface finish and decoration: Striations on the body below the shoulder. Finer striations on the lower body. Unslipped, smoothed neck. Form: Jar with outcurved neck. Exterior-folded rim and squared lip. Rounded base. Use-wear: The base is fragmentary, and use-wear is not clear.

WVS No.: 20A-44; Catalog No.: 310268 (Figure 8.25a and 8.25b)
Bag No.: Rim: 638 (11-3-2), 1465 (43-3-4), 1427 (42-3-1), 1107 (41-1-1); Body: 638, 1427, 1465, 1464 (43-3-4); Base: 1427, 1428 (42-3-2), 1464. Provenience: 20A11-3-2. Context: Floor. On the floor of the north addition. Fragments of one section of the vessel (half the rim) were found inside the north addition (Units 11 and 43) whereas fragments of another section (the base and a small portion of the rim) were outside the northern wall of the north addition (Unit 42). Although the sections from inside and outside the room do not fit together, their forms are identical and we assume that they were parts of the same vessel. One possibility is that the residents kept fragments of a broken vessel inside. Another possibility is that a complete vessel was placed outside and that some fragments fell inside the north addition when the structure collapsed. Condition: Reconstructible (65% present). Fragments from inside the north addition are relatively well preserved, but those from outside are more eroded. Part of the rim from inside is darkened. The exterior of most fragments has a reddish color while their interiors are darker. It is not clear whether this color pattern is due to the original firing of the vessel or the fire at the time of abandonment. Dimensions: Rim diameter: 38 cm (estimate); Height: 6.0 cm (measured); Wall thickness: 0.9–1.3 cm; Sample weight: 1,618 g; Original weight: 2,489 g; Volume: 3,224 cm³. Coordinates: (33.78, 12.06) (estimate). Type: Encanto Striated. Paste, temper, and firing: Reddish yellow paste (7.5YR6/6). Medium grain. A medium amount of calcite temper (0.3–1.5 mm diameter). Common paste for Encanto/Cambio jars. The paste is completely oxidized. Surface finish and decoration: The interior is polished and probably had thin cream wash, which is barely preserved on some parts of the interior rim. The entire exterior, except for the rim, is striated (the same striations as in most Encanto jars). Form: Plate with round

sides. Direct rim and flat lip. Slightly incurved base. Use-wear: Not clear because of erosion. The exterior base appears to be slightly worn. The exterior does not have soot, which would have resulted from cooking.

WVS No.: 20A-45; Catalog No.: 310176 (Figures 8.25c and 8.60s)
Bag No.: Rim: 1499 (41-3-4), 603 (13-3-3), 606 (13-3-3); Body: 1499, 1407 (41-2-2). Provenience: 20A41-3-4. Context: Floor. On the floor of the north addition, near its northwestern corner. A significant portion of the recovered fragments was found in one concentration. Condition: Reconstructible (60% present). Relatively well preserved. No recognizable traces of burning. It is missing the base. Dimensions: Rim diameter: [exterior] 16.2 cm, [top] 15.9 cm (measured); Maximum diameter: 40 cm (rough estimate); Minimum opening: 8.6 cm (measured); Height: 40 cm (rough estimate); Neck height: 5.8 cm (measured); Wall thickness: 0.5–0.8 cm; Sample weight: 2,334 g; Original weight: 3,890 g; Volume: 22,033 cm³. Coordinates: (34.39, 7.55) (measured). Type: Pantano Impressed. Paste, temper, and firing: Pink paste (7.5YR7/4). Medium grain. A medium amount of calcite temper (0.1–1.0 mm diameter) and a medium amount of ferruginous temper (0.5–1.0 mm diameter). The paste is completely oxidized. Surface finish and decoration: Red slip on the exterior surface. Very weak slip on the interior neck. Cross-and-dots stamps and triangular punctuations below the neck-body juncture. Form: Jar with outcurved neck. Direct rim and grooved lip. Use-wear: Not clear.

WVS No.: 20A-46; Catalog No.: 310174
Bag No.: Rim: 599 (13-3-3), 416 (13-2-2), 214 (11-3-4), 606 (13-3-3); Body: 599, 660 (13-3-2), 214, 416; Base: 599. Provenience: 20A13-3-3. Context: Floor. On the floor of the north addition. A significant portion of the recovered fragments was found in one concentration. Others were scattered in an area 2 × 2 m to the north of the concentration. Condition: Reconstructible (70% present). Eroded. The vessel appears to be darkened from burning. Fragments were not refitted. Dimensions: Rim diameter: 38 cm (estimate); Maximum diameter: 41 cm (estimate); Height: 13 cm (rough estimate); Wall thickness: 0.6–0.7 cm; Sample weight: 1,317 g; Original weight: 1,881 g; Volume: 8,028 cm³. Coordinates: (32.80, 8.33) (measured). Type: Chaquiste Impressed. Paste, temper, and firing: Pink paste (7.5YR7/4). Medium grain. A medium amount of calcite temper (0.3–1.0 mm diameter), a small

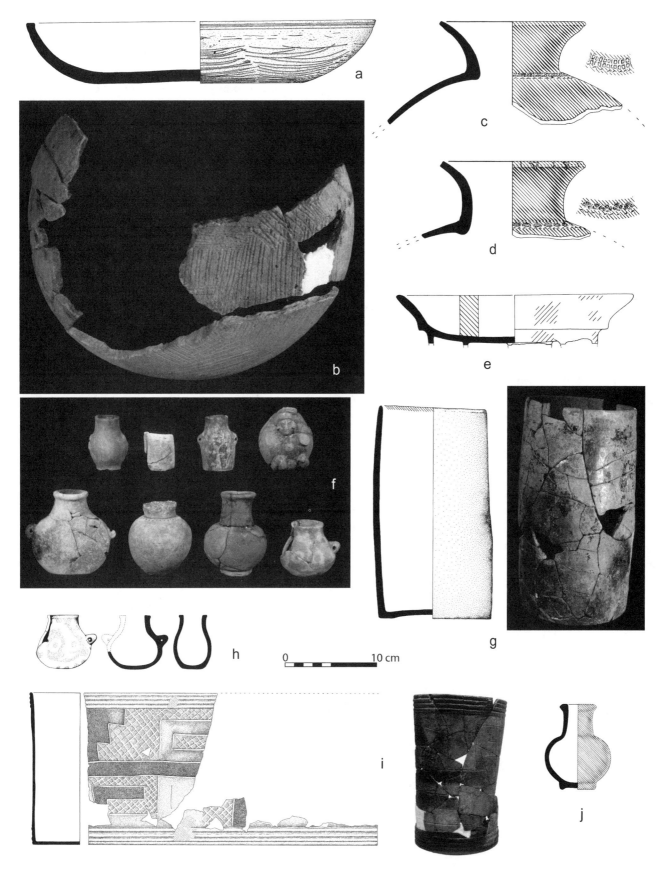

FIGURE 8.25. Complete and reconstructible vessels from the north addition of Structure M8-8. (a, b) Encanto Striated, 20A11-3-2, Cat. 310268, WVS 20A-44. (c, d) Pantano Impressed. (c) 20A41-3-4, Cat. 310176, WVS 20A-45. (d) 20A43-3-3, Cat. 310175, WVS 20A-48. (e) Saxche-Palmar Polychrome, 20A12-3-1, Cat. 310010, WVS 20A-49. (f) Miniature vessels from Structure M8-8: *top from left:* WVS 20A-67, 20A-76, 20A-74, 20A-77; *bottom from left:* WVS 20A-5, 20A-6, 20A-47, 20A-52. (g) Saxche-Palmar Polychrome, 20A12-3-1, Cat. 310011, WVS 20A-50. (h) Undetermined, 20A14-3-1, Cat. 310019, WVS 20A-52. (i) Chicxulub Incised, 20A13-3-2, Cat. 310054, WVS 20A-51. (j) Tinaja Undetermined, 20A13-3-4, Cat. 310029, WVS 20A-47.

amount of ferruginous temper (0.3–1.5 mm diameter), and a small amount of black particles (0.3–0.8 mm diameter). The paste is completely oxidized. Surface finish and decoration: Remains of red slip on the exterior rim above the ridge and on the interior surface. Wide stamps with a three-dots-and-X motif on the ridge. Form: Shallow bowl with incurved sides. Exterior-thickened rim and rounded lip. Ridge below the rim. Ring base. Use-wear: Not clear because of erosion.

WVS No.: 20A-47; Catalog No.: 310029 (Figure 8.25f and 8.25j)
Bag No.: Rim: 1406 (42-2-2); Body: 620 (13-3-4), 1406; Base: 661 (13-3-4). Provenience: 20A13-3-4. Context: Floor. On the floor of the north addition. Fragments were scattered in a small area. Some pieces were found in the northern part of Unit 13, and some were in the wall-fall layer of Unit 42. Condition: Reconstructible (70% present). Burned and eroded. Dimensions: Rim diameter: [exterior] 4.0 cm, [top] 3.2 cm (measured); Maximum transversal measurement: 6.9 cm (measured); Height: 8.9 cm (measured); Wall thickness: 0.6 cm; Sample weight: 98 g; Original weight: 140 g; Volume: 100 cm³. Coordinates: (33.90, 9.56) (estimate). Type: Tinaja Undetermined. Paste, temper, and firing: Very pale brown paste (10YR7/4). Fine. A small amount of calcite temper (0.1–0.3 mm diameter). The paste is completely oxidized. Surface finish and decoration: Orange slip on the entire exterior wall. Probably no paint on the base. Form: Miniature jar with vertical neck. Body with oval cross section. Exterior-thickened rim and squared lip. Ring base. Use-wear: Not clear because of erosion.

WVS No.: 20A-48; Catalog No.: 310175 (Figures 8.25d and 8.60t)
Bag No.: Rim: 1466 (43-3-3); Body: 1466, 1464 (43-3-4), 1398 (43-2-2), 1465 (43-3-4); Base: 1466, 1464. Provenience: 20A43-3-3. Context: Floor. On the floor of the north addition, near its north wall. Most fragments were found in one concentration. Condition: Reconstructible (90% present). Eroded. Some parts are darkened, possibly from burning. Most fragments, except the neck, were not refitted. Dimensions: Rim diameter: [exterior] 15.9 cm, [top] 15.0 cm (measured); Maximum diameter: 27 cm (rough estimate); Minimum opening: 9.2 cm (measured); Height: 27 cm (rough estimate); Neck height: 6.4 cm (measured); Wall thickness: 0.6–0.8 cm; Sample weight: 2,763 g; Original weight: 3,070 g; Volume: 6,589 cm³. Co-

ordinates: (34.34, 10.84) (measured). Type: Pantano Impressed. Paste, temper, and firing: Reddish yellow paste (5YR7/6). Medium grain. A medium amount of calcite temper (0.2–1.0 mm diameter) and a small amount of ferruginous temper (0.5–1.5 mm diameter). The paste is completely oxidized. Surface finish and decoration: Red slip on the exterior surface, including the base. Weak red slip on the interior neck. X-and-dots stamps and triangular punctuations below the neck-body juncture. Notches and triangular excisions on the lip. Form: Jar with outcurved neck. Direct rim and squared lip. Incurved base. Use-wear: The edge of the base is worn.

WVS No.: 20A-49; Catalog No.: 310010 (Figure 8.25e)
Bag No.: Rim: 812 (12-3-1); Body: 812, 804 (13-3-1); Base: 812, 804. Provenience: 20A12-3-1. Context: Floor. On the floor of the north addition. Fragments were found in one concentration. Condition: Reconstructible (80% present). Severely burned and eroded. Different fragments were burned differently, indicating that the vessel was exposed to fire after it broke. We did not find fragments of the feet. It appears that the plate was used without feet. Dimensions: Rim diameter: [exterior] 26.0 cm, [top] 25.3 cm (measured); Height without feet: 4.9 cm (measured); Wall thickness: 0.7–0.9 cm; Sample weight: 718 g; Original weight: 898 g; Volume: 1,061 cm³. Coordinates: (32.14, 10.55) (measured). Type: Saxche-Palmar Polychrome. Paste, temper, and firing: Reddish yellow paste (7.5YR7/6). Fine. A small amount of calcite temper (0.1–0.3 mm diameter). The paste is completely oxidized. Surface finish and decoration: Orange slip over cream underslip on the entire interior and the exterior wall. The exterior base seems to have orange slip without underslip. Red paint on the rim. Painting in the interior is almost completely eroded. Form: Plate with flared sides and slightly rounded base. Plain basal ridge. Direct rim and flat lip. The vessel originally had three hollow feet with two openings. Use-wear: Not clear because of erosion.

WVS No.: 20A-50; Catalog No.: 310011 (Figure 8.25g)
Bag No.: Rim: 648 (12-3-1), 216 (12-2-2); Body: 648; Base: 648. Provenience: 20A12-3-1. Context: Floor. On the floor of the north addition. Fragments were found in one concentration. Condition: Reconstructible (90% present). Heavily eroded. Severely burned in orange and black colors. Mainly burned while the vessel was complete. Some fragments received further heat after the vessel broke. Dimensions: Rim diameter: [exterior] 11.8 cm,

[top] 11.6 cm (measured); Maximum diameter: 12.6 cm; Height: 22.1 cm (measured); Wall thickness: 0.6–0.7 cm; Sample weight: 715 g; Original weight: 794 g; Volume: 2,066 cm³. Coordinates: (32.77, 10.73) (measured). Type: Saxche-Palmar Polychrome. Paste, temper, and firing: Yellow paste (10YR8/6). Very fine. A very small amount of ferruginous temper (0.1–0.3 mm diameter). The paste is completely oxidized. Surface finish and decoration: Black, red, and orange paints over cream underslip on the exterior wall. Figurative designs are almost completely eroded. Form: Vase with slightly incurved sides and slightly incurved base. Direct rim and rounded lip. Use-wear: Not clear because of erosion.

WVS No.: 20A-51; Catalog No.: 310054 (Figure 8.25i) Bag No.: Rim: 616 (13-3-2); Body: 616; Base: 816 (12-3-1). Provenience: 20A13-3-2. Context: Floor. On the floor of the north addition. Fragments were found in two 1-×-1-m lots (the rim and body in 13-3-2 and the base in 12-3-1). Condition: Reconstructible (60% present). Since this is a thin-walled Fine Gray vessel, small fragments may not have been preserved. Burned and eroded. Different fragments are burned in different colors, indicating that they were exposed to fire after the vessel broke. Most of the stucco is lost. Dimensions: Rim diameter: 10 cm (estimate); Height: 15.8 cm (measured); Wall thickness: 0.3–0.4 cm; Sample weight: 175 g; Original weight: 292 g; Volume: 991 cm³. Coordinates: (32.67, 9.92) (estimate). Type: Chicxulub Incised. Paste, temper, and firing: Gray paste (5YR6/1). Where it is burned and oxidized, it is reddish yellow (5YR6/8). Fine. A very small amount of white particles (0.1–0.3 mm diameter). The core is dark. Surface finish and decoration: Horizontal grooves below the rim and above the base. Geometric zoning by incision. Some zones have black paints, and others are filled with cross-hatch incisions. The entire exterior wall appears to have been covered with stucco with red paint, although only small pieces of stucco are preserved now. Form: Cylinder vase with flat base. Direct rim and rounded lip. Use-wear: Not clear because of erosion.

WVS No.: 20A-52; Catalog No.: 310019 (Figure 8.25f and 8.25h) Bag No.: Rim: 597 (14-3-1); Body: 597; Base: 597. Provenience: 20A14-3-1. Context: Floor. On the floor of the north addition near the southwestern corner. Fragments were found in one concentration. Condition: Reconstructible (65% present). Eroded. Darkened probably

from fire. Dimensions: Rim diameter: [exterior] 3.5 cm, [top] 3.0 cm (measured); Maximum transversal measurement: 6.1 cm (measured); Height: 5.7 cm (measured); Wall thickness: 0.5 cm; Sample weight: 56 g; Original weight: 86 g; Volume: 53 cm³. Coordinates: (32.15, 7.58) (measured). Type: Undetermined. Paste, temper, and firing: Very pale brown paste (10YR7/3). Fine. A medium amount of calcite temper (0.1–1.0 mm diameter) and a small amount of ferruginous temper (1.0–2.0 mm diameter). The core is not oxidized. Surface finish and decoration: Negative decoration. The line (negative part) has the color of the paste, and the other parts are darkened. It does not seem to have paint. A face on each side. Form: Miniature jar with insloped neck. Body with oval cross section. Exterior-thickened rim and squared lip. Two strap handles. Flat base. Use-wear: Not clear because of erosion.

South Addition and South Exterior

WVS No.: 20A-53; Catalog No.: 310309 Bag No.: Body: 1602 (35-3-1), 1481 (32-3-2); Base: 1602. Provenience: 20A35-3-1. Context: Floor. On the floor of the southern addition near its entrance. Most of the recovered fragments were found in one concentration. Only one side of the lower body and base was found. The vessel may have been broken and scattered in the disturbance during or after the abandonment. Condition: Reconstructible (18% present). Eroded. Some parts appear to be burned and darkened. Most of the recovered fragments were refitted. Dimensions: Maximum diameter: 46 cm (estimate); Height: 45 cm (rough estimate); Wall thickness: 0.7–0.8 cm; Sample weight: 1,604 g; Original weight: 8,911 g; Volume: 36,849 cm³. Coordinates: (19.96, 12.67) (measured). Type: Cambio Unslipped with red wash. Paste, temper, and firing: Light brown paste (7.5YR6/4). Coarse grain. A large amount of calcite temper (0.3–2.0 mm diameter). The paste is completely oxidized. Surface finish and decoration: Red wash on the upper body. Smoothed, unslipped lower body. Form: Jar. Slightly rounded base with prominent ring. Use-wear: The ring base has no clear use-wear.

WVS No.: 20A-54; Catalog No.: 310274 Bag No.: Rim: 1600 (31-3-4), 1321 (33-2-2), 1502 (32-3-4), 1183; Body: 1621 (31-3-2), 1600, 1582 (45-3-2), 1502, 1393 (31-2-1), 1565 (45-3-4), 1313 (32-2-1), 1481 (32-3-2), 1383 (32-2-2), 1523 (31-3-1), 1571 (46-3-3), 1321, 1561 (45-3-1), 1450 (33-3-4), 1180 (45-1-1), 1409 (45-2-1), 1580 (46-3-1), 1093 (32-1-1), 1410 (46-2-1), 1084 (31-1-1), 1508 (32-3-2), 1659

(31-3-4), 1179 (46-1-1), 1617 (31-3-2), 1183 (47-1-1); Base: 1621, 1313, 1481. Provenience: 20A31-3-2. Context: Floor. On the floor of the south addition. A significant part of the vessel, including a large part of the neck and body, was found in one concentration. The nearly entire base and a substantial part of the body were found 0.5 m to the north. A small portion of the vessel was scattered on the exterior floor to the south and west of the south addition. Fragments may have been scattered in the disturbance during or after the abandonment. Condition: Reconstructible (85% present). Eroded. The vessel is burned and blackened. A significant part of the neck and base was reconstructed, but most body sherds were not refitted. Dimensions: Rim diameter: [exterior] 31 cm, [top] 29.3 cm (measured); Maximum diameter: 49 cm (estimate); Minimum opening: 20.4 cm (measured); Height: 47 cm (rough estimate); Neck height: 9.5 cm (measured); Wall thickness: 0.8–1.1 cm; Sample weight: 9,175 g; Original weight: 10,794 g; Volume: 30,265 cm³. Coordinates: (18.89, 11.54) (measured). Type: Encanto Striated. Paste, temper, and firing: Pink paste (7.5YR7/4). Coarse grain. A large amount of calcite temper (0.3–2.0 mm diameter). The paste is completely oxidized. Surface finish and decoration: Striation on the body below the shoulder. Unslipped, smoothed neck. Form: Jar with outcurved neck. Exterior-folded rim and beveled-in lip. Rounded base. Use-wear: Not clear because of erosion.

WVS No.: 20A-55; Catalog No.: 310307 (Figure 8.26a)
Bag No.: Rim: 1508 (32-3-2), 1502 (32-3-4), 1523 (31-3-1), 1383 (32-2-2); Body: 1508, 1502, 1523, 1503 (32-3-4), 1383; Base: 1502. Provenience: 20A32-3-2. Context: Floor. On the exterior floor west of the south addition. Most fragments were found in an area 1.5 × 1 m. Condition: Reconstructible (40% present). Eroded. The vessel is burned and darkened. The nearly entire neck was reconstructed, but most body sherds were not refitted. Dimensions: Rim diameter: [exterior] 29.5 cm, [top] 28.6 cm (measured); Maximum diameter: 45 cm (rough estimate); Minimum opening: 17.8 cm (measured); Height: 50 cm (rough estimate); Neck height: 10.5 cm (measured); Wall thickness: 0.6–0.8 cm; Sample weight: 3,360 g; Original weight: 8,400 g; Volume: 38,600 cm³. Coordinates: (19.51, 9.80) (measured). Type: Encanto Striated. Paste, temper, and firing: Reddish yellow paste (5YR7/6). Coarse grain. A large amount of calcite temper (0.3–1.5 mm diameter) and a small amount of ferruginous temper (0.5–1.5 mm diameter). In some parts the core of the paste is dark. Sur-

face finish and decoration: Striation on the body below the shoulder. Unslipped, smoothed body. Form: Jar with outcurved neck. Exterior-folded rim and beveled-in lip. Rounded base. Use-wear: Not clear because of erosion.

WVS No.: 20A-56; Catalog No.: 310311 (Figure 8.26b and 8.26c)
Bag No.: Rim: 1602 (35-3-1), 1349 (29-3-3), 1177 (29-2-2); Body: 1602, 1621 (31-3-2), 1358 (29-3-4), 1383 (32-2-2), 1565 (45-3-4), 1600 (31-3-4), 1582 (45-3-2), 1393 (31-2-1), 1561 (45-3-1), 1580 (46-3-1), 1093 (32-1-1), 1349, 1571 (46-3-3); Base: 1602, 1358. Provenience: 20A35-3-1. Context: Floor. On the floor of the south addition. The entire rim and a significant part of the body were in one concentration at the entrance of the south addition. A small portion of the body was in the western half of the chamber (Unit 31). A small number of fragments, which were not refitted but are most likely parts of this vessel, were on the exterior floor to the west and south of the south addition (Units 32, 45, and 46). Both the pieces found inside and outside are burned on the exterior. Fragments may have been scattered in the disturbance after abandonment. Condition: Reconstructible (70% present). Eroded. The lower body is particularly heavily eroded. A large part of the body is burned and darkened on the exterior. A significant number of the recovered fragments were refitted. Dimensions: Rim diameter: [exterior] 24.4 cm, [top] 23.4 cm (measured); Maximum diameter: 36 cm (estimate); Minimum opening: 15.9 cm (measured); Height: 40 cm (estimate); Neck height: 9.5 cm (measured); Wall thickness: 0.6–1.4 cm; Sample weight: 3,701 g; Original weight: 5,287 g; Volume: 18,100 cm³. Coordinates: (19.91, 12.63) (measured). Type: Encanto Striated. Paste, temper, and firing: Reddish yellow paste (5YR6/6). Coarse grain. A large amount of calcite temper (0.2–2.0 mm diameter). The paste is completely oxidized. Surface finish and decoration: Striations on the body below the shoulder. Although striations on the upper body are deep and well defined, those on the lower body are shallow and poorly executed. Unslipped, smoothed neck. Form: Jar with outcurved neck. Exterior-folded rim and rounded lip. Rounded base. Use-wear: Not clear because of erosion.

WVS No.: 20A-57; Catalog No.: 310305 (Figure 8.26d and 8.26e)
Bag No.: Rim: 1617 (31-3-2); Body: 1617; Base: 1617. Provenience: 20A31-3-2. Context: Floor. On the floor of the south addition. Most fragments were found in one

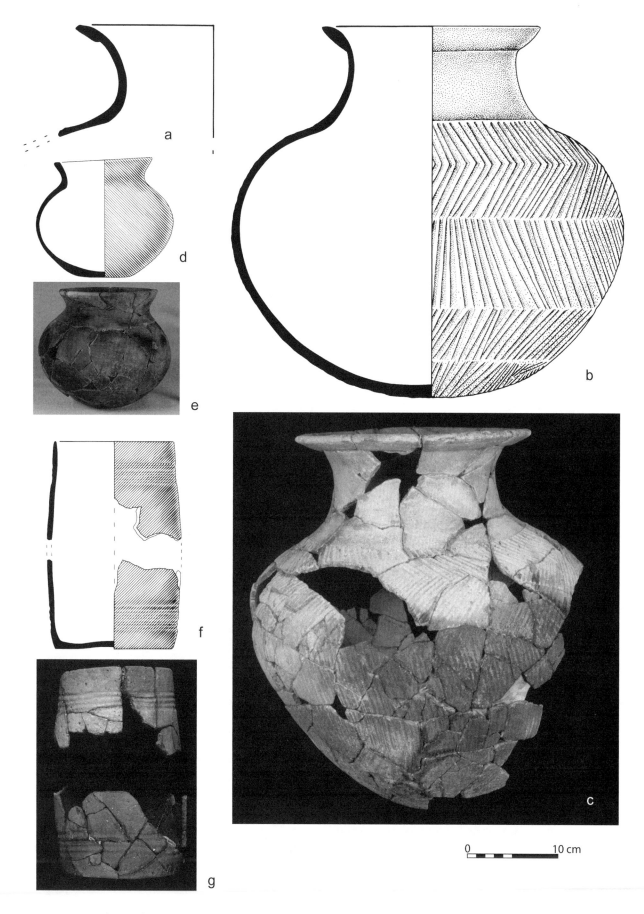

FIGURE 8.26. Complete and reconstructible vessels from the south addition and the southern exterior of Structure M8-8. (a–c) Encanto Striated. (a) 20A32-3-2, Cat. 310307, WVS 20A-55. (b, c) 20A35-3-1, Cat. 310311, WVS 20A-56. (d, e) Tinaja Red, 20A31-3-2, Cat. 310305, WVS 20A-57. (f, g) Matu Incised, 20A31-3-4, Cat. 310304, WVS 20A-62.

concentration. Condition: Reconstructible (90% present). Slightly eroded. The vessel appears to have been burned, and some parts are darkened. Dimensions: Rim diameter: [exterior] 10.7 cm, [top] 10.1 cm (measured); Maximum diameter: 14.7 cm (measured); Minimum opening: 7.6 cm (measured); Height: 12.4 cm (measured); Neck height: 2.1 cm (measured); Wall thickness: 0.3–0.5 cm; Sample weight: 502 g; Original weight: 558 g; Volume: 969 cm^3. Coordinates: (19.80, 11.70) (measured). Type: Tinaja Red. Paste, temper, and firing: Reddish yellow paste (7.5YR7/6). Medium grain. A medium amount of calcite temper (0.2–1.0 mm diameter) and a small amount of ferruginous temper (0.5–1.2 mm diameter). The paste is completely oxidized. Surface finish and decoration: Light red slip on the entire exterior, including the base, and the interior neck. Form: Jar with outflared neck. Smooth neck-body juncture. Direct rim and flat lip. Flat base. Use-wear: Not clear.

WVS No.: 20A-58; Catalog No.: 310163
Bag No.: Rim: 1358 (29-3-4); Body: 1358; Base: 1358. Provenience: 20A29-3-4. Context: Floor. On the exterior floor in front (north) of the south addition. All the recovered fragments were found in one concentration. Condition: Reconstructible (35% present): Eroded. Traces of burning not clear. Most of the recovered fragments were of the lower body. A small number of fragments were of the rim and upper body. Dimensions: Rim diameter: 15 cm (estimate); Maximum diameter: 24 cm (rough estimate); Height: 24 cm (rough estimate); Wall thickness: 0.5–0.6 cm; Sample weight: 775 g; Original weight: 2,214 g; Volume: 5,081 cm^3. Coordinates: (20.37, 12.80) (measured). Type: Pantano Impressed. Paste, temper, and firing: Reddish yellow paste (5YR7/6). Medium grain. A medium amount of calcite temper (0.3–1.3 mm diameter) and a small amount of ferruginous temper (0.5–1.3 mm diameter). The paste is completely oxidized. Surface finish and decoration: Red slip on the exterior, including the base. It is not clear whether the interior neck was slipped. Vertical incisions on the lip. Stamps (motif unclear) and triangular punctuations below the neck-body juncture. Form: Jar with outcurved neck. Direct rim and squared lip. Incurved base. Use-wear: The edge of the base is worn.

WVS No.: 20A-59; Catalog No.: 310313 (Figures 8.27a and 8.60u)
Bag No.: Rim: 1438 (33-3-1); Body: 1438, 1450 (33-3-4), 1321 (33-2-2), 1448 (33-3-3), 1503 (32-3-4), 1090 (33-1-2), 1481

(32-3-2), 1383 (32-2-2), 1435 (33-3-5), 1085 (33-1-1); Base: 1450, 1438, 1448. Provenience: 20A33-3-1. Context: Floor. On the exterior floor south of the structure. Most fragments were found in an area 2 × 3 m in Units 33 and 32. Condition: Reconstructible (50% present). Eroded. Some parts appear to be burned and darkened. A significant portion of the recovered fragments was refitted. Dimensions: Rim diameter: [exterior] 15.4 cm, [top] 15.0 cm (measured); Maximum diameter: 46 cm (estimate); Minimum opening: 8.9 cm (measured); Height: 43 cm (estimate); Neck height: 5.6 cm (measured); Wall thickness: 0.6–0.9 cm; Sample weight: 3,385 g; Original weight: 6,770 g; Volume: 40,761 cm^3. Coordinates: (19.11, 6.99) (measured). Type: Pantano Impressed. Paste, temper, and firing: Reddish yellow paste (7.5YR7/6). Medium grain. A medium amount of calcite temper (0.2–1.0 mm diameter) and a small amount of ferruginous temper (0.5–1.0 mm diameter). The paste is completely oxidized. Surface finish and decoration: Red slip on the exterior surface, including the base. Weak red slip on the interior neck. Cross-hatch stamps and arc-shaped incisions below the neck-body juncture. Form: Jar with outcurved neck. Direct rim and pointed lip. Incurved base. Use-wear: The base is relatively well preserved, and the edge is only slightly worn.

WVS No.: 20A-60; Catalog No.: 310308
Bag No.: Rim: 1585 (46-3-4), 1622 (31-3-2); Body: 1622, 1585, 1565 (45-3-4), 1185 (48-1-1), 1571 (46-3-3), 1180 (45-1-1), 1410 (46-2-1). Provenience: 20A31-3-2. Context: Floor. On the floor of the south addition. A significant portion of the recovered fragments was found in one concentration inside the south addition. Other fragments were scattered on the exterior floor to the south and east of the south addition. The vessel may have been broken and scattered in the disturbance during or after abandonment. Condition: Reconstructible (20% present). Eroded. Traces of burning not clear. Dimensions: Rim diameter: 25 cm (estimate); Maximum diameter: 46 cm (estimate); Height: 33 cm (rough estimate); Wall thickness: 0.7–0.9 cm; Sample weight: 2,250 g; Original weight: 11,250 g; Volume: 31,428 cm^3. Coordinates: (19.44, 11.30) (measured). Type: Chaquiste Impressed. Paste, temper, and firing: Light reddish brown paste (5YR6/4). Medium grain. A medium amount of calcite temper (0.3–1.5 mm diameter) and a small amount ferruginous temper (0.5–1.0 mm diameter). The paste is completely oxidized. Surface finish and decoration: Red slip on the exterior surface above the ridge. Dot-circle stamps below the thickened rim, and larger

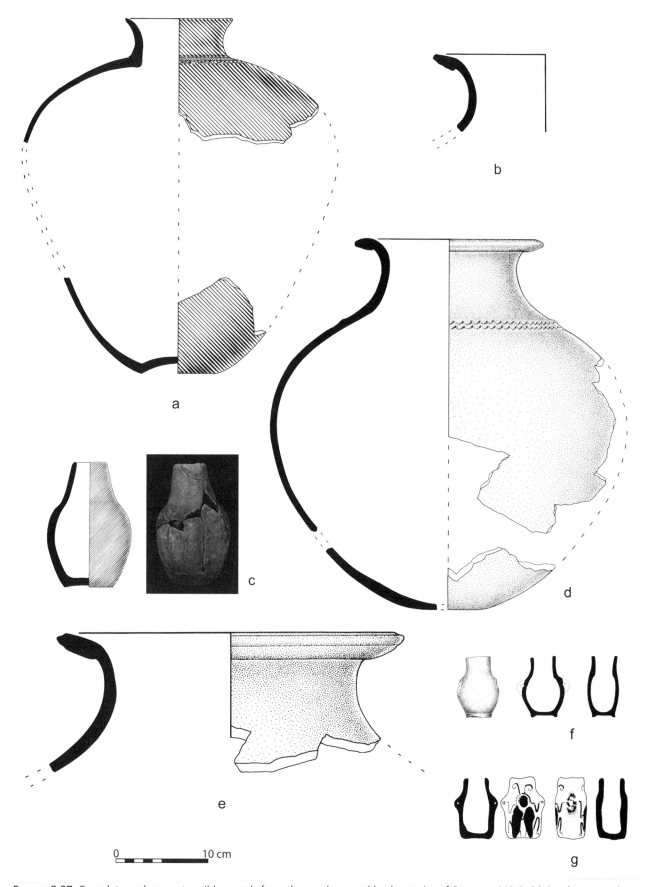

FIGURE 8.27. Complete and reconstructible vessels from the southern and back exterior of Structure M8-8. (a) Southern exterior, Pantano Impressed, 20A33-3-1, Cat. 310313, WVS 20A-59. (b–g) Back exterior. (b) Encanto Striated, 20A17-3-4, Cat. 310151, WVS 20A-65. (c) Tinaja Red, 20A9-2-1, Cat. 310157, WVS 20A-66. (d) Manteca Impressed, 20A39-3-2, Cat. 310169, WVS 20A-63. (e) Encanto Striated, 20A8-3-4, Cat. 310156, WVS 20A-64. (f) 20A6-3-3, Cat. 310018, WVS 20A-67. (g) Saxche-Palmar Poly-chrome, 20A24-3-4, Cat. 310046, WVS 20A-74.

dots-and-cross stamps on the ridge. It is not clear whether the interior was slipped. Form: Bowl with markedly incurved sides and restricted orifice. Exterior-thickened rim and rounded lip. Ridge on the shoulder. Use-wear: Not clear because of the fragmentary state.

WVS No.: 20A-61; Catalog No.: 310314
Bag No.: Rim: 1542 (48-3-3), 1321 (33-2-2), 1410 (46-2-1), 1093 (32-1-1), 1421 (48-2-1), 1135 (38-2-1), 1501 (48-3-1), 1675 (35-3-2), 1571 (46-3-3); Body: 1321, 1565 (45-3-4), 1580 (46-3-1), 1582 (45-3-2), 1313 (32-2-1), 1622 (31-3-2), 1233 (22-3-2), 1410, 1093, 1450 (33-3-4), 1571 (46-3-3), 1180 (45-1-1), 1185 (48-1-1), 1383 (32-2-2), 1085 (33-1-1), 1675, 1409 (45-2-1), 1129 (22-2-2), 1621, 1393 (31-2-1), 1568 (47-3-1), 1472 (33-3-2), 1530 (4-3-3), 1542 (48-3-3), 1410, 1336 (31-2-2), 1561 (45-3-1), 1569 (47-3-3), 1438 (33-3-1), 1570 (47-3-4), 1530 (45-3-3), 1564 (45-3-1), 1521 (32-3-1), 1502 (32-3-4), 1617 (31-3-2); Base: 1321, 1283 (33-2-1), 1580, 1410, 1622 (31-3-2). Provenience: 20A33-2-1. Context: Floor. On the exterior floor south of the structure. Fragments were scattered all along the southern side of the structure, from Unit 33 to Unit 48. A small number of sherds were found inside the south addition and behind the structure. It is not clear whether the fragments were intentionally scattered. Condition: Reconstructible (40% present). Eroded. The vessel appears to have been burned and darkened. Most fragments were not glued together. Dimensions: Rim diameter: 36 cm (estimate); Maximum diameter: 64 cm (rough estimate); Height: 40 cm (rough estimate); Wall thickness: 0.7–0.9 cm; Sample weight: 3,672 g; Original weight: 9,180 g; Volume: 75,422 cm³. Coordinates: (18.90, 7.84) (estimate). Type: Chaquiste Impressed. Paste, temper, and firing: Light reddish brown paste (5YR6/4). Coarse grain. A large amount of calcite temper (0.3–1.8 mm diameter) and a small amount of ferruginous temper (0.5–1.0 mm diameter). The paste is completely oxidized. Surface finish and decoration: Red slip on the exterior surface above the ridge and on the interior surface. Cross-hatch stamps and triangular punctuations below the thickened rim. Cross-hatch stamps on the ridge. Form: Bowl with markedly incurved sides and restricted orifice. Exterior-thickened rim and rounded lip. Ridge on the shoulder. Ring base. Use-wear: Not clear because of erosion.

WVS No.: 20A-62; Catalog No.: 310304 (Figure 8.26f and 8.26g)
Bag No.: Rim: 1383 (32-2-2), 1565 (45-3-4), 1313 (32-2-1),

1093 (32-1-1); Body: 1659 (31-3-4), 1383, 1336 (31-2-2), 1313, 1582 (45-3-2), 1093, 1621 (31-3-2), 1503 (32-3-4), 1502 (32-3-4), 1391 (31-2-3), 1600 (31-3-4), 1565, 1410 (46-2-1), 1393 (31-2-1); Base: 1659. Provenience: 20A31-3-4. Context: Floor. On the floor of the southern addition. The base and a small portion of the body were found in the southwestern quadrant of the south addition. Other fragments were scattered on the exterior floor to the west and south of the south addition (Units 32 and 45). The pieces may have been scattered in disturbance during and after abandonment. Some fragments that were found inside and outside the south addition and were glued together show the same continuous burning pattern. This suggests that fragments were scattered after they were burned. Condition: Reconstructible (60% present). Badly eroded. Heavily burned and darkened. Dimensions: Rim diameter: [exterior] 12.4 cm, [top] 12.1 cm (measured); Height: 22 cm (rough estimate); Wall thickness: 0.5–0.7 cm; Sample weight: 552 g; Original weight: 920 g; Volume: 2,395 cm³. Coordinates: (18.52, 11.61) (estimate). Type: Matu Incised. Paste, temper, and firing: Reddish yellow paste (7.5YR7/6) (Burning may have changed the paste color.) Fine grain. A small amount of calcite temper (0.3–1.2 mm diameter), a very small amount of ferruginous temper (0.5–1.5 mm diameter), and a very small amount of volcanic ash temper (0.1 mm length). The paste is completely oxidized. Surface finish and decoration: Red slip on the exterior. Four horizontal grooves near the rim and near the base. Incised lines on the body, but motifs are not clear. Form: Cylinder vase with vertical sides. Direct rim and rounded lip. Flat base. Use-wear: Not clear because of erosion.

Behind the Structure

WVS No.: 20A-63; Catalog No.: 310169 (Figure 8.27d)
Bag No.: Rim: 1253 (39-3-2); Body: 1253; Base: 1253, 1150 (39-2-2). Provenience: 20A39-3-2. Context: Floor. On the exterior floor behind the structure, close to the back wall. All fragments were found in one concentration. Condition: Reconstructible (90% present). Eroded. Burned and blackened. Dimensions: Rim diameter: [exterior] 19.6 cm, [top] 17.6 cm (measured); Maximum diameter: 44 cm (estimate); Minimum opening: 12.5 cm (measured); Height: 49 cm (estimate); Neck height: 6.3 cm (measured); Wall thickness: 0.8–1.3 cm; Sample weight: 4,993 g; Original weight: 5,547 g; Volume: 23,182 cm³. Coordinates: (22.80, 6.32) (measured). Type: Manteca Impressed with red wash. Paste, temper, and firing: Reddish yellow paste (7.5YR7/6). Coarse grain. A very large amount of calcite

temper (0.3–2.0 mm diameter). The paste is completely oxidized. Surface finish and decoration: Smoothed surface. Some remains of red wash on the interior rim and the exterior upper body. The neck and the upper body probably had red wash. Two lines of triangular stamps below the neck-body juncture. Form: Jar with outcurved neck. Exterior-folded rim and rounded lip. Rounded base. Use-wear: Not clear because of erosion.

WVS No.: 20A-64; Catalog No.: 310156 (Figure 8.27e)
Bag No.: Rim: 693 (8-3-4), 727 (9-3-4); Body: 727, 744 (8-3-4), 550 (8-2-2), 557 (9-2-1), 693, 712 (9-3-1), 743 (8-3-3). Provenience: 20A8-3-4. Context: Floor. On the exterior floor behind the structure. Fragments were found in an area 2 × 1.5 m. Condition: Reconstructible (30% present). Eroded. Traces of burning not clear. Most fragments, except for the rim, were not refitted. Dimensions: Rim diameter: [exterior] 36.9 cm, [top] 35.1 cm (measured); Maximum diameter: 60 cm (rough estimate); Minimum opening: 23.7 cm (measured); Height: 65 cm (rough estimate); Neck height: 12.0 cm (measured); Wall thickness: 0.9–1.5 cm; Sample weight: 7,235 g; Original weight: 24,116 g; Volume: 85,492 cm³. Coordinates: (27.45, 6.10) (measured). Type: Encanto Striated. Paste, temper, and firing: Light brown paste (7.5YR6/3). Very coarse grain. A very large amount of calcite temper (0.5–2.5 mm diameter). A large part of the paste is dark. Surface finish and decoration: Striation on the body below the shoulder. Form: Jar with outcurved neck. Exterior-thickened rim and beveled-in lip with a shallow groove. Thick-walled. Use-wear: Not clear because of the fragmentary state.

WVS No.: 20A-65; Catalog No.: 310151 (Figure 8.27b)
Bag No.: Rim: 754 (17-3-4), 739 (16-3-2), 554 (16-2-1); Body: 754, 554, 729 (17-3-4); Base: 754, 544. Provenience: 20A17-3-4. Context: Floor. On the exterior floor behind the structure, near the back wall. Fragments were found in an area 2 × 2 m. Condition: Reconstructible (70% present). Eroded. Some parts are slightly darkened. Most fragments, except the rim sherds, were not refitted. Body sherds may be mixed with those of other Encanto vessels. Dimensions: Rim diameter: 25 cm (estimate); Maximum diameter: 33 cm (rough estimate); Minimum opening: 15 cm (estimate); Height: 35 cm (rough estimate); Neck height: 8.0 cm (measured); Wall thickness: 0.8–1.0 cm; Sample weight: 2,869 g; Original weight: 4,099 g; Volume: 12,781 cm³. Coordinates: (29.66, 6.30) (estimate). Type: Encanto Striated. Paste, temper, and firing: Light

brown paste (7.5YR6/3). Coarse grain. A large amount of calcite temper (0.3–1.5 mm diameter). The paste is completely oxidized. Surface finish and decoration: Striations on the body below the shoulder. Unslipped, smoothed neck. Form: Jar with outcurved neck. Exterior-folded rim and beveled-in lip. Rounded base. Use-wear: The base is relatively well preserved and does not show clear use-wear.

WVS No.: 20A-66; Catalog No.: 310157 (Figure 8.27c)
Bag No.: Rim: 557 (9-2-1); Body: 557, 713 (9-3-3), 1123 (24-2-1), 1193 (24-3-4), 130 (9-1-1). Provenience: 20A9-2-1. Context: Floor. On the exterior floor behind the central room. Fragments were found in the wall-fall and floor layers of two adjacent units (Units 9 and 24). The vessel was probably stored in a high location near the back wall behind the structure. Condition: Reconstructible (70% present). Eroded. Some parts are blackened, probably from fire. Dimensions: Rim diameter: [exterior] 3.6 cm, [top] 3.1 cm (measured); Maximum diameter: 8.8 cm (measured); Minimum opening: 2.7 cm (measured): Height: 12.9 cm (measured); Neck height 4.1 cm (measured); Wall thickness: 0.6–0.9 cm; Sample weight: 299 g; Original weight: 427 g; Volume: 266 cm³. Coordinates: (26.01, 4.84) (estimate). Type: Tinaja Red. Paste, temper, and firing: Reddish yellow paste (5Y6/8). Medium grain. A large amount of calcite temper (0.1–0.5 mm diameter) and a small amount of round ferruginous temper (0.8–2.0 mm diameter). The paste is completely oxidized. Surface finish and decoration: Red slip on the entire exterior. Form: Jar with insloped neck. Narrower body than most Tinaja jars. Smooth neck-body juncture. Direct rim with rounded lip. It appears to have had an open spout, which was not recovered. Incurved base. Use-wear: Although the observation of use-wear is difficult because of erosion, the edge of the base and the rim appear to be worn from use.

WVS No.: 20A-67; Catalog No.: 310018 (Figures 8.25f and 8.27f)
Bag No.: Rim: 776 (6-3-3); Body: 776; Base: 776. Provenience: 20A6-3-3. Context: Floor. On the exterior floor behind the north room. Condition: Complete (98% present). Handles are lost. It is not clear whether the handles were damaged from use or from the collapse of the building. Some parts are blackened from fire. Dimensions: Rim diameter: [exterior] 2.9 cm, [top] 2.5 cm (measured); Maximum transversal measurement: 4.9 cm (measured); Height: 6.4 cm (measured); Wall thickness: 0.4 cm;

Sample weight: 56 g; Original weight: 57 g; Volume: 28 cm³. Coordinates: (30.64, 6.46) (measured). Type: Tinaja Red. Paste, temper, and firing: Very pale brown paste (10Y7/4). Fine. A small amount of calcite temper (0.1–0.4 mm diameter). It is not clear whether the paste is oxidized. Surface finish and decoration: Orange slip on the entire exterior except the base. The slip is more orange than common Tinaja Red. Form: Miniature jar with vertical neck. Direct rim and squared lip. Ring base. Two strap handles. Use-wear: The base is heavily worn from use. The handles are lost, possibly from use. The rim is well preserved.

WVS No.: 20A-68; Catalog No.: 310051 (Figures 8.28a–c and 8.60v)
Bag No.: Rim: 1191 (22-3-2); Body: 1191; Base: 1191. Provenience: 20A22-3-2. Context: Floor. On the exterior floor behind the structure, near the back wall. All fragments were found in one concentration, and it was recognized as a reconstructible vessel in the field. Condition: Reconstructible (98% present). Eroded. One side is severely burned and eroded. The other side is relatively well preserved. The vessel was completely reconstructed except for small holes. Dimensions: Rim diameter: [exterior] 14.8 cm, [top] 14.5 cm (measured); Maximum diameter: 26.3 cm (measured); Minimum opening: 8.9 cm (measured); Height: 26.2 cm (measured); Neck height: 5.3 cm (measured); Wall thickness: 0.5–0.8 cm; Sample weight: 2,226 g; Original weight: 2,271 g; Volume: 6,335 cm³. Coordinates: (24.35, 6.04) (measured). Type: Pantano Impressed. Paste, temper, and firing: Reddish yellow paste (5YR7/6). Medium grain. A large amount of calcite temper (0.1–1.0 mm diameter) and a small amount of ferruginous temper (0.5–1.5 mm diameter). The paste is completely oxidized. Surface finish and decoration: Red slip on the body, including the base. The interior neck has weak red slip. Cross-hatch stamps and small triangular punctuations below the neck-body juncture. Square notches on the lip. Form: Jar with outcurved neck. Direct rim and squared lip. Incurved base. Use-wear: The edge of the base is heavily worn. Small hole (2 cm diameter) on the midbody, which appears to have been made by percussion from the exterior with a pointed object. There is a similar hole at 90 degrees counterclockwise from the other hole on the lower body. It is not clear whether these holes were made when the vessel fell or whether the vessel was used with the holes.

WVS No.: 20A-69; Catalog No.: 310178 (Figures 8.28d and 8.60w)
Bag No.: Rim: 754 (17-3-4); Body: 754, 790 (17-3-3), 753 (17-3-4), 786 (6-3-3); Base: 754, 790. Provenience: 20A17-3-3. Context: Floor. On the exterior floor behind the structure, on the step of coarse stones. Most fragments were found in an area 1 × 0.5 m. Several pieces were 2 m to the north along the back wall of the structure. Condition: Reconstructible (90% present). Eroded. Some fragments are blackened. Most pieces, except the neck and base, were not refitted. Dimensions: Rim diameter: [exterior] 13.5 cm, [top] 13.0 cm (measured); Maximum diameter: 40 cm (rough estimate); Minimum opening: 8.2 cm (measured); Height: 40 cm (rough estimate); Neck height: 5.9 cm (measured); Wall thickness: 0.7–0.8 cm; Sample weight: 4,268 g; Original weight: 4,742 g; Volume: 27,666 cm³. Coordinates: (28.71, 6.33) (estimate). Type: Pantano Impressed. Paste, temper, and firing: Light red paste (2.5YR7/6). Medium grain. A medium amount of calcite temper (0.1–0.4 mm diameter), a medium amount of ferruginous temper (0.5–2.0 mm diameter), and a small amount of sand of various minerals (0.5–2.0 mm diameter). The paste is completely oxidized. Surface finish and decoration: Red slip on the entire exterior, including the base, and the interior neck. Stamps below the neck-body juncture. Form: Jar with outcurved neck. Direct rim and rounded lip. Incurved base. Use-wear: The edge of the base is heavily worn.

WVS No.: 20A-70; Catalog No.: 310012 (Figure 8.29a)
Bag No.: Rim: 702 (9-3-3), 699 (9-3-2), 705 (16-3-2), 713 (9-3-3), 724 (17-3-4), 727 (9-3-4); Body: 727, 702, 713; Base: 702, 699, 705, 713, 724, 727, 728 (9-3-2). Provenience: 20A9-3-3. Context: Floor. On the exterior floor behind the room partition between the central and north rooms under wall fall. Fragments were scattered over an area 3 × 2 m in Units 9, 16, and 17. It appears that the vessel was originally placed in a high location next to the back wall of the structure. Condition: Reconstructible (95% present). The interiors of pieces from Lot 9-3-3 are badly eroded. Other parts are also somewhat eroded, but a significant portion of the painting is visible. Some pieces are blackened from burning. Dimensions: Rim diameter: [exterior] 34.4 cm, [top] 33.4 cm (measured); Height: 10.7 cm (measured); Height without feet: 5.4 cm (measured); Wall thickness: 0.6–0.8 cm; Sample weight: 1,727 g; Original weight: 1,818 g; Volume: 2,200 cm³. Coordinates: (27.82,

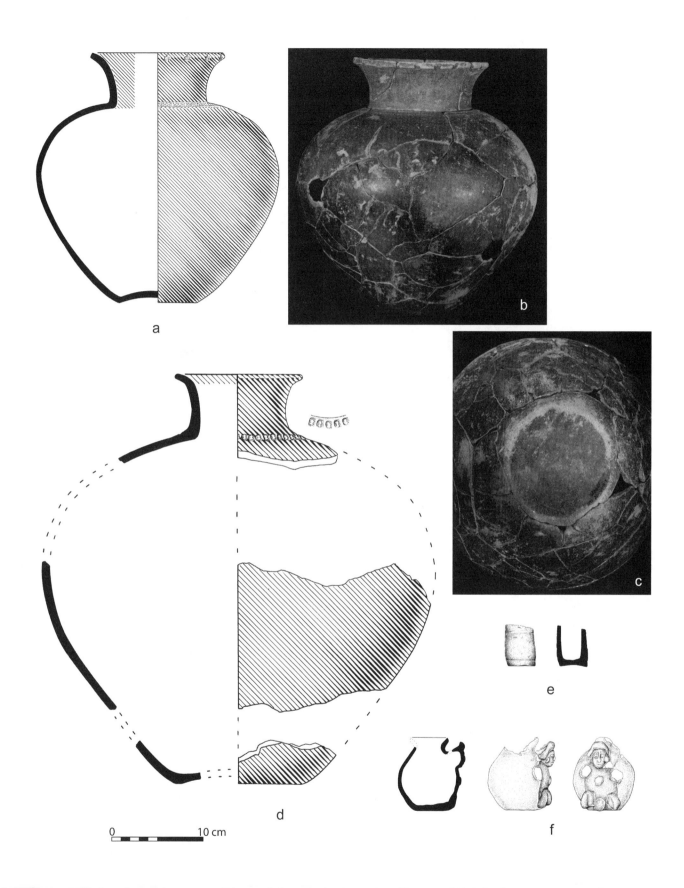

Figure 8.28. Complete and reconstructible vessels from the back exterior of Structure M8-8. (a–d) Pantano Impressed. (a–c) 20A2-3-2, Cat. 310051, WVS 20A-68. Note the worn base. (d) 20A17-3-3, Cat. 310178, WVS 20A-69. (e, f) Undetermined. (e) 20A17-3-4, Cat. 310047, WVS 20A-76. (f) 20A39-3-1, Cat. 310049, WVS 20A-77.

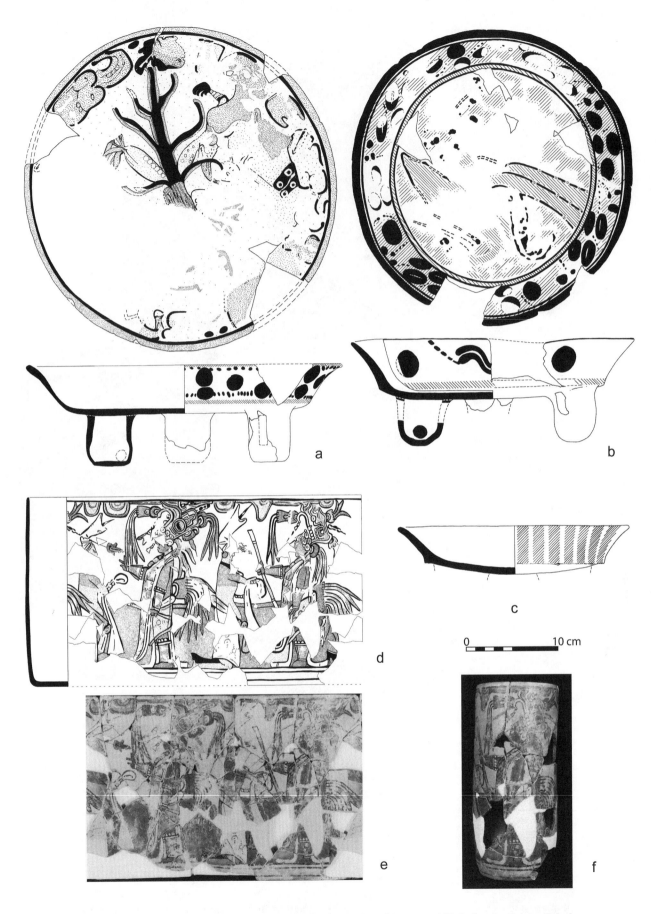

Figure 8.29. Complete and reconstructible vessels from the back exterior of Structure M8-8. Saxche-Palmar Polychrome. (a) 20A9-3-3, Cat. 310012, WVS 20A-70. (b) 20A6-3-3, Cat. 310015, WVS 20A-71. (c) 20A10-3-1, Cat. 310033, WVS 20A-72. (d–f) 20A22-3-1, Cat. 310042, WVS 20A-73. Rollout photograph by Inga E. Calvin (K30076).

4.84) (estimate). Type: Saxche-Palmar Polychrome. Paste, temper, and firing: Pinkish white paste (5Y8/2). Fine. A small amount of calcite temper (0.1–1.0 mm diameter) and a very small amount of ferruginous temper (0.3–1.5 mm diameter). The paste is completely oxidized. Surface finish and decoration: The entire exterior, including the base and feet, has cream slip. A red band above the exterior basal angle. A band of small black dots above the red band and below the rim. Large black dots in between, which probably represent jaguar skin. The entire interior has cream underslip and orange slip. A band of red and black on the lip. Glyphs on the interior wall, consisting of black outlines and reddish brown and red fill. Glyphs are eroded and not legible. The interior base has a depiction of a maize plant. It is painted with red and black, with white paint over them. Form: Plate with outcurved sides and flat base. Slightly outflared everted rim and rounded lip. Three hollow oven feet with two openings and a rattle. Use-wear: None recognizable.

WVS No.: 20A-71; Catalog No.: 310015 (Figure 8.29b)
Bag No.: Rim: 761 (6-3-3), 544 (6-2-2), 705 (16-3-2), 128 (10-1-1), 754 (17-3-4), 844 (14-3-3); Body: 544; Base: 544, 761, 183 (14-2-2), 724 (17-3-4), 154 (17-1-1). Provenience: 20A6-3-3. Context: Floor. On the exterior floor behind the north room. Fragments were scattered in five units (Units 6, 10, 14, 16, and 17) in an area roughly 4 × 2 m. Some were mixed in wall fall. The vessel was probably put in the exterior in a high place near the back wall. Condition: Reconstructible (92% present). The outside is very eroded, but on the interior some paintings are preserved. Dimensions: Rim diameter: [exterior] 30.8 cm, [top] 30.3 cm (measured); Height: 11.1 cm (measured); Height without feet: 6.3 cm (measured); Wall thickness: 0.8–1.0 cm; Sample weight: 1,432 g; Original weight: 1,557 g; Volume: 1,980 cm^3. Coordinates: (30.23, 6.67) (measured). Type: Saxche-Palmar Polychrome. Paste, temper, and firing: Light red paste (2.5YR7/8). Fine. A small amount of calcite temper (0.1–2.0 mm diameter). The paste is completely oxidized. Surface finish and decoration: Cream slip on the exterior wall, and orange slip over cream slip on the interior. The exterior base and feet are unslipped. Black bands on the interior lip, and a red band bordered by black on the interior corner of the wall and base. Black dots, which may represent jaguar skin, on the interior wall. A design on the interior base is painted with red and black and may represent a tree. A red band above the exterior corner of the wall and base. Black dots on the exterior

wall. Form: Plate with outcurved sides and slightly rounded base. Direct rim and rounded lip. Three hollow oven feet with two openings and a rattle. Use-wear: None recognizable. The bases of the feet are not worn.

WVS No.: 20A-72; Catalog No.: 310033 (Figure 8.29c)
Bag No.: Rim: 747 (10-3-1), 128 (2-3-3), 749 (10-3-3), 130 (2-3-3), 557 (9-2-1); Body: 130; Base: 747, 749. Provenience: 20A10-3-1. Context: Floor. On the exterior floor behind the north room. A significant portion of the vessel was found in an area 1 × 2 m in Unit 10, but a few fragments were found in Unit 9, which is about 4 m away. No fragments of feet were recovered. It is not clear whether the residents discarded the vessel after it broke or whether the vessel was complete; it appears to have been burned when it was still complete. The vessel might have been used without feet. Condition: Reconstructible (60% present). Heavily eroded and burned. Dimensions: Rim diameter: [exterior] 26.1 cm, [top] 25.4 cm (measured); Height without feet: 4.6 cm (measured); Wall thickness: 0.5–0.7 cm; Sample weight: 503 g; Original weight: 838 g; Volume: 908 cm^3. Coordinates: (30.22, 4.41) (estimate). Type: Saxche-Palmar Polychrome. Paste, temper, and firing: Pink paste (7.5Y7/4). Fine. A small amount of calcite temper (0.1–0.3 mm diameter) and a small amount of ferruginous temper (0.3–0.8 mm diameter). The paste is completely oxidized. Surface finish and decoration: The surface is heavily eroded. In some parts cream slip is preserved. Some orange paint over cream slip. Orange vertical lines over cream slip on the exterior wall. Form: Plate with outcurved sides and slightly rounded base. Direct rim and flat lip. Plain basal ridge. The vessel originally had three hollow feet. Use-wear: The interior base is pitted, possibly from use.

WVS No.: 20A-73; Catalog No.: 310042 (Figure 8.29d–f)
Bag No.: Rim: 1397 (22-3-1); Body: 1397; Base: 1397. Provenience: 20A22-3-1. Context: Floor. On and between flagstones of the exterior floor behind the central room under wall fall. Fragments were found in a small concentration. Condition: Reconstructible (75% present). Broken into small fragments. Parts of the painting are eroded, but most decorations are present. No traces of burning. Dimensions: Rim diameter: [exterior] 8.8 cm, [top] 8.4 cm (measured); Maximum diameter: 9.5 cm (measured); Height: 19.7 cm (measured); Wall thickness: 0.4–0.5 cm; Sample weight: 346 g; Original weight: 461 g; Volume: 839 cm^3. Coordinates: (25.82, 6.38) (measured). Type:

Saxche-Palmar Polychrome. Paste, temper, and firing: Pink paste (7.5Y7/4). Fine. A small amount of calcite temper (0.1 mm diameter) and a small amount of ferruginous temper (0.3–0.8 mm diameter). The paste is completely oxidized. Surface finish and decoration: No slip. Paintings were applied to the well-polished surface of pink paste. Paintings consist of black outlines filled with gray (or weak black), orange, and red. In some parts fugitive (possibly postfiring) green color was applied over these paints. Four human figures in elaborate ceremonial attire under possible curtain motifs. Black on the interior rim. Form: Vase with slightly incurved sides. Direct rim with rounded lip. Flat base. Use-wear: The base is slightly worn from use. Parts of the lip also appear worn, which may be due to use.

WVS No.: 20A-74; Catalog No.: 310046 (Figures 8.25f and 8.27g)
Bag No.: Rim: 1214 (24-3-4); Body: 1214; Base: 1214. Provenience: 20A24-3-4. Context: Floor. On the exterior floor behind the central room under wall fall. Condition: Complete (100% present). Eroded. Slightly darkened from fire. Dimensions: Rim diameter: [exterior] 2.6 cm, [top] 2.4 cm (measured); Maximum transversal measurement: 4.2 cm (measured); Height: 6.4 cm (measured); Wall thickness: 0.4–0.5 cm; Sample weight: 60 g; Original weight: 60 g; Volume: 28 cm^3. Coordinates: (24.66, 5.67) (measured). Type: Saxche-Palmar (bichrome). Paste, temper, and firing: Very pale brown paste (10YR7/4). Fine. A small amount of calcite temper (0.1–0.5 mm diameter). Because the vessel is complete, it is not clear whether the paste is oxidized. Surface finish and decoration: Orange slip on the entire exterior except for the base. Black paint (bland on the rim; an insect motif on each side). The original color of the paint before it was burned may have been red. Form: Miniature jar with vertical neck. Body with oval cross section. Direct rim and rounded lip. Flat base. Two strap handles. Use-wear: Not clear due to erosion.

WVS No.: 20A-75; Catalog No.: 310032
Bag No.: Rim: 551 (17-2-2), 747 (10-3-1); Body: 747, 551; Base: 551. Provenience: 20A17-2-2. Context: Floor. On the exterior floor behind the north room. A significant portion of the vessel was found in the lower part of wall fall in Unit 17, and some pieces were found at the floor level in Unit 10. The vessel appears to have been stored in a high location along the back wall behind the structure. Con-

dition: Reconstructible (40% present). Heavily eroded and burned. Dimensions: Rim diameter: 18 cm (estimate); Height: 7.5 cm (measured); Wall thickness: 0.7–0.8 cm; Sample weight: 264 g; Original weight: 660 g; Volume: 814 cm^3. Coordinates: (29.83, 6.13) (estimate). Type: Undetermined (probably Saxche-Palmar Polychrome). Paste, temper, and firing: Reddish yellow paste (7.5Y7/6). Fine. A medium amount of calcite temper (0.3–1.0 mm diameter) and a small amount of ferruginous temper (0.8–1.3 mm diameter). The paste is completely oxidized. Surface finish and decoration: The surface is completely eroded. Form: Bowl with flared sides and flat base. Direct rim and rounded lip. Use-wear: Not clear because of erosion.

WVS No.: 20A-76; Catalog No.: 310047 (Figure 8.25f and 8.28e)
Bag No.: Rim: 1056; Body: 1056; Base: 1056. Provenience: 20A17-3-4. Context: Floor. On the exterior floor behind the north room under wall fall. Condition: Reconstructible (60% present). Badly eroded. Severely burned. Dimensions: Rim diameter: [exterior] 3.4 cm, [top] 2.9 cm (measured); Maximum diameter: 3.6 cm (measured); Height: 4.2–4.5 cm (measured); Wall thickness: 0.4–0.7 cm; Sample weight: 36 g; Original weight: 60 g; Volume: 12 cm^3. Coordinates: (29.42, 6.24) (estimate). Type: Undetermined. Paste, temper, and firing: Very pale brown paste (10YR7/4). Most parts appear to have been heavily reoxidized in white by fire. Fine. A large amount of calcite temper (0.1 mm diameter). Because the vessel is severely burned, it is not clear whether the paste is originally oxidized. Surface finish and decoration: Because of erosion, it is not clear whether the vessel was slipped. Form: Miniature vase with vertical sides with slanted rim. Direct rim and rounded lip. Incurved base. Use-wear: Not clear due to erosion. There are remains of white material on the interior surface, which may be residues or burned slip. They are similar to the material found on a miniature vase from Operation 23B (WVS 23B9, Cat. 310182).

WVS No.: 20A-77; Catalog No.: 310049 (Figure 8.25f and 8.28f)
Bag No.: Rim: 1693 (39-3-1); Body: 1693; Base: 1693. Provenience: 20A39-3-1. Context: Floor. On the exterior floor behind the room partition between the center and south rooms under wall fall. All fragments were found close together, and it was recognized as a reconstructible vessel in the field. Condition: Reconstructible (80% present).

Eroded. The back part is blackened from fire. Dimensions: Rim diameter: 4.5 cm (estimate); Maximum diameter: 7.0 cm (measured); Height: 7.5 cm (measured); Wall thickness: 0.4–0.6 cm; Sample weight: 133 g; Original weight: 166 g; Volume: 113 cm³. Coordinates: (23.67, 6.72) (measured). Type: Undetermined. Paste, temper, and firing: Reddish yellow paste (7.5Y6/6). Medium grain. A small amount of calcite temper (0.1–0.5 mm diameter) and a medium amount of ferruginous temper (0.4–2.0 mm diameter). The paste is completely oxidized. The same paste as for figurines. Surface finish and decoration: Modeled male or half-animal figure on the frontal part of the body. Most of the vessel is unslipped. Red paint on the modeled figure. Form: Miniature effigy jar with short outflared neck. Direct rim (the lip is lost). Flat base. Use-wear: Not clear due to erosion.

STRUCTURE M8-10 (HOUSE OF THE SCRIBE): OPERATION 14A

Catalog No.: 310006 (Figure 8.30a and 8.30b)
Bag No.: Rim: 147 (4-4-2); Body: 147; Base: 147. Provenience: 14A4-4-2. Context: Burial 9. Under the room floor in the center room. Found next to cranium. Condition: Reconstructible (94% present). Paint is relatively well preserved in the interior. One-third of the exterior is badly eroded. Dimensions: Rim diameter: [exterior] 16.5 cm, [top] 16.2 cm (measured); Maximum diameter: 16.5 cm (measured); Height: 8.4–9.7 cm (measured); Wall thickness: 0.4–0.5 cm; Sample weight: 566 g; Original weight: 602 g; Volume: not calculated. Type: Saxche-Palmar Polychrome. Paste, temper, and firing: Reddish yellow paste (5YR6/8). Fine. A very small amount of calcite temper (0.2–1.0 mm diameter). The paste is completely oxidized. Surface finish and decoration: The interior is painted in red. Oblique paint strokes by a wide brush (c. 5 cm wide?) are visible. The interior bottom is eroded, and it is not clear whether this part was originally painted. A thin black band on the interior lip over the red paint. The exterior is not slipped. Painting is executed directly on well-polished natural surface. Outlines were drawn first in black, and some parts were filled in red. The design consists of two very similar motifs. Form: Bowl with slightly rounded sides and a small incurved base. The rim is visibly slanted. It was probably made in this shape intentionally. Direct rim and rounded lip. Use-wear: The exterior base is worn, probably from use. The interior base is eroded and has numerous small pits, probably from use. It appears that the vessel was not made specifi-

cally for funerary use but underwent a significant period of use before it was buried. The vessel was probably used for serving.

STRUCTURE M8-13: OPERATION 14B AND C
West Room

WVS No.: 14B-1; Catalog No.: 310144 (Figure 8.30c)
Bag No.: Rim: 561 (7-3-2), 423 (7-2-1), 184 (14-2-1), 598 (7-3-3); Body: 561, 723 (2-5-4), 164 (7-1-2). Provenience: 14B7-3-2. Context: Floor. On the exterior floor in front of the entrance of the west room. Condition: Reconstructible (40% present). Eroded. Some fragments are blackened, but it is not clear whether that was caused by the fire at the time of abandonment. Dimensions: Rim diameter: [exterior] 34 cm (estimate); Maximum diameter: 34 cm (estimate); Height: 5.5 cm (estimate); Wall thickness: 0.8–1.3 cm; Sample weight: 684 g; Original weight: 1,710 g; Volume: 1,720 cm³. Coordinates: (−1.69, 11.59) (measured). Type: Encanto Striated. Paste, temper, and firing: Reddish yellow paste (7.5YR7/6). Coarse. A large amount of calcite temper (0.5–3.0 mm diameter) and a small amount of silicate temper (1.0–3.0 mm diameter). Dark core is present in some parts. The paste is identical with that of some Encanto jars. Surface finish and decoration: Striation on the exterior except for the rim. Striation is finer and shallower than on most Encanto jars. The interior is smoothed. Form: Shallow plate with slightly rounded base. Almost no sides. A shape similar to that of *comales*. Slightly exterior-thickened rim and flat lip with a groove. Use-wear: Not clear, partly because of the eroded and fragmentary condition. There is no marked burning on the exterior, and it does not seem to have been used as a *comal*.

WVS No.: 14B-2; Catalog No.: 310136 (Figure 8.30d)
Bag No.: Rim: 415 (9-3-1); Body: 415. Provenience: 14B9-3-1. Context: Floor. In the northern part of the bench of the west room. Condition: Partial (20% present). Eroded. A significant part of the rim and neck is present, but a large portion of the body is missing. Many fragments may have fallen outside the room and remained unexcavated. Dimensions: Rim diameter: [exterior] 36 cm (estimate); Maximum diameter: 49 cm (rough estimate); Minimum opening: 20 cm (estimate); Wall thickness: 0.7–1.2 cm; Sample weight: 2,029 g; Original weight: 10,145 g; Volume: 57,249 cm³. Coordinates: (−2.79, 9.84) (measured). Type: Encanto Striated. Paste, temper, and firing: Strong brown paste (7.5YR5/6).

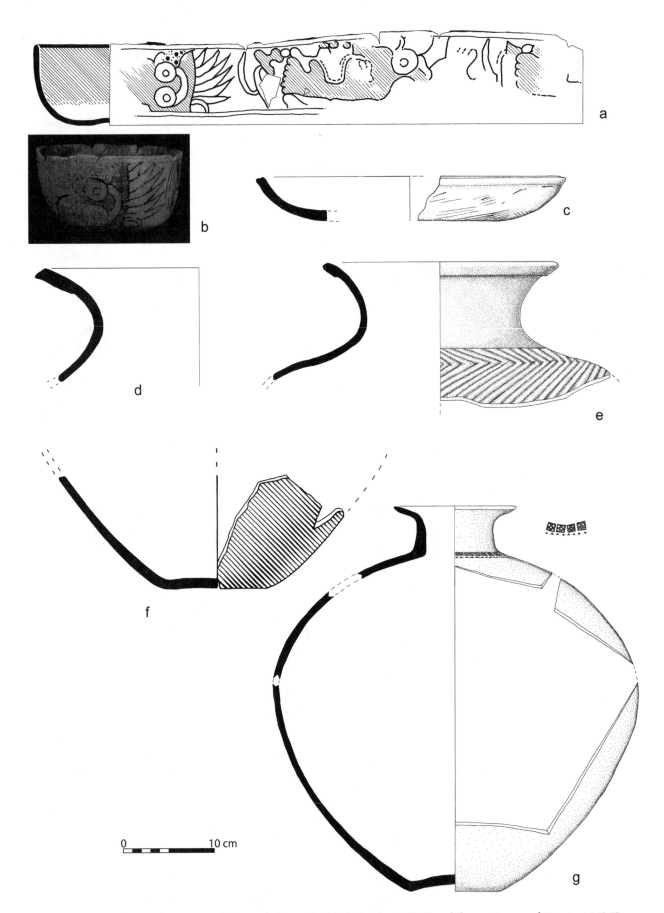

FIGURE 8.30. Complete and reconstructible vessels from a burial of Structure M8-10 and the west room of Structure M8-13. (a, b) Structure M8-10, Burial 9, Saxche-Palmar Polychrome, 14A4-4-2, Cat. 310006. (c–g) Structure M8-13, west room. (c–e) Encanto Striated. (c) 14B7-3-2, Cat. 310144, WVS 14B-1. (d) 14B9-3-1, Cat. 310136, WVS 14B-2. (e) 14B14-3-3, Cat. 310152, WVS 14B-4. (f) Tinaja Red or Pantano Impressed, 14B3-3-1, Cat. 310098, WVS 14B-5. (g) Pantano Impressed, 14B3-3-1, Cat. 310099, WVS 14B-6.

Coarse. A large amount of calcite temper (0.3–2.0 mm diameter). The paste is completely oxidized. Surface finish and decoration: Striation on the exterior body. Form: Jar with outcurved neck. Slightly exterior-thickened rim and beveled-in lip. Use-wear: Not clear because of the eroded and fragmentary condition.

WVS No.: 14B-3; Catalog No.: 310107
Bag No.: Body: 530 (16-3-1). Provenience: 14B16-3-1. Context: Floor. In the southeastern corner of the room floor of the west room. All present fragments were found in one concentration. Condition: Partial (10% present). Eroded. Most fragments are from the body, and one is from the neck. It is missing a rim. It is possible that other body sherds found in the room belong to this vessel. The vessel may have been used without a rim. Dimensions: Maximum diameter: 52 cm (estimate); Wall thickness: 0.7–1.0 cm; Sample weight: 1,439 g; Original weight: 14,390 g; Volume: not calculated. Coordinates: (–4.03, 12.41) (measured). Type: Encanto Striated. Paste, temper, and firing: Reddish yellow paste (7.5YR7/6). Coarse. A large amount of calcite temper (0.5–3.0 mm diameter). The paste is completely oxidized. Surface finish and decoration: Striation on the exterior body below the neck. The exterior neck is smoothed. Form: Jar with outcurved neck. Use-wear: Not clear because of the eroded and fragmentary condition.

WVS No.: 14B-4; Catalog No.: 310152 (Figure 8.30e)
Bag No.: Rim: Body: 578 (14-3-3), 317 (7-1-3), 423 (7-2-1), 411 (14-2-2); Body: 598 (7-3-3), 216 (1-3-1), 594 (14-3-3), 578 (14-3-3), 592 (14-3-1), 423. Provenience: 14B14-3-3. Context: Floor. On the exterior floor in front of the eastern front wall of the west room. Condition: Partial (20% present). Eroded. It is not clear whether the vessel is burned. Dimensions: Rim diameter: 25 cm (estimate); Maximum diameter: 42 cm (rough estimate); Minimum opening: 16 cm (estimate); Height: 42 cm (rough estimate); Wall thickness: 0.7–0.8 cm; Sample weight: 1,534 g; Original weight: 7,670 g; Volume: 26,739 cm^3. Coordinates: (–0.53, 12.84) (measured). Type: Encanto Striated. Paste, temper, and firing: Light brown paste (7.5YR6/4). Coarse. A large amount of calcite temper (0.3–2.0 mm diameter). The paste is completely oxidized. Surface finish and decoration: Striation on the exterior body below the neck. The exterior neck is smoothed. Form: Jar with outcurved neck. Exterior-folded rim and beveled-in lip. Use-wear: Not clear because of the eroded and fragmentary condition.

WVS No.: 14B-5; Catalog No.: 310098 (Figure 8.30f)
Bag No.: Body: 545 (1-3-4), 523 (3-3-1), 537 (12-3-2), 314 (3-3-1), 586 (16-3-1), 431 (16-2-2); Base: 587 (12-3-2), 499 (3-3-2), 416 (10-3-1), 586, 537, 523. Provenience: 14B3-3-1. Context: Floor. Fragments were scattered throughout the room floor of the west room. The vessel was probably placed in a high place originally, and it smashed when it fell. Condition: Partial (30% present). Eroded. Some fragments are blackened from fire. Only the base is present; it may have been reused as a bowl. Dimensions: Maximum diameter: 40 cm (rough estimate); Height: 40 cm (rough estimate); Wall thickness: 0.6–1.0 cm; Sample weight: 1,178 g; Original weight: 3,927 g; Volume: 24,277 cm^3. Coordinates: (–4.01, 10.75) (measured). Type: Tinaja Red or Pantano Impressed. Paste, temper, and firing: Reddish yellow paste (7.5YR6/6). Medium grain. A moderate amount of calcite temper (0.3–2.0 mm diameter) and a small amount of ferruginous temper (0.5–1.5 mm diameter). The paste is completely oxidized. Surface finish and decoration: Red slip on the exterior, including the base. Form: Jar with incurved base. Use-wear: The base is worn from use. No clear use-wear inside.

WVS No.: 14B-6; Catalog No.: 310099 (Figures 8.30g and 8.60x)
Bag No.: Rim: 501 (1-2-3), 589 (1-3-4), 555 (1-3-4); Body: 523 (3-3-1), 238 (1-3-1), 545 (1-3-4), 230 (3-3-1), 501 (1-2-3), 354 (3-1-2), 555; Base: 523. Provenience: 14B3-3-1. Context: Floor. In the southwestern corner of the room floor of the west room, near the bench and back wall. The base and a substantial portion of the body were found in one concentration in the southwestern corner of the room floor (523). Smaller but significant portions of the body were in two different concentrations about 2 m away from the first one: one in the central northern part (545) and the other in the northwestern part (238) of the room floor. The neck and a small portion of the body were in Lot 1-3-4, 1–1.5 m to the northeast of the first concentration. The vessel was probably placed in a high location originally, and it smashed when it fell; it probably fell before the structure walls collapsed. Condition: Reconstructible (80% present). Eroded. Some fragments are blackened from fire. Dimensions: Rim diameter: [exterior] 14 cm (estimate); Maximum diameter: 39 cm (estimate); Minimum opening: 6.3 cm (measured); Height: 41 cm (rough estimate); Neck height: 4.9 cm (measured); Wall thickness: 0.5–0.8 cm; Sample weight: 3,368 g; Original weight: 4,210 g; Volume: 25,244 cm^3. Coordinates: (–4.22, 10.29) (measured). Type: Pantano Impressed. Paste, temper, and

firing: Reddish yellow paste (7.5YR7/6). Medium grain. A large amount of calcite temper (0.3–2.0 mm diameter) and a small amount of ferruginous temper (0.5–1.5 mm diameter). The paste is completely oxidized. Surface finish and decoration: Red slip on the exterior. The base does not seem to be slipped. Stamped impressions below the neck-body juncture. Form: Jar with markedly outcurved neck and incurved base. Direct rim and pointed lip. Use-wear: The base is worn from use.

WVS No.: 14B-7; Catalog No.: 310100 (Figures 8.31a and 8.60y)
Bag No.: Body: 516 (1-3-3), 219 (1-3-2), 238 (1-3-1), 513 (1-3-2), 523 (3-3-1), 222 (1-3-3), 589 (1-3-4), 307 (1-3-2), 555 (1-3-4), 305 (1-3-3), 230 (3-3-1), 302 (2-3-1); Base: 516. Provenience: 14B1-3-3. Context: Floor. Near the center of the west room, on the room floor in front of the bench. The base and a large part of the lower half of the body were found in one concentration on the room floor at the base of the bench (516). Other parts were scattered around this concentration in an area 2 × 1.5 m on the room floor. The vessel was probably placed on the bench or in a high place originally. It appears to have fallen where the base was found (516). Since pieces are scattered all around this concentration, the vessel probably fell before the structure walls collapsed rather than with them. Condition: Reconstructible (80% present). Eroded. Some sherds appear to have been burned and reoxidized. The entire neck is missing. It is not clear whether the vessel was used without the neck. Dimensions: Maximum diameter: 38 cm (rough estimate); Height: 43 cm (rough estimate); Wall thickness: 0.5–0.8 cm; Sample weight: 4,170 g; Original weight: 5,213 g; Volume: 25,960 cm³. Coordinates: (−3.49, 10.23) (measured). Type: Pantano Impressed. Paste, temper, and firing: Reddish yellow paste (7.5YR7/6). Medium grain. A large amount of calcite temper (0.2–2.0 mm diameter) and a small amount of ferruginous temper (0.5–1.5 mm diameter). The paste is completely oxidized. Surface finish and decoration: Red slip on the exterior including the base. Stamped impressions and incisions below the neck-body juncture. Form: Jar with slightly incurved base. Use-wear: The base is worn from use.

WVS No.: 14B-8; Catalog No.: 310147 (Figure 8.31d)
Bag No.: Rim: 415 (9-3-1); Body: 415, 699 (9-4-1); Base: 699. Provenience: 14B9-3-1. Context: Floor. In the northern part of the bench of the west room. Some sherds appear to have fallen into the loose fill through the broken

surface of the bench. Condition: Reconstructible (70% present). Eroded. It is not clear whether the vessel was burned. Dimensions: Rim diameter: [exterior] 14.0 cm (measured), [top] 13.7 cm (measured); Maximum diameter: 40 cm (rough estimate); Minimum opening: 8.5 cm (measured); Height: 38 cm (rough estimate); Neck height: 5.1 cm (measured); Wall thickness: 0.6–1.1 cm; Sample weight: 2,915 g; Original weight: 4,164 g; Volume: 20,253 cm³. Coordinates: (−3.35, 9.38) (measured). Type: Pantano Impressed. Paste, temper, and firing: Reddish yellow paste (5YR6/6). Medium grain. A moderate amount of calcite temper (0.2–3.0 mm diameter) and a small amount of ferruginous temper (0.5–3.0 mm diameter). The paste is completely oxidized. Surface finish and decoration: Red slip on the exterior. The rim and neck are heavily eroded. Stamped impressions and incisions below the neck-body juncture. Form: Jar with outcurved neck and slightly incurved base. Direct rim and pointed lip. Use-wear: Not clear because of the eroded and fragmentary condition.

WVS No.: 14B-9; Catalog No.: 310043 (Figure 8.31e and 8.31f)
Bag No.: Rim: 548 (1-3-4), 537 (12-3-2); Body: 548, 537, 431 (16-2-2), 432 (3-2-2); Base: 537, 499 (3-3-2), 534 (16-3-1). Provenience: 14B1-3-4. Context: Floor. Near the center of the room floor of the west room. Roughly half the vessel was found in one concentration (548-551). Other fragments were found to the east of the concentration in an area 1 × 1.5 m. It is probable that the vessel was originally placed in a high location and that it broke when it fell. Condition: Reconstructible (90% present). Eroded. Many fragments are blackened from fire. Dimensions: Rim diameter: [interior] 23.5 cm, [top] 24.1 cm (measured); Maximum diameter: 26.3 cm (measured); Minimum opening: 23.5 cm (measured); Height: 11.7 cm (measured); Wall thickness: 0.6–0.7 cm; Sample weight: 1,110 g; Original weight: 1,233 g; Volume: 2,627 cm³. Coordinates: (−3.81, 11.74) (measured). Type: Chaquiste Impressed. Paste, temper, and firing: Reddish yellow paste (5YR6/6). Medium grain. A moderate amount of calcite temper (0.2–0.8 mm diameter) and a small amount of ferruginous temper (0.5–2.0 mm diameter). The paste is completely oxidized. Surface finish and decoration: Red slip on the exterior rim (above the ridge) and remains of weak reddish slip on the body. Nail impressions on the ridge. Form: Bowl with incurved walls and slightly restricted orifice. Exterior-thickened rim and pointed lip.

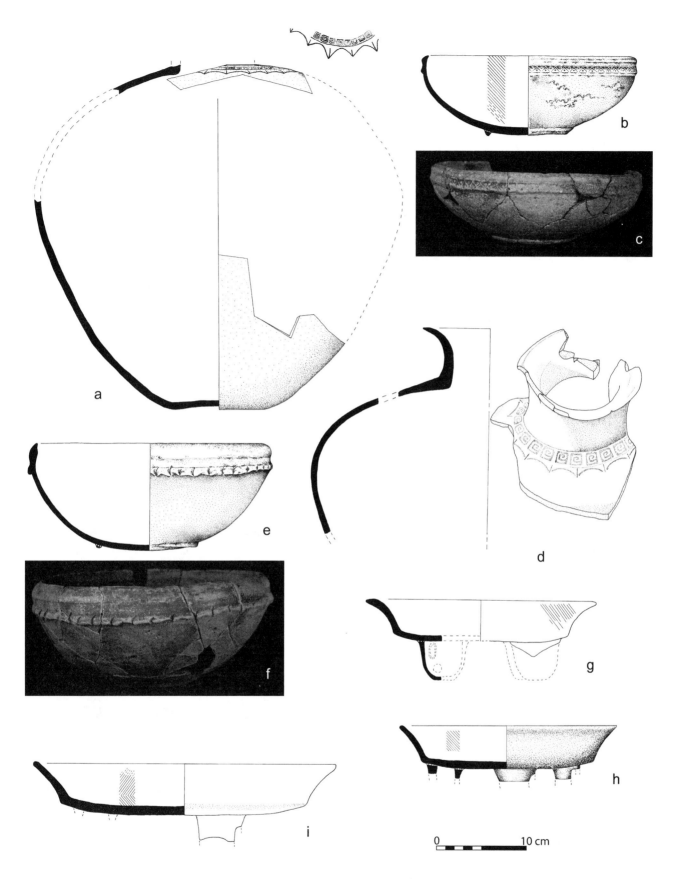

Figure 8.31. Complete and reconstructible vessels from the west room of Structure M8-13. (a) Pantano Impressed, 14B1-3-3, Cat. 310100, WVS 14B-7. (b, c) Chaquiste Impressed, 14B12-3-2, Cat. 310045, WVS 14B-10. (d) Pantano Impressed, 14B9-3-1, Cat. 310147, WVS 14B-8. (e, f) Chaquiste Impressed, 14B1-3-4, Cat. 310043, WVS 14B-9. (g–i) Saxche-Palmar Polychrome. (g) 14B10-3-1, Cat. 310024, WVS 14B-11. (h) 14B14-2-1, Cat. 310141, WVS 14B-12. (i) 14B14-2-1, Cat. 310142, WVS 14B-13.

Ridge below the rim. Ring base. Use-wear: The interior base is rough, possibly from use.

WVS No.: 14B-10; Catalog No.: 310045 (Figures 8.31b, 8.31c, and 8.6oz)
Bag No.: Rim: 537 (12-3-2); Body: 537; Base: 537. Provenience: 14B12-3-2. Context: Floor. In the central eastern part of the room floor of the west room near the room division with the center room. All fragments were found in one concentration and were recognized as part of a reconstructible vessel in the field. Condition: Reconstructible (85% present). Relatively well preserved. Some parts of the vessel are blackened, but it is not clear whether that was caused by the fire at the time of abandonment. Dimensions: Rim diameter: [interior] 22.0 cm, [top] 22.3 cm (measured); Maximum diameter: 23.8 cm (measured); Minimum opening: 22.0 cm (measured); Height: 8.2 cm (measured); Wall thickness: 0.4–0.7 cm; Sample weight: 730 g; Original weight: 859 g; Volume: 1,964 cm³. Coordinates: (–3.58, 12.71) (measured). Type: Chaquiste Impressed. Paste, temper, and firing: Reddish yellow paste (5YR6/6). Medium grain. A large amount of calcite temper (0.2–2.0 mm diameter). The paste is completely oxidized. Surface finish and decoration: Red slip on the exterior rim (above the ridge) and the entire interior. Stamped impressions on the ridge. Form: Bowl with incurved walls and slightly restricted orifice. Exterior-thickened rim and pointed lip. Ridge below the rim. Ring base. Use-wear: The interior is smooth, and there is no recognizable wear. The ring base is barely worn, and the vessel may have been relatively new.

WVS No.: 14B-11; Catalog No.: 310024 (Figure 8.31g)
Bag No.: Rim: 416 (10-3-1), 475 (1-2-2); Base: 475, 104 (1-1-1), 589 (1-3-4), 416, 187 (1-2-1). Provenience: 14B10-3-1. Context: Floor. In the southern part of the bench of the west room. Condition: Reconstructible (40% present). Very eroded. Some fragments may have fallen outside the room and remained unexcavated. Dimensions: Rim diameter: 24 cm (estimate); Height: 9.1 cm (measured); Height without feet: 4.2 cm (measured); Wall thickness: 0.7–0.8 cm; Sample weight: 292 g; Original weight: 730 g; Volume: 726 cm³. Coordinates: (–4.26, 9.19) (measured). Type: Saxche-Palmar Polychrome. Paste, temper, and firing: Reddish yellow paste (7.5YR6/6). Fine. A small amount of calcite temper (0.1–0.3 mm diameter) and ferruginous temper (0.5–1.3 mm diameter). The paste is completely oxidized. Surface finish and decoration: Re-

mains of red paint over white underslip on the interior and exterior. Form: Plate with markedly outcurved sides and flat base. Direct rim and flat lip. Three hollow oven feet with two openings. Use-wear: Not clear because of erosion.

WVS No.: 14B-12; Catalog No.: 310141 (Figure 8.31h)
Bag No.: Rim: 160 (14-2-1), 184 (14-2-1); Base: 160, 184. Provenience: 14B14-2-1. Context: Floor. In front of the front wall between the center and west rooms. Most fragments were found in one concentration next to the front wall. It is probable that the vessel was originally placed in front of the front wall. Condition: Reconstructible (80% present). Eroded. Some fragments are blackened from fire. Dimensions: Rim diameter: [exterior] 23.7 cm (measured), [top] 23.1 cm (measured); Height: 9.5 cm (rough estimate); Height without feet: 4.6 cm (measured); Wall thickness: 0.6–0.9 cm; Sample weight: 550 g; Original weight: 688 g; Volume: 1,053 cm³. Coordinates: (–1.59, 13.21) (measured). Type: Saxche-Palmar Polychrome. Paste, temper, and firing: Reddish yellow paste (7.5YR6/6). Fine. A small amount of calcite temper (0.1–0.5 mm diameter). The paste is completely oxidized. Surface finish and decoration: Remains of red paint over white underslip on the interior. The exterior is completely eroded. Form: Plate with outcurved sides and flat base. Direct rim and rounded lip. Three hollow feet with two openings. Use-wear: Not clear because of erosion.

WVS No.: 14B-13; Catalog No.: 310142 (Figure 8.31i)
Bag No.: Rim: 184 (14-2-1), 160 (14-2-1); Base: 184, 160. Provenience: 14B14-2-1. Context: Floor. In the wall fall in front of the front wall between the center and west rooms. It is probable that the vessel was originally placed in front of the front wall. Condition: Partial (40% present). Eroded. It is not clear whether the vessel is burned. Dimensions: Rim diameter: 33 cm (estimate); Height: 9.5 cm (rough estimate); Height without feet: 5.1 cm (measured); Wall thickness: 0.9–1.2 cm; Sample weight: 549 g; Original weight: 1,373 g; Volume: 2,044 cm³. Coordinates: (–1.30, 12.60) (estimate). Type: Saxche-Palmar Polychrome. Paste, temper, and firing: Reddish yellow paste (7.5YR7/6). Fine. A medium amount of calcite temper (0.1–0.5 mm diameter). The paste is completely oxidized. Surface finish and decoration: Remains of red and orange paint on the interior. The exterior is completely eroded, and its surface is uneven. Form: Plate with outcurved sides and flat base. Direct rim and rounded lip. Three hollow

feet with two openings. Use-wear: Not clear because of erosion.

WVS No.: 14B-14; Catalog No.: 310154
Bag No.: Rim: 222 (1-3-3), 468 (12-2-2), 432 (3-2-2), 356 (1-1-2), 499 (3-3-2), 589 (1-3-4), 501 (1-2-3); Base: 222, 432, 356, 499, 589. Provenience: 14B1-3-3. Context: Floor. In the central western part of the room floor of the west room. A significant portion of the vessel was found in one concentration, but other fragments were scattered in other parts of the room floor. It is probable that the vessel was originally placed in a high location and broke when it fell. Condition: Reconstructible (50% present). Very eroded and fragmentary, though three feet are complete. Many small pieces were probably lost. Some fragments appear to have been reoxidized in red by fire. Dimensions: Rim diameter: 28 cm (estimate); Height: 9.5 cm (estimate); Height without feet: 5.5 cm (estimate); Wall thickness: 0.7–0.8 cm; Sample weight: 455 g; Original weight: 910 g; Volume: 1,555 cm^3. Coordinates: (–3.69, 10.78) (measured). Type: Saxche-Palmar Polychrome. Paste, temper, and firing: Yellow paste (10YR7/6). Fine. A moderate amount of calcite temper (0.5–3.0 mm diameter). The paste is completely oxidized. Surface finish and decoration: Remains of red paint. Form: Plate with slightly outcurved sides and flat base. Direct rim and rounded lip. Three hollow oven feet with two openings and a rattle. Use-wear: Not clear because of erosion.

Center Room

WVS No.: 14B-15; Catalog No.: 310066 (Figure 8.32a)
Bag No.: Rim: 166 (2-2-2), 898 (24-3-2), 144 (14-1-2), 105 (2-1-2). Provenience: 14B2-2-2. Context: Floor. On the room floor of the center room. Adjoining pieces were found apart from each other, some from Unit 24 (the eastern part of the room floor), some from Unit 2 (the western part of the room floor), and some from Unit 14 (the exterior in front of the division between the center and west rooms). Condition: Partial (7% present, 60% of the rim). There do not appear to be enough body fragments of a Cambio/Encanto jar in nearby areas to indicate the presence of a reconstructible vessel. The joints between fragments from different units are relatively well preserved. It is not clear whether the broken rim was refuse or was reused for unknown purposes. It is also possible that it was deposited at the time of the destruction of the structure or that other parts of the vessel were removed at the time of abandonment. Dimensions: Rim

diameter: [exterior] 36.0 cm, [top] 35.4 cm (measured); Minimum opening: 22.5 cm (measured); Wall thickness: 1.1–1.5 cm (for the rim); Sample weight: 1,582 g; Original weight: 22,600; Volume: not calculated. Coordinates: (–2.10, 14.88) (estimate). Type: Cambio Unslipped or Encanto Striated. Paste, temper, and firing: Reddish yellow paste (7.5YR7/6). Coarse. A large amount of calcite and silicate sand temper (0.3–4.0 mm diameter). The paste is completely oxidized. Surface finish and decoration. Unslipped. Form: Jar with outcurved neck. Exterior-folded rim and squared lip. Use-wear: Not clear.

WVS No.: 14B-16; Catalog No.: 310094 (Figure 8.32b)
Bag No.: Rim: 672 (20-2-1), 687 (24-2-1), 892 (23-3-1), 901 (20-3-3); Body: 898 (24-3-2), 901, 672, 894 (19-3-1), 854 (19-3-2), 885 (19-3-4); Base: 898. Provenience: 14B24-3-2. Context: Floor. In the eastern part of the room floor of the center room near the wall and on the exterior floor in front of it. Most fragments were found in an area 2 × 2 m. It was probably placed on the floor in the corner in front of the bench. Condition: Reconstructible (50% present). Eroded. It is not clear whether the vessel was burned. Many pieces may have been lost because of a large tree fall. Dimensions: Rim diameter: [exterior] 24 cm (estimate); Maximum diameter: 40 cm (rough estimate); Minimum opening: 16 cm (rough estimate); Height: 47 cm (measured); Wall thickness: 0.7–0.9 cm; Sample weight: 3,547 g; Original weight: 7,094 g; Volume: 24,900 cm^3. Coordinates: (–2.49, 18.32) (measured). Type: Encanto Striated. Paste, temper, and firing: Reddish yellow paste (7.5YR7/6). Coarse. A large amount of calcite temper (0.5–2.0 mm diameter) and a moderate amount of quartz sand temper (0.5–2.0 mm diameter). The paste is completely oxidized. Surface finish and decoration: Unslipped. Striation on the shoulder and base, not on the rest of the body. Form: Jar with outcurved neck and rounded base. Exterior-thickened rim and beveled-in lip. Use-wear: Not clear, partly because of erosion.

WVS No.: 14B-17; Catalog No.: 310079 (Figures 8.32c and 8.60a')
Bag No.: Rim: 250 (2-3-4); Body: 186 (2-2-2), 172 (2-2-2), 244 (2-3-3), 250, 901 (20-3-3), 247 (2-3-3), 328 (2-3-6), 302 (2-3-1). Provenience: 14B2-3-4. Context: Floor. In the western part of the room floor of the center room. Most fragments were found close together in an area 2 × 2 m. Condition: Partial (30% present). Eroded. It is not clear whether it was burned. Dimensions: Rim diameter:

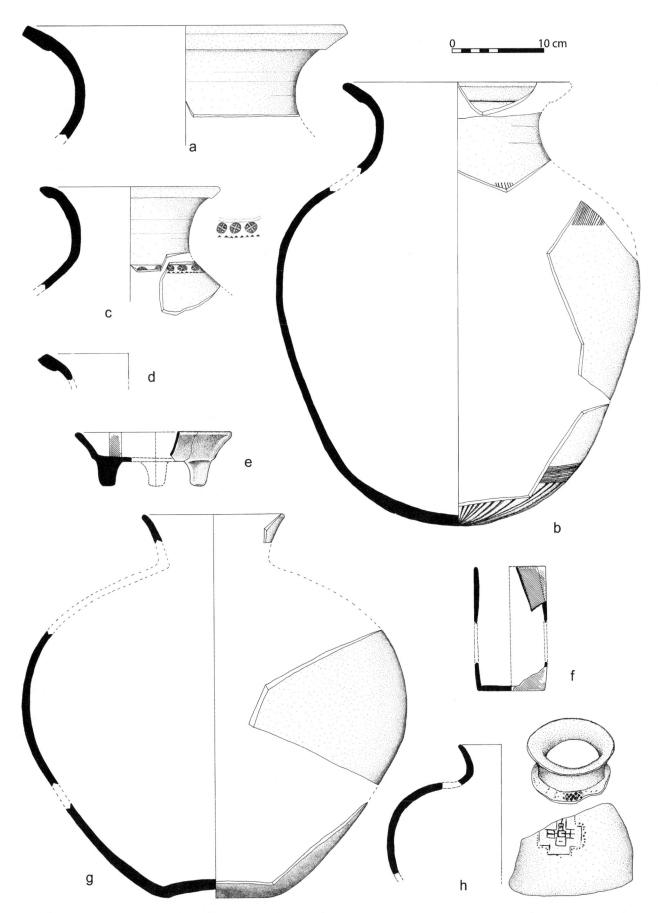

FIGURE 8.32. Complete and reconstructible vessels from the center room of Structure M8-13. (a) Cambio Unslipped or Encanto Striated, 14B2-2-2, Cat. 310066, WVS 14B-15. (b) Encanto Striated, 14B24-3-2, Cat. 310094, WVS 14B-16. (c) Manteca Impressed, 14B2-3-4, Cat. 310079, WVS 14B-17. (d) Encanto Striated, 14B2-3-4, Cat. 310115, WVS 14B-18. (e, f) Tinaja Red. (e) 14B20-2-1, Cat. 310057, WVS 14B-19. (f) 14B6-2-2, Cat. 310059, WVS 14B-20. (g) Tinaja Red or Pantano Impressed, 14B2-3-4, Cat. 310114, WVS 14B-21. (h) Pantano Impressed, 14B19-3-4, Cat. 310073, WVS 14B-22.

[exterior] 21 cm (estimate); Maximum diameter: 42 cm (rough estimate); Minimum opening: 13.7 cm (measured); Wall thickness: 0.7–1.4 cm; Sample weight: 1,337 g; Original weight: 4,457 g; Volume: 33,060 cm³. Coordinates: (–2.47, 14.57) (estimate). Type: Manteca Impressed. Paste, temper, and firing: Reddish yellow paste (7.5YR8/6). Coarse. A large amount of calcite temper (0.1–3.0 mm diameter) and a large amount of silicate sand temper (1.0–3.0 mm diameter). The paste is mostly oxidized. The paste is basically the same as in many Cambio Unslipped and Encanto Striated vessels. Surface finish and decoration: Red slip on the exterior neck and body. Stamp and triangular impressions below the neck-body juncture. Impressions are similar to those of Pantano Impressed, but the stamped impressions are more spaced than in most Pantano Impressed. Form: Jar with outcurved neck. Exterior-thickened and pointed lip. The neck-body juncture is smooth. The form is similar to those of Cambio Unslipped and Encanto Striated jars, but the thickening of the rim is smoother than in common Cambio and Encanto jars. Use-wear: Not clear.

WVS No.: 14B-18; Catalog No.: 310115 (Figure 8.32d)
Bag No.: Rim: 259 (2-3-4); Body: 259, 151 (4-1-3), 905 (19-3-3), 449 (5-2-3), 885 (19-3-4). Provenience: 14B2-3-4. Context: Floor. In the western part of the room floor of the central room. Most sherds were found in an area 2 × 3 m. Condition: Partial (30% present). Eroded. It is not clear whether it was burned. It is not clear whether it is reconstructible. Dimensions: Rim diameter: [exterior] 20 cm (estimate); Maximum diameter: 43 cm (rough estimate); Wall thickness: 0.8–1.1 cm; Sample weight: 1,555 g; Original weight: 5,183 g; Volume: 27,132 cm³. Coordinates: (–2.20, 14.35) (measured). Type: Encanto Striated. Paste, temper, and firing: Very pale brown paste (10YR7/4). Coarse. A large amount of calcite temper (0.5–2.0 mm diameter) and a large amount of silicate temper (0.5–2.0 mm diameter). Surface finish and decoration: Striation below the shoulder. The interior is smoothed but porous. Form: Jar with outcurved neck. Exterior-folded rim and beveled-in lip. Use-wear: Not clear because of the eroded and fragmentary condition.

WVS No.: 14B-19; Catalog No.: 310057 (Figure 8.32e)
Bag No.: Rim: 672 (20-2-1), 901 (20-3-3), 328 (2-3-6), 890 (19-3-2); Base: 672. Provenience: 14B20-2-1. Context: Floor. In the central and eastern parts of the room floor in the center room. Most fragments were found in the wall

fall and on the floor in an area 1 × 2 m. Condition: Reconstructible (60% present). Many pieces are eroded. Some fragments are blackened from fire. Dimensions: Rim diameter: [exterior] 17.5 cm, [top] 16.9 cm (measured); Height: 5.7 cm (measured); Height without feet: 3.7 cm (measured); Wall thickness: 0.6–1.0 cm; Sample weight: 257 g; Original weight: 428 g; Volume: 319 cm³. Coordinates: (–3.10, 17.10) (estimate). Type: Tinaja Red. Paste, temper, and firing: Reddish yellow paste (5YR7/6). Fine. A small amount of calcite temper (0.3–1.0 mm diameter) and a small amount of ferruginous temper (0.8–1.5 mm diameter). The paste is completely oxidized. Surface finish and decoration: Red slip on the interior. It is not clear whether the exterior is eroded or is not slipped. Form: Plate with outcurved sides and flat base. Direct rim and beveled-in lip. Three solid oven feet. Use-wear: None recognizable, partly because of erosion.

WVS No.: 14B-20; Catalog No.: 310059 (Figure 8.32f)
Bag No.: Rim: 208 (6-2-2); Body: 208; Base: 118 (4-4-1). Provenience: 14B6-2-2. Context: Floor. In the western part of the bench in the center room. Condition: Partial (30% present). Relatively well preserved. Some fragments are blackened from fire. Dimensions: Rim diameter: [exterior] 8.0 cm, [top] 7.6 cm (estimate); Maximum diameter: 8.4 cm (estimate); Wall thickness: 0.5–0.7 cm; Sample weight: 87 g; Original weight: 290 g; Volume: 402 cm³. Coordinates: (–4.20, 15.40) (estimate). Type: Tinaja Red. Paste, temper, and firing: Reddish yellow paste (7.5YR7/6). Fine, hard. A small amount of calcite temper (0.3–1.5 mm diameter). Dark core. Surface finish and decoration: Red slip on the exterior. The exterior base and the interior are unslipped. Form: Vase with slightly incurved sides and flat base. Direct rim and rounded lip. Use-wear: None recognizable.

WVS No.: 14B-21; Catalog No.: 310114 (Figure 8.32g)
Bag No.: Rim: 262 (2-3-4); Body: 253 (2-3-4), 186 (2-2-2), 324, 169 (2-2-2), 177 (2-2-2), 320 (2-3-3), 262; Base: 253. Provenience: 14B2-3-4. Context: Floor. In the western part of the room floor of the center room. Many sherds were found in an area 1 × 1 m. Condition: Reconstructible (40% present). Eroded. It is not clear whether the vessel was burned. It is missing the entire neck. It is possible that one of the isolated necks found in other units belongs to this vessel (one in 14B Unit 4, one in 14C Unit 6, and two in 14C Unit 5). Dimensions: Maximum diameter: 40 cm (rough estimate); Height: 43 cm (rough estimate); Wall

thickness: 0.6–1.0 cm (for the body and base); Sample weight: 2,248 g; Original weight: 5,620 g; Volume: 28,320 cm³. Coordinates: (–2.65, 14.34) (measured). Type: Tinaja Red or Pantano Impressed. Paste, temper, and firing: Reddish yellow paste (7.5YR7/6). Medium grain. A large amount of calcite temper (0.2–1.0 mm diameter) and a small amount of ferruginous temper (0.5–2.0 mm diameter). The paste is completely oxidized. Surface finish and decoration: Red slip on the exterior, including the base. Form: Jar with incurved base. Use-wear: The base is worn from use.

WVS No.:14B-22; Catalog No.: 310073 (Figure 8.32h)
Bag No.: Rim: 169 (2-2-2); Body: 885 (19-3-4), 892 (23-3-1), 898 (24-3-2), 629 (26-1-1). Provenience: 14B19-3-4. Context: Floor. Scattered in the eastern part of the room floor of the center room and on the exterior floor in front of it. It probably fell from a high location. Condition: Reconstructible (40% present). Other Tinaja Red sherds from the area may be part of this vessel. Eroded. It is not clear whether it is burned. Dimensions: Rim diameter: [exterior] 9.5 cm, [top] 9.0 cm (measured); Maximum diameter: 25 cm (estimate); Minimum opening: 5.7 cm (measured); Height: 20 cm (rough estimate); Neck height: 3.0 cm (measured); Wall thickness: 0.7–0.8 cm; Sample weight: 490 g; Original weight: 1,225 g; Volume: 5,049 cm³. Coordinates: (–0.60, 17.70) (estimate). Type: Pantano Impressed. Paste, temper, and firing: Pink paste (7.5YR8/4). Medium grain paste. A large amount of calcite temper (0.3–3.0 mm diameter). The paste is almost completely oxidized, but the interior is dark. Surface finish and decoration: Red slip on the exterior. Stamped impressions below the neck-body juncture. Incisions on the body. Remains of blue paint on the neck. Form: Jar with outcurved neck. The base form is not clear. Direct rim and squared lip. Use-wear: None recognizable.

WVS No.: 14B-23; Catalog No.: 310090 (Figure 8.33a)
Bag No.: Rim: 672 (20-2-1), 105 (2-1-2), 253 (2-3-4), 708 (2-4-1); Body: 262 (2-3-4), 250 (2-3-4), 169 (2-2-2), 177 (2-2-2), 253; Base: 262. Provenience: 14B2-3-4. Context: Floor. In the western part of the room floor of the center room. Most fragments were found in an area 1 × 1 m. Condition: Reconstructible (75% present). Eroded. It is not clear whether the vessel was burned. Dimensions: Rim diameter: [exterior] 13.6 cm, [top] 12.8 cm (measured); Maximum diameter: 26 cm (estimate); Minimum opening: 7.5 cm (measured); Height: 27.2 cm (measured);

Neck height: 5.0 cm (measured); Wall thickness: 0.7–0.9 cm; Sample weight: 2,286 g; Original weight: 3,048 g; Volume: 6,465 cm³. Coordinates: (–2.07, 14.44) (measured). Type: Pantano Impressed. Paste, temper, and firing: Reddish yellow paste (7.5YR7/6). Medium grain. A large amount of calcite temper (0.2–2.0 mm diameter) and a small amount of ferruginous temper (0.5–2.0 mm diameter). The paste is completely oxidized. Surface finish and decoration: Red slip on the exterior. There appear to be impressions below the neck-body juncture, but they are heavily eroded. Form: Jar with outcurved neck and incurved base. Direct rim and rounded lip. Use-wear: The base is worn from use.

WVS No.:14B-24; Catalog No.: 310091 (Figure 8.33b)
Bag No.: Rim: 672 (20-2-1), 901 (20-3-3); Body: 672, 901, 611 (23-1-1); Base: 672, 901. Provenience: 14B20-2-1. Context: Floor. In the eastern part of the room floor of the center room. Condition: Reconstructible (50% present). Severely eroded. It is not clear whether the vessel is burned. Dimensions: Rim diameter: [exterior] 9.5 cm, [top] 9.0 cm (measured); Maximum diameter: 15 cm (rough estimate); Minimum opening: 6.1 cm (measured); Height: 15 cm (rough estimate); Neck height: 3.4 cm (measured): Wall thickness: 0.7–0.9 cm; Sample weight: 565 g; Original weight: 1,130 g; Volume: 1,874 cm³. Coordinates: (–2.30, 17.90) (estimate). Type: Pantano Impressed. Paste, temper, and firing: Light red paste (10R6/8). Medium grain paste. A moderate amount of calcite temper (0.1–1.5 mm diameter). The paste is completely oxidized. Surface finish and decoration: Red slip on the exterior. Impressions below the neck-body juncture. Form: Jar with outcurved neck and incurved base. Outflared everted rim and pointed lip. Use-wear: None recognizable.

WVS No.:14B-25; Catalog No.: 310092 (Figures 8.33c and 8.60b')
Bag No.: Rim: 901 (20-3-3), 898 (24-3-2), 850 (20-3-4); Body: 672 (20-2-1), 901, 894 (19-3-1), 898, 850, 697 (23-2-1), 926 (25-3-4). Provenience: 14B20-3-4. Context: Floor. In the eastern part of the room floor of the center room. Condition: Reconstructible (40% present). Other Tinaja Red sherds from the area may be part of this vessel. Eroded. It is not clear whether the vessel is burned. Dimensions: Rim diameter: [exterior] 12.8 cm, [top] 11.4 cm (measured); Maximum diameter: 23 cm (rough estimate); Minimum opening: 8.7 cm (measured); Height: 20 cm (rough estimate); Neck height: 5.1 cm (measured): Wall

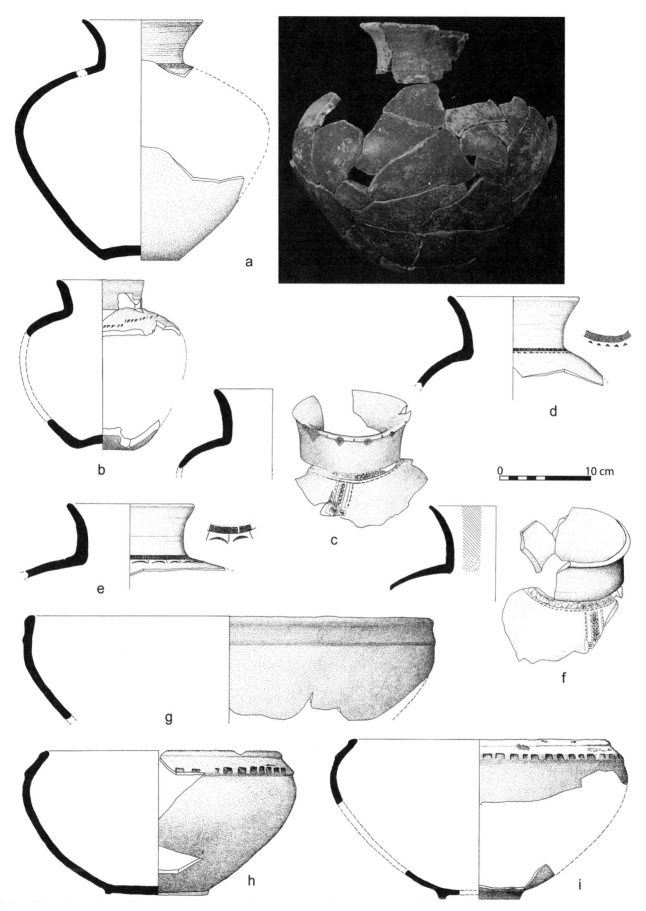

FIGURE 8.33. Complete and reconstructible vessels from the center room of Structure M8-13. (a–f) Pantano Impressed.
(a) 14B2-3-4, Cat. 310090, WVS 14B-23. (b) 14B20-2-1, Cat. 310091, WVS 14B-24. (c) 14B20-3-4, Cat. 310092, WVS 14B-25.
(d) 14B19-3-1, Cat. 310095, WVS 14B-26. (e) 14B19-3-1, Cat. 310096, WVS 14B-27. (f) 14B20-3-4, Cat. 310025, WVS 14B-28.
(g) Subin Red, 14B2-3-3, Cat. 310083, WVS 14B-29. (h, i) Chaquiste Impressed. (h) 14B2-3-4, Cat. 310082, WVS 14B-30.
(i) 14B2-3-4, Cat. 310084, WVS 14B-31.

thickness: 0.8–1.1 cm; Sample weight: 434 g; Original weight: 1,085 g; Volume: 3,129 cm³. Coordinates: (–2.49, 17.45) (estimate). Type: Pantano Impressed. Paste, temper, and firing: Light red paste (10R7/6). Medium grain paste. A large amount of calcite temper (0.1–1.3 mm diameter). The paste is completely oxidized. Surface finish and decoration: Red slip on the exterior. Impressions below the neck-body juncture. Incisions on the body. Dents around the rim. Form: Jar with outcurved neck. Exterior-thickened rim and pointed lip. Use-wear: None recognizable.

WVS No.: 14B-26; Catalog No.: 310095 (Figures 8.33d and 8.60c')
Bag No.: Rim: 894 (19-3-1); Body: 888 (19-3-1), 890 (19-3-2), 697 (23-2-1), 672 (20-2-1), 687 (24-2-1), 609 (19-1-1), 894. Provenience: 14B19-3-1. Context: Floor. On the exterior floor in front of the center room. Condition: Reconstructible (30% present). Many sherds are heavily eroded. It is not clear whether it was burned. Many pieces may have been lost because of a large tree fall. Dimensions: Rim diameter: [exterior] 14.8 cm, [top] 14.1 (measured); Maximum diameter: 36 cm (rough estimate); Minimum opening: 9.2 cm (measured); Neck height: 5.4 cm (measured); Wall thickness: 0.9–1.1 cm; Sample weight: 1,239 g; Original weight: 4,130 g; Volume: 15,541 cm³. Coordinates: (–1.4, 16.3) (estimate). Type: Pantano Impressed. Paste, temper, and firing: Very pale brown paste (10YR7/4). Medium grain. A moderate amount of calcite temper (0.3–2.0 mm diameter) and a small amount of ferruginous temper (0.5–2.0 mm diameter). Some parts of the paste are dark. Surface finish and decoration: Red slip on the exterior and on the interior of the neck. Stamped impressions and incisions below the neck-body juncture. Form: Jar with outcurved neck. Direct rim and rounded lip. Use-wear: Not clear, partly because of erosion.

WVS No.: 14B-27; Catalog No.: 310096 (Figures 8.33e and 8.60d')
Bag No.: Rim: 609 (19-1-1), 894 (19-3-1); Body: 894, 885 (19-3-4), 494 (4-3-1), 888 (19-3-1), 609, 107(14C4-1-1). Provenience: 14B19-3-1. Context: Floor. On the exterior floor in front of the center room. Condition: Reconstructible (40% present). Many sherds are heavily eroded. It is not clear whether the vessel was burned. Many pieces may have been lost because of a large tree fall. Dimensions: Rim diameter: [exterior] 14 cm (estimate); Maximum diameter: 28 cm (rough estimate); Minimum opening:

9.2 cm (measured); Neck height: 5.5 cm (measured); Wall thickness: 0.9–1.1 cm; Sample weight: 1,073 g; Original weight: 2,683 g; Volume: 8,289 cm³. Coordinates: (–1.0, 16.6) (estimate). Type: Pantano Impressed. Paste, temper, and firing: Pink paste (7.5YR7/4). Medium grain. A moderate amount of calcite temper (0.2–0.5 mm diameter) and a small amount of ferruginous temper (1.0–4.0 mm diameter). The paste is completely oxidized. Surface finish and decoration: Red slip on the exterior. Stamped impressions and incisions below the neck-body juncture. Form: Jar with outcurved neck. Direct rim and rounded lip. Use-wear: Not clear, partly because of erosion.

WVS No.: 14B-28; Catalog No.: 310025 (Figures 8.33f and 8.60e')
Bag No.: Rim: 850 (20-3-4); Body: 850, 901 (20-3-3), 672 (20-2-1), 609 (19-1-1); Base: 882 (23-3-2). Provenience: 14B20-3-4. Context: Floor. In the eastern part of the room floor of the center. Condition: Partial (25% present). Many sherds are heavily eroded. The erosion makes it difficult to recognize body sherds belonging to this vessel. It is not clear whether it was burned. Some pieces may have been lost because of a large tree fall in front of the room. Dimensions: Rim diameter: [exterior] 14.3 cm (measured), [top] 13.8 cm (measured); Maximum diameter: 24 cm (rough estimate); Minimum opening: 8.9 cm (measured); Height: 27 cm (rough estimate); Neck height: 5.3 cm (measured); Wall thickness: 0.5–0.7 cm; Sample weight: 471 g; Original weight: 1,884 g; Volume: 7,261 cm³. Coordinates: (–2.76, 17.77) (estimate). Type: Pantano Impressed. Paste, temper, and firing: Pink paste (7.5YR7/4). Medium grain. A large amount of calcite temper (0.2–1.0 mm diameter). The paste is completely oxidized. Surface finish and decoration: Red slip on the exterior and the interior of the neck. Stamped impressions and incisions below the neck-body juncture. Indentation on the exterior rim. Some incisions and impressions on the shoulder. Form: Jar with outcurved neck and incurved base. Exterior-thickened rim and rounded lip. Use-wear: Not clear, partly because of erosion.

WVS No.: 14B-29; Catalog No.: 310083 (Figure 8.33g)
Bag No.: Rim: 247 (2-3-3), 186 (2-2-2), 324 (2-3-4), 105 (2-1-2), 265 (2-3-3), 320 (2-3-3), 901 (20-3-3); Body: 324, 247, 186, 105, 265, 102 (2-1-1), 327 (2-3-5), 328 (2-3-6), 172 (2-2-2); Base: 901. Provenience: 14B2-3-3. Context: Floor. In the western part of the room floor of the center room. Most fragments were found in an area 1.5 × 2 m. Condi-

tion: Reconstructible (50% present). Eroded. It is not clear whether the vessel is burned. Dimensions: Rim diameter: [interior] 44 cm (estimate); Maximum diameter: 47 cm (estimate); Minimum opening: 44 cm (estimate); Height: 16 cm (rough estimate); Wall thickness: 0.7–0.9 cm; Sample weight: 2,031 g; Original weight: 4,062 g; Volume: 12,985 cm³. Coordinates: (−3.13, 14.60) (measured). Type: Subin Red. Paste, temper, and firing: Reddish yellow paste (5YR6/6). Coarse. A large amount of calcite temper (0.3–2.0 mm diameter) and a small amount of silicate sand (0.5–2.0 mm diameter). The paste is mostly oxidized. Surface finish and decoration: Remains of red paint on the rim and the interior. The exterior body was smoothed but probably not slipped. Form: Bowl with incurved sides and restricted orifice. Ring base. Exterior-thickened rim and rounded lip. Small ridge. Use-wear: Not clear, partly because of erosion.

WVS No.: 14B-30; Catalog No.: 310082 (Figure 8.33h)
Bag No.: Rim: 256 (2-3-4), 324 (2-3-4); Body: 256, 253 (2-3-4), 186 (2-2-2), 299 (2-3-4), 324; Base 299. Provenience: 14B2-3-4. Context: Floor. In the western part of the room floor of the center room. Most fragments were found in an area 1 × 1 m. Condition: Partial (50% present). Eroded. It is not clear whether the vessel is burned. Dimensions: Rim diameter: [interior] 25 cm, [top] 26 cm (estimate); Maximum diameter: 30 cm (estimate); Minimum opening: 25 cm (estimate); Height: 15 cm (estimate); Wall thickness: 0.8–0.9 cm; Sample weight: 587 g; Original weight: 1,174 g; Volume: 5,245 cm³. Coordinates: (−2.52, 14.34) (measured). Type: Chaquiste Impressed. Paste, temper, and firing: Yellow paste (10YR7/6). Coarse paste. A large amount of calcite temper (0.1–0.5 mm diameter). Some large ferruginous and calcite inclusions (2.0–4.0 mm diameter). The paste is completely oxidized. Surface finish and decoration: Light reddish cream slip on the exterior. Stamped impressions on the ridge. Form: Bowl with incurved sides and restricted orifice. Ring base. Exterior-thickened rim and rounded lip. Ridge below the rim. Use-wear: The interior base is rough, but it is not clear whether the roughness resulted from erosion.

WVS No.: 14B-31; Catalog No.: 310084 (Figure 8.33i)
Bag No.: Rim: 324 (2-3-4), 186 (2-2-2), 256 (2-3-4), 265 (2-3-3), 708 (2-4-1); Body: 186, 256, 324, 166 (2-2-2), 172 (2-2-2), 177 (2-2-2), 253 (2-3-4), 265, 614 (21-1-1), 901 (20-3-3), 927 (24-3-3), 932 (25-3-1), 928 (25-3-3), 162 (6-3-4); Base: 927. Provenience: 14B2-3-4. Context: Floor. In the

western part of the room floor of the center room. Most fragments were found in an area 1.5 × 2 m. Condition: Reconstructible (50% present). Eroded. It is not clear whether the vessel is burned. Dimensions: Rim diameter: [interior] 27 cm (estimate); Maximum diameter: 33 cm (estimate); Minimum opening: 27 cm (estimate); Height: 17 cm (rough estimate); Wall thickness: 0.7–0.9 cm; Sample weight: 1,025 g; Original weight: 2,050 g; Volume: 6,306 cm³. Coordinates: (−2.62, 14.44) (estimate). Type: Chaquiste Impressed. Paste, temper, and firing: Yellowish brown paste (10YR5/4). Relatively coarse. A large amount of calcite temper (0.3–1.5 mm diameter). Some part of the paste is dark. Surface finish and decoration: Orange slip above the ridge. Stamped impressions on the ridge. Form: Bowl with incurved sides and restricted orifice. Ring base. Exterior-thickened rim and rounded lip. Ridge below the rim. Use-wear: The interior base is rough, but it is not clear whether that is due to erosion.

WVS No.: 14B-32; Catalog No.: 310058 (Figure 8.34a)
Bag No.: Rim: 328 (2-3-6), 732 (2-5-3); Body: 328, 716 (2-5-1), 184 (14-2-1); Base: 328, 732, 184. Provenience: 14B2-3-6. Context: Floor. In the central and western parts of the room floor in the center room. Fragments were scattered in an area 2 × 2 m. A few pieces were in front of the structure 2–3 m apart from others. The vessel was probably stored in a high location originally and smashed when it fell. Condition: Reconstructible (30% present). Some pieces are eroded. Some fragments are blackened from fire. Dimensions: Rim diameter: [exterior] 10 cm (estimate); Height: 6.5 cm (measured); Height without feet: 6.0 cm (measured); Wall thickness: 0.4–0.6 cm; Sample weight: 53 g; Original weight: 177 g; Volume: 169 cm³. Coordinates: (−2.24, 15.40) (estimate). Type: Nanzal Red (or Tinaja Red). Paste, temper, and firing: Reddish yellow paste (7.5YR7/6). Medium grain paste, hard. A moderate amount of calcite temper (0.3–1.5 mm diameter). The paste is completely oxidized. Surface finish and decoration: Thin, light red slip on the exterior. The exterior is unslipped and well polished. Form: Bowl with slightly outcurved sides and flat base. Direct rim and flat lip. Possibly three solid nubbin feet (only one is present). Use-wear: None recognizable, partly because the base is very fragmented.

WVS No.: 14B-33; Catalog No.: 310056 (Figure 8.34b)
Bag No.: Rim: 105 (2-1-2), 186 (2-2-2), 102 (2-1-1), 324 (2-3-4); Body: 324; Base: 177 (2-2-2), 716, 206 (6-2-1), 324,

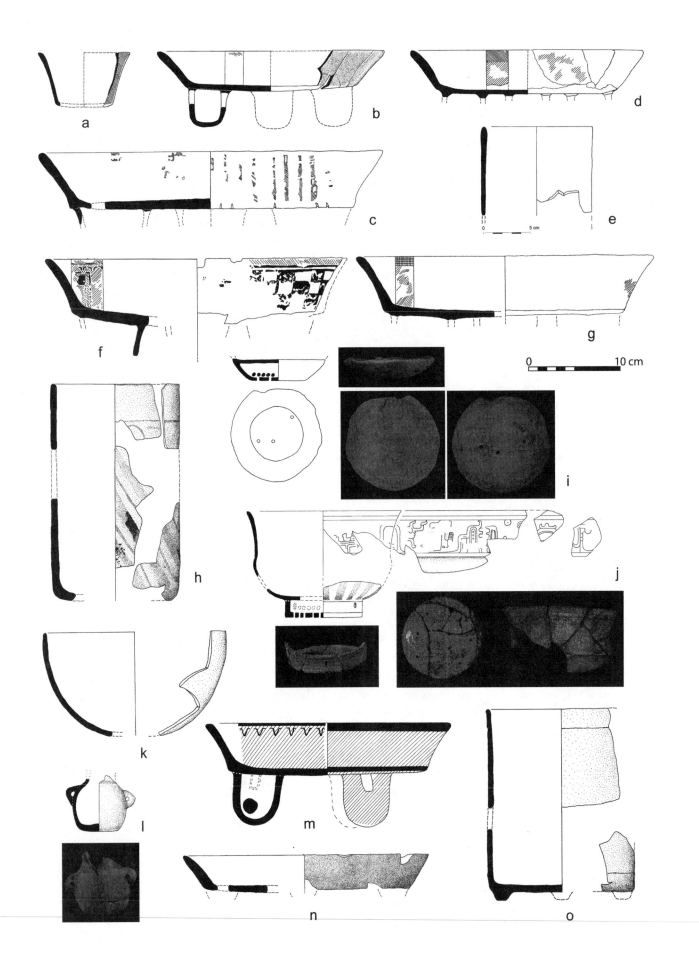

102, 105, 186. Provenience: 14B2-1-2. Context: Floor. In the western part of the room floor in the center room. Most fragments were found in the humus and wall-fall layers in an area 1 × 2 m. The vessel was probably stored on the bench or in a higher place originally. Condition: Reconstructible (70% present). Most pieces are heavily eroded, and the paints are almost completely gone. Some fragments are blackened from fire. Dimensions: Rim diameter: [exterior] 25.1 cm, [top] 24.0 cm (measured); Height: 8.2 cm (measured); Height without feet: 4.2 cm (measured); Wall thickness: 0.6–0.9 cm; Sample weight: 456 g; Original weight: 651 g; Volume: 874 cm³. Coordinates: (−2.51, 15.09) (estimate). Type: Saxche-Palmar Polychrome. Paste, temper, and firing: Reddish yellow paste (5YR7/8). Fine. A small amount of calcite temper (0.1–0.4 mm diameter). The paste is completely oxidized. Surface finish and decoration: Remains of red paint on the lip. Form: Plate with slightly outcurved sides and flat base. Direct rim and beveled-in lip. Three hollow oven feet with two openings. Use-wear: None recognizable, partly because of erosion.

WVS No.: 14B-34; Catalog No.: 310061 (Figure 8.34c)
Bag No.: Rim: 890 (19-3-2), 894 (19-3-1), 177 (2-2-2), 609 (19-1-1), 672 (20-2-1), 854, 888 (19-3-1); Body: 894; Base: 894. Provenience: 14B19-3-2. Context: Floor. On the exterior floor in front of the entrance of the center room. Many fragments were found in an area 1 × 2 m. A few sherds were found scattered in an area 4 × 4 m. Condition: Reconstructible (80% present). Many pieces are eroded. Some fragments are blackened from fire. Missing feet. Dimensions: Rim diameter: [exterior] 38.0 cm, [top] 37.4 cm (measured); Height: 11 cm (estimate); Height without feet: 5.6 cm (measured); Wall thickness: 0.9–1.1 cm; Sample weight: 1,674 g; Original weight: 2,093 g; Volume: 3,275 cm³. Coordinates: (−1.20, 17.60) (estimate). Type: Saxche-Palmar Polychrome. Paste, temper, and firing: Reddish yellow paste (5YR7/8). Fine. A very small amount of calcite temper (0.1–0.5 mm diameter). The paste is completely oxidized. Surface finish and decoration: Red vertical stripes over orange slip on the exterior. Red paint on the lip and a black band below it. The dec-

oration on the body and base is not clear because of erosion. Form: Plate with slightly outcurved sides and flat base. Incisions and dents on the basal ridge. Direct rim and rounded lip. Three hollow feet. Use-wear: None recognizable, partly because of erosion.

WVS No.: 14B-35; Catalog No.: 310063 (Figure 8.34d)
Bag No.: Rim: 324 (2-3-4), 328 (2-3-6), 105 (2-1-2), 177 (2-2-2), 615 (20-1-2), 708 (2-4-1), 901 (20-3-3); Body: 901; Base: 901, 324, 327, 708, 716 (2-5-1). Provenience: 14B2-3-4. Context: Floor. In the western part of the room floor of the center room. Many fragments were found in an area 2 × 2 m. Condition: Reconstructible (90% present). Severely eroded. Some fragments are severely burned. Dimensions: Rim diameter: [exterior] 25.5 cm, [top] 24.5 cm (measured); Height without feet: 4.2 cm (measured); Wall thickness: 0.7–0.8 cm; Sample weight: 678 g; Original weight: 753 g; Volume: 1,042 cm³. Coordinates: (−2.63, 15.09) (estimate). Type: Saxche-Palmar Polychrome. Paste, temper, and firing: Yellow paste (10YR8/6). Fine. A very small amount of calcite temper (0.1–0.5 mm diameter). The paste is completely oxidized. Surface finish and decoration: Red paint on the lip. Orange slip on the exterior and interior. Form: Plate with slightly outcurved sides and flat base. Direct rim and rounded lip. Three hollow feet. Use-wear: Numerous small dents on the interior base, possibly from use.

WVS No.: 14B-36; Catalog No.: 310075 (Figure 8.34f)
Bag No.: Rim: 901 (20-3-3), 184 (14-2-1), 320 (2-3-3), 672 (20-2-1), 743 (2-5-4), 885 (19-3-4), 888 (24-3-2); Body: 901, 244 (2-3-3), 888, 411 (14-2-2); Base: 888, 184, 320, 328 (2-3-6), 609 (19-1-1), 694 (19-2-1), 708 (2-4-1). Provenience: 14B20-3-3. Context: Floor. In the central part of the room floor of the center room and on the exterior floor in front of it. Fragments were scattered in an area 4 × 4 m. Condition: Reconstructible (70% present). Eroded. Some pieces appear to be burned and reoxidized. Dimensions: Rim diameter: [exterior] 33 cm, [top] 32 cm (estimate); Height: 14 cm (rough estimate); Height without feet: 6.0 cm (measured); Wall thickness: 0.8–1.0 cm; Sample weight: 669 g; Original weight: 956 g; Volume: 2,631 cm³.

FIGURE 8.34. (*opposite*) Complete and reconstructible vessels from the center and east rooms of Structure M8-13. (a–l) Center room. (a) Nanzal Red, 14B2-3-6, Cat. 310058, WVS 14B-32. (b–h) Saxche-Palmar Polychrome, 14B2-1-2, Cat. 310056, WVS 14B-33. (c) 14B19-3-2, Cat. 310061, WVS 14B-34. (d) 14B2-3-4, Cat. 310063, WVS 14B-35. (e) 14B8-2-1, Cat. 310088, WVS 14B-38. (f) 14B20-3-3, Cat. 310075, WVS-36. (g) 14B21-1-1, Cat. 310076, WVS 14B-37. (h) 14B19-1-1, Cat. 310097, WVS 14B-39. (i) Fine Gray, 14B2-3-2, Cat. 310110, WVS 14B-40. (j) Unnamed red-orange paste, incised, white paint, 14B2-3-1, Cat. 310109, WVS 14B-41. (k, l) Undetermined. (k) 14B20-2-1, Cat. 310108, WVS 14B-42. (l) 14B6-1-1, Cat. 310048, WVS 14B-43. (m–o) East room. (m, n) Saxche-Palmar Polychrome. (m) 14B24-3-3, Cat. 310026, WVS 14B-44. (n) 14B29-3-4, Cat. 310102, WVS 14B-45. (o) Unnamed volcanic ash undetermined, 14B28-2-1, Cat. 310104, WVS 14B-46.

Coordinates: (–2.73, 16.77) (measured). Type: Saxche-Palmar Polychrome. Paste, temper, and firing: Pink paste (7.5YR8/4). Fine. A small amount of fine calcite temper (0.1–0.2 mm diameter), and a small amount of larger calcite, ferruginous, and quartz (0.5–2.0 mm diameter). The paste is completely oxidized. Surface finish and decoration: Cream slip. Red band on the lip. Black checker patterns on the exterior. The interior is eroded. Form: Plate with outcurved sides and flat base. Direct rim and flat lip. Three hollow feet. Use-wear: None recognizable, partly because of erosion.

WVS No.: 14B-37; Catalog No.: 310076 (Figure 8.34g) Bag No.: Rim: 244 (2-3-3), 614 (21-1-1), 909 (22-3-4), 829 (27-3-2), 890 (19-3-2), 908 (26-3-1); Body: 186 (2-2-2), 265; Base: 186, 244, 265 (2-3-3), 614, 676 (26-2-1), 908. Provenience: 14B21-1-1. Context: Floor. In the center room. Fragments are scattered on the bench and on the room floor of the center room, as well as in the wall fall behind the structure. The vessel was probably stored on the bench or in a higher location originally. Condition: Reconstructible (50% present). Eroded. Some pieces appear to have been burned and reoxidized. Dimensions: Rim diameter: [exterior] 32.7 cm (measured), [top] 31.8 cm (measured); Height: 14 cm (rough estimate); Height without feet: 6.9 cm (measured); Wall thickness: 0.9–1.0 cm; Sample weight: 698 g; Original weight: 1,396 g; Volume: 2,479 cm^3. Coordinates: (–5.10, 17.20) (estimate). Type: Saxche-Palmar Polychrome. Paste, temper, and firing: Pink paste (7.5YR8/4). Fine. A small amount of calcite temper (0.1–2.0 mm diameter). The paste is completely oxidized. Surface finish and decoration: Orange slip. Black or red band on the lip. Form: Plate with outcurved sides and flat base. Direct rim and flat lip. Three hollow feet. Use-wear: None recognizable, partly because of erosion.

WVS No.: 14B-38; Catalog No.: 310088 (Figure 8.34e) Bag No.: Rim: 277 (8-2-1), 623 (22-1-1), 679 (22-2-1); Body: 277, 679, 438 (8-2-3), 184 (14-2-1); Base: 679. Provenience: 14B8-2-1. Context: Floor. Many fragments were found in the humus and wall-fall layers behind the center room. It is probable that the vessel was originally placed in the center room, on the bench or in a higher place near the back wall. Other pieces may be in nearby unexcavated areas. Condition: Reconstructible (35% present). Very eroded. Some fragments are blackened from fire. Dimensions: Rim diameter: [exterior] 12.1 cm, [top] 11.6 cm

(measured); Height: 18 cm (rough estimate); Wall thickness: 0.4 (wall)–0.6 (base) cm; Sample weight: 256 g; Original weight: 731 g; Volume: 1,428 cm^3. Coordinates: (–6.70, 14.80) (estimate). Type: Saxche-Palmar Polychrome. Paste, temper, and firing: Reddish yellow paste (7.5YR7/8). Some parts of the vessel are blackened or oxidized in orange color by fire. Fine. A very small amount of calcite temper (0.1–0.4 mm diameter) and volcanic ash temper (0.1 mm diameter). Surface finish and decoration: Remains of red paint on the rim. Form: Vase with vertical sides and flat base. Direct rim and rounded lip. Use-wear: Not clear because of the eroded and fragmentary condition.

WVS No.: 14B-39; Catalog No.: 310097 (Figure 8.34h) Bag No.: Rim: 898 (24-3-2), 672 (20-2-1), 697 (23-2-1), 694 (19-2-1), 885 (19-3-4), 888 (19-3-1); Body: 609 (19-1-1), 892 (23-3-1), 888, 697, 672, 611 (23-1-1), 411 (14-2-2), 890 (19-3-2), 840 (27-3-3), 649 (28-1-1), 692 (28-2-1), 932 (25-3-1), 854 (19-3-2), 901 (20-3-3), 894 (19-3-1). Provenience: 14B19-1-1. Context: Floor. In the eastern part of the room floor of the center room and on the exterior floor in front of it. Fragments were scattered in an area 4 × 4 m. Many fragments were probably moved by a large tree fall. Condition: Reconstructible (50% present). Many fragments may not have been recovered because of tree disturbance. Severely eroded. Some pieces are blackened from fire. Dimensions: Rim diameter: [exterior] 14 cm (estimate); Maximum diameter: 14 cm (estimate); Height: 23 cm (rough estimate); Wall thickness: 0.6–0.8 cm; Sample weight: 491 g; Original weight: 982 g; Volume: 2,218 cm^3. Coordinates: (–1.20, 16.90) (estimate). Type: Saxche-Palmar Polychrome. Paste, temper, and firing: Yellow paste (10YR7/6). Fine. A small amount of calcite temper (0.1–0.3 mm diameter). Dark core. Surface finish and decoration: A black band on the rim. Below are red and black paints over cream underslip. Diagonal flutes. Form: Vase with slightly flared sides and flat base. Direct rim and rounded lip. Use-wear: None recognizable, partly because of erosion.

WVS No.: 14B-40; Catalog No.: 310110 (Figure 8.34i) Bag No.: Base: 243 (2-3-2). Provenience: 14B2-3-2. Context: Floor. In the northwestern corner of the room floor of the center room. Condition: Partial (20% present). Eroded. Only the rattle base part is present. It is not clear whether the body parts disintegrated or the residents just kept the base and used it as a rattle. Dimensions: Wall thickness: 0.7 cm; Sample weight: 88 g; Original weight:

440 g; Volume: not calculated. Coordinate: (-2.55, 13.63) (measured). Type: Fine Gray. Paste, temper, and firing: Pale red paste (2.5YR7/2). Very fine. A very small amount of very fine volcanic ash temper (0.1 mm diameter). The paste is completely oxidized. Surface finish and decoration: Possible remains of black paint on the exterior. Form: Possibly a bowl, although the body part is missing. Hollow rattle base. Use-wear: Not clear, partly because of erosion.

WVS No.: 14B-41; Catalog No.: 310109 (Figure 8.34j)
Bag No.: Rim: 458 (5-3-1), 311 (11-2-1), 129 (11-1-1), 461 (11-3-1), 615 (20-1-2); Body: 311, 461, 334 (5-2-1), 448 (5-2-3), 679 (22-2-1), 111 (5-1-2), 458, 901 (20-3-3), 129; Base: 242, 334, 463 (11-3-2), 411 (14-2-2). Provenience: 14B2-3-1. Context: Floor. The lower part of the hollow base was found in the southwestern corner of the room floor of the center room. Other parts of the vessels, including the upper part of the hollow base, were found in various parts of the structure: Unit 5 (in front of the center room), Unit 20 (eastern part of the center room), Unit 11 (midden behind the west room), and Unit 22 (behind the center room). Some fragments from these units fit together. It appears that after the vessel broke, only the lower part of the hollow base was kept in the center room, while other fragments were scattered in various areas. Since only the lower part of the hollow base was kept, it was not used as a rattle. It is not clear whether the original complete vessel was owned by the residents of Structure M8-13 or by those of nearby buildings. Condition: Partial (40% present). Eroded. A large portion of the lower part of the hollow base is present. Roughly one-third of the rim, body, and upper part of the hollow base was recovered. No rattle balls were found. The lower part of the hollow base was burned. It is not clear whether other parts were burned. Dimensions: Wall thickness: 0.5 cm; Sample weight: 196 g; Original weight: 490 g; Volume: not calculated. Coordinates: (-3.17, 13.71) (estimate). Type: Unnamed red-orange paste, Incised, White Paint. Paste, temper, and firing: Strong brown paste (7.5YR5/8). Medium grain. A small amount of calcite temper (0.1–0.3 mm diameter). The paste is completely oxidized. Surface finish and decoration: White paint on the entire interior. White paint and fine incisions on the rim and upper exterior body and on the base. White vertical stripes on the lower exterior body. Form: Bowl with hollow base, which probably contained rattle balls. Use-wear: Not clear. The interior base is not worn.

WVS No.: 14B-42; Catalog No.: 310108 (Figure 8.34k)
Bag No.: Rim: 672 (20-2-1), 105 (2-1-2), 104 (14C1-1-1); Body: 672, 105, 328 (2-3-6), 888 (19-3-1), 494 (4-3-1). Provenience: 14B20-2-1. Context: Floor. In the central part of the room floor of the center room. Fragments were scattered in an area 4 × 4 m. A few sherds were scattered in an even wider area. Pieces were probably moved by a large tree fall. Condition: Partial (20% present). Very eroded. Some pieces were blackened from fire. Many pieces may have been lost because of tree disturbance. Dimensions: Rim diameter: [exterior] 20 cm (estimate); Height: 12 cm (rough estimate); Wall thickness: 0.6–0.7 cm; Sample weight: 180 g; Original weight: 900 g; Volume: 1,422 cm^3. Coordinates: (-2.10, 17.30) (estimate). Type: Undetermined, possibly eroded Saxche-Palmar Polychrome. Paste, temper, and firing: Reddish yellow paste (5YR6/6). Coarse. A small amount of calcite and ferruginous temper (0.1–0.3 mm diameter). The paste is completely oxidized. Surface finish and decoration: Remains of red paint on the interior. The exterior is completely eroded. Form: Bowl with slightly incurved sides. The base is missing. Direct rim and rounded lip. Use-wear: Not clear, partly because of erosion.

WVS No.: 14B-43; Catalog No.: 310048 (Figure 8.34l)
Bag No.: Body: 123 (6-1-1), 208 (6-2-2); Base: 123, 277 (8-2-1). Provenience: 14B6-1-1. Context: Floor. In the western part of the bench of the center room. Condition: Reconstructible (80% present). Eroded. It is not clear whether the vessel is burned. Dimensions: Rim diameter: [exterior] 3.8 cm (rough estimate); Maximum diameter: 3.3–6.0 cm (measured); Minimum opening: 2.4 cm (estimate); Height: 7.3 cm (estimate); Neck height: 2.1 cm (estimate); Wall thickness: 0.6–0.7 cm; Sample weight: 63 g; Original weight: 79 g; Volume: 76 cm^3. Coordinates: (-4.70, 14.40) (estimate). Type: Undetermined. Paste, temper, and firing: Very pale brown paste (10YR7/4). Fine. A very small amount of calcite temper (0.1–0.3 mm diameter). Some black core. Surface finish and decoration: Eroded. Form: Miniature jar. Two small handles, each with a hole. Flat base. Use-wear: Not clear, partly because of erosion.

East Room

WVS No.: 14B-44; Catalog No.: 310026 (Figure 8.34m)
Bag No.: Rim: 857 (24-3-3), 816 (28-3-1); Body: 857; Base: 857. Provenience: 14B24-3-3. Context: Floor. In the western part of the east room. Most fragments were found in

one concentration. Condition: Reconstructible (50% present). The exterior is relatively well preserved, while the interior is eroded. About half the plate is present. It is possible that the other half fell out of the room and was lost in a tree fall or eroded beyond recognition. The interior base is blackened from fire. The patterns of erosion and fire blackening suggest that the present portion of the plate fell face-up and was covered by burning materials. Dimensions: Rim diameter: [exterior] 27 cm (estimate); Height: 9.8 cm (measured); Height without feet: 5.5 cm (measured); Wall thickness: 0.6–0.9 cm; Sample weight: 720 g; Original weight: 1,440 g; Volume: 1,260 cm^3. Coordinates: (–3.33, 19.88) (measured). Type: Saxche-Palmar Polychrome. Paste, temper, and firing: Reddish yellow paste (7.5YR7/6). Fine. A small amount of calcite temper (0.3–1.0 mm diameter). The paste is completely oxidized. Surface finish and decoration: Black band on the rim. Orange slip on the exterior, interior, and feet. Black band above the wall-base juncture on the exterior. There seem to be designs on the interior base, but they are very eroded. Form: Plate with slightly outcurved sides and flat base. Direct rim and beveled-in lip. Three hollow oven feet with two openings and a rattle. Use-wear: Not clear, partly because of erosion.

WVS No.: 14B-45; Catalog No.: 310102 (Figure 8.34n)
Bag No.: Rim: 808 (29-3-4), 827 (28-3-4), 619 (24-1-1), 638 (27-1-1), 927 (24-3-3); Body: 808; Base: 808. Provenience: 14B29-3-4. Context: Floor. In the western part of the room floor of the east room. Condition: Partial (30% present). Other pieces may be in unexcavated areas. Heavily eroded. Some pieces are blackened from fire. Dimensions: Rim diameter: [exterior] 27 cm (estimate); Height without feet: 4.7 cm (estimate): Wall thickness: 0.9–1.2 cm; Sample weight: 259 g; Original weight: 863 g; Volume: 1,072 cm^3. Coordinates: (–4.80, 21.40) (estimate). Type: Saxche-Palmar Polychrome. Paste, temper, and firing: Reddish yellow paste (5YR7/6). Fine. A moderate amount of calcite temper (0.3–3.0 mm diameter) and ferruginous temper (0.5–4.0 mm diameter). The paste is completely oxidized. Surface finish and decoration: Paints are almost completely eroded. Form: Plate with flared sides and flat base. Direct rim and rounded lip. Feet are missing. Use-wear: None recognizable, partly because of erosion.

WVS No.: 14B-46; Catalog No.: 310104 (Figure 8.34o)
Bag No.: Rim: 819 (28-3-3), 692 (28-2-1), 680 (29-2-1), 806 (29-3-2); Body: 692, 808 (29-3-4), 680, 827 (28-3-4), 816

(28-3-1), 819; Base 692. Provenience: 14B28-2-1. Context: Floor. In the western part of the room floor of the east room. Condition: Partial (30% present). There may be more pieces in unexcavated areas. Relatively well preserved. Some fragments are blackened from fire. Dimensions: Rim diameter: [exterior] 16 cm (estimate); Maximum diameter: 16 cm (estimate); Wall thickness: 0.5–0.6 cm; Sample weight: 234 g; Original weight: 780 g; Volume: 2,837 cm^3. Coordinates: (–3.10, 20.90) (estimate). Type: Unnamed volcanic ash undetermined. Paste, temper, and firing: Reddish brown paste (5YR5/4). Fine, hard. A small amount of fine volcanic ash temper (0.1–0.5 mm long). Surface finish and decoration: Light orange slip on the exterior. Polished. Form: Vase with slightly outcurved sides and flat base. Exterior-thickened rim and rounded lip. Possibly three solid nubbin feet. Use-wear: None recognizable.

In Front of the Structure

WVS No.: 14B-47; Catalog No.: 310101 (Figures 8.34a and 8.61a)
Bag No.: Rim: 834 (23-3-2), 830 (27-3-1); Body: 834, 830, 882 (23-3-2), 833 (27-3-4), 697 (23-2-1). Provenience: 14B23-3-2. Context: Floor. On the exterior floor in front of the room division between the center and east rooms. Condition: Partial (35% present). Eroded. Some blackened areas, but it is not clear whether they were caused by the burning of the building. Dimensions: Rim diameter: [interior] 31 cm, [top] 29 cm (estimate); Maximum diameter: 51 cm (estimate); Height: 26 cm (rough estimate); Wall thickness: 0.8–0.9 cm; Sample weight: 1,412 g; Original weight: 4,034 g; Volume: 30,142 cm^3. Coordinates: (–1.20, 19.40) (estimate). Type: Chaquiste Impressed. Paste, temper, and firing: Yellow paste (10YR8/6). Coarse paste. A large amount of calcite temper (0.1–0.5 mm diameter). Some large ferruginous and calcite inclusions (2.0–4.0 mm diameter). The paste is completely oxidized. Surface finish and decoration: Red slip on the exterior above the ridge. Stamped impressions below the rim and on the ridge. Form: Bowl with incurved sides and restricted orifice. The base form is not clear. Exterior-thickened rim and rounded lip. Ridge below the rim. Use-wear: None recognizable.

WVS No.: 14B-48; Catalog No.: 310124 (Figures 8.35b and 8.60b)
Bag No.: Rim: 149 (14C5-3-1), 145 (14C-5-3-2), 153 (14C5-3-3), 155 (14C6-3-1), 157 (14C6-3-2); Body: 155, 149;

Base: 158 (14C5-3-4), 150 (14C4-3-1), 156 (14C4-3-2). Provenience: 14C6-3-1. Context: exterior floor in front of the east room. Condition: Reconstructible (50% present). Very eroded. It is not clear whether it is burned. Dimensions: Rim diameter: [interior] 31 cm (estimate); Maximum diameter: 35 cm (estimate); Height: 12 cm (rough estimate); Wall thickness: 0.8–1.0 cm; Sample weight: 731 g; Original weight: 1,462 g; Volume: 4,179 cm³. Coordinates: (0.74, 20.23) (estimate). Type: Chaquiste Impressed. Paste, temper, and firing: Reddish yellow paste (7.5YR7/6). Coarse. A moderate amount of calcite temper (0.1–0.5 mm diameter). Part of the paste is dark. Surface finish and decoration: Remains of red paint on the rim and the interior. It is not clear whether the exterior body was slipped. Stamped impressions on the ridge. Form: Bowl with incurved sides and restricted orifice. Ring base. Exterior-thickened rim and rounded lip. A ridge below the rim. Use-wear: The interior base is rough, but it is not clear whether that is due to erosion.

Behind the Structure

WVS No.: 14B-49; Catalog No.: 310077 (Figure 8.35c–e) Bag No.: Rim: 912 (22-3-3), 909 (22-3-4); Body: 912, 909. Provenience: 14B22-3-3. Context: Floor. On the exterior floor behind the back wall of the center room. Most fragments were found in an area 1 × 2 m. Other pieces may be in nearby unexcavated areas. Condition: Reconstructible (85% present). Very eroded. Some sherds are blackened from fire. Dimensions: Rim diameter: [exterior] 11.9 cm, [top] 11.5 cm (measured); Maximum diameter: 20.5 cm (measured); Minimum opening: 7.9 cm (measured); Height: 19 cm (rough estimate); Neck height: 3.1 cm (measured); Wall thickness: 0.8–1.0 cm; Sample weight: 1,152 g; Original weight: 1,355 g; Volume: 3,082 cm³. Coordinates: (–6.74, 16.73) (measured). Type: Pantano Impressed. Paste, temper, and firing: Pink paste (7.5YR7/4). Medium grain. A large amount of calcite temper (0.2–2.0 mm diameter) and a moderate amount of ferruginous temper (0.5–4.0 mm). The paste is completely oxidized. Surface finish and decoration: Red slip on the exterior. Circular and long triangle impressions around the neck-body juncture. Form: Jar with outcurved neck. Unlike the case in common Tinaja/Pantano jars, the neck-body juncture is smooth. Direct rim and rounded lip. Use-wear: Not clear because of erosion.

WVS No.: 14B-50; Catalog No.: 310078 (Figures 8.35f and 8.61c)

Bag No.: Rim: 909 (22-3-4); Body: 909; Base: 909. Provenience: 14B22-3-4. Context: Floor. On the exterior floor behind the back wall of the center room. Most fragments were found close together in an area 1 × 1 m. Condition: Reconstructible (80% present). Many sherds are heavily eroded. Some sherds are blackened, possibly from fire. Dimensions: Rim diameter: [exterior] 13.0 cm, [top] 12.5 (measured); Maximum diameter: 37 cm (estimate); Minimum opening: 7.5 cm (measured); Height: 34 cm (rough estimate); Neck height: 5.2 cm (measured): Wall thickness: 0.6–0.9 cm; Sample weight: 2,740 g; Original weight: 3,425 g; Volume: 16,647 cm³. Coordinates: (–6.75, 17.36) (measured). Type: Pantano Impressed. Paste, temper, and firing: Reddish yellow paste (7.5YR7/6). Medium grain. A large amount of calcite temper (0.2–1.0 mm diameter) and a small amount of ferruginous temper (0.5–3.0 mm diameter). The paste is mostly oxidized. Surface finish and decoration: Red slip on the exterior. Stamp and triangular impressions below the neck-body juncture. Form: Jar with outcurved neck and incurved base. Direct rim and beveled-in lip. Use-wear: The base is slightly worn from use.

WVS No.: 14B-51; Catalog No.: 310080 (Figures 8.36a and 8.61d)

Bag No.: Rim: 941 (30-3-3); Body: 941; Base: 791 (30-3-1). Provenience: 14B30-3-3. Context: Floor. On the exterior floor behind the back wall of the east room. Most fragments were found in an area 1 × 2 m. Other pieces may be in nearby unexcavated areas. Condition: Partial (20% present). Very eroded. Some sherds appear to be blackened from fire. Dimensions: Rim diameter: [exterior] 12.0 cm, [top] 11.6 cm (measured); Maximum diameter: 36 cm (estimate); Minimum opening: 6.7 cm (measured); Height: 36 cm (rough estimate); Neck height: 5.1 cm (measured); Wall thickness: 0.6–0.7 cm; Sample weight: 846 g; Original weight: 4,230 g; Volume: 18,994 cm³. Coordinates: (–6.40, 20.90) (estimate). Type: Pantano Impressed. Paste, temper, and firing: Pink paste (7.5YR7/4). Medium grain. A large amount of calcite temper (0.2–2.0 mm diameter) and a small amount of ferruginous temper (0.5–3.0 mm). The paste is completely oxidized. Surface finish and decoration: Red slip on the exterior. Stamp and triangular impressions just below the neck-body juncture, but because of erosion the design of the stamp is not clear. Form: Jar with outcurved neck. Direct rim and rounded lip. Use-wear: Not clear because of the eroded and fragmentary condition.

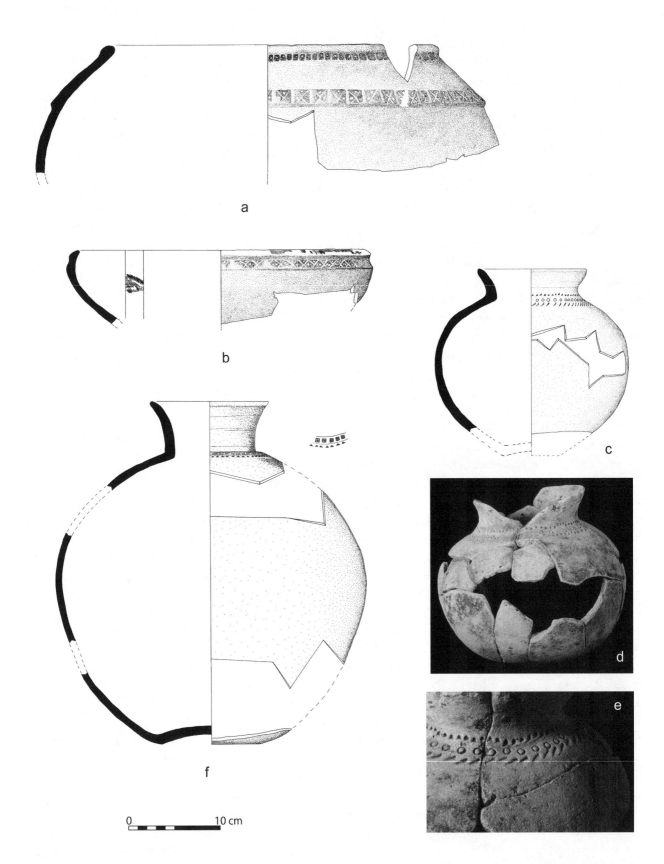

Figure 8.35. Complete and reconstructible vessels from the front and back exterior of Structure M8-13. (a, b) Front exterior, Chaquiste Impressed. (a) 14B23-3-2, Cat. 310101, WVS 14B-47. (b) 14C6-3-1, Cat. 310124, WVS 14B-48. (c–f) Back exterior, Pantano Impressed. (c–e) 14B22-33, Cat. 310077, WVS 14B-49. (e) Close-up of WVS 14B-49 (not to scale). (f) 14B22-3-4, Cat. 310078, WVS 14B-50.

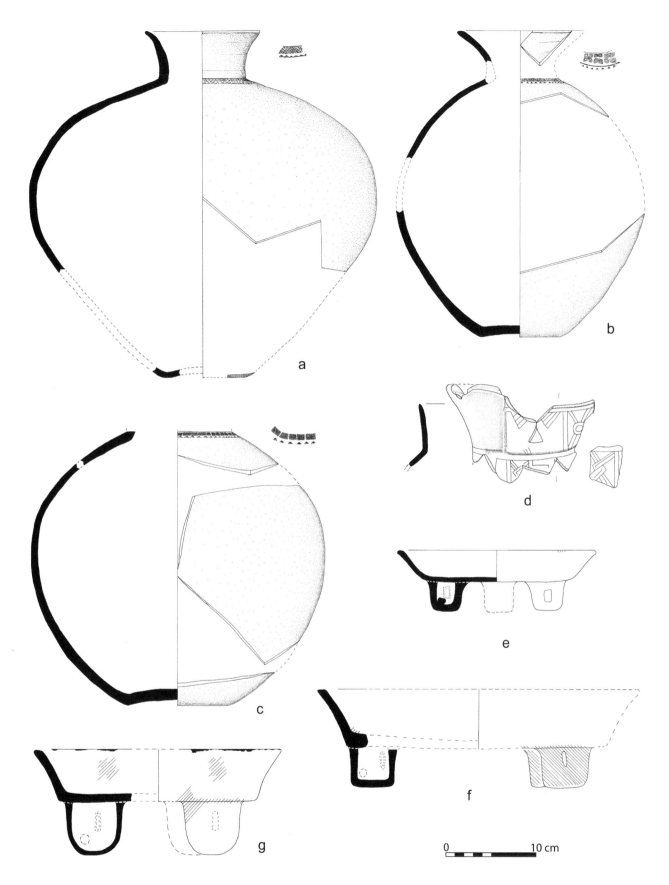

FIGURE 8.36. Complete and reconstructible vessels from the back exterior of Structure M8-13. (a–c) Pantano Impressed.
(a) 14B30-3-3, Cat. 310080, WVS 14B-51. (b) 14B30-3-4, Cat. 310081, WVS-14B-52. (c) 14B30-3-3, Cat. 310130, WVS 14B-53.
(d) Corozal Incised, 14B26-3-4, Cat. 310131, WVS 14B-56. (e–g) Saxche-Palmar Polychrome. (e) 14B26-3-2, Cat. 310062, WVS
14B-57. (f) 14B30-3-1, Cat. 310064, WVS 14B-58. (g) 14B26-3-1, Cat. 310065, WVS 14B-59.

WVS No.: 14B-52; Catalog No.: 310081 (Figures 8.36b and 8.61e)

Bag No.: Rim: 621 (25-1-1); Body: 647 (30-1-1), 705 (30-2-1), 780 (30-3-4), 792 (30-3-4), 793 (30-3-2), 777 (30-3-2), 625 (30-1-1), 791 (30-3-1); Base: 647. Provenience: 14B30-3-4. Context: Floor. On the exterior floor behind the back wall of the east room. Most fragments were found in an area 2 × 2 m. Condition: Reconstructible (50% present). Heavily eroded. It is not clear whether the vessel was burned. Probably there are more fragments in unexcavated areas. Dimensions: Rim diameter: [exterior] 13 cm (estimate); Maximum diameter: 28 cm (rough estimate); Minimum opening: 8 cm (estimate); Height: 30 cm (rough estimate); Wall thickness: 0.6–1.0 cm; Sample weight: 1,651 g; Original weight: 3,302 g; Volume: 8,547 cm³. Coordinates: (−6.30, 21.60) (estimate). Type: Pantano Impressed. Paste, temper, and firing: Red paste (2.5YR6/8). Medium grain. A large amount of fine calcite temper (0.1 mm diameter) and a small amount of ferruginous temper (0.2–0.7 mm diameter). The paste is completely oxidized. Unusual paste for Pantano Impressed. Surface finish and decoration: Red slip on the exterior. Stamp and triangular impressions below the neck-body juncture. Form: Jar with outcurved neck and slightly incurved base. Direct rim and pointed lip. Use-wear: The base is slightly worn from use.

WVS No.: 14B-53; Catalog No.: 310130 (Figures 8.36c and 8.60f)

Bag No.: Body: 792 (30-3-4), 783 (30-3-3), 941 (30-3-3), 936 (30-3-1), 791 (30-3-1), 766 (30-3-1), 777 (30-3-2), 647 (30-1-1), 793 (30-3-2), 705 (30-2-1); Base: 792, 791. Provenience: 14B30-3-3. Context: Floor. Behind the back wall of the east room. Most fragments were found in an area 2 × 2 m. Condition: Reconstructible (40% present). Eroded. It is not clear whether the vessel was burned. The entire neck is missing. It is possible that there are more pieces in nearby unexcavated areas (outside the units and underneath a tree). Dimensions: Maximum diameter: 33 cm (estimate); Height: 33 cm (rough estimate); Wall thickness: 0.6–0.9 cm; Sample weight: 1,555 g; Original weight: 3,888 g; Volume: 13,511 cm³. Coordinates: (−6.90, 20.90) (estimate). Type: Pantano Impressed. Paste, temper, and firing: Reddish yellow paste (5YR7/6). Medium grain. A moderate amount of calcite temper (0.3–2.0 mm diameter) and a small amount of ferruginous temper (0.5–2.0 mm diameter). The paste is completely oxidized. Surface finish and decoration: Red slip on the exterior, including the base. Stamp and triangular impression below the neck-body juncture. Form: Jar with incurved base. Use-wear: The base is worn from use.

WVS No.: 14B-54; Catalog No.: 310085 (Figure 8.37a)

Bag No.: Rim: 908 (26-3-1); Body: 915 (26-3-3), 946, 915; Base: 946 (26-3-4), 910 (26-3-4). Provenience: 14B26-3-1. Context: Floor. On the exterior floor behind the back wall near the division between the center and east rooms. Most fragments were found in an area 2 × 2 m. Other pieces may be in nearby unexcavated areas. Condition: Partial (20% present). Eroded. It is not clear whether the vessel was burned. Dimensions: Rim diameter: [interior] 40 cm (estimate); Maximum diameter: 44 cm (estimate); Height: 21 cm (rough estimate); Wall thickness: 0.6–0.7 cm; Sample weight: 631 g; Original weight: 3,155 g; Volume: 9,500 cm³. Coordinates: (−7.13, 18.77) (measured). Type: Subin Red. Paste, temper, and firing: Reddish yellow paste (7.5YR6/6). Coarse. A large amount of calcite temper (0.2–1.5 mm diameter). Dark core. Surface finish and decoration: It is not clear whether there is red slip. Form: Bowl with incurved side, restricted orifice. Ring base. Exterior-thickened rim and rounded lip. A ridge below the rim. Use-wear: Not clear because of the eroded and fragmentary condition.

WVS No.: 14B-55; Catalog No.: 310003 (Figure 8.37b and 8.37c)

Bag No.: Rim: 868 (22-3-4); Body: 868, 909 (22-3-4); Base: 868, 909. Provenience: 14B22-3-4. Context: Floor. On the exterior floor behind the back wall of the center room. Most fragments were found in one concentration, and the shape of the vessel was almost recognizable in the field. Condition: Reconstructible (85% present). Eroded. It is not clear whether the vessel was burned. Dimensions: Rim diameter: [interior] 39.5 cm (measured), [top] 41.5 cm (measured); Maximum diameter: 44.2 cm (measured); Minimum opening: 39.5 cm (estimate); Height: 18.2 cm (measured); Wall thickness: 0.8–0.9 cm; Sample weight: 4,220 g; Original weight: 4,964 g; Volume: 11,396 cm³. Coordinates: (−6.33, 17.44) (measured). Type: Subin Red. Paste, temper, and firing: Reddish yellow paste (7.5YR7/6). Coarse. A large amount of calcite temper (0.2–1.3 mm diameter) and a small amount of ferruginous temper (0.5–3.0 mm diameter). Surface finish and decoration: Remains of red paint on the rim. No remains of paint on the interior or on the body. Form: Bowl with slightly incurved side, restricted orifice. Flat base. Exterior-thickened rim and rounded lip. A ridge below

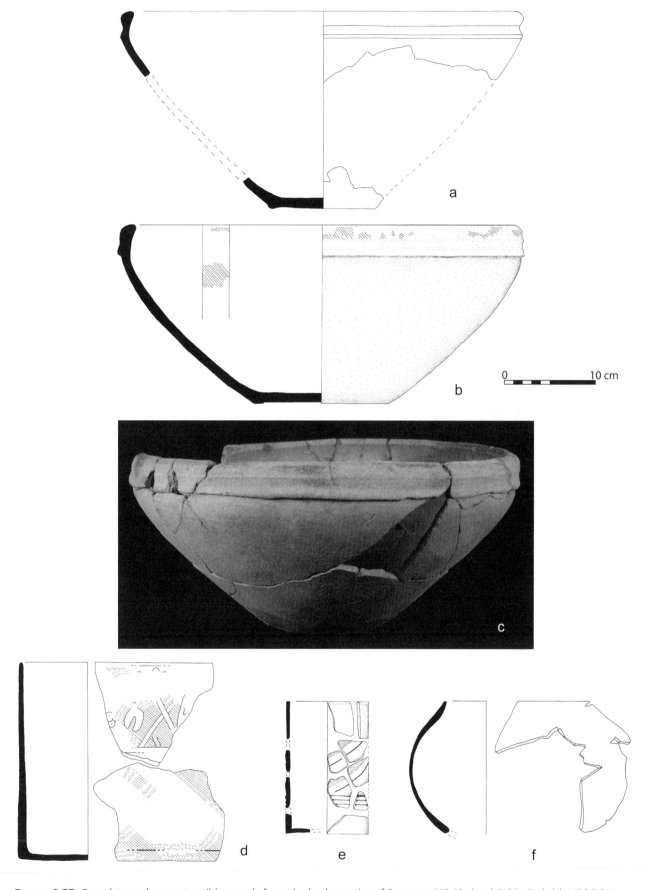

Figure 8.37. Complete and reconstructible vessels from the back exterior of Structure M8-13. (a–c) Subin Red. (a) 14B26-3-1, Cat. 310085, WVS 14B-54. (b, c) 14B22-3-4, Cat. 310003, WVS 14B-55. (d) Saxche-Palmar Polychrome, 14B8-2-1, Cat. 310089, WVS 14B-60. (e) Chicxulub Incised, 14B26-2-1, Cat. 310133, WVS 14B-61. (f) Undetermined, 14B26-3-3, Cat. 310007, WVS 14B-62.

the rim. Use-wear: Not clear. Some fire smudge on the exterior and interior, but it is not clear whether that was caused by the fire at the time of abandonment.

WVS No.: 14B-56; Catalog No.: 310131 (Figure 8.36d)
Bag No.: Rim: 946 (26-3-4); Body: 946. Provenience: 14B26-3-4. Context: Floor. On the exterior floor behind the back wall near the division between the center and east rooms. Most sherds were found in an area 1 × 1 m. Condition: Partial (15% present). Severely eroded. It is not clear whether the vessel was burned. Other pieces may be in nearby unexcavated areas. Dimensions: Rim diameter: [exterior] 11 cm (estimate); Maximum diameter: 18 cm (rough estimate); Minimum opening: 10 cm (estimate); Height: 25 cm (rough estimate); Neck height: 4.9 cm (measured); Wall thickness: 0.3–0.6 cm; Sample weight: 210 g; Original weight: 1,400 g; Volume: 2,974 cm^3. Coordinates: (–6.21, 19.15) (measured). Type: Corozal Incised. Paste, temper, and firing: Red paste (2.5YR6/8). Medium grain. A moderate amount of calcite temper (0.3–2.0 mm diameter), a moderate amount of ferruginous temper (0.5–3.0 mm diameter), and a small amount of silicate sand temper (0.5–1.0 mm diameter). Surface finish and decoration: Although the fragments are heavily eroded, some remains of red slip are present on the exterior. Fine incisions in geometric designs on the neck and body. Form: Pitcher (jar with vertical neck, globular body, and an open spout; possibly with a handle, although it is missing). Use-wear: Not clear because of the fragmentary and eroded condition. Note: Very similar to a completely reconstructible vessel found in the center room of Structure M8-10 during the Petexbatun Project (Petexbatun Cat. 306888) (Foias 1996:511, Fig. 6.38; Inomata 1995). This vessel has similar geometric incisions on the neck and upper body. It also has an open spout and a whistle handle.

WVS No.: 14B-57; Catalog No.: 310062 (Figure 8.36e)
Bag No.: Rim: 911 (26-3-2); Body: 911; Base: 911. Provenience: 14B26-3-2. Context: Floor. On the exterior floor behind the back wall near the division between the center and east rooms. Most fragments were found in an area 1 × 1 m. Other pieces may be in nearby unexcavated areas. Condition: Reconstructible (30% present). Very eroded. It is not clear whether the vessel was burned. Dimensions: Rim diameter: [exterior] 21 cm (estimate); Height: 7.2 cm (measured); Wall thickness: 0.5–0.6 cm; Sample weight: 262 g; Original weight: 873 g; Volume: 1,084 cm^3. Coor-

dinates: (–7.66, 19.15) (measured). Type: Saxche-Palmar Polychrome. Paste, temper, and firing: Reddish yellow paste (7.5YR7/6). Fine. A moderate amount of ferruginous temper (0.5–3.0 mm diameter) and silicate temper (0.5–3.0 mm diameter). The paste is completely oxidized. Surface finish and decoration: Remains of red paint on the lip. Form: Plate with outcurved sides and flat base. Slightly exterior-thickened rim and rounded lip. Three hollow oven feet with two opening and a rattle. Use-wear: Not clear because of erosion.

WVS No.: 14B-58; Catalog No.: 310064 (Figure 8.36f)
Bag No.: Rim: 936 (30-3-1), 647 (30-1-1); Body: 936, 911 (26-3-2); Base: 936, 791 (30-3-1), 792 (30-3-4), 793 (30-3-2), 783 (30-3-3), 941 (30-3-3). Provenience: 14B30-3-1. Context: Floor. On the exterior floor behind the back wall of the east room. Most sherds were found in an area 2 × 2 m. Other pieces may be in nearby unexcavated areas. Condition: Reconstructible (35% present). Very eroded. The body and rim are badly fragmented, but all three feet are preserved. It is not clear whether the vessel was burned. Dimensions: Rim diameter: [exterior] 33 cm (estimate); Height: 10.3 cm (measured); Height without feet: 5.8 cm (measured); Wall thickness: 0.8–0.9 cm; Sample weight: 577 g; Original weight: 1,649 g; Volume: 3,368 cm^3. Coordinates: (–7.45, 20.10) (estimate). Type: Saxche-Palmar Polychrome. Paste, temper, and firing: Reddish yellow paste (5YR7/8). Fine. A very small amount of calcite temper (0.3–0.8 mm diameter), ferruginous temper (0.5–1.5 mm diameter), and quartz sand temper (0.1–1.0 mm diameter). The paste is completely oxidized. Surface finish and decoration: The surface is almost completely eroded, but there are remains of orange paint on the interior and red paint on the feet. Form: Plate with outcurved sides and flat base. Direct rim and flat lip. Three hollow square feet with two openings. Use-wear: Not clear because of the eroded and fragmentary condition.

WVS No.: 14B-59; Catalog No.: 310065 (Figure 8.36g)
Bag No.: Rim: 908 (26-3-1), 915 (26-3-3), 932 (25-3-1); Body: 908, 915, 932; Base: 908, 764 (26-2-1), 915. Provenience: 14B26-3-1. Context: Floor. On the exterior floor behind the back wall near the division between the center and east rooms. Other pieces may be in nearby unexcavated areas. Condition: Reconstructible (50% present). Very eroded. It is not clear whether the vessel was burned. Dimensions: Rim diameter: [exterior] 27 cm (estimate); Height: 10.4 cm (measured); Height without feet: 5.6 cm

(measured); Wall thickness: 0.7–0.8 cm; Sample weight: 758 g; Original weight: 1,516 g; Volume: 1,376 cm³. Coordinates: (−7.60, 18.45) (estimate). Type: Saxche-Palmar Polychrome. Paste, temper, and firing: Light red paste (2.5YR7/8). Fine. A small amount of calcite temper (0.3–1.0 mm diameter), a small amount of ferruginous temper (0.5–2.0 mm diameter), and a very small amount of silicate temper (0.3–0.8 mm diameter). The paste is completely oxidized. Surface finish and decoration: A black band on the lip. Orange slip on the interior and exterior walls, as well as on the feet and the exterior base. The interior base is completely eroded. White underslip is recognizable on the interior wall-base juncture, but not in other parts. Form: Plate with slightly outcurved sides and flat base. Direct rim and flat lip. Three hollow oven feet with one opening and a rattle. Use-wear: Not clear because of the eroded and fragmentary condition.

WVS No.: 14B-60; Catalog No.: 310089 (Figure 8.37d)
Bag No.: Rim: 737 (22-2-1), 679 (22-2-1), 912 (22-3-3), 946 (26-3-4); Body: 277 (8-2-1), 946; Base: 277, 908 (26-3-1). Provenience: 14B8-2-1. Context: Floor. Behind the back wall of the center room. Most fragments were found in an area 5 × 2 m (Units 8, 22, and 26). Other pieces may be in nearby unexcavated areas. Some fragments were mixed in the wall fall, while others were on the exterior floor. It is not clear whether the vessel was originally placed behind the structure or in the center room. Condition: Reconstructible (60% present). Very eroded. Many pieces are blackened from fire. Dimensions: Rim diameter: [exterior] 15 cm (estimate); Maximum diameter: 15 cm (estimate); Height: 20.8 cm (measured); Wall thickness: 0.6–0.9 cm; Sample weight: 786 g; Original weight: 1,310 g; Volume: 2,352 cm³. Coordinates: (−7.60, 15.80) (estimate). Type: Saxche-Palmar Polychrome. Paste, temper, and firing: Reddish yellow paste (7.5YR6/6). Fine. A moderate amount of ferruginous temper (0.1–0.5 mm diameter). There is a slightly dark core. Surface finish and decoration: Painting on the exterior. Remains of red and black paint over cream underslip. There appear to be iconographic designs, but they are not clear. Form: Vase with vertical sides and flat base. Direct rim and rounded lip. Use-wear: Not clear because of erosion.

WVS No.: 14B-61; Catalog No.: 310133 (Figure 8.37e)
Bag No.: Rim: 676 (26-2-1), 910 (26-3-4), 915 (26-3-3); Body: 676, 915, 653 (21-2-1), 908 (26-3-1); Base: 915. Provenience: 14B26-2-1. Context: Floor. On the exterior floor

behind the back wall near the division between the center and east rooms. Most sherds were found in an area 2 × 2 m. Condition: Reconstructible (40% present). Eroded. It is not clear whether the vessel was burned. Other pieces may be in nearby unexcavated areas. Dimensions: Rim diameter: [exterior] 8 cm (estimate); Height: 11 cm (rough estimate); Wall thickness: 0.4–0.5 cm; Sample weight: 103 g; Original weight: 258 g; Volume: 621 cm³. Coordinates: (−6.70, 19.10) (estimate). Type: Chicxulub Incised/Groove-Incised variety. Paste, temper, and firing: Gray to Orange paste (2.5Y5/1 - 5YR6/8), depending on the degree of oxidation (the orange does not have an exact match in the Munsell color chart). Fine, but coarser than most other Fine Gray. Also, it contains more temper than common Fine Gray. A small amount of calcite temper (0.1–0.3 mm diameter) and a small amount of ferruginous temper (0.3–1.0 mm diameter). It also contains a very small amount of very fine, shiny inclusions, but their identity is not clear. While a large part of the core is oxidized in orange color, the interior surface is reduced in black. Surface finish and decoration: Black slip on the exterior. The interior is also black, but it may be because of reduced firing. Horizontal grooves and diagonal flutes and grooves on the body. Form: Vase with vertical sides with slightly incurved base. Direct rim and squared lip. Use-wear: Not clear.

WVS No.: 14B-62; Catalog No.: 310071 (Figure 8.37f)
Bag No.: Rim: 915 (26-3-3); Body: 915; Base: 915. Provenience: 14B26-3-3. Context: Floor. On the exterior floor behind the back wall near the division between the center and east rooms. Other pieces may be in nearby unexcavated areas. Condition: Partial (20% present). Very eroded. It is not clear whether the vessel was burned. Dimensions: Rim diameter: [interior] 10 cm (estimate); Maximum diameter: 15 cm (rough estimate); Height: 16 cm (rough estimate); Wall thickness: 0.4–0.7 cm; Sample weight: 135 g; Original weight: 675 g; Volume: 1,797 cm³. Coordinates: (−6.89, 18.60) (measured). Type: Undetermined, possibly Saxche-Palmar Polychrome. Paste, temper, and firing: Pink paste (7.5YR7/4). Fine. A moderate amount of calcite temper (0.2–2.0 mm diameter) and a small amount of ferruginous temper (0.5–2.0 mm diameter). The paste is completely oxidized. Surface finish and decoration: Remains of red paint. Form: Bowl with markedly incurved sides and restricted orifice. Direct rim and rounded lip. Use-wear: Not clear because of the eroded and fragmentary condition.

STRUCTURES M8-2 AND M8-3: OPERATION 23B

Inside Structure M8-2

WVS No.: 23B-1; Catalog No.: 310212

Bag No.: Rim: 390 (24-3-4); Body: 390, 416 (18-3-4), 388 (24-3-2). Provenience: 23B24-3-4. Context: Floor. Most fragments were found outside the east wall of Structure M8-2. Some pieces were inside the structure (Unit 18). It is not clear whether the vessel was stored inside or outside the structure. Condition: Reconstructible (20% present). Slightly eroded. Some fragments are darkened, but it is not clear whether that was caused by fire at the time of abandonment. Some fragments probably remained in unexcavated areas. Dimensions: Rim diameter: 31 cm (estimate); Maximum diameter: 50 cm (rough estimate); Minimum opening: 19 cm (estimate); Height: 48 cm (rough estimate); Wall thickness: 0.5–0.9 cm; Sample weight: 3,003 g; Original weight: 15,015 g; Volume: 44,071 cm³. Coordinates: (54.55, 41.80) (estimate). Type: Encanto Striated. Paste, temper, and firing: Yellowish red paste (5YR6/6). Coarse. A large amount of calcite temper (0.3–2.0 mm diameter) and a small amount of ferruginous temper (0.3–0.5 mm diameter). The thin core remained dark in some fragments. Surface finish and decoration: The surface is smoothed and unslipped. The shoulder has a band of striation between nail-like impressions that were made in a clockwise direction. Form: Jar with outcurved neck. Exterior-folded rim with beveled-in lip. Use-wear: Not clear. No clear signs that the vessel was used on fire for cooking.

WVS No.: 23B-2; Catalog No.: 310194 (Figures 8.38a and 8.61g)

Bag No.: Rim: 417 (18-3-1), 413 (18-3-1); Body: 417, 413. Provenience: 23B18-3-1. Context: Floor. In the northwestern part of Structure M8-2. All fragments were found in an area 1 × 1 m. Condition: Partial (25% present). Eroded. Some fragments, including the interior neck, are darkened. It is not clear whether fire clouding was caused by fire at the time of abandonment. It is not clear whether the upper part of the vessel was reused after it broke or whether it was used as a complete vessel. Dimensions: Rim diameter: [exterior] 14.4 cm, [top] 14.0 cm (measured); Maximum diameter: 32 cm (rough estimate); Minimum opening: 8.9 cm (measured); Height: 33 cm (rough estimate); Neck height: 6.0 cm (measured); Wall thickness: 0.7–0.9 cm; Sample weight: 591 g; Original weight: 2,364 g; Volume: 12,050 cm³. Coordinates: (56.12, 38.39) (measured). Type: Pantano Impressed. Paste, temper, and

firing: Pink paste (5YR7/4). Medium grain. A medium amount of calcite temper (0.1–1.2 mm diameter) and a small amount of ferruginous temper (0.3–1.0 mm diameter). The paste is completely oxidized. Surface finish and decoration: The exterior has red slip whereas the interior neck does not appear to be slipped. Four-dots stamps and triangular impressions below the neck-body juncture. Form: Jar with outcurved neck. Direct rim and rounded lip. Use-wear: Not clear.

WVS No.: 23B-3; Catalog No.: 310196 (Figures 8.38b and 8.60h)

Bag No.: Rim: 192 (24-1-1); Body: 388 (24-3-2); Base: 388. Provenience: 23B24-3-2. Context: Floor. Most fragments were found outside the east wall of Structure M8-2 in an area 0.6 × 1 m. It is not clear whether the vessel was stored inside or outside the structure. Condition: Reconstructible (90% present). Eroded. It is not clear whether the fire clouding on the lower exterior body was caused by the original firing of the vessel. Some fragments probably remained in unexcavated areas. Dimensions: Rim diameter: [exterior] 13.9 cm, [top] 13.6 cm (measured); Maximum diameter: 38 cm (rough estimate); Minimum opening: 8.0 cm; Height: 38 cm (rough estimate); Neck height: 5.5 cm (measured); Wall thickness: 0.6–0.9 cm; Sample weight: 3,604 g; Original weight: 4,004 g; Volume: 21,871 cm³. Coordinates: (55.60, 41.80) (estimate). Type: Pantano Impressed. Paste, temper, and firing: Pink paste (7.5YR7/4). Medium grain. A medium amount of calcite temper (0.3–1.3 mm diameter) and a small amount of ferruginous temper (0.5–2.0 mm diameter). The paste is completely oxidized. Surface finish and decoration: The exterior has red slip whereas the interior neck does not appear to be slipped. Cross-hatch stamps and triangular impressions below the neck-body juncture. Form: Jar with outcurved neck. Direct rim and rounded lip. Incurved base. Use-wear: Not clear.

WVS No.: 23B-4; Catalog No.: 310183 (Figure 8.38c and 8.38d)

Bag No.: Rim: 388 (24-3-2), 416 (18-3-4); Body: 388; Base: 388, 416. Provenience: 23B24-3-2. Context: Floor. Although most fragments were found outside the east wall, a few pieces were in the central part of the structure. It is probable that the vessel was stored in a high location inside the structure near the east wall. Condition: Reconstructible (90% present). Eroded. Some parts of the vessel appear to be burned in reddish color. No fragments of

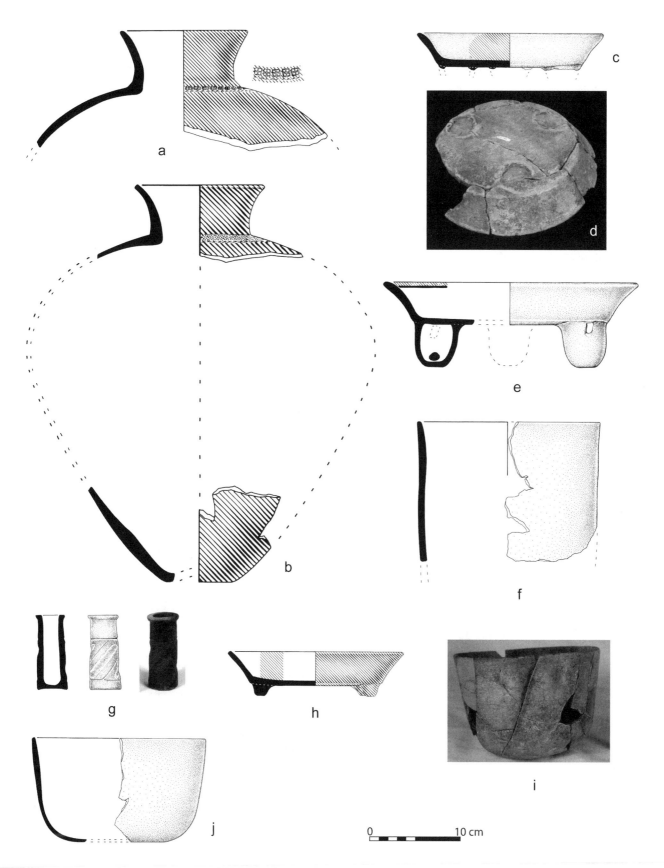

FIGURE 8.38. Complete and reconstructible vessels from Structure M8-2. (a–f) Inside the structure. (a, b) Pantano Impressed.
(a) 23B18-3-1, Cat. 310194, WVS 23B-2. (b) 23B24-3-2, Cat. 310196, WVS 23B-3. (c–e) Saxche-Palmar Polychrome. (c, d) 23B24-3-2,
Cat. 310183, WVS 23B-4. (e) 23B18-3-1, Cat. 310192, WVS 23B-5. (f) Unnamed volcanic ash undetermined, 23B18-3-3, Cat. 310207,
WVS 23B-6. (g–j) West exterior. (g) Salada Fluted, 23B6-3-1, Cat. 310182, WVS 23B-9. (h–i) Saxche-Palmar Polychrome. (h) 23B5-3-1,
Cat. 310184, WVS 23B-10. (i) 23B5-3-1, Cat. 310189, WVS 23B-11. (j) Unnamed red-orange paste, 23B13-3-1, Cat. 310191, WVS 23B-12.

feet were recovered. It is not clear whether the vessel was used without feet. Dimensions: Rim diameter: [exterior] 20.5 cm, [top] 19.7 cm (measured); Height: 4.5 cm (measured); Height without feet: 3.5 cm (measured); Wall thickness: 0.7–0.9 cm; Sample weight: 480 g; Original weight: 533 g; Volume: 419 cm^3. Coordinates: (55.56, 41.42) (estimate). Type: Saxche-Palmar Polychrome. Paste, temper, and firing: Light reddish brown paste (5YR6/4). Fine. A small amount of calcite temper (0.1–0.3 mm diameter) and a small amount of ferruginous temper (0.5–1.5 mm diameter). The paste is completely oxidized. Surface finish and decoration: The surface is mostly eroded. Red paint over cream underslip on the interior wall. Remains of cream underslip on the exterior wall. Form: Plate with slightly outcurved sides and flat base. Direct rim and rounded lip. Traces of three hollow feet. Use-wear: Not clear because of erosion.

WVS No.: 23B-5; Catalog No.: 310192 (Figure 8.38e)
Bag No.: Rim: 413 (18-3-1), 238 (19-2-1); Body: 413; Base: 413, 238. Provenience: 23B18-3-1. Context: Floor. In the northwestern part of Structure M8-2. Condition: Reconstructible (55% present). Eroded. A significant part of the vessel is burned in dark color. Fragments were found in an area 1 × 2 m. Two feet are present. Dimensions: Rim diameter: [exterior] 26.5 cm, [top] 26.0 cm (measured); Height: 8.7 cm (measured); Height without feet: 4.2 cm (measured); Wall thickness: 0.6–0.9 cm; Sample weight: 501 g; Original weight: 911 g; Volume: 1,188 cm^3. Coordinates: (55.89, 38.66) (estimate). Type: Saxche-Palmar Polychrome. Paste, temper, and firing: Reddish yellow paste (5YR6/8). Fine. A small amount of calcite temper (0.1–0.7 mm diameter) and a small amount of ferruginous temper (0.5–1.0 mm diameter). The paste is completely oxidized. Surface finish and decoration: The surface is mostly eroded. Remains of red paint over cream underslip on the rim. Form: Plate with slightly outcurved sides and flat base. Direct rim and rounded lip. Three hollow oven feet with two openings and a rattle. Use-wear: Not clear because of erosion.

WVS No.: 23B-6; Catalog No.: 310207 (Figure 8.38f)
Bag No.: Rim: 415 (18-3-3), 414 (18-3-2), 413 (18-3-1), 167 (18-1-1); Body: 415, 414, 416, 188 (23-1-1). Provenience: 23B18-3-3. Context: Floor. In the southwestern part of Structure M8-2. Condition: Partial (20% present). Eroded. No clear traces of burning. The base was not recovered. Fragments were found in an area 3 × 3 m (Units 18, 19, and 23). It is not clear whether these fragments are

parts of a reconstructible vessel, parts of a reused partial vessel, or refuse. Dimensions: Rim diameter: [exterior] 20.1 cm, [top] 19.6 cm (measured); Wall thickness: 0.8–0.9 cm; Sample weight: 440 g; Original weight: 2,200 g; Volume: 3,100 cm^3. Coordinates: (54.37, 38.75) (estimate). Type: Unnamed volcanic ash undetermined. Paste, temper, and firing: Only a thin surface layer (1 mm) of the paste is oxidized in light brown color (7.5YR6/4), and the core remained black (7.5YR2.5/1). Fine. A small amount of volcanic ash (0.1 mm length). Identical to common Andres Red paste. Surface finish and decoration: The surface is mostly eroded. Remains of red and white paints on the exterior wall. Form: Vase with vertical sides. Direct rim and squared lip. Use-wear: Not clear because of erosion.

West of Structure M8-2

WVS No.: 23B-7; Catalog No.: 310215
Bag No.: Rim: 358 (5-3-1), 382 (6-3-3), 380 (6-3-1), 398 (13-3-2), 365 (5-3-3); Body: 358, 359 (5-3-1), 365, 369 (5-3-4), 104 (5-1-1), 131 (10-1-1). Provenience: 23B5-3-1. Context: Floor. On the exterior floor to the southwest of Structure M8-2. Most fragments were found in Unit 5, and a small number of pieces were from Units 6 and 13 to the north. It is not clear whether a complete vessel was placed on the exterior floor, whether a partially broken vessel was kept outside, or whether the pieces are discarded fragments. Condition: Reconstructible (80% present). Badly eroded. No clear traces of burning. The vessel was not reconstructed, except for part of the rim. We judged that the pieces are from the same vessel, based on similarities in paste and striation. It is not clear whether the base is present. Dimensions: Rim diameter: 33 cm (estimate); Maximum diameter: 49 cm (rough estimate); Minimum opening: 21 cm (estimate); Height: 47 cm (rough estimate); Neck height: 12 cm (estimate); Wall thickness: 1.0–1.2 cm; Sample weight: 7,691 g; Original weight: 9,613 g; Volume: 39,232 cm^3. Coordinates: (53.60, 36.37) (estimate). Type: Encanto Striated. Paste, temper, and firing: Light brown paste (7.5YR6/4). Coarse grain. A large amount of calcite temper (0.3–2.0 mm diameter) and a small amount of quartz temper (0.5 mm diameter). The paste is completely oxidized. Surface finish and decoration: Striation on the body. Form: Jar with outcurved neck. Exterior-folded rim and beveled-in lip. Use-wear: Not clear.

WVS No.: 23B-8; Catalog No.: 310218
Bag No.: Rim: 350 (10-3-4), 349 (10-3-3), 215 (10-2-1); Body: 350, 215, 349, 131 (10-1-1); Base: 350. Provenience:

23B10-3-4. Context: Floor. On the platform to the west of Structure M8-2. Fragments were found in an area 0.5 × 1 m. Condition: Reconstructible (90% present). Eroded. Traces of burning are not clear. Dimensions: Rim diameter: [exterior] 14.0 cm, [top] 13.8 cm (measured); Maximum diameter: 36 cm (rough estimate); Minimum opening: 8.6 cm (measured); Height: 36 cm (rough estimate); Neck height: 5.6 cm (measured); Wall thickness: 0.6–1.0 cm; Sample weight: 3,507 g; Original weight: 3,897 g; Volume: 16,260 cm³. Coordinates: (52.68, 34.93) (estimate). Type: Pantano Impressed. Paste, temper, and firing: Reddish yellow paste (5YR6/6). Medium grain. A medium amount of calcite temper (0.3–1.5 mm diameter) and a small amount of ferruginous temper (0.5–1.3 mm diameter). The paste is completely oxidized. Surface finish and decoration: Red slip on the exterior. It is not clear whether the interior neck and the exterior base were slipped. Stamps and triangular impressions below the neck-body juncture. Form: Jar with outcurved neck and incurved base. Direct rim and rounded lip. Use-wear: Not clear because of erosion.

WVS No.: 23B-9; Catalog No.: 310182 (Figure 8.38g)
Bag No.: Rim: 162 (6-3-1); Body: 162; Base: 162. Provenience: 23B6-3-1. Context: Floor. In the dense deposit on the exterior floor between Structure M8-2 and the platform. Condition: Complete (100% present). Eroded. Severely burned in black color. Dimensions: Rim diameter: [exterior] 3.3 cm, [top] 2.6 cm (measured); Height: 7.8 cm (measured); Wall thickness: 0.4 cm; Sample weight: 43 g; Original weight: 43 g; Volume: 34 cm³. Coordinates: (55.65, 35.92) (measured). Type: Salada Fluted. Paste, temper, and firing: Light brown paste (7.5YR6/4). This color may be due to oxidation during burning; the original paste color may have been darker. Medium grain. Different from the common Saxche-Palmar Polychrome paste. A small amount of ferruginous temper (0.3–1.0 mm diameter) and a very small amount of quartz temper (0.2–0.7 mm length). There appears to have been calcite temper, which has mostly eroded away. Because the vessel is complete, it is not clear whether the paste is completely oxidized. Surface finish and decoration: Remains of slip on the exterior, which is burned in black color. It may originally have been red or orange. Diagonal incisions and fluting, commonly seen on Salada Fluted cylinders. Form: Miniature vase with vertical sides and flat base. Exterior-thickened rim and squared lip. Use-wear: Not clear because of erosion. There are remains of white material on the exterior, which may be a residue or burned

slip. It seems similar to the material found on the interior surface of a miniature cylinder from Structure M8-8 (Cat. 310047).

WVS No.: 23B-10; Catalog No.: 310184 (Figure 8.38h)
Bag No.: Rim: 360 (5-3-1); Body: 360; Base: 360. Provenience: 23B5-3-1. Context: Floor. On the exterior floor to the southwest of Structure M8-2. Condition: Reconstructible (65% present). Badly eroded. The interior base is darkened. It is not clear whether this is due to the fire at the time of abandonment. Dimensions: Rim diameter: [exterior] 19.8 cm, [top] 19.4 cm (estimate); Height: 4.5 cm (measured); Height without feet: 3.3 cm (measured); Wall thickness: 0.6 cm; Sample weight: 234 g; Original weight: 360 g; Volume: 379 cm³. Coordinates: (53.40, 36.00) (estimate). Type: Saxche-Palmar Polychrome. Paste, temper, and firing: Reddish yellow paste (5YR6/6). Medium grain. Different from the common Saxche-Palmar Polychrome paste. A medium amount of ferruginous temper (0.5–2.5 mm diameter) and a small amount of shiny, glass-like particles (0.1 mm diameter). The paste is completely oxidized. The paste and temper do not react to weak acid. Surface finish and decoration: The surface is mostly eroded. Traces of red paint over cream underslip on the exterior wall. Form: Plate with flared sides and flat base. Direct rim and squared lip. Three nubbin feet. The vessel is not well shaped, and its outlines and wall thickness are uneven. Use-wear: Not clear because of erosion.

WVS No.: 23B-11; Catalog No.: 310189 (Figure 8.38i)
Bag No.: Rim: 361 (5-3-1), 382 (6-3-3), 104 (5-1-1); Body: 361, 382, 358 (5-3-1), 232 (6-2-1); Base: 382. Provenience: 23B5-3-1. Context: Floor. On the exterior floor to the southwest of Structure M8-2. Fragments were found in an area 1 × 2 m. Condition: Reconstructible (85% present). Badly eroded. Some parts are burned in dark color. Some fragments were exposed to fire after the vessel broke. Dimensions: Rim diameter: [exterior] 16.1 cm, [top] 15.9 cm (measured); Height: 10.2–11.3 cm (measured); Wall thickness: 0.5–0.6 cm; Sample weight: 380 g; Original weight: 447 g; Volume: 731 cm³. Coordinates: (53.33, 36.39) (estimate). Type: Saxche-Palmar Polychrome. Paste, temper, and firing: Reddish yellow paste (5YR6/6). Fine grain. A small amount of calcite temper (0.1–0.3 mm diameter) and a medium amount of ferruginous temper (0.3–1.3 mm diameter). The paste is completely oxidized. Surface finish and decoration: The surface is mostly eroded. Some traces of red paint on cream underslip on the interior. Form: Open bowl with flared sides and flat base. Direct rim and

rounded lip. Slanted rim. Use-wear: Not clear because of erosion.

WVS No.: 23B-12; Catalog No.: 310191 (Figure 8.38j)
Bag No.: Rim: 584 (13-3-1); Body: 584; Base: 584. Provenience: 23B13-3-1. Context: Floor. On the floor of the platform. Condition: Partial (40% present). Badly eroded. Burned in red and black colors. Some fragments were exposed to fire after the vessel broke. Some fragments may have remained in unexcavated areas. Dimensions: Rim diameter: 18 cm (estimate); Height: 11.3 cm (measured); Wall thickness: 0.3–0.5 cm; Sample weight: 171 g; Original weight: 428 g; Volume: 996 cm³. Coordinates: (57.80, 34.15) (estimate). Type: Unnamed red-orange paste. Paste, temper, and firing: Red paste (2.5YR5/8). Very fine, compact, and hard. The paste and temper do not react to weak acid. A small amount of white temper (0.1–0.4 mm diameter) and a very small amount of shiny, glass-like particles (volcanic ash? 0.1 mm length). The paste is completely oxidized. Surface finish and decoration: Remains of slip or paint on the interior, which is burned in black color. The original color of the paint is not clear. Form: Bowl with slightly flared sides. Direct rim and rounded lip. Slightly rounded base. Use-wear: Not clear because of erosion.

Behind Structure M8-2

WVS No.: 23B-13; Catalog No.: 310198 (Figure 8.39a)
Bag No.: Rim: 334 (12-3-1), 343 (12-3-2); Body: 334, 344 (12-3-2); Base: 334, 344. Provenience: 23B12-3-1. Context: Floor. On the exterior floor behind Structure M8-2. Condition: Reconstructible (40% present). Some fragments are heavily eroded. No clear traces of burning. Some fragments may have remained in unexcavated areas. Dimensions: Rim diameter: [exterior] 14.8 cm, [top] 14.1 cm (measured); Maximum diameter: 36 cm (rough estimate); Minimum opening: 8.4 cm (measured); Height: 34 cm (rough estimate); Neck height: 5.2 cm (measured); Wall thickness: 0.6–0.9 cm; Sample weight: 1,290 g; Original weight: 3,225 g; Volume: 15,874 cm³. Coordinates: (57.41, 36.98) (estimate). Type: Tinaja Red or Pantano Impressed. Paste, temper, and firing: Reddish yellow paste (7.5YR7/6). Medium grain. A medium amount of calcite temper (0.3–1.0 mm diameter). The paste is completely oxidized. Surface finish and decoration: The entire exterior, including the base, is slipped in red. The interior neck does not seems to be slipped. The exterior body is polished, but the neck is smoothed. Fragments directly below the neck-body juncture were not recovered. Form: Jar

with outcurved neck and incurved base. Direct rim and squared lip. Use-wear: Not clear because of erosion.

WVS No.: 23B-14; Catalog No.: 310199
Bag No.: Rim: 334 (12-3-1); Body: 334; Base: 335 (12-3-2). Provenience: 23B12-3-2. Context: Floor. On the exterior floor behind Structure M8-2. Condition: Reconstructible (50% present). Badly eroded. No clear traces of burning. Some fragments may have remained in unexcavated areas. Dimensions: Rim diameter: [exterior] 13.3 cm, [top] 12.9 cm (measured); Maximum diameter: 29 cm (rough estimate); Minimum opening: 7.9 cm (measured); Height: 31 cm (rough estimate); Neck height: 5.3 cm (measured); Wall thickness: 0.7–0.8 cm; Sample weight: 1,443 g; Original weight: 2,886 g; Volume: 9,881 cm³. Coordinates: (57.56, 37.17) (estimate). Type: Pantano Impressed. Paste, temper, and firing: Pink paste (7.5YR7/4). Medium grain. A medium amount of calcite temper (0.3–1.2 mm diameter) and a small amount of ferruginous temper (0.5–1.3 mm diameter). The paste is completely oxidized. Surface finish and decoration: The exterior has red slip. It is not clear whether the exterior base and interior neck are slipped. Cross-and-dots stamps and triangular impressions below the neck-body juncture. Form: Jar with outcurved neck and incurved base. Direct rim and rounded lip. Use-wear: Not clear because of erosion.

WVS No.: 23B-15; Catalog No.: 310282
Bag No.: Rim: 335 (12-3-2), 140 (12-1-2); Body: 335, 333 (12-3-1); Base: 333. Provenience: 23B12-3-1. Context: Floor. On the exterior floor behind Structure M8-2. Condition: Reconstructible (45% present). Badly eroded. It is not clear whether the fire clouding on the exterior base was caused during the original firing of the vessel or during the fire at the time of abandonment. Some fragments may have remained in unexcavated areas. Dimensions: Rim diameter: [exterior] 12.3 cm, [top] 12.1 cm (measured); Maximum diameter: 40 cm (rough estimate); Minimum opening: 8.5 cm (measured); Height: 40 cm (rough estimate); Neck height: 5.0 cm (measured), Wall thickness: 0.7–1.2 cm; Sample weight: 2,120 g; Original weight: 4,711 g; Volume: 22,759 cm³. Coordinates: (57.43, 36.56) (measured). Type: Pantano Impressed. Paste, temper, and firing: Reddish yellow paste (7.5YR7/6). Medium grain. A medium amount of calcite temper (0.1–1.3 mm diameter) and a small amount of ferruginous temper (0.5–1.3 mm diameter). The paste is completely oxidized. Surface finish and decoration: The exterior has red slip. It is not clear

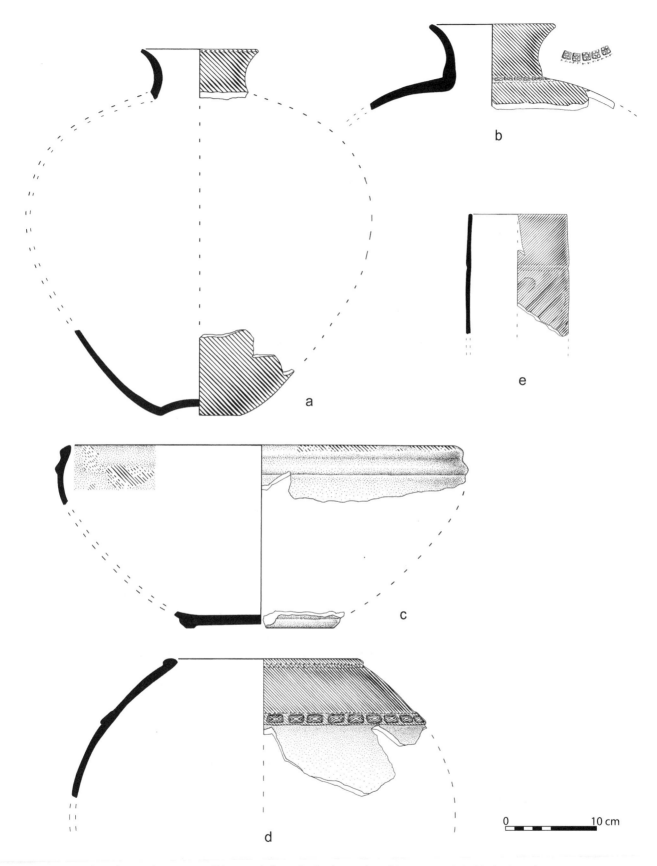

FIGURE 8.39. Complete and reconstructible vessels from the back exterior of Structure M8-2. (a) Tinaja Red or Pantano Impressed, 23B12-3-1, Cat. 310198, WVS 23B-13. (b) Pantano Impressed, 23B12-3-3, Cat. 310460, WVS 23B-16. (c) Subin Red, 23B19-3-2, Cat. 310203, WVS 23B-17. (d) Chaquiste Impressed, 23B19-3-2, Cat. 310195, WVS 23B-18. (e) Salada Fluted, 23B19-3-2, Cat. 310206, WVS 23B-19.

whether the exterior base and interior neck are slipped. There are stamps below the neck-body juncture, but their patterns are not clear. Form: Jar with outcurved neck and incurved base. Direct rim and rounded lip. Use-wear: Not clear because of erosion.

WVS No.: 23B-16; Catalog No.: 310460 (Figures 8.39b and 8.61i)
Bag No.: Rim: 376 (12-3-3); Body: 376; Base: 376. Provenience: 23B12-3-3. Context: Floor. On the exterior floor behind Structure M8-2. Fragments were found in an area 1 × 1 m. Condition: Reconstructible (25% present). Eroded. Traces of burning are not clear. Dimensions: Rim diameter: [exterior] 14 cm, [top] 13.4 cm (measured); Maximum diameter: 34 cm (rough estimate); Minimum opening: 7.9 cm (measured); Height: 34 cm (rough estimate); Neck height: 5.4 cm (measured); Wall thickness: 0.6–0.8 cm; Sample weight: 1,213 g; Original weight: 4,852 g; Volume: 14,761 cm³. Coordinates: (56.80, 36.45) (measured). Type: Pantano Impressed. Paste, temper, and firing: Reddish yellow paste (5YR7/6). Medium grain. A large amount of calcite temper (0.1–2.0 mm diameter) and a small amount of ferruginous temper (0.5–1.0 mm diameter). The paste is completely oxidized. Surface finish and decoration: Red slip on the exterior, including the base. It is not clear whether the interior neck was slipped. Quincunx stamps and triangular punctuations below the neck-body juncture. Form: Jar with outcurved neck. Direct rim and rounded lip. Incurved base. Use-wear: Not clear because of erosion.

WVS No.: 23B-17; Catalog No.: 310203 (Figure 8.39c)
Bag No.: Rim: 373 (19-3-2), 172 (19-1-1), 356 (19-3-1); Body: 373, 356; Base: 356, 240 (19-2-2). Provenience: 23B19-3-2. Context: Floor. On the exterior floor behind Structure M8-2. Condition: Reconstructible (60% present). Severely eroded. Some parts appear to be burned in dark color. Dimensions: Rim diameter: [interior] 40.0 cm, [top] 39.0 cm (measured); Maximum diameter: 43.5 cm (estimate); Height: 14 cm (rough estimate); Wall thickness: 0.6–1.0 cm; Sample weight: 1,644 g; Original weight: 2,740 g; Volume: 16,317 cm³. Coordinates: (57.25, 39.35) (measured). Type: Subin Red. Paste, temper, and firing: Reddish yellow paste (7.5YR6/6). Medium grain. A large amount of calcite temper (0.3–1.5 mm diameter) and a small amount of ferruginous temper (0.5–1.3 mm diameter). The paste is completely oxidized. Surface finish and decoration: The surface is mostly eroded. Some remains of red slip on the rim and on the interior. Ridge below

the rim. Form: Open bowl with incurved sides. Exterior-thickened rim and rounded lip. Flat base and ring. Use-wear: The ring base is worn. The worn surface on the base is blackened from fire. There is no indication that the vessel was used on fire.

WVS No.: 23B-18; Catalog No.: 310195 (Figures 8.39d and 8.61j)
Bag No.: Rim: 375 (19-3-2); Body: 375. Provenience: 23B19-3-2. Context: Floor. On the exterior floor behind Structure M8-2. Condition: Reconstructible (20% present). Relatively well preserved. Some parts are burned in black color. Some fragments may have remained in unexcavated areas. Dimensions: Rim diameter: [interior] 16.9 cm, [top] 18.5 cm (measured); Maximum diameter: 43 cm (estimate); Height: 29 cm (rough estimate); Wall thickness: 0.6–0.8 cm; Sample weight: 527 g; Original weight: 2,635 g; Volume: 17,561 cm³. Coordinates: (57.53, 39.54) (measured). Type: Chaquiste Impressed. Paste, temper, and firing: Reddish yellow paste (7.5YR6/6). Medium grain. A medium amount of calcite temper (0.1–0.8 mm diameter). The paste is completely oxidized. Surface finish and decoration: The exterior rim and wall above the ridge are slipped in red. The exterior wall below the ridge was mostly unslipped, although small areas have thin red slip. The interior was unslipped. Two lines of triangular impressions below the rim. Triangular impressions and rectangular stamps on the ridge. Form: Closed bowl with markedly incurved sides and restricted orifice. Thin wall. Exterior-thickened rim and rounded lip. Ridge in the upper body. Use-wear: Not clear.

WVS No.: 23B-19; Catalog No.: 310206 (Figure 8.39e)
Bag No.: Rim: 375 (19-3-2), 240 (19-2-2), 356 (19-3-1); Body: 375, 240, 356. Provenience: 23B19-3-2. Context: Floor. On the exterior floor behind Structure M8-2. Condition: Reconstructible (50% present). Eroded. Parts of the vessel are severely burned in red color. The base was not recovered. Some fragments may have remained in unexcavated areas. Dimensions: Rim diameter: [exterior] 10.6 cm, [top] 10.2 cm (measured); Wall thickness: 0.4–0.5 cm; Sample weight: 210 g; Original weight: 420 g; Volume: 1,390 cm³. Coordinates: (57.30, 39.20) (estimate). Type: Salada Fluted. Paste, temper, and firing: Yellowish red paste (5YR5/8). Fine, compact, and hard. A small amount of white particles (0.1–0.5 mm diameter) and a very small amount of shiny, glass-like particles (0.1 mm length). The paste and temper do not react to weak acid. Dark core. Surface finish and decoration: The surface is

mostly eroded, but it appears to have been well polished. Remains of orange slip on the exterior wall. Diagonal incisions and fluting on the body. Form: Vase with vertical sides. Direct rim and rounded lip. Use-wear: Not clear.

In Front of Structure M8-2 and Behind Structure M8-3

WVS No.: 23B-20; Catalog No.: 310283
Bag No.: Rim: 289 (16-3-1); Body: 289, 294 (16-3-2); Base: 289. Provenience: 23B16-3-1. Context: Floor. On the exterior floor behind Structure M8-3. Most fragments were found in one concentration. Other fragments were in the next lot (16-3-2). We did not reconstruct the vessel, but the concentration of sherds and their similarity suggest that they were parts of the same jar. Only a small portion of the rim was recovered. It is not clear whether we did not recognize other parts of the rim mixed in different lots or whether the vessel was used with a broken rim. Condition: Reconstructible (60% present). Eroded. No clear traces of burning. Dimensions: Rim diameter: 35 cm (rough estimate); Maximum diameter: 48 cm (rough estimate); Minimum opening: 25 cm (rough estimate); Height: 46 cm (rough estimate); Wall thickness: 0.6–1.2 cm; Sample weight: 5,349 g; Original weight: 8,915 g; Volume: 39,283 cm^3. Coordinates: (51.67, 38.22) (measured). Type: Encanto Striated. Paste, temper, and firing: Light brown paste (7.5YR6/4). Coarse. A large amount of calcite temper (0.5–1.5 mm diameter). The paste is completely oxidized. Surface finish and decoration: Unslipped. Striation on the exterior body. The neck is smoothed. Form: Jar with outcurved neck. Exterior-folded rim and beveled-in lip. It appears to have a rounded base. Use-wear: Not clear.

WVS No.: 23B-21; Catalog No.: 310205 (Figure 8.40a)
Bag No.: Rim: 290 (16-3-1), 294 (16-3-2); Body: 290, 293 (16-3-2), 294; Base: 290, 294, 293, 129 (8-1-1), 128 (7-1-1). Provenience: 23B16-3-1. Context: Floor. On the exterior floor behind Structure M8-3. Most fragments (half the rim, parts of the body and base) were found in an area 1 × 2 m next to the back wall of Structure M8-3. A few pieces of the base were found in Units 8 and 9, to the west of the structure. Although fragments from Unit 16 and those from Units 8 and 9 do not fit together, they seem to be parts of the same vessel. The pattern of fire clouding that covers parts of the base also appears similar. It is not clear whether the fire clouding was caused during the original firing of the vessel or during the fire at the time of abandonment. One possibility is that after the vessel broke, half of it was used or kept behind the structure. Another possibility is that the vessel was used as a complete

piece and was disturbed after it broke in the fire. Condition: Partial (40% present). Eroded. No clear traces of burning besides the fire clouding on the base and on a part of the rim. Dimensions: Rim diameter: 35 cm (estimate); Maximum diameter: 38 cm (estimate); Height: 17 cm (estimate); Wall thickness: 0.7–0.9 cm; Sample weight: 1,451 g; Original weight: 3,628 g; Volume: 9,015 cm^3. Coordinates: (51.96, 38.39) (estimate). Type: Subin Red. Paste, temper, and firing: Strong brown paste (7.5YR5/6). Medium grain. A large amount of calcite temper (0.1–1.0 mm diameter). The paste is completely oxidized. Surface finish and decoration: Remains of red slip on the interior and on the exterior rim above the ridge. Form: Open bowl with rounded sides. Exterior-thickened rim and rounded lip. Ridge below the rim. Flat base with ring. Use-wear: Not clear because of erosion.

Inside Structure M8-3

WVS No.: 23B-22; Catalog No.: 310211 (Figure 8.40b)
Bag No.: Rim: 186 (22-1-1), 219 (16-2-1), 226 (22-2-2), 152 (16-1-1), 217 (22-2-1); Body: 186, 219, 152, 217; Base: 186. Provenience: 23B16-3-3. Context: Floor. Near the northeast corner of the bench of Structure M8-3. Most fragments were found in the humus and wall-fall layer. The vessel may have been stored in a high location. Condition: Reconstructible (70% present). Eroded. Traces of burning not clear. Some fragments probably remained in unexcavated areas. Dimensions: Rim diameter: 44 cm (estimate); Height: 3.5 cm (estimate); Wall thickness: 0.7–0.8 cm; Sample weight: 1,414 g; Original weight: 2,020 g; Volume: 2,183 cm^3. Coordinates: (50.80, 40.50) (estimate). Type: Cambio Unslipped. Paste, temper, and firing: Reddish yellow paste (7.5YR6/6). Coarse. A large amount of calcite temper (0.6–1.3 mm diameter). The paste is completely oxidized. Surface finish and decoration: The interior is polished, but the exterior is smoothed. Unslipped. Form: Plate with no sides and slightly rounded base (*comal*). Direct rim and grooved lip. Use-wear: None clear on the interior. The exterior is more heavily eroded. The exterior of some base fragments is darkened, but it may be from the original firing of the vessel. Most fragments are not darkened. Thus, there are no clear signs that it was used on fire as a griddle.

WVS No.: 23B-23; Catalog No.: 310181 (Figure 8.40c)
Bag No.: Rim: 286 (16-3-3), 219 (16-2-1), 287 (16-3-3); Body: 286; Base: 286. Provenience: 23B16-3-3. Context: Floor. Near the center of the bench surface. Most fragments were found in one concentration. Condition: Reconstructible

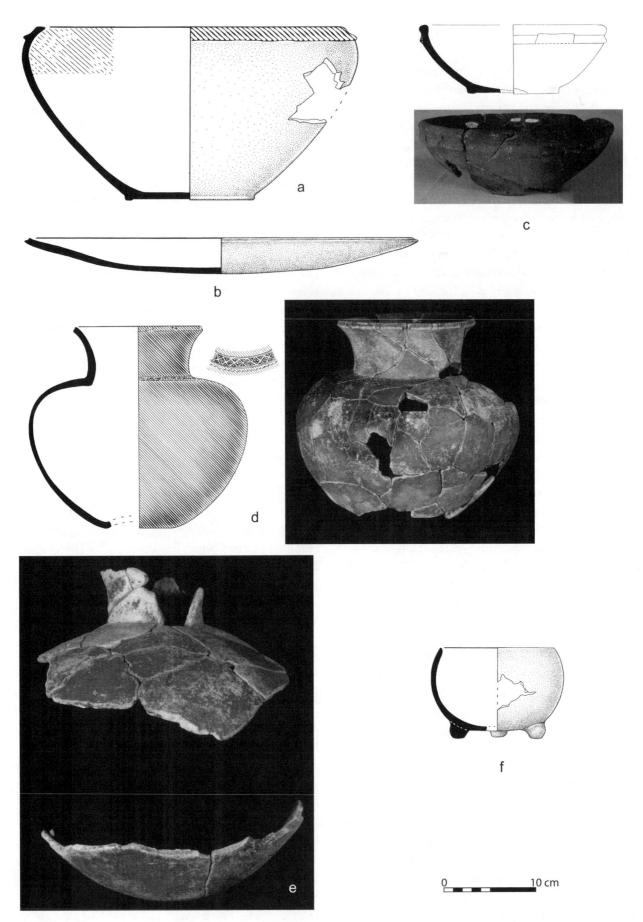

FIGURE 8.40. Complete and reconstructible vessels from Structures M8-2 and M8-3. (a) Area in front of Structure M8-2 and behind Structure M8-3, Subin Red, 23B16-3-1, Cat. 310205, WVS 23B-21. (b–f) Inside Structure M8-3. (b) Cambio Unslipped, 23B16-3-3, Cat. 310211, WVS 23B-22. (c) Subin Red, 23B16-3-3, Cat. 310181, WVS 23B-23. (d, e) Pantano Impressed. (d) 23B21-3-3, Cat. 310188, WVS 23B-24. (e) 23B15-3-1, Cat. 310200, WVS 23B-25. (f) Saxche-Palmar Polychrome, 23B3-3-2, Cat. 310201, WVS 23B-26.

(80% present). Badly eroded. Burned in dark color. A significant part of the ridge broke off, probably due to fire. Dimensions: Rim diameter: [exterior] 20.1 cm, [top] 19.1 cm (measured); Height: 6.7 cm (measured); Wall thickness: 0.4–0.6 cm; Sample weight: 476 g; Original weight: 595 g; Volume: 706 cm³. Coordinates: (50.20, 38.55) (measured). Type: Subin Red. Paste, temper, and firing: Strong brown paste (7.5YR5/6). Medium grain. A large amount of calcite temper (0.3–1.5 mm diameter) and a small amount of ferruginous temper (0.5–1.2 mm diameter). The paste is completely oxidized. Surface finish and decoration: The surface is mostly eroded. Some traces of red slip on the interior and on the exterior rim above the ridge. Form: Open bowl with incurved sides. Exterior-thickened rim and rounded lip. Flat base and ring. Ridge below the rim. Use-wear: The interior base and the ring base are heavily worn, probably from use.

WVS No.: 23B-24; Catalog No.: 310188 (Figures 8.40d and 8.61k)
Bag No.: Rim: 274 (21-3-3), 280 (21-3-4); Body: 274, 248 (20-3-2), 280, 181, 216 (21-2-1); Base: 204 (20-2-1). Provenience: 23B21-3-3. Context: Floor. Fragments were found near the southeastern corner of the eastern wing of the bench and on the exterior floor in front of it. The vessel was probably placed on the bench or in a higher place. Condition: Reconstructible (55% present). Slightly eroded. The lower body appears to be burned in reddish color. Some fragments probably remained in unexcavated areas. Dimensions: Rim diameter: [exterior] 14.1 cm, [top] 13.8 cm (measured); Maximum diameter: 23.8 cm (measured); Minimum opening: 9.2 cm (measured); Height: 21.0 cm (measured); Neck height: 5.3 cm (measured); Wall thickness: 0.4–0.7 cm; Sample weight: 943 g; Original weight: 1,715 g; Volume: 4,294 cm³. Coordinates: (48.85, 41.00) (estimate). Type: Pantano Impressed. Paste, temper, and firing: Reddish yellow paste (7.5YR7/6). Medium grain. A medium amount of calcite temper (0.3–1.5 mm diameter) and a small amount of ferruginous temper (0.5–1.5 mm diameter). The paste is completely oxidized. Surface finish and decoration: Red slip on the exterior and on the interior neck. It is not clear whether the exterior base was slipped. The exterior body is polished, but the exterior and interior neck are smoothed. A series of two notches on the rim. Cross-and-dots stamps and triangular impressions below the neck-body juncture. Form: Jar with outcurved neck. Direct rim and squared lip. Incurved base. Use-wear: Not clear.

WVS No.: 23B-25; Catalog No.: 310200 (Figure 8.40e)
Bag No.: Rim: 262 (15-3-1), 151 (15-1-1); Body: 262, 408 (15-3-3), 151; Base: 262. Provenience: 23B15-3-1. Context: Floor. Near the northwestern corner of the room floor in front of the bench of Structure M8-3. Most fragments were found in one concentration. It appears that the vessel was placed on the room floor. Condition: Reconstructible (93% present). Badly eroded. The vessel appears to be darkened from fire. Dimensions: Rim diameter: 11 cm (estimate); Maximum diameter: 36 cm (rough estimate); Minimum opening: 8.7 cm (measured); Height: 36 cm (rough estimate); Neck height: 5.7 cm (measured); Wall thickness: 0.7–0.9 cm; Sample weight: 3,622 g; Original weight: 3,894 g; Volume: 17,849 cm³. Coordinates: (49.38, 38.11) (measured). Type: Pantano Impressed. Paste, temper, and firing: Pink paste (7.5YR7/4). Medium grain. A medium amount of calcite temper (0.3–1.5 mm diameter) and a small amount of ferruginous temper (0.5–2.0 mm diameter). The paste is completely oxidized. Surface finish and decoration: Red slip on the exterior, including the exterior base. It is not clear whether the interior neck is slipped. Stamps with dots below the neck-body juncture, but their pattern is not clear. Triangular impressions below it. Form: Jar with outcurved neck. Rim is damaged. Incurved base. Use-wear: The edge of the exterior base is worn.

WVS No.: 23B-26; Catalog No.: 310201 (Figure 8.40f)
Bag No.: Rim: 105 (3-1-1), 275 (2-3-1), 314 (3-3-2); Body: 105, 210 (3-2-1), 275, 314; Base: 105, 275. Provenience: 23B3-3-2. Context: Floor. Near the southern end of the west wing of the bench of Structure M8-3. A significant portion of fragments was found in the humus layer, and some were found in front of the bench outside the structure. Condition: Reconstructible (60% present). Badly eroded. Fragments appear to be burned in dark color. Broken into small fragments. Dimensions: Rim diameter: 12 cm (estimate); Maximum diameter: 13 cm (estimate); Height: 9.5 cm (estimate); Height without feet: 9.0 cm (estimate); Wall thickness: 0.5 cm; Sample weight: 259 g; Original weight: 432 g; Volume: 481 cm³. Coordinates: (48.38, 36.95) (estimate). Type: Saxche-Palmar Polychrome. Paste, temper, and firing: Yellowish red paste (5YR5/6). Medium grain. A medium amount of ferruginous temper (0.8–3.0 mm diameter) and a medium amount of white temper (0.5–1.3 mm length). The paste and temper do not react to weak acid. The paste is different from common Saxche-Palmar paste. The paste is completely oxidized. Surface finish and

decoration: The surface is mostly eroded. Some traces of red paint on the interior and of orange paint over cream underslip on the exterior. Form: Open bowl with rounded sides and flat base. Direct rim and rounded lip. Flat base and ring. Three nubbin feet. Use-wear: The feet are worn. Use-wear on the interior is not clear because of erosion.

In Front of Structure M8-3

WVS No.: 23B-27; Catalog No.: 310209 (Figure 8.41a and 8.41b)

Bag No.: Body: 253 (20-3-3), 254 (20-3-3), 204 (20-2-1). Provenience: 23B20-3-3. Context: Floor. The exterior floor in front of Structure M8-3. The vessel may have fallen from Structure M8-5. Condition: Reconstructible (25% present). Relatively well preserved. Traces of burning are not clear. Other fragments may have remained in unexcavated areas. The rim and base were not recovered. Dimensions: Maximum diameter: 41 cm (rough estimate); Height: 42 cm (rough estimate); Wall thickness: 0.7 cm; Sample weight: 1,503 g; Original weight: 6,012 g; Volume: 23,295 cm³. Coordinates: (46.47, 40.41) (estimate). Type: Encanto Striated. Paste, temper, and firing: Brown paste (7.5YR5/4). Coarse. A large amount of calcite temper (0.5–1.5 mm diameter). The core remained dark. Surface finish and decoration: The exterior and interior surfaces are unslipped and smoothed. A band of striation on the shoulder bordered by nail-like impressions that were made in a clockwise direction. Form: Jar. Use-wear: Not clear.

WVS No.: 23B-28; Catalog No.: 310210

Bag No.: Body: 270 (7-3-2), 266 (7-3-1), 259 (14-3-3), 258 (14-3-2). Provenience: 23B7-3-2. Context: Floor. The exterior floor in front of Structure M8-3. The vessel may have fallen from Structure M8-5. Condition: Reconstructible (20% present). Slightly eroded. It is not clear whether some fire clouding was caused during the original firing of the vessel. Other fragments may have remained in unexcavated areas. The rim and base were not recovered. Dimensions: Maximum diameter: 53 cm (rough estimate); Wall thickness: 0.8 cm; Sample weight: 1,698 g; Original weight: 8,490 g; Volume: 57,443 cm³. Coordinates: (47.68, 35.36) (estimate). Type: Encanto Striated. Paste, temper, and firing: Light brown paste (7.5YR6/4). Coarse. A large amount of calcite temper (0.3–1.3 mm diameter) and a medium amount of probable crushed ceramic temper (0.5–1.3 mm diameter). The wide core remained black. Surface finish and decoration: Most parts

of the exterior and interior surfaces appear to be unslipped and smoothed. There are possible remains of red wash on the shoulder near the striated band. A band of striation on the shoulder bordered by nail-like impressions that were made in a counterclockwise direction. Form: Jar. Use-wear: Not clear.

WVS No.: 23B-29; Catalog No.: 310202 (Figures 8.41c and 8.61l)

Bag No.: Rim: 253 (20-3-3); Body: 253 (20-3-3). Provenience: 23B20-3-3. Context: Floor. In front of Structure M8-3. Although a significant portion of the vessel is missing, all fragments were found in one concentration. The vessel may have fallen from Structure M8-5. Condition: Reconstructible (50% present). Eroded. Some fragments appear to have been burned. Some fragments probably remained in unexcavated areas. Dimensions: Rim diameter: [exterior] 15.5 cm, [top] 14.9 cm (measured); Maximum diameter: 25 cm (estimate); Minimum opening: 10.1 cm (measured); Height: 25 cm (rough estimate); Neck height: 4.9 cm (measured); Wall thickness: 0.7–0.8 cm; Sample weight: 794 g; Original weight: 1,588 g; Volume: 5,668 cm³. Coordinates: (46.47, 41.07) (measured). Type: Pantano Impressed. Paste, temper, and firing: Light reddish brown paste (5YR6/4). Medium grain. A large amount of calcite temper (0.3–1.3 mm diameter) and a small amount of ferruginous temper (0.5–2.0 mm length). The paste is completely oxidized. Surface finish and decoration: Red slip on the exterior and on the interior neck. Cross-and-dots stamps and triangular impressions below the neck-body juncture. Incised motifs on two opposite sides of the shoulder. Notches on the rim. Form: Jar with outcurved neck. Exterior-thickened rim and squared lip. Use-wear: Not clear.

WVS No.: 23B-30; Catalog No.: 310193 (Figures 8.41d and 8.61m)

Bag No.: Rim: 248 (20-3-2); Body: 248, 176 (20-1-1), 204 (20-2-1), 280 (21-3-4), 258 (14-3-2), 253 (20-3-3); Base: 248, 176. Provenience: 23B20-3-2. Context: Floor. In front of the eastern wing of the bench of Structure M8-3. A significant portion of the vessel was found in one concentration, and other fragments were in an area 2 × 3 m. Condition: Reconstructible (45% present). Eroded. Some fragments appear to be burned in red and black colors. Some fragments probably remained in unexcavated areas. Dimensions: Rim diameter: 28 cm (estimate); Maximum diameter: 46 cm (estimate); Height: 40 cm (estimate); Wall

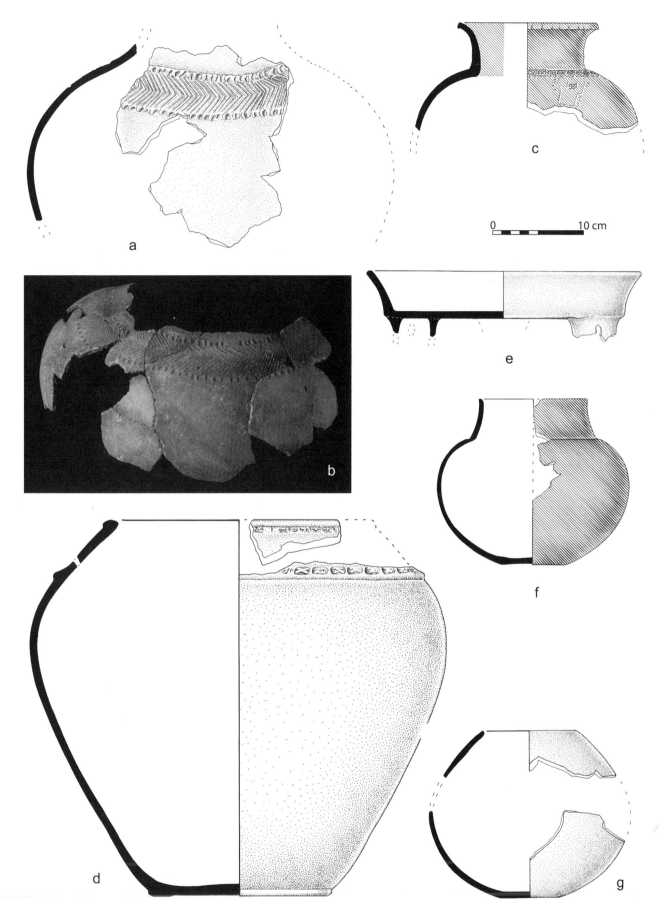

FIGURE 8.41. Complete and reconstructible vessels from the front exterior of Structure M8-3. (a, b) Encanto Striated, 23B20-3-3, Cat. 310209, WVS 23B-27. (c) Pantano Impressed, 23B20-3-3, Cat. 310202, WVS 23B-29. (d) Chaquiste Impressed, 23B20-3-2, Cat. 310193, WVS 23B-30. (e) Saxche-Palmar Polychrome, 23B7-3-2, Cat. 310190, WVS 23B-31. (f) Andres Red, 23B2-3-2, Cat. 310186, WVS 23B-32. (g) Unnamed volcanic ash undetermined, 23B2-3-3, Cat. 310204, WVS 23B-33.

thickness: 0.8–1.0 cm; Sample weight: 3,680 g; Original weight: 8,178 g; Volume: 29,174 cm³. Coordinates: (48.12, 41.54) (measured). Type: Chaquiste Impressed. Paste, temper, and firing: Yellowish red paste (5YR5/6). Medium grain. A medium amount of calcite temper (0.1–0.3 mm diameter). The paste is completely oxidized. Surface finish and decoration: The surface is mostly eroded. Some traces of red slip on the interior and on the upper exterior. Stamps below the rim and on the ridge, but their patterns are not clear. Form: Open bowl with markedly incurved sides and restricted orifice. Flat base with ring. Exterior-thickened rim and rounded lip. Ridge on the shoulder. Use-wear: The ring base is worn. Use-wear on the interior surface is not clear because of erosion. No clear signs that the vessel was used on fire for cooking.

WVS No.: 23B-31; Catalog No.: 310190 (Figure 8.41e)
Bag No.: Rim: 268 (7-3-2), 125 (7-1-1), 119 (2-1-1), 200 (2-2-1); Body: 268, 125; Base: 268, 198 (27-2-1), 125, 272 (7-3-3), 270 (7-3-2). Provenience: 23B7-3-2. Context: Floor. A significant portion of the vessel was found in one concentration on the exterior floor near the southwestern corner of Structure M8-3. Other pieces were found in an area 2 × 2 m. Condition: Reconstructible (50% present). Badly eroded. Burned in dark and reddish colors. Some pieces may have remained in unexcavated areas. Dimensions: Rim diameter: [exterior] 29.5 cm, [top] 28.9 cm (measured); Height: 11 cm (rough estimate); Height without feet: 4.5 cm (measured); Wall thickness: 0.7–0.9 cm; Sample weight: 647 g; Original weight: 1,294 g; Volume: 1,735 cm³. Coordinates: (47.81, 35.47) (measured). Type: Saxche-Palmar Polychrome. Paste, temper, and firing: Reddish yellow paste (5YR7/6). Fine. A small amount of calcite temper (0.1–0.5 mm diameter) and a very small amount of shiny, glass-like particles (0.1 mm length). The paste is completely oxidized. Surface finish and decoration: The surface is mostly eroded. Remains of red paint over cream underslip on the interior wall and remains of red paint on the exterior base. Form: Plate with outcurved sides and flat base. Direct rim and rounded lip. Three hollow feet with two openings and possibly a rattle. The openings were made while the clay was still soft after the feet were attached to the base. Use-wear: Not clear because of erosion.

WVS No.: 23B-32; Catalog No.: 310186 (Figure 8.41f)
Bag No.: Rim: 277 (2-3-2), 276 (2-3-2), 247 (20-3-1); Body: 277, 257 (14-3-1), 119 (2-1-1), 200 (2-2-1), 203 (14-2-1); Base:

277. Provenience: 23B2-3-2. Context: Floor. On the exterior in front of Structure M8-3. About half the vessel was found in one concentration right in front of the structure. Other fragments were scattered in an area 2 × 4 m. The vessel may have been placed on the western wing of the bench or in a higher location. Condition: Reconstructible (80% present). Some fragments are heavily eroded, but others are better preserved. Burned. Some parts were burned and blackened after the vessel broke. Dimensions: Rim diameter: [exterior] 12.2 cm, [top] 11.8 cm (measured); Maximum diameter: 19.4 cm (measured); Minimum opening: 10.8 cm (measured); Height: 16.6 cm (measured); Neck height: 3.8 cm (measured); Wall thickness: 0.5–0.7 cm; Sample weight: 692 g; Original weight: 865 g; Volume: 3,016 cm³. Coordinates: (47.81, 37.74) (measured). Type: Andres Red. Paste, temper, and firing: Reddish yellow paste (7.5YR7/6). Fine grain. A small amount of volcanic temper (0.1 mm length) and a very small amount of black and red particles (0.3–1.0 mm diameter). The paste is completely oxidized. Surface finish and decoration: Red slip on the exterior wall and the interior neck. It is not clear whether the base was slipped. Form: Jar with slightly insloped, outcurved neck. Direct rim and squared lip. Flat base. A shallow groove along the neck-body juncture. Use-wear: Not clear because of erosion.

WVS No.: 23B-33; Catalog No.: 310204 (Figure 8.41g)
Bag No.: Rim: 203 (14-2-1), 259 (14-3-3); Body: 254 (20-3-3), 253 (20-3-3), 200 (2-2-1), 259, 275 (2-3-1), 119 (2-1-1), 203 (14-2-1); Base: 254, 253, 200. Provenience: 23B2-3-3. Context: Floor. On the exterior floor in front of Structure M8-3. Fragments were found in an area 1 × 5 m (Units 2, 14, and 20). The vessel may have fallen from Structure M8-5. Condition: Reconstructible (40% present). Eroded. No clear traces of burning. It is likely that some fragments remained in unexcavated areas. Dimensions: Rim diameter: 10 cm (estimate); Maximum diameter: 24 cm (estimate); Height: 20 cm (rough estimate); Wall thickness: 0.4–0.7 cm; Sample weight: 378 g; Original weight: 945 g; Volume: 3,883 cm³. Coordinates: (46.70, 36.70) (estimate). Type: Unnamed volcanic ash undetermined. Paste, temper, and firing: Only the thin layer of the exterior surface and of the upper interior surface is oxidized in reddish yellow color (7.5YR6/6). The wide core remained black (7.5YR2.5/1). Fine. A small amount of volcanic ash temper (0.1 mm length). Common paste for Andres Red. Surface finish and decoration: The surface is almost completely eroded. Form: Closed bowl with

markedly incurved sides and restricted orifice. Direct rim and rounded lip. Flat base. Use-wear: Not clear because of erosion.

STRUCTURE M7-34 (HOUSE OF METATES): OPERATION 21A

North Room

WVS No.: 21A-1; Catalog No.: 310240
Bag No.: Rim: 364 (2-3-1), 163 (1-2-1); Body: 364, 365 (2-3-1); Base: 364, 365. Provenience: 21A2-3-1. Context: Floor. In the area between the front wall and the internal division in the northern part of the north room. Most of the recovered fragments were found in one concentration. Condition: Reconstructible (30% present). Eroded. Some fragments appear to be burned and blackened. Other fragments may have been scattered in the disturbance at the time of abandonment. Only some pieces of the shoulder and lower body were glued together. Dimensions: Rim diameter: 38 cm (rough estimate); Maximum diameter: 57 cm (rough estimate); Minimum opening: 21 cm (estimate); Height: 53 cm (rough estimate); Neck height: 12 cm (rough estimate); Wall thickness: 0.8–1.1 cm; Sample weight: 4,502 g; Original weight: 15,006 g; Volume: 58,565 cm³. Coordinates: (22.12, 8.11) (measured). Type: Encanto Striated with red wash. Paste, temper, and firing: Reddish yellow paste (5YR7/6). Coarse grain. A very large amount of calcite temper (0.5–2.5 mm diameter) and a small amount of ferruginous temper (0.5–1.2 mm diameter). The paste is completely oxidized. Surface finish and decoration: Relatively wide striation on the body and base below the shoulder. There are some remains of red wash on the exterior neck. Form: Jar with outcurved neck. Exterior-folded rim and rounded lip. Rounded base. Use-wear: Not clear because of the fragmentary state.

WVS No.: 21A-2; Catalog No.: 310437
Bag No.: Rim: 309 (8-3-3), 368 (16-3-1), 117 (8-1-1), 204 (6-2-2), 127 (8-1-2), 776 (50-3-2), 144 (20-1-2); Body: 309, 368, 380 (8-3-4); Base: 309, 368. Provenience: 21A8-3-3. Context: Floor. On the exterior floor in front of the north room. A significant portion of the recovered fragments were found in a loose concentration. Other pieces were scattered in an area 4 × 4 m. Condition: Reconstructible (25% present). Eroded. Traces of burning not clear. Dimensions: Rim diameter: 35 cm (estimate); Maximum diameter: 54 cm (rough estimate); Minimum opening: 25 cm (estimate); Height: 50 cm (rough estimate); Neck height: 10.5 cm (measured); Wall thickness: 0.7–0.8 cm;

Sample weight: 3,833 g; Original weight: 15,332 g; Volume: 49,001 cm³. Coordinates: (20.52, 5.26) (measured). Type: Encanto Striated. Paste, temper, and firing: Light brown paste (7.5YR6/4). Coarse grain. A large amount of calcite temper (0.5–2.0 mm diameter). The core is slightly dark. Surface finish and decoration: Striation on the body and base below the shoulder. The neck is unslipped. Form: Jar with outcurved neck. Exterior-folded rim and lip with a shallow groove. Rounded base. Use-wear: The base does not appear to be worn.

WVS No.: 21A-3; Catalog No.: 310418 (Figure 8.42a)
Bag No.: Rim: 351 (20-3-2), 392 (20-3-2); Body: 351, 392, 144 (20-1-2), 138 (20-1-1), 397 (20-3-3). Provenience: 21A20-3-2. Context: Floor. On the exterior floor in front of the north room. Most of the recovered fragments were found in a loose concentration. Condition: Reconstructible (35% present). Eroded. Traces of burning are not clear. The entire rim and a significant part of the neck were recovered, but only a small part of the body was found. Dimensions: Rim diameter: [exterior] 30.3 cm, [top] 29.3 cm (measured); Maximum diameter: 46 cm (rough estimate); Minimum opening: 19.9 cm (measured); Height: 54 cm (rough estimate); Neck height: 9.0 cm (measured); Wall thickness: 0.7–0.9 cm; Sample weight: 3,284 g; Original weight: 9,383 g; Volume: 37,997 cm³. Coordinates: (19.32, 5.37) (measured). Type: Encanto Striated. Paste, temper, and firing: Pink paste (5YR7/4). Coarse grain. A large amount of calcite temper (0.5–2.5 mm diameter). The paste is completely oxidized. Surface finish and decoration: Striation on the body below the shoulder. The neck and the interior are smoothed and unslipped. Form: Jar with outcurved neck. Exterior-folded rim and beveled-in lip. Use-wear: Not clear because of the fragmentary state.

WVS No.: 21A-4; Catalog No.: 310438
Bag No.: Rim: 380 (8-3-4), 309 (8-3-3), 232 (8-2-2), 378 (8-3-1), 397 (20-3-3), 237 (20-2-2), 127 (8-1-2), 138 (20-1-1); Body: 380, 309, 237, 127. Provenience: 21A8-3-4. Context: Floor. On the exterior floor in front of the north room. The recovered sherds were found in an area 2 × 2 m. Other fragments of the vessel may have been scattered in other areas. Condition: Partial (10% present). Badly eroded. Traces of burning not clear. Only the rim and neck are present. Dimensions: Rim diameter: 35 cm (estimate); Minimum opening: 21 cm (estimate); Neck height: 10 cm (estimate); Wall thickness: 0.8–1.0 cm; Sample weight: 1,881 g; Original weight: 18,810 g; Volume: not calculated.

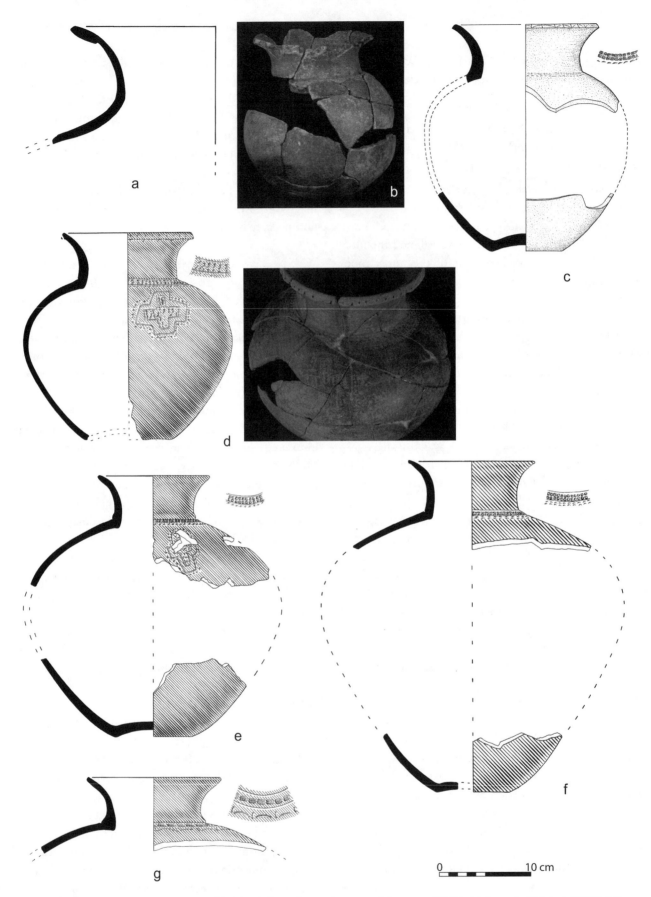

Figure 8.42. Complete and reconstructible vessels from the north room of Structure M7-34. (a) Encanto Striated, 21A20-3-2, Cat. 310418, WVS 21A-3. (b) Tinaja Red, 21A50-3-3, Cat. 310431, WVS 21A-5. c–g. Pantano Impressed. (c) 21A3-2-1, Cat. 310262, WVS 21A-6. (d) 21A2-2-3, Cat. 310239, WVS 21A-7. (e) 21A47-3-4, Cat. 310429, WVS 21A-8. (f) 21A48-3-1, Cat. 310430, WVS 21A-9. (g) 21A20-3-2, Cat. 310420, WVS 21A-10.

Coordinates: (20.48, 5.65) (estimate). Type: Cambio Unslipped or Encanto Striated. Paste, temper, and firing: Pink paste (5YR7/4). Coarse grain. A large amount of calcite temper (0.3–2.0 mm diameter). The core of the paste is dark. Surface finish and decoration: Unslipped, smoothed neck. Form: Jar with outcurved neck. Exterior-folded rim and beveled-in lip. Use-wear: Not clear because of the fragmentary state.

WVS No.: 21A-5; Catalog No.: 310431 (Figure 8.42b)
Bag No.: Rim: 937 (50-2-2); Body: 937, 1383 (51-3-4); Base: 1340 (50-3-3), 1383, 769 (50-3-1), 957 (51-2-2). Provenience: 21A50-3-3. Context: Floor. On the exterior floor in front of the north room. Fragments were found in an area 2 × 2 m. Condition: Reconstructible (80% present). Eroded. Burned and darkened. Dimensions: Rim diameter: [exterior] 14.8 cm, [top] 14.5 cm (measured); Maximum diameter: 18.6 cm (measured); Minimum opening: 8.0 cm (measured); Height: 16.9 cm (measured); Wall thickness: 0.7–0.8 cm; Sample weight: 1,068 g; Original weight: 1,335 g; Volume: 2,114 cm^3. Coordinates: (21.27, 2.62) (estimate). Type: Tinaja Red. Paste, temper, and firing: Reddish yellow paste (7.5YR7/6). Medium grain. A medium amount of calcite temper (0.3–1.5 mm diameter) and a very small amount of ferruginous temper (0.3–1.0 mm diameter). The paste appears to have darkened during burning. Surface finish and decoration: Red slip on the exterior. It is not clear whether the exterior base and the interior neck were slipped. Form: Jar with outcurved neck. Direct rim and squared lip. Incurved base. Use-wear: The edge of the base appears to be worn.

WVS No.: 21A-6; Catalog No.: 310262 (Figures 8.42c and 8.61n)
Bag No.: Rim: 404 (3-2-1), 169 (3-2-1); Body: 404, 169; Base: 775 (3-3-2), 404. Provenience: 21A3-2-1. Context: Floor. On the floor between the front wall and the front partition in the southern part of the north room. A significant portion of the fragments was in the wall-fall layer. The vessel was probably stored in a high location. Condition: Reconstructible (35% present). Relatively well preserved. Fire clouding on the exterior body, which may have been caused during the fire at the time of abandonment. Some fragments may have remained in an unexcavated area under a tree. Dimensions: Rim diameter: [exterior] 16.0 cm, [top] 14.8 cm (measured); Maximum diameter: 22 cm (estimate); Minimum opening: 9.0 cm (measured);

Height: 24 cm (rough estimate); Neck height: 5.2 cm (measured); Wall thickness: 0.5–1.0 cm; Sample weight: 923 g; Original weight: 2,637 g; Volume: 4,265 cm^3. Coordinates: (19.50, 7.90). Type: Pantano Impressed. Paste, temper, and firing: Reddish yellow paste (5YR6/6). Medium grain. A medium amount of calcite temper (0.5–1.8 mm diameter) and a small amount of ferruginous temper (0.5–2.0 mm diameter). The paste is completely oxidized. Surface finish and decoration: The entire exterior, including the base, and the interior neck have red slip. The exterior body is polished, but the interior and exterior neck surfaces are brushed or combed, leaving fine, horizontal lines. An incised line along the neck-body juncture. Cross-and-dots stamps and triangular impressions below it. Incisions on the lip. Form: Jar with outcurved neck and incurved base. Slightly interior thickened rim and squared lip. Use-wear: The edge of the exterior base is worn.

WVS No.: 21A-7; Catalog No.: 310239 (Figures 8.42d and 8.61o)
Bag No.: Rim: 164 (2-2-3); Body: 164, 377 (2-3-1). Provenience: 21A2-2-3. Context: Floor. In the area between the front wall and the internal division in the northern part of the north room. Most fragments were found in the wall-fall layer. The base and a part of the lower body may have been lost during the disturbance at the time of abandonment. Condition: Reconstructible (70% present). Relatively well preserved. No recognizable traces of burning. Most recovered sherds were glued together, and one side reaches to the edge of the base. Dimensions: Rim diameter: [exterior] 15.1 cm, [top] 14.3 cm (measured); Maximum diameter: 23.1 cm (measured); Minimum opening: 9.8 cm (measured); Height: 21.9 cm (measured); Neck height: 5.2 cm (measured); Wall thickness: 0.5–0.9 cm; Sample weight: 1,247 g; Original weight: 1,781 g; Volume: 3,716 cm^3. Coordinates: (22.55, 8.03) (estimate). Type: Pantano Impressed. Paste, temper, and firing: Light red paste (2.5YR7/6). Medium grain. A medium amount of calcite temper (0.3–1.5 mm diameter) and a small amount of ferruginous temper (0.5–2.0 mm diameter). The paste is completely oxidized. Surface finish and decoration: Red slip on the exterior surface and the interior neck. Rectangular stamps with two dots and a line, as well as triangular punctuations, below the neck-body juncture. Cross-shaped motifs defined by incised lines and filled with the same stamps on two sides of the shoulder. A series of small perforations through the exterior-thickened rim. Form:

Jar with outcurved neck. Exterior-thickened rim with perforations and squared lip. Probably incurved base. Use-wear: The top of the lip is worn, possibly from use.

WVS No.: 21A-8; Catalog No.: 310429 (Figures 8.42d and 8.61p)
Bag No.: Rim: 579 (47-3-4); Body: 579, 641 (48-2-1), 642 (48-2-2), 542 (48-1-2); Base: 579. Provenience: 21A47-3-4. Context: Floor. On the exterior floor northwest of the north room. Fragments were found in an area 1 × 3 m. Condition: Reconstructible (60% present). Badly eroded. Traces of burning are not clear. Dimensions: Rim diameter: [exterior] 11.4 cm, [top] 11.2 cm (measured); Maximum diameter: 28 cm (rough estimate); Minimum opening: 7.3 cm (measured); Height: 26 cm (rough estimate); Neck height: 4.6 cm (measured); Wall thickness: 0.4–0.8 cm; Sample weight: 1,512 g; Original weight: 2,520 g; Volume: 7,754 cm^3. Coordinates: (24.76, 5.14) (estimate). Type: Pantano Impressed. Paste, temper, and firing: Pink paste (5YR7/4). Medium grain. A medium amount of calcite temper (0.3–1.5 mm diameter) and a small amount of ferruginous temper (0.5–1.0 mm diameter). The paste is completely oxidized. Surface finish and decoration: Red slip on the exterior. It is not clear whether the exterior base and the interior neck were slipped. Cross-and-dots stamps and triangular punctuations below the neck-body juncture. Cross shape defined by incised lines and filled with triangular punctuations on one side of the shoulder. The other side of the shoulder, which is missing, may have had the same decoration. Form: Jar with outcurved neck. Direct rim and rounded lip. Incurved base. Thin-walled. Use-wear: Not clear because of erosion.

WVS No.: 21A-9; Catalog No.: 310430 (Figures 8.42f and 8.61q)
Bag No.: Rim: 749 (48-3-1); Body: 749, 542 (48-1-2), 642 (48-2-2); Base: 749, 542. Provenience: 21A48-3-1. Context: Floor. On the exterior floor northwest of the north room, near the corner of the peripheral wall. Fragments were found in a loose concentration. Condition: Reconstructible (40% present). Eroded. Traces of burning are not clear. Dimensions: Rim diameter: [exterior] 13.4 cm, [top] 13.3 cm (measured); Maximum diameter: 33 cm (rough estimate); Minimum opening: 7.9 cm (measured); Height: 33 cm (rough estimate); Neck height: 5.1 cm (measured); Wall thickness: 0.5–0.8 cm; Sample weight: 1,523 g; Original weight: 3,807 g; Volume: 13,790 cm^3. Coordinates: (24.33, 2.42) (measured). Type: Pantano Im-

pressed. Paste, temper, and firing: Pink paste (5YR8/4). Medium grain. A medium amount of calcite temper (0.2–1.2 mm diameter) and a small amount of ferruginous temper (0.8–2.0 mm diameter). The paste is completely oxidized. Surface finish and decoration: Red slip on the exterior. It is not clear whether the exterior base and the interior neck were slipped. Cross-and-dots stamps and triangular punctuations below the neck-body juncture. Form: Jar with outcurved neck. Direct rim and beveled-out lip. Incurved base. Use-wear: The edge of the base appears to be worn.

WVS No.: 21A-10; Catalog No.: 310420 (Figures 8.42g and 8.61r)
Bag No.: Rim: 350 (20-3-2), 138 (20-1-1), 397 (20-3-3); Body: 350, 392 (20-3-2), 138; Base: 237 (20-2-2). Provenience: 21A20-3-2. Context: Floor. On the exterior floor in front of the north room. Fragments were found in an area 1.5 × 1 m. Condition: Reconstructible (35% present). Eroded. Traces of burning are not clear. Dimensions: Rim diameter: [exterior] 14.4 cm, [top] 14.3 cm (measured); Maximum diameter: 33 cm (rough estimate); Minimum opening: 8.0 cm (measured); Height: 33 cm (rough estimate); Neck height: 4.7 cm (measured); Wall thickness: 0.6–0.8 cm; Sample weight: 1,268 g; Original weight: 3,622 g; Volume: 13,300 cm^3. Coordinates: (19.51, 5.44) (measured). Type: Pantano Impressed. Paste, temper, and firing: Pink paste (5YR7/4). Medium grain. A medium amount of calcite temper (0.1–1.2 mm diameter) and a small amount of ferruginous temper (0.5–2.0 mm diameter). The paste is completely oxidized. Surface finish and decoration: Red slip on the exterior. It is not clear whether the exterior base and the interior neck were slipped. Cross-and-dots stamps and incised lines below the neck-body juncture. Form: Jar with outcurved neck. Direct rim and pointed lip. Incurved base. Use-wear: Not clear because of erosion.

WVS No.: 21A-11; Catalog No.: 310241 (Figure 8.43a)
Bag No.: Rim: 365 (2-3-1); Body: 365, 364 (2-3-1); Base: 365, 364. Provenience: 21A2-3-1. Context: Floor. On the floor of the north room, near the northern front wall. Condition: Partial (20% present). Eroded. It appears to be burned and darkened. One side is reconstructed from the rim to the base. Dimensions: Rim diameter: 41 cm (estimate); Maximum diameter: 44 cm (estimate); Height: 18.2 cm (measured); Wall thickness: 0.7–0.9 cm; Sample weight: 1,110 g; Original weight: 5,550 g; Volume:

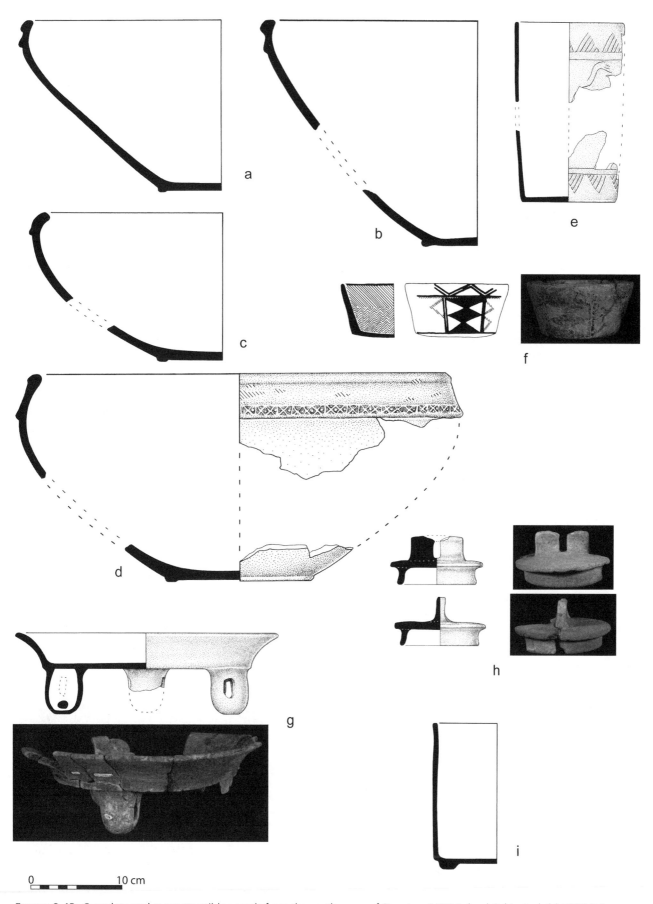

FIGURE 8.43. Complete and reconstructible vessels from the north room of Structure M7-34. (a–c) Subin Red. (a) 21A2-3-1, Cat. 310241, WVS 21A-11. (b) 21A49-3-2, Cat. 310427, WVS 21A-12. (c) 21A8-3-2, Cat. 310422, WVS 21A-13. (d) Chaquiste Impressed, 21A17-2-2, Cat. 310344, WVS 21A-14. (e) Corozal Incised, 21A50-3-2, Cat. 310435, WVS 21A-15. (f, g) Saxche-Palmar Polychrome. (f) 21A1-3-2, Cat. 310044, WVS 21A-16. (g) 21A50-2-2, Cat. 310433, WVS 21A-17. (h) Peten Gloss group undetermined, 21A50-3-3, Cat. 310434, WVS 21A-18. (i) Unnamed micaceous paste, 21A7-2-2, Cat. 310365, WVS 21A-19.

10,080 cm³. Coordinates: (21.49, 7.73) (measured). Type: Subin Red. Paste, temper, and firing: Light reddish brown paste (5YR6/4). Medium grain. A large amount of calcite temper (0.2–0.4 mm diameter) and a small amount of ferruginous temper (0.5–1.0 mm diameter). The paste is completely oxidized. Surface finish and decoration: The exterior rim and the interior surface are polished and have red slip. The exterior surface below the rim is only smoothed. Form: Bowl with incurved sides. Exterior-thickened rim and rounded lip. A ridge below the rim. Ring base. Use-wear: The ring base appears to be worn.

WVS No.: 21A-12; Catalog No.: 310427 (Figure 8.43b)
Bag No.: Rim: 304 (16-3-2), 874 (50-1-2), 368 (16-3-1); Body: 308 (8-3-4), 304, 764 (49-3-2), 757 (48-3-1), 127 (8-1-2), 379 (8-3-2); Base: 757, 764, 874. Provenience: 21A49-3-2. Context: Floor. On the exterior floor in front of the north room. Recovered fragments were scattered in an area 4 × 3 m, perhaps a result of the disturbance at the time of or after the abandonment. Condition: Reconstructible (25% present). Badly eroded. The base is heavily burned in black and reddish color. Dimensions: Rim diameter: 44 cm (estimate); Height: 24 cm (estimate); Wall thickness: 0.8–0.9 cm; Sample weight: 1,254 g; Original weight: 5,016 g; Volume: 25,069 cm³. Coordinates: (22.56, 3.77) (estimate). Type: Subin Red. Paste, temper, and firing: Pink paste (7.5YR7/4). Medium grain. A medium amount of calcite temper (0.2–0.8 mm diameter) and a small amount of ferruginous temper (0.5–1.0 mm diameter). The paste is completely oxidized. Surface finish and decoration: The surface is almost completely eroded. Form: Bowl with slightly incurved sides. Exterior-thickened rim and rounded lip. A ridge below the rim. Ring base. Use-wear: Not clear because of erosion.

WVS No.: 21A-13; Catalog No.: 310422 (Figure 8.43c)
Bag No.: Rim: 307 (8-3-2), 308 (8-3-4), 379 (8-3-2), 232 (8-2-2), 380 (8-3-4); Body: 307, 379, 308, 304 (16-3-2), 780 (51-3-2), 375 (16-3-4), 380, 214 (16-2-1); Base: 780. Provenience: 21A8-3-2. Context: Floor. On the exterior floor in front of the north room. Most of the recovered fragments were in two concentrations found against the front step of the room. Other pieces were scattered in an area 4 × 3 m. Condition: Reconstructible (55% present). Eroded. Traces of burning are not clear. Dimensions: Rim diameter: [interior] 38.7cm, [top] 40.0 cm (measured); Maximum diameter: 41.9 cm (measured); Height: 15.7 cm (estimate); Wall thickness: 0.7–0.9 cm; Sample weight:

2,140 g; Original weight: 3,890 g; Volume: 9,160 cm³. Coordinates: (21.72, 5.96) (measured). Type: Subin Red. Paste, temper, and firing: Reddish yellow paste (7.5YR7/6). Medium grain. A medium amount of calcite temper (0.3–0.8 mm diameter). In some parts the core is slightly dark. Surface finish and decoration: There are no visible traces of slip, probably due to erosion. Form: Bowl with incurved sides. Exterior-thickened rim and rounded lip. A ridge below the rim. Ring base. Use-wear: Not clear because of erosion.

WVS No.: 21A-14; Catalog No.: 310344 (Figures 8.43d and 8.61s)
Bag No.: Rim: 206 (17-2-2), 199 (6-2-1), 197 (17-2-1), 204 (6-2-2); Body: 197, 199, 121 (6-1-2), 134 (17-1-1); Base: 199, 206, 121. Provenience: 21A17-2-2. Context: Floor. On the floor of the north room near the southern front wall. Condition: Reconstructible (60% present). Badly eroded. Traces of burning are not clear. Dimensions: Rim diameter: 43 cm (estimate); Maximum diameter: 46 cm (estimate); Height: 22 cm (rough estimate); Wall thickness: 0.6–1.0 cm; Sample weight: 3,011 g; Original weight: 5,018 g; Volume: 18,853 cm³. Coordinates: (19.69, 7.87) (estimate). Type: Chaquiste Impressed. Paste, temper, and firing: Pink paste (7.5YR7/4). Medium grain. A medium amount of calcite temper (0.2–2.0 mm diameter) and a small amount of ferruginous temper (0.5–1.5 mm diameter). The paste is completely oxidized. Surface finish and decoration: The exterior surface above the ridge, the ridge, and the interior are polished, and there are some remains of red slip. The exterior below the ridge is smoothed and unslipped. Crosshatch-and-dots stamps on the ridge. Form: Bowl with incurved sides. Exterior-thickened rim and rounded lip. Ridge below the rim. Ring base. Use-wear: Not clear because of erosion.

WVS No.: 21A-15; Catalog No.: 310435 (Figure 8.43e)
Bag No.: Rim: 776 (50-3-2), 397 (20-3-3), 778 (51-3-1); Body: 776, 778, 138 (20-1-1), 237 (20-2-2), 937 (50-2-2), 780 (51-3-2), 602 (51-1-1), 860 (53-1-2), 239 (21-2-1), 861 (51-1-2), 146 (21-1-1), 228 (20-2-1), 1004 (54-2-1); Base: 776, 138, 239, 861, 602, 780. Provenience: 21A50-3-2. Context: Floor. Fragments were scattered in an area 5 × 4 m. Condition: Reconstructible (50% present). Eroded. Heavily burned and blackened. Dimensions: Rim diameter: 9.5 cm (estimate); Height: 19 cm (rough estimate); Wall thickness: 0.3–0.5 cm; Sample weight: 349 g; Original weight: 698 g; Volume: 919 cm³. Coordinates: (20.38, 3.68) (esti-

mate). Type: Corozal Incised. Paste, temper, and firing: Light reddish brown paste (5YR6/4). The paste color in most parts appears to have changed as a result of burning. Medium grain. A medium amount of calcite temper (0.2–0.8 mm diameter) and a medium amount of ferruginous temper (0.5–2.0 mm diameter). Surface finish and decoration: Red slip on the exterior. It is not clear whether the base was slipped. Striped triangles made by incised lines on the exterior. Form: Cylinder vase with vertical sides. Direct rim and rounded lip. Flat base. Use-wear: Not clear because of erosion.

WVS No.: 21A-16; Catalog No.: 310044 (Figure 8.43f). Bag No.: Rim: 446 (1-3-2); Body: 446; Base: 446. Provenience: 21A1-3-2. Context: Floor. On the floor in front of the bench of the north room. Condition: Reconstructible (97% present). Broken into one large fragment and two small pieces. All pieces were found together. No recognizable traces of burning. Dimensions: Rim diameter: [exterior] 11.6 cm, [top] 11.2 cm (measured); Height: 5.5 cm (measured); Wall thickness: 0.7 cm; Sample weight: 231 g; Original weight: 238 g; Volume: 276 cm³. Coordinates: (21.22, 9.00) (measured). Type: Saxche-Palmar Polychrome. Paste, temper, and firing: Reddish yellow paste (5YR6/6). Fine. A very small amount of calcite temper (0.1–0.3 mm diameter) and a very small amount of ferruginous temper (0.1 mm diameter). Dark core. Surface finish and decoration: The entire vessel, including the base, has cream underslip. Red and orange paints on the interior. Black paint on the rim. Red and black paints on the exterior wall. Form: Bowl with outflared sides. Direct rim and rounded lip. Slightly rounded base. Use-wear: Not clear because of erosion.

WVS No.: 21A-17; Catalog No.: 310433 (Figure 8.43g) Bag No.: Rim: 937 (50-2-2), 117 (8-1-1), 764 (49-3-2), 956 (49-2-2); Body: 937, 956; Base: 937, 117, 219 (8-2-1). Provenience: 21A50-2-2. Context: Floor. On the exterior floor in front of the north room. Fragments were found in an area 3 × 3 m. Condition: Reconstructible (80% present). Badly eroded. Some fragments are burned and darkened. Dimensions: Rim diameter: [exterior] 28.4 cm, [top] 28.1 cm (measured); Height: 8.5 cm (measured); Wall thickness: 0.6–0.8 cm; Sample weight: 636 g; Original weight: 795 g; Volume: 1,066 cm³. Coordinates: (21.33, 3.83) (estimate). Type: Saxche-Palmar Polychrome. Paste, temper, and firing: Pale red paste (2.5YR7/4). Fine grain. A small amount of calcite temper (0.1–0.7 mm diameter)

and a small amount of ferruginous temper (0.5–1.2 mm diameter). The paste is completely oxidized. Surface finish and decoration: Remains of orange paint over cream underslip. Form: Plate with outcurved sides. Direct rim and rounded lip. Flat base. Three hollow oven feet with two openings and a rattle. Use-wear: Not clear because of erosion.

WVS No.: 21A-18; Catalog No.: 310434 (Figure 8.43h) Bag No.: 1341 (50-3-3). Provenience: 21A50-3-3. Context: Floor. On the exterior floor in front of the north room, near the peripheral wall. It is not clear which vessel belonged to this lid. The diameter of a cylinder vase (Cat. 310435) found nearby is close to that of this lid, but its paste and surface decoration are different. Condition: Reconstructible (70% present). Eroded. One fragment is burned and darkened. Dimensions: Diameter: 10.3 cm (measured); Internal ridge diameter: 8.6 cm (measured); Wall thickness: 0.8 cm; Sample weight: 118 g; Original weight: 169 g. Coordinates: (21.39, 2.44) (estimate). Type: Peten Gloss group undetermined. Paste, temper, and firing: Pink paste (5YR7/4). Fine grain. A small amount of calcite temper (0.3–0.8 mm diameter) and a small amount of ferruginous temper (0.7–1.5 mm diameter). The paste is completely oxidized. Surface finish and decoration: Remains of red paint over thick cream underslip on the exterior. Form: Lid with a slab-shaped knob. Use-wear: Not clear.

WVS No.: 21A-19; Catalog No.: 310365 (Figure 8.43i) Bag No.: Rim: 194 (7-2-2), 257 (18-2-2); Body: 194; Base: 194. Provenience: 21A7-2-2. Context: Floor. In the wall fall behind the north room. The vessel was probably stored in the north room along the back wall. Missing pieces probably fell down the slope. Condition: Reconstructible (25% present). Badly eroded and burned. Dimensions: Rim diameter: 15 cm (estimate); Height: 15.3 cm (measured); Height without feet: 14.7 cm (measured); Wall thickness: 0.5–0.7 cm; Sample weight: 264 g; Original weight: 1,056 g; Volume: 1,775 cm³. Coordinates: (20.51, 13.45) (estimate). Type: Unnamed micaceous paste. Paste, temper, and firing: Reddish yellow paste (5YR7/6). Fine grain. A small amount of mica temper (0.2–0.4 mm diameter), a small amount of volcanic ash temper (0.1 mm length), and a very small amount of black particles (0.1 mm diameter). The paste is completely oxidized. Surface finish and decoration: Remains of red slip on the exterior. Form: Cylinder vase with vertical sides. Direct rim and rounded lip. Flat base. Three solid nubbin feet. Use-wear: Not clear because of erosion.

WVS No.: 21A-20; Catalog No.: 310050 (Figure 8.44)
Bag No.: Rim: 294 (16-3-4), 304 (16-3-2), 579 (47-2-4); Body: 294, 375 (16-3-4), 304, 214 (16-2-1), 215 (16-2-2), 130 (16-1-1), 178 (5-4-1), 295 (16-3-3), 574 (47-3-3), 141 (10-1-2); Base: 294, 375, 215. Provenience: 21A16-3-4. Context: Floor. On the exterior floor in front of the north room. Most fragments were found in one concentration. Several sherds were found in an area 3 × 2 m. One fragment came from Unit 10, over the back wall of the central room. This piece was surrounded by fragments found in Unit 16, and it is highly unlikely that just this part broke off. The piece was probably moved by a rodent or other animals post-depositionally. The vessel may have been stored in a high location along the exterior face of the front wall of the north room. Condition: Reconstructible (95% present). The slip is mostly eroded, but the modeled surface is rel-atively well preserved. Traces of burning are not clear ex-cept for some darkened parts of the exterior. Dimensions: Rim diameter: [interior] 11.6 cm, [top] 12.1 cm (mea-sured); Maximum diameter: [side to side] 16.7 cm, [front to back] 20.7 cm (measured); Height: 23.8 cm (measured); Wall thickness: 0.5 cm; Sample weight: 1,658 g; Original weight: 1,745 g; Volume: 5,932 cm³. Coordinates: (22.83, 5.42) (measured). Type: Unnamed modeled. Paste, tem-per, and firing: Very pale brown paste (10YR7/4). Fine grain. A small amount of calcite temper (0.1–0.3 mm di-ameter), a small amount of ferruginous temper (0.5–1.0 mm diameter), a very small amount of probable quartz temper (0.4–0.8 mm length), and a very small amount of volcanic ash temper (0.1 mm length). The paste is oxi-dized in most parts, but in some areas the core of the paste is dark. Surface finish and decoration: The front part is modeled into the shape of an old deity. There are some re-mains of orange slip. The entire exterior surface, except the base, was probably polished and slipped. There is a small perforation at each of the lower cheeks where some kind of decoration, such as a beard, was probably hung. Form: Model cylinder shape. Probably an incense burner. Direct rim and rounded lip. Flat base. Use-wear: The interior sur-face, except the interior base, is blackened, probably from use as an incense burner.

Center Room
WVS No.: 21A-21; Catalog No.: 310269 (Figure 8.45a)
Bag No.: Rim: 771 (4-3-1), 521 (3-2-4); Body: 771, 521, 260

(4-2-2). Provenience: 21A4-3-1. Context: Floor. On the floor of the central room in front of the northern front partition. A significant portion of the vessel may have been lost due to the disturbance at the time of aban-donment or may have remained in the unexcavated area under a tree. Condition: Reconstructible (40% present). Slightly eroded and burned. Some parts are reoxidized in red color whereas others are blackened. Only the neck and a part of the upper body are reconstructed. Dimensions: Rim diameter: [exterior] 19.6 cm, [top] 19.5 cm (mea-sured); Maximum diameter: 30 cm (estimate); Minimum opening: 12.8 cm (measured); Height: 30 cm (rough esti-mate); Neck height: 3.2 cm (measured); Wall thickness: 0.4–0.7 cm; Sample weight: 1,164 g; Original weight: 2,910 g; Volume: 11,445 cm³. Coordinates: (17.60, 8.41) (measured). Type: Cambio Unslipped. Paste, temper, and firing: Reddish yellow paste (5YR7/6). Coarse grain. A large amount of calcite temper (0.3–2.5 mm diameter) and a small amount of ferruginous temper (1.0–2.0 mm diam-eter). The core of the paste is dark in some parts. Surface finish and decoration: The surface is smoothed and un-slipped. Form: Jar with outcurved neck. Direct rim and beveled-out lip. Thin-walled. The short neck and direct rim are not commonly found in Cambio jars. Use-wear: Not clear because of the fragmentary state.

WVS No.: 21A-22; Catalog No.: 310263 (Figure 8.45b)
Bag No.: Body: 521 (3-2-4), 771 (4-3-1), 163 (1-2-1). Prove-nience: 21A3-2-4. Context: Floor. In the northern part of the central room between the front wall and the front par-tition. All fragments were found in the wall-fall layer. The vessel was probably placed in a high location. Condition: Reconstructible (40% present). Eroded. The exterior is darkened, possibly from fire. Some fragments probably re-mained in an unexcavated area under a tree. Dimensions: Maximum diameter: 42 cm (rough estimate); Minimum opening: 16 cm (estimate); Wall thickness: 0.8–1.0 cm; Sample weight: 2,044 g; Original weight: 5,110 g; Vol-ume: 28,483 cm³. Coordinates: (18.30, 8.30) (estimate). Type: Encanto Striated with angled neck and fine stria-tion. Paste, temper, and firing: Brown paste (7.5YR5/4). Coarse. A large amount of calcite temper, including shiny crystals. The paste is completely oxidized. Surface finish and decoration: The interior and exterior neck surfaces are smoothed. Striations right below the neck-body junc-ture. Striations are finer and shallower than those of com-mon Encanto jars. The outline of the striated area below the neck is better defined than in common Encanto jars.

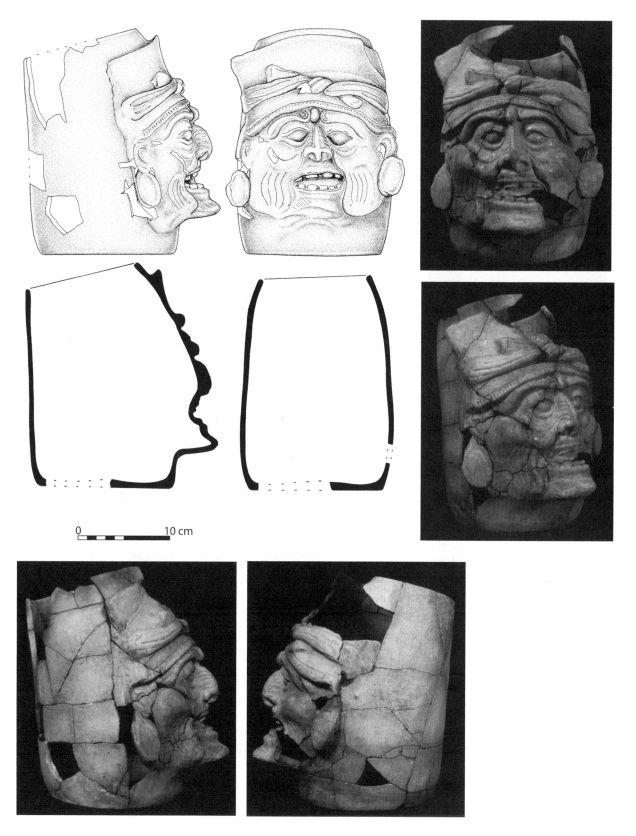

FIGURE 8.44. Reconstructible vessel from the north room of Structure M7-34. Unnamed modeled, 21A16-3-4, Cat. 310050, WVS 21A-20.

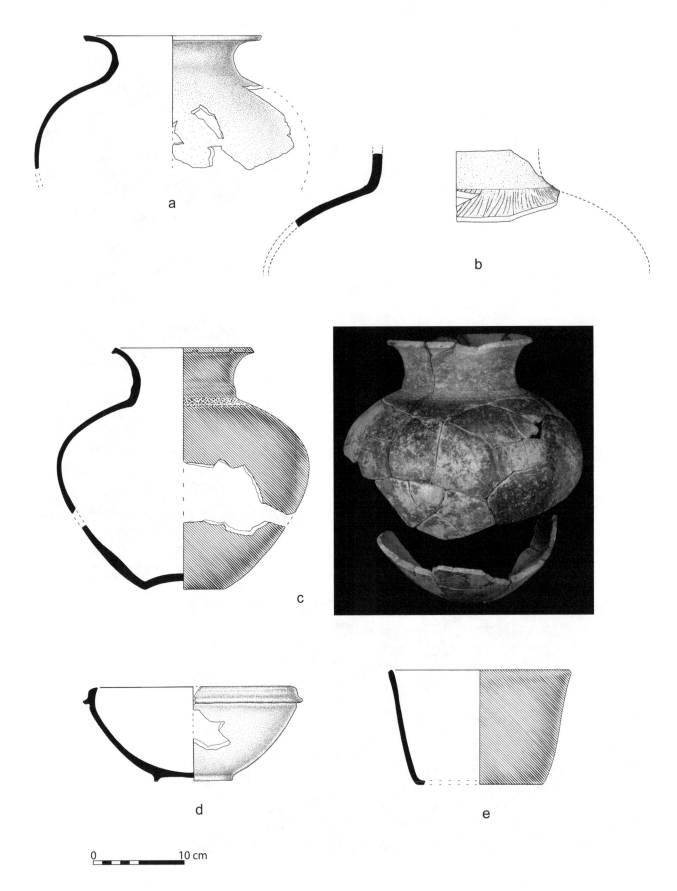

FIGURE 8.45. Complete and reconstructible vessels from the center room of Structure M7-34. (a) Cambio Unslipped, 21A4-3-1, Cat. 310269, WVS 21A-21. (b) Encanto Striated, 21A3-2-4, Cat. 310263, WVS 21A-22. (c) Pantano Impressed, 21A25-3-1, Cat. 310270, WVS 21A-23. (d) Subin Red, 21A4-3-1, Cat. 310342, WVS 21A-25. (e) Saxche-Palmar Polychrome, 21A20-1-2, Cat. 310432, WVS 21A-26.

Form: Jar. The neck shape is not clear. Angular neck-body juncture. The vessel probably had a rounded base. Use-wear: Not clear.

WVS No.: 21A-23; Catalog No.: 310270 (Figures 8.45c and 8.61t)
Bag No.: Rim: 743 (30-3-1), 744 (30-3-1); Body: 643 (25-3-1), 743, 487 (24-2-2), 746 (30-3-3); Base: 643, 744, 487. Provenience: 21A25-3-1. Context: Floor. On the room floor between the front wall and the front partition near the division between the center and south rooms. Most fragments were found in an area 1 × 0.5 m. Condition: Reconstructible (70% present). Eroded. No clear recognizable traces of burning. Dimensions: Rim diameter: [exterior] 15.8 cm, [top] 15.2 cm (measured); Maximum diameter: 27.2 cm (measured); Minimum opening: 9.3 cm (measured); Height: 27.4 cm (measured); Neck height: 5.8 cm (measured); Wall thickness: 0.7–1.1 cm; Sample weight: 1,727 g; Original weight: 2,467 g; Volume: 6,734 cm^3. Coordinates: (14.40, 8.22) (estimate). Type: Pantano Impressed. Paste, temper, and firing: Reddish yellow paste (5YR7/6). Medium grain. A large amount of calcite temper (0.1–1.5 mm diameter) and a small amount of ferruginous temper (0.5–1.2 mm diameter). The paste is completely oxidized. Surface finish and decoration: Red slip on the entire exterior, including the base, and on the interior neck. The interior and exterior neck surfaces are smoothed. Cross-hatch stamps and triangular impressions below the neck-body juncture. Form: Jar with outcurved neck and incurved base. Slightly exterior-thickened rim and squared lip. Use-wear: The edge of the exterior base is worn.

WVS No.: 21A-24; Catalog No.: 310229 (Figure 8.46a and 8.46b)
Bag No.: Rim: 643, 120 (4-1-2), 487 (24-2-2); Body: 643, 120, 249 (13-2-2), 457 (25-2-1); Base: 643 (25-3-1), 457. Provenience: 21A25-3-1. Context: Floor. In the southern part of the front area of the center room between the front wall and the dividing wall. Most fragments were found in one concentration. A small amount was found in nearby units (Units 4 and 13). Condition: Reconstructible (55% present). Slightly eroded. Some fragments were darkened by fire after the vessel broke. The darkening of one side of the base appears to have been caused during the original firing because the dark surface on the ring base is worn by use. Dimensions: Rim diameter: 41 cm (estimate); Maximum diameter: 46 cm (estimate); Height: 21.3 cm (measured);

Wall thickness: 0.8–0.9 cm; Sample weight: 2,758 g; Original weight: 5,015 g; Volume: 15,703 cm^3. Coordinates: (15.06, 8.29) (measured). Type: Subin Red. Paste, temper, and firing: Light brown paste (7.5YR6/4). Medium grain. A large amount of calcite temper, including shiny crystals (0.3–1.5 mm diameter). The paste is completely oxidized. Surface finish and decoration: The interior is well smoothed, but the exterior is roughly smoothed. Red slip on the exterior rim above the ridge. It is not clear whether the interior was slipped. Form: Open bowl with incurved sides. Exterior-thickened rim and rounded lip. Flat base with ring. Use-wear: The ring base is worn. Use-wear on the interior is not clear because of erosion. No traces of use on fire.

WVS No.: 21A-25; Catalog No.: 310342 (Figure 8.45d)
Bag No.: Rim: 771 (4-3-1), 260 (4-2-2), 521 (3-2-4), 775 (3-3-2); Body: 771, 260; Base: 771, 260. Provenience: 21A4-3-1. Context: Floor. On the floor of the center room between the front wall and the front partition. A significant portion of the recovered fragments was in one concentration. Some parts may have been lost because of disturbance during or after the abandonment, or may have remained in the unexcavated area under a tree. Condition: Reconstructible (30% present). Slightly eroded. Burned and blackened. Dimensions: Rim diameter: 22 cm (estimate); Maximum diameter: 24 cm (estimate); Height: 9.8 cm (measured); Wall thickness: 0.5–0.6 cm; Sample weight: 558 g; Original weight: 1,860 g; Volume: 1,544 cm^3. Coordinates: (17.92, 8.49) (measured). Type: Subin Red. Paste, temper, and firing: Pink paste (5YR7/4). Medium grain. A large amount of calcite temper (0.1–1.2 mm diameter) and a small amount of ferruginous temper (0.5–1.0 mm diameter). The paste is completely oxidized. Surface finish and decoration: The interior surface and the exterior rim above the ridge are polished and appear to have had weak red slip. The exterior surface below the ridge is only smoothed. Form: Bowl with incurved sides. Exterior-thickened rim and pointed lip. A ridge below the rim. Ring base. Use-wear: The interior surface and the ring base do not appear to be worn.

WVS No.: 21A-26; Catalog No.: 310432 (Figure 8.45e)
Bag No.: Rim: 397 (20-3-3), 380 (8-3-4), 144 (20-1-2), 138 (20-1-1), 392 (20-3-2); Body: 138, 237 (20-2-2), 397, 144, 380, 645 (53-3-1), 146 (21-1-1), 232 (8-2-2), 1291 (60-3-1); Base: 138, 645, 237, 144. Provenience: 21A20-1-2. Context: Floor. On the exterior floor in front of the center room. Recovered

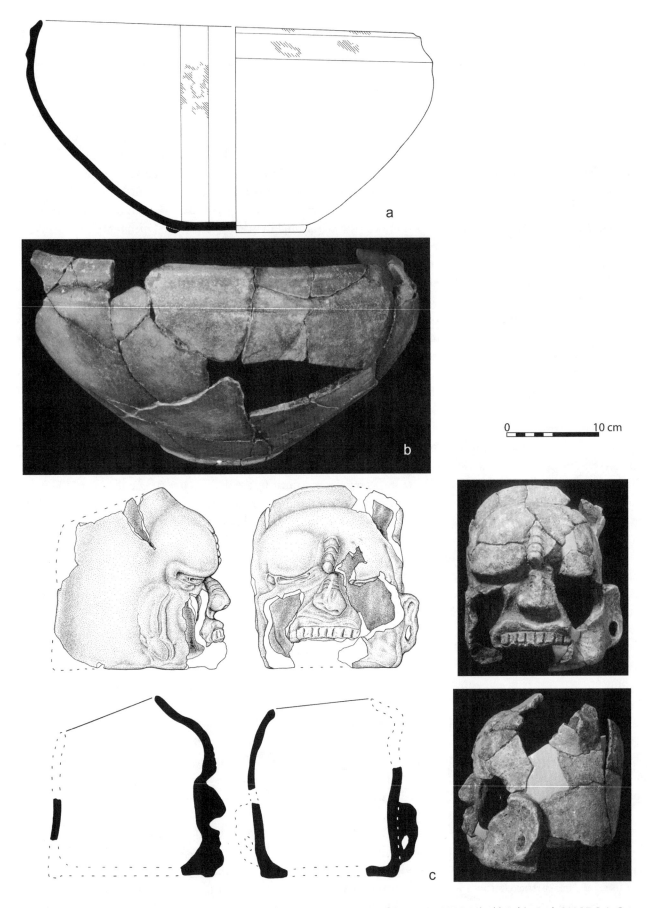

Figure 8.46. Complete and reconstructible vessels from the center room of Structure M7-34. (a, b) Subin Red, 21A25-3-1, Cat. 310229, WVS 21A-24. (c) Peten Gloss group undetermined, 21A21-3-3, Cat. 310385, WVS 21A-27.

0   10 cm

fragments were scattered in an area 6 × 4 m, perhaps a result of disturbance at the time of or after abandonment. Condition: Reconstructible (60% present). Badly eroded. Some pieces appear to be burned and darkened. Dimensions: Rim diameter: 20 cm (estimate); Height: 12.2 cm (measured); Wall thickness: 0.6–0.8 cm; Sample weight: 548 g; Original weight: 913 g; Volume: 1,461 cm³. Coordinates: (18.14, 4.18) (estimate). Type: Saxche-Palmar Polychrome. Paste, temper, and firing: Red paste (2.5YR5/8). Fine grain. A small amount of calcite temper (0.1–0.3 mm diameter) and small amount of ferruginous temper (0.5–1.5 mm diameter). The paste is completely oxidized. The paste is redder than in common Saxche-Palmar vessels. Surface finish and decoration: Some remains of weak red paint over cream underslip on the exterior. Form: Bowl with outflared sides. Direct rim and rounded lip. Flat base. Use-wear: Not clear because of erosion.

WVS No.: 21A-27; Catalog No.: 310385 (Figure 8.46c)
Bag No.: Rim: 1391 (52-3-3), 138 (20-1-1), 144 (20-1-2), 226 (39-1-1); Body: 138, 407 (21-3-3), 451 (24-1-2), 181 (33-1-1), 228 (20-2-1), 144, 1391, 722 (28-3-4); Base: 1398 (83-3-1), 226, 414 (23-1-2). Provenience: 21A21-3-3. Context: Floor. On the exterior in front of the structure, inside the peripheral walls. Fragments were found in an area 12 × 4 m in front of the north, central, and south rooms. They may have been intentionally scattered or they may be refuse. Condition: Reconstructible (70% present). Dimensions: Rim diameter: 10–12.5 cm (estimate); Maximum diameter: 16.0–18.5 cm (measured); Height: 14.1–18.1 cm (measured); Wall thickness: 0.9 cm; Sample weight: 1,163 g; Original weight: 1,661 g; Volume: 2,590 cm³. Coordinates: (16.50, 4.76) (estimate). Type: Peten Gloss group undetermined. Paste, temper, and firing: Pink paste (7.5YR7/4). Medium grain. A medium amount of calcite temper (0.3–1.5 mm diameter) and a small amount of ferruginous temper (0.8–1.5 mm diameter). The paste is completely oxidized. Surface finish and decoration: Remains of red slip on the exterior. Form: Modeled incense burner. The face of the Death God. Direct rim and rounded lip. Flat base. Use-wear: Not clear because of erosion.

South Room
WVS No.: 21A-28; Catalog No.: 310273 (Figure 8.24d)
Bag No.: Rim: 739 (29-3-2), 738 (29-3-1), 261 (29-1-2); Body: 746 (30-3-3), 738, 739, 156 (29-1-1), 261, 525 (30-2-3); Base: 746. Provenience: 21A30-3-3. Context: Floor. On the room floor in front of the bench of the south room. The

base and a significant portion of the body were found in one concentration in the area between the front partitions. The rim was found 2 m to the west of this concentration near the front wall. The vessel may have been placed on the floor between the front partitions and have fallen forward when the building collapsed. Condition: Reconstructible (40% present). Eroded. Traces of burning not clear. We reconstructed the rim and the base but not the body. Dimensions: Rim diameter: [exterior] 41.0 cm, [top] 38.9 cm (measured); Maximum diameter: 60 cm (rough estimate); Minimum opening: 26.4 cm (measured); Height: 70 cm (rough estimate); Neck height: 12 cm (estimate); Wall thickness: 0.9–1.1 cm; Sample weight: 10,351 g; Original weight: 25,878 g; Volume: 93,194 cm³. Coordinates: (12.62, 8.95) (measured). Type: Cambio Unslipped with red wash. Paste, temper, and firing: Light brown paste (7.5YR6/4). Coarse. A large amount of calcite temper (0.5–1.8 mm diameter) and a small amount of ferruginous temper (0.5–2.5 mm diameter). The core is dark. Surface finish and decoration: Red wash on the exterior neck. The body is smoothed and unslipped. Form: Jar with outcurved neck. Exterior-folded rim and pointed lip. Flat base with ring. Use-wear: The base is barely worn, perhaps because the vessel was rarely moved.

WVS No.: 21A-29; Catalog No.: 310416 (Figure 8.24e)
Bag No.: Rim: 755 (43-3-3); Body: 755, 754 (43-3-3), 493 (43-2-3), 477 (43-2-2). Provenience: 21A43-3-3. Context: Floor. On the exterior floor in front of the south room. Condition: Reconstructible (50% present). Eroded. Traces of burning not clear. Missing parts may be in unexcavated areas. Dimensions: Rim diameter: 17 cm (rough estimate); Maximum diameter: 40 cm (rough estimate); Minimum opening: 11.5 cm (estimate); Height: 48 cm (rough estimate); Neck height: 7 cm (estimate); Wall thickness: 0.7–1.2 cm; Sample weight: 2,565 g; Original weight: 5,130 g; Volume: 33,947 cm³. Coordinates: (8.55, 6.12) (estimate). Type: Cambio Unslipped, angled neck, scratched. Paste, temper, and firing: Pink paste (7.5YR7/4). Coarse grain. A large amount of calcite temper, including shiny crystals (0.3–2.0 mm diameter). The paste is completely oxidized. The paste is similar to that of common Cambio/Encanto jars. Surface finish and decoration: Rough surface with irregular scratched patterns on the body. Smoothed neck and interior surface. Form: Jar with outcurved neck. Angular neck-body juncture. Use-wear: Not clear because of the fragmentary state.

WVS No.: 21A-30; Catalog No.: 310417 (Figure 8.47a)
Bag No.: Rim: 755 (43-3-3); Body: 755, 752 (43-3-1), 271 (43-1-1), 475 (43-2-1), 400 (43-1-2). Provenience: 21A43-3-3. Context: Floor. On the exterior floor in front of the south room. Most of the recovered fragments were found in a loose concentration. Missing parts may have remained in unexcavated areas. Condition: Reconstructible (30% present). Eroded. Traces of burning not clear. Dimensions: Rim diameter: [exterior] 22.5 cm, [top] 21.0 cm (measured); Maximum diameter: 42 cm (rough estimate); Minimum opening: 15.5 cm (measured); Height: 51 cm (rough estimate); Neck height: 10.4 cm (measured); Wall thickness: 0.6–0.7 cm; Sample weight: 1,571 g; Original weight: 5,236 g; Volume: 32,869 cm^3. Coordinates: (9.02, 6.16) (measured). Type: Encanto Striated. Paste, temper, and firing: Pink paste (7.5YR7/4). Medium grain. A medium amount of calcite temper, including shiny crystals (0.3–1.2 mm diameter). The paste is completely oxidized. The paste is finer than that of common Encanto jars. Surface finish and decoration: Striations below the neck-body juncture. Striations are shallower than those of common Encanto jars, but their patterns are similar. Form: Jar with outcurved neck. Exterior-thickened rim and rounded lip. The rim and neck shapes are different from those of common Encanto jars. Thin-walled. Use-wear: Not clear because of the incomplete state.

WVS No.: 21A-31; Catalog No.: 310267 (Figure 8.47b)
Bag No.: Rim: 525 (30-2-3), 250 (30-1-2); Body: 525, 518 (30-2-2); Base: 525. Provenience: 21A30-2-3. Context: Floor. In the wall-fall layer in front of the central part of the bench of the south room. Most fragments were found in one concentration. The vessel was probably placed on the bench and fell forward. Condition: Reconstructible (70% present). We did not reconstruct the body part. Many fragments are darkened, which may have been caused by burning. A horizontal breakage on the shoulder where the striation ends. Dimensions: Rim diameter: [exterior] 34.5 cm, [top] 33.5 cm (measured); Maximum diameter: 54 cm (rough estimate); Minimum opening: 19.8 cm (measured); Height: 58 cm (rough estimate); Neck height: 11.5 cm (measured); Wall thickness: 0.8–1.1 cm; Sample weight: 9,231 g; Original weight: 13,187 g; Volume: 58,002 cm^3. Coordinates: (13.40, 9.61) (estimate). Type: Encanto Striated. Paste, temper, and firing: Reddish yellow paste (5YR6/6). Coarse. A large amount of calcite temper, including shiny crystals (0.3–1.5 mm diameter). In some parts the interior wall is dark. Surface finish

and decoration: Unslipped. Striation below the shoulder. The exterior neck is smoothed. Form: Jar with outcurved neck and probably with rounded base. Exterior-folded rim and grooved lip. Use-wear: None clear on the rim.

WVS No.: 21A-32; Catalog No.: 310228 (Figure 8.47c)
Bag No.: Rim: 736 (42-3-1), 728 (33-3-3), 735 (42-3-2); Body: 736, 1318 (55-3-3). Provenience: 21A42-3-1. Context: Floor. On the exterior floor in front of the south room. Recovered fragments were found in an area 4 × 4 m. Missing pieces may have remained in unexcavated areas. Only the rim and neck were reconstructed. The vessel may have been placed on the exterior floor near some metates. Condition: Reconstructible (20% present). Badly eroded. Some parts appear to be burned and darkened. Dimensions: Rim diameter: [exterior] 31.4 cm, [top] 30.4 cm (measured); Maximum diameter: 53 cm (rough estimate); Minimum opening: 21.4 cm (measured); Height: 62 cm (rough estimate); Neck height: 10.0 cm (measured); Wall thickness: 0.8–1.0 cm; Sample weight: 3,698 g; Original weight: 18,490 g; Volume: 70,061 cm^3. Coordinates: (9.65, 4.49) (estimate). Type: Encanto Striated. Paste, temper, and firing: Pink paste (7.5YR7/4). Coarse grain. A large amount of calcite temper (0.3–2.5 mm diameter). The paste is completely oxidized. Surface finish and decoration: Striation on the body below the shoulder. Form: Jar with outcurved neck. Exterior-folded rim and beveled-in lip. Use-wear: Not clear because of the fragmentary state.

WVS No.: 21A-33; Catalog No.: 310404 (Figure 8.47d)
Bag No.: Rim: 1318 (55-3-3), 975 (55-2-2); Body: 1318, 975. Provenience: 21A55-33-3. Context: Floor. On the exterior floor in front of the south room. The recovered fragments were found in an area 2 × 2 m. It is probable that other parts of the vessel were scattered in other areas. Condition: Reconstructible (20% present). Eroded. Some parts appear to be burned and darkened. Dimensions: Rim diameter: [exterior] 17.3 cm, [top] 16.6 cm (measured); Maximum diameter: 32 cm (estimate); Minimum opening: 11.4 cm (measured); Height: 32 cm (rough estimate); Neck height: 4.0 cm (measured); Wall thickness: 0.7–0.8 cm; Sample weight: 655 g; Original weight: 3,275 g; Volume: 13,668 cm^3. Coordinates: (11.72, 2.52) (estimate). Type: Encanto Striated. Paste, temper, and firing: Reddish yellow paste (5YR6/8). Coarse grain. A large amount of calcite temper (0.2–1.0 mm diameter). The paste is completely oxidized. Surface finish and decoration: Striations on the

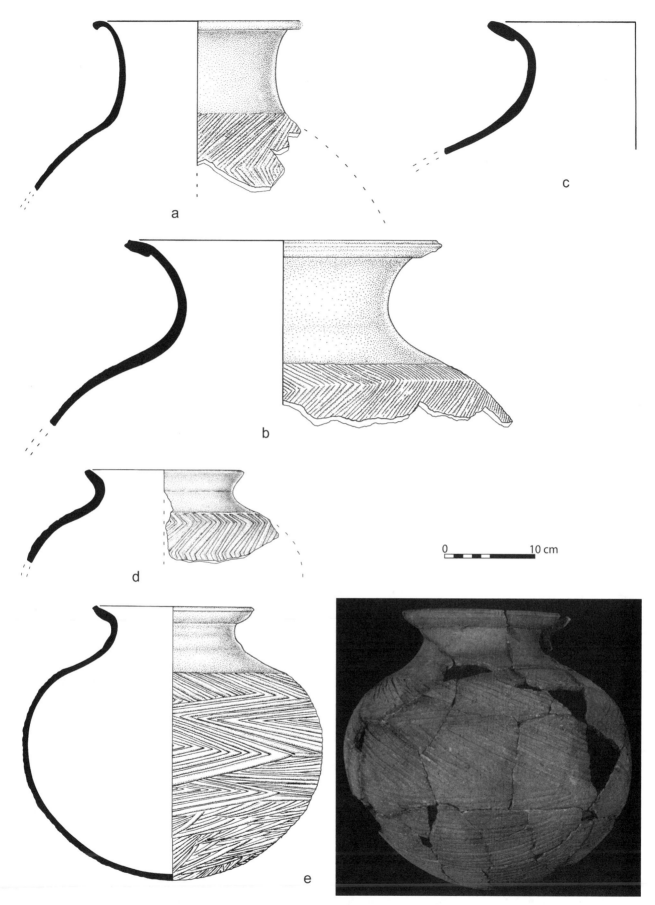

FIGURE 8.47. Complete and reconstructible vessels from the south room of Structure M7-34. Encanto Striated. (a) 21A43-3-3, Cat. 310417, WVS 21A-30. (b) 21A30-2-3, Cat. 31A30-2-3, WVS 21A-31. (c) 21A42-3-1, Cat. 310228, WVS 21A-32. (d) 21A55-3-3, Cat. 310404, WVS 21A-33. (e) 21A33-1-1, Cat. 310482, WVS 21A-35.

0   10 cm

body below the shoulder. Unslipped, smoothed neck. Form: Jar with outcurved neck. Shorter neck than in common Encanto jars. Exterior-folded rim and beveled-in lip. Use-wear: Not clear because of the fragmentary state.

WVS No.: 21A-34; Catalog No.: 310394

Bag No.: Rim: 725 (42-3-4); Body: 725, 475 (43-2-1). Provenience: 21A42-3-4. Context: Floor. On the exterior floor in front of the south room. The recovered fragments were found in an area 1 × 2 m. Other sherds may have been scattered in other areas, or the remaining parts may have been kept as a partial vessel. Condition: Partial (15% present). Eroded. Traces of burning not clear. Only the neck and upper body were recovered. Dimensions: Rim diameter: 30 cm (estimate); Maximum diameter: 42 cm (rough estimate); Minimum opening: 22 cm (estimate); Height: 45 cm (rough estimate); Neck height: 10.0 cm (measured); Wall thickness: 0.7–1.3 cm; Sample weight: 1,512 g; Original weight: 10,080 g; Volume: 30,001 cm³. Coordinates: (8.45, 5.72) (estimate). Type: Encanto Striated. Paste, temper, and firing: Pink paste (7.5YR7/4). Coarse grain. A large amount of calcite temper (0.2–2.0 mm diameter). The paste is completely oxidized. Surface finish and decoration: Striations on the body below the shoulder. Unslipped, smoothed neck. Form: Jar with outcurved neck. Exterior-folded rim and beveled-in lip. Use-wear: Not clear because of the fragmentary state.

WVS No.: 21A-35; Catalog No.: 310482 (Figure 8.47e)

Bag No.: Rim: 181 (33-1-1), 720 (33-3-1); Body: 181, 150 (28-1-1), 714 (28-3-3), 739 (29-3-2), 722 (28-3-4), 720, 156 (29-1-1), 231 (34-1-2); Base: 719 (23-3-3), 722, 714, 150. Provenience: 21A33-1-1. Context: Floor. On the exterior floor in front of the south room. Fragments were found in an area 4 × 4 m. A small portion was on the front step of the room, and a large part was in an area in front of it. The base is broken into small fragments. It appears that the vessel was originally hung and fell on the base. Condition: Reconstructible (85% present). Eroded. Some parts are burned. All fragments were refitted. Dimensions: Rim diameter: [exterior] 17.4 cm, [top] 16.7 cm (measured); Maximum diameter: 30.8 cm (measured); Minimum opening: 11.7 cm (measured); Height: 29.0 cm (measured); Neck height: 6.0 cm (measured); Wall thickness: 0.5–0.6 cm; Sample weight: 2,641 g; Original weight: 3,107 g; Volume: 12,131 cm³. Coordinates: (11.90, 5.90) (estimate). Type: Encanto Striated. Paste, temper, and firing: Reddish yellow paste (7.5YR6/6). Medium grain.

A medium amount of calcite temper (0.3–1.0 mm diameter). The paste is completely oxidized. The paste is finer than that of common Cambio/Encanto vessels. Surface finish and decoration: Striations on the body below the shoulder. The base has parallel striations, not radiating ones. Form: Jar with outcurved neck. Exterior-folded rim and beveled-in lips. Rounded base. Use-wear: None clearly recognizable on the base.

WVS No.: 21A-36; Catalog No.: 310402 (Figures 8.49d and 8.61w)

Bag No.: Rim: 728 (33-3-3), 1358 (55-3-4); Body: 1317 (55-3-3), 728, 785 (55-3-2); Base: 1358. Provenience: 21A55-3-3. Context: Floor. On the exterior floor in front of the south room. Recovered fragments were found in an area 2 × 3 m. Condition: Reconstructible (50% present). Eroded. Traces of burning not clear. Dimensions: Rim diameter: [exterior] 13.8 cm, [top] 13.5 cm (measured); Maximum diameter: 40 cm (rough estimate); Minimum opening: 8.2 cm (measured); Height: 39 cm (rough estimate); Neck height: 5.4 cm (measured); Wall thickness: 0.5–1.1 cm; Sample weight: 1,938 g; Original weight: 3,876 g; Volume: 23,647 cm³. Coordinates: (11.30, 2.27) (estimate). Type: Pantano Impressed. Paste, temper, and firing: Pink paste (7.5YR7/4). Medium grain. A medium amount of calcite temper (0.3–1.3 mm diameter) and a small amount of ferruginous temper (0.5–1.3 mm diameter). The paste is completely oxidized. Surface finish and decoration: Red slip on the exterior, including the base. The interior neck does not appear to be slipped. Cross-and-dots stamps and triangular punctuations below the neck-body juncture. Form: Jar with outcurved neck. Direct rim and rounded lip. Use-wear: The edge of the exterior base is worn.

WVS No.: 21A-37; Catalog No.: 310280 (Figures 8.48a, 8.48b, and 8.61u)

Bag No.: Rim: 760 (30-2-4), 525 (30-2-3), 518 (30-2-2), 248 (31-1-2); Body: 760, 525, 518, 248, 250 (30-1-2), 746 (30-3-3), 470 (25-2-3), 781 (30-3-4); Base: 760. Provenience: 21A30-2-4. Context: Floor. In the northern part of the south room between the bench face and the front partition. Most fragments were found in the wall-fall layer. A few pieces were found on the bench. The vessel was probably placed on the bench or in a higher location. Condition: Reconstructible (85% present). Eroded. One side of the exterior base and parts of the exterior body are darkened. It is not clear whether the fire clouding was caused during the fire at the time of abandonment. Dimensions:

Rim diameter: [exterior] 15.5 cm, [top] 14.5 cm (estimate); Maximum diameter: 37.9 cm (measured); Minimum opening: 8.0 cm (measured); Height: 35.3 cm (rough estimate); Neck height: 5.4 cm (measured); Wall thickness: 0.6–1.1 cm; Sample weight: 4,004 g; Original weight: 4,711 g; Volume: 18,942 cm^3. Coordinates: (13.31, 9.62) (estimate). Type: Pantano Impressed. Paste, temper, and firing: Reddish yellow paste (5YR6/6). Medium grain. A large amount of calcite temper (0.3–0.6 mm diameter) and a small amount of ferruginous temper (0.5–1.3 mm diameter). The paste is completely oxidized. Surface finish and decoration: Red slip on the entire exterior, including the base. It is not clear whether the interior neck is slipped. Cross-hatch stamps and triangular punctuations below the neck-body juncture. Form: Jar with outcurved neck and incurved base. Rim is slightly everted horizontally. Rounded lip. Use-wear: The edge of the base appears to be worn.

WVS No.: 21A-38; Catalog No.: 310272 (Figures 8.48c, 8.48d, and 8.61v)
Bag No.: Rim: 746 (30-3-3); Body: 765 (34-3-2), 766 (34-3-3), 738 (29-3-1), 739 (29-3-2), 740 (29-3-3); Base: 765. Provenience: 21A34-3-2. Context: Floor. On the front step of the south room. A significant portion of the fragments was found in a loose concentration. Other pieces were found in an area 2 × 2 m. Condition: Reconstructible (70% present). Badly eroded. Severely burned. One side of the vessel was completely reconstructed. Dimensions: Rim diameter: [exterior] 13.4 cm, [top] 12.9 cm (measured); Maximum diameter: 36.3 cm (measured); Minimum opening: 7.2 cm (measured); Height: 33.7 cm (measured); Neck height: 5.2 cm (measured); Wall thickness: 0.6–1.7 cm; Sample weight: 3,681 g; Original weight: 5,258 g; Volume: 15,452 cm^3. Coordinates: (11.63, 7.13) (measured). Type: Pantano Impressed. Paste, temper, and firing: Pink paste (5YR7/4). Medium grain. A medium amount of calcite temper (0.2–1.3 mm diameter) and a small amount of ferruginous temper (0.5–2.0 mm diameter). The paste is slightly dark in some parts, which may be due to burning. Surface finish and decoration: Red slip on the exterior. It is not clear whether the exterior base and the interior neck were slipped. Quincunx stamps and triangular punctuations along (not below) the neck-body juncture. The placement of stamps is unique. Form: Jar with outcurved neck. Direct rim and rounded lip. Incurved base. Less angular neck-body juncture than in common Pantano. The wall of the lower body is thicker

than in common Pantano jars. Use-wear: The edge of the base appears to be worn.

WVS No.: 21A-39; Catalog No.: 310410 (Figure 8.49a and 8.49b)
Bag No.: Rim: 475 (43-2-1); Body: 475, 751 (34-3-1), 755 (43-3-3), 770 (43-3-5); Base: 765 (34-3-2). Provenience: 21A43-3-2. Context: Floor. On the front step in front of the front wall of the south room. A significant part of the recovered fragments was found in one concentration. Others were scattered in an area 1.5 × 1 m along the front step. Condition: Reconstructible (35% present). Eroded. Traces of burning not clear. Dimensions: Rim diameter: [exterior] 14.5 cm, [top] 14.3 cm (measured); Maximum diameter: 30 cm (rough estimate); Minimum opening: 8.7 cm (measured); Height: 30 cm (rough estimate); Neck height: 4.4 cm (measured); Wall thickness: 0.5–0.7 cm; Sample weight: 1,054 g; Original weight: 3,011 g; Volume: 10,541 cm^3. Coordinates: (9.50, 6.89) (estimate). Type: Pantano Impressed. Paste, temper, and firing: Light red paste (2.5YR7/6). Medium grain. A large amount of calcite temper (0.2–1.0 mm diameter) and a small amount of ferruginous temper (0.5–1.2 mm diameter). The paste is completely oxidized. Surface finish and decoration: Red slip on the exterior surface, including the base. It is not clear whether the interior neck was slipped. Two lines of triangular punctuations below the neck-body juncture. Form: Jar with outcurved sides. Direct rim and squared lip. Incurved base. Use-wear: The edge of the base appears to be worn.

WVS No.: 21A-40; Catalog No.: 310409 (Figure 8.49c)
Bag No.: Rim: 754 (43-3-3); Body: 755 (43-3-3), 754, 475 (43-2-1), 493 (43-2-3); Base: 755. Provenience: 21A43-3-3. Context: Floor. On the exterior in front of the south room. Most of the recovered fragments were found in one concentration. Missing parts may have remained in the nearby unexcavated area. Condition: Reconstructible (40% present). Eroded. It appears to be burned and darkened. Dimensions: Rim diameter: 48 cm (estimate); Maximum diameter: 50 cm (estimate); Height: 16.7 cm (measured); Wall thickness: 0.7–0.8 cm; Sample weight: 2,370 g; Original weight: 5,925 g; Volume: 14,987 cm^3. Coordinates: (8.70, 6.46) (measured). Type: Chaquiste Impressed. Paste, temper, and firing: Reddish yellow paste (5YR6/6). Medium grain. A medium amount of calcite temper (0.2–1.0 mm diameter) and a small amount of ferruginous temper (0.3–0.8 mm diameter). The paste is

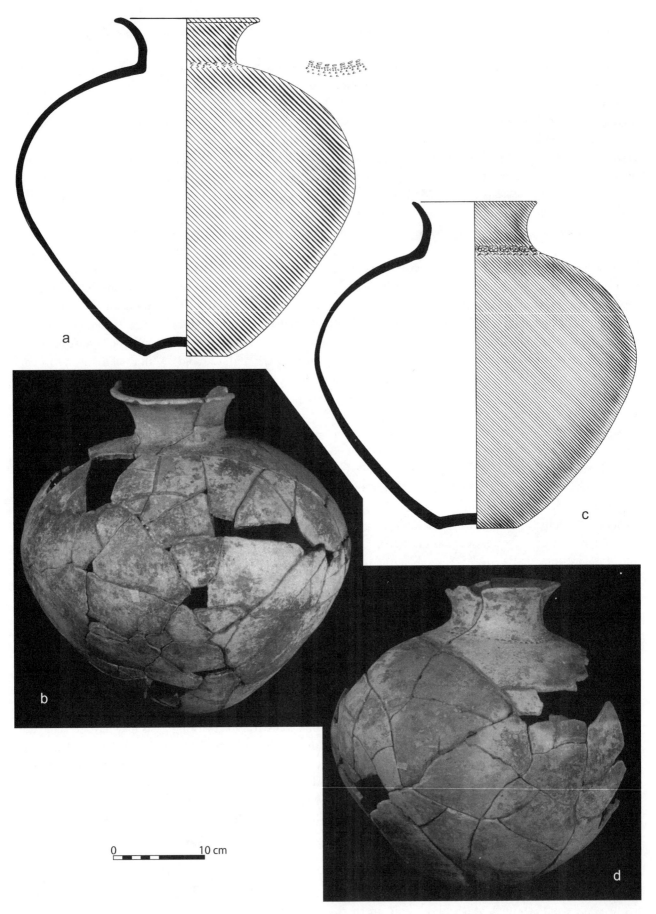

FIGURE 8.48. Complete and reconstructible vessels from the south room of Structure M7-34. Pantano Impressed. (a, b) 21A30-2-4, Cat. 310280, WVS 21A-37. (c, d) 21A34-3-2, Cat. 310272, WVS 21A-38.

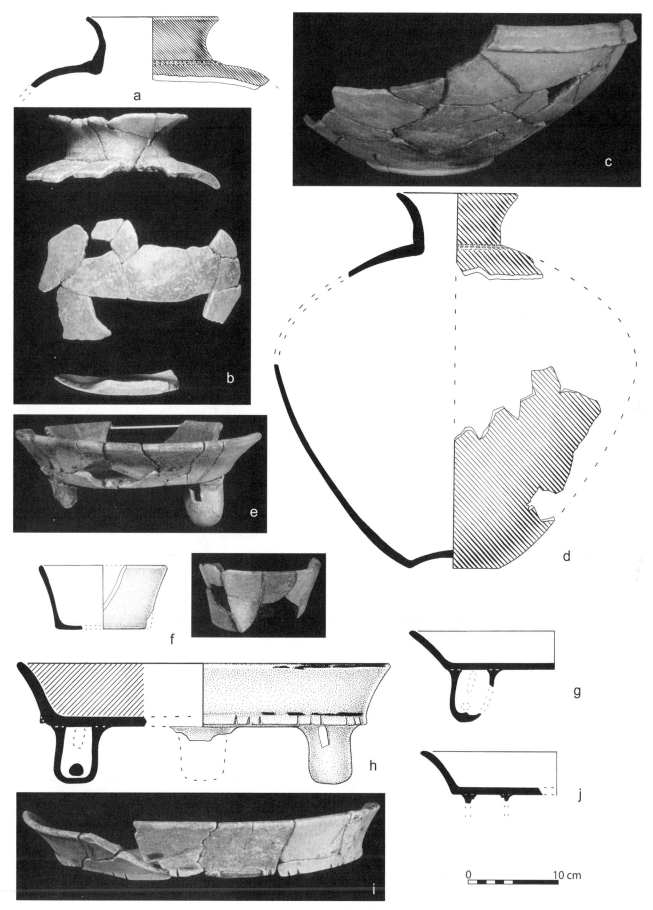

FIGURE 8.49. Complete and reconstructible vessels from the south room of Structure M7-34. (a, b) Pantano Impressed, 21A43-3-2, Cat. 310410, WVS 21A-39. (c) Chaquiste Impressed, 21A43-3-3, Cat. 310409, WVS 21A-40. (d) Pantano Impressed, 21A55-3-3, Cat. 310402, WVS 21A-36. (e–j) Saxche-Palmar Polychrome. (e) 21A33-3-2, Cat. 310387, WVS 21A-42. (f) 21A36-1-1, Cat. 310271, WVS 21A-41. (g) 21A56-3-2, Cat. 310375, WVS 21A-43. (h, i) 21A56-3-2, Cat. 310374, WVS 21A-44. (j) 21A54-3-4, Cat. 310389, WVS 21A-45.

completely oxidized. Surface finish and decoration: No recognizable remains of slip. Stamps on the ridge. Form: Bowl with slightly incurved sides. Exterior-thickened rim and pointed lip. Ridge below the rim. Ring base. Use-wear: Not clear because of erosion.

WVS No.: 21A-41; Catalog No.: 310271 (Figure 8.49f)
Bag No.: Rim: 241 (36-1-2), 535 (35-2-2); Body: 227 (35-1-1), 241, 535; Base: 241, 535. Provenience: 21A36-1-1. Context: Floor. In the southern part of the bench of the south room. A few fragments were found in the wall-fall layer in front of the bench. Condition: Reconstructible (65% present). Badly eroded. Severely burned in dark color. Dimensions: Rim diameter: [exterior] 12.3 cm, [top] 12.0 cm (measured); Height: 6.7 cm (measured); Wall thickness: 0.4–0.5 cm; Sample weight: 140 g; Original weight: 215 g; Volume: 485 cm^3. Coordinates: (10.90, 10.10) (estimate). Type: Saxche-Palmar Polychrome. Paste, temper, and firing: Reddish yellow paste (7.5YR6/6). Fine. A small amount of calcite temper (0.1–0.3 mm diameter) and a very small amount of possible volcanic ash temper (0.1 mm length). The paste is completely oxidized. Surface finish and decoration: The surface is mostly eroded. Remains of red paint over cream underslip on the interior surface. Form: Open bowl with flared sides and flat base. Direct rim and rounded lip. Use-wear: Not clear because of erosion.

WVS No.: 21A-42; Catalog No.: 310387 (Figure 8.49e)
Bag No.: Rim: 720 (33-3-1), 724 (33-3-2); Body: 181 (33-1-1); Base: 181, 724. Provenience: 21A33-3-2. Context: Floor. On the exterior floor in front of the south room. Fragments were found in an area 2 × 2 m. Condition: Reconstructible (40% present). Badly eroded. Some parts are burned and darkened. Dimensions: Rim diameter: [exterior] 28.6 cm, [top] 28.1 cm (measured); Height: 10.0 cm (estimate); Height without feet: 4.1 cm (measured); Wall thickness: 0.7–0.9 cm; Sample weight: 534 g; Original weight: 1,335 g; Volume: 1,250 cm^3. Coordinates: (11.30, 5.03) (estimate). Type: Saxche-Palmar Polychrome. Paste, temper, and firing: Reddish yellow paste (7.5YR8/6). Fine grain. A small amount of calcite temper (0.1–0.3 mm diameter) and a small amount of ferruginous temper (0.5–2.0 mm diameter). The paste is completely oxidized. Surface finish and decoration: The surface is completely eroded. Form: Plate with outflared sides. Direct rim and rounded lip. Flat base. Use-wear: Not clear because of erosion.

WVS No.: 21A-43; Catalog No.: 310375 (Figure 8.49g)
Bag No.: Rim: 1287 (56-3-2), 1288 (56-3-2), 400 (43-1-2), 412 (42-1-2), 606 (42-2-1), 265 (42-1-1); Base: 1287, 1283 (56-3-1), 940 (56-2-1), 1288, 412, 728 (33-3-3), 181 (33-1-1), 534 (33-2-2), 609 (42-2-2), 617 (55-1-1). Provenience: 21A56-3-2. Context: Floor. On the exterior floor in front of the south room. Fragments were scattered in an area 3 × 4 m, which may be due to disturbance during or after abandonment. Condition: Reconstructible (80% present). Eroded. Burned and darkened. The vessel appears to have been burned when it was complete, and then it was broken. A few sherds were differentially burned after the vessel broke. Dimensions: Rim diameter: [exterior] 25.7 cm, [top] 25.2 cm (measured); Height: 8.9 cm (measured); Height without feet: 5.1 cm (measured); Wall thickness: 0.6–0.8 cm; Sample weight: 640 g; Original weight: 800 g; Volume: 1,256 cm^3. Coordinates: (9.54, 3.66) (estimate). Type: Saxche-Palmar Polychrome. Paste, temper, and firing: Pink paste (7.5YR8/4). Fine grain. A small amount of calcite temper (0.2–1.5 mm diameter) and a small amount of ferruginous temper (0.8–1.2 mm diameter). The paste is completely oxidized. Surface finish and decoration: Remains of red and orange paints over cream underslip. Form: Plate with outflared sides. Direct rim and rounded lip. Flat base. Three hollow oven feet with two openings and a rattle. Use-wear: Not clear because of erosion.

WVS No.: 21A-44; Catalog No.: 310374 (Figure 8.49h and 8.49i)
Bag No.: Rim: 1283 (56-3-1), 784 (55-3-1), 1358 (55-3-4), 975 (55-2-2), 1004 (54-2-1), 412 (42-1-2), 728 (33-3-3); Body: 1283, 784, 1358, 1365 (53-3-2), 720 (33-3-1), 236 (33-1-2); Base: 1283. Provenience: 21A56-3-2. Context: Floor. On the exterior floor in front of the south room. Some fragments were found in a small concentration, and others were scattered in an area 6 × 4 m. Condition: Reconstructible (50% present). Eroded. Slightly burned. Dimensions: Rim diameter: 40 cm (estimate); Height: 11.9 cm (measured); Height without feet: 6.5 cm (measured); Wall thickness: 0.9–1.4 cm; Sample weight: 1,649 g; Original weight: 3,298 g; Volume: 4,161 cm^3. Coordinates: (9.72, 2.79) (measured). Type: Saxche-Palmar Polychrome. Paste, temper, and firing: Reddish yellow paste (5YR6/8). Fine grain. A small amount of calcite temper (0.1–0.5 mm diameter) and a small amount of ferruginous temper (0.5–1.5 mm diameter). The paste is completely oxidized. Surface finish and decoration: Remains of red, black, and

orange paints over cream underslip on the interior surface. Form: Plate with outflared sides. Direct rim and rounded lip. Flat base. Three hollow oven feet with two openings and a rattle. Use-wear: Not clear because of erosion.

WVS No.: 21A-45; Catalog No.: 310389 (Figure 8.49j)
Bag No.: Rim: 1303 (54-3-4), 156 (29-1-1), 534 (33-2-2), 1358 (55-3-4), 1288 (56-3-2); Body: 1303; Base: 1303, 1358. Provenience: 21A54-3-4. Context: Floor. On the exterior floor in front of the south room. Fragments were found in an area 4 × 6 m. Condition: Reconstructible (40% present). Eroded. Some fragments were burned and darkened after the vessel broke. No fragments of feet were recovered, and the broken facets of feet are heavily worn or eroded. The vessel may have been used after the feet broke off. Dimensions: Rim diameter: 32 cm (estimate); Height: 10 cm (rough estimate); Height without feet: 5.4 cm (measured); Wall thickness: 0.7–0.8 cm; Sample weight: 656 g; Original weight: 1,640 g; Volume: 1,597 cm^3. Coordinates: (12.49, 3.83) (estimate). Type: Saxche-Palmar Polychrome. Paste, temper, and firing: Pink paste (5YR8/4). Fine grain. A small amount of calcite temper (0.1–0.5 mm diameter) and a small amount of ferruginous temper (0.3–0.8 mm diameter). The core of the paste is slightly dark in some parts, which may be due to burning. Surface finish and decoration: Remains of red and orange paints over cream underslip on the interior surface. Form: Plate with slightly outcurved sides. Direct rim and rounded lip. Flat base. Three hollow feet with two openings. Use-wear: Broken edges of feet appear to be worn.

WVS No.: 21A-46; Catalog No.: 310379
Bag No.: Rim: 1314 (56-3-4), 947 (77-2-2), 724 (33-3-2); Body: 1314, 728 (33-3-3), 735 (42-3-2), 784 (55-3-1). Provenience: 21A56-3-4. Context: Floor. On the exterior floor in front of the south room. Fragments were found in an area 5 × 4 m. Condition: Reconstructible (50% present). Eroded. Burned and darkened. Dimensions: Rim diameter: 15 cm (estimate); Height: 7 cm (estimate); Wall thickness: 0.5–0.6 cm; Sample weight: 155 g; Original weight: 310 g; Volume: 648 cm^3. Coordinates: (8.62, 3.64) (measured). Type: Saxche-Palmar Polychrome. Paste, temper, and firing: Reddish yellow paste (5YR7/6). Fine grain. A small amount of calcite temper (0.1–0.5 mm diameter) and a small amount of ferruginous temper (0.5–0.8 mm diameter). The paste is completely oxidized. Surface finish and decoration: Remains of red paint over cream underslip on the interior surface. The exterior surface is

eroded. Form: Bowl with incurved sides. Direct rim and rounded lip. Use-wear: Not clear because of the fragmentary state.

North of the Structure

WVS No.: 21A-47; Catalog No.: 310367 (Figure 8.50a)
Bag No.: Rim: 562 (38-3-3), 561 (38-3-3); Body: 561, 562, 517 (38-2-1), 262 (40-1-1). Provenience: 21A38-3-3. Context: Floor. On the exterior floor north of the structure. Most fragments were found in one loose concentration. The vessel may have been placed on the exterior floor. Condition: Reconstructible (60% present). Eroded. Traces of burning not clear. The vessel was not reconstructed. Dimensions: Rim diameter: 26 cm (estimate); Maximum diameter: 35 cm (rough estimate); Height: 39 cm (rough estimate); Wall thickness: 0.6–0.7 cm; Sample weight: 2,126 g; Original weight: 3,543 g; Volume: 17,082 cm^3. Coordinates: (24.71, 7.43) (measured). Type: Manteca Impressed. Paste, temper, and firing: Pink paste (7.5YR7/4). Coarse grain. A very large amount of calcite temper (0.8–2.5 mm diameter). The paste is completely oxidized. Surface finish and decoration: The surface is plain except for a line of small impressions made with a nail. Form: Jar with outcurved neck. Folded rim and beveled-in lip. Use-wear: Not clear because of the fragmentary state.

WVS No.: 21A-48; Catalog No.: 310231 (Figure 8.50b)
Bag No.: Rim: 575 (40-3-3), 591 (40-3-4), 580 (40-3-1), 571 (39-3-4), 494 (40-2-4); Body: 575, 580, 494, 591, 478 (40-2-2), 485 (40-2-3). Provenience: 21A40-3-3. Context: Floor. On the exterior floor and on the side step north of the structure. Most of the recovered fragments were found in a loose concentration in an area 2 × 2 m. Missing pieces may have remained in the unexcavated area. The vessel may have been placed on the side step or on the exterior floor. Condition: Reconstructible (50% present). Eroded. Some parts appear to be burned and darkened. Only the rim and neck were reconstructed. Dimensions: Rim diameter: [exterior] 32.1 cm, [top] 30.6 cm (measured); Maximum diameter: 55 cm (rough estimate); Minimum opening: 21.8 cm (measured); Height: 60 cm (rough estimate); Neck height: 11.5 cm (measured); Wall thickness: 0.8–1.0 cm; Sample weight: 8,449 g; Original weight: 16,898 g; Volume: 64,595 cm^3. Coordinates: (24.76, 10.38) (estimate). Type: Encanto Striated. Paste, temper, and firing: Pink paste (7.5YR7/4). Coarse grain. A large amount of calcite temper (0.3–2.0 mm diameter). The paste is completely oxidized. Surface finish and

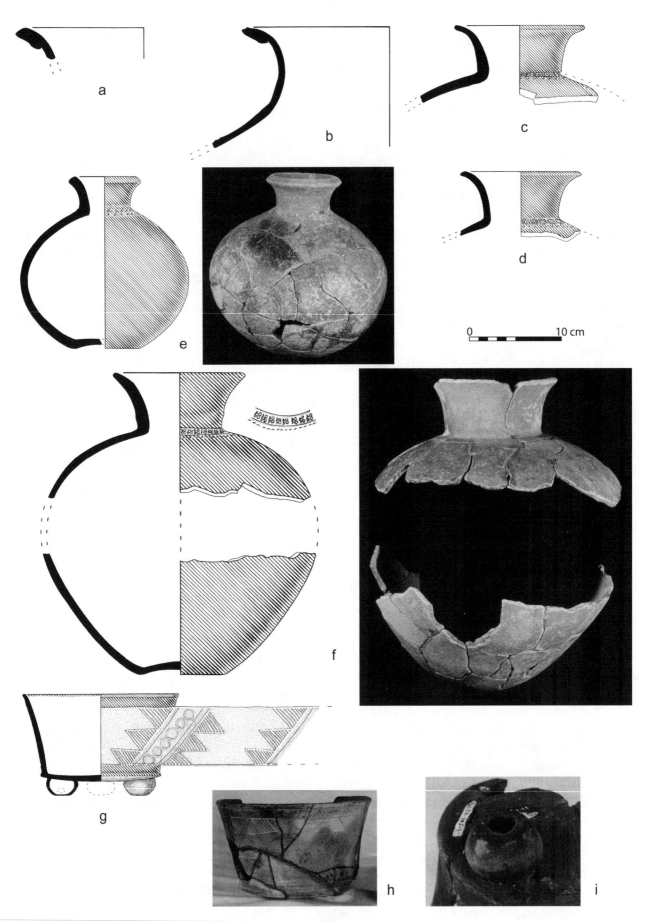

FIGURE 8.50. Complete and reconstructible vessels from the north exterior of Structure M7-34. (a) Manteca Impressed, 21A38-3-3, Cat. 310367, WVS 21A-47. (b) Encanto Striated, 21A40-3-3, Cat. 310231, WVS 21A-48. (c–f) Pantano Impressed. (c) 21A39-3-3, Cat. 310395, WVS 21A-49. (d) 21A39-3-4, Cat. 310398, WVS 21A-50. (e) 21A39-3-3, Cat. 310226, WVS 21A-51. (f) 21A40-3-3, Cat. 310392, WVS 21A-52. (g–i) Corozal Incised, 21A39-3-3, Cat. 310399, WVS 21A-53. (i) Close-up of a worn foot of WVS 21A-53 (not to scale).

decoration: Striation on the body and base below the shoulder. Form: Jar with outcurved neck. Folded rim and beveled-in lip. Rounded base. Use-wear: The center of the base appears to be slightly worn.

WVS No.: 21A-49; Catalog No.: 310395 (Figures 8.50c and 8.61x)
Bag No.: Rim: 564 (39-3-3); Body: 564, 565 (39-3-3), 571 (39-3-4), 591 (40-3-4); Base: 564, 571, 591. Provenience: 21A39-3-3. Context: Floor. On the exterior floor north of the structure. A significant portion of the recovered fragments was found in one concentration. Condition: Reconstructible (30% present). Eroded. Traces of burning not clear. Dimensions: Rim diameter: 13.5 cm (estimate); Maximum diameter: 30 cm (rough estimate); Minimum opening: 7.1 cm (measured); Height: 30 cm (rough estimate); Neck height: 5.6 cm (measured); Wall thickness: 0.7–1.1 cm; Sample weight: 1,104 g; Original weight: 3,680 g; Volume: 9,337 cm^3. Coordinates: (25.86, 8.59) (measured). Type: Pantano Impressed. Paste, temper, and firing: Reddish yellow paste (5YR7/6). Medium grain. A medium amount of calcite temper (0.1–1.3 mm diameter) and a small amount of ferruginous temper (0.5–1.8 mm diameter). The paste is completely oxidized. Surface finish and decoration: Red slip on the exterior, including the base. It is not clear whether the interior neck was slipped. Cross-and-dots stamps and triangular punctuations below the neck-body juncture. Incised decoration on the shoulder, but it is only partially preserved. Form: Jar with outcurved neck. Direct rim and rounded lip. Incurved base. Use-wear: Not clear because of erosion.

WVS No.: 21A-50; Catalog No.: 310398 (Figures 8.50d and 8.61y)
Bag No.: Rim: 571 (39-3-4), 581 (41-2-1); Body: 571, 564 (39-3-3); Base: 571. Provenience: 21A39-3-4. Context: Floor. On the exterior floor north of the structure. Most fragments were found in a loose concentration. Condition: Reconstructible (70% present). Badly eroded. Some parts of the vessel are darkened and appear to be burned. Only the neck and base were restored. Dimensions: Rim diameter: [exterior] 13.5 cm, [top] 12.9 cm (measured); Maximum diameter: 34 cm (rough estimate); Minimum opening: 7.3 cm (rough estimate); Height: 33 cm (rough estimate); Neck height: 4.6 cm (measured); Wall thickness: 0.5–0.8 cm; Sample weight: 2,356 g; Original weight: 3,365 g; Volume: 13,907 cm^3. Coordinates: (24.80, 9.35) (measured). Type: Pantano Impressed. Paste, temper, and

firing: Reddish yellow paste (5YR7/6). Coarse grain. A large amount of calcite temper (0.3–1.5 mm diameter) and a small amount of ferruginous temper (0.5–1.5 mm diameter). The paste is completely oxidized. The paste is coarser than that of common Tinaja/Pantano jars but finer than that of Cambio/Encanto jars. Surface finish and decoration: Red slip on the exterior. It is not clear whether the exterior base and the interior neck are slipped. X-and-dots stamps and triangular punctuations below the neck-body juncture. Form: Jar with outcurved neck. Direct rim and rounded lip. Incurved base. Use-wear: Although the base is badly eroded, its edge appears to be heavily worn and rounded.

WVS No.: 21A-51; Catalog No.: 310226 (Figure 8.50e)
Bag No.: Rim: 564 (39-3-3); Body: 564, 512 (39-2-4); Base: 564. Provenience: 21A39-3-3. Context: Floor. On the exterior floor north of the structure. Most fragments were found in one concentration. The vessel appears to have broken in an upside-down position, but the rim is not damaged. It is probable that the vessel was placed upside-down on the exterior or rolled from a nearby place. Condition: Reconstructible (95% present). The upper body is relatively well preserved whereas the lower body is eroded, reflecting its upside-down position. Dimensions: Rim diameter: [exterior] 8.0 cm, [top] 6.6 cm (measured); Maximum diameter: 18.3 cm (measured); Minimum opening: 3.6 cm (measured); Height: 18.2 cm (measured); Neck height: 3.6 cm (measured); Wall thickness: 0.9–1.1 cm; Sample weight: 1,195 g; Original weight: 1,258 g; Volume: 2,016 cm^3. Coordinates: (25.78, 8.72) (measured). Type: Pantano Impressed. Paste, temper, and firing: Pink paste (5YR7/4). Medium grain. A medium amount of calcite temper (0.2–1.0 mm diameter) and a small amount of ferruginous temper (0.5–1.3 mm diameter). The paste is completely oxidized. Surface finish and decoration: Red slip on the exterior. It is not clear whether the base was slipped. The interior neck is unslipped. Triangular punctuations below the neck-body juncture. Form: Jar with outcurved neck. Direct rim and squared lip. Incurved base. Use-wear: The base is eroded, but its edge appears to be worn.

WVS No.: 21A-52; Catalog No.: 310392 (Figures 8.50f and 8.61z)
Bag No.: Rim: 591 (40-3-4); Body: 591, 575 (40-3-3), 571 (39-3-4), 235 (39-1-2), 244 (39-2-1); Base: 575, 591. Provenience: 21A40-3-3. Context: Floor. On the exterior floor north of the structure. Condition: Reconstructible (75%

present). Eroded. Traces of burning not clear. Dimensions: Rim diameter: 13.5cm (estimate); Maximum diameter: 31 cm (estimate); Minimum opening: 8.2 cm (measured); Height: 29 cm (estimate); Neck height: 6.1 cm (measured); Wall thickness: 0.6–1.0 cm; Sample weight: 2,475 g; Original weight: 3,300 g; Volume: 9,686 cm³. Coordinates: (25.27, 10.53) (estimate). Type: Pantano Impressed. Paste, temper, and firing: Pink paste (5YR7/4). Medium grain. A medium amount of calcite temper (0.3–1.2 mm diameter) and a small amount of ferruginous temper (0.5–1.5 mm diameter). The paste is completely oxidized. Surface finish and decoration: Red slip on the exterior, including the base. Weak red slip on the interior neck. Quincunx stamps and triangular punctuations below the neck-body juncture. Form: Jar with outcurved neck. Direct rim and rounded lip. Incurved base. Use-wear: The edge of the base is worn.

WVS No.: 21A-53; Catalog No.: 310399 (Figure 8.50g–i)
Bag No.: Rim: 565 (39-3-3); Body: 565, 508 (39-2-3), 512 (39-2-4), 571 (39-3-4), 575 (40-3-3); Base: 565, 561 (38-3-3). Provenience: 21A39-3-3. Context: Floor. On the exterior floor north of the structure. Fragments were found in an area 1 × 3 m. Condition: Reconstructible (80% present). Eroded. Burned and blackened. Dimensions: Rim diameter: [exterior] 16.5 cm, [top] 16.1 cm (measured); Height: 10.6 cm (measured); Height without feet: 9.0 cm (measured); Wall thickness: 0.6 cm; Sample weight: 393 g; Original weight: 491 g; Volume: 904 cm³. Coordinates: (25.15, 8.74) (estimate). Type: Corozal Incised. Paste, temper, and firing: Pink paste (7.5YR7/4). Fine grain. A small amount of calcite temper (0.3–0.8 mm diameter). The paste is completely oxidized. Surface finish and decoration: Red bands on the rim and above the body-base juncture. The rest of the exterior wall is unslipped. Incisions on the wall depicting circles and striped triangles. Form: Bowl with slightly outcurved sides. Exterior-thickened rim and rounded lip. Flat base. Three hollow spherical feet, each with a small perforation. Use-wear: The base of a foot appears to be worn through.

WVS No.: 21A-54; Catalog No.: 310368 (Figure 8.51a)
Bag No.: Rim: 563 (38-3-3), 512 (39-2-4), 517 (38-2-1); Body: 563, 512, 516 (38-2-2); Base: 563. Provenience: 21A38-3-3. Context: Floor. On the exterior floor north of the structure. A significant part of the recovered fragments was found in one concentration. Condition: Reconstructible (60% present). Eroded. The vessel is black, which is

probably its original color. Dimensions: Rim diameter: 12.5 cm (estimate); Height: 5.6 cm (measured); Height without feet: 5.0 cm (measured); Wall thickness: 0.4–0.6 cm; Sample weight: 153 g; Original weight: 255 g; Volume: 358 cm³. Coordinates: (25.93, 8.00) (measured). Type: Infierno Black. Paste, temper, and firing: Red paste (2.5YR6/6). Medium grain. A medium amount of calcite temper (0.3–1.2 mm diameter) and a small amount of ferruginous temper (1.0–2.0 mm diameter). The core of the paste is oxidized, but the surface is black. Surface finish and decoration: The vessel appears to be unslipped and polished. Its black surface probably resulted from firing in a reduced atmosphere. Notches on the basal ridge. Form: Bowl with outflared sides. Direct rim and rounded lip. Flat base. Small basal ridge. Three solid nubbin feet. Use-wear: The interior base is heavily pitted from use. The feet appear to be worn.

WVS No.: 21A-55; Catalog No.: 310400 (Figure 8.51b and 8.51c)
Bag No.: Rim: 575 (40-3-3), 591 (40-3-4), 494 (40-2-4); Body: 575; Base: 575, 591. Provenience: 21A40-3-3. Context: Floor. On the exterior floor north of the structure. Most fragments were found in an area 1 × 1 m. Condition: Reconstructible (60% present). Badly eroded. It appears to be burned and slightly darkened. Dimensions: Rim diameter: [exterior] 23.8 cm, [top] 22.7 cm (measured); Height: 7.0 cm (measured); Height without feet: 3.8 cm (measured); Wall thickness: 0.7–0.8 cm; Sample weight: 505 g; Original weight: 841 g; Volume: 615 cm³. Coordinates: (25.40, 10.89) (estimate). Type: Saxche-Palmar Polychrome. Paste, temper, and firing: Reddish yellow paste (7.5YR7/6). Fine grain. A small amount of calcite temper (0.2–0.8 mm diameter) and a very small amount of ferruginous temper (0.5–1.2 mm diameter). The paste is completely oxidized. Surface finish and decoration: Remains of red and orange paints over cream underslip on the interior and the exterior wall. Form: Plate with slightly outcurved sides. Direct rim and flat lip. Flat base. Three hollow oven feet with two openings and a rattle. Use-wear: The bases of the feet appear to be worn through from use.

WVS No.: 21A-56; Catalog No.: 310326 (Figure 8.51e–g)
Bag No.: Rim: 846 (39-3-2), 575 (40-3-3), 571 (39-3-4); Body: 846, 575, 485 (40-2-3), 494 (40-2-4); Base: 575, 571. Provenience: 21A39-3-2. Context: Floor. On the side step north of the structure. Most fragments were found in an area 0.5 × 2 m. The vessel may have been placed on the step

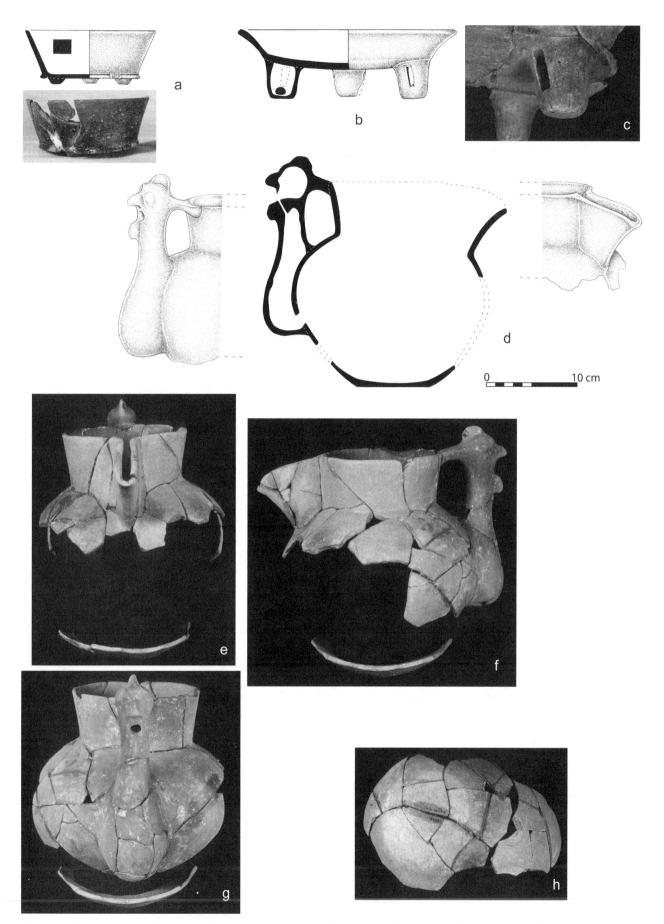

FIGURE 8.51. Complete and reconstructible vessels from the north exterior of Structure M7-34. (a) Infierno Black, 21A38-3-3, Cat. 310368, WVS 21A-54. (b, c) Saxche-Palmar Polychrome, 21A40-3-3, Cat. 310400, WVS 21A-55. (c) Close-up of the heavy worn feet (not to scale). (d–h) Undetermined. (d–g). 21A39-3-2, Cat. 310326, WVS 21A-56. (h) 21A40-3-4, Cat. 310391, WVS 21A-57 (photograph of its base).

or in a higher place along the north wall of the structure. Condition: Reconstructible (85% present). Eroded. The vessel appears to be burned and darkened. The interior of the vessel is darkened, but it is not clear whether this coloring resulted from the original firing or from burning at the time of abandonment. Dimensions: Rim diameter: [exterior] 13.0 cm, [top] 12.5 cm (measured); Maximum diameter: 21 cm (estimate); Minimum opening: 10.0 cm (measured); Height: 20.5 cm (measured); Neck height: 5.0 cm (measured); Wall thickness: 0.5–0.7 cm; Sample weight: 1,124 g; Original weight: 1,322 g; Volume: 3,468 cm³. Coordinates: (24.37, 9.80) (estimate). Type: Undetermined. Paste, temper, and firing: Red paste (2.5YR6/8). Fine grain. Compact. A small amount of volcanic ash temper (0.1 mm length) and a small amount of black and red particles (0.1 mm diameter). The paste is completely oxidized. Surface finish and decoration: The surface is mostly eroded, but the vessel appears to be unslipped. The surface was polished. The top part of the handle was modeled into what appears to be the head of a turkey. There are no incisions on the neck and body. Form: Jar-shaped pitcher with slightly outflared neck, open spout, and whistle handle. Direct rim and rounded lip. Flat base. Use-wear: Not clear because of erosion.

WVS No.: 21A-57; Catalog No.: 310391 (Figure 8.51h)
Bag No.: Rim: 591 (40-3-4), 494 (40-2-4); Body: 591, 494; Base: 591. Provenience: 21A40-3-4. Context: Floor. On the exterior floor north of the structure. Most fragments were found in an area 1 × 1 m. Missing pieces probably remained in the unexcavated area. The paste and the vessel shape appear to be identical to those of WVS 21A56 (Cat. 310326), found in a nearby unit. They were probably used together. Condition: Reconstructible (37% present). Eroded. The vessel appears to be burned and darkened. Dimensions: Maximum diameter: 21 cm (rough estimate); Height: 21 cm (rough estimate); Wall thickness: 0.5–0.7 cm; Sample weight: 491 g; Original weight: 1,327 g; Volume: 3,317 cm³. Coordinates: (25.69, 11.56) (estimate). Type: Undetermined. Paste, temper, and firing: Red paste (2.5YR6/8). Fine grain. Compact. A small amount of volcanic ash temper (0.1 mm length) and a small amount of black and red particles (0.1 mm diameter). The paste is completely oxidized. Surface finish and decoration: The surface is mostly eroded, but the vessel appears to be unslipped. The surface was polished. Form: Probable whistle-handle pitcher. Although the vessel is fragmentary and only the base was reconstructed, it most

likely had the same shape as WVS 21A56 (Cat. 310326). Use-wear: Not clear because of erosion.

South of the Structure

WVS No.: 21A-58; Catalog No.: 310408 (Figures 8.52a, 8.52b, and 8.61a')
Bag No.: Rim: 1448 (77-3-2), 949 (80-2-1); Body: 1448, 915 (77-1-2), 945 (77-2-1), 947 (77-2-2), 949, 1267 (77-3-2), 1270 (77-3-3); Base: 1448. Provenience: 21A77-3-2. Context: Floor. On the exterior floor southwest of the structure. Most of the recovered fragments were found in a loose concentration. Missing pieces probably remained in unexcavated areas. Condition: Reconstructible (45% present). Eroded. Some parts appear to be burned and darkened. Nearly half the vessel is reconstructed. Dimensions: Rim diameter: 16 cm (estimate); Maximum diameter: 34 cm (estimate); Minimum opening: 11 cm (estimate); Height: 33.2 cm (measured); Neck height: 6.7 cm (measured); Wall thickness: 0.6–1.2 cm; Sample weight: 1,675 g; Original weight: 3,722 g; Volume: 12,789 cm³. Coordinates: (7.32, 3.53) (measured). Type: Pantano Impressed. Paste, temper, and firing: Reddish yellow paste (5YR7/6). Medium grain. A medium amount of calcite temper (0.2–1.5 mm diameter) and a small amount of ferruginous temper (0.5–2.0 mm diameter). The paste is completely oxidized. Surface finish and decoration: Red slip on the exterior, including the base. The interior neck does not appear to be slipped. Cross-and-dots stamps and triangular punctuations below the neck-body juncture. Form: Jar with outcurved neck. Direct rim and beveled-in lip. Incurved base. Use-wear: The edge of the base appears to be heavily worn.

WVS No.: 21A-59; Catalog No.: 310230 (Figures 8.52c and 8.61b')
Bag No.: Rim: 777 (45-3-1), 527 (45-2-1); Body: 777, 527; Base: 777, 527, 779 (45-3-2). Provenience: 21A45-3-1. Context: Floor. On the side step south of the structure. Most of the recovered fragments were found in one concentration. Missing pieces may have remained in unexcavated areas. Condition: Reconstructible (30% present). Slightly eroded. Some parts are blackened, but it is not clear whether this coloration is due to burning. Dimensions: Rim diameter: 41 cm (estimate); Maximum diameter: 45 cm (estimate); Height: 15 cm (estimate); Wall thickness: 0.8–1.0 cm; Sample weight: 1,237 g; Original weight: 4,123 g; Volume: 7,949 cm³. Coordinates: (8.67, 10.30) (measured). Type: Chaquiste Impressed. Paste, temper, and firing: Pink paste (7.5YR7/4). Medium grain. A me-

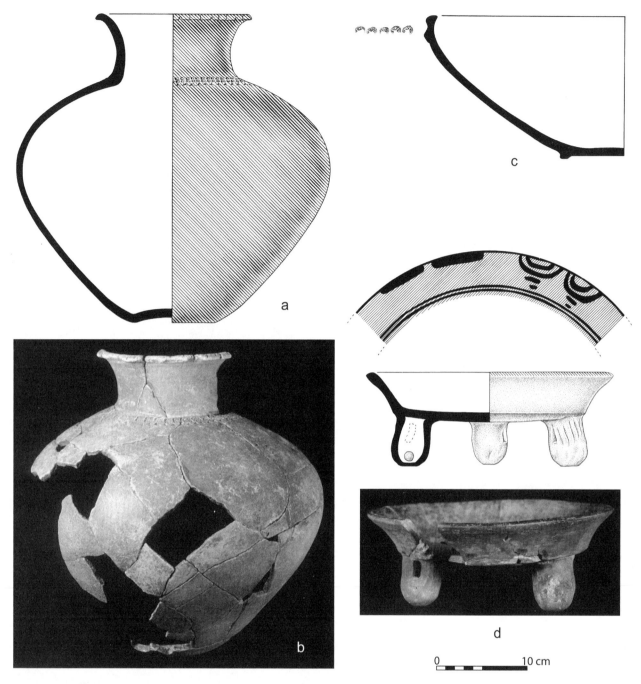

FIGURE 8.52. Complete and reconstructible vessels from the south exterior of Structure M7-34. (a, b) Pantano Impressed, 21A77-3-2, Cat. 310408, WVS 21A-58. (c) Chaquiste Impressed, 21A45-3-1, Cat. 310230, WVS 21A-59. (d) Saxche-Palmar Polychrome, 21A44-3-1, Cat. 310238, WVS 21A-60.

dium amount of calcite temper (0.3–1.0 mm diameter) and a small amount of black particles (0.3–0.6 mm diameter). The paste is completely oxidized. Surface finish and decoration: Weak red slip on the exterior rim above the ridge and on the interior. X-and-dots stamps on the ridge. Form: Bowl with incurved sides. Exterior-thickened rim and rounded lip. Ring base. Ridge below the rim. Usewear: Not clear.

WVS No.: 21A-60; Catalog No.: 310238 (Figure 8.52d) Bag No.: Rim: 773 (44-3-1); Body: 773; Base: 773. Provenience: 21A44-3-1. Context: Floor. On the side porch to the south of the structure. All fragments were found in one concentration. Condition: Reconstructible (90% present). Slightly eroded. Burned in dark color. Dimensions: Rim diameter: [exterior] 26.7 cm, [top] 25.7 cm (measured); Height: 9.3 cm (measured); Height without feet: 5.3 cm (measured); Wall thickness: 0.6–1.0 cm; Sample weight: 1,031 g; Original weight: 1,146 g; Volume: 1,148 cm³. Coordinates: (8.91, 8.46) (measured). Type: Saxche-Palmar Polychrome. Paste, temper, and firing: Reddish yellow paste (5YR6/6). Fine. A medium amount of calcite temper (0.1–0.3 mm diameter) and a small amount of ferruginous temper (0.3–0.8 mm diameter). The paste is completely oxidized. Surface finish and decoration: The interior is polished, but the exterior is smoothed and the exterior surface is uneven. Traces of thin red slip on the exterior wall. Orange slip over cream underslip on the interior. Black and red paint on the interior. Red on the lip. Form: Plate with outcurved sides and flat base. Direct rim and flat lip. Three hollow oven feet with two openings and a rattle. Use-wear: The feet are slightly worn. Use-wear on the interior is not clear because of erosion.

Structure M7-91

WVS No.: 21A-61; Catalog No.: 310451 (Figure 8.53a)
Bag No.: Rim: 1177 (81-3-2), 980 (81-2-1), 927 (81-1-1), 1186 (81-3-4), 977 (81-2-2); Body: 1177, 980, 927, 977, 1186. Provenience: 21A81-3-2. Context: Floor. On the floor of Structure M7-91. Fragments were found in an area 2 × 2 m. Missing pieces may have remained in unexcavated areas. Condition: Reconstructible (50% present). Eroded. Traces of burning not clear. Dimensions: Rim diameter: [exterior] 25.1 cm, [top] 23.8 cm (measured); Maximum diameter: 37 cm (rough estimate); Minimum opening: 15.6 cm (measured); Height: 43 cm (rough estimate); Neck height: 7.5 cm (measured); Wall thickness: 0.7–0.8 cm; Sample weight: 3,235 g; Original weight: 6,470 g; Volume: 21,988 cm³. Coordinates: (5.48, 1.42) (estimate). Type: Encanto Striated. Paste, temper, and firing: Pink paste (5YR7/4). Medium grain. A medium amount of calcite temper (0.3–2.5 mm diameter) and a small amount of ferruginous temper (0.5–1.2 mm diameter). The paste is completely oxidized. The paste is finer than that of common Encanto jars. Surface finish and decoration: Striation on the body. Form: Jar with outcurved neck. Exterior-folded rim and rounded lip. Use-wear: Not clear because of the fragmentary state.

WVS No.: 21A-62; Catalog No.: 310466 (Figure 8.53b)
Bag No.: Rim: 1229 (82-3-4), 1206 (82-3-1), 1212 (82-3-2), 1223 (82-3-3); Body: 1229, 1206, 980 (81-2-1), 1000 (82-2-1), 1206, 929 (82-1-2), 1177 (81-3-2). Provenience: 21A82-3-4. Context: Floor. On the floor of Structure M7-91. Fragments were found in an area 3 × 3 m. Missing pieces may

have remained in unexcavated areas. Condition: Reconstructible (20% present). Eroded. The vessel appears to be burned and darkened. Dimensions: Rim diameter: [exterior] 33.1 cm, [top] 31.7 cm (measured); Maximum diameter: 40 cm (estimate); Minimum opening: 19 cm (estimate); Height: 47 cm (rough estimate); Neck height: 10.5 cm (measured); Wall thickness: 0.7–1.0 cm; Sample weight: 2,161 g; Original weight: 10,805 g; Volume: 26,150 cm³. Coordinates: (4.78, −0.40) (estimate). Type: Encanto Striated. Paste, temper, and firing: Light reddish brown paste (5YR6/3). Coarse grain. A large amount of calcite temper (0.3–2.0 mm diameter). The paste is completely oxidized. Surface finish and decoration: Striation on the body. Form: Jar with outcurved neck. Exterior-folded rim and beveled-in lip. Use-wear: Not clear because of the fragmentary state.

WVS No.: 21A-63; Catalog No.: 310465 (Figure 8.53c)
Bag No.: Rim: 1212 (82-3-2), 1177 (81-3-2), 927 (81-1-1), 1229 (82-3-4); Body: 1212, 1177, 927, 1229, 930 (82-1-1), 1000 (82-2-1). Provenience: 21A82-3-2. Context: Floor. On the floor of Structure M7-91. Fragments were found in an area 2 × 2 m. The rim and neck are nearly complete. Missing pieces may have remained in unexcavated areas. Condition: Reconstructible (30% present). Badly eroded. Some parts are burned and darkened. Dimensions: Rim diameter: [exterior] 27.4 cm, [top] 26.6 cm (measured); Maximum diameter: 38 cm (estimate); Minimum opening: 17.0 cm (measured); Height: 41 cm (rough estimate); Neck height: 9.0 cm (measured); Wall thickness: 0.7–0.8 cm; Sample weight: 2,759 g; Original weight: 9,197 g; Volume: 21,845 cm³. Coordinates: (5.11, −0.27) (estimate). Type: Encanto Striated. Paste, temper, and firing: Pink paste (5YR7/4). Coarse grain. A very large amount of calcite temper (0.3–2.5 mm diameter). The paste is completely oxidized. Surface finish and decoration: Striation on the body. Form: Jar with outcurved neck. Exterior-folded rim and squared lip. Use-wear: Not clear because of the fragmentary state.

WVS No.: 21A-64; Catalog No.: 310440 (Figure 8.53d)
Bag No.: Rim: 1243 (57-3-2); Body: 1315 (73-3-3), 1320 (73-3-4), 1003 (73-2-1), 917 (74-1-1), 1221 (74-3-3), 968 (74-2-1), 1320, 919 (57-1-2); Base: 1315, 917. Provenience: 21A73-3-3. Context: Floor. On the Causeway floor north of Structure M7-91. Fragments were found in an area 4 × 3 m. Condition: Reconstructible (40% present). Eroded. Traces of burning are not clear. Dimensions: Rim diameter: [exterior] 14.8 cm, [top] 14.3 cm (measured);

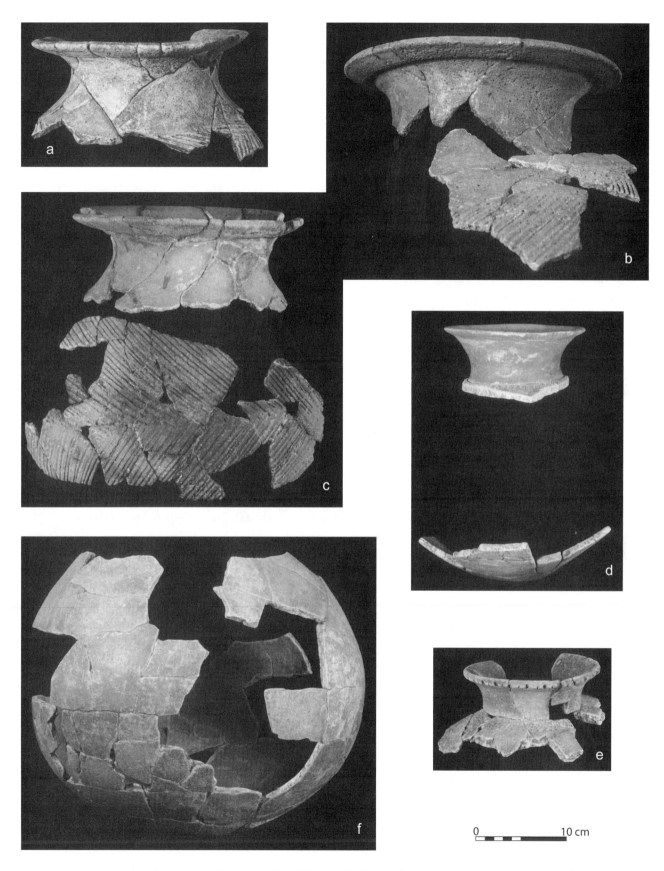

FIGURE 8.53. Complete and reconstructible vessels from Structure M7-91. (a–c) Encanto Striated. (a) 21A81-3-2, Cat. 310451, WVS 21A-61. (b) 21A82-3-4, Cat. 310466, WVS 21A-62. (c) 21A82-3-2, Cat. 310465, WVS 21A-63. (d, e) Pantano Impressed. (d) 21A73-3-3, Cat. 310440, WVS 21A-64. (e) 21A78-3-3, Cat. 310476, WVS 21A-66. (f) Tinaja Red or Pantano Impressed, 21A79-3-2, Cat. 310243, WVS 21A-67.

Maximum diameter: 35 cm (rough estimate); Minimum opening: 7.0 cm (measured); Height: 35 cm (rough estimate); Neck height: 4.8 cm (measured); Wall thickness: 0.7–0.8 cm; Sample weight: 1,520 g; Original weight: 3,800 g; Volume: 14,662 cm³. Coordinates: (10.40, –1.23) (estimate). Type: Pantano Impressed. Paste, temper, and firing: Pink paste (7.5YR7/4). Relatively fine grain. A medium amount of calcite temper (0.1–1.5 mm diameter) and a small amount of ferruginous temper (0.5–1.8 mm diameter). The paste is completely oxidized. Surface finish and decoration: Red slip on the exterior. It is not clear whether the exterior base was slipped. The interior neck does not appear to have been slipped. Half-circles-and-dots stamps below the neck-body juncture. Form: Jar with outcurved neck. Direct rim and pointed lip. Incurved base. Use-wear: Not clear because of erosion.

WVS No.: 21A-65; Catalog No.: 310441
Bag No.: Rim: 1236 (57-3-1); Body: 1236, 1001 (58-2-1), 1243 (57-3-2), 926 (57-1-1); Base: 1001. Provenience: 21A57-3-1. Context: Floor. On the Causeway floor north of Structure M7-92. Fragments were found in an area 1.5 × 1.5 m. Missing parts may be in unexcavated areas. Condition: Reconstructible (25% present). Badly eroded. The base appears to be burned and darkened. Dimensions: Rim diameter: 14.5 cm (estimate); Maximum diameter: 33 cm (rough estimate); Minimum opening: 8.1 cm (measured); Height: 33 cm (rough estimate); Neck height: 5.3 cm (measured); Wall thickness: 0.6–1.1 cm; Sample weight: 867 g; Original weight: 3,468 g; Volume: 13,335 cm³. Coordinates: (9.63, 0.23) (estimate). Type: Pantano Impressed. Paste, temper, and firing: Pink paste (5YR7/4). Medium grain. A medium amount of calcite temper (0.1–1.5 mm diameter) and a small amount of ferruginous temper (0.5–1.5 mm diameter). The paste is completely oxidized. Surface finish and decoration: Red slip on the exterior. It is not clear whether the exterior base and the interior neck were slipped. Quincunx stamps and triangular punctuations below the neck-body juncture. Form: Jar with outcurved neck. Direct rim and squared lip. Incurved base. Use-wear: Not clear because of erosion.

WVS No.: 21A-66; Catalog No.: 310476 (Figure 8.53e)
Bag No.: Rim: 977 (81-2-2); Body: 1224 (78-3-3), 1227 (78-3-1), 977, 1186 (81-3-4), 1145 (81-3-1), 925 (78-1-2), 1201 (79-3-2), 1203 (79-3-4), 980 (81-2-1). Provenience: 21A78-3-3. Context: Floor. On the floor of Structure M7-91. Fragments were found in an area 3 × 3 m. Miss-

ing pieces may have remained in unexcavated areas. Condition: Reconstructible (40% present). Eroded. Traces of burning not clear. Dimensions: Rim diameter: [exterior] 15.3 cm, [top] 15.0 cm (measured); Maximum diameter: 27 cm (rough estimate); Minimum opening: 9.5 cm (measured); Height: 27 cm (rough estimate); Neck height: 4.3 cm (measured); Wall thickness: 0.7–0.8 cm; Sample weight: 643 g; Original weight: 1,607 g; Volume: 7,131 cm³. Coordinates: (6.26, 0.33) (estimate). Type: Pantano Impressed. Paste, temper, and firing: Light red paste (10R6/6). Medium grain. A medium amount of calcite temper (0.1–0.4 mm diameter) and a small amount of ferruginous temper (0.5–1.0 mm diameter). The paste is completely oxidized. The paste color is different from that of common Pantano jars. Surface finish and decoration: Red slip on the exterior. It is not clear whether the internal neck was slipped. X-and-dots stamps and triangular punctuations below the neck-body juncture. Rectangular areas filled with the same stamps on two sides of the shoulder. Notches on the lip. Form: Jar with outcurved neck. Direct rim and beveled-out lip. Use-wear: Not clear because of the fragmentary state.

WVS No.: 21A-67; Catalog No.: 310243 (Figure 8.53f)
Bag No.: Body: 1201 (79-3-2), 1238 (78-3-2), 1162 (49-3-4), 972 (78-2-1), 1224 (78-3-3), 1203 (79-3-4), 1240 (78-3-4), 982 (79-2-1), 1227 (78-3-1), 931 (79-1-1), 928 (79-1-2), 978 (78-2-2), 1185 (81-3-3), 970 (57-2-2), 930 (82-1-1); Base: 972, 1238. Provenience: 21A79-3-2. Context: Floor. On the floor of Structure M7-91. Fragments were found in an area 4 × 4 m. Condition: Reconstructible (70% present). Eroded. Some parts appear to be burned and blackened. The neck was not recovered. Dimensions: Maximum diameter: 39.3 cm (measured); Height: 42 cm (estimate); Wall thickness: 0.7–0.8 cm; Sample weight: 2,819 g; Original weight: 4,027 g; Volume: 27,403 cm³. Coordinates: (7.29, –0.53) (estimate). Type: Tinaja Red or Pantano Impressed. Paste, temper, and firing: Pink paste (5YR7/4). Relatively fine grain. A relatively small amount of calcite temper (0.1–0.3 mm diameter) and a small amount of ferruginous temper (0.5–2.5 mm diameter). The paste is completely oxidized. Surface finish and decoration: Red slip on the exterior, including the base. Form: Jar. Incurved base. Use-wear: The edge of the base is worn.

WVS No.: 21A-68; Catalog No.: 310445 (Figure 8.54a)
Bag No.: Rim: 1007 (59-2-1), 1259 (59-3-1), 1011 (60-2-2); Body: 1007, 1260 (59-3-2), 1259; Base: 1007. Provenience:

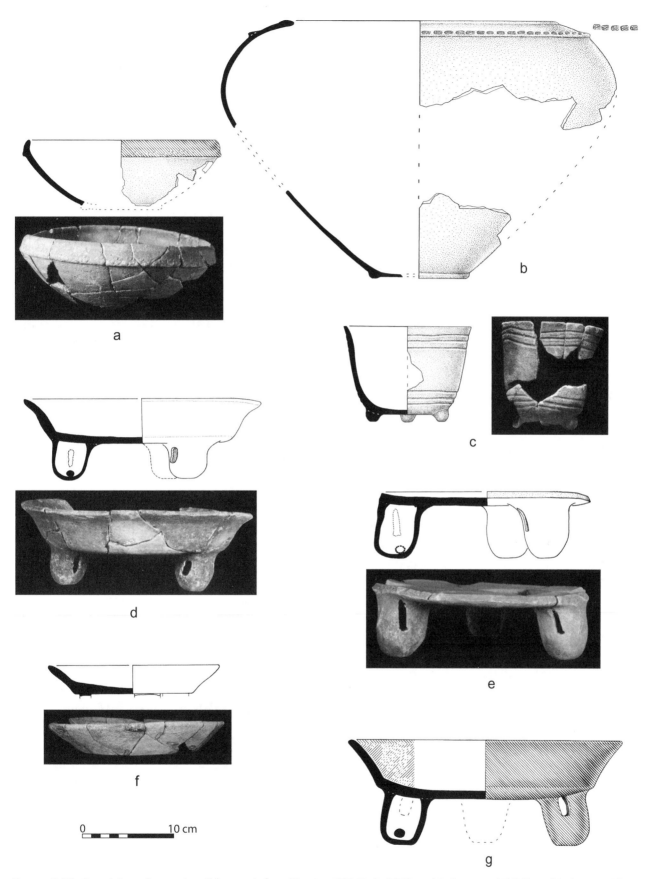

FIGURE 8.54. Complete and reconstructible vessels from Structure M7-91. (a, b) Chaquiste Impressed. (a) Chaquiste Impressed, 21A59-2-1, Cat. 310445, WVS 21A-68. (b) 21A82-3-1, Cat. 310453, WVS 21A-69. (c) Corozal Incised, 21A81-3-2, Cat. 310444, WVS 21A-70. (d–g) Saxche-Palmar Polychrome. (d) 21A78-3-2, Cat. 310234, WVS 21A-71. (e) 21A78-3-2, Cat. 310235, WVS 21A-72. (f) 21A78-3-2, Cat. 310236, WVS 21A-73. (g) 21A59-3-4, Cat. 310442, WVS 21A-74.

21A59-2-1. Context: Floor. On the Causeway floor north of Structure M7-91. Condition: Reconstructible (50% present). Eroded. Some parts are burned and darkened. Dimensions: Rim diameter: [interior] 20.2 cm, [top] 20.6 cm (measured); Maximum diameter: 22.4 cm (measured); Height: 7.0 cm (estimate); Wall thickness: 0.5–0.6 cm; Sample weight: 349 g; Original weight: 698 g; Volume: 1,160 cm³. Coordinates: (13.52, 0.84) (estimate). Type: Chaquiste Impressed. Paste, temper, and firing: Red paste (2.5YR5/6). Medium grain. A medium amount of calcite temper (0.1–0.4 mm diameter) and a very small amount of ferruginous temper (0.5–1.5 mm diameter). The paste is completely oxidized. Surface finish and decoration: Red slip on the rim above the ridge and on the interior surface. The exterior surface below the ridge does not appear to have been slipped. Stamps on the ridge. Form: Bowl with slightly incurved sides. Exterior-thickened rim and rounded lip. A ridge below the rim. The base is missing. Use-wear: Not clear because of the fragmentary state.

WVS No.: 21A-69; Catalog No.: 310453 (Figures 8.54b and 8.61c')

Bag No.: Rim: 1205 (82-3-1), 1202 (79-3-3); Body: 1205, 1000 (82-2-1), 1145 (81-3-1), 1177 (81-3-2), 1185 (81-3-3), 1203 (79-3-4), 923 (78-1-1), 929 (82-1-2), 1202; Base: 1205. Provenience: 21A82-3-1. Context: Floor. On the floor of Structure M7-91 and on the exterior floor next to it. Half the recovered fragments were found in one concentration. Other pieces were scattered in an area 4 × 4 m. Some fragments probably remained in the nearby unexcavated area. Condition: Reconstructible (60% present). Eroded. The vessel appears to be burned and darkened. Dimensions: Rim diameter: 31 cm (estimate); Maximum diameter: 44 cm (estimate); Height: 28 cm (estimate); Wall thickness: 0.5–0.7 cm; Sample weight: 3,661 g; Original weight: 6,102 g; Volume: 47,504 cm³. Coordinates: (5.81, –1.80) (measured). Type: Chaquiste Impressed. Paste, temper, and firing: Light reddish brown paste (5YR6/4). Coarse grain. A large amount of calcite temper (0.1–3.0 mm diameter) and a small amount of ferruginous temper (0.5–2.0 mm). The paste is completely oxidized. Surface finish and decoration: Weak red slip on the exterior surface above the ridge and on the interior surface. Quincunx stamps on the ridge. Form: Bowl with markedly incurved sides and restricted orifice. Exterior-thickened rim and rounded lip. Ridge below the rim. Ring base. Use-wear: Not clear because of erosion.

WVS No.: 21A-70; Catalog No.: 310444 (Figure 8.54c)

Bag No.: Rim: 1177 (81-3-2), 977 (81-2-2), 1224 (78-3-3), 933 (81-1-2), 1145 (81-3-1); Body: 1177, 980 (81-2-1), 1186 (81-3-4), 1211 (82-3-2), 927 (81-1-1), 1206 (82-3-1), 977; Base: 1177, 1224. Provenience: 21A81-3-2. Context: Floor. On the floor of Structure M7-91. Fragments were found in an area 3 × 3 m. Missing pieces may have remained in unexcavated areas. Condition: Reconstructible (50% present). Eroded. The vessel is burned and darkened. Dimensions: Rim diameter: 12 cm (estimate); Height: 10 cm (rough estimate); Wall thickness: 0.4–0.6 cm; Sample weight: 242 g; Original weight: 484 g; Volume: 435 cm³. Coordinates: (5.24, 1.34) (estimate). Type: Corozal Incised. Paste, temper, and firing: Reddish yellow paste (5YR7/6). Medium grain. A medium amount of calcite temper (0.3–1.0 mm diameter) and a small amount of ferruginous temper (0.5–1.0 mm diameter). The paste is completely oxidized. Surface finish and decoration: Remains of red slip on the interior surface. The exterior surface is completely eroded. Grooved lines on the exterior rim and near the base. Form: Bowl with outflared side. Direct rim and squared lip. Rounded base. Three solid nubbin feet. Use-wear: Not clear because of erosion.

WVS No.: 21A-71; Catalog No.: 310234 (Figure 8.54d)

Bag No.: Rim: 1238 (78-3-2), 978 (78-2-2), 1248 (77-3-1); Body: 1238; Base: 1238, 922 (78-1-1), 978, 970 (57-2-2). Provenience: 21A78-3-2. Context: Floor. Inside Structure M7-91. Most fragments were found in an area 1 × 1 m. Condition: Reconstructible (80% present). Badly eroded. Although traces of burning are not clear because of erosion, part of the rim appears to have laminated due to fire. Dimensions: Rim diameter: [exterior] 25.9 cm, [top] 25.3 cm (measured); Height: 8.1 cm (measured); Height without feet: 4.3 cm (measured); Wall thickness: 0.5–0.9 cm; Sample weight: 701 g; Original weight: 876 g; Volume: 1,015 cm³. Coordinates: (7.48, 1.21) (estimate). Type: Saxche-Palmar Polychrome. Paste, temper, and firing: Reddish yellow paste (7.5YR6/6). Fine. A small amount of calcite temper (0.1 mm diameter) and a very small amount of ferruginous temper (0.5 mm diameter). The paste is completely oxidized. Surface finish and decoration: Although it was most likely a polychrome vessel, all paints are eroded. Form: Plate with outcurved sides and flat base. Direct rim and rounded lip. Three hollow oven feet with two openings and a rattle. Use-wear: Not clear because of erosion.

WVS No.: 21A-72; Catalog No.: 310235 (Figure 8.54e)
Bag No.: Base: 1238 (78-3-2), 972 (78-2-1). Provenience: 21A78-3-2. Context: Floor. Inside Structure M7-91. Fragments were found in an area 1 × 1 m. Condition: Partial (40% present). We found a significant portion of the base with three feet. It was broken neatly all along the wall-base juncture, and we did not find any fragments of the wall and rim. The vessel appears to have been used without the wall. The vessel is eroded and slightly darkened, probably from burning. Dimensions: Diameter of the base: 23.5 cm (measured); Height without wall: 6.6 cm (measured); Wall thickness: 0.7 cm; Sample weight: 834 g; Original weight: 2,085 g; Volume: not calculated. Coordinates: (7.20, 1.52) (estimate). Type: Saxche-Palmar Polychrome. Paste, temper, and firing: Reddish yellow paste (7.5YR6/6). Fine. A small amount of calcite temper (0.1–0.2 mm diameter), a small amount of ferruginous temper (0.5–1.0 mm diameter), and a very small amount of shiny, glassy particles (0.1 mm length). The paste is completely oxidized. Surface finish and decoration: The surface is mostly eroded. Traces of cream underslip and red paint on the interior base. Form: Plate with flat base. Three hollow oven feet with two openings and a rattle. Use-wear: Not clear because of erosion.

WVS No.: 21A-73; Catalog No.: 310236 (Figure 8.54f)
Bag No.: Rim: 1238 (78-3-2), 972 (78-2-1), 1224 (78-3-3), 1227 (78-3-1); Body: 1238; Base: 1238, 1224. Provenience: 21A78-3-2. Context: Floor. Inside Structure M7-91. Fragments were found in an area 2 × 2 m. Condition: Reconstructible (80% present). Although a significant portion of the vessel is present, we did not find any feet. It appears that one foot broke off during firing. The users may have broken the two remaining feet intentionally and used the rest of the vessel. Eroded. Part of the vessel appears to have been burned in red color. Dimensions: Rim diameter: [exterior] 18.7 cm, [top] 18.3 cm (measured); Height without feet: 3.0 cm (measured); Wall thickness: 0.6–0.8 cm; Sample weight: 375 g; Original weight: 469 g; Volume: 225 cm³. Coordinates: (7.17, 1.12) (estimate). Type: Saxche-Palmar Polychrome. Paste, temper, and firing: Reddish yellow paste (7.5YR6/6). Fine. A medium amount of calcite temper (0.1–0.3 mm diameter) and a small amount of ferruginous temper (0.5–1.3 mm diameter). The paste is completely oxidized. Surface finish and decoration: The surface is mostly eroded. Traces of cream slip on the interior and on the exterior wall. Small traces of orange paint

on the interior. Form: Plate with flared sides and flat base. Direct rim and rounded lip. There appear to have been three slab feet. Use-wear: The parts of the base where two feet were attached are worn.

WVS No.: 21A-74; Catalog No.: 310442 (Figure 8.54g)
Bag No.: Rim: 1262 (59-3-4), 1007 (59-2-1); Body: 1262, 1007; Base: 1262, 1007, 877 (60-1-1). Provenience: 21A59-3-4. Context: Floor. On the Causeway floor north of Structure M7-91. Fragments were found in an area 2 × 1 m. Condition: Reconstructible (40% present). Eroded. No recognizable traces of burning. Dimensions: Rim diameter: 30 cm (estimate); Height: 9.7 cm (measured); Height without feet: 5.5 cm (measured); Wall thickness: 0.8–0.9 cm; Sample weight: 622 g; Original weight: 1,555 g; Volume: 1,876 cm³. Coordinates: (12.84, 1.46) (measured). Type: Saxche-Palmar Polychrome. Paste, temper, and firing: Pink paste (7.5YR8/4). Fine grain. A small amount of calcite temper (0.1–0.3 mm diameter) and a small amount of ferruginous temper (0.5–1.5 mm diameter). The paste is completely oxidized. Surface finish and decoration: Red and orange paints on the interior surface. Red paint on the exterior wall. Weak red paint on the exterior base. Form: Plate with outflared sides. Direct rim and rounded lip. Flat base. Three hollow oven feet with two openings and a rattle. Use-wear: The bases of the feet appear to be slightly worn.

Structure M7-92

WVS No.: 21A-75; Catalog No.: 310443
Bag No.: Body: 1198 (72-3-1), 1276 (71-3-3), 1200 (72-3-2), 1251 (72-3-3); Base: 1198. Provenience: 21A72-3-1. Context: Floor. On the Causeway floor south of Structure M7-92. Recovered fragments were found in a loose concentration. Condition: Reconstructible (50% present). Badly eroded. Traces of burning not clear. Dimensions: Rim diameter: 31 cm (rough estimate); Maximum diameter: 52 cm (rough estimate); Minimum opening: 21 cm (estimate); Height: 58 cm (rough estimate); Neck height: 7 cm (estimate); Wall thickness: 1.0–1.5 cm; Sample weight: 8,037 g; Original weight: 16,074 g; Volume: 65,104 cm³. Coordinates: (13.37, –1.03) (measured). Type: Manteca Impressed Ridged variety. Paste, temper, and firing: Reddish yellow paste (5YR6/6). Coarse grain. A very large amount of calcite temper, including shiny crystals (0.5–2.0 mm diameter). The paste is completely oxidized. Surface finish and decoration: A ridge with simple impressions on the

shoulder. Form: Jar with outcurved neck. Slightly angular neck-body juncture. Flat base. Use-wear: Not clear because of erosion.

WVS No.: 21A-76; Catalog No.: 310458 (Figure 8.55a)
Bag No.: Rim: 1332 (63-3-2), 1330 (63-3-2), 1327 (69-3-3); Body: 1330, 1354 (62-3-1), 1452 (63-3-2). Provenience: 21A63-3-2. Context: Floor. On the floor of Structure M7-92. Fragments were found in an area 2 × 2 m. Condition: Reconstructible (60% present). Eroded. Traces of burning not clear. Dimensions: Rim diameter: [exterior] 26.6 cm, [top] 24.7 cm (measured); Maximum diameter: 40 cm (rough estimate); Minimum opening: 17.2 cm (measured); Height: 45 cm (rough estimate); Neck height: 7.9 cm (measured); Wall thickness: 0.6–1.0 cm; Sample weight: 3,367 g; Original weight: 5,611 g; Volume: 28,429 cm³. Coordinates: (20.18, 0.22) (measured). Type: Cambio Unslipped, angled neck, scratched. Paste, temper, and firing: Pink paste (7.5YR7/4). Coarse grain. A large amount of calcite temper, including shiny crystals (0.3–2.0 mm diameter) and a small amount of ferruginous temper (0.5–1.5 mm diameter). The core of the paste is dark. Surface finish and decoration: Very shallow striations on the body. Striations are clearer and more regular than the scratched patterns of WVS 21A29, 21A76, or 22A3 (Cat. 310416, 310458, 310299). A small ridge where striations begin. Some remains of red wash on the rim. Form: Jar with outcurved neck. Slightly angular neck-body juncture, which has smoother, more curved connection than other vessels of this type. Exterior-folded rim and rounded lip. The folded part is smaller than that of common Cambio/Encanto vessels. The striation, rim shape, and neck shape of this vessel represent a middle way between common Encanto jars and other Cambio vessels with angular neck-body junctures and scratched patterns. Use-wear: Not clear because of the fragmentary state.

WVS No.: 21A-77; Catalog No.: 310481
Bag No.: Rim: 1335 (64-3-2). Provenience: 21A64-3-2. Context: Floor. On the exterior floor north of Structure M7-92. The complete rim and parts of the neck were analyzed. Encanto body sherds found in nearby areas may be parts of this vessel. Condition: Reconstructible (20% present). Eroded. Traces of burning not clear. Dimensions: Rim diameter: [exterior] 24.2 cm, [top] 22.7 cm (measured); Maximum diameter: 40 cm (rough estimate); Minimum opening: 12 cm (estimate); Height: 38 cm (rough estimate); Neck height: 10 cm (estimate);

Wall thickness: 0.8–1.1cm; Sample weight: 1,153 g; Original weight: 5,765 g; Volume: 18,996 cm³. Coordinates: (23.75, 1.79) (estimate). Type: Cambio Unslipped or Encanto Striated (probably Encanto Striated). Paste, temper, and firing: Reddish yellow paste (5YR7/6). Coarse grain. A very large amount of calcite temper (0.3–2.0 mm diameter). The paste is completely oxidized. Surface finish and decoration: Unslipped, smoothed neck. Form: Jar with outcurved neck. Exterior-folded rim and beveled-in lip. Use-wear: Not clear because of the fragmentary state.

WVS No.: 21A-78; Catalog No.: 310450 (Figure 8.55b)
Bag No.: Rim: 1309 (70-3-2), 1327 (69-3-3); Body: 1309, 869 (66-1-1), 1215 (66-3-2), 1214 (66-3-2), 1305 (70-3-1), 1363 (70-3-4); Base: 1309, 901 (70-1-2). Provenience: 21A70-3-2. Context: Floor. On the floor of Structure M7-92. A significant portion of fragments was found in an area 3 × 1 m. A few pieces that fitted to the rest of the vessel were found in Unit 66, which was 6 m to the north. Condition: Reconstructible (60% present). Eroded. Traces of burning are not clear. Dimensions: Rim diameter: [exterior] 14.1 cm, [top] 13.6 cm (measured); Maximum diameter: 21.1 cm (measured); Minimum opening: 9.1 cm (measured); Height: 17.8 cm (measured); Neck height: 4.2 cm (measured); Wall thickness: 0.7–0.8 cm; Sample weight: 1,071 g; Original weight: 1,785 g; Volume: 2,612 cm³. Coordinates: (17.86, −0.29) (estimate). Type: Pantano Impressed. Paste, temper, and firing: Pink paste (5YR8/4). Medium grain. A medium amount of calcite temper (0.1–0.5 mm diameter) and a small amount of ferruginous temper (0.5–1.0 mm). The paste is completely oxidized. Surface finish and decoration: Red slip on the exterior. It is not clear whether the exterior base and the interior neck were slipped. X-and-dots stamps and triangular punctuations below the neck-body juncture. Notched on the lip. Stamps and punctuations placed in the shape of a cross on two sides of the shoulder. Form: Jar with outcurved neck. Direct rim and squared lip. Incurved base. Use-wear: Not clear because of erosion.

WVS No.: 21A-79; Catalog No.: 310449
Bag No.: Rim: 997 (69-2-1), 1313 (70-3-3); Body: 1363 (70-3-4), 1373 (61-3-3), 1367 (61-3-1), 1370 (61-3-2), 1313, 962 (62-2-1); Base: 1363, 1291 (60-3-1). Provenience: 21A70-3-4. Context: Floor. On the floor of Structure M7-92. Condition: Reconstructible (60% present). Eroded. Traces of burning not clear. Dimensions: Rim diameter: 13 cm (estimate); Maximum diameter: 24 cm (rough estimate);

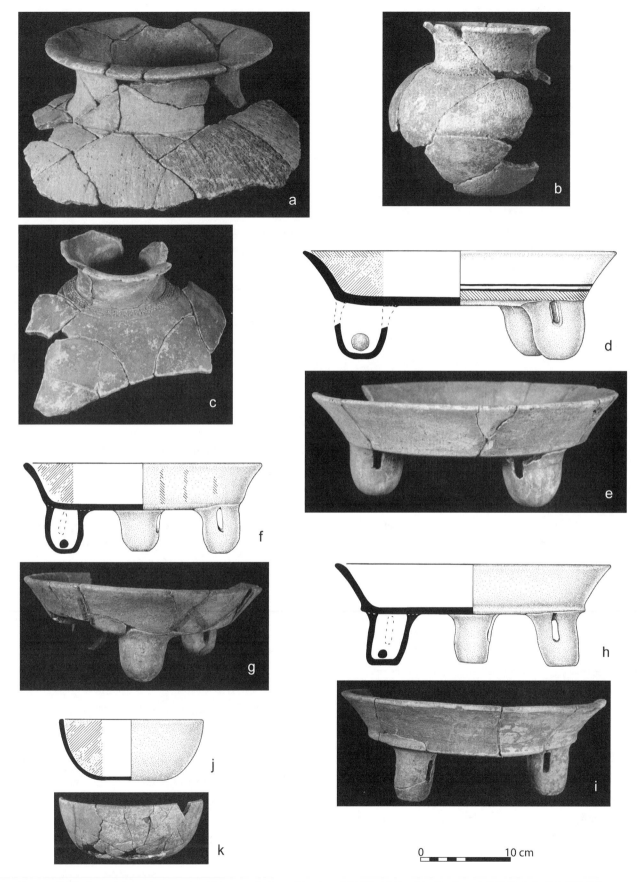

FIGURE 8.55. Complete and reconstructible vessels from Structure M7-92. (a) Cambio Unslipped, 21A63-3-2, Cat. 310458, WVS 21A-76. (b, c) Pantano Impressed. (b) 21A70-3-2, Cat. 310450, WVS 21A-78. (c) 21A63-3-2, Cat. 310456, WVS 21A-80. (d–k) Saxche-Palmar Polychrome. (d, e) 21A63-3-2, Cat. 310233, WVS 21A-81. (f, g) 21A61-3-1, Cat. 310455, WVS 21A-82. (h, i) 21A62-3-3, Cat. 310232, WVS 21A-83. (j, k) 21A62-3-1, Cat. 310454, WVS 21A-84.

Minimum opening: 9 cm (estimate); Height: 22 cm (estimate); Neck height: 4.4 cm (measured); Wall thickness: 0.6–0.9 cm; Sample weight: 1,381 g; Original weight: 2,302 g; Volume: 4,353 cm^3. Coordinates: (16.27, −0.36) (estimate). Type: Pantano Impressed. Paste, temper, and firing: Pink paste (5YR7/4). Medium grain. A medium amount of calcite temper (0.2–1.5 mm diameter) and a small amount of ferruginous temper (0.5–1.5 mm diameter). The paste is completely oxidized. Surface finish and decoration: Red slip on the exterior. It is not clear whether the exterior base and the interior neck were slipped. Notches on the lip. Form: Jar with outcurved neck. Direct rim and grooved lip. Incurved base. Use-wear: Not clear because of erosion.

WVS No.: 21A-80; Catalog No.: 310456 (Figure 8.55c)
Bag No.: Rim: 1452 (63-3-2), 1332 (63-3-2); Body: 1452, 1330 (63-3-2); Base: 1452. Provenience: 21A63-3-2. Context: Floor. On the floor of Structure M7-92. Fragments were found in an area 1.5 × 1.5 m. Condition: Reconstructible (35% present). Eroded. Traces of burning not clear. Dimensions: Rim diameter: 13 cm (estimate); Maximum diameter: 34 cm (rough estimate); Minimum opening: 7.4 cm (measured); Height: 34 cm (rough estimate); Neck height: 5.4 cm (measured); Wall thickness: 0.6–0.7 cm; Sample weight: 1,360 g; Original weight: 3,885 g; Volume: 16,184 cm^3. Coordinates: (19.70, −0.25) (estimate). Type: Pantano Impressed. Paste, temper, and firing: Pink paste (5YR7/4). Medium grain. A medium amount of calcite temper (0.1–0.3 mm diameter) and a small amount of ferruginous temper (0.5–1.8 mm diameter). The paste is completely oxidized. Surface finish and decoration: Red slip on the exterior. Weak red slip on the interior neck. It is not clear whether the base was slipped. Quincunx stamps and impressed lines below the neck-body juncture. Form: Jar with outcurved neck. Direct rim and rounded lip. Incurved base. Use-wear: Not clear because of erosion.

WVS No.: 21A-81; Catalog No.: 310233 (Figure 8.55d and 8.55e)
Bag No.: Rim: 1331 (63-3-2), 1357 (62-3-1), 1452 (63-3-2); Body: 1331, 1357; Base: 1331, 1357, 1330 (63-3-2), 1327 (69-3-3). Provenience: 21A63-3-2. Context: Floor. The vessel appears to have been inside Structure M7-82. A large portion of fragments was found in one concentration. Others were found in an area 2 × 2 m. Condition: Reconstructible (85% present). Eroded. Traces of burning not clear. Dimensions: Rim diameter: [exterior] 34.6 cm, [top]

33.8 cm (measured); Height: 11.1 cm (measured); Height without feet: 5.3 cm (measured); Wall thickness: 0.9–1.3 cm; Sample weight: 1,923 g; Original weight: 2,262 g; Volume: 2,231 cm^3. Coordinates: (20.28, 0.29) (estimate). Type: Saxche-Palmar Polychrome. Paste, temper, and firing: Light red paste (2.5YR6/6). Fine. A small amount of calcite temper (0.1–1.0 mm diameter) and a small amount of ferruginous temper (0.5–1.5 mm diameter). Some fragments show thin dark core. Surface finish and decoration: The surface is mostly eroded. Traces of red paint on cream underslip on the interior and on the rim. Traces of red horizontal band and black horizontal lines on cream underslip on the exterior wall. Form: Plate with slightly outcurved sides and flat base. Direct rim and rounded lip. Three hollow oven feet with two openings and a rattle. Use-wear: Not clear because of erosion.

WVS No.: 21A-82; Catalog No.: 310455 (Figure 8.55f and 8.55g)
Bag No.: Rim: 1368 (61-2-1), 885 (69-1-1), 1309 (70-3-2), 870 (62-1-1), 1321 (69-3-1), 1327 (69-3-3), 994 (62-2-2); Body: 1368; Base: 1368, 1367 (61-3-1), 1309, 997 (69-2-1). Provenience: 21A61-3-1. Context: Floor. On the floor of Structure M7-72. Fragments were found in an area 3 × 3 m. Condition: Reconstructible (75% present). Badly eroded. Burned and darkened. Dimensions: Rim diameter: [exterior] 27.0 cm, [top] 26.5 cm (measured); Height: 9.2 cm (measured); Height without feet: 4.9 cm (measured); Wall thickness: 0.5–0.6 cm; Sample weight: 742 g; Original weight: 989 g; Volume: 1,276 cm^3. Coordinates: (17.82, 0.15) (estimate). Type: Saxche-Palmar Polychrome. Paste, temper, and firing: Reddish yellow paste (5YR7/6). Fine grain. A small amount of calcite temper (0.1–0.5 mm diameter) and a small amount of ferruginous temper (0.5–1.3 mm diameter). The paste is completely oxidized. Surface finish and decoration: Remains of orange paint over cream underslip on the interior wall and base. Vertical red stripes on the exterior wall. It is not clear whether the exterior base and feet were slipped. Form: Plate with outflared sides. Direct rim and rounded lip. Flat base. Three hollow oven feet with two openings and a rattle. Use-wear: Not clear because of erosion.

WVS No.: 21A-83; Catalog No.: 310232 (Figure 8.55h and 8.55i)
Bag No.: Rim: 1379 (62-3-3); Body: 1379, 1375 (61-3-4); Base: 1379, 1361 (62-3-3), 870 (62-1-1), 959 (68-2-2), 1281 (68-3-4). Provenience: 21A62-3-3. Context: Floor. On the floor of

Structure M7-92. Fragments were scattered over nearly the entire floor of the platform. Condition: Reconstructible (45% present). Eroded. Some fragments appear to have been burned after the vessel broke. Dimensions: Rim diameter: [exterior] 30.1 cm, [top] 29.3 cm (measured); Height: 10.4 cm (measured); Height without feet: 4.9 cm (measured); Wall thickness: 0.6–0.8 cm; Sample weight: 641 g; Original weight: 1,424 g; Volume: 1,752 cm³. Coordinates: (18.92, 0.16) (estimate). Type: Saxche-Palmar Polychrome. Paste, temper, and firing: Reddish yellow paste (5YR7/6). Fine grain. A small amount of calcite temper (0.1–0.4 mm diameter) and a small amount of ferruginous temper (0.5–1.3 mm diameter). The paste is completely oxidized. Surface finish and decoration: Remains of red paint over cream underslip on the exterior wall. Form: Plate with outflared sides. Direct rim and flat lip. Flat base. Three hollow oven feet with two openings and a rattle. Use-wear: Not clear because of erosion.

WVS No.: 21A-84; Catalog No.: 310454 (Figure 8.55j and 8.55k)
Bag No.: Rim: 1354 (62-3-1), 962 (62-2-1); Body: 1354, 870 (62-1-1), 997 (69-2-1); Base: 1354. Provenience: 21A62-3-1. Context: Floor. On the floor of Structure M7-92. Most of the recovered fragments were found in an area 1 × 1 m. Condition: Reconstructible (45% present). Badly eroded and heavily burned. Dimensions: Rim diameter: 15.5 cm (estimate); Height: 6.7 cm (measured); Wall thickness: 0.3–0.6 cm; Sample weight: 122 g; Original weight: 271 g; Volume: 667 cm³. Coordinates: (19.43, 0.11) (estimate). Type: Saxche-Palmar Polychrome. Paste, temper, and firing: Pink paste (5YR7/4). Fine grain. A small amount of calcite temper (0.2–0.5 mm diameter). The paste is completely oxidized. Surface finish and decoration: Remains of orange paint over cream underslip on the interior surface. Only cream underslip is left on the exterior. Form: Bowl with slightly incurved sides. Direct rim and rounded lip. Flat base. Use-wear: Not clear because of erosion.

WVS No.: 21A-85; Catalog No.: 310446
Bag No.: Rim: 1282 (71-3-4), 1363 (70-3-4), 1273 (71-3-2); Body: 1282, 1273, 1291 (60-3-1); Base: 1282. Provenience: 21A71-3-4. Context: Floor. On the exterior floor south of Structure M7-92 and in front of the entrance to Structure M7-34. Fragments were found in an area 4 × 4 m. Condition: Reconstructible (50% present). Eroded. Burned and blackened. Dimensions: Rim diameter: 11 cm (estimate); Height: 4.1 cm (measured); Height without feet: 3.5 cm

(measured); Wall thickness: 0.3–0.5 cm; Sample weight: 55 g; Original weight: 110 g; Volume: 196 cm³. Coordinates: (14.73, –0.63) (estimate). Type: Peten Gloss group undetermined (may have been Infierno Black, Tinaja Red, or Saxche/Palmar Polychrome). Paste, temper, and firing: Red paste (2.5YR5/8). Fine grain. A small amount of calcite temper (0.1–0.3 mm diameter). The paste is completely oxidized. Surface finish and decoration: The exterior and interior surfaces are slipped, but they are burned black and the original color is not clear. Form: The bowl with slightly outcurved sides. Direct rim and rounded lip. Flat base. Three small, solid nubbin feet. Use-wear: Not clear because of erosion.

Around the Stairway to the North

WVS No.: 21A-86; Catalog No.: 310469 (Figure 8.56a and 8.56b)
Bag No.: 1398 (83-3-1). Provenience: 21A83-3-1. Context: Floor. In the area between the stairway of the Palace Group platform and the peripheral wall of Structure M7-34, an area that may be a midden. Condition: Reconstructible (70% present). Eroded. It appears to be burned. The upper side, including where an appendage was attached, is partially blackened. It may have been burned after the appendages broke off. Dimensions: Rim diameter: [exterior] 18.8 cm (measured); Height without appendages: 3.0 cm (measured); Wall thickness: 1.1 cm; Sample weight: 569 g; Original weight: 813 g; Volume: not calculated. Coordinates: (26.02, 2.48) (estimate). Type: Cambio group undetermined. Paste, temper, and firing: Light reddish brown paste (5YR6/4). Coarse grain. A very large amount of calcite temper (0.2–2.0 mm diameter) and a small amount of ferruginous temper (0.5–1.0 mm diameter). The paste is completely oxidized. Surface finish and decoration: Smoothed, unslipped surface. Form: Probable three-pronged censor lid. On the top there are traces of three probable prongs. We did not find any incense burns connected with this lid. Use-wear: None recognizable.

WVS No.: 21A-87; Catalog No.: 310480 (Figure 8.56c)
Bag No.: Rim: 1266 (68-3-1), 1215 (66-3-2); Body: 1215, 895 (66-1-2), 998 (66-2-1), 1444 (66-3-3), 1233 (66-3-3), 894 (67-1-1), 868 (65-1-1), 960 (65-2-1), 987 (65-2-3), 1405 (65-3-1), 1407 (65-3-3), 1247 (67-3-4), 959 (68-2-2), 1266, 902 (68-1-2); Base: 1207 (66-3-1), 1215. Provenience: 21A66-3-1. Context: Floor. On the exterior floor in front of the stairway of the platform of the Palace Group, north of Structure M7-92. Fragments were scattered in an area 5 × 3 m.

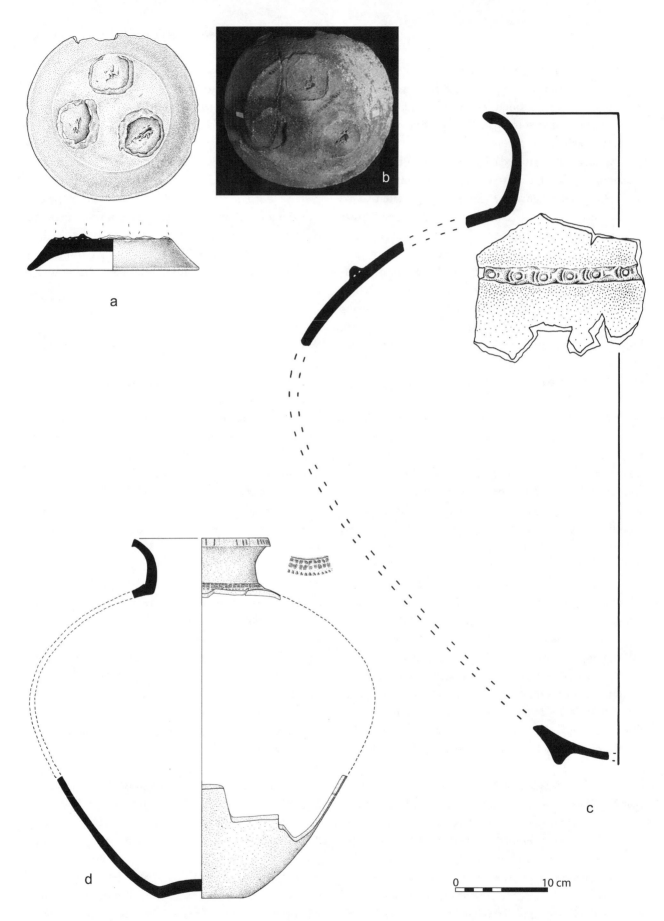

FIGURE 8.56. Complete and reconstructible vessels from the area around the stairway to the north of Structure M7-92. (a, b) Cambio group undetermined, 21A83-3-1, Cat. 310496, WVS 21A-86. (c) Manteca Impressed, 21A66-3-1, Cat. 310480, WVS 21A-87. (d) Pantano Impressed, 21A83-3-1, Cat. 310261, WVS 21A-88.

Some pieces probably remained in the unexcavated area. Condition: Reconstructible (30% present). Eroded. Traces of burning not clear. The rim and base were not refitted with body parts. There remains a possibility that they are not parts of the same vessel. Dimensions: Rim diameter: 31 cm (estimate); Maximum diameter: 67 cm (rough estimate); Minimum opening: 21 cm (estimate); Height: 70 cm (rough estimate); Neck height: 11.0 cm (measured); Wall thickness: 1.2–1.6 cm; Sample weight: 8,815 g; Original weight: 29,383 g; Volume: 225,186 cm³. Coordinates: (25.30, –1.59) (estimate). Type: Manteca Impressed Ridged variety. Paste, temper, and firing: Reddish yellow paste (7.5YR6/6). Coarse grain. A large amount of calcite temper, including shiny crystals (0.3–2.0 mm diameter). The paste is completely oxidized. Surface finish and decoration: Unslipped, smoothed surface. Fillet (1.7 cm wide) with concentric-circle stamps. Form: Jar with outcurved neck. Somewhat angular neck-body juncture. Relatively vertical neck. The shape of the neck is different from that of common Cambio/Encanto jars. Exterior-thickened rim and rounded lip. Flat base with prominent ring. The ring is 1.4 cm high. Use-wear: Not clear because of erosion.

WVS No.: 21A-88; Catalog No.: 310261 (Figures 8.56d and 8.61d')
Bag No.: Rim: 1396 (83-3-1); Body: 1396; Base: 1396. Provenience: 21A83-3-1. Context: Floor. On the exterior floor between the stairway and the circumferential wall. Fragments were found in an area 1 × 1 m. The area may have been a midden. Condition: Reconstructible (70% present). Eroded. No clear traces of burning. Dimensions: Rim diameter: [exterior] 15.1 cm, [top] 14.8 cm (measured); Maximum diameter: 38 cm (rough estimate); Minimum opening: 9.8 cm (measured); Height: 38 cm (rough estimate); Neck height: 4.8 cm (measured); Wall thickness: 0.6–1.0 cm; Sample weight: 2,753 g; Original weight: 3,933 g; Volume: 19,422 cm³. Coordinates: (26.11, 2.83) (estimate). Type: Pantano Impressed. Paste, temper, and firing: Pink paste (5YR7/4). Medium grain. A medium amount of calcite temper (0.3–0.8 mm diameter) and a small amount of ferruginous temper (0.5–1.0 mm diameter). The paste is completely oxidized. Some fire clouding on the exterior. Surface finish and decoration: Red slip on the entire exterior, including the base, and on the interior neck surface. The interior and exterior neck surfaces are smoothed whereas the exterior body is polished. Cross-and-dots stamps and triangular impressions below the

neck-body juncture. Vertical incision on the lip. Form: Jar with slightly outcurved sides and incurved base. Exterior-thickened rim and squared lip. Use-wear: The edge of the exterior base is worn.

WVS No.: 21A-89; Catalog No.: 310471 (Figures 8.57a and 8.61e')
Bag No.: Rim: 1214 (66-3-2), 1215 (66-3-2), 869 (66-1-1); Body: 1214, 1215, 1405 (65-3-1), 895; Base: 1210 (66-3-2), 869. Provenience: 21A66-3-2. Context: Floor. On the Causeway floor north of Structure M7-92 and the south of the stairway of the Palace Group platform. Fragments were found in an area 2 × 3 m. Condition: Reconstructible (50% present). Eroded. Some parts appear to be burned and darkened. Dimensions: Rim diameter: [exterior] 15.3 cm, [top] 14.9 cm (measured); Maximum diameter: 22 cm (rough estimate); Minimum opening: 10.0 cm (measured); Height: 24 cm (rough estimate); Neck height: 5.0–5.3 cm (measured); Wall thickness: 0.5–0.7 cm; Sample weight: 813 g; Original weight: 1,626 g; Volume: 4,262 cm³. Coordinates: (25.56, –0.56) (estimate). Type: Pantano Impressed. Paste, temper, and firing: Pink paste (5YR7/4). Medium grain. A medium amount of calcite temper (0.3–1.3 mm diameter) and a small amount of ferruginous temper (0.8–1.5 mm diameter). The paste is completely oxidized. Surface finish and decoration: Red slip on the exterior surface, including the base and the interior neck. Cross-and-dots stamps and triangular punctuations below the neck-body juncture. A cross-shaped area defined by incised lines on a shoulder. There may have been the same decoration on the other side of the shoulder. Incisions on the lip. Form: Jar with outcurved neck. Direct rim and grooved lip. Incurved base. Use-wear: The edge of the base appears to be slightly worn.

WVS No.: 21A-90; Catalog No.: 310473 (Figures 8.57c–d and 8.61f')
Bag No.: Rim: 1405 (65-3-1); Body: 1405; Base: 1405. Provenience: 21A65-3-1. Context: Floor. On the Causeway floor in front of the stairway of the Palace Group platform, near the corner of the peripheral wall of Structure M7-34. Fragments were found in an area 1 × 1 m. It may be a midden. Condition: Reconstructible (90% present). Slightly eroded. The vessel appears to be burned and darkened. There is a hole in the center of the base (7 cm diameter). The edge of the hole is rounded. It appears that the hole was made intentionally and the vessel was used

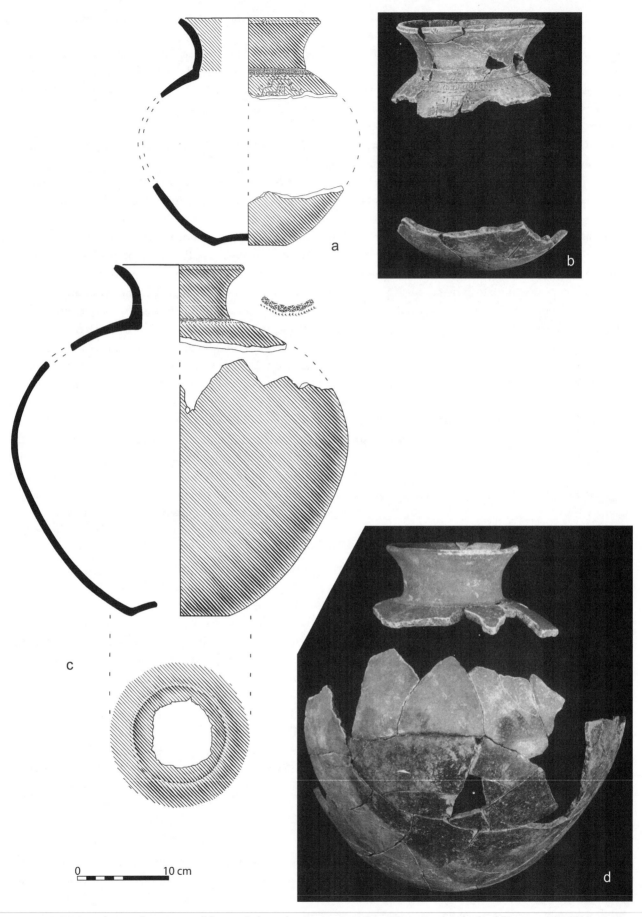

Figure 8.57. Complete and reconstructible vessels from the area around the stairway to the north of Structure M7-92. Pantano Impressed. (a, b) 21A66-3-2, Cat. 310471, WVS 21A-89. (c, d) 21A65-3-1, Cat. 310473, WVS 21A-90.

with the hole. Dimensions: Rim diameter: [exterior] 14.0 cm, [top] 13.7 cm (measured); Maximum diameter: 36.2 cm (measured); Minimum opening: 8.2 cm (measured); Height: 36.1 cm (measured); Neck height: 5.5 cm (measured); Wall thickness: 0.6–0.9 cm; Sample weight: 4,181 g; Original weight: 4,645 g; Volume: 17,544 cm³. Coordinates: (25.50, 0.48) (estimate). Type: Pantano Impressed. Paste, temper, and firing: Pink paste (5YR7/4). Medium grain. A relatively large amount of calcite temper (0.3–1.0 mm diameter) and a small amount of ferruginous temper (0.5–2.0 mm diameter). The paste is completely oxidized. Surface finish and decoration: Red slip on the exterior surface, including the base. It is not clear whether the interior neck was slipped. X-and-dots stamps and triangular punctuations below the neck-body juncture. Form: Jar with outcurved neck. Direct rim and squared lip. Incurved base. Use-wear: The edge of the base is only slightly worn.

WVS No.: 21A-91; Catalog No.: 310475 (Figure 8.58a and 8.58b)
Bag No.: Rim: 1405 (65-3-1); Body: 1405, 1403 (65-3-2), 987 (65-2-3), 960 (65-2-1), 1215 (66-3-2); Base: 1403, 1405, 987. Provenience: 21A65-3-2. Context: Floor. On the exterior outside the northern peripheral wall of Structure M7-34, in front of the stairway of the Palace Group platform. Most fragments were found in an area 1 × 2 m. The deposit may be a midden. Condition: Reconstructible (90% present). Eroded. Traces of burning not clear. A significant portion of the fragments were not refitted. Dimensions: Rim diameter: [exterior] 14.2 cm, [top] 14.0 cm (measured); Maximum diameter: 38 cm (rough estimate); Minimum opening: 9.0 cm (measured); Height: 38 cm (rough estimate); Neck height: 6.0 cm (measured); Wall thickness: 0.7–1.1 cm; Sample weight: 4,532 g; Original weight: 5,035 g; Volume: 20,448 cm³. Coordinates: (26.01, 1.14) (estimate). Type: Pantano Impressed. Paste, temper, and firing: Pink paste (5YR7/3). Medium grain. A medium amount of calcite temper (0.2–2.0 mm diameter) and a small amount of ferruginous temper (0.5–1.5 mm diameter). The paste is completely oxidized. Surface finish and decoration: Red slip on the exterior surface, including the base. The interior neck also appears to have been slipped. Scroll-motif stamps and triangular punctuations below the neck-body juncture. Form: Jar with outcurved neck. Direct rim and lip with a shallow groove. Incurved base. Use-wear: The edge of the base is worn.

WVS No.: 21A-92; Catalog No.: 310242 (Figure 8.58c and 8.58d)
Bag No.: Rim: 1403 (65-3-2), 1405 (65-3-1), 1234 (67-3-1); Body: 1403, 1405, 1234, 985 (65-2-2), 1407 (65-3-3); Base: 1403. Provenience: 21A65-3-2. Context: Floor. In the area in front of the stairway of the Palace Group platform, near the corner of the peripheral wall of Structure M7-34. The area may be a midden. Condition: Reconstructible (80% present). Eroded. Traces of burning not clear. Dimensions: Rim diameter: 35 cm (estimate); Maximum diameter: 37 cm (estimate); Height: 15.2 cm (measured); Wall thickness: 0.7–1.0 cm; Sample weight: 2,220 g; Original weight: 2,775 g; Volume: 8,061 cm³. Coordinates: (26.08, 1.26) (estimate). Type: Subin Red. Paste, temper, and firing: Reddish yellow paste (5YR7/6). Medium grain. A medium amount of calcite temper (0.1–0.5 mm diameter) and small amount of ferruginous temper (0.5–1.3 mm diameter). The core of the paste is slightly dark. Surface finish and decoration: Weak red slip on the interior surface and on the exterior rim. Form: Bowl with incurved sides. Exterior-thickened rim and pointed lip. Ridge below the rim. Flat base with ridge. Use-wear: The interior base is irregular and nearly worn through. The upper part of the interior is well preserved.

WVS No.: 21A-93; Catalog No.: 310472 (Figure 8.58e)
Bag No.: Rim: 1436 (76-3-4), 1430 (76-3-2), 1427 (76-3-1); Body: 1436, 1430, 1427, 889 (75-1-1); Base: 1436. Provenience: 21A76-3-4. Context: Floor. On the platform of the Palace Group. Fragments were found in an area 3 × 2 m. Condition: Reconstructible (70% present). Badly eroded. Traces of burning not clear. Dimensions: Rim diameter: [exterior] 15.2 cm, [top] 14.8 cm (measured); Maximum diameter: 15.4 cm (measured); Height: 8.1 cm (measured); Wall thickness: 0.5–0.7 cm; Sample weight: 237 g; Original weight: 339 g; Volume: 686 cm³. Coordinates: (28.68, –0.38) (estimate). Type: Saxche-Palmar Polychrome. Paste, temper, and firing: Pink paste (5YR7/4). Fine grain. A small amount of calcite temper (0.1–0.4 mm diameter) and a small amount of ferruginous temper (0.4–1.3 mm diameter). The paste is completely oxidized. Surface finish and decoration: Red paint over cream underslip on the interior surface. The exterior surface is badly eroded, but there are small remains of red paint. Form: Bowl with incurved sides. Direct rim and rounded lip. Most parts of the base are missing. Use-wear: Not clear because of erosion.

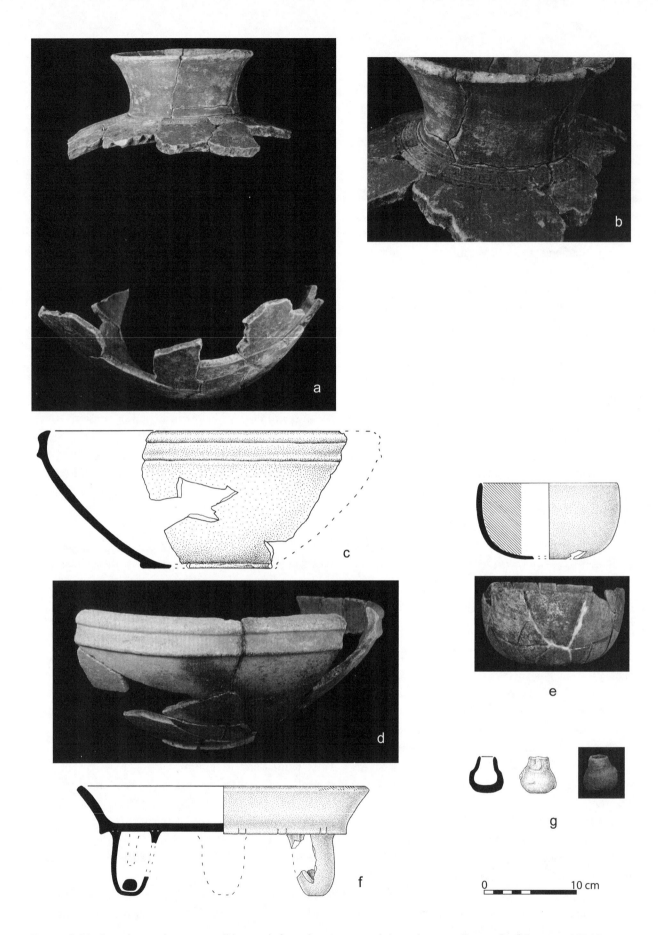

FIGURE 8.58. Complete and reconstructible vessels from the area around the stairway to the north of Structure M7-92. (a, b) Pantano Impressed, 21A65-3-2, Cat. 310475, WVS 21A-91. (b) Close-up (not to scale). (c, d) Subin Red, 21A65-3-2, Cat. 310242, WVS 21A-92. (e, f) Saxche-Palmar Polychrome. (e) 21A76-3-4, Cat. 310472, WVS 21A-93. (f) 21A75-3-4, Cat. 310470, WVS 21A-94. (g) Unslipped undetermined, 21A65-3-2, Cat. 310237, WVS 21A-95.

WVS No.: 21A-94; Catalog No.: 310470 (Figure 8.58f)
Bag No.: Rim: 1433 (75-3-3), 1440 (75-3-4), 1429 (75-3-2), 889 (75-1-1); Body: 1433; Base: 1433, 1440, 889, 1440, 1456 (65-3-2). Provenience: 21A75-3-4. Context: Floor. On the platform of the Palace Group and below its stairway. Fragments were found in an area 3 × 3 m. Condition: Reconstructible (50% present). Badly eroded. No recognizable traces of burning. Most of the recovered fragments were glued together. Dimensions: Rim diameter: 33 cm (estimate); Height: 10.8 cm (measured); Height without feet: 5.0 cm (measured); Wall thickness: 0.9–1.0 cm; Sample weight: 851 g; Original weight: 1,702 g; Volume: 2,082 cm³. Coordinates: (26.69, –0.55) (estimate). Type: Saxche-Palmar Polychrome. Paste, temper, and firing: Pink paste (7.5YR8/4). Fine grain. A small amount of calcite temper (0.3–0.8 mm diameter) and a small amount of ferruginous temper (0.5–1.5 mm diameter). The paste is completely oxidized. Surface finish and decoration: The surface is almost completely eroded, but there are some remains of red paint over cream underslip on the exterior wall. Form: Plate with outflared sides. Direct rim and squared lip. Flat base. A ridge with notches at the base. Three hollow oven feet with two openings and a rattle. Use-wear: Not clear because of erosion.

WVS No.: 21A-95; Catalog No.: 310237 (Figure 8.58g)
Bag No.: Rim: 1179 (65-3-2); Body: 1179; Base: 1179. Provenience: 21A65-3-2. Context: Floor. On the exterior floor between the stairway and the circumferential wall. The area may have been a midden. Condition: Complete (98% present). Eroded. The exterior is darkened. It is not clear whether the darkening was caused during the fire at the time of abandonment. Dimensions: Rim diameter: [exterior] 1.9 cm, [top] 1.7 cm (measured); Maximum diameter: 3.8 cm (measured); Minimum opening: 1.4 cm (measured); Height: 4.0 cm (measured); Wall thickness: 0.5 cm; Sample weight: 38 g; Original weight: 39 g; Volume: 10 cm³. Coordinates: (25.50, 1.01) (estimate). Type: Unslipped undetermined. Paste, temper, and firing: Strong brown paste (7.5YR5/6). Medium grain. A medium amount of calcite temper (0.1–0.3 mm diameter) and a small amount of probable quartz temper (0.1–0.2 mm diameter). Because the vessel is complete, it is not clear whether the paste is oxidized. Surface finish and decoration: Rough, uneven surface. Unslipped. Form: Miniature jar with insloped neck and flat base. Direct rim and rounded lip. Crudely shaped. There appears to have been one handle. Use-wear: Not clear.

BARRANCA ESCONDIDA: OPERATION 24
Knoll (Op. 24B)

WVS No.: 24A-1; Catalog No.: 310219 (Figure 8.59a)
Bag No.: Rim: 189 (6-2-1); Body: 189; Base: 189. Provenience: 24B6-2-1. Context: Ritual deposit on the knoll. Condition: Complete (100% present). Well preserved. Dimensions: Rim diameter: [top] 2.1–2.4 cm (measured); Transversal dimensions: 4.2 × 4.7 cm (measured); Height: 5.0 cm (measured); Wall thickness: 0.4 cm; Sample weight: 71 g; Volume: not calculated. Type: Pedregal Modeled. Paste, temper, and firing: Yellowish red paste (5YR5/6). Very coarse. A large amount of quartz temper (1.0–3.0 mm length), a medium amount of calcite temper (0.5–1.0 mm diameter), and a small amount of ferruginous temper (0.8–1.5 mm diameter). Surface finish and decoration: The surface is unslipped and rough. One side has a roughly modeled image of an owl. Form: Miniature asymmetrical bowl with round sides and flat base. The rim shape is irregular. Use-wear: None recognizable. No traces of burning in the interior. The vessel may have contained a small amount of perishable materials.

Chasm (Op. 24A Unit 18)

WVS No.: 24A-2; Catalog No.: 310221 (Figure 8.59b and 8.59d)
Bag No.: Rim: 217 (18-1-1); Body: 217; Base: 217. Provenience: 24A18-1-1. Context: Ritual deposit at the bottom of the chasm. Condition: Complete (100% present). Well preserved. Dimensions: Rim diameter: [exterior] 2.4 cm, [top] 2.1 cm (measured); Horizontal dimensions: 5.0 × 2.9 cm (measured); Height: 5.0 cm (measured); Wall thickness: 0.6 cm; Sample weight: 51 g; Volume: not calculated. Type: Cambio Unslipped. Paste, temper, and firing: Very pale brown paste (10YR7/4). Medium grain. A small amount of calcite temper (0.2–1.0 mm diameter). The paste is finer than that of common Cambio Unslipped vessels. The paste is identical to that of WVS 24A4 (Cat. 310222). Surface finish and decoration: The surface is rough and is not well smoothed. Unslipped. Form: Miniature jar with a short insloped neck. Direct rim and rounded lip. A unique shape with two conically shaped bases. The vessel is not completely symmetrical and appears to have been roughly shaped. The shape is similar to that of WVS 24A-4 (Cat. 310222) but slightly different. It was most likely used with a lid (WVS 24A-3, Cat. 310291). Use-wear: No clear use-wear. The vessel may have been made specifically for a ritual and may have been deposited soon after its manufacture. No identifiable

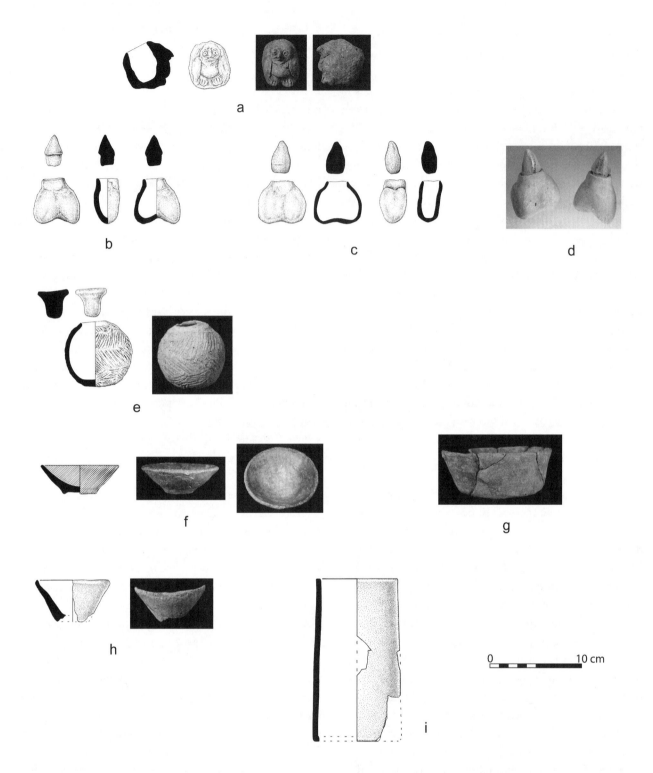

FIGURE 8.59. Complete and reconstructible vessels from the Barranca Escondida and Structure L8-5. (a–e) Barranca Escondida. (a) Pedregal Modeled, 24B6-2-1, Cat. 310219, WVS 24B6-2-1. (b–d) Cambio Unslipped. (b) 24A18-1-1, Cat. 310221, WVS 24A-2 (jar) and Cat. 310291, WVS 24A-3 (lid). (c) 24A18-1-1, Cat. 310222, WVS 24A-4 (jar) and Cat. 310461, WVS 24A-5 (lid). (d) *left*, WVS 24A-4 and 24A-5; *right*, WVS 24A-2 and 24A-3. (e) 24A18-1-1, Encanto Striated, Cat. 310220, WVS 24A-6 (bowl), and Cambio Unslipped, Cat. 310292, WVS 24A-7 (lid). (f–i). Structure L8-5. (f–h) Cambio Unslipped. (f) 25A5-2-1, Cat. 310484, WVS 25A-1. (g) 25A1-2-1, Cat. 310487, WVS 25A-2. (h) 25A6-1-1, Cat. 310488, WVS 25A-3. (i) Peten Gloss group undetermined, 25A1-3-1, Cat. 310486, WVS 25A-4.

residues were recovered from the interior. One side is darkened, and the vessel may have been burned during a ritual. There are no clear traces of soot or burning in the interior.

WVS No.: 24A-3; Catalog No.: 310291 (Figure 8.59b and 8.59d)

Bag No.: 211 (18-1-1). Provenience: 24A18-1-1. Context: Ritual deposit at the bottom of the chasm. Condition: Complete (100% present). Well preserved. Dimensions: Maximum diameter: 2.0 cm (measured); Diameter of the lower part: 1.6 cm (measured); Height: 3.3 cm (measured); Sample weight: 8 g. Type: Cambio Unslipped. Paste, temper, and firing: Pale brown paste (10YR6/3). Medium grain. A small amount of calcite temper (0.2–1.0 mm diameter). The paste is identical to that of WVS 24A2 and 24A4 (Cat. 310221 and 310222). Surface finish and decoration: The surface is rough and is not well smoothed. Unslipped. Form: The upper part is in a conical shape, and the lower part has a cylindrical shape. It was probably a lid for WVS 24A-2 (Cat. 310221), although it is slightly too large for WVS 24A-2 and the base of the conical part does not touch the jar's lip. It is also possible that other, similar vessels remained unexcavated. Use-wear: No clear use-wear. One side is darkened. It was probably burned while it was placed on WVS 24A-2.

WVS No.: 24A-4; Catalog No.: 310222 (Figure 8.59c and 8.59d)

Bag No.: Rim: 217 (18-1-1); Body: 217; Base: 217. Provenience: 24A18-1-1. Context: Ritual deposit at the bottom of the chasm. Condition: Complete (100% present). Well preserved. Dimensions: Rim diameter: [exterior] 2.6 cm, [top] 2.4 cm (measured); Horizontal dimensions: 5.2 × 2.8 cm (measured); Height: 4.7 cm (measured); Wall thickness: 0.6 cm; Sample weight: 48 g; Volume: not calculated. Type: Cambio Unslipped. Paste, temper, and firing: Very pale brown paste (10YR7/4). Medium grain. A small amount of calcite temper (0.2–1.0 mm diameter). The paste is finer than that of common Cambio Unslipped vessels. The paste is identical to that of Cat. 310221. Surface finish and decoration: The surface is rough and is not well smoothed. Unslipped. Form: Miniature jar with short insloped neck. Direct rim and rounded lip. A unique shape with two conically shaped bases. The vessel is not completely symmetrical and appears to have been roughly shaped. The shape is similar to that of WVS 24A-2 (Cat. 310221) but slightly different. It might have

been used with a lid (WVS 24A-5, Cat. 310461). Use-wear: No clear use-wear. The vessel may have been made specifically for a ritual and may have been deposited soon after its manufacture. No identifiable residues were recovered from the interior. One side is darkened, and the vessel may have been burned during a ritual. There are no clear traces of soot or burning in the interior.

WVS No.: 24A-5; Catalog No.: 310461 (Figure 8.59c and 8.59d)

Bag No.: 212 (18-1-1). Provenience: 24A18-1-1. Context: Ritual deposit at the bottom of the chasm. Condition: Complete (100% present). Well preserved. Dimensions: Maximum diameter: [wider side] 2.1 cm, [narrower side] 1.6 cm (measured); Height: 3.6 cm (measured); Sample weight: 12 g. Type: Cambio Unslipped. Paste, temper, and firing: Pale brown paste (10YR6/3). Medium grain. A small amount of calcite temper (0.2–1.0 mm diameter). The paste is identical to that of WVS 24A2 and 24A4 (Cat. 310221 and 310222). Surface finish and decoration: The surface is rough and is not well smoothed. Unslipped. Form: A conical shape. It was most likely a lid for WVS 24A-4, as it fits well. Use-wear: No clear use-wear. One side is darkened. It was probably burned while it was placed on WVS 24A-4.

WVS No.: 24A-6; Catalog No.: 310220 (Figure 8.59e)

Bag No.: Rim: 214 (18-1-1); Body: 214; Base: 214. Provenience: 24A18-1-1. Context: Ritual deposit at the bottom of the chasm. Condition: Complete (100% present). Well preserved. Dimensions: Rim diameter: [interior] 2.4 cm, [top] 2.6 cm (measured); Maximum diameter: 7.2 cm (measured); Height: 6.8 cm (measured); Wall thickness: 0.4–0.5 cm; Sample weight: 167 g; Volume: 93 cm³. Type: Encanto Striated. Paste, temper, and firing: Pale brown paste (10YR6/3). Coarse. A large amount of calcite temper (0.3–2.0 mm diameter). The paste is similar to that of common Cambio and Encanto vessels. Surface finish and decoration: The surface is unslipped and striated. The striations are finer than those on common Encanto jars. Form: Miniature bowl with round sides and restricted orifice. Direct rim and slightly rounded beveled-in lip. Rounded base. Use-wear: None recognizable. The vessel may have been made specifically for a ritual and may have been deposited soon after its manufacture. The interior is blackened, but no identifiable residues were recovered. One side is darkened. It is not clear whether the vessel was burned during a ritual.

WVS No.: 24A-7; Catalog No.: 310292 (Figure 8.59e)
Bag No.: 211 (18-1-1). Provenience: 24A18-1-1. Context: Ritual deposit at the bottom of the chasm. Condition: Almost complete (95% present). Well preserved. Dimensions: Maximum diameter: 3.5 cm (measured); Height: 3.0 cm (measured); Sample weight: 21 g; Original weight: 22 g. Type: Cambio Unslipped. Paste, temper, and firing: Reddish yellow paste (5YR6/6). Medium grain. A large amount of calcite temper (0.2–1.5 mm diameter). The paste is different from that of 24A-2, 24A-4, or 24A-6 (Cat. 310221, 310222, 310220). Surface finish and decoration: The surface is roughly smoothed and unslipped. Form: Rounded conical shape with a wide, flat base. It was probably a lid for a miniature vessel, but it does not fit well on WVS 24A-2, 24A-4, or 24A-6 (Cat. 310221, 310222, or 310220). It may have been used with WVS 24A-6, or it may belong with an unexcavated miniature vessel. Cambio Unslipped lids of similar shapes are found at Dos Pilas (Foias 1996:773, Fig. 6.15 b–d). Use-wear: None clear.

STRUCTURE L8-5: OPERATION 25A

WVS No.: 25A-1; Catalog No.: 310484 (Figure 8.59f)
Bag No.: Rim: 128 (5-2-1); Body: 128; Base: 128. Provenience: 25A5-2-1. Context: Floor. On the front step of the temple near the northern wall. Condition: Complete (100% present). Not broken. The upper part of the interior wall is blackened, and the exterior wall is darkened. It is not clear whether that reflects its use as an incense burner or was caused by the burning of the building. Dimensions: Rim diameter: [exterior] 8.8 cm, [top] 8.4 cm (measured); Height: 3.0 cm (measured); Wall thickness: 0.4 cm; Sample weight: 82 g; Volume: not calculated. Coordinates: (9.49, 11.78) (measured). Type: Cambio Unslipped. Paste, temper, and firing: Light brown paste (7.5YR6/4). Medium grain. A medium amount of calcite temper (0.1–0.8 mm diameter). The paste is similar to that of Subin/Chaquiste bowls. Surface finish and decoration: The surface is smoothed but irregular. Light red color on the lower (central) part of the interior. It appears to be original slip rather than remains of red pigment placed in the vessel. Form: Miniature bowl with flared sides. Probably an incense burner. The vessel is roughly shaped. Direct rim and rounded lip. Flat base with ring. Use-wear: The darkening of the upper interior wall may have been caused by use as an incense burner. The ring base is slightly worn. No clear wear on the interior and the rim.

WVS No.: 25A-2; Catalog No.: 310487 (Figure 8.59g)
Bag No.: Rim: 116 (1-2-1); Body: 116; Base: 116. Prove-

nience: 25A1-2-1. Context: Floor. Inside the temple near the north wall. All fragments come from one unit, but it was not recognized as a reconstructible vessel in the field. Condition: Reconstructible (40% present). Eroded. It is not clear whether the vessel was burned. Dimensions: Rim diameter: [exterior] 11.5 cm, [top] 11.2 cm (measured); Height: 4.3 cm (measured); Wall thickness: 0.5–0.7 cm; Sample weight: 99 g; Original weight: 248 g; Volume: not calculated. Coordinates: (9.40, 15.70) (estimate). Type: Cambio Unslipped. Paste, temper, and firing: Reddish yellow paste (5YR7/6). Medium grain. A medium amount of calcite temper (0.1–0.7 mm diameter) and a small amount of ferruginous temper (0.5–1.5 mm diameter). The paste is completely oxidized. The paste is similar to that of Subin/Chaquiste bowls. Surface finish and decoration: Irregular, smoothed surface. Unslipped. Form: Small bowl with slightly outcurved sides. Probably an incense burner or ritual container. The vessel is roughly shaped. Direct rim and rounded lip. Flat base. Use-wear: Not clear because of erosion.

WVS No.: 25A-3; Catalog No.: 310488 (Figure 8.59h)
Bag No.: Rim: 114 (6-1-1), 129 (5-2-1); Body: 114; Base: 114. Provenience: 25A6-1-1. Context: Floor. In front of the temple. Fragments were found in an area 2 × 2 m. Condition: Reconstructible (40% present). Eroded. It is not clear whether the vessel is burned. Dimensions: Rim diameter: 8.2 cm (estimate); Height: 4.9 cm (estimate); Wall thickness: 0.6–0.8 cm; Sample weight: 40 g; Original weight: 100 g; Volume: 43 cm^3. Coordinates: (7.62, 11.31) (estimate). Type: Cambio Unslipped. Paste, temper, and firing: Light reddish brown paste (5YR6/4). Medium grain. A medium amount of calcite temper (0.1–1.0 mm diameter) and a small amount of ferruginous temper (0.5–1.3 mm diameter). The paste is completely oxidized. The paste is similar to that of Subin/Chaquiste bowls. Surface finish and decoration: Irregular surface. Unslipped. Form: Miniature bowl with flared sides. The vessel is roughly shaped. Probably an incense burner or ritual container. Direct rim and rounded lip. Use-wear: Not clear because of erosion.

WVS No.: 25A-4; Catalog No.: 310486 (Figure 8.59i)
Bag No.: Rim: 135 (1-3-1), 116 (1-2-1); Body: 135, 116; Base: 105 (5-1-1), 116. Provenience: 25A1-3-1. Context: Floor. Inside the temple. Fragments were found in an area 2 × 4 m along the north wall. Condition: Reconstructible (50% present). Heavily eroded. Burned. Some parts are darkened and some reoxidized. Dimensions: Rim diameter:

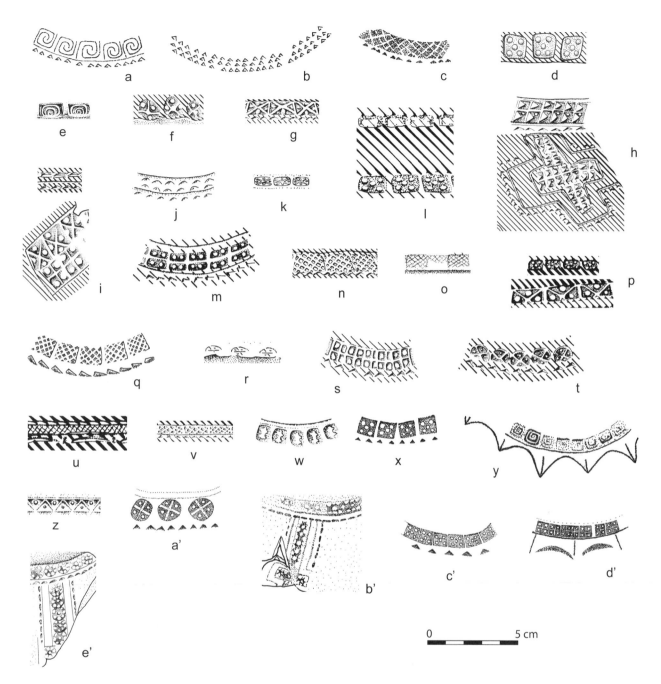

Figure 8.60. Impressed motifs (½ scale). (a–c) Pantano Impressed. (a) Cat. 310036, WVS 22A-4. (b) Cat. 310052, WVS 22A-5. (c) Cat. 310053, WVS 22A-6. (d–f) Chaquiste Impressed. (d) Cat. 310256, WVS 22A-8. (e) Cat. 310295, WVS 22A-9. (f) Cat. 310296, WVS 22A-10. (g–j) Pantano Impressed. (g) Cat. 310279, WVS 23A-7. (h) Cat. 310301, WVS 23A-11. (i) Cat. 310300, WVS 23A-14. (j) Cat. 310370, WVS 23A-16. (k, l) Chaquiste Impressed. (k) Cat. 310361, WVS 23A-19. (l) Cat. 310366, WVS 23A-67. (m, n) Pantano Impressed. (m) Cat. 310022, WVS 20A-8. (n) Cat. 310027, WVS 20A-9. (o, p) Chaquiste Impressed. (o) Cat. 310128, WVS 20A-12. (p) Cat. 310023, WVS 20A-13. (q) Pantano Impressed, Cat. 310140, WVS 20A-28. (r) Chaquiste Impressed, Cat. 310038, WVS 20A-29. (s–y) Pantano Impressed. (s) Cat. 310176, WVS 20A-45. (t) Cat. 310175, WVS 20A-48. (u) Cat. 310313, WVS 20A-59. (v) Cat. 310051, WVS 20A-68. (w) Cat. 310178, WVS 20A-69. (x) Cat. 310099, WVS 14B-6. (y) Cat. 310100, WVS 14B-7. (z) Chaquiste Impressed, Cat. 310045, WVS 14B-10. (a′) Manteca Impressed, Cat. 310079, WVS 14B-17. (b′–e′) Pantano Impressed. (b′) Cat. 310092, WVS 14B-25. (c′) Cat. 310095, WVS 14B-26. (d′) Cat. 310096, WVS 14B-27. (e′) Cat. 310025, WVS 14B-28.

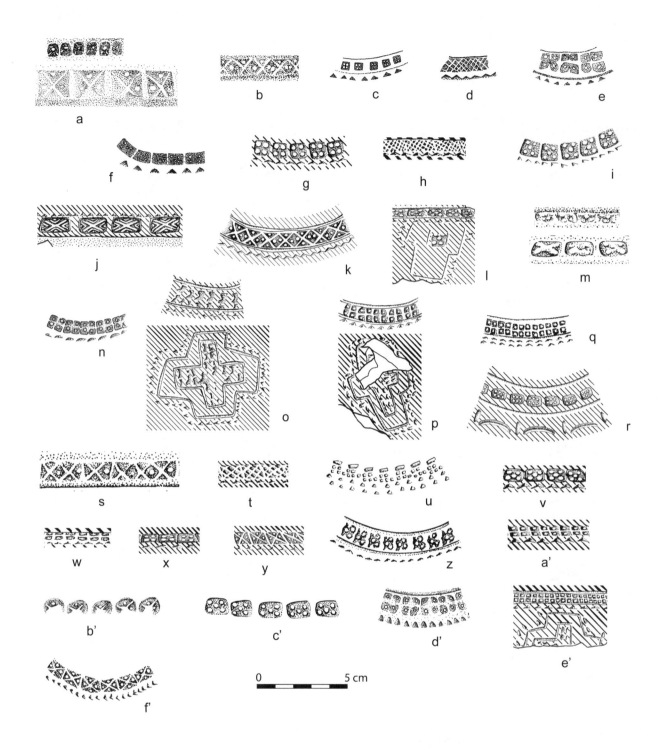

Figure 8.61. Impressed motifs (½ scale). (a, b) Chaquiste Impressed. (a) Cat. 310101, WVS 14B-47. (b) Cat. 310124, WVS 14B-48. (c–i) Pantano Impressed. (c) Cat. 310078, WVS 14B-50. (d) Cat. 310080, WVS 14B-51. (e) Cat. 310081, WVS-14B-52. (f) Cat. 310130, WVS 14B-53. (g) Cat. 310194, WVS 23B-2. (h) Cat. 310196, WVS 23B-3. (i) Cat. 310460, WVS 23B-16. (j) Chaquiste Impressed, Cat. 310195, WVS 23B-18. (k, l) Pantano Impressed. (k) Cat. 310188, WVS 23B-24. (l) Cat. 310202, WVS 23B-29. (m) Chaquiste Impressed, Cat. 310193, WVS 23B-30. (n–r) Pantano Impressed. (n) Cat. 310262, WVS 21A-6. (o) Cat. 310239, WVS 21A-7. (p) Cat. 310429, WVS 21A-8. (q) Cat. 310430, WVS 21A-9. (r) Cat. 310420, WVS 21A-10. (s) Chaquiste Impressed, Cat. 310344, WVS 21A-14. (t–a′) Pantano Impressed. (t) Cat. 310270, WVS 21A-23. (u) Cat. 310280, WVS 21A-37. (v) Cat. 310272, WVS 21A-38. (w) Cat. 310402, WVS 21A-36. (x) Cat. 310395, WVS 21A-49. (y) Cat. 310398, WVS 21A-50. (z) Cat. 310392, WVS 21A-52. (a′) Cat. 310408, WVS 21A-58. (b′, c′) Chaquiste Impressed. (b′) Cat. 310230, WVS 21A-59. c′. Cat. 310453, WVS 21A-69. (d′–f′) Pantano Impressed. (d′) Cat. 310261, WVS 21A-88. (e′) Cat. 310471, WVS 21A-89. (f′) Cat. 310473, WVS 21A-90.

[exterior] 8.8 cm, [top] 8.3 cm (measured); Maximum diameter: 9.0 cm (measured); Height: 17.2 cm (measured); Wall thickness: 0.5–0.6 cm; Sample weight: 260 g; Original weight: 520 g; Volume: 771 cm^3. Coordinates: (9.30, 14.15) (estimate). Type: Peten Gloss group undetermined (Saxche/Palmar Polychrome or Cream-slipped). Paste, temper, and firing: Reddish yellow paste (5YR6/6). Fine grain. A medium amount of calcite temper (0.1–0.3 mm diameter) and a small amount of ferruginous temper (0.5–1.5 mm diameter). Dark core in some parts. Surface finish and decoration: Well-polished surface. Cream slip in some parts. It is not clear whether the vessel had paint. Form: Cylinder vase. Direct rim and squared lip. Flat base. Use-wear: Not clear because of erosion.

9

Complete and Reconstructible Drums

Takeshi Inomata, Daniela Triadan, and Estela Pinto

Table 9.1 summarizes the data from this chapter.

STRUCTURE M7-22 (HOUSE OF MASKS): OPERATION 22A

WDR No.: 22A-1; Catalog No.: 310264 (Figure 9.1a and 9.1d)

Bag No.: Upper rim: 784 (14-3-3); Body: 784; Lower rim: 784, Provenience: 22A14-3-3, Context: Floor. Floor in front of the bench of the easternmost room. All fragments were found close together, and the drum's original shape was recognizable in the field. Condition: Reconstructible (95% present). Eroded. Some parts are darkened by fire. Dimensions (Drum 1): Rim diameter: [exterior] 6.0 cm, [top] 5.7 cm (measured); Height: 11.7 cm (measured); Wall thickness: 0.5 cm. Dimensions (Drum 2): Rim diameter: [exterior] 4.8 cm, [top] 4.5 cm (measured); Height: 7.5 cm (measured); Wall thickness: 0.5 cm. Sample weight: 176 g; Original weight 185 g. Coordinates: (20.71, 23.67) (measured). Type: Unnamed white slipped. Paste, temper, and firing: Reddish yellow paste (5YR6/8). Medium grain. Paste different from that of most polychrome vessels. Contains a medium amount of calcite temper (0.1–0.5 mm diameter) and a small amount of hematite temper (0.5–1.0 mm diameter). The paste is completely oxidized. Surface finish and decoration: Large parts of the exterior were probably covered with white slip, which is mostly eroded. No white slip along the upper rims, which are blackened, probably by fire. The lack of slip along the rims is probably for the attachment of heads. Form: Double drums. The upper and lower rims of both drums have direct rims and squared lips. Use-wear: Not clear because of erosion. Comment: Identical to WDR 22A-2 (Cat. 319265)

WDR No.: 22A-2; Catalog No.: 310265 (Figure 9.1b and 9.1d)

Bag No.: Upper rim: 786 (10-3-2); Body: 786; Lower rim: 786. Provenience: 22A10-3-2. Context: Floor. Floor in front of the bench of the easternmost room. All fragments were found close together, and the drum's original shape was recognizable in the field. Condition: Reconstructible (98% present). Eroded. Some parts are darkened by fire. Dimensions (Drum 1): Rim diameter: [exterior] 6.5 cm, [top] 6.1 cm (measured); Height: 12.1 cm (measured); Wall thickness: 0.4–0.5 cm. Dimensions (Drum 2): Rim diameter: [exterior] 4.9 cm, [top] 4.5 cm (measured); Height: 7.5 cm (measured); Wall thickness: 0.4–0.5 cm. Sample weight: 181 g; Original weight 185 g. Coordinates: (19.67, 23.69) (measured). Type: Unnamed white slipped. Paste, temper, and firing: Reddish yellow paste (5YR6/8). Medium grain. Paste different from that of most polychrome vessels. Contains a medium amount of calcite temper (0.1–0.5 mm diameter) and a small amount of hematite temper (0.5–1.0 mm diameter). The paste is completely oxidized. Surface finish and decoration: The exterior, except the upper rims, is covered with white slip. No slip along the upper rims. The lack of slip along the rims is probably for the attachment of heads. Form: Double drums. The upper and lower rims of both drums have direct rims and squared lips. Use-wear: Not clear because of erosion. Comment: Identical to WDR 22A-1 (Cat. 319264).

WDR No.: 22A-3; Catalog No.: 310266 (Figure 9.1c and 9.1d)

Bag No.: Upper rim: 815 (14-3-2); Body: 815; Lower rim: 815. Provenience: 22A14-3-2. Context: Floor. Floor in front of the bench of the easternmost room. All fragments were found close together. Condition: Reconstructible (85% present). Some parts are darkened by fire. Dimensions (Drum 1): Rim diameter: [exterior] 6.1 cm, [top] 5.8 cm (measured); Height: 12.3 cm (measured);

TABLE 9.1. Summary of Reconstructible Drum Data.

STRUCTURES WDR	CATALOG	PROV.	PRESENT PORTION (%)	RIM DIA. (cm) EX/IN	RIM DIA. (cm) TOP	MAX DIA. (cm)	HT. DIA (cm)	WALL THICK. (cm) THIN	WALL THICK. (cm) THICK	WEIGHT (g) SAMPLE	WEIGHT (g) ORIGINAL	TYPE
M7-22 (House of Bones)												
22A-1	310264	22A14-3-3	95	6.0	5.7		11.7	0.5		176	185	Unnamed White Slipped
22A-2	310265	22A10-3-2	98	6.5	6.1		12.1	0.4	0.5	181	185	Unnamed White Slipped
22A-3	310266	22A14-3-2	85	6.1	5.8		12.3	0.4	0.5	145	171	Azote Orange
M8-4 (House of Mirrors)												
23A-1	310316	23A43-3-3	75	7.7	7.3		15.5	0.5		172	229	Unnamed Incised
23A-2	310405	23A18-3-4	90	8.9	8.5		23.0	0.5		295	327	Saxche-Palmar Poly.
23A-3	310317	23A14-3-4	75	9.5			24.0	0.6		313	417	Saxche-Palmar Poly.
23A-4	310315	23A32-3-1	90	8.7	8.3		11.8	0.5		187	208	Unnamed White Slipped
M8-3												
23B-1	310180	23B3-3-1	30					0.5		128	427	Saxche-Palmar Poly.
M7-34 (House of Metates)												
21A-1	310411	21A42-2-1	70	15.8	15.4	19.0	37.0	0.5	0.8	1039	1484	Saxche-Palmar Poly.
21A-2	310412	21A42-3-1	70	11.0		14.7	40.0	0.4	0.6	755	1078	Saxche-Palmar Poly.
21A-3	310413	21A54-3-2	60	16.9	16.5	21.0	40.0	0.5	0.8	875	1458	Saxche-Palmar Poly.
21A-4	310390	21A33-3-1	30			19.0	37.0	0.3	0.5	354	1180	Saxche-Palmar Poly.
21A-5	310227	21A39-3-4	80	11.1	10.7		30.0	0.5	0.7	784	980	Saxche-Palmar Poly.
21A-6	310477	21A65-3-2	95	12.0	11.6	16.5	34.7	0.3	0.5	943	993	Saxche-Palmar Poly.
21A-7	310478	21A83-3-1	90	14.2	14.0	21.0	40.0	0.5	0.8	1737	1930	Saxche-Palmar Poly.

Wall thickness: 0.4–0.5 cm. Dimensions (Drum 2): Rim diameter: [exterior] 4.5 cm, [top] 4.3 cm (measured); Height: 10.3 cm; Wall thickness: 0.4 cm. Sample weight: 145 g; Original weight 171 g. Coordinates: (20.11, 23.66) (measured). Type: Azote Orange. Paste, temper, and firing: Yellow paste (10YR7/6). Fine. Contains a very small amount of black particles (0.1 mm diameter). The paste is completely oxidized. Surface finish and decoration: Large parts of the exterior are covered with brownish orange slip. No slip along the upper rims, probably for the attachment of heads. Form: Double drums. The upper and lower rims of both drums have direct rims and squared lips. Use-wear: The lower rim of the smaller drum is worn.

STRUCTURE M8-4 (HOUSE OF MIRRORS): OPERATION 23A

WDR No.: 23A-1; Catalog No.: 310316 (Figure 9.1e–f)
Bag No.: Upper rim: 1376 (43-3-3); Body: 1376; Lower rim: 1376. Provenience: 23A43-3-3. Context: Floor. On the floor of the front area of the north room in front of the front bench. Although the drum was badly smashed, most fragments were found in one concentration. Condition: Reconstructible (75% present). Eroded. Burned and

reoxidized. Dimensions: Rim diameter: [exterior] 7.7 cm, [top] 7.3 cm (measured); Height: 15.5 cm (estimate); Wall thickness: 0.5 cm; Sample weight: 172 g; Original weight: 229 g. Coordinates: (46.82, 17.32) (measured). Type: Unnamed incised. Paste, temper, and firing: Dark red paste (2.5YR4/8). Medium paste. A small amount of ferruginous temper (0.5–1.3 mm diameter), a very small amount of calcite temper (0.1–0.3 mm diameter), and a very small amount of volcanic ash temper (0.1 mm length). The paste is completely oxidized. Surface finish and decoration: The surface does not appear to have been slipped. A horizontal band of incisions with a series of animal heads and striped triangles. Form: Drum. Direct upper rim and squared lip. Exterior-thickened lower rim and flat lip. Use-wear: Not clear because of erosion.

WDR No.: 23A-2; Catalog No.: 310405 (Figure 9.1g)
Bag No.: Upper rim: 1116 (18-3-4); Body: 1116; Lower rim: 1116. Provenience: 23A18-3-4. Context: Floor. On the floor in front of the rear bench of the north room. All recovered fragments were found in one concentration. Condition: Reconstructible (90% present). Eroded. Burned and darkened. Some parts of the ridge below the

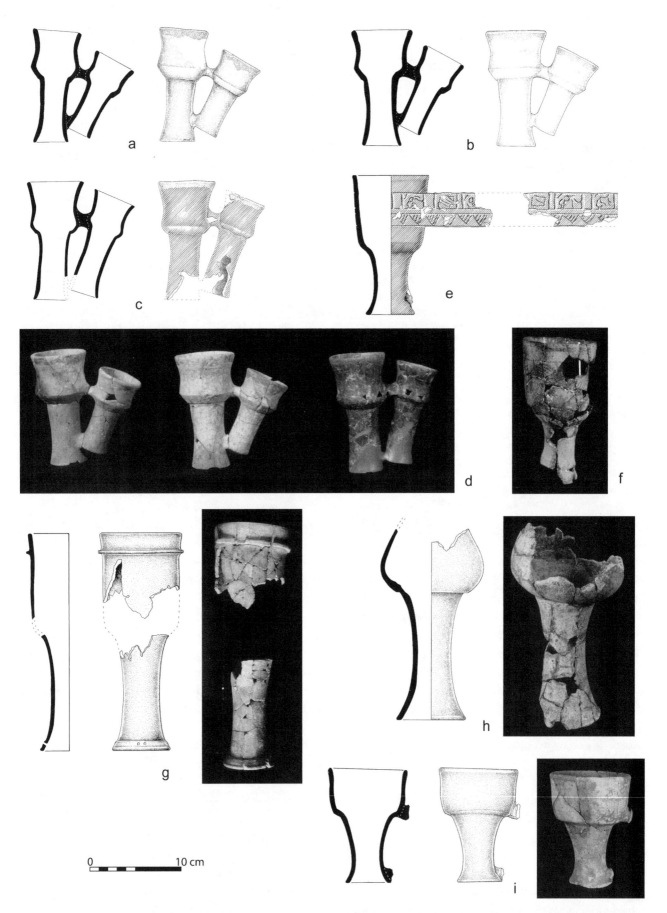

FIGURE 9.1. Complete and reconstructible ceramic drums. (a–d) Structure M7-22. (a, b) Unnamed white slipped. (a) 22A14-3-3, Cat. 310264, WDR 22A-1. (b) 22A10-3-2, Cat. 310265, WDR 22A-2. (c) Azote Orange, 22A14-3-2, Cat. 310266, WDR 22A-3. (d) *From left:* WDR-1, 2, and 3. (e–i) Structure M8-4. (e, f) Unnamed incised, 23A43-3-3, Cat. 310316, WDR 23A-1. (g, h) Saxche-Palmar Polychrome. (g) 23A18-3-4, Cat. 310405, WDR 23A-2. (h) 23A14-3-4, Cat. 310317, WDR 23A-3. (i) Unnamed white slipped, 23A32-3-1, Cat. 310315, WDR 23A-4.

rim had broken off, probably in the fire. Broken into small fragments. Dimensions: Rim diameter: [exterior] 8.9 cm, [top] 8.5 cm (measured); Height: 23 cm (estimate); Wall thickness: 0.5 cm; Sample weight: 295 g; Original weight: 327 g. Coordinates: (50.77, 17.47) (measured). Type: Saxche-Palmar Polychrome. Paste, temper, and firing: Reddish yellow paste (5YR7/6). Medium grain. A medium amount of calcite temper (0.1–0.5 mm diameter) and a small amount of ferruginous temper (1.0–2.0 mm diameter). The paste is dark from burning. Surface finish and decoration: Some remains of cream slip. It is not clear whether there was polychrome painting. Form: Drum. Direct upper rim and rounded lip. Ridge below the rim. Exterior-thickened lower rim and rounded lip. Three pairs of small perforations through the lower rim. There appear to be three holes that do not go through below the upper rim. There may be similar holes in the mid-body. Use-wear: Not clear.

WDR No.: 23A-3; Catalog No.: 310317 (Figure 9.1h)
Bag No.: Upper rim: 1400 (15-2-1), 1975 (14-3-2); Body: 2096 (14-3-4), 1400, 1975, 2006, 1218 (14-2-2); Lower rim: 2096, 2006 (47-3-4), 1218. Provenience: 23A14-3-4. Context: Floor. On the floor of the central room in front of the bench. Most fragments of the mid and lower bodies were found in one concentration, but others were scattered in an area 2 × 2 m. The drum may have been stored on the bench surface or in a higher location. Condition: Reconstructible (75% present). Badly eroded. Burned and reoxidized. Dimensions: Rim diameter: 9.5 cm (rough estimate); Height: 24 cm (rough estimate); Wall thickness: 0.6 cm; Sample weight: 313 g; Original weight: 417 g. Coordinates: (46.82, 17.32) (measured). Type: Saxche-Palmar Polychrome. Paste, temper, and firing: Red paste (2.5YR5/8). Medium paste. A medium amount of calcite temper (0.3–1.0 mm diameter) and a small amount of ferruginous temper (0.5–1.3 mm diameter). The paste is completely oxidized. Surface finish and decoration: The surface is mostly eroded. Some remains of red paint. Form: Drum. Direct upper rim and rounded lip. Direct lower rim and squared lip. Use-wear: Not clear because of erosion.

WDR No.: 23A-4; Catalog No.: 310315 (Figure 9.1i)
Bag No.: Upper rim: 1880 (32-3-1), 1482 (32-3-1); Body: 1880; Lower rim: 1880. Provenience: 23A32-3-1. Context: Floor. On the exterior floor east of the north addition. Most fragments were found in one concentration. Con-

dition: Reconstructible (90% present). Badly eroded and burned. It was a double drum or a drum with a handle, but it was apparently used without the attachment. Dimensions: Rim diameter: [exterior] 8.7 cm, [top] 8.3 cm (measured); Height: 11.8 cm (measured); Wall thickness: 0.5 cm; Sample weight: 187 g; Original weight: 208 g. Coordinates: (55.69, 20.50) (measured). Type: Unnamed white slipped. Paste, temper, and firing: Reddish yellow paste (7.5YR7/6). Medium grain. A large amount of calcite temper (0.1–0.3 mm diameter) and a small amount ferruginous temper (0.5–2.0 mm). The paste is completely oxidized. The paste is similar to that of Tinaja Red. Surface finish and decoration: Cream slip on the exterior. The interior is unslipped. Form: Drum. Direct rim and rounded lip. Use-wear: Not clear.

STRUCTURE M8-3: OPERATION 23B

WDR No.: 23B-1; Catalog No.: 310180
Bag No.: Body: 313 (3-3-1); Lower rim: 313. Provenience: 23B3-3-1. Context: Floor. On the western wing of the bench of Structure M8-3. Only the support of a drum was recovered. All fragments were found in one concentration. It appears that the support was reused. Condition: Partial (30% present). Badly eroded. Fragments appear to be burned in dark color. Dimensions: Height of support: 11.9 cm (measured); Wall thickness: 0.5 cm; Sample weight: 128 g; Original weight 427 g. Coordinates: (49.61, 36.60) (measured). Type: Saxche-Palmar Polychrome. Paste, temper, and firing: Reddish yellow paste (7.5YR6/6). Fine. Contains a small amount of calcite temper (0.1–0.5 mm diameter) and a small amount of hematite temper (0.5–1.5 mm diameter). The core is slightly dark. Surface finish and decoration: The surface is mostly eroded. Remains of red paint on cream underslip. Form: Drum. Exterior-thickened lower rim and rounded lip. Use-wear: Not clear.

STRUCTURE M7-34 (HOUSE OF METATES): OPERATION 21A

WDR No.: 21A-1; Catalog No.: 310411 (Figure 9.2a)
Bag No.: Upper rim: 940 (56-2-1), 735 (42-3-2), 736 (42-3-1), 271 (43-1-1), 725 (42-3-4), 265 (42-1-1), 728 (33-3-3), 1288; Body: 736, 725, 271, 735, 732 (42-3-3), 181 (33-1-1), 1288, 943 (56-2-2), 736, 496 (43-2-4); Lower rim: 728, 1288 (56-3-2), 534 (33-2-2), 940. Provenience: 21A42-2-1. Context: Floor. On the exterior floor in front of the south room and on the front step of the south room. Fragments were found in an area 5 × 3 m. Some pieces probably remained in the

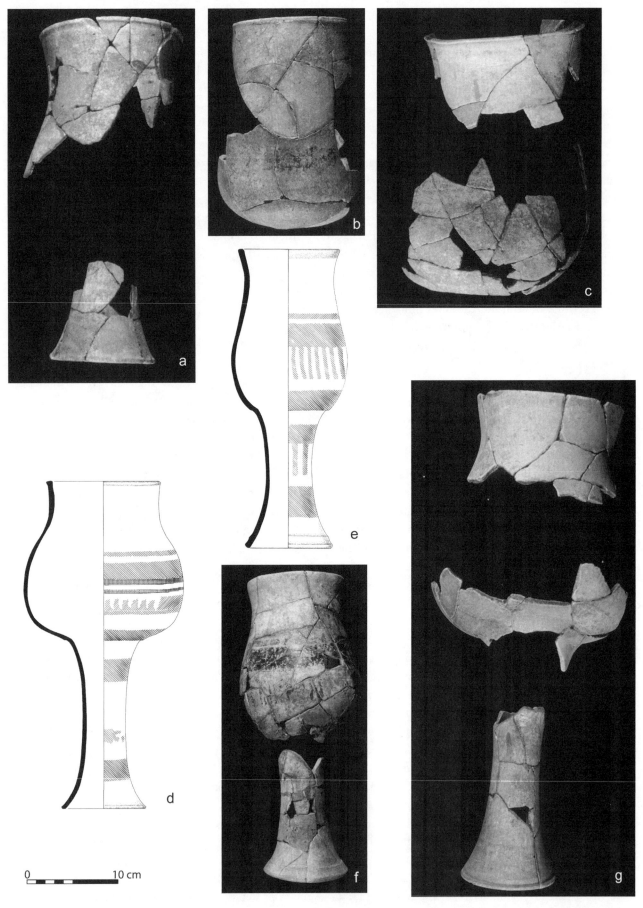

FIGURE 9.2. Complete and reconstructible ceramic drums from Structure M7-34. Saxche-Palmar Polychrome. (a) 21A42-2-1, Cat. 310411, WDR 21A-1. (b) 21A42-3-1, Cat. 310412, WDR 21A-2. (c) 21A54-3-2, Cat. 310413, WVS 21A-3. (d) 21A65-3-2, Cat. 310477, WDR 21A-6. (e, f) 21A39-3-4, Cat. 310227, WDR 21A-5. (g) 21A83-3-1, Cat. 310478, WDR 21A-7.

0   10 cm

unexcavated area. Condition: Reconstructible (70% present). Badly eroded. Burned and darkened. Dimensions: Rim diameter: [exterior] 15.8 cm, [top] 15.4 cm (measured); Maximum diameter: 19 cm (estimate); Height: 37 cm (rough estimate); Wall thickness: 0.5–0.8 cm; Sample weight: 1,039 g; Original weight: 1,484 g. Coordinates: (9.17, 5.74) (estimate). Type: Saxche-Palmar Polychrome. Paste, temper, and firing: Reddish yellow paste (7.5YR7/6). Fine grain. A small amount of calcite temper (0.1–0.5 mm diameter) and a small amount of ferruginous temper (0.5–1.5 mm diameter). In some parts the core of the paste is dark. Surface finish and decoration: Remains of red paint over cream underslip. Form: Drum. Slightly exterior-thickened upper rim and flat lip. Slightly exterior-thickened lower rim and rounded lip. Use-wear: Not clear because of erosion.

WDR No.: 21A-2; Catalog No.: 310412 (Figure 9.2b)
Bag No.: Upper rim: 609 (42-2-2), 736 (42-3-1), 412 (42-1-2); Body: 412, 736, 735 (42-3-2), 943 (56-2-2), 475 (43-2-1), 940 (56-2-1), 728 (33-3-3), 785 (55-3-2), 739 (29-3-2), 740 (29-3-3); Lower rim: 609. Provenience: 21A42-3-1. Context: Floor. On the exterior floor in front of the south room. Fragments were found in an area 1.5 × 4 m. Condition: Reconstructible (70% present). Badly eroded. Burned and darkened. Dimensions: Rim diameter: 11 cm (estimate); Maximum diameter: 14.7 cm (measured); Height: 40 cm (rough estimate); Wall thickness: 0.4–0.6 cm; Sample weight: 755 g; Original weight: 1,078 g. Coordinates: (9.23, 4.64) (estimate). Type: Saxche-Palmar Polychrome. Paste, temper, and firing: Reddish yellow paste (7.5YR7/6). Fine grain. A small amount of calcite temper (0.1–0.5 mm diameter) and a small amount of ferruginous temper (0.5–1.0 mm diameter). The paste is completely oxidized. Surface finish and decoration: Some remains of red horizontal bands and orange paint over cream underslip. Form: Drum. Exterior-thickened upper rim and flat lip. Use-wear: Not clear.

WDR No.: 21A-3; Catalog No.: 310413 (Figure 9.2c)
Bag No.: Rim: 1300 (54-3-2), 1283 (56-3-1), 920 (56-1-2), 975 (55-2-2), 181 (33-1-1), 784 (55-3-1); Body: 1300, 1358 (55-3-4), 730 (33-3-4), 728 (33-3-3). Provenience: 21A54-3-2. Context: Floor. On the exterior floor in front of the south room, near the peripheral wall. Fragments were found in an area 5 × 3 m. Condition: Reconstructible (60% present). Badly eroded. Burned and darkened. Only part of the rim was reconstructed. Dimensions: Rim diameter:

[exterior] 16.9 cm, [top] 16.5 cm (measured); Maximum diameter: 21 cm (estimate); Height: 40 cm (rough estimate); Wall thickness: 0.5–0.8 cm; Sample weight: 875 g; Original weight: 1,458 g. Coordinates: (11.33, 3.48) (estimate). Type: Saxche-Palmar Polychrome. Paste, temper, and firing: Pink paste (7.5YR7/4). Fine grain. A small amount of calcite temper (0.1–0.4 mm diameter) and a small amount of ferruginous temper (0.5–1.5 mm diameter). In some parts the core of the paste is dark. Surface finish and decoration: Remains of red paint over cream underslip. Form: Drum. Exterior-thickened upper rim and flat lip. Use-wear: Not clear because of the fragmentary state.

WDR No.: 21A-4; Catalog No.: 310390
Bag No.: Body: 1007 (59-2-1), 1011 (60-2-2), 720 (33-3-1), 736 (42-3-1). Provenience: 21A33-3-1. Context: Floor. On the exterior floor in front of the south room. A small portion was found in an area 2 × 1 m in front of the south room inside the peripheral wall (Units 33 and 42). A larger portion was in an area 3 × 2 m outside the peripheral wall, near the entrance (Units 59 and 60). Pieces from those two areas were refitted. They are burned in similar ways, which suggests that the drum was burned when it was complete and then was scattered. The drum may have been stored with other drums in or near the south room and then scattered in the disturbance after abandonment. Condition: Reconstructible (30% present). Eroded. Burned and darkened. Most of the recovered fragments were glued together. Dimensions: Maximum diameter: 19 cm (rough estimate); Height: 37 cm (rough estimate); Wall thickness: 0.3–0.5 cm; Sample weight: 354 g; Original weight: 1,180 g. Coordinates: (11.31, 4.61) (estimate). Type: Saxche-Palmar Polychrome. Paste, temper, and firing: Reddish yellow paste (7.5YR7/6). Fine grain. A small amount of calcite temper (0.1–0.3 mm diameter) and a small amount of ferruginous temper (0.3–1.0 mm diameter). The core of the paste in some parts is dark. Surface finish and decoration: Remains of red paint over cream underslip. Form: Drum. Use-wear: Not clear.

WDR No.: 21A-5; Catalog No.: 310227 (Figure 9.2e and 9.2f)
Bag No.: Upper rim: 571 (39-3-4), 846 (39-3-2), 193 (38-2-1), 508 (39-2-3); Body: 571, 234 (39-1-2), 565 (39-3-3), 262 (40-1-1), 227 (35-1-1), 494 (40-2-4), 273 (40-1-2). Provenience: 21A39-3-4. Context: Floor. On the exterior floor between the north wall of Structure M7-34 and the

circumferential wall. A significant portion of fragments was found in one concentration. Other pieces were scattered in an area 2 × 4 m (Units 38, 39, and 40). The drum may have been stored in a high location near the north wall of the structure. Condition: Reconstructible (80% present). Eroded. Severely burned in black color. Dimensions: Rim diameter: [exterior] 11.1 cm, [top] 10.7 cm (measured); Height: 30.0 cm (measured); Wall thickness: 0.5–0.7 cm; Sample weight: 784 g; Original weight: 980 g. Coordinates: (24.80, 9.35) (measured). Type: Saxche-Palmar Polychrome. Paste, temper, and firing: Reddish yellow paste (7.5YR6/6). Fine. Contains a small amount of calcite temper (0.3–0.8 mm diameter) and a small amount of hematite temper (0.5–1.5 mm diameter). The core is slightly dark. Surface finish and decoration: The surface is mostly eroded. Cream underslip and red horizontal bands. Form: Drum. Direct upper rim and squared lip. Exterior-thickened lower rim and rounded lip. Use-wear: Not clear because of erosion.

WDR No.: 21A-6; Catalog No.: 310477 (Figure 9.2d)
Bag No.: Upper rim: 1456 (65-3-2), 987 (65-2-3), 1396 (83-3-1), 1403 (65-3-2); Body: 1455 (65-3-2), 987, 1456, 1416 (83-3-1), 1403, 1207 (66-3-1); Lower rim: 1401 (65-3-2), 1455, 1403. Provenience: 21A65-3-2. Context: Floor. On the exterior floor outside the peripheral wall of Structure M7-34, in front of the stairway of the Palace Group platform. The fragments were found in an area 1 × 3 m. The deposit may be a midden. Condition: Reconstructible (95% present). Eroded. The lower part was blackened after the vessel broke. Dimensions: Rim diameter: [exterior] 12.0 cm, [top] 11.6 cm (measured); Maximum diameter: 16.5 cm (measured); Height: 34.7 cm (measured); Wall thickness: 0.3–0.5 cm; Sample weight: 943 g; Original weight: 993 g. Coordinates: (25.92, 1.65) (estimate). Type: Saxche-Palmar Polychrome. Paste, temper, and firing: Reddish yellow paste (7.5YR7/6). Fine grain. A small amount of calcite temper (0.1–0.3 mm diameter) and a small amount of ferruginous temper (0.5–0.8 mm diameter). The core of the paste is dark. Surface finish and decoration: Horizontal bands of red, orange, and brown over cream underslip. One band contains wavy motifs. Form: Drum. Slightly exterior-thickened upper rim and squared lip. Slightly exterior-thickened lower rim and rounded lip. Use-wear: Not clear because of erosion.

WDR No.: 21A-7; Catalog No.: 310478 (Figure 9.2g)
Bag No.: Upper rim: 1453 (83-3-1), 1396 (83-3-1), 1015 (83-2-1); Body: 1453, 1396, 1015, 1416 (83-3-1), 987 (65-2-3); Lower rim: 1401 (65-3-2), 1453, 1396, 1455 (65-3-2), 1416. Provenience: 21A83-3-1. Context: Floor. On the exterior floor outside the peripheral wall of Structure M7-34, in front of the stairway of the Palace Group platform. The fragments were found in an area 1 × 3 m. The deposit may be a midden. Condition: Reconstructible (90% present). Eroded. The lower part was darkened after the vessel broke. Many of the fragments were not refitted. Dimensions: Rim diameter: [exterior] 14.2 cm, [top] 14.0 cm (measured); Maximum diameter: 21 cm (estimate); Height: 40 cm (estimate); Wall thickness: 0.5–0.8 cm; Sample weight: 1,737 g; Original weight: 1,930 g. Coordinates: (25.97, 2.43) (estimate). Type: Saxche-Palmar Polychrome. Paste, temper, and firing: Reddish yellow paste (5YR7/6). Fine grain. A small amount of calcite temper (0.1–0.3 mm diameter) and a small amount of ferruginous temper (0.3–1.0 mm diameter). The core of the paste is dark. Surface finish and decoration: Some remains of a red horizontal band over cream underslip. Form: Drum. Direct upper rim and rounded lip. Exterior-thickened lower rim and squared lip. Use-wear: Not clear because of erosion.

10 | Formation Processes of the Ceramic Assemblages

Takeshi Inomata

ALTHOUGH WE HAVE ample evidence indicating that the epicenter of Aguateca was abandoned rapidly, certain objects were probably removed or added and their locations were changed at the time of abandonment. The examination of such formation processes of the archaeological record is a critical step in understanding the social and cultural implications of the assemblages (Inomata and Webb 2003; Schiffer 1987). The ceramic remains, with their large numbers and varying sizes, provide particularly important information in this regard. Our investment of a substantial time and effort in refitting ceramic vessels during the lab seasons was geared significantly toward this issue.

THE PALACE GROUP

Structure M7-22 (House of Masks): Operation 22A

In Structure M7-22, all reconstructible vessels derive from the sealed easternmost room and the area in front of it. They were most likely stored in this room as complete pieces. After the room was opened, probably by the invading enemies, many objects were broken and thrown out of the room. These fragments were found on the layer of stones that had sealed the entrance and under the collapse layer of the building. The fragments found in this area were generally larger than those from the dense deposits in the other areas. Fragments of WVS 22A-3 (Cat. 310299) and WVS 22A-9 (Cat. 310295) were found both inside and outside the room, further supporting the interpretation that these vessels were intentionally broken and scattered after the room was opened. Despite our best efforts, we could probably not refit many of the scattered vessels. The original number of vessels stored in the easternmost room may have been substantially larger than that listed in Chapter 8. We did not find any other reconstructible vessels in the dense deposits around the building. It appears that participants in the terminal rituals deposited already-broken vessels instead of breaking complete vessels and scattering their fragments.

Structure M7-32 (House of Bones): Operation 22B

All ceramics found in and around Structure M7-32 were parts of termination ritual deposits. Like those of Structure M7-22, most of them were broken, nonreconstructible objects. Nonetheless, a small number of reconstructible vessels were found, both inside the center room and on the northern side of the building. It is probable that they were deposited as whole objects or were intentionally broken at the time of deposition. For example, fragments of WVS 22B-3 were scattered in the central room, and the vessel was nearly completely reconstructed. Pieces of this vessel were found in the broken part of the bench floor and in the broken niche, as well as on the room floor in front of the bench, indicating that the materials in the broken bench floor and the broken niche were deposited at the same time as the rest of the termination ritual materials.

THE CAUSEWAY AREA

In evaluating the formation processes in the rapidly abandoned structures, we may examine how successful our effort of refitting fragments was by comparing the weight of refitted fragments and the estimated weights of original vessels with the total weight of excavated ceramics (Table 10.1). Table 10.1 shows that the total estimated weight of original vessels is somewhat lower than the weight of all ceramics. Three factors may be responsible for this pattern. First, it is possible that we could not recognize a certain number of reconstructible vessels. Second, the original assemblages may have included fragments and sherds that were kept before the abandonment or were added at the time of abandonment. Third, we may have underestimated the original weights of many vessels. In

TABLE 10.1. Comparison of the Weights of All Ceramics with Those of Complete, Reconstructible, and Partial Vessels.

SUB-OPERATIONS	STRUCTURES	ROOMS/AREAS	ALL CERAMICS	RECONSTRUCTIBLE PRESENT SAMPLES	WEIGHT (g) % OF ALL CERAMICS	RECONSTRUCTIBLE ESTIMATED ORIGINAL	% OF ALL CERAMICS
23A							
	M8-4	North addition	106458	13017	12.2	19176	18.0
	M8-4	North room	145910	97985	67.2	138822	95.1
	M8-4	Center room	23239	3911	16.8	6306	27.1
	M8-4	South room	71674	43312	60.4	84174	117.4
	M8-4	South side	29069	16238	55.9	42636	146.7
	M8-4	Front	8928	0	0.0	0	0.0
	Subtotal		385278	174463	45.3	291114	75.6
20A							
	M8-8	North addition	67764	56428	83.3	75159	110.9
	M8-8	North room	84521	66114	78.2	82704	97.9
	M8-8	Center room	59906	52480	87.6	70007	116.9
	M8-8	South room	19638	9267	47.2	14258	72.6
	M8-8	South addition	19020	17784	93.5	37720	198.3
	M8-8	North side	9595	0	0.0	0	0.0
	M8-8	South side	27090	10417	38.5	24350	89.9
	M8-8	Back	86757	26183	30.2	46219	53.3
	Subtotal		374291	238673	63.8	350417	93.6
14B							
	M8-13	West room	63693	19904	31.3	55161	86.6
	M8-13	Center room	77148	28201	36.6	81162	105.2
	M8-13	East room	20732	2625	12.7	7117	34.3
	M8-13	Back	58968	14840	25.2	30690	52.0
	Subtotal		220541	65570	29.7	174130	79.0
23B							
	M8-2		182314	35892	19.7	73827	40.5
	M8-3		46715	16234	34.8	36455	78.0
21A							
	M7-34	North room	50810	22077	43.5	77994	153.5
	M7-34	Center room	38672	12973	33.5	24954	64.5
	M7-34	South room	97648	46383	47.5	108248	110.9
	M7-34	North side	36115	22667	62.8	39780	110.1
	M7-34	South side	4011	1031	25.7	1146	28.6
	M7-34	Front	74859	14344	19.2	35964	48.0
	M7-34	Back	1082	264	24.4	1056	97.6
	M7-91		42711	19817	46.4	49390	115.6
	M7-92		72277	20024	27.7	38146	52.8
	Causeway terrace		136288	27689	20.3	53213	39.0
	Subtotal		554473	187269	33.8	429891	77.5
Total			1763612	718101	40.7	1355834	76.9

The table does not include ceramics from construction fills and middens.

The table does not include ceramics from the central part of the patio of Suboperation 23A and 23B and those from Suboperations 14C and 14D.

Materials found directly in front of a room were combined with those from inside the room, but those found in the side or back areas were counted separately.

The data for Structures M8-2, M8-3, M7-91, and M7-92 include ceramics found in the immediate surroundings of the buildings.

The Causeway terrace refers to the northwestern corner of Operation 21A.

particular, only small portions of large vessels were usually refitted, and the estimates of their original weight probably have a substantial range of error.

Despite these uncertainties, it appears significant that the estimated weight of original vessels for Structure M8-8 is fairly close to the total weight of ceramics. Compared with the other structures in the Causeway area, this building was relatively well preserved. In particular, its north addition and north room contained many vessels within their high standing walls. It appears that under these favorable conditions it is easier to achieve a better success in reconstructing vessels. If so, the disturbance at the time of and after abandonment may be a major factor contributing to the larger discrepancies seen in other buildings.

Structure M8-4 (House of Mirrors): Operation 23A

In the north addition of Structure M8-4, the weight of refitted sherds and the estimated weight of original vessels are markedly lower than that of all sherds. It is probable that many fragments found there fell from the platform of the Palace Group to the north. In the north room, fragments of most vessels were found in tight concentrations, and it was easy to recognize them as reconstructible objects in the field. There was little indication of disturbance during the abandonment.

The situation of the center room is quite different. Reconstructible vessels account for only a small portion of the excavated ceramics. Whereas fragments of some vessels were found close together, others were scattered in wide areas. It is not clear whether this pattern was caused by disturbance during or after abandonment. In the south room, pieces of many vessels were scattered in wide areas, although the estimated weight of original vessels is close to the amount of all excavated ceramics. It appears that the room was disturbed at the time of abandonment, which is also indicated by the wide distribution of pyrite pieces. In the extramural area to the south of the building, the estimated weight of original vessels is substantially higher than that of all ceramics, probably because many pieces remained in unexcavated areas.

Structure M8-8 (House of Axes): Operation 20A

As mentioned above, the ceramic assemblage in Structure M8-8 appears relatively undisturbed. In the north addition and north room, in particular, reconstructed vessels account for substantial portions of the excavated ceramics. The southwestern section of the center room was unexcavated because of a large tree, and some reconstructible vessels may have remained in this area. In other parts of the room, many vessels were found relatively undisturbed. In the south room, however, many sherds were not refitted although the total amount of excavated ceramics was small. This may be partly due to the disturbance caused by the roots of the tree standing in the room, but it is also possible that the area was disturbed at the time of abandonment.

The pattern in the south addition was anomalous, as the estimated weight of original vessels was twice as large as the weight of excavated ceramics. This is because substantial parts of some vessels were found in the area outside the south addition. It is highly unlikely that this pattern was caused by post-abandonment processes. The vessels appear to have been scattered before or during abandonment. Behind the buildings, fragments of many vessels were found in relatively tight concentrations, but there was a substantial quantity of sherds that were not accounted for by these reconstructible vessels. Many of them appear to have fallen from Structures M7-34 and M8-9.

Structure M8-13: Operation 14B

In Structure M8-13, only a small portion of excavated ceramics was refitted. The building appears to have been substantially disturbed by tree roots and tree falls. The turned-up bedrock found in front of the center room was most likely caused by an old tree fall. Such post-abandonment disturbances probably contributed considerably to the difficulty of refitting ceramics from this operation. It is not clear whether the assemblages were disturbed significantly at the time of abandonment.

Structures M8-2 and M8-3: Operation 23B

Many the ceramics from Operation 23B were not refitted. The ratio of refitted fragments to all ceramics and that of the estimated weight of original vessels to all ceramics are particularly low for Structure M8-2. There were four necks of Tinaja/Pantano jars without bases, which were not counted as reconstructible or partial (2 in Unit 5, 1 in Unit 3, and 1 in Unit 23). There was a significant portion of a Chaquiste bowl in Unit 6 that was not counted as reconstructible. The small ratio of refitted pieces may support the interpretation that the dense deposit to the west of Structure M8-2 was a midden. In addition, the masonry parts of the walls of these buildings were low, and artifacts were probably susceptible to various processes of disturbance after abandonment. Moreover, some objects found behind Structure M8-2 probably had fallen from the platform of the Palace Group.

Structures M7-34 (House of Metates), M7-91, and M7-92: Operation 21A

A relatively small portion of the ceramics was refitted in Operation 21A. Unlike Structures M8-4 and M8-8, where differences between preserved areas and disturbed ones are relatively clear, Structure M7-34 shows rather consistently low ratios of refitting. We would expect that the objects found in the front part of each room were protected by masonry walls, but many of them also show low rates of refitting. It thus appears that this building was substantially disturbed at the time of abandonment or was scavenged afterward. If so, it is difficult to determine whether the vessels found in the area in front of Structure M7-34 and inside the circumferential walls were originally placed there or were thrown there during the disturbance. Still, the general distribution pattern appears meaningful. Many of the objects were found in the areas in front of the north and south rooms, and the area in front of the center room, which provided the main access from outside, had a smaller quantity of ceramics. This pattern may indicate that the general distribution pattern of ceramics approximates the original distribution of the vessels. There are several Cambio/Encanto necks apparently without bodies on the exterior floor in front of the rooms. It is not clear whether the occupants kept the broken necks or whether we could reconstruct only the necks of the reconstructible vessels because their pieces were so badly scattered.

References

Adams, Richard E. W.

1971 *The Ceramics of Altar de Sacrificios, Guatemala*. Papers of the Peabody Museum Vol. 63, No. 1. Harvard University, Cambridge.

1981 Settlement Patterns of the Central Yucatan and Southern Campeche Regions. In *Lowland Maya Settlement Patterns*, edited by Wendy Ashmore, pp. 211–257. University of Mexico Press, Albuquerque.

Anglo, Sydney

1977 The Courtier: The Renaissance and Changing Ideals. In *The Courts of Europe: Politics, Patronage, and Royalty, 1400–1800*, edited by A. G. Dickens, pp. 33–53. Thames and Hudson, London.

Aoyama, Kazuo

2000 La especialización artesanal y las actividades cotidianas en la sociedad clásica maya: Análisis preliminar de las microhuellas de uso sobre la lítica de Aguateca. In *XIII simposio de investigaciones arqueológicas en Guatemala*, edited by Juan Pedro Laporte, Héctor L. Escobedo, Ana Claudia de Suasnavar, and Bárbara Arroyo, pp. 21–232. Ministerio de Cultura y Deportes, Instituto de Antropología e Historia, and Asociación Tikal, Guatemala City.

2005 Classic Maya Warfare and Weapons: Spear, Dart and Arrow Points of Aguateca and Copán. *Ancient Mesoamerica* 16:291–304.

2007 Elite Artists and Craft Producers in Classic Maya Society: Lithic Evidence from Aguateca, Guatemala. *Latin American Antiquity* 18:3–26.

2009 *Elite Craft Producers, Artists, and Warriors at Aguateca: Lithic Analysis*. Monographs of the Aguateca Archaeological Project First Phase, vol. 2. University of Utah Press, Salt Lake City.

Ashmore, Wendy

1992 Deciphering Maya Architectural Plans. In *New Theories on the Ancient Maya*, edited by Elin Darien and Robert Sharer, pp. 173–184. University Museum Monograph 77. University of Pennsylvania, Philadelphia.

Ashmore, Wendy (editor)

1981 *Lowland Maya Settlement Patterns*. School of American Research Advanced Seminar Series. University of New Mexico Press, Albuquerque.

Ashmore, Wendy, and Richard R. Wilk

1988 Household and Community in the Mesoamerican Past. In *Household and Community in the Mesoamerican Past*, edited by Wendy Ashmore and Richard R. Wilk, pp. 1–28. University of New Mexico Press, Albuquerque.

Austin, J. L.

1962 *How to Do Things with Words*. Oxford University Press, Oxford.

Bachand, Bruce R.

2006 Preclassic Excavations at Punta de Chimino, Petén, Guatemala: Investigating Social Emplacement on an Early Maya Landscape. Unpublished Ph.D. dissertation, University of Arizona, Tucson.

2007 The Pre-Classic Ceramic Sequence of Punta de Chimino, Petén, Guatemala. *Mayab* 19:5–26.

Baker, Charles M.

1975 Site Abandonment and the Archaeological Record: An Empirical Case for Anticipated Return. *Proceedings of the Arkansas Academy of Science* 29:10–11.

Ball, Joseph, W., and Richalene G. Kelsay

1992 Prehistoric Intrasettlement Land Use and Residual Soil Phosphate Levels in the Upper Belize Valley, Central America. In *Gardens of Prehistory: The Archaeology of Settlement Agriculture in Greater Mesoamerica*, edited by Thomas W. Killion, pp. 234–262. University of Alabama Press, Tuscaloosa.

Barba, Luis, and Agustín Ortiz

1992 Análisis químico de pisos de ocupación: Un caso etnográfico en Tlaxcala, México. *Latin American Antiquity* 3:63–82.

Bawden, Garth

1982 The Household: A Study of Pre-Columbian Social Dynamics. *Journal of Field Archaeology* 9:165–181.

Beaubien, Harriet F.

2001 *Use Analysis of Stone Implements from Aguateca, Guatemala*. Report filed at the Smithsonian Center for Materials Research and Education, Washington, D.C.

Becquelin, Pierre, and Dominique Michelet

1994 Demografía en la zona puuc: El recurso del método. *Latin American Antiquity* 5:289–311.

Bender, Donald R.

1967 A Refinement of the Concept of Household: Families, Co-Residence, and Domestic Functions. *American Anthropologist* 69:493–504.

Bermann, Marc

1994 *Lukurmata: Household Archaeology in Prehispanic Bolivia*. Princeton University Press, Princeton.

Blanton, Richard E.

1994　*Houses and Households: A Comparative Study*. Interdisciplinary Contributions to Archaeology. Plenum Press, New York.

Bourdieu, Pierre

1977　*Outline of a Theory of Practice*. Cambridge Studies in Social Anthropology 16. Cambridge University Press, Cambridge.

Brumfiel, Elizabeth M.

1991　Weaving and Cooking: Women's Production in Aztec Mexico. In *Engendering Archaeology: Women and Prehistory*, edited by Joan M. Gero and Margaret W. Conkey, pp. 224–251. Blackwell, Oxford.

Cameron, Catherine M., and Steve A. Tomka

1993　*Abandonment of Settlements and Regions: Ethnoarchaeological and Archaeological Approaches*. Cambridge University Press, Cambridge.

Carr, C.

1984　The Nature of Organization of Intrasite Archaeological Records and Spatial Analytic Approaches to Their Investigation. *Advances in Archaeological Method and Theory* 7:103–221.

Chase, Diane Z., and Arlen F. Chase

2000　Inferences about Abandonment: Maya Household Archaeology and Caracol, Belize. *Mayab* 13:67–77.

Cogolludo, Diego López de

1971　[1654] *Los tres siglos de la dominación española en Yucatán o sea historia de esta provincia*. 2 vols. Akademische Druck- und Verlangsanstalt, Graz.

Culbert, T. Patrick

1993　*Tikal Report No. 25, Part A: The Ceramics of Tikal; Vessels from the Burials, Caches and Problematical Deposits*. University Museum Monograph 81. University of Pennsylvania, Philadelphia.

Culbert, T. Patrick (editor)

1991　*Classic Maya Political History: Hieroglyphic and Archaeological Evidence*. Cambridge University Press, Cambridge.

Culbert, T. Patrick, and Don S. Rice (editors)

1990　*Precolumbian Population History in the Maya Lowlands*. University of New Mexico Press, Albuquerque.

David, Nicholas, and Carol Kramer

2001　*Ethnoarchaeology in Action*. Cambridge World Archaeology. Cambridge University Press, New York.

Deal, Michael

1985　Household Pottery Disposal in the Maya Highlands: An Ethnoarchaeological Interpretation. *Journal of Anthropological Archaeology* 4:243–291.

1998　*Pottery Ethnoarchaeology in the Central Maya Highlands*. Foundations of Archaeological Inquiry. University of Utah Press, Salt Lake City.

Deetz, James J. F.

1982　Households: A Structural Key to Archaeological Explanation. *American Behavioral Scientist* 25(6):717–724.

de la Garza, Mercedes, Ana Luisa Izquierdo, María del Carmen León, and Tolita Figueroa

1983　*Relaciones histórico-geográficas de la gobernación de Yucatán (Mérida, Valladolid y Tabasco)*. 2 vols. Universidad Nacional Autónoma de México, Mexico City.

Demarest, Arthur A.

1997　The Vanderbilt Petexbatun Regional Archaeological Project 1989–1994: Overview, History, and Major Results of a Multidisciplinary Study of the Classic Maya Collapse. *Ancient Mesoamerica* 8(2):209–228.

2006　*The Petexbatun Regional Archaeological Project: A Multidisciplinary Study of the Collapse of a Classic Maya Kingdom*. Vanderbilt Institute of Mesoamerican Archaeology Series 1. Vanderbilt University Press, Nashville, Tennessee.

Demarest, Arthur, Kim Morgan, Claudia Wolley, and Héctor Escobedo

2003　The Political Acquisition of Sacred Geography: The Murciélagos Complex at Dos Pilas. In *Maya Palaces and Elite Residences: An Interdisciplinary Approach*, edited by Jessica Joyce Christie, pp. 120–153. University of Texas Press, Austin.

Demarest, Arthur A., Matt O'Mansky, Claudia Wolley, Dirk Van Tuerenhout, Takeshi Inomata, Joel Palka, and Héctor Escobedo

1997　Classic Maya Defensive Systems and Warfare in the Petexbatun Region: Archaeological Evidence and Interpretation. *Ancient Mesoamerica* 8(2):229–254.

Douglas, Mary

1972　Symbolic Orders in the Use of Domestic Space. In *Man, Settlement and Urbanism*, edited by Peter J. Ucko, Geoffrey W. Dimbleby and Ruth Tringham, pp. 513–521. Duckworth, London.

Drennan, Robert D.

1988　Household Location and Compact versus Dispersed Settlement in Prehispanic Mesoamerica. In *Household and Community in the Mesoamerican Past*, edited by Richard R. Wilk and Wendy Ashmore, pp. 273–294. University of New Mexico Press, Albuquerque.

Eberl, Markus

2007　Community Heterogeneity and Integration: The Maya Sites of Nacimiento, Dos Ceibas, and Cerro de Cheyo (El Peten, Guatemala) during the Late Classic. Unpublished Ph.D. dissertation, Tulane University, New Orleans.

Elias, Norbert

1983　*The Court Society*. Translated by Edmund Jephcott. Pantheon, New York. Originally published as *Die höfische Gesellschaft*, 1969.

Emery, Kitty, and Kazuo Aoyama

2007　Bone, Shell and Lithic Evidence for Crafting in Elite Maya Households at Aguateca, Guatemala. *Ancient Mesoamerica* 18:69–89.

Engels, Friedrich

1942　*The Origin of the Family, Private Property and the State*. International Publishers, New York.

Fahsen, Federico

2003　La Escalinata 2 de Dos Pilas, Petén: Los nuevos escalones. In *XVI Simposio de Investigaciones Arqueológicas en Guatemala, 2002*, edited by Juan Pedro Laporte, Barbara Arroyo, Héctor L. Escobedo, and Héctor Mejía, pp. 687–700. Ministerio de Cultura y Deportes, Instituto de Antropología e Historia, and Asociación Tikal, Guatemala City.

Fash, Barbara, William Fash, Sheree Lane, Rudy Larios, Linda Schele, Jeffrey Stomper, and David Stuart
1992   Investigations of a Classic Maya Council House at Copán, Honduras. *Journal of Field Archaeology* 19:419–442.

Fladmark, K. R.
1982   Microdebitage Analysis: Initial Considerations. *Journal of Archaeological Science* 9:205–220.

Foias, Antonia E.
1996   Changing Ceramic Production and Exchange Systems and the Classic Maya Collapse in the Petexbatun Region. Unpublished Ph.D. dissertation, Vanderbilt University, Nashville, Tennessee.

Freeman, J. D.
1958   The Family System of the Iban of Borneo. In *The Developmental Cycle in Domestic Groups*, edited by Jack Goody, pp. 15–52. Cambridge University Press, Cambridge.

Freidel, David A.
1990   The Jester God: The Beginning and End of a Maya Royal Symbolism. In *Vision and Revision in Maya Studies*, edited by Flora S. Clancy and Peter D. Harrison, pp. 67–76. University of New Mexico Press, Albuquerque.

Freidel, David A., and Robin Robertson
1986   *Archaeology at Cerros, Belize, Central America*. Southern Methodist University Press, Dallas.

Freidel, David, and Linda Schele
1988   Symbol and Power: A History of the Lowland Maya Cosmogram. In *Maya Iconography*, edited by Elizabeth P. Benson and Gillett G. Griffin, pp. 44–93. Princeton University Press, Princeton.
1989   Dead Kings and Living Temples: Dedication and Termination Rituals among the Ancient Maya. In *Word and Image in Maya Culture*, edited by William F. Hanks and Don S. Rice, pp. 233–243. University of Utah Press, Salt Lake City.

Freidel, David A., Charles K. Suhler, and Rafael Cobos Palma
1998   Termination Ritual Deposits at Yaxuna: Detecting the Historical in Archaeological Contexts. In *The Sowing and the Dawning: Termination, Dedication, and Transformation in the Archaeological and Ethnographic Record of Mesoamerica*, edited by Shirley Boteler Mock, pp. 135–144. University of New Mexico Press, Albuquerque.

Garber, James F.
1983   Patterns of Jade Consumption and Disposal at Cerros, Northern Belize. *American Antiquity* 48:800–807.

Gardiner, Michael
1992   *The Dialogics of Critique: M. M. Bakhtin and the Theory of Ideology*. Routledge, New York.

Geertz, Clifford
1980   *Negara: The Theatre State in Nineteenth-Century Bali*. Princeton University Press, Princeton.

Giddens, Anthony
1984   *The Constitution of Society: Outline of the Theory of Structuration*. Polity Press, Cambridge.

Gillespie, Susan D.
2000   Rethinking Ancient Maya Social Organization: Replacing "Lineage" with "House." *American Anthropologist* 102: 467–484.

Glassie, Henry H.
1975   *Folk Housing in Middle Virginia: A Structural Analysis of Historic Artifacts*. University of Tennessee Press, Knoxville.

Goodenough, Ward H.
1970   *Description and Comparison in Cultural Anthropology*. Aldine, Chicago.

Goody, Jack
1958   The Fission of Domestic Groups among the LoDagaba. In *The Developmental Cycle in Domestic Groups*, edited by Jack Goody, pp. 53–91. Cambridge University Press, Cambridge.

Graham, Ian
1967   *Archaeological Explorations in El Peten, Guatemala*. Middle American Research Institute Publication 33. Tulane University, New Orleans.
1978   *Corpus of Maya Hieroglyphic Inscriptions, Volume 2, Part 2: Naranjo*. Peabody Museum of Archaeology and Ethnology, Harvard University, Cambridge.

Guenter, Stanley
2003   The Inscriptions of Dos Pilas Associated with B'ajlaj Chan K'awiil. Electronic document, www.mesoweb.com/features/guenter/DosPilas.pdf.

Hammel, E. A.
1980   Household Structure in Fourteenth-Century Macedonia. *Journal of Family History* 5:242–273.

Hammel, E. A., and Peter Laslett
1974   Comparing Household Structure over Time and between Cultures. *Comparative Studies in Society and History* 16(1):73–109.

Harrison, Peter D.
1970   The Central Acropolis, Tikal, Guatemala: A Preliminary Study of the Functions of Its Structural Components during the Late Classic Period. Unpublished Ph.D. dissertation, University of Pennsylvania.

Haviland, William Arthur
1972   Family Size, Prehistoric Population Estimates, and the Ancient Maya. *American Antiquity* 37:135–139.
1985   *Excavations in Small Residential Groups of Tikal: Groups 4F-1 and 4F-2*. Tikal Report No. 19. University Museum, University of Pennsylvania, Philadelphia.

Hayden, Brian, and Aubrey Cannon
1983   Where the Garbage Goes: Refuse Disposal in the Maya Highlands. *Journal of Anthropological Archaeology* 2:117–163.

Hellmuth, Nicholas M.
1977   Cholti-Lacandon (Chiapas) and Petén—Ytzá Agriculture, Settlement Pattern and Population. In *Social Process in Maya Prehistory*, edited by Norman Hammond, pp. 421–448. Academic Press, London.

Hendon, Julia A.
1996   Archaeological Approaches to the Organization of Domestic Labor: Household Practice and Domestic Relations. *Annual Review of Anthropology* 25:45–61.
1997   Women's Work, Women's Space, and Women's Status

among the Classic-Period Maya Elite of the Copan Valley, Honduras. In *Women in Prehistory: North America and Mesoamerica*, edited by Cheryl Claassen and Rosemary A. Joyce, pp. 33–46. University of Pennsylvania Press, Philadelphia.

Herbich, Ingrid, and Michael Dietler

1993　Space, Time and Symbolic Structure in the Luo Homestead: An Ethnoarchaeological Study of "Settlement Biography" in Africa. In *Actes du XIIe Congrès International des Sciences Préhistoriques et Protohistoriques, Bratislava, Czechoslovakia, September 1–7, 1991, Vol. 1*, edited by J. Pavúk, pp. 26–32. Archaeological Institute of the Slovak Academy of Sciences, Nitra.

Hirth, G. Kenneth

1993　The Household as an Analytical Unit: Problems in Method and Theory. In *Prehispanic Domestic Units in Western Mesoamerica: Studies of the Household, Compound, and Residence*, edited by Robert Santley and Kenneth G. Hirth, pp. 21–36. CRC Press, Boca Raton, Florida.

Hodder, Ian

1990　*The Domestication of Europe: Structure and Contingency in Neolithic Societies*. Blackwell, Oxford.

Horne, Lee

1982　The Household in Space: Dispersed Holdings in an Iranian Village. *American Behavioral Scientist* 25:677–685.

Houston, Stephen D.

1987　The Inscriptions and Monumental Art of Dos Pilas, Guatemala: A Study of Classic Maya History and Politics. Unpublished Ph.D. dissertation, Yale University, New Haven.

1993　*Hieroglyphs and History at Dos Pilas: Dynastic Politics of the Classic Maya*. University of Texas Press, Austin.

Houston, Stephen D., and Takeshi Inomata

2009　*The Classic Maya*. Cambridge University Press, Cambridge.

Houston, Stephen D., and David Stuart

1996　Of Gods, Glyphs and Kings: Divinity and Rulership among the Classic Maya. *Antiquity* 70:289–312.

Hymes, Dell H.

1975　Breakthrough into Performance. In *Folklore: Performance and Communication*, edited by Dan Ben-Amos and Kenneth S. Goldstein, pp. 11–74. Mouton, The Hague.

Inomata, Takeshi

1995　Archaeological Investigations at the Fortified Center of Aguateca, El Petén, Guatemala: Implications for the Study of the Classic Maya Collapse. Unpublished Ph.D. dissertation, Vanderbilt University, Nashville, Tennessee.

1997　The Last Day of a Fortified Classic Maya Center: Archaeological Investigations at Aguateca, Guatemala. *Ancient Mesoamerica* 8:337–351.

2001a　The Classic Maya Royal Palace as a Political Theater. In *Reconstruyendo la ciudad maya: El urbanismo en las sociedades antigua*, edited by Andrés Ciudad Ruiz, María Josefa Iglesias Ponce de León, and María del Carmen Martínez Martínez, pp. 341–362. Sociedad Española de Estudios Mayas, Madrid.

2001b　King's People: Classic Maya Royal Courtiers in a Comparative Perspective. In *Royal Courts of the Ancient Maya,*

Volume 1: Theory, Comparison, and Synthesis, edited by Takeshi Inomata and Stephen D. Houston, pp. 27–53. Westview Press, Boulder, Colorado.

2001c　The Power and Ideology of Artistic Creation: Elite Craft Specialists in Classic Maya Society. *Current Anthropology* 42:321–349.

2003　War, Destruction, and Abandonment: The Fall of the Classic Maya Center of Aguateca, Guatemala. In *The Archaeology of Settlement Abandonment in Middle America*, edited by Takeshi Inomata and Ronald W. Webb, pp. 43–60. University of Utah Press, Salt Lake City.

2007　*Warfare and the Fall of a Fortified Center: Archaeological Investigations at Aguateca*. Vanderbilt Institute of Mesoamerican Archaeology Series, Vol. 3. Vanderbilt University Press, Nashville, Tennessee.

2009　*Settlements and Fortifications of Aguateca: Archaeological Maps of a Petexbatun Center*. Vanderbilt Institute of Mesoamerican Archaeology Series, Vol. 4. Vanderbilt University Press, Nashville, Tennessee.

Inomata, Takeshi, and Lawrence S. Coben (editors)

2006　Overture: An Invitation to the Archaeological Theater. In *Archaeology of Performance: Theaters of Power, Community, and Politics*, edited by Takeshi Inomata and Lawrence S. Coben, pp. 11–46. AltaMira Press, Lanham, Maryland.

Inomata, Takeshi, and Stephen D. Houston

2001　Opening the Royal Maya Court. In *Royal Courts of the Ancient Maya, Volume 1: Theory, Comparison, and Synthesis*, edited by Takeshi Inomata and Stephen D. Houston, pp. 3–23. Westview Press, Boulder, Colorado.

Inomata, Takeshi, and Stephen Houston (editors)

2001a　*Royal Courts of the Ancient Maya, Volume 1: Theory, Comparison, and Synthesis*. Westview Press, Boulder, Colorado.

2001b　*Royal Courts of the Ancient Maya, Volume 2: Data and Case Studies*. Westview Press, Boulder, Colorado.

Inomata, Takeshi, Erick Ponciano, Oscar Santos, Oswaldo Chinchilla, Otto Román, and Véronique Breuil-Martínez

2004　An Unfinished Temple at the Classic Maya Center of Aguateca, Guatemala. *Antiquity* 78(302):798–811.

Inomata, Takeshi, and Payson Sheets

2000　Mesoamerican Households Viewed from Rapidly Abandoned Sites: An Introduction. *Mayab* 13:5–10.

Inomata, Takeshi, and Laura R. Stiver

1998　Floor Assemblages from Burned Structures at Aguateca, Guatemala: A Study of Classic Maya Households. *Journal of Field Archaeology* 25(4):431–452.

Inomata, Takeshi, and Daniela Triadan (editors)

In preparation *Life and Politics at the Royal Court of Aguateca: Artifacts, Analytical Data, and Synthesis*. Monographs of the Aguateca Archaeological Project First Phase Volume 3.

Inomata, Takeshi, Daniela Triadan, Erick Ponciano, and Kazuo Aoyama (editors)

2009　*La política de lugares y comunidades en la antigua sociedad maya de Petexbatun: Las investigaciones del Proyecto Arqueológico Aguateca Segunda Fase*. Ministerio de Cultura y Deportes, Dirección General del Patrimonio Cultural y Natural, and Instituto de Antropología e Historia, Guatemala. In press.

Inomata, Takeshi, Daniela Triadan, Erick Ponciano, Richard Terry, and Harriet F. Beaubien
2001 In the Palace of the Fallen King: The Royal Residential Complex at Aguateca, Guatemala. *Journal of Field Archaeology* 28:287–306.

Inomata, Takeshi, and Ronald W. Webb
2003 Archaeological Studies of Abandonment in Middle America. In *The Archaeology of Settlement Abandonment in Middle America*, edited by Takeshi Inomata and Ronald W. Webb, pp. 1–10. University of Utah Press, Salt Lake City.

Inomata, Takeshi, and Ronald W. Webb (editors)
2003 *The Archaeology of Settlement Abandonment in Middle America*. University of Utah Press, Salt Lake City.

Ishihara, Reiko
2007 Bridging the Chasm between Religion and Politics: Archaeological Investigations of the Grietas at the Late Classic Maya Site of Aguateca, Peten, Guatemala. Unpublished Ph.D. dissertation, University of California, Riverside.
2009 Grietas. In *La política de lugares y comunidades en la antigua sociedad maya de Petexbatun: Las investigaciones del Proyecto Arqueológico Aguateca Segunda Fase*, edited by Takeshi Inomata, Daniela Triadan, Erick Ponciano, and Kazuo Aoyama, pp. 52–112. Ministerio de Cultura y Deportes, Dirección General del Patrimonio Cultural y Natural, Instituto de Antropología e Historia, Guatemala City.

Iwamoto, Hiro, and Takeshi Inomata
2009 Petroglifos de la Barranca Escondida. In *La política de lugares y comunidades en la antigua sociedad maya de Petexbatun: Las investigaciones del Proyecto Arqueológico Aguateca Segunda Fase*, edited by Takeshi Inomata, Daniela Triadan, Erick Ponciano, and Kazuo Aoyama, pp. 312–313. Ministerio de Cultura y Deportes, Dirección General del Patrimonio Cultural y Natural, Instituto de Antropología e Historia, Guatemala City.

Jackson, Sarah
2005 Deciphering Classic Maya Political Hierarchy: Epigraphic, Archeological, and Ethnohistoric Perspectives on the Courtly Elite. Unpublished Ph.D. dissertation, Harvard University, Cambridge.
2009 Imagining Courtly Communities: An Exploration of Classic Maya Experiences of Status and Identity through Painted Vessels. *Ancient Mesoamerica* 20:71–85.

Joyce, Rosemary
1993 Women's Work: Images of Production and Reproduction in Pre-Hispanic Southern Central America. *Current Anthropology* 34:255–274.
2000 *Gender and Power in Prehispanic Mesoamerica*. University of Texas Press, Austin.

Kent, Susan
1984 *Analyzing Activity Areas: An Ethnoarchaeological Study of the Use of Space*. University of New Mexico Press, Albuquerque.

Kent, Susan (editor)
1990 *Domestic Architecture and the Use of Space: An Interdisciplinary Cross-Cultural Study*. Cambridge University Press, Cambridge.

Kramer, Carol
1979 *Ethnoarchaeology: Implications of Ethnography for Archaeology*. Columbia University Press, New York.

Lange, F. W., and C. R. Rydberg
1972 Abandonment and Post-abandonment at a Rural Central American House-Site. *American Antiquity* 37:419–432.

Laslett, Peter
1969 Size and Structure of the Household in England over Three Centuries. *Population Studies* 23:199–223.

Laslett, Peter, and Richard Wall (editors)
1972 *Household and Family in Past Time*. Cambridge University Press, Cambridge.

Lawrence, Denise L., and Setha M. Low
1990 The Built Environment and Spatial Form. *Annual Review of Anthropology* 19:453–505.

Loades, David
1986 *The Tudor Court*. Batsford, London.

Lohse, Jon C., and Fred Valdez (editors)
2004 *Ancient Maya Commoners*. University of Texas Press, Austin.

Longacre, William A. (editor)
1991 *Ceramic Ethnoarchaeology*. University of Arizona Press, Tucson.

Manzanilla, Linda (editor)
1993 *Anatomía de un conjunto residencial teotihuacano en Oztoyahualco*. Universidad Nacional Autónoma de México, Instituto de Investigaciones Antropológicas, Mexico City.

Manzanilla, Linda, and Luis Barba
1990 The Study of Activities in Classic Households: Two Case Studies from Coba and Teotihuacan. *Ancient Mesoamerica* 1:41–49.

Martin, Simon
2000 At the Periphery: The Movement, Modification and Re-use of Early Monuments in the Environs of Tikal. In *Sacred and the Profane: Architecture and Identity in the Maya Lowlands*, edited by Pierre Robert Colas, Kai Delvendahl, Marcus Kuhnert, and Annette Schubart, pp. 51–61. Verlag Anton Saurwein, Markt Schwaben, Germany.

Martin, Simon, and Nikolai Grube
2000 *Chronicle of the Maya Kings and Queens: Deciphering the Dynasties of the Ancient Maya*. Thames and Hudson, London.

McAnany, Patricia Ann
1995 *Living with the Ancestors: Kinship and Kingship in Ancient Maya Society*. University of Texas Press, Austin.

McGovern, T. H., P. C. Buckland, D. Savory, G. Sveinbjarnardottir, C. Andreasen, and P. Skidmore
1983 A Study of the Faunal and Floral Remains from Two Norse Farms in the Western Settlement, Greenland. *Arctic Anthropology* 20:93–111.

McGuire, Randall H.
1992 *A Marxist Archaeology*. Academic Press, San Diego.

Meskell, Lynn
1999 *Archaeologies of Social Life: Age, Sex, Class et cetera in Ancient Egypt*. Blackwell, Oxford.

Miller, Mary
1986 *The Murals of Bonampak*. Princeton University Press, Princeton.

Miller, Mary, and Simon Martin (editors)

2004 *Courtly Art of the Ancient Maya*. Thames and Hudson, New York.

Moholy-Nagy, Hattula

2003 *Tikal Report No. 27, Part B: The Artifacts of Tikal: Utilitarian Artifacts and Unworked Material*. University Museum Monograph 118. University of Pennsylvania, Philadelphia.

Morgan, Lewis Henry

1871 *Systems of Consanguinity and Affinity of the Human Family*. Smithsonian Contributions to Knowledge No. 218. Smithsonian Institution, Washington, D.C.

1965 [1881] *Houses and House-Life of the American Aborigines*. University of Chicago Press, Chicago.

Nakane, Chie

1970 *Kazokuno kouzou: Shakaijinruigakuteki bunseki* [Structure of Households: Social Anthropological Analyses]. University of Tokyo Press, Tokyo.

Netting, Robert M.

1965 Household Organization and Intensive Agriculture: The Kofyar Case. *Africa* 35:422–429.

1993 *Smallholders, Householders: Farm Families and the Ecology of Intensive, Sustainable Agriculture*. Stanford University Press, Stanford, California.

Netting, Robert McC., Richard R. Wilk, and Eric J. Arnould

1984 Introduction. In *Households: Comparative and Historical Studies of the Domestic Group*, edited by Robert McC. Netting, Richard R. Wilk, and Eric J. Arnould, pp. xiii–xxxviii. University of California Press, Berkeley.

Netting, Robert McC., Richard R. Wilk, and Eric J. Arnould (editors)

1984 *Households: Comparative and Historical Studies of the Domestic Group*. University of California Press, Berkeley.

Palka, Joel W.

1997 Reconstructing Classic Maya Socioeconomic Differentiation and the Collapse at Dos Pilas, Peten, Guatemala. *Ancient Mesoamerica* 8:293–306.

Pearson, Michael Parker, and Colin Richards (editors)

1994 *Architecture and Order: Approaches to Social Space*. Routledge, London.

Ponciano, Erick, Takeshi Inomata, Estela Pinto, and Marco Antonio Monroy

2009 Excavaciones en la Plaza Principal: Estructuras L8-6 (Operación AG32A) y L8-7 (Operación AG33A). In *La política de lugares y comunidades en la antigua sociedad maya de Petexbatun: Las investigaciones del Proyecto Arqueológico Aguateca Segunda Fase*, edited by Takeshi Inomata, Daniela Triadan, Erick Ponciano, and Kazuo Aoyama, pp. 27–38. Ministerio de Cultura y Deportes, Dirección General del Patrimonio Cultural y Natural, and Instituto de Antropología e Historia, Guatemala City. In press.

Puleston, Dennis

1973 *Ancient Maya Settlement Patterns and Environment at Tikal, Guatemala: Implications for Subsistence Models*. Tikal Report No. 13. University Museum Monograph 48. University of Pennsylvania, Philadelphia.

Rapoport, Amos

1969 *House Form and Culture*. Foundations of Cultural Geography Series. Prentice-Hall, Englewood Cliffs, New Jersey.

1982 *The Meaning of the Built Environment: A Nonverbal Communication Approach*. Sage Publications, Beverly Hills, California.

Rapp, Rayna

1991 Family and Class in Contemporary America: Notes Towards an Understanding of Ideology. In *Family, Household and Gender Relations in Latin America*, edited by Elizabeth Jelin, pp. 197–215. Kegan Paul International, London.

Rathje, William L.

1983 To the Salt of the Earth: Some Comments on Household Archaeology among the Maya. In *Prehistoric Settlement Patterns: Essays in Honor of Gordon R. Willey*, edited by Evon Z. Vogt and Richard M. Leventhal, pp. 23–34. University of New Mexico Press, Albuquerque.

Redfield, Robert, and A. Villa Rojas

1934 *Chan Kom: A Maya Village*. Publication 448. Carnegie Institution of Washington, Washington, D.C.

Rice, Don S., and T. Patrick Culbert

1990 Historical Contexts for Population Reconstruction in the Maya Lowlands. In *Precolumbian Population History in the Maya Lowlands*, edited by T. Patrick Culbert and Don S. Rice, pp. 1–36. University of New Mexico Press, Albuquerque.

Ringle, William M., and E. Wyllys Andrews V

1990 Demography of Komchen, an Early Maya Town in Northern Yucatan. In *Precolumbian Population History in the Maya Lowlands*, edited by T. Patrick Culbert and Don S. Rice, pp. 215–243. University of New Mexico Press, Albuquerque.

Ringle, William M., and George J. Bey III

2001 Post-Classic and Terminal Classic Courts of the Northern Maya Lowlands. In *Royal Courts of the Ancient Maya, Volume 2: Data and Case Study*, edited by Takeshi Inomata and Stephen D. Houston, pp. 266–307. Westview Press, Boulder, Colorado.

Robertson, Robin

1983 Functional Analysis and Social Process in Ceramics: The Pottery from Cerros, Belize. In *Civilization in the Ancient Americas: Essays in Honor of Gordon R. Willey*, edited by Richard M. Leventhal and Alan L. Kolata, pp. 105–142. University of New Mexico Press, Albuquerque.

Robin, Cynthia

2003 New Directions in Classic Maya Household Archaeology. *Journal of Archaeological Research* 11:307–356.

2006 Gender, Farming, and Long-Term Change: Maya Historical and Archaeological Perspective. *Current Anthropology* 47:409–433.

Rosen, Arlene M.

1986 *Cities of Clay: The Geoarchaeology of Tells*. University of Chicago Press, Chicago.

Roys, Ralph L., France V. Scholes, and Eleanor B. Adams

1940 *Report and Census of the Indians of Cozumel, 1570*. Contributions to American Anthropology and History No. 30. Publication 523. Carnegie Institution of Washington, Washington, D.C.

1959 Census and Inspection of the Town of Pencuyut, Yucatan, in 1583 by Diego García de Palacio, Oider of the Audiencia of Guatemala. *Ethnohistory* 6:195–225.

Sabloff, Jeremy A.

1975 *Excavations at Seibal, Department of Peten, Guatemala: Ceramics*. Memoirs of the Peabody Museum of Archaeology and Ethnology Vol. 13, No. 2. Harvard University, Cambridge.

Sahlins, Marshall D.

1985 *Islands of History*. University of Chicago Press, Chicago.

Samson, Ross

1990 *The Social Archaeology of Houses*. Edinburgh University Press, Edinburgh.

Sanders, William T., and David Webster

1988 Mesoamerican Urban Tradition. *American Anthropologist* 90:521–546.

Santley, Robert S., and Kenneth G. Hirth (editors)

1993 *Prehispanic Domestic Units in Western Mesoamerica: Studies of the Household, Compound, and Residence*. CRC Press, Boca Raton, Florida.

Schele, Linda, and Mary Ellen Miller

1986 *The Blood of Kings: Dynasty and Ritual in Maya Art*. Kimbell Art Museum, Fort Worth, Texas.

Schiffer, Michael B.

1976 *Behavioral Archeology*. Studies in Archeology. Academic Press, New York.

1987 *Formation Processes of the Archaeological Record*. University of New Mexico Press, Albuquerque.

Schwartz, Glenn M., and Steven E. Falconer (editors)

1994 *Archaeological Views from the Countryside: Village Communities in Early Complex Societies*. Smithsonian Institution Press, Washington, D.C.

Sheets, Payson D.

1992 *The Ceren Site: A Prehistoric Village Buried by Volcanic Ash in Central America*. Case Studies in Archaeology Series. Harcourt Brace Jovanovich College Publishers, Fort Worth, Texas.

Sheets, Payson D. (editor)

2002 *Before the Volcano Erupted: The Ancient Cerén Village in Central America*. University of Texas Press, Austin.

Smith, Michael E.

1987 Household Possessions and Wealth in Agrarian States: Implications for Archaeology. *Journal of Anthropological Archaeology* 6:297–335.

Smith, Robert E.

1955 *Ceramic Sequence at Uaxactun, Guatemala*. Middle American Research Institute, Publication 20. Tulane University, New Orleans.

Smith, Robert E., and James C. Gifford

1966 *Maya Ceramic Varieties, Types, and Wares at Uaxactun: Supplement to "Ceramic Sequence at Uaxactun, Guatemala."* Middle American Research Institute, Middle American Research Record, Vol. 3. Tulane University, New Orleans.

Stevenson, Marc G.

1982 Toward an Understanding of Site Abandonment Behavior: Evidence from Historical Mining Camps in the Southwest Yukon. *Journal of Anthropological Archaeology* 1:237–265.

Stuart, David

2005 *The Inscriptions from Temple XIX at Palenque: A Commentary*. Pre-Columbian Art Research Institute, San Francisco.

Tambiah, Stanley Jeyaraja

1976 *World Conqueror and World Renouncer: A Study of Buddhism and Polity in Thailand against a Historical Background*. Cambridge Studies in Social Anthropology 15. Cambridge University Press, Cambridge.

Terry, Richard E., Fabian G. Fernández, J. Jacob Parnell, and Takeshi Inomata

2004 The Story in the Floors: Chemical Signatures of Ancient and Modern Maya Activities at Aguateca, Guatemala. *Journal of Archaeological Science* 31:1237–1250.

Therborn, Göran

1980 *The Ideology of Power and the Power of Ideology*. NLB, London.

Tourtellot, Gair

1983 Assessment of Classic Maya Household Composition. In *Prehistoric Settlement Patterns: Essays in Honor of Gordon R. Willey*, edited by Evon Z. Vogt and Richard M. Leventhal, pp. 35–54. University of New Mexico Press, Albuquerque.

1988a Developmental Cycles of Households and Houses at Seibal. In *Household and Community in the Mesoamerican Past*, edited by Richard R. Wilk and Wendy Ashmore, pp. 97–120. University of New Mexico Press, Albuquerque.

1988b *Excavations at Seibal, Department of Peten, Guatemala: Peripheral Survey and Excavation, Settlement and Community Patterns*. Memoirs of the Peabody Museum of Archaeology and Ethnology Vol. 16. Harvard University, Cambridge.

Tourtellot, Gair, III, Jeremy A. Sabloff, and Michael P. Smyth

1990 Room Counts and Population Estimation for Terminal Classic Sayil in the Puuc Region, Yucatan, Mexico. In *Precolumbian Population History in the Maya Lowlands*, edited by T. Patrick Culbert and Don S. Rice, pp. 245–262. University of New Mexico Press, Albuquerque.

Triadan, Daniela

2000 Elite Household Subsistence at Aguateca, Guatemala. *Mayab* 13:46–56.

2007 Warriors, Nobles, Commoners, and Beasts: Figurines from Elite Buildings at Aguateca, Guatemala. *Latin American Antiquity* 18:269–294.

Tringham, Ruth

1991 Households with Faces: The Challenge of Gender in Prehistoric Architectural Remains. In *Engendering Archaeology: Women and Prehistory*, edited by Joan M. Gero and Margaret W. Conkey. Blackwell, Oxford.

Valdés, Juan Antonio, Mónica Urquizú, Carolina Díaz Samayoa, and Horacio Martínez Paíz

1999 *Informe anual del Proyecto de Restauración Aguateca*. Report presented to the Instituto de Antropología e Historia de Guatemala, Guatemala City.

Villagutierre Soto-Mayor, J. de

1933 [1701] *Historia de la conquista de la provincia de el Itzá*. Biblioteca Guatemala, Guatemala City.

Villa Rojas, A.

1945 *The Maya of East Central Quintana Roo*. Publication 559. Carnegie Institution of Washington, Washington, D.C.

1969 The Maya of Yucatan. In *Ethnology, Part 1*, edited by

Evon Z. Vogt, pp. 244–297. Handbook of Middle American Indians, Robert Wauchope, general editor. University of Texas Press, Austin.

Walker, Debra S.

1998   Smashed Pots and Shattered Dreams: The Material Evidence for an Early Classic Maya Site Termination at Cerros, Belize. In *The Sowing and the Dawning: Termination, Dedication, and Transformation in the Archaeological and Ethnographic Record of Mesoamerica*, edited by Shirley Boteler Mock, pp. 81–99. University of New Mexico Press, Albuquerque.

Wauchope, Robert

1934   *House Mounds of Uaxactun, Guatemala*. Contributions to American Archaeology 7, Publication 436. Carnegie Institution of Washington, Washington, D.C.

1938   *Modern Maya Houses: A Study of Their Archaeological Significance*. Publication 502. Carnegie institution of Washington, Washington, D.C.

Weber, Max

1978   *Economy and Society*. University of California Press, Berkeley.

Webster, David (editor)

1989   *The House of the Bacabs, Copan, Honduras*. Studies in Pre-Columbian Art and Archaeology 29. Dumbarton Oaks Research Library and Collection, Washington, D.C.

Webster, David, and AnnCorrine Freter

1990   The Demography of Late Classic Copan. In *Precolumbian Population History in the Maya Lowlands*, edited by T. Patrick Culbert and Don S. Rice, pp. 37–61. University of New Mexico Press, Albuquerque.

Wilk, Richard R.

1983   Little House in the Jungle: The Causes of Variation in House Size among Modern Kekchi Maya. *Journal of Anthropological Archaeology* 2:99–116.

1991   *Household Ecology: Economic Change and Domestic Life among the Kekchi Maya in Belize*. University of Arizona Press, Tucson.

Wilk, Richard R., and Wendy Ashmore (editors)

1988   *Household and Community in the Mesoamerican Past*. University of New Mexico Press, Albuquerque.

Wilk, Richard R., and Robert McC. Netting

1984   Households: Changing Forms and Functions. In *Households: Comparative and Historical Studies of the Domestic Group*, edited by Robert McC. Netting, Richard R. Wilk, and Eric J. Arnould, pp. 1–28. University of California Press, Berkeley.

Wilk, Richard R., and William L. Rathje (editors)

1982   Archaeology of the Household: Building a Prehistory of Domestic Life. Special issue, *American Behavioral Scientist* 25(6).

Willey, Gordon R.

1978   *Excavations at Seibal, Department of Peten, Guatemala: Artifacts*. Memoirs of the Peabody Museum of Archaeology and Ethnology Vol. 14, No. 1. Harvard University, Cambridge.

1981   Maya Lowland Settlement Patterns: A Summary Review. In *Lowland Maya Settlement Patterns*, edited by Wendy Ashmore, pp. 385–415. University of New Mexico Press, Albuquerque.

Willey, Gordon R., William R. Bullard Jr., John B. Glass, and James C. Gifford

1965   *Prehistoric Maya Settlements in the Belize Valley*. Papers of the Peabody Museum of Archaeology and Ethnology Vol. 54. Harvard University, Cambridge.

Wright, Rita P.

1991   Women's Labor and Pottery Production in Prehistory. In *Engendering Archaeology: Women and Prehistory*, edited by Joan M. Gero and Margaret W. Conkey, pp. 93–131. Blackwell, Oxford.

Yaeger, Jason

2003   Small Settlements in the Upper Belize River Valley: Local Complexity, Household Strategies of Affiliation, and the Changing Organization. In *Perspectives on Ancient Maya Rural Complexity*, edited by Gyles Iannone and Samuel V. Connell, pp. 42–58. Monograph 49. Cotsen Institute of Archaeology, University of California, Los Angeles.

Yanagisako, Sylvia Junko

1979   Family and Household: The Analysis of Domestic Groups. *Annual Review of Anthropology* 8:161–205.

Index

Numbers in *italics* refer to figures and tables.